Alexander Mackenzie: Clear Grit

DALE C. THOMSON

Alexander Mackenzie

CLEAR GRIT

1960

THE MACMILLAN COMPANY

OF CANADA LIMITED

TORONTO

DESIGNER: LESLIE SMART

PRINTER: T. H. BEST PRINTING COMPANY LIMITED

PRINTED IN CANADA

PREFACE

Alexander Mackenzie: Clear Grit is the story of a young Scottish stonemason who left his native land to seek a brighter future for himself and his family. An ardent Liberal, he was shocked to find in Canada a system of government as reactionary as the one he had learned to hate at home. Settling on the outskirts of civilization in Port Sarnia, he developed a prosperous business as a builder, but his main interest throughout his life was the reform of political and social abuses.

Despite the handicap of a very limited formal education, Mackenzie proved to be a natural leader, and was largely responsible for launching the great George Brown on his parliamentary career in 1851. Ten years later he himself joined the ranks of the Liberals in the Parliament of United Canada as the member for Lambton, and gave Brown loyal support in his struggle to achieve Confederation. On Brown's defeat in the 1867 elections, Alexander Mackenzie succeeded him as federal leader for Ontario, and in 1873 became the first Dominion-wide Leader of the Liberal Party. Within a year he had defeated John A. Macdonald on the Pacific scandal, and become Prime Minister of Canada.

Mackenzie's life is a tale of triumph; it is also a story of disappointment and defeat. The ex-stonemason was able to accomplish much, and many of his accomplishments marked the path to Canadian nationhood. Fate dealt unkindly with him, however, and after five years as Prime Minister he was relegated to the political sidelines. In failing health, he had to watch for fourteen years as his life-long political opponent, the genial but somewhat unscrupulous Macdonald, held sway over the Dominion's affairs. Worse, Mackenzie was stricken by paralysis of the throat, and was scarcely able to speak out for his principles.

The period of history covered in this volume extends from the Union of Upper and Lower Canada in 1840 to the end of the Macdonald era half a century later. They were critical years for Canada, years which saw the introduction of responsible government, the development of the party system, the achievement of Confederation, and the extension of the Dominion "from sea to sea". Canadians shook off their colonial status, accepted their rights and responsibilities as free-born men and women, and set their feet irrevocably on the path of independent nationhood. Alexander Mackenzie played a vital part in every stage of that development.

What justifies a fresh biography of Alexander Mackenzie at this time? Shortly after his death in 1892, two loyal friends, his former private secretary William Buckingham, and George W. Ross, later Premier of Ontario, wrote *The Honourable Alexander Mackenzie, His Life and Times*. Although a useful document, the partisan character of this volume, and the lack of historical perspective now available, have lessened its interest to present-day readers. As a consequence, Mackenzie has become one of the least known, and certainly the most underrated, of Canada's Prime Ministers. In a period when Canadians are becoming much more conscious of their national heritage, a fresh examination of Mackenzie's life and works seems appropriate.

Happily for students of Canadian history, a number of valuable collections of personal papers have been made available in recent years that throw fresh light on Alexander Mackenzie and his contemporaries. The *Mackenzie Letterbooks*, composed principally of letters written as Prime Minister, have been in the Public Archives of Canada for some years. However, it was only recently that the *Mackenzie Papers*, a collection of private and confidential correspondence, were presented to Queen's University by the late Mrs. John Thompson of Ottawa. Mr. John Thompson, grandson of Alexander Mackenzie, had planned to write a biography of his famous ancestor after retiring from the federal civil service, but time ran out, and death prevented the realization of this project. In 1959 Mrs. B. R. Morgan of Ottawa, great-grand-daughter of Mackenzie, made available to the author some additional private papers passed down by the Thompsons which are listed in this volume as the *Mackenzie-Thompson Papers*. For this valuable material I have been very grateful, as they have given a new insight into Mackenzie's personality.

Other relevant collections have appeared in recent years. Professor J. M. S. Careless, Chairman of the Department of History of the University of Toronto, discovered and brought back to Canada from Scotland the *George Brown Papers*. These he gave me permission to consult in the Public Archives of Canada before they were made available to the public, and before completing his own two-volume study of the period, *Brown of the Globe*. I am most indebted to Professor Careless for this disinterested assistance.

While this biography was in preparation Dr. W. Kaye Lamb, Dominion Archivist, secured for the Public Archives of Canada a microfilm set of the *Earl of Dufferin Papers* from the Dufferin estate of Clandeboye in Northern Ireland. This material complemented the *Dufferin-Carnarvon Correspondence* published by De Kiewiet and Underhill in 1955. A glance at the references at the end of this volume will show how extensively I have used this material.

The *Edward Blake Papers* have also been made available in microfilm at the Public Archives of Canada in recent years, and were of great importance in reconstructing the story of the Liberal Administration of 1873-8. In 1952 the Public Archives of Nova Scotia published a series of letters from Mackenzie to Alfred Jones which provide a valuable insight into the public life of the period. The *W. L. Mackenzie-Lindsey Papers* at the Public Archives of Ontario and the *David Mills Papers* at the University of Western Ontario were important sources of information. Mr. Edmond Joly de Lotbinière of Ottawa granted me permission to consult the *Joly de Lotbinière Papers* in the family archives at Leclercville, Quebec.

It is impossible to list all the persons who have contributed to the successful completion of this project. I acknowledge with gratitude the patient and courteous co-operation of Dr. W. Kaye Lamb and the staff of the Public Archives of Canada, and of Dr. G. W. Spragge and the staff of the Public Archives of Ontario. To the staff of the Library of Parliament, whose friendly help has made my research so enjoyable, I express my heartfelt thanks. Dr. F. H. Underhill, Dr. J. M. S. Careless, Dr. Blair Neatby, and Mr. Patrick Daniel have all read this study at various stages of its preparation and made helpful comments and suggestions. The Canada Council and the Social Science Research Council of Canada have granted me financial assistance which I am pleased to acknowledge. The Canada Council and the Humanities Research Council of Canada made a most useful grant in aid of publication. In particular, I wish to express my warm thanks to Dr. John Robbins who, as Secretary-Treasurer of the Social Science and Humanities Research Councils, was instrumental in enabling me to obtain the above assistance. Dr. Robbins' constant kindness and understanding were of immeasurable value in giving me the courage to push this project to completion.

This series of acknowledgments would not be complete without an expression of respect and gratitude to my former employer, the Right Honourable Louis S. St. Laurent, whose inspiring example, both as a man and a statesman, gave me a closer insight into the life and work of his predecessor. The expressions "sterling statesman" and "honest politician" apply equally well to both men.

Finally, may all those whose names are not mentioned here rest assured that their contributions are neither ignored nor forgotten.

ILLUSTRATIONS

All illustrations courtesy of the Public Archives of Canada, with the exception of the photograph of Edward Blake (facing p. 148), courtesy of the Ontario Department of Travel and Publicity.

CONTENTS

This book is dedicated
to my mother

CHAPTER 1

In the Forests of the Far West

Moderate winds filled the sails of the *Monarch* and drove her forward at a steady pace. The captain picked his way gingerly through the ice-filled Cabot Strait between Nova Scotia and Newfoundland and into the Gulf of St. Lawrence. The first vessel of the 1842 shipping season had broken through the floes of pack ice and dodged around the icebergs just four days ahead of them. Despite some strong winds shortly after they had lifted anchor in Greenock on April 15, the voyage had not been a hard one. With one exception, when they had come dangerously close to an iceberg, the seventy passengers had little cause for complaint. On deck, a sandy-haired, bright-eyed youth of barely twenty years scanned the horizon for the first glimpse of his new home. Like many thousands of his fellow-Scots in the early 1840's, the young stonemason Alexander Mackenzie was on his way to seek his fortune in the virgin forests of the New World.

The Perthshire lad had not embarked on this great adventure from love of fame or conquest; in depression-ridden Britain he had heard tales of better hourly wages in the colony across the Atlantic. He was not casting off his allegiance to his youthful sovereign, Queen Victoria, just three years his senior; he wore proudly the title of British freeman. He was not fleeing his home and family; he had left them with an aching heart. He was not on board the *Monarch* because she was the best or cheapest vessel sailing to Canada; he was aboard because he was in love and his sweetheart was there.

To Alexander Mackenzie the quiet, fertile little valley of the Tummel and Tay rivers in the Perthshire Highlands was home.[1] Three generations of Mackenzies had been born and grown up there since his great-grandfather Donald came down from Ross-shire and settled at the foot of the Pass of Killiecrankie over a century before. His peaceful migration had been in marked contrast to the raids of the marauding bands that used to sweep through the Pass, murdering, pillaging, burning, and carrying off livestock, women, and hostages.

Donald Mackenzie was more likely drawn to the Tummel valley by the rich soil and the prosperous farming community. Finding ready employment, he married a local lass and settled near the spot where the Garry flows into the Tummel. Here his sons Malcolm and Donald were born, here he lived out his days, and died. Grandfather Malcolm was equally sedentary. He obtained from the Duke of Athol, who owned a good part of the land in the area, a lease to the old stone mill of Kincraigie which stood nearby. With the mill went the right of "thirlage", the right to compel the tenants of the neighbouring lands to bring their grain to him for grinding. As payment, Malcolm Mackenzie was to perform certain services for the Duke, and to pay the "Tack" or taxes. Thus he became the district miller and millwright, a respectable and reasonably remunerative occupation that he practised for some half a century.

Alexander Mackenzie Sr., the father of the young emigrant of 1842, was born in the old Miln of Kincraigie in the parish of Logierait in 1784. Like his ancestors for many generations, he learned at an early age to work with his hands. By the time he was ready to practise his trade of carpenter, Britain was again at war with France, her age-old enemy across the English Channel. Tradesmen were needed in the south to make ready the great fleets that would sail under Admiral Nelson and other naval heroes. Stirred by patriotism and the lure of good wages, the young carpenter moved south to Portsmouth for the duration of the hostilities. Only when the battle of Waterloo put an end to the French Emperor's career, and threw the British ship-building industry into a slump, did he return to Scotland.

After more than a decade of absence, it was not easy to find suitable employment in the quiet, rural community. Like the rest of Britain, Perthshire was suffering from the post-war economic collapse. Of an enterprising and adventurous mind, the ex-shipbuilder tried his hand at a variety of activities. He supervised the construction of some manorial houses, took contracts and hired his own men for building projects, and entered into agreements to cut timber on the land of local lairds. In 1817, he was married to Mary Fleming, daughter of the local schoolmaster and clerk of the church.

The children began arriving in rapid succession, and were duly recorded in a notebook entitled "Chronology of Remarkable Occurrences relating to me, Alexander Mackenzie".[2] In

1818 the first son, Robert, was born; in 1820 a second, Hope Fleming; and in 1822, a third, who was to bear his name. "1822 – at Logierait Monday 28th January," wrote the proud father, "Born to me at quarter past twelve Sunday night or three quarters before one in the morning my third son – Babtized [*sic*] on Friday 8th of Feby. Named Alexander." It was a "remarkable occurrence" for the Mackenzie family, but outside the solid grey stone house on the river's edge it caused scarcely a ripple in the placid village life. Nothing indicated it was more worthy of note than any of the other births that occurred at frequent intervals.

Despite his initiative, the former ship-joiner never again attained the prosperity of the war years. Yielding to the lure of distant horizons, he moved about Scotland in search of greater opportunities. When Alexander was three, the fast-growing family was living in Edinburgh. It was there that the fourth son died in infancy, and the three older boys contracted the measles. Hope was so ill that he had to be bled, leeched, and blistered, but Robert and Alexander "got them easily over".[3]

The following year found them in Leith, and in 1828 they lived in both Dundee and Perth. The family was growing at a steady pace. In Perth, Mrs. Mackenzie gave birth to her sixth son in a row. To simplify the problem of accommodation and relieve the financial strain, the two eldest of the "bairns" were sent back to the valley to stay with their aunt, Anne Fleming, on the modest estate of Cluny. There they were "to attend school and learn the galic".[4] Alexander remained with his mother, the babies, and the family furniture.

When the seventh son arrived in 1830, the Mackenzies were back at the foot of Killiecrankie. At forty-six and in failing health, Alexander Sr. was forced to abandon the quest for brighter fortunes in distant fields. With his remaining resources, he built himself a house in the little town of Pitlochry, a few miles from Logierait. "Removed back to Pitlochry to our new house", he noted in his "Chronology" in October of 1829. For little Alex, the return to his birthplace was a happy event. Nearly eight years old, he could appreciate the freedom of country life, far from the cramped quarters and dirty streets of the towns through which they had passed. If he did not know many of the people in the valley, most of them knew him. The area abounded with relatives and friends of the family. Grandfather Fleming was dead, and buried in the Logierait graveyard, but Grandfather Mackenzie, well over eighty years old, and grey and wrinkled with age, was still alive. He had a seemingly inexhaustible fund of stories of life in the old mill and the history-rich countryside around it. Many of the tales of the mill inspired more fear than affection. Alexander became convinced that it was haunted by ghosts, and always went by it on a dead run with the terrifying feeling that a swarm of sheeted creatures was about to swoop down and carry him off to horrible tortures.

Other stories of the area were hardly less blood-chilling. The name "Logierait" was Gaelic for "the hollow of the fortress", and was a seat of justice when the Dukes of Athol reigned supreme in that part of the country. One small elevation in the village was known as "Gallows Hill", and it was there that harsh justice was meted out to offenders against the law. In fact, the house where Alexander was born stood on the very place where the prisoners used to pause and say goodbye to their loved ones. It was for this reason that it was known as "Clais-'n-deoir", the "Hollow of Weeping". One of the most stirring epics of the valley's past was the famous battle of Killiecrankie that took place at the foot of the Pass in 1689. Every youth in the area knew before he could read about it in the history books that Viscount Dundee had placed himself at the head of the Jacobites who were attempting to put the Catholic Stuarts back on the throne. The royalist forces under General Mackay had met him at the foot of the Pass and half of the royalists had been killed. The battle was lost, but the "Deil of Dundee" had been slain as well, and that was a great victory. As a direct consequence, "popery" was soon eradicated from Scottish soil.

Like all healthy young boys, the Mackenzies were full of fun and mischief. Fifty years later Alexander could still identify the cherry tree from which he had fallen as a lad when trying to make off with some of its fruit; he could also recall the punishment he had received for the damage done to his jacket in the process. The new-found freedom of rural life did not extend to the classroom. The school was a one-room structure with thick stone walls, situated beside the church at Moulin about a mile from Pitlochry. To the pupils it seemed ageless. One part of it extended into the graveyard, where the accumulation of bodies throughout the centuries had raised the level of the ground several feet. As a result, the back windows of the school were half covered by the soil, and a rich growth of grass and flowers beckoned to them as they sat on their hard benches. To Alexander, the building looked as though it had stood there since the flood, and might have been used by Noah and his family.[5]

The schoolmaster, Mr. Robertson, ruled with a stern discipline reminiscent of the earlier Athols. An adept at handling the tawse, a pedagogue's cat-o'-nine-tails, he brooked no scepticism about his authority or his teachings. To supplement his meagre wages, he doubled as the village watch-maker, and tinkered with his watches and clocks while the children committed their lessons to memory. His secondary occupation did not prevent him from keeping a sharp eye out for the slightest disturbance, and putting an end to it in the most summary manner.

The move to Pitlochry was not quite the end of the aging shipbuilder's peregrinations. Fighting off increasing poverty and ill health, he moved his family a few miles along the river to Little Dunkeld, and the following year to the old cathedral town of Dunkeld itself. It was here, not a dozen miles from the old mill, that he died at the age of fifty-two. Of ten sons, seven had survived to bear his name. The eldest was seventeen, the youngest still in his mother's arms.

Robert, Hope, and Alexander had already learned to work. Robert was apprenticed to a carpenter in Dunkeld, and contributing to the support of the family. Alex had begun earning a few pence at the age of ten by tending the sheep and cattle on neighbouring farms. For three winters he returned to school, but in the last year of his father's life he was obliged to spend his full time in the fields, or at any other occupation that would add to the family income. At thirteen he put an end to his formal education. At fourteen he was one of three full-time young breadwinners with eight mouths to feed.

Young Alexander had not yet learned the proper use of the words "was" and "were", and he was never certain when the letter "i" preceded "e". He had learned no other languages, and spoke even Gaelic with difficulty. Literature and mathematics and science were nearly completely foreign to him. In one field, however, he did have a sound grounding. He was a thorough, practising Christian. He had learned that the church was the keystone of society, and that the Sabbath was truly a day of rest and prayer, to be observed with both morning and evening services. No day was complete without a session of Bible reading, and without the entire family praying on their knees for forgiveness and guidance. Convinced of His indomitable will, the Mackenzies were God-fearing, sober-minded folk.

Alexander reacted well to responsibility. Displaying great energy and single-mindedness, he was determined to bear his full share of the burden of caring for his mother and younger brothers. While Hope followed Robert into the carpenter's shop, he continued to work in the fields, and before long was doing a man's work behind the plough. As the younger boys grew, they, too, were able to contribute to the upkeep of the home. Drawn still closer in adversity, Mary Mackenzie and her sons were a united family and even found time to enjoy happy hours together. Before they were out of their teens, the older boys had climbed nearly all heather-clad peaks within view, including Ben Vrackie, Craig-a-Cruith, Faragon, and even distant and towering Schiehallem. Together they traced and re-lived the Battle of Killiecrankie, and sang the songs of Bonnie Prince Charlie and other Scottish heroes. Ever ready for fun and frolic, Alex proved a natural leader in these excursions and displayed all the mischievous instincts of a lad of his age.[6]

He and his mother had always harboured a dream that he would be able to resume his education, but as long as there were small mouths to feed this was out of the question. Alexander resigned himself to becoming a tradesman, and was apprenticed to a local builder to learn the art of stone-cutting and masonry. Of medium height, lithe, strong, and agile, he adapted well to the heavy work, and finished his training before his twentieth birthday.

Like his father, the young stonemason found himself seeking employment in a time of financial depression. Britain seemed to be wallowing helplessly in a morass of economic stagnation. The beginnings of industrialization had brought more human misery instead of less. Along the Tummel, building was almost completely at a standstill. Anxious to put his newly acquired knowledge and ability to use, he looked about for other opportunities. It was the beginning of the railroad era, and a line was being built along the west coast of Scotland between Glasgow and Ayr. This meant that stone bridges and culverts were needed. Alexander packed his tools and set off for the land of Robert Burns. His initiative was well rewarded. Hours after his arrival in the town of Irvine, he was at work on the railway project.

Burns had been a craftsman in Irvine as well. It wasn't long before Mackenzie was strolling through the streets of neighbouring Ayr, and along the "banks and braes o' bonnie Doon", trying to re-capture the life and spirit of the Scottish bard whose poems every lad his age knew by heart. Life in the humble farm cottage, the hours of monotonous labour in the fields, the frustrations of poverty – these were all subjects he could understand from personal experience. Perhaps he could even understand, if he could not condone, the search for relief in alcohol.

Imbued with a strong social consciousness, it was not long before the young Perthshireman was taking an interest in politics. Like many another youth anxious to make his way in the world, he could not accept without question the human misery and lack of opportunities about him. How was it possible, he and many others asked, that Britain could emerge from the Napoleonic wars as the most powerful nation in the world, and then allow so many of her subjects to languish in semi-starvation? How was it possible that great leaders such as the Duke of Wellington, so adept in war, could not assure the basic requirements of their fellow-citizens: work at fair wages; food and shelter at reasonable prices? Why was it necessary for so many of Britain's fairest sons to seek their fortune in the United States, the former colonies that had turned their backs on the Motherland?

Out of the ferment of misery came many answers, both revolutionary and peaceful. Some sought solutions in the field of trade; others attributed their sorry fate to the greed and lust for power of the upper classes. Some called for a popular uprising; others suggested pleading their case at the foot of the throne.

The largest group of discontented people were the Chartists. They supported a six-point "charter" calling for universal suffrage, vote by ballot, annual Parliaments, equal electoral areas, payment and abolition of property qualifications for members of Parliament. A petition bearing 1,280,000 signatures in favour of these six points was submitted to Parliament, and rejected, in 1839. Throughout 1841 and 1842, a much larger petition was being prepared that would include not only workers but also large numbers from the middle classes. The burgeoning trade unions were giving it their active support.

Within the Chartist movement, there were conservative, moderate and radical groups. In Paisley, not far from Irvine, a Reverend Patrick Bunster advocated a brand he called Christian Chartism. It was this more moderate form that attracted Alexander Mackenzie rather than the violent alternatives of the starving handloom weavers and cotton-spinners in the Glasgow area. He had even some hesitation about accepting all six points of the Charter, and was repelled by the disloyal and unpatriotic utterances of the rougher elements. Of a practical turn of mind, he was more inclined to seek solutions through an examination of the economic factors of the problem.

Ardent and zealous in everything he undertook to do, the young stonemason attended many of the Chartist meetings and took part in the public debates. Always attracted by a good argument, he gradually hammered out a point of view of his own on social, economic, and even political questions. Though not yet eligible to vote, he found himself in sympathy with the

Whig party, and was deeply impressed by the Liberal doctrines of free trade and *laissez-faire*. To him, as to many others, the protective Corn Laws were iniquitous legislation designed to raise the price of the working-man's bread, and to increase the power and wealth of a few at the expense of the masses. Abolition of the barriers to trade would lower prices at home, and give the British workers an opportunity to show that they could compete in the markets of the world.

Chartism was not a movement dedicated solely to parliamentary reform. One of the solutions it adopted to relieve the suffering was to engage ships and send some of the unemployed to the colonies. "Is it consonant with His beneficent purposes", wrote a Paisley citizen in an open letter to the Prime Minister,[7] "that the inhabitants of these Islands shall be cooped up at the rate of 300 to the square mile, and that millions of them, notwithstanding all their energy, skill, and perseverance, shall be doomed to idleness, poverty, and starvation, while it is in the power of the Government of the country to transfer them, and find scope for their exertions and industry in the new and untrodden regions of our Colonial possessions? . . . Yes! the destiny of Great Britain is to be the instrument, under Divine Providence, of spreading civilization and Christianity, by means of Colonization and the Emigration of her Anglo-Saxon children over the whole globe. . . ." They were sentiments in keeping with Mackenzie's, and offered a challenge which suited his inclinations.

This was a point of view shared by the Governor General's Executive Council in Canada. Canadian politicians, officials and agents toured Britain, extolling the advantages of life in the North American colony, and offering reduced fares of three to five pounds sterling to prospective emigrants. In contrast to the inequality and hopeless distress at home, they promised boundless opportunities with millions of acres of land waiting to be settled, and visions of roads, railways, and entire new cities about to spring up in the wilderness. "I will furnish you with mail coach roads, macadamized roads, plank roads, nay, even railroads, from Gaspé to the Rocky Mountains," promised one Canadian Minister, ". . . our frontier towns like Toronto, London, Hamilton and Bytown will prosper . . . our lakes will be covered with vessels, our streets filled with shops, our artisans masters of large establishments (and) then we can speak of rivalry with our neighbours . . ."[8] Beyond the Great Lakes was a vast plain through which the Saskatchewan River ran without obstruction for fifteen hundred miles, said the Canadian propagandists, and was navigable for boats carrying ten to twelve tons. The soil and climate were equal to any in Canada, and coal could be gathered without even a spade. The size of the Russian Empire, which had a population of seventy millions, this great expanse would be lost to Britain if it were not filled soon with loyal settlers.

A good season's work behind him, and a few pounds in his pocket, Alexander Mackenzie was ready to try his fortune across the seas. There was another factor which prompted his decision. In Irvine he had met a family named Neil. William Neil and his eldest son were stonemasons, and his son-in-law was a carpenter. They had befriended their young fellow "mechanic", and offered him the hospitality of their home. There he had met and fallen in love with the seventeen-year-old daughter of the family, Helen. When the Neils spoke of moving to Canada, Alexander was more than willing to go along.

The year spent in Irvine was important in still another way. Young Mackenzie had been shocked and disturbed by the disregard for religion among his fellow-workers. The stern, cold discipline of the Church of Scotland had provoked an adverse reaction among many people, and driven them into revolt against its teachings. This was a serious matter to a young man whose whole life depended on harmony with God, and who continued to kneel in prayer and read the Bible every evening. In Irvine he met a group of zealous Baptists of the Haldane school who were struggling to bring the people back into the sheltering arms of religion. Alexander attended their meetings, studied their teachings, and was baptized again into their community. It was an important decision, and one from which he never deviated. Though he liked to joke in later years that the only real difference was that some people liked to be sprinkled while others preferred immersion, he remained a loyal Baptist all his life.

There was neither time nor money to return to Pitlochry before sailing. His mother and brothers sent him a chest of clothes and other necessities, and he had a good set of tools; any other possessions he would have to earn in Canada. The *Monarch* was more expensive than an ordinary emigrant ship, but the Neils were reluctant to submit the women to the primitive conditions aboard the latter. On emigrant ships only water was provided, and that in limited quantities.[9] It was necessary to take along huge amounts of ham, biscuits, oatmeal, potatoes, and other provisions for a voyage of several weeks. This food had to be prepared and eaten among a crowded mass of seasick humanity, either in the stuffy hold or exposed to the biting northerly winds on deck. Violence and theft were common, and the crew treated the passengers more like animals than human beings. It was worth an extra fortnight's wages to avoid such an experience.

In addition to the seventy passengers, there was a full load of cargo aboard.[10] The hold was stocked with bales of woollens, cottons, linens, some sixty hogsheads of liquor, sixty tons of pig-iron, and fifteen of coal.

Besides his clothing and, of course, his tools, Alexander Mackenzie had a good supply of books in his travelling chest. While the others played games to pass the time, he sought out a quiet corner on deck and absorbed himself in his reading. Some passengers interpreted his love of solitude to shyness or to an unfriendly personality. It was neither. He realized the handicap of his abbreviated formal education and was anxious to take every opportunity to compensate for it. For this struggle he had several assets: a quick, penetrating mind, a natural inclination to get to the bottom of every subject he attacked, and an exceptional memory that enabled him to retain an amazing amount of everything he read.[11] His schedule of study accomplished for the day, he became more sociable, and revealed the warmer side of his character, too often suppressed by his determination to overcome the disadvantages of his youth. In the evenings he joined the group who were singing the Scottish songs he had learned as a lad, and thought nostalgically of home and family receding ever farther beyond the stern of the vessel. Before bedtime, he and the Neils met for daily worship, including Bible reading, prayers, and the singing of hymns.

The first Canadian soil they sighted was the long, low, windswept island of Anticosti at the mouth of the St. Lawrence River. Patches of snow still covered the jagged rocks and weather-beaten trees. It was hardly an impressive sight from the ice-encircled ship, and a jarring contrast to the green fields they had seen as they sailed down the Clyde. Mackenzie remarked dourly that he had seen better heather on the hillsides at home. It was a homesick lad who mailed his first letter back to Scotland from Quebec in early May.

The old French capital was interesting enough. Having read of the Battle of the Plains of Abraham, he was able to lead a group of comrades up the cliff near the site of Wolfe's ascent, and give a vivid description of the decisive contest that had delivered Canada into British hands. Snow still covered the former battlefield, and a cold, north breeze cut through their rough tweeds, but the enthusiastic young sightseer led them on until he had both generals prostrate and dying, and the victory won. While wandering over the historic site, he made the acquaintance of a Scottish soldier who took him on a tour of the Citadel itself. "If ye can imagine the Craig of Ailsa on the banks of a river a mile broad," wrote another Scottish emigrant from Irvine in the same fortnight,[12] "ye may have some notion of it – only it has houses stuck to it like swallows' nests to a wall, and fortifications bristling with cannons to the very top."

After a day's pause, the *Monarch* continued up the river. On either side the tin-covered church steeples, regularly spaced about three or four miles apart, glistened in the warm May sun. From the neat, white farm-houses near the banks, narrow fields extended inland as far as the eye could see. Not a square yard of arable soil near the water appeared to remain untilled, as the French-Canadian settlers struggled to maintain at least a foothold on the great waterway. It was hardly the view the new arrivals expected of a vast, empty semi-continent.

The voyage ended in Montreal on the morning of May 6, 1842. The weather was still unusually cold as the Neils and Alexander Mackenzie gathered up their earthly belongings and left the ship. The young stonemason had sixteen shillings in his pocket when he stepped ashore.[13] The first impressions of the bilingual city were favourable. With a population of some twenty-five thousand, the dock area was filled with jostling men and horse-drawn carts. Montreal had all the appearance of a transportation centre on the edge of a rich and promising hinterland. Above St. Anne's market, a Government agent dispensed advice on employment opportunities. The new arrivals did not have to go even that far for their first offer of employment. Hearing that there were stonemasons on board, some contractors met them at the ship and offered immediate employment to the three men at seven shillings a day.[14] They were canny. If their abilities were so much in demand near the sea, they reasoned, opportunities and wages should be even better further inland. Their inclination to push on was reinforced by the discovery that a large number of the men around the harbour were unemployed. Many were unskilled emigrants who had arrived the previous year, or even earlier. Some had found temporary employment, but had been thrown back on the streets with the arrival of winter, and were wandering aimlessly about in the hope of finding any form of work. The majority were Irishmen who had been brought over on emigrant ships and dumped at the first port of call. A few were hired from time to time to work on the Lachine Canal project a few miles up the St. Lawrence; the others continued to mill around the docks and the market square. It was soon evident to the newcomers that Canada, too, was in the midst of just such an economic depression as they had left at home.

Mackenzie made arrangements with the French-Canadian skipper of a flat-bottomed freight barge to take them deeper into the land of opportunity.[15] Though the Lachine Canal locks had been opened earlier in the month, they took the longer route up the Ottawa River to the little lumbering village of Bytown, and through the Rideau Canal to the new colonial capital of Kingston at the foot of the Great Lakes. If there was no work there, they would be able to move along the shore of Lake Ontario toward the vast unclaimed expanses of virgin soil about which they had heard so much. Seated on their precious boxes and bundles, they had ample opportunity to enjoy the scenery from the low deck. The steamer towing them puffed along at a leisurely pace, stopping frequently for fuel, and to load and discharge cargo. The day of their departure, the weather turned beautifully warm, and they watched the countryside spring to life before their eyes. The small cabin provided shelter for the women against the cool night air; the men wrapped themselves in blankets on the deck. "I never spent such a delightful week as that I spent coming from Montreal to Kingston up the Ottawa River for nearly a hundred miles and then through the Rideau Canal, river and locks," Alex wrote enthusiastically to Scotland a few days later, "we was [*sic*] towed by a steamboat the whole way, and we had plenty of time at the locks to examine the country."[16]

Kingston was a bustling town of some five thousand souls. Situated at the beginning of the Great Lakes waterways system, it was no unusual sight to see thirty or forty vessels, from large square-rigged three-masters to fore-and-aft schooners, at anchor in the harbour. Even with the completion of the Lachine Canal, large lake vessels could not descend as far as Montreal; at Kingston their cargoes were transferred to barges for the rest of the journey. The huge Queen's Wharf was piled high with goods of every description, and foremen shouted and cursed at sweating stevedores as the trans-shipments were completed as quickly as possible. At the other end of the long series of wharves, new keels were being laid in the shipyard, and new vessels made ready to join the Canadian merchant fleet. But there was more. The little town had been chosen recently as the new capital of United Canada. Down on the lake-front, other crews were completing the transformation of the old hospital into the new Parliament Buildings. Everywhere, houses and shops were mushrooming to meet the demands of the imminent influx of parliamentarians and administrators. Despite the depression, Kingston was booming.

Having been in Canada more than a fortnight, the young stonemason was anxious to get to work. Ice the thickness of window-pane covered the puddles on Princess Street as he set off on the morning following his arrival to find a job. A disappointment awaited him. The tools that he had kept by his side during the long journey were not hard enough to cut the stone of the Kingston quarries. The rocks of the Canadian Shield would not be hewn so easily to the will of the immigrant Scot.

To purchase a set of cast steel tools was impossible. "This staggered me a little," he reported to his brother Robert, "but as I had a hammer and trowel with me I resolved not to be outdone, so I commenced builder."[17] Even in his father's trade it was not all clear sailing. The town was crowded with tradesmen and labourers who had converged on the new capital in search of employment, many of them from the depression-ridden United States. As a result, wages were not any higher than in Montreal, and little more than at home. But there was no turning back. He persisted, and two days after his arrival in Kingston he was at work on a new building being erected on Princess Street. His employer watched him for a few hours, and then, convinced he knew his business, left him on his own.

On the whole, Kingston was a satisfactory jumping-off place for the Scottish emigrants. Food was very cheap and they soon discovered that by buying wholesale in large quantities, provisions could be obtained one-third cheaper still. Board and lodgings were expensive, but as long as he continued to live with the Neils that was not a problem for Mackenzie. He soon calculated that a man and his wife could live more cheaply than a single man could do by boarding in a tavern, a heartening conclusion for a young man in the daily company of his bride-to-be. The town itself was as handsome as any he had seen in Scotland, with Mechanics Societies, a Total Abstinence Society, and frequent meetings and lectures to suit the most varied tastes. There were several churches, including a new Baptist church with less than twenty members on Rear Street. The Sabbath appeared to him to be well enough respected, although he found "little true religion amongst the great mass of population".

On the second day after his arrival Alex sought out a friend of his brother Hope. They soon became cronies, and met after the morning sermon on Sunday to explore the area. "I feel very happy till I begin to think of home and its inmates . . ." he confessed to his family. ". . . I only wish Mother and all the rest were out here with me, I assure you we would live here very happy, and if we had some land (as I expect to have soon) we might soon make ourselves independent."[18] It would be hard work, for Canada was obviously no place for idlers, but they would be working for themselves, and "there would be no tax gatherers standing over us thrusting his hand into our pockets."

It was a precious dream; he steeled himself to the challenge of making it come true, of uniting them in this wide new land. ". . . When you are all gathered together under the Maternal roof," the twenty-year-old stonemason concluded his first letter home from Kingston, "and see (as the poet says) the vacant seat, the empty spoon, forget not that there is one of your number (who could duly appreciate the happiness of the family circle) plodding in the forests of the far west. Often am I, in fond, though in delusive imagination, transported among you enjoying the presence of a fond Mother and no less fond Brothers, but I hope we may yet meet in reality once more on earth, and if not, God grant that we may all meet in that happy Land which is the promised inheritance of all believers, and the anticipation of which is the greatest happiness given us on earth."

* * * * *

Once settled into his new surroundings, Mackenzie was able to take a closer look at his adopted land. There were some disappointing parallels with the political situation that had driven him to the New World. Canadians were still struggling to free themselves from the Family Compact, a group of prominent families who passed the reins of office and the privileges of power back and forth within their restricted circle. Professing undying loyalty to Queen and Empire, they had the support of the British Government, which was imbued, in Mackenzie's view, with the same selfish and retrogade spirit. In desperation, some of the colonists had risen in rebellion in 1837, but the uprisings had been suppressed, and the leaders, including William Lyon Mackenzie and Louis-Joseph Papineau, had taken refuge in the United States. The most beneficial result had been the mission of the liberal-minded Lord Durham to investigate the causes of the trouble, and his recommendations for uniting the two Canadas, and introducing responsible government. The union was accomplished, but responsible government was still not a political reality in British North America when Alexander arrived.

The young Scot found two principal political camps in Canada. On the one hand were the Conservatives or Tories, the supporters of the old Family Compact. On the other hand were the proponents of change, who called themselves Reformers in Upper Canada and Patriotes in Lower Canada. The Reformers ranged from radical followers of William Lyon Mackenzie to the moderates led by progressive-minded men of reason and integrity such as W. W. Baldwin and his son Robert. Although a reform-minded man, Alexander Mackenzie was a loyal British subject, and deplored the extremist talk of secession and annexation to the United States. His only desire, he insisted, was to enjoy the full rights and advantages of a British freeman. Certainly, he could have no patience with the Tory leader, Sir Allan MacNab, who boasted in London that spring that he was opposing the introduction of responsible government at every stage.[19] Before many weeks had passed, Mackenzie found that his views were closest to the Baldwin Reform group.

By the time the young stonemason arrived, the Reformers had won a few skirmishes. Governor General Sydenham had introduced representatives of their group into his Executive Council, although he had refused to have any of the Patriotes at the Council table. Under his successor, Sir Charles Bagot, that, too, was accomplished. Two days after Mackenzie wrote his first letter home, Francis Hincks, a dynamic young man who had brought the Reformers and the Patriotes together in a loose political alliance, was named Inspector General of Public Accounts. His campaign for re-election was the first political contest witnessed in Canada by the Perthshire Scot. During the summer, both Robert Baldwin and his French-speaking counterpart, Hippolyte Lafontaine, entered the Executive Council.

The rudest shock to Mackenzie's political sensitivities was the position of the Anglican church as the "Established" church of Upper Canada.* This state churchism was completely contrary to his concept of religious and political freedom. Worse still, blocks of land were set aside for the use of the officially recognized clergy, and payments were made from the public purse to support its activity. One such "clergy reserve" was situated beyond the Parliament Buildings on a choice section of Ontario lake-front. The Church of Scotland had succeeded in obtaining a thin slice of the public monies, but the other religious groups received nothing. As a member of one such minority group, Alexander Mackenzie resented strongly the privileged position and wealth of the Anglicans. He associated them with the Family Compact and the Imperial Government as his natural enemies. Before he had been in Canada many weeks, the young stonemason was an outspoken and highly partisan advocate of the Reform cause.[20]

One of the leading Kingston Conservatives was absent in the Old Country during the first part of the summer.[21] He was John

*Under the Act of Union, Upper and Lower Canada were officially designated Canada West and Canada East, but we have preserved the older designation which remained in popular use.

A. Macdonald, a bright young lawyer of twenty-seven years, with his own law office not far from the Princess Street building site. He, too, was a Scotsman, born in Glasgow, midway between Logierait and Irvine. However, since he had arrived in Canada at the age of five, he passed pretty much for a native. Urbane in manner and dress, he moved in the best social circles of the capital. After a heavy win in a gambling game at the lake-front mansion of the wealthy arch-Tory, John Cartwright, Macdonald had left for an extended holiday in Britain. While the immigrant stonemason struggled to gain his feet in Canada, Macdonald was enjoying Edinburgh society, spending his winnings, and courting the cousin he was to marry the following year. In his absence, a young lawyer apprentice, Alexander Campbell, laboured over the weighty statute books in the Kingston law office.

One of Macdonald's former apprentices had just returned from Toronto and opened an office in the capital. Oliver Mowat, son of a local business man, specialized in legal work that required him to be near Parliament. When the Legislature moved from Toronto, he followed it back to his native town. Neither Macdonald nor Campbell had any reason to be aware of the arrival of a future opponent, nor Mowat of a future ally.

Oliver Mowat's father had earlier contact with the young immigrant. Mackenzie worked steadily at the building trade for a good part of the summer. Most of the men on the site were married, and accepted provisions from their employer's store in lieu of wages, but the determined Scot wanted payment in cash. Every farthing in his pocket was a step nearer the farm he and his loved ones would occupy together. It was a mistake. At the end of the season he discovered that the contractor was bankrupt, and that the promissory note he had in his pocket was just another worthless piece of paper. He had spent the precious summer months working for nothing. The dream of land, marriage, and family reunion, faded.

The story came to the ears of John Mowat, father of the young lawyer.[22] A sergeant in the Imperial army during the Napoleonic wars, he and his Scottish bride had homesteaded on a two-hundred-acre land grant twenty-two miles north of Kingston. However, after clearing a small patch of forest, he had abandoned rural life for the greater comforts of the city, and had become a prosperous business man. As the construction season was well advanced and employment still scarce, he offered Mackenzie and his friends the use of the farm, with an option to purchase it later if they desired, and were financially able. The grateful newcomers accepted. They would still have a piece of property to call their own!

Life on the farm was primitive. The log house squatting in the middle of a two-acre clearing consisted of a single room, eighteen feet long and sixteen wide, and a primitive lean-to about twelve feet square. In a sadly dilapidated condition, it was hardly adequate for seven adults, including two married couples. Still, it was rent-free, and that was a vitally important consideration.

The Mowat homestead was the only occupied piece of land in the densely wooded area. The nearest settlement was the tiny village of Sydenham, some three miles away. After helping to patch up the old house, Alexander hired himself out to the owner of the flour and oatmeal mill there, in order to provide a bit of cash for the communal budget. His second job in Canada consisted of building foundations and chimneys for some employees' homes, and doing various work around the mill. With the arrival of winter, he ceased his morning and evening hikes to the village, and took to the woods with the other men to clear some land for seeding in the spring.

The tragi-comical experiences of the small band of pioneers have been repeated in every part of Canada. Alexander Mackenzie was the only one who could claim any knowledge of farming, and that knowledge was hardly applicable to conditions in the Canadian backwoods. Helen's brother-in-law, Steed, was not only a ship's carpenter by trade but a philosopher by inclination; his contribution toward the economic survival of the group was negligible. Helen's brother was considering a change from stonemasonry to the pulpit, and was more interested in discussing the questions of revelation and the restoration of the Jews than in felling trees. Mr. Neil remained a stonemason, even with an axe in his hand. The three ladies were equally ill-suited to the harsh realities of life on the Canadian Shield.

With all its hardships and cares, it was a pleasant winter. The clearing grew gradually to a respectable eight or ten acres. On one occasion, Mackenzie's pioneering days in Canada were nearly cut short by a falling tree, but he escaped from its path in the nick of time. The outdoor life was invigorating, and everyone was healthy and in good spirits. An astonishing amount of the wood that was felled went to stoke the cavernous fireplace around which they spent the long winter evenings. Reading material was scarce, but lively discussions were commonplace, and lasted often well into the night. The politician of the group, Alex had an "awfu' tongue" as he laid about his adversaries.[23] When the lights were at last extinguished and the embers burned low, he would lie back on his primitive bed, listening to the regular breathing of the other occupants of the room and the snapping of the trees in the cold night air. Directly above him, through the cracks between the rough planks of the roof, he could see the myriad stars of a Canadian winter night.

The young stonemason was an incorrigible practical joker, and the butt of his jokes was more often than not the hapless Steed. To grant them a bit more privacy, the young couple had been allocated the lean-to room at the back of the building. One night Alex stuffed their chimney and brought them coughing and sputtering into the main part of the building. As soon as he could recover his voice, the would-be philosopher launched into a lengthy discourse on the principles of air currents, declaring that it was useless to resist the forces of nature, and they must endure the smoke until the wind changed. The next morning the wind did change, but the smoke still refused to rise. The trick was discovered and the chimney cleared.[24]

Alexander Mackenzie's Canadian farming experience ended with the winter. Funds were needed desperately after the long unproductive months in the backwoods. Said a contemporary: "The land around it [Kingston] was formed whereon to place the wicked for the punishment of their sins."[25] It was not punishment he was seeking; he walked off the farm and never returned. In Kingston the Government was inviting tenders to construct a stone bomb-proof arch at Fort Henry, on the outskirts of town. It was a stonemason's work. He placed a bid and won the contract. In one step he was not only at work; he was also in business as an independent contractor!

Though only twenty years old, he won the respect and admiration of the stonemasons he employed. Clear-cut in temperament and in physical appearance, he knew exactly what he wanted, and could express himself with force and precision. His bright, penetrating eyes, straight nose, and the determined set of mouth and chin, lent authority to his demeanour. Completely devoid of artifice, "Sandy" was, in the words of one of his men, "a clear Scotchman, plain and true".[26]

In addition to being a deeply religious man, Alex Mackenzie was a total abstainer from alcohol. In this respect he differed sharply from the majority of his fellow-workers and artisans. Drinking vied with religion as a solace and a distraction for pioneer Canadians. Whiskey was so cheap that it was often served as a beverage at meal times. Obliviousness to the cares of the world cost less than a shilling. The lad from Logierait did not falter; no drop passed his lips.[27]

As he laboured at Fort Henry, two men arrived in Kingston. The first came from the United States. An unusually tall, broad-shouldered Scot of twenty-five with a lantern jaw, he introduced himself as the travelling agent of the New York *British Chronicle*, published by his father. His name was George Brown. Finding the atmosphere in New York hostile to British sentiments, he was attempting to extend the circulation of the newspaper in Canada, and investigating the possibilities of transferring the operation to the colony. He was pleased with what he found. Many Reform-minded Canadians were anxious to see in Canada a newspaper such as he proposed to publish. Returning to New York, Brown abandoned the *Chronicle* and moved to Toronto. In August 1843, the Presbyterian *Banner* appeared, to be followed several months later by the outspoken Reform weekly, the *Globe*.

Although Brown was unaware of Mackenzie's existence, the other new arrival in Kingston sought him out. It was his brother Hope. Encouraged by the reports from Alex and his friend Robert Urquhart, he, too, decided to try his luck in Canada. It was a joyful reunion. The budding contractor had seen no member of the family since he left Dunkeld at the end of his apprenticeship. Hope found work in his trade of carpenter and cabinet-maker, and moved into the same boarding-house as his brother. Canada was suddenly a less lonesome place for Alexander; his hopes of reunion with the entire family soared.

From Fort Henry or the boarding-house to the Parliament Buildings, the hub of Canadian politics, was just a few minutes' walk. The vice-regal offices were occupied by the third Governor General in less than a year. Lord Sydenham's career had been cut short the previous summer by a riding accident. His successor, Sir Charles Bagot, was lying on his death bed, and Sir Charles Metcalfe had arrived in April to take over from him in turn. To superstitious minds, there seemed to be almost a curse on Reform-minded nominees. Durham had died not long after his return to England; both Sydenham and Bagot were struck down before their work was fairly begun.

The appointment of Metcalfe delighted the Tories as much as it displeased the Reformers. A stern and self-righteous colonial administrator, he had risen through the ranks of the colonial service to the Governorship of India, and subsequently of Jamaica. Those colonies were poor training grounds for a responsible Governor; he had not found it necessary before to accommodate himself to the intricacies of party politics. In

Kingston, he soon made it clear that he did not have the same conception of responsible government as the Reform-minded advisers that he inherited, and that he did not intend to be bound by their advice. Equally sceptical of the ability of the colonists to manage their own affairs, the Colonial Office encouraged him in this anti-progressive attitude.

The delicate balance of interests around the Council table could not long survive such a tense situation. Bagot was not yet dead before Sir Allan MacNab delivered a blistering attack on his Administration, and proclaimed his successor as Canada's saviour. The Reformers replied by flooding the sick room with addresses of appreciation and support. Tension increased when the Orangemen, a solidly Tory organization, prepared their annual July 12 "walk" through the streets of the capital. On the night of the 11th, shooting broke out between Orangemen and Catholics, and a youth was killed in front of the new Roman Catholic Church. Many Reformers demanded that the "walks" be forbidden, and their instigators disqualified from public office.

Alexander Mackenzie threw himself into the renewed battle for popular rights, attacking the "fossil Tories" and the man who found himself recognized as their leader, the Governor General. Mackenzie's bluntness outraged his adversaries. On one occasion, while dressing stone for the doorway of St. Mary's Cathedral, he got into a bitter argument over the clergy reserves. Unable to defeat him in argument, they returned at night and destroyed the blocks of limestone he had so carefully prepared.[28]

The inevitable break between the Governor General and the Reform Ministers came over the manner of making appointments to government offices. Backed by a majority in Parliament, Baldwin and Lafontaine insisted that their advice should be accepted. Metcalfe maintained that this would place him in a subordinate position to the Executive Council, and, worse still, at the mercy of Canadian politicians. On September 30, 1843, the Ministry, with the exception of one renegade Reformer, Dominick Daly, resigned. Unable to form a new Council that would have the confidence of Parliament and still accept his views, Sir Charles governed for nearly a year with advisers incapable of winning a vote from the people's representatives. Descending from his non-partisan pinnacle, he toured the Colony, showering it with pamphlets and letters and denouncing the Reformers as enemies of British Sovereignty.

At a meeting in Toronto in March, 1844, his opponents replied by creating the Reform Association of Canada "for the constitutional defence of your guaranteed and acknowledged privileges."[29] They rejected the accusation of disloyalty, and demanded "the practical application of the principles of the Constitution of our beloved Mother Country". "Not one hair's breadth further do we go, or desire to go", said Robert Baldwin, "but not with one hair's breadth short of that will we ever be satisfied . . . Born under the protection of the British standard, – under the protection of that standard I wish to live and die, and to leave that protection as an inheritance to my children after me."

The list of prominent personalities at the Reform meeting included the brilliant jurist, William Hume Blake, and the dynamic newcomer, George Brown. Alexander Mackenzie read of the meeting in the local press. The construction season of 1843 had been a successful one, but in November the decision was taken to move the seat of government to Montreal. The Kingston boom collapsed. Fortunately there were other works in progress. Down the St. Lawrence near Montreal, the Beauharnois canal was under construction. The general foreman, a fellow-Scot, hired him to set the huge stones that were to form the sides of the lock.[30]

Stone-setting was not the most difficult part of the operation. The gang of workers allotted to him were about as rough and motley a crew as existed in the province. Many were illiterate Irish refugees continually on the verge of open revolt against authority in any form. Beside them were rugged French-Canadians from the tiny farms or the logging camps of Lower Canada, Yankees from south of the border, Orangemen, and United Empire Loyalists. To avoid clashes, Mackenzie divided them into two groups along religious lines. It was of little use. Fights broke out continually, one so serious that a company of soldiers had to be sent from Montreal to restore order.

Some two months later, misfortune struck again. One of the huge stone blocks, over a ton in weight, fell on the young stonemason's leg. Fortunately the blow was cushioned by the bed of soft cement into which he was thrown when the block fell, and it was not hopelessly crushed. Nevertheless, the damage was severe. Despite the intense pain, he did not utter a cry as he was lifted out of the work-site and carried to his boarding-house. It was several weeks before he was able to walk; the leg never regained its former strength.

Unable to stand hard labour for a few months, Mackenzie accepted a position under the same contractor as a foreman on the Welland Canal project at the other end of Lake Ontario. The trip gave him his first opportunity to visit the muddy but prospering city of Toronto. An agglomeration of some hundred buildings in 1830, it had grown rapidly to a thriving centre of over fifteen thousand population, with handsome brick houses and shops extending north from the harbour along Yonge Street.

Alex Mackenzie's return to Kingston at the end of the construction season coincided with the October elections. It had been a bitter campaign all the way, with the Governor General declaring openly that a vote for the Reformers was a vote against the Queen. With such powerful backing, the Conservatives won a narrow majority. John A. Macdonald was elected as the member for Kingston.

While Macdonald went down to his first session of Parliament in Montreal, the tradesman took a job for the winter on Wolfe's Island, across the bay from the abandoned capital. During the week he supervised the cutting of stone for use on the Welland Canal; on Saturday night he picked his way across the frozen channel to see Helen Neil, who was waiting in Kingston to become his wife. Such romantic ardour very nearly ended in tragedy. Once he appeared at her door, wet and half-frozen, after falling through the ice in the darkness. He persisted in making the dangerous crossing, but the lesson did not go completely unheeded. The next time he fell through he had a long pole to help himself out of the hole in the ice.

The years of waiting were ended at St. George's Anglican church on March 28, 1845.[31] The wedding could not be performed in the tiny Baptist chapel as the battle of religious freedom had not yet been won in Upper Canada, and the "Established" Anglican Church alone was allowed to perform the ceremony. There was only one part of the Anglican vows to which the twenty-three-year-old bridegroom objected. Neither clergyman, nor best man Hope, nor friends, could induce him to say, "With this body I thee worship." The vow was omitted.

The newly-weds spent the summer at Matilda, near present-day Morrisburg, where Alexander had found employment. It was a happy time, except for a rather severe attack of fever and ague contracted by Helen in the marshy riverside area. When the works closed there, they returned to Kingston. With United States relations still tense and hostile, the Imperial Government had decided to strengthen the defences at Fort Henry and other points along the border. When construction started on the series of martello towers around Kingston, Alexander Mackenzie was in charge of the one being built on Cedar Island. It was a group of his men who tried to cross the bay to their families one stormy Saturday night in an overcrowded boat, and were thrown into the lake a short distance from shore. Seventeen drowned, leaving seventy-two children fatherless and destitute. The scene of the tragedy was re-named Deadman's Bay.

Mackenzie, too, crossed the bay at every opportunity. Helen was expecting her first baby in June. Her pregnancy was complicated by recurring attacks of the previous summer's illness, so severe that she required medical attention. Ironically, the doctor who attended her suffered from another early Canadian malady, drunkenness, which the Mackenzies held in such horror and disgust. The baby was safely delivered, but the excessive doses of calomel that had been administered left the young mother's health permanently impaired.

Relegated to the status of just another provincial town, Kingston was no longer the ideal place for a group of ambitious immigrants to seek their fortunes. While Alexander laboured on the Cedar Island tower, Hope and Steed set off on a reconnaissance trip to the west. One of the ships that called regularly at Kingston came from the extreme limit of Canada, the frontier town of Port Sarnia, near the base of Lake Huron. It was operated by a dynamic Lanark-born Scot named Malcolm Cameron. The tales of Cameron's accomplishments in the far west were almost legendary. Among his many enterprises was a burgeoning ship-building industry. Steed was already a qualified ship's carpenter, and Hope was willing to try his hand at a trade his father had practised during the Napoleonic Wars. Shortly after their arrival at Sarnia, they signed contracts with Cameron and went to work.

Alexander and Helen followed in the summer of 1847. After the completion of the martello towers, he had found work on the Montreal harbour basin, but Helen was not well enough to accompany him. In May, their daughter fell ill and he returned to his wife's side.[32] After the baby died, they decided to follow the migration west.

The Port Sarnia area had vast potential. Situated beside the St. Clair River, it was on the water route between Lake Erie and Lake Huron. Across the river was the busy little American town of Port Huron, Michigan. The hinterland was a treasure-house of the richest lowland soil and magnificent stands of hardwood timber. In 1807, a small French-speaking settlement had been founded there, but it was not until 1832 that the first English settler arrived. He was Lieutenant Vidal, formerly of the Royal Navy. A year later, Malcolm Cameron arrived. The town was built on the original farms of the two men.

A man of energy and vision, Cameron divided his land into lots and started a campaign to bring in the sturdy Scottish farmers from his native Lanark. The swamps of the west, he argued with justice, offered a brighter future than the rocks of the Canadian Shield. Expanding his activity, he acquired large tracts of land and timber, and entered the lumber business. On the banks of the St. Clair he built his sawmills. To grind the grain grown on the tiny clearings in the forest he brought in a flour mill. To move the produce of field and forest he built ships. To supply the needs of the community, he built a store. By 1847, he was the undisputed ruler of the bustling outport.

The Mackenzies found a town of several hundred souls, and thread-like wagon roads leading to small clearings and farmsteads farther inland. A stage route to London was under construction through the dense forests and swamps, but in the meantime the only means of communication with the outside world was the steamship service down the St. Clair to Windsor and points east. Spiritual needs were well provided for. There were Presbyterian, Anglican, Methodist, and Roman Catholic churches in town, and a Baptist place of worship a few miles inland.[33]

As in most frontier towns, liquor and passions ran freely. Cameron was trying to control at least part of that situation as well. He founded a Temperance Society, and led the struggle to combat heavy drinking in his realm. His political influence was even stronger. A Reformer, like so many Scots, he had represented Lanark for twelve years in the Legislative Assembly, and served as Inspector General of Revenue under Sir Charles Bagot. The year the Mackenzies arrived, he decided to consolidate his interests by running in Kent county, where Port Sarnia was located. He crushed his Conservative opponent by more than two to one.

With its Scottish leader, religious overtones, temperance movement, Reform inclinations, and an undoubted economic future, the little town on the St. Clair had much to recommend it to the energetic stonemason. He decided to make it their home. Having several years of practical experience behind him, he set himself up as a building contractor and prospered. By the end of the first summer, he and Hope had saved enough money to make a precious dream come true. With their pooled resources, Hope sailed for Scotland to bring out the rest of the family.[34] Although Robert had steady work in Edinburgh, he soon agreed to the plan. The others were not more difficult to persuade. Disposing of their fixed possessions, the mother and six brothers sailed from Glasgow in October. With them was Hope's new wife, Vera, to whom he had become engaged before he left for Canada in 1843. When they arrived in Sarnia at the outset of winter, Alexander had their new home ready for them. They had come to stay.

CHAPTER 2

"Heelanders" on the St. Clair

Port Sarnia rewarded well the confidence placed in her by the immigrant Scots. They found abundant work and prospered. Robert and Hope opened a carpenter and cabinet-maker's shop on Front Street; James found work as a carpenter as well; John as a tin- and copper-smith; and Adam as a druggist. Charles, the youngest of the seven, had interrupted his apprenticeship in the tin- and copper-smith trade to follow the rest of the family to Canada. Just fourteen, he drove a water cart between the river and the centre of the town for a few months, then was sent to Toronto and apprenticed to the *Globe* to become a printer. The work and the distance from home displeased him, and he returned to Port Sarnia to continue his first calling under the guidance of his twenty-year-old brother, John.

Alexander succeeded best of all. From modest beginnings such as the Episcopal Church he constructed in Port Sarnia in 1848 for seven hundred and sixty-six dollars, he expanded to bigger projects.[1] He built the first Bank of Upper Canada in the busy frontier town, the court-house and gaol in Chatham and Sandwich, the county buildings when Port Sarnia became the seat of Lambton County. From Lake Erie to the shores of Lake Huron, the solid, flat-roofed brick and stone structures marked his progress. He built well; over a century later, some were still in use.* Life on the St. Clair was far from dull. Still trying to continue his education, the energetic contractor read voraciously. During the long winter evenings, or in brief hours of respite from other activities, he abused his eyes unmercifully in the quest for knowledge. The classics of English literature, historical works, philosophic, scientific, and political treatises – he

*In 1959, a resident of Sarnia remarked, in commenting on a rumour that the old gaol was to be torn down: "What foolishness! Alex Mackenzie built it over a century ago and no one ever got out of it yet!"

studied them all, and retained an amazing amount of what he read. In addition, he took an active part in the work of local organizations, such as the Temperance, St. Andrew's, and Debating Societies, and even ran for municipal office on a prohibitionist ticket. It was his only personal defeat at the polls.

Whenever possible, he and a comrade walked eight miles into the country on Sunday to worship with their fellow-Baptists. After the service, a local Scottish farmer, Robert Sym, who had moved from Lanark under the influence of Malcolm Cameron's persuasive tongue, offered hospitality to the members of the little congregation. Helen's health did not allow her to make the excursions with her husband. In their second summer in Port Sarnia, she gave birth to another daughter, who was baptized Mary, after Alexander's mother. In the spring of 1850 a son was born; he survived only a brief four months.[2]

Like most western Canadians, the Mackenzies followed political events through the *Globe*. George Brown had succeeded in expanding his newspaper into a tri-weekly, and supplementing it with a special western edition aimed at rural readers. Fearlessly outspoken, he waged constant war on all who disagreed with his views. Although he declared "the limited Monarchy of Great Britain is the best system of Government yet devised by the wisdom of man," he denounced Metcalfe and his Ministers for refusing to practise the system in its full sense.[3]

Alexander Mackenzie was an ardent *Globe* reader. When his work took him away from home, he made sure that every issue was kept for his return. He shared Brown's confidence in the supremacy of British institutions, and his view that Britons must be free, whether they lived on the fringe or at the hub of the Empire. He approved of the *Globe*'s crusade for responsible government, religious and civil liberty, and separation of church and state.

Down in Montreal, the political pendulum was swinging in favour of the Reformers. In 1847, the new Governor General, Lord Elgin, veered away from the old Family Compact and brought the more moderate Conservative, John A. Macdonald, into the Cabinet. When the 1847-8 year's-end election gave the Opposition a clear majority in both Upper and Lower Canada, Elgin formed a new Executive Council, which included Baldwin, Lafontaine, Hincks, and Blake. Malcolm Cameron, returned for Kent constituency, became Assistant Commissioner of Public Works.

It was the Tories' turn to abuse the Queen's representative. They resented his signature on legislation passed by the Reform majority to curb the Orange Societies, and to free the University in Toronto from the control of the Anglican Church. They were outraged when he signed the Rebellion Losses Bill in 1849, thus authorizing compensation to Lower Canadians for losses incurred during the uprising of the 1830's such as Upper Canadians had received a few years earlier. Conservative spokesmen maintained that former rebels would be paid for damage they themselves had caused by the revolt against Imperial authority. After the Bill was passed, words gave way to action. Lord Elgin was stoned, rotten-egged, and narrowly avoided being almost beaten. He remained firm. In his view, it was not too great a price to pay for responsible government. In a frenzy of frustration, a Tory-led mob set fire to the Parliament Buildings and burned them to the ground. In Toronto, the homes of Baldwin, Blake and Brown were attacked, and their owners burned in effigy.

In Kingston, an association known as the British American League met and gave expression to the feelings of the discontented elements in a motley conglomeration of proposals ranging from a protective tariff policy to an elective Legislative Council, from British North American federation to annexation to the United States.[4] An Annexation Manifesto was sent up from Montreal, but John A. Macdonald and others refused to sign, and it was soon abandoned.

The storm passed, and the "Great Ministry" settled down to a peaceful course. By the end of the third session, most of the reforms on which a majority of the Government supporters could agree had been accomplished. The crusade against abuses gave way to the compromises of a responsible administration. As the Reformers moved in toward the centre of the political scale, they left their flank exposed. Ministerial supporters like the *Globe* found themselves harassed not only by the traditional enemy, but also by the radical elements re-grouping round William Lyon Mackenzie, recently returned from exile, and the Clear Grit or Simon-pure Reformers.[5]* Procrastination in settling the clergy reserves question, and the maintenance of a system of separate schools, aroused widespread discontent among liberal-minded English Canadians.

As rigid in his adherence to principle as any man, George Brown clung to the belief that reforms could only be accomplished if the Ministry survived. In his defence of the Government, he soon found himself in open conflict with the Clear Grits,* whom he derided as "bunkum-talking cormorants", and

*The expression "clear grit" may have been coined by David Christie, who told Brown the Reformers wanted no half-hearted supporters, "only men who are clear grit".

with William McDougall, the editor of their new organ, the *North American.* One of his most bitter opponents was Malcolm Cameron, who resigned from the Ministry in a huff in 1849, and allied himself with the Grits.

Stung by the attacks of his fellow-Reformers, Brown decided in early 1851 to step into the political arena himself, and to goad the Government into action within the caucus. William Lyon Mackenzie chose the same time and the same place, the Haldimand by-election, to begin his political comeback. Brown ran as a Government supporter, advocating separation of church and state, a nation-wide system of education free from sectarian teaching, free trade, and reciprocity with the United States. Mackenzie ran on his somewhat romanticized reputation as a man of the people who had dared to defy the authorities. The vote was split between three Reformers and a Tory. Anathema to Catholics because of his outspoken "anti-popery" statements, opposed by the Clear Grits, and even eyed askance by some of the Ministers, the *Globe* publisher met a decisive defeat at the hands of the former rebel.

Shortly after the Haldimand by-election, both Baldwin and Lafontaine announced their intention to retire, and Francis Hincks and Augustus Morin prepared to take their places. Brown's reluctance to attack the Ministry decreased. A few weeks later, a new Hincksite-Clear Grit combination was formed. Malcolm Cameron re-entered the Government as President of the Council, and William McDougall turned the *North American* into the official organ of the Government. George Brown was in political limbo.

Back at his editorial desk, the *Globe* publisher declared his independence, and lashed out with vigour and venom at Conservative and Reformer alike. In defeat, he clung more tenaciously than ever to his principles, and expanded his list of objectives. He declared that the Lower Canadian Ministers were blocking settlement of the religious questions, and condemned Hincks for stating his readiness to join any combination to maintain the union. He called for a re-distribution of parliamentary seats to take into account the new preponderance of population in the English-speaking West. "Party or no Party, Reform Ministry or Tory Ministry," he wrote, "we go for British connection and responsible government. We shall not sit quietly and see the foundations sapped from under the only party honestly working our constitutional system."[6] It was a sentiment that found an echo in many hearts in Canada West. The new Secretary of the Central Reform Association of Lambton, Alexander Mackenzie, heartily concurred.

Like Brown, and an increasing number of other Reformers, Mackenzie was growing impatient with the compromises and manoeuvres going on in the capital. The fact that the local member was one of the Ministers did not prevent him from giving expression to that impatience. The busy contractor owed nothing to Cameron, and was not inclined to accept his domination. His sympathy was wholly with George Brown, and the latter's defeat had been a personal disappointment to him.

General elections were held shortly after the Haldimand contest. Malcolm Cameron announced his intention to run in Huron constituency, another area where he had great interests and influence. Mackenzie and other *Globe* fans decided to defy the Minister, and asked George Brown to be their candidate in Kent and Lambton.

Having burned his fingers in his first grasp for parliamentary honours, Brown hesitated to expose himself to a second humiliation. The name Alexander Mackenzie meant little to him, and the Counties of Kent and Lambton were associated in his mind with the President of the Council. In his reply to the Reform Secretary, he enumerated the reasons why he should not run. Only with the last paragraph did he open the door a trifle. "Notwithstanding all this it would be a high honour to sit for Kent, and it would be a loud testimony in favour of the cause in which I am enlisted were the convention to give me the nomination without solicitation on my part. I fear I would not have the courage to refuse such an offer, were there a likelihood of success."[7]

To deliver the nomination on a silver platter, without Brown making so much as a single appearance in the constituency, was a tall order. Determined to have the *Globe* publisher and no other as their candidate, Mackenzie and his friends fanned out into the townships to collect signatures for a requisition asking him to stand. There was only time enough to cover the area superficially; some of the lists were obtained by passing a sheet of paper from one neighbour to another. Still, the result was impressive and interest was aroused. When nomination day arrived, George Brown became the Reform candidate without having lifted a finger on his own behalf. "Unless some extraordinary change takes place in public matters and private opinion, Lambton will indicate her character," reported the jubilant contractor.[8] But the fight was not yet won. "For all that you would be astonished at the want of principle manifested in many quarters, and disgusted also," he warned.

Brown hesitated. The news from Kent was much less favourable than from Lambton, and there were indications that Cameron was determined to do everything in his power to squelch the revolt. There were other constituencies which might be less risky. He finally decided to go west to see for himself how the land lay. "There will be great opposition against me," he wrote Mackenzie on his return to Toronto. "Unless Lambton goes almost unanimously for me, it will be all up . . . Look at it fairly and if you say so – I am with you."[9] The Lambtonites insisted it could be done. The *Globe* publisher waited another fortnight and then cast caution to the winds. "I will run for Kent and Lambton," he told Mackenzie, "Scatcherd will run for Oxford, and we will, without a doubt, put out the Hyena* . . . Put plenty of work on me. I can speak 6 or 8 hours a day easily."[10]

The fight was on. Mackenzie took charge of the campaign in Lambton, and another Scot, Archibald McKellar, in Kent. McKellar was a stocky, good-natured man with a brogue still broader than Mackenzie's, and an inexhaustible fund of humorous stories to match. Despite his easy manner, which contrasted with the puritan earnestness of the other two members of the Scottish Reform triumvirate, he was an efficient organizer. At one point in the campaign, he accepted an invitation for "Geordie Broon" to stay at the homestead of an admirer. The log building, it turned out, consisted of only one room, with living-room furniture at one end and a row of beds, sufficient to accommodate eighteen people, at the other. As the hour of bedtime approached, the embarrassed bachelor-candidate doubled and redoubled his efforts to keep the conversation alive, in order to put off the dreaded moment of undressing in public. Finally, in desperation, he called McKellar outside, and asked how they were to get out of the predicament. He was told it would be a gross breach of Highland hospitality if he did not stay. They re-entered the house, and Brown, screwing up his courage, according to McKellar's version of the incident, stripped and made a plunge for his bed "so wild and ungraceful that it might be imagined but could never be described".[11]

On the platform, the towering newspaperman was not embarrassed. Malcolm Cameron had boasted that he would give him a "Coon hunt on the Wabash",[12] and would deal once and for all with the upstarts who dared to challenge his authority. Dubbing the President of the Council "the Coon", Brown traded blow for blow at every school-house and street corner where they met. When roused, words seemed to block in his throat for an instant, and then cascaded forth in a great torrent that drowned all other noises for hundreds of yards around. There was an impression of pent-up indignation in the performance.

*Francis Hincks, so called because of his fierceness in debate.

HONOURABLE MALCOLM CAMERON
Canadian Illustrated News: October 2, 1875

No one doubted his sincerity, least of all his travelling partner, Alexander Mackenzie.

For the duration of the campaign, the Reform Secretary dropped all other activity and devoted himself to getting his candidate elected. He recruited volunteers, set up poll organizations, distributed propaganda, and spoke at the public meetings. His efforts were well rewarded. The voting took place in mid-December, and Brown won a comfortable majority over the Tory and Hincks-Cameron candidates. The *Globe* publisher had made his entry into public life, and Alexander Mackenzie had become a person of consequence in the western counties.

Bursting with renewed energy and confidence, Brown returned to his editorial desk and preparations for his first session of Parliament. Mackenzie returned home to a sadder, more difficult role. Helen had never recovered from the overdoses of calomel administered by the drunken doctor during their honeymoon summer six years before. Wracked by pain, her body had weakened steadily and with terrifying inevitability. Nevertheless, she had borne him three children, although only little three-year-old Mary had survived.

As Christmas approached, it was obvious that the end was near. The best of modern medicine and science was unable to repair the damage done, or halt the course of events. The little family waited and prayed. The end came on the fourth day of the New Year. The twenty-nine-year-old widower recorded the event on the back of their marriage certificate. "Our earthly separation took place on the fourth day of January, 1852 at ¼ to 8 o'clock p.m. when my dear Helen was taken home by her Heavenly Father. She was born on 21st October, 1826. She will meet in heaven, her husband Alexander Mackenzie."[13]

* * * * *

Before they separated, Brown, Mackenzie and the other Reformers had decided that it would be advisable to have a newspaper in Port Sarnia to propagate their views. A printer named William Robertson was sent from Toronto to look after the mechanical side of the operation, and the leading Brownite Reformers were to furnish material for the four seven-column pages. In fact, the work fell to the trustworthy Association Secretary, now considered one of the educated men of the community.

The first issue of the *Lambton Shield* appeared from a little office on Front Street opposite Copeland's Bakery, on January 9, 1852.[14] ". . . The *Lambton Shield* will be a constitutional but unflinching advocate of Progressive Reform . . .", the lead editorial proclaimed. It would advocate responsible government "so as to establish and secure civil and religious equality, and the severance of the existing union between Church and State . . . Each man is bound to discharge his obligations to the Church to which he belongs in the same way as he is bound to discharge his civil obligations, and he has no right to put his hand into the public purse to save himself from this obligation . . ." The *Shield* opposed the sectarian school legislation, and advocated a system of free common schools. It stood for free trade, reciprocity, extension of the suffrage, retrenchment of government spending, temperance, improvement of the judicial system, and investigation of the affairs of the Grand Trunk Railway. It declared that its influence would be used "to consolidate and strengthen the party with which we have taken our stand", but confessed that it regarded some members of the Cabinet with suspicion. The best it would promise was that it would support the Administration "in every liberal measure". Brown's first speech in the Legislature a few months later followed precisely the same line.[15]

In addition to publishing the *Shield*, there was a multitude of small tasks of which Mackenzie could relieve the busy politician. A constituency needs to be cultivated constantly in order to keep it fertile and productive of the right kind of votes. Brown's heavy schedule made it necessary to leave that task largely to his friends. The best he could do was to send copies of the *Globe* containing his speeches, and the occasional letter. "Do you Heelanders keep your blood warm on the banks of the St. Clair," he urged Mackenzie from Quebec, where the Legislature was sitting. "I am half a Mackenzie man myself."[16]

One of the most delicate tasks was the handling of patronage. With no personnel officers or recruiting organization, government positions were filled usually on the recommendation of the local member, or, if he was not a Government supporter, some sources favourable to the Administration. Alexander Mackenzie assured Brown that the Committee was "alive and ready for action".[17] The newspaperman was not at all certain that his recommendations would be accepted by Ministers he had designated with such uncomplimentary titles as the "Hyena" and the "Coon". His support might even do harm. Still, "if the county member's nominee is *the right man*", Brown wrote in early September of 1852, "it is hard to resist his application – and we must try to have always the right man".[18] He was not averse to following the recognized practice of giving first consideration to political friends, and was willing to receive names from the Reform committee. ". . . I go dead for getting every office for Reformers – especially *Brownies*. But we must not forget the public interest. Where a man is decidedly better for the office even the Brownies should go to the wall."[19]

No public man ever had a more loyal supporter. Alex Mackenzie covered the county from one end to the other, singing

Brown's praise and arguing their common causes. After labouring on his construction projects during the day, he exchanged the hammer and chisel for the editorial pen in the evening. His style was clear, precise, and matter-of-fact. He aimed straight at his target and there was plenty of muscle in the blows. His motto was blunt and fearless:

> "With or without offence to friends or foes,
> I sketch your world exactly as it goes".[20]

Besides "shoaling" petitions and arguments on the *Globe* publisher for use in debate or in his columns, Mackenzie spurred him on with declarations of loyalty and support. In mid-1853, he ridiculed Cameron's boast that Brown was "a used-up man in Kent and Lambton".[21] "A public reception now . . . would be more enthusiastic than even the last if that were possible . . . As old Mr. Watson said one day to me lately, 'I could not tell you how proud I feel that we have such a member, the only honest consistent man in the house!' So they all feel . . . I feel fully as proud as anyone."

There was one major difference between Mackenzie's letters and the general run that Brown received. Most coupled their assurances of support with requests for favours; he asked only to serve. "I have been afraid that political life may have proved a burden to you financially," he sympathized in one letter, "but you must not let that trouble your mind . . . Christians will feel it a duty and a privilege to sustain truth and righteousness . . ."[22] In the envelope he enclosed five dollars from the sale of memberships in the Reform Association. Two were from himself.

Despite his many activities, the young contractor still hiked to the little Baptist community east of town as often as possible. In addition to their common origin, politics, and religion, he had now something more in common with Robert Sym, his host after the Sabbath service. They were both widowers. Mrs. Sym was dead and the eldest daughter, Jane, had assumed the heavy responsibility of looking after the household and caring for the rest of the children. A short, slight girl, her appearance and demeanour already bore evidence of the hard labour that seemed her lot in life. However, she went about her daily tasks with a quiet cheerfulness that struck a responsive chord in the young contractor, as he recalled the loss of one of his own parents in his youth. His admiration for the dutiful young girl grew to affection, and from affection to love. On June 17, 1853, she became his second wife.[23]

The career of the *Lambton Shield* was a brief and stormy one. As the months passed and no satisfactory legislation was introduced on the clergy reserves, the university, and other issues, the paper became increasingly outspoken. Not a man to use a feather if a sledge-hammer would be equally effective, Mackenzie was soon in open opposition to the Reform Ministry. To Malcolm Cameron it was an intolerable affront to have such Brownite propaganda appearing in his own back yard. In late 1853, he persuaded J. R. Gemmill, publisher of the *Lanark Observer*, to transfer his operations to Sarnia and set up in opposition to the *Shield* as the *Sarnia Observer*.* Backed by Cameron's wealth and prestige, and the printing contracts at his disposal, Gemmill was in an excellent position to compete with a part-time editor operating with one paid employee. And Robertson, it turned out, was a drunkard.

Gemmill launched his attack at once. "The *Shield* honours us with a kind of left-handed compliment . . . aimed at the character of the Proprietor of the *Observer*", he wrote in his first issue. ". . . It is an old saying . . . 'you can't expect anything from a sow but a grunt!' Our friend can therefore grunt on!! He is scarcely worthy of any other notice."[24] The battle was on.

Malcolm Cameron had further arms at his disposal. The *Shield* had reproduced an article from another newspaper alleging that an ex-member of the Baldwin-Lafontaine Government had received a petition for some seventeen thousand acres of marshy land in a certain township in western Canada, that he had pocketed the petition and applied to the Government for the land in his own name, along with a grant for drainage expenses. The Commissioner of Crown Land was supposed to have opposed the application and to have been so annoyed at the insistence of his colleague that he had threatened to resign. He had, in fact, resigned shortly afterwards. "The Minister who thus acted so corruptly," said the article, "is one of the leading men of Hincks administration!!"

The *Shield* published the article with a short footnote. " 'The certain township', we have reason to believe, is situated in the County of Kent, the Minister applying for the land was then connected with that County, the 'ex-member of Mr. Baldwin's Government' was, in all likelihood, Mr. Price himself, at least so *we guess*. The story is no new one to many in the west. Ed. *Shield*."[25] The implication was obvious. Cameron sued for libel.

Mackenzie put on a bold front, and condemned the suit as a "miserable exercise of personal malice".[26] With regard to the thousand-pound claim for damages, which he termed "the pre-

*In the initial period called the *Lambton Observer*.

cise value of the Hon. Malcolm Cameron's character", he teased the Minister for being too modest. ". . . We declare upon the gospels we believe he has made at least three times that sum by his character since 1851! . . ." In private it was a very different matter. He confessed to Brown that he was worried, and asked if the Honourable J. H. Price could be made to appear at the trial to prove the statement about the marsh lands. "If *proof* can be had I will walk into Malcolm as I have never done yet," he wrote the *Globe* publisher vengefully, ". . . a triumph on my part *will finish him*". [27] Brown was reassuring. "I do not see that you run any risk in the matter," he replied.[28] Mr. Price would bear him out, and it would not even be necessary to call other witnesses.

The trial was held on a fine spring Saturday in April, 1854.[29] Three Ministers or former Ministers, Baldwin, Price, and Merritt, were on hand as witnesses; over five hundred spectators gathered to see the fun. The *Shield* editor had thought of pleading his own case, but changed his mind in view of his limited legal knowledge, and hired three lawyers as counsel for the defence. Fate was not on his side. When the trial opened, his main lawyer, a Mr. Vankoughnet of Toronto, was nowhere to be seen. Only afterwards was it learned that he had been delayed in Hamilton. The next lawyer stepped into the breach. He pleaded that the statements were true, and that it was for the public good that they should be known. To prove their veracity, he explained, the defence had planned to call on certain members of the Executive Council. However, they had learned for the first time half an hour earlier that the Ministers considered themselves bound by their oath of office not to divulge what had taken place in the Council Chamber, and he wished the judge to decide the point. Price appeared on the witness stand and confirmed that he and his colleagues refused to break their vow of Cabinet secrecy. He was on solid ground. Even if he had not been, he had no inclination to harm his former colleagues for the sake of saving a henchman of Brown, who had made his life so uncomfortable in the Legislature and through the press. Justice Draper, a former Conservative Cabinet Minister, agreed with Price's stand. The ground taken by the defence collapsed under their feet. The jury returned a verdict of twenty pounds in Cameron's favour.

The *Shield* editor was furious. "Mr. Mackenzie immediately paid over this valuation of Mr. Cameron's character to his Counsel," he reported in the next edition of his paper.[30] The concluding portion of the report of the trial was almost as libellous as the one that had brought him into court. "Price told me if he'd been consulted he'd have advised to settle . . ., implying very distinctly he *never was* asked about it," Mackenzie grumbled to Brown. "It is very clear that Price was willing to injure Cameron by circulating the story but only in the dark. How he could act in such a manner is more than I can understand. He told you 'it is all true and more' except as to the quantity of land. It was a real blessing he did not have to give evidence *on oath*. . . ." That Brown might have exaggerated in reporting the statement was beyond belief; Mackenzie had placed the Toronto newspaperman on too high a pedestal to doubt his word or his judgment. "I believe I have succeeded in my article on the suit to clean myself and keep C. pretty dirty," he assured his friend ". . . Above all your name never appeared . . ."[31]

The fine and the jury's condemnation were not so serious. A good portion of the Upper Canadian newspapers had come to his defence with strong articles on the freedom of the press, and the iniquities of politicians. More important were the costs of the trial, which had to be borne by the loser. His pride at stake, Mackenzie insisted on paying the whole six or seven hundred dollars himself. It was a large sum just six years after his arrival in the west, as much as the entire cost of the Episcopal church that he had built in 1848. It would take some scraping, but he would not allow anyone else to pay for his mistakes. However, the *Shield* would have to be stopped. "I can not keep it up any longer with such a contemptible wretch as Robertson to deal with," he told Brown a few days after the trial. ". . . I am of the opinion still that the stoppage will do us harm but I cannot keep it on. R. won't walk a step or say a word to get subscribers or do anything. He tells me if you pay me I will print. On this system *I have printed* all winter at a cost out of my own pocket of $172. I know a good hand could make it pay, but it is not my professional business.[32]

The valedictory issue of the *Shield* was published in early May. "We suffer peculiarly from our outspokenness," stated the lead editorial. ". . . However, we leave the profession as we entered it, with clean hands, and it was not because we had not the opportunity to follow an evil practice that we kept our hands clean in the management of a public journal. We deemed it a sacred duty to seek no man's favour or to be regardless of any man's frown."[33]

The victorious *Observer* could not resist a final parting blow. "Died the death of a rattle snake – stung itself to death", it crowed.[34] The *Globe* was suitably complimentary, as were many other Reform-minded papers. William Lyon Mackenzie, veteran of many a battle of the quill, not to mention the spoken word and the sword, was highly eulogistic. "One word about the man who penned the above noble sentiments," he wrote of the last *Shield* editorial in his own newspaper, the *Weekly Message*. "His name is Alexander Mackenzie, by birth a Scotchman, and by trade a labouring mason. He is every whit a self-made, self-educated man. Has large mental capacity and indomitable energy."[35] He took the time to write a sympathetic letter from Quebec to the retiring editor:

> I see you are a Scotsman and I fear that you have been sacrificed. For many years the knaves in authority in this infant colony harassed me, almost to death, with libel suits. The first grey hair that I ever saw in my own head was when preparing to defend, without legal aid, a heavy civil action for libel. I merely write because I cannot call upon you, to express good-will and sympathy, and to express a hope that when the elections come you will stir yourself up to return capable and honest men – so that tho' we be working apart we may be working for one and the same good object.
>
> The Hincks-Elgin-Cameron gov't sent us summarily to the right about yesterday. Now is the time to work.
>
> Your faithful admirer,
>
> and I wish I might be permitted to add – friend,
>
> W. L. Mackenzie.[36]

The "right about" was a snap election. The Government had put off calling Parliament for one day short of a year, the legal limit between sessions. When the members met, settlement of the clergy reserves question, and the equally thorny problem of abolishing the seigneurial system in Lower Canada, was nowhere in sight. Attacked by the Tories under MacNab and his chief lieutenant John A. Macdonald, by Brownites, by Lower Canada Liberals or "Rouges", by Clear Grits, and by William Lyon Mackenzie, the Ministry was defeated twice in the first week of the session. They dissolved the House and went to the country.

The news took Canadians by surprise. Politicians scurried to prepare for the struggle. For Mackenzie and his friends, the situation was serious. Lambton had just been separated from Kent, and made a constituency in its own right; Malcolm Cameron, buoyed up by his victory in the libel suit, was returning home to claim the ground as his own. Since the 1851 election three years before, George Brown had scarcely appeared in the county; there was much work to be done. "You must be here every day M. Cameron is," his chief organizer warned.[37] The Central Reform Committee sprang into action, collecting signatures for requisitions and arguing the Brownite cause. The Orangemen refused to allow their names to appear on a list, but promised their votes if no Tory candidate appeared.

It was a two-way fight between the dynamic Reformers. Both were capable men, and their political futures were at stake. The bitterness of the intra-party struggle, culminating in the libel suit, had brought personal animosities to a white heat. Politics was on everyone's lips. The *Observer* insisted until the morning of the nomination that the *Globe* publisher would not have the courage to appear. Mackenzie and his associates, operating without the advantage of a local newspaper, insisted that he would be there.

The platform for the nomination proceedings was erected near the northern end of the Court House that Mackenzie had completed a short time before.[38] It was a fine July day, and many farmers had left their haying to hear the famous candidates outline their views. Cameron was the older by several years, and wore the dignity of office well, without letting his listeners forget that he, too, was a man of the west. His sentences were well considered for maximum effect; sincerity, abuse, and humour were carefully balanced. His tone was paternal and confident. Despite his urban background, Brown was almost as rough and ready as the farmers before him. Deadly earnest and boundlessly sincere, his righteous indignation at the "sins" of his opponents recalled the scene of Christ driving the merchants from the temple. Every farmer could sympathize as the great arms flailed, and he tried to force out of his throat words adequate to express his moral indignation. Having themselves often failed to find words to express their own pent-up emotions, it was an experience they could understand.

The campaign was short, but the Brownites did their work well. The air was tense around the polls as the citizens of Lambton stood up in turn and called out the name of their choice. When all had spoken, "Sandy" Mackenzie's man was the victor by nearly two hundred votes. The king of Lambton had fallen to the upstart immigrant; the death of the *Shield* was avenged.

CHAPTER 3

Reform Secretary

With Brown back in Parliament, Mackenzie returned to the quieter life of a local contractor. The political causes he espoused were in good hands, the best political hands. For the first time since his marriage a year before, he could take time to enjoy the family life he had missed so much during Helen's illness, and since her death. Jane, unobtrusive but efficient, had taken charge of the household, including wee six-year-old Mary, and provided him with a real home again.

Britain was at war once more, this time with Russia. The causes of the Crimean conflict were somewhat obscure to most Upper Canadians, but that was of little importance; the Mother Country was fighting, and Canada's place was at her side. At a meeting organized by the Presbyterian church, the thirty-two-year-old contractor moved a resolution of loyalty and coupled it with assurances of material and moral support. The Imperial Government was interested most of all in obtaining farm products and other supplies for the troops in the Black Sea area. This new demand for Canadian goods gave further impetus to the period of growth and prosperity the Colony was enjoying. For the first time since the arrival of Mackenzie, the price of wheat rose to two dollars a bushel. Farmers were able to purchase the newly invented mowers to replace their scythes, and oxen were giving way to horses in the fields. The Great Western Railway had completed a line from Toronto to Windsor, and another was under construction through the swamps that would link Port Sarnia to London. Already many Sarnians preferred taking the boat to Windsor to catch the train, rather than endure the eighteen- or twenty-hour ordeal bouncing along the London Plank Road in the horse-drawn stage coach.

The economic climate was excellent for a contractor, and Mackenzie worked hard at his trade. The solid, functional, brick homes, rapidly becoming his trade-mark, were in great demand by newcomers and older residents alike. One he built on the corner of Cromwell and Christina streets for his own little family. When the municipal elections came around, he helped Hope into the Mayor's chair; he himself continued to build.

The Hincks-Morin Government lasted four days in the new Parliament, and was then replaced by a Liberal-Conservative combination under MacNab and Morin. The real power behind the throne was the Attorney General West, John A. Macdonald, soon to be joined by the dynamic, terrier-like Georges-Etienne Cartier. Occasionally the names of the front men changed; but the Kingston lawyer's influence remained and grew. Brownites, Clear Grits, Rouges, and the irrepressible William Lyon Mackenzie, found themselves side by side in opposition.

Disillusioned with Canadian politics, Francis Hincks accepted a position as a British Governor in the West Indies. By sheer energy and will-power, Brown became the outstanding personality of the anti-ministerial benches. With reciprocity achieved in the dying days of the Hincks régime, he centred his attack on the clergy reserve and the seigneurial questions. Before these controversial issues were settled, he was already attacking the separate school legislation, and demanding a redistribution of seats in order to provide parliamentary representation according to population, instead of a fixed number of seats for each section of the province. "Rep by pop" was a natural cry for a group of people who paid the largest share of the taxes, constituted the largest portion of the population, and yet saw legislation imposed upon them by the minority. When the Lower Canadians were in the majority in the 1840's, they had made a similar suggestion. Now that the roles were reversed, they saw it as a threat to their institutions, and such strong feelings were aroused that Brown's friends feared for his safety in the streets of Quebec. Even the courageous new Rouge leader, Antoine-Aimé Dorion, was careful not to associate himself too closely with the belligerent newspaperman.

Alexander Mackenzie followed political events with keen and partisan interest. When his work took him to the Windsor area during the summer of 1856, he had the *Globe* and the *Weekly Message* sent to his temporary address. In Sandwich his religious sensitivities were outraged when he learned that in one district there was a separate school but no common school, and the one Protestant child there had to be taught by the Catholic clergy or go without an education. As long as the Ministry depended for its existence on the Lower Canadian votes, there was little hope for a solution to such problems, and still less hope of increased representation for the Reform-minded west. "I thought when we gained so complete a victory in Canada West over Hincks' ministry that a final blow had been dealt at wickedness in high places," he wrote the "little rebel" when renewing his subscription to the *Message*, "but somehow the victory has been sadly barren of results. . . . If this session ends as it has begun I shall become a convert to what I still think an unwise measure, the dissolution of the union."[1]

The 1856 session brought him no hope of reforms under the existing system. It seemed to be a "matter of moonshine", he commented, what men occupied the different portfolios, the result was the same, and a return to Reformers like Baldwin, Cameron, and Price seemed equally unlikely to provide favourable results. "There must be a radical change before we can fairly hope for a good ministry," the contractor told his namesake in June. ". . . all pray for a dissolution. Who can say that a new batch of traitors and hypocrites will not be returned unless some way can be devised to prevent the wholesale system of plundering the public chest?"[2]

There was only one constitutional solution – to rally greater support to the Brownite cause, and win more seats in Parliament at the next election. Already Brown had succeeded in gaining the confidence of some of the former supporters of Francis Hincks, and he had taken over the Clear Grits – with the exception, of course, of the pro-American inclinations of the radical wing – name and all. He had purchased the other Reform newspapers in Toronto, the *North American* and the *Examiner*, and set the editor of the former, William McDougall, to work writing articles for the *Globe*. In December, he sent out a circular letter inviting Reformers who agreed with his views to send delegates to a meeting in Toronto "for the purpose of forming an Association for carrying out these ends".[3] The circular called for representation by population, a national system of education free from sectarianism, and refusal of all government grants for sectarian purposes. There should be uniform legislation in both sections of the Colony, and gradual elimination of differences in local institutions. Constitutional restraints should be placed on the Administration "to curb run-away expenditures and the reckless legislation of late years". The eight-point programme included the adoption of free trade, registration of parliamentary votes, and incorporation of the vast Hudson's Bay Territory west of Lake Superior as Canadian soil.

It was an attractive package of reforms for Upper Canadians.

Even former opponents like J. R. Gemmill of the *Sarnia Observer* were pleased. In a sudden conciliatory outburst, he expressed the hope that it would form a basis of co-operation among all anti-Ministerialists, Cameron and Brown supporters alike.

As Secretary of the Reform Association of Lambton, Mackenzie made certain that a full quota from the county attended the meeting, and worked to have the eight points accepted as Reform policy. Everything went off smoothly; all points were adopted, even the one concerning incorporation of the western prairies, which was not so much a reform demanded by the people, as a cherished dream of the *Globe* publisher and of his editorial writer, William McDougall. To ensure that the gains were consolidated and extended, a "Reform Alliance" was brought into being to replace the old Association that had been formed in 1844, and allowed to die of atrophy and misuse when the Reformers were in power.[4]

Immediately following the meeting, the aggressive contractor organized a "Brown Dinner" in Sarnia to "manifest at once their cordial approval of your entire course in Parliament as their representative, and their indignation at the base – but futile – attempts made by the Ministerial leaders to blast your reputation and thus mar your usefulness."[5] His programme adopted, the Reform leader spoke with still more confidence and vigour. While in the West, he addressed other meetings arranged by Mackenzie and McKellar in their respective counties. In Wallaceburg, near the border between Lambton and Kent, the Presbyterian church was filled to overflowing, and a huge crowd stood outside in the nippy January air, straining their ears to catch every word of the deep rumbling flow of argument echoing through the portals. The meeting in Mooretown, the heart of Lambton's farming community, was a similar success, and the Grit leader was presented with an official request to continue as the local member of Parliament.[6] There was no doubt about it: the West was the hard core of Reformism, and it was there that Brown could find the surest support for his crusade.

Alexander Mackenzie was not content merely to keep the constituency safe; he was anxious to see the anti-Government forces unite under Brown in order to make certain of expelling the "corruptionists" at the coming election. One man who could not be bent to this view was William Lyon Mackenzie, by nature an individualist, by instinct an opponent of conciliation and compromise. His attacks on the new Reform Alliance were taken by the Sarnia contractor almost as a personal affront. Writing "as a sincere friend of yours", he told the eternal rebel that the party had reason to expect better treatment at his hands.[7] "Opposition from Tories is natural, the more the better for that matter but opposition from you is a very different matter and must result in either depriving you of all influence politically, or in killing of a laudable attempt to unite all reformers under a close consistent organization. . . . If Mr. Brown is considered by yourself and the body of reformers unsafe and unprincipled attack him openly by all means. If he is not so considered, ally yourselves with him. For my own part I can say that he has entirely fulfilled all the pledges he made at the two elections here. Like yourself he has laboured unceasingly for the good of the party and the public interest; and now it seems to me quite possible to make our principles and party the dominant party in the state if you and other reformers fall in heartily with us in the recent movement. If this is not done there will be nothing left for us to do but battle against professed friend and open foe alike." It was too late. At sixty-five, the fiery little Scot would heed neither threats nor flattery. A rebel he had lived, and a rebel he would die, even if it meant a permanent break with his fellow-Reformers.

The year 1857 was one of those years known as "l'année terrible". Everything seemed to go wrong. In March, the greatest railway accident to that date occurred near Hamilton, taking some seventy lives. In June a steamer bearing immigrants up the St. Lawrence took fire, and about two hundred and fifty lives were lost. The harvest was only half the normal size, and the end of the Crimean war brought a sharp fall in farm prices. The autumn ushered in the most serious economic crisis Canadians had ever experienced. By the time the first snow fell, business was practically at a standstill.

As they had done since the burning of the Parliament Buildings, the Colony's law makers were still peregrinating back and forth between Quebec and Toronto every four years, alternating the site of the capital between the two towns. The Legislative Assembly finally decided by a small majority to fix Quebec as the permanent capital, but the Legislative Council defeated the proposal. The wily Macdonald suggested leaving the choice to Queen Victoria. From the Ministerial point of view, that solution had the advantage of silencing the Opposition out of respect for the Sovereign, and at the same time enabling him to direct the choice behind closed doors. Despite Reform protests that such a procedure constituted an unnecessary interference by the Crown in local affairs, and was contrary to the principles of responsible government, the proposal was adopted.

Reinforced by the resolutions adopted in January by the new Reform Alliance, Brown returned to the attack. The Government showed signs of weakness at times, but it did not fall; the resolutions for representation by population, separation of church and state, and the other cardinal points in the Reform platform, were rejected. The only hopeful sign for the Opposition was the rapprochment between the *Globe* publisher and A.-A. Dorion, the Rouge leader. An eminently reasonable man, Dorion declared himself in favour of the federal union that was being discussed by Brown and Luther Holton of Montreal, but said he would accept representation based upon population if that could not be obtained.[8]

The 1857 session over, politicians began to prepare for another election. In an attempt to broaden the popular support of the Administration, Macdonald invited into the Cabinet, first Dorion, then John Sandfield Macdonald, a leading Reformer who did not accept Brown's leadership, and finally Alexander Galt, the representative of Montreal's English-speaking business interests. All refused. In Sarnia, a correspondent reported peevishly in October that the Secretary of the Reform Association and a few intimates were meeting nearly every night in Archibald Young's store on Front Street to plot campaign strategy.[9] He suggested that Mackenzie and his friends were scheming to frustrate a movement to work out a compromise that would enable Malcolm Cameron to run in Lambton, while Brown took one of the other nominations offered to him. Having received some indications that Cameron's hostility to him personally was subsiding, Brown was not averse to such an agreement. It would keep Lambton in the fold, leaving him free to win a more doubtful seat, and possibly one to which he could devote more personal attention. Mackenzie was violently opposed.

The Reform Secretary's objections to the former Minister were twofold. He had never endorsed the programme of the Reform Alliance, and he had insisted on judging the Government measures on their merits rather than voting on party lines. To the distrustful Mackenzie, this "loose-fish" attitude was a clever manoeuvre designed to keep the door open for an invitation to re-enter the Council Chamber. Such a consideration was of less importance to Brown. He himself was already counting the Reform members there would be in the new legislature, and envisaging the Reform Council that would cure the Colony's ills. The situation was further complicated by the fact that Brown had stated on several occasions the previous winter that Lambton was too large and too far from Toronto for him to serve adequately, and that he would not be a candidate there again. As October advanced, Mackenzie denied flatly the rumours that the *Globe* publisher would not let his name stand.[10] The Cameronites scoffed at Mackenzie's assertion, repudiated the authority of the Central Reform Association to speak for Lambton Reformers, and issued a requisition asking the former Minister to be the Reform candidate. Only one man could settle the dispute. On November 14, the *Globe* carried a statement, presumably written by George Brown himself, stating that "the matter is entirely with Mr. Brown's friends in Lambton. . . . If . . . they want him to come to the poll at the next election, he will be there." Privately, he was less definite. "If Cameron were only repentant and thoroughly covenanted to go for the points (of the Alliance) and against the Ministry," he urged Mackenzie, "it would be no loss to let him in."[11]

Mackenzie and his friend Archibald Young decided reluctantly to have a talk with the "Coon".[12] Alexander Vidal, son of the naval officer who had pioneered on the town site, negotiated the meeting. Cameron's first reaction to the request for an interview was that he was willing to see Mackenzie and Young on personal matters, but it was useless to talk politics as he was determined not to give any pledge, nor to be questioned on political matters. After trudging back to Young's general store, Vidal was told to reply that there were no private matters to be discussed, but that his views were being sought on public issues. Would he vote for representation by population, and the abolition of separate schools? they wanted to know; would he oppose the ecclesiastical corporations, and cast his weight against the Coalition Ministry? Vidal went back to the ex-Minister again; when he returned a few minutes later, he had Cameron in tow.

Already tense, the atmosphere grew quickly tenser. Mackenzie and Young explained that they wanted to see if the veteran politician's views were "such as would justify us, as a party, in uniting with him, and thereby avoiding a contest". The implication was clear that they considered themselves the representatives of the Reform Party, and the former Minister a renegade. Cameron replied haughtily that he had been twenty years in public life, that everyone knew what he had done, that he would continue to do exactly as before, and that he "had never done anything he regretted in his political career". His interrogators pressed for his views on current issues. There were two versions of what then transpired. "Mr. Cameron then referred to events connected with the last election," reported Mackenzie later in a statement to the *Observer*, "and told us that he lost his [last] election by lies. He told us that Brown lied, that we lied, that it was lies, lies, all over! . . . Mr. Mackenzie here said the whole statement was an infamous falsehood . . . [and that] he would not sit there and be abused in that manner from any man living, and accused Mr. Cameron of continually calling every person liars. Mr. Cameron continued for a moment to remark that they [the Hincks Ministry] ought to have had an opportunity to show their willingness to go ahead with the [Clergy] Reserve Bill – when we remarked that they had already been tried and found wanting. At this moment Mr. Cameron abruptly left the apartment." Cameron's version, carried in the same edition of the *Observer*, was somewhat different. He had agreed to the meeting on the understanding that Mackenzie and his friends felt a few words of explanation would enable them to support him. However, he had hardly begun when the Central Reform Association Secretary said, "It is an infamous lie." "As I have long condemned the brutality of knocking a fool down because he was also a brute and thus putting yourself on a par with him," stated the ex-Minister, "I took my hat and walked out."[13]

Thus ended the negotiations. The gloves-off fight began. Mackenzie reported to Brown the failure of the talks and preparations for the contest. In suggesting the negotiations with Cameron, the *Globe* publisher had said that he still preferred to run in Lambton and that if they wanted him, his address to the electorate would be published at once "and then for a thorough fight".[14] The pugnacious contractor needed no further encouragement. The constituency organization swung into action for a repeat performance of the 1854 two-way battle. "Your late member George Brown, Esquire, will present himself for re-election," he announced in the Dec. 3 issue of the *Observer*.[15] ". . . Mr. Brown will be in the County as soon as possible to visit the Electors. His Address will be published immediately." With evident relief, Mackenzie fell upon his old opponent. "Mr. Malcolm Cameron has commenced to canvas the County as a supporter of the Coalition Ministry," he told the electorate, "he is also the nominee of the Roman Catholics who know that he will uphold the Sectarian Schools now enjoyed by the Romish Church, as granted by the Ministry of which Mr. Cameron was a member. Remember that Mr. Cameron expressly declares that he will, if elected, do exactly as he formerly did; that he justifies all the acts for which you rejected him in 1854 . . . and to crown all he is now the recognized candidate of the present unprincipled Ministry who have, in three years, DOUBLED YOUR TAXES! and brought the whole country into contempt."

Cameron rejected the accusation of being associated with Catholics or the Coalition, but insisted he would oppose or support measures of the Macdonald Government on their merit. He also repeated the rumour that Brown was going to back out of the fight and run in another constituency. He was right. Preparations were well advanced for Brown's speaking tour when the December 3 issue of the *Globe* arrived. It contained a requisition asking the newspaperman to run in Oxford County. Below the list of names appeared his unconditional acceptance. The Mackenzie camp was thrown into consternation; a special messenger was sent to implore Brown to run in Lambton. The *Globe* of December 4 brought still worse news. The Reformers of Toronto, too, had issued a requisition asking for him, and he accepted that one as well! Not a word about Lambton appeared. The Tories having declined to put forward a candidate, the Cameronites rubbed their hands with glee at the prospect of a unanimous decision for their man.

The messenger returned from Toronto, and the Brown supporters had to accept the facts. He preferred to run in his own home constituency, and had accepted the Oxford requisition as an alternative in case the bid for Toronto failed. Girded for the struggle, they refused to accept defeat, and looked around frantically for another candidate. Archibald Young was considered. He had been Warden several years before, but unfortunately he was not well known outside the town of Sarnia. Alexander Mackenzie himself preferred the role of king-maker to king. One local resident with undoubted popular appeal was his brother, Hope. As Mayor of Sarnia until a short time before, he had been so successful that George Brown had expressed the hope of seeing him in Parliament one day.[16] His bland, open face bespoke honesty, and inspired both confidence and affection. Unquestionably upright and sincere, he shared his brother's high principles, but lacked the aggressiveness that made Alexander a precious ally but a bitter opponent. In short, the affable Hope was the better vote-getter of the two. Moreover, he was a widower, and it was easier for him to attend the session of Parliament away from home.*

After the Central Reform Committee decided to run him, Hope was given no opportunity to decline. From the time the requisition appeared, there were but twelve days to campaign. He ran on a strong Brownite line. He condemned the Ministry as "the very embodiment of corrupt and dishonest government", and declared the time had come "when all sound Protestants who value the blood-bought privileges handed down to us by our

*Hope Mackenzie's first wife died in 1849.

forefathers should be banded together to defend them".[17] The first means to that end, he explained, was representation by population.

With two campaigns behind him, Alexander directed the battle, wrote propaganda, arranged polls and speaking tours, and took the platform himself when the occasion arose. For a county where no contest was expected a fortnight before, commented the *Observer*, "in no County in the Province has there been so much done in the way of canvassing".[18] On nomination day, the heat of partisan feeling contrasted with the cold December wind sweeping in from Lake Huron. Hope's nominator was interrupted so frequently that he abandoned his prepared speech, and contented himself with yelling defiantly that the "Coon" could have nomination day, election day would belong to the Mackenzie clan. Two days before Christmas the voters gave their verdict. Cameron was victorious with a majority of one hundred and fifty-eight out of over three thousand votes.

The result was not a total disappointment to the Mackenzies. Running a complete novice in a short campaign, they had given the veteran politician a close race. With a few more days, the result might have been very different. Even Gemmill was treating them with a new respect. He avowed that he had backed Cameron "with all his faults", and warned him to keep clear of the Ministry and conduct himself "as a good sound honest clear Grit Protestant Reformer should and as he did in days of yore."[19] The Mackenzies had lost the election, but won the battle of principle. There was another consolation. The next day they learned that Archibald McKellar had taken Kent constituency.

The election of 1857 was one of the stalemates that led to Confederation. The Clear Grits were undoubtedly making progress in Upper Canada, and three English-speaking Ministers went down to defeat. Brown was successful in both Toronto and North Oxford. Faced with the choice, he declined the latter, but managed to secure it for his editorial writer, William McDougall. In Lower Canada, the friends of the Reformers were less successful. Labelling Dorion as a friend of Brown, and reading long extracts from the "Rep by Pop" and secularization statements of the Clear Grit leader, Cartier defeated all but a handful of the Rouges candidates. The new Legislature was divided more than ever along racial and religious lines.

It was a treacherous mount for even such a dexterous rider as John A. Macdonald to control.[20] With a majority of the Upper Canadian representatives behind him, Brown made every detail a pretext for a full-scale debate. Attacks on election corruption were commonplace. On one occasion, the Opposition kept the House sitting for thirty-six hours merely to prevent Thursdays, normally private members days, being used to discuss Government business. Another sitting lasted one hundred and twenty-eight hours! The cauldron boiled over on the discussions over the site for the new capital. With due prompting, Queen Victoria had been "graciously pleased" to choose Bytown as the future site. "The second worse place in all Canada," thundered Brown, the worst being Quebec. He moved a resolution to cancel the choice. It carried. The "corruptionists" were beaten![21]

The Governor General, Sir Edmund Head, followed the constitutional practice of asking the leading member of the Opposition to form a Government, but soon followed the request with a written warning that he made "no pledge or promise, express or implied, with reference to dissolving Parliament".[22] Having accepted a task, Brown was not the man to withdraw. He decided that there would be time to discuss dissolution or other steps when he was sworn in as official adviser to His Excellency. "A prudent fish will play around with the bait some time before he takes it," commented the watchful Macdonald, "but in this instance the fish scarcely waited till the bait was let down. He jumped out of the water to catch it."[23] The Brown-Dorion Cabinet was sworn in on August 2, 1858. Included in the list of Ministers were the independent-minded Reformer from Cornwall, J. S. Macdonald, Oliver Mowat, and Luther Holton of Montreal. Having accepted office, the new Ministers automatically vacated their seats and had to be re-elected.

With the Ministers watching helplessly from a bench near the Speaker's chair, the House met after lunch to authorize writs for their re-election. It was a routine procedure, but John A. Macdonald and his followers opposed it. With no Ministers to speak for the new Administration, some Reformers convinced that a defeat would lead to dissolution and a new election that would give them a clear majority, and a special Grand Trunk train to bring Tory supporters to the Legislature, the Conservative amendment carried. Brown advised dissolution. Head refused on grounds of cost and inconvenience.[24] The Ministers had no alternative but to resign. The Tory trick had worked! Taking advantage of a technicality that Ministers who resigned and accepted other offices within one month did not automatically vacate their seats, Macdonald juggled the Cabinet posts, then the following day he juggled them back again. To avoid the appearance – on paper at least – of making the "double shuffle" too precipitate, the Governor General met the Conservatives shortly before midnight, swore them into new portfolios, chatted with them until the clock struck twelve, then accepted their resignations and swore them into their old offices again. After being Premier for forty-eight hours, Brown was not only defeated but did not even have a seat in Parliament. The Coalition Ministers were back at their jobs and stronger than before.

To the Clear Grits, the "double shuffle" was another example of Tory intrigue and dishonesty, and the Governor General, who had ruined the Reformers' chances, yet co-operated in Macdonald's adroit manoeuvre, was an "unscrupulous partisan".[25] Like Brown, Mackenzie was convinced that Head was in constant touch with Macdonald during the crisis, and accepted advice from him instead of from his constitutional advisers. "Either the Governor had back-stairs advisers, whom he had consulted and whose advice he followed," he wrote later, "or he had determined from the first that if Mr. Brown should undertake the tasks imposed upon him he [the Governor] would prevent him fulfilling his duty. . . . On either ground the action of the Governor was disgraceful, and manifestly the proceeding of a shameless partisan. . . . The transaction will be ever remembered as a shameful violation of constitutional usage on the part of a Governor General, apparently entered upon for the benefit of the Tory party."[26]

The "double shuffle" was not a complete disaster for the Reformers; it united them in opposition and defined party lines. Cameron-type fence-sitting became almost impossible. In addition, a basis of agreement between Grits and Rouges had been established. When the Ministry was formed, Brown and Dorion had agreed to try to work out a system of representation according to population, with adequate constitutional checks to safeguard the rights of French Canada. On this understanding, six Catholics had agreed to serve in the same Cabinet with Brown, whose name symbolized the antithesis of Catholicism on the St. Lawrence.

Discouraged and disgruntled, the Grit leader collapsed. "I am . . . out of health, worn out, driven to death – I cannot bring my mind to the most ordinary exertion," he wrote to Luther Holton in September.[27] He had not even the strength to go down to Montreal to discuss a memorandum of complaint to the Colonial Office concerning the Governor General's conduct. Instead, he headed west to the St. Catharines baths. For him, the West was the most refreshing and invigorating place in Canada. "You have no idea how earnest and general the enthusiasm is for the Brown-Dorion Government all over Western Canada, west of Kingston," he told Holton, "I have never seen anything like it. Head and his fellow-conspirators are proportionately condemned."

The "double shuffle" marked the final triumph of the Mackenzies in Lambton County. Not even Malcolm Cameron dared defend it, and the *Observer* swung solidly behind Brown and his friends. It was just a matter of time before the County would send a thorough Clear Grit to his side.

* * * * *

As 1858 drew to an end, another item of news sent a thrill of excitement through Sarnia. The new railway line direct from London was to be opened at Christmas time! Gone forever the long, bumpy ride on the stage-coach over the Plank Road! Gone the long detour via Windsor that landed passengers in Toronto at three or four o'clock in the morning! Sarnia was about to be really integrated into Canada! A public meeting was called to discuss plans for a celebration to mark the great occasion. It had to be the biggest event of its kind ever staged. Alexander Mackenzie suggested a mammoth excursion on a special train to London, to be followed by a reception for the Railway Directors in Sarnia. Hope Mackenzie agreed to serve on the Arrangements Committee.[28]

When the first train puffed into the new station on the waterfront the day after Christmas, most of the town's population was on hand.[29] The men waved their hats in the air and cheered, the children clapped and screamed, and the dogs barked at the strange, snorting, black monster. In addition to the locomotive and coal tender, there were only three passenger cars and a baggage car, but to the spectators it was a beautiful sight to behold. When the ticket office opened at six o'clock the following morning, the waiting room was already crowded with people, including several Americans from across the river in Port Huron, all anxious to exchange the $2.37 in their hands for one of the first tickets to London.

Its coarse, metallic whistle in jarring contrast to the shrill echoing horn of the stage-coach, the train moved out of town on schedule at 6:45 a.m. Much of the ballasting was still incomplete, and the engineer moved slowly and cautiously through the marshy lowland. The number of clearings soon diminished, and the heavy stands of trees crowded in on either side of the track. After lunch, openings began to appear again, and families standing before farm-houses waved excitedly as if they were witnessing the arrival of some strange new race out of the depths of the primeval forest. The sun was completing its daily course through the winter sky as they pulled into London at four in the afternoon. Lambton was integrated into Canada at last.

Early in 1859 there was another excursion to London, or as

one Englishman of the period called it, the "burlesque on its namesake". The Sarnia Volunteer Fire Brigade, accompanied by the Port Huron Volunteers, made the day-long journey to visit their fellow fire-fighters at the other end of the line. At their head as they marched through the streets behind the Phoenix Band was one of the best known of their number, Alexander Mackenzie. He was glad to see the rail service established, he told the Mayor at the reception, with a wink in the direction of the Port Huron fire chief; Sarnia was in danger of becoming "Yankeefied" by its neighbours across the St. Clair.[30]

Both Hope and Alexander were moving noticeably to the fore in the western community. Hope was undoubtedly the more popular of the two. He exuded warmth and sincerity, and could create just the right atmosphere of friendly conviviality at a civic ceremony, a St. Andrew's Day dinner, or a church supper. Audiences listened with the same rapt attention whether he sang "Auld Lang Syne" or "Canada the Land We Live In", whether he spoke on the humanity and genius of Robert Burns or the inadequacies of the local garbage-disposal system.[31]

Alexander was certainly as honest and public-spirited as his brother, but his sharp tongue and decided opinions had offended many a lukewarm ally, and alienated many a potential friend. Vitally interested in all that went on about him, he abhorred subterfuge and rationalization. Once his mind was made up on any subject, it took an exceptional man to change his views. When he espoused a public cause or a community project, he applied to it the same energy and keen judgment that had won him such success as a business man. As a member of the Temperance Society, he was not so fanatic that he believed, like one member, that "the man who would sell liquor, would pick the pearly gates of Paradise with a rusty nail and steal the tinsel from the angels' wings"; but he was willing to help to buy up the only two barrels of liquor in town and hold a burning ceremony in the public square. (They wouldn't burn!) He was too good a democrat – though he disdained that word as a symbol of the mob rule and political corruption across the border – to try to impose prohibition by law until a majority of public opinion favoured such a step, but he asserted the right of the majority to close the bars if they chose to do so.[32]

The unschooled Perthshire immigrant was winning recognition in the intellectual field as well as in politics and business. He took a prominent part in the discussions of the Dialectic Society, and was on hand in May 1859 when the young Liberal member of Parliament, D'Arcy McGee, came to speak on Robert

Burns and Thomas Moore.[33] He was a member of the school board, and an ardent supporter of a national university free from religious influence. When he delivered a speech, his remarks bore evidence of an extensive background and careful preparation. In a lecture, "The Anglo-Saxon Race", at the Mechanics' Institute, he showed that he had transferred the proud confidence of his Highland background to all of Britain.[34] In his view, the Anglo-Saxons were a "chosen" people, with a great mission to carry the message of Christian civilization throughout the world. Their capacity for self-government was a superior trait not possessed in like degree by any others, and a "grand requisite for political power". In Anglo-Saxon countries, local government was administered by pen and ink, in others by sword and musket. Public opinion was the ruling power over English-speaking people, and the heads of government were administrators, not despots. No other people had to such an extent God's eternal laws as the foundation of their own. In Britain, the steam-engine and the Bible went hand in hand. There were still problems, conceded the ex-stonemason. Along with their great qualities, the Anglo-Saxons excelled in the vices of drunkenness and prostitution, particularly in the great new manufacturing cities. Insufficient attention had been paid to the needs of the people in these new centres. However, these social problems did not blur the Sarnia contractor's vision of the future. Putting aside old animosities, as the Scots had done in their relations with England, he argued, Anglo-Saxons of the United States and Britain should advance side by side to their destiny, the universality of Anglo-Saxon influence, just as their language was fast becoming universal throughout the world.

Alexander Mackenzie's faith in his people and the Empire was as firm as his faith in God and the Church to which he belonged. It was a foundation for his life more unshakeable even than the sturdy architecture for which he was known.

* * * * *

Back in charge of the Colony's affairs, Macdonald succeeded in having Ottawa adopted as the new capital, and introduced a "national policy" tariff to protect Canadian manufacturers. When he recovered from the fatigue and humiliation of the events of 1858, Brown decided to submerge the representation question in a more all-embracing concept: federal union. The idea was at least a century old. A good many people who studied the map of British North America, and saw the Colonies scattered along the northern border of its great federated neighbour, had wondered why they did not follow suit. Brown, Holton, and Dorion had been discussing the pros and cons of such a move at least since 1857, and Galt, the new Minister of Finance, had introduced a resolution urging federation when a private member in 1858. He had even made it a condition of joining the new Administration that a mission should go to London to discuss the project. The mission had gone, but the British leaders had been too preoccupied with other matters, and it had returned empty handed.

The Clear Grit leader was less interested in a great continent-wide federation than in a constitutional change that would allow Upper and Lower Canada to control their own affairs, sharing only those matters common to both. A federal system would remove friction over local issues, he told *Globe* readers, maintain access to the St. Lawrence, increase the chances of acquiring the North West, and further the Reform aims of cheap and simple government. To Holton he added a further reason: "It will . . . be a tremendous card at next election, come when it may."[35] He decided to call another Reform Convention to have his new policy endorsed.

When the Convention was announced, and talk of another election began to circulate, Malcolm Cameron decided to make a desperate effort to heal the breach left by the last campaign. Caught between Tories and Clear Grits, his only alternative was political oblivion. A meeting of Reformers was called in October, a few weeks before the 1859 Convention. Nearly every adult male in Sarnia attended. Cameron outlined his position, declaring that he was now opposed to the Administration because of its inaction on the representation question, and that he favoured wholeheartedly the idea of a federal union. Hope Mackenzie welcomed the statement of his recent opponent and assured him that as long as they agreed, they could co-operate in serving the Reform cause. The conciliatory spirit evinced by Hope was not shared by his brother. He could not forgive and forget so easily. It was with serious misgivings that he called the Central Reform Committee together the next day so that a resolution could be passed, accepting Cameron back into the Reform ranks "in view of the alarming state of the country, – arising out of the dishonest working of the Union with Lower Canada by the party now in power – and the consequent necessity for an immediate change in our relations with the other portion of the Province."[36] The inference was clear; Cameron was allowed back, but it took a national emergency to do it.

The Toronto Reform Convention, said one observer, was a

political avalanche of outraged virtue unique in the annals of British North America. The five hundred delegates were told that Upper Canada was a helpless victim at the mercy of a dishonest Ministry that maintained itself in office by the "cohesive power of public plunder". "There is no creature more despicable", railed the *Globe*, "than the Western Canadian who at this moment aids the hierarchy and the dominant clique to fasten upon our necks the French yoke."[37] History does not record if John A. Macdonald's ears burned.

George Brown was in control of the meeting all the way. The existing Union was condemned, and with it the "double majority" principle, according to which a majority from each section should approve every item of legislation. The delegates decided to work for a system of two or more local governments, "to which shall be committed the control of all matters of a local or sectional character, and some joint authority charged with such matters as are necessarily common to both sections of the Province." The vague expression, "joint authority", instead of an outright demand for a federal system, was an amendment agreed upon to secure the approval of some delegates who favoured separation from Lower Canada. The wording did not alter Brown's goal for an instant; the "general" government, or "joint authority", would be organized on the principle of representation by population. During the discussions, Hope Mackenzie threw the full support of the Lambton Reformers behind the federal plan, and supported his leader in suppressing a movement in the direction of separation from Great Britain. Separation was akin to annexation, said Brown, and "I have no fear that the people of Upper Canada would ever desire to become the fag-end of the neighbouring republic".[38]

The reception of Brown's resolution in favour of federation early in the 1860 session was disappointing. The Government's supporters opposed it solidly. They were joined by all but four Lower Canadians, and by a group of Reformers under J. S. Macdonald who still clung to the double majority principle.

Against such odds, the federal plan did not have a chance. Intense as ever, Alexander Mackenzie reacted bitterly against the Reformers who opposed the resolution. "I have thought you gave them undue prominence, in fact they were both warmed into life solely by you," he wrote Brown of two of the mavericks.[39] "You are mistaken about Mr. Cameron," he told his leader at the same time. "I firmly believe he is all the time plotting against you in private and pretending to work with you in public, and I entreat you to keep him at arm's length." The other party members could do what they liked; he and his friends would not support the "Coon" for the vacant seat in the Legislative Council he was known to be seeking.

Regardless of his personal views, Alexander Mackenzie's position as Secretary of the Lambton Reform Association imposed on him the duty of organizing the Convention to choose a Reform candidate for the Legislative Council seat. After trying in vain to withdraw from the position, he did his duty. When Cameron was victorious over eight other candidates, he and his father-in-law, Robert Sym, who had presided at the meeting, signed the requisition asking him to stand.[40] "Systematic spoliation for the benefit of the Lower Province, and the maintenance of a necessarily corrupt Administration," they stated in the familiar language of the contractor, "compel us to demand the immediate dissolution of the Legislative Union and the substitution of a Federal Union . . . Accepting your profession of devotion to that policy and having every confidence . . . in your desire to maintain generally the principles for which the Reform party has long struggled, we invite you to accept the nomination".[41] Cameron accepted the requisition and the policy dictated to him. He was elected, and gave his loyal support to George Brown.

Despite the depression, Alexander Mackenzie's construction business continued to thrive. He had no handsome store on Front Street like Robert and Hope, or like John and Charles, but he was never idle. From construction, he entered the real estate business, and began selling lots as the little town expanded.[42] In late 1859, the Sarnia contractor missed one of the greatest opportunities of his career as a builder. Despite his objection to Ottawa as the site of the new capital, he decided to tender for some of the construction work to be done there. He joined forces with a fellow-contractor named James Stewart and a plumber named Neil McNeil from Kingston, and went down to study the plans and location.[43] The Parliament Buildings were to be set on a rock ledge known as Barrack Hill, overlooking the Ottawa River. After clambering over the snow-covered ground and studying the specifications for several days, the three business men retired to a hotel to decide their course. Mackenzie and his brother Robert, who joined the group in Ottawa, joined with Stewart in submitting a tender for the main building for four hundred and fifty thousand dollars.[44] Among the names they listed as security guarantees was that of George Brown. Alexander Mackenzie shared in an additional tender of three hundred and fifty-one thousand, five hundred dollars for the East and West Departmental Blocks, and a third one for the Governor General's residence. When the decisions had been taken and the business concluded, the Mackenzies and Stewart, to the surprise of their companion, drew Bibles from their travelling cases and invited him to join in a session of religious reading.

The group's tenders were reasonable, but not reasonable enough. The one for the Parliament Buildings was sixth out of twenty-one, the other still farther down the list. The work was awarded to a Lower Canadian recommended by a former Minister, Joseph Cauchon. Alexander Mackenzie went back to his contracting in the West.

In October, Hope Mackenzie was asked to stand for the Legislative Assembly seat vacated by Cameron. With the split in Reform ranks healed, at least on the surface, it was likely to be an easy fight, but he hesitated. He had recently remarried, and felt no desire to go tilting at Tory windmills in Quebec or Ottawa. Moreover, his health, always indifferent since childhood, had recently taken a turn for the worse. It was only the call of duty that forced him to accept the nomination, and to campaign for the "joint authority" and the other aims outlined at the Toronto Convention.

Hope's second try for office went off smoothly. Notwithstanding the occasional heckler, and several opponents on nomination day, he won an easy victory.[45] The downcast Grit leader was delighted at the achievement of the Lambton "bricks", as he loved to call them. "I cannot tell you how rejoiced I was at Hope's return," Brown wrote to Alexander.[46] "He will be invaluable in the Lower House . . . Tell him he must take hold from the start or he will find it tenfold more difficult afterwards. It is just like 'dooking'."*

The political struggle, and even the final compromise with Cameron, had not been in vain. Lambton was a pure Brownite county again. Hope would be as devoted a servant of the cause as the master himself. Alexander returned contentedly to his family, to his community activities, to his curling matches with his brothers and friends on the St. Clair River, and to his work. That year little Mary, already twelve years old, presented her school trustee father with a Christmas present that filled his heart with pride: a first prize for writing from the Senior Common School.[47]

* * * * *

Hope's first session was a discouraging one for the Clear Grits. Brown's massive body refused to be driven on and on at such a ruthless pace. Exhausted by his herculean efforts, and depres-

*A cold plunge.

sed from fatigue and frustration, he had to miss the entire session, even though a general election was expected to follow immediately. With the *Globe* publisher out of the way, the John Sandfield Macdonald wing of the party surged forward. Instead of pursuing the battle for federal union, they continued to support the double majority principle. The only memorable moment of the session was a brisk exchange between John A. Macdonald and Oliver Mowat, fast moving into prominence as a Clear Grit. Stung by the aggressiveness of his former pupil, the Tory leader walked across the aisle and shook his fist in Mowat's face, roaring, "You damned young pup, I'll slap your chops!"[48] John Sandfield Macdonald intervened before the onlookers had an opportunity to see if he really would.

Hope found the law-making interesting and made his views known in some able speeches, but he was ill much of the time. Some weeks he was in such bad health that his friend, D'Arcy McGee, who stayed at the same boarding-house, had to nurse him before leaving for the Legislature in the morning and on his return at night. There was one frightful occasion when Hope fell ill while crossing the river from Point Lévis to Quebec City in a small boat, with ice floes crunching ominously against the fragile bark. McGee had to hold him in his arms and carry him ashore.

When the election was announced, Hope refused to continue. The disconcerted Reformers had no alternative but to ballot for another candidate. The choice fell almost unanimously on the Secretary and general work-horse of the Central Reform Association. Alexander Mackenzie protested that he preferred to continue in his familiar supporting role.[49] Beneath the protective layer of self-confidence, the former stonemason was still unable to convince himself that he had overcome the disadvantage of the lack of a formal education. Proud and sensitive, he did not feel he could compete with orators like Brown or Cameron or McGee. His love for Hope had convinced him that his brother was worthy to stand in such company; he himself was but a working-man. He had many contracts on hand; he was interested in the development of the new oil industry a few miles out of town; and he wanted to stay near his cozy home where Jane and Mary awaited him when he returned from work.

There was only one argument that could break his resistance – the call of duty to a cause greater than himself. A severe critic of the faults and weaknesses of others as well as of his own, he was brought to see that the young county had no abler and truer hands to which the task could be entrusted. Surely he was not willing to let the mantle of Brown fall on weak or even enemy shoulders? He gave in. "Personally, I would much rather you had chosen some other . . . but I cannot see the way clear to refuse under the circumstances," he said finally. ". . . Thanking you very cordially for your generous confidence – the more so, because unsought."[50]

The choice met with general approval. Even his old opponent, J. R. Gemmill, sang his praise. "There cannot be any doubt Mr. Mackenzie is thoroughly reliable as a Reformer," he told his readers, "is a good speaker as many of us well know; while for knowledge of the political position of the Province and acquaintance with its political history for the past fifteen or twenty years we are free to assert, and do so without fear of contradiction, his equal is not to be found within the County."

The decision taken, the candidate cast all doubts and hesitations aside. "I believe the present Coalition Government to have been the most mischievous and corrupt Administration which has swayed the destiny of United Canada," he told the electors in his written address, and therefore, if you honour me by electing me as your representative, I shall . . . vote want of confidence in them."[51] He condemned "that infamous trick", the "double shuffle", and praised "the enlightened *sober* statesmen" of Lower Canada, such as Dorion and McGee, who conceded the justice of the demands of Upper Canada, and only demanded guarantees that any increased power should not be used to interfere with the ecclesiastical privileges and laws of their area. He stood for cheap, honest government, free trade, and an active immigration and colonization policy.

Opposition to Hope had been divided among several candidates; this time it united behind the County Treasurer, Alexander Vidal. Vidal ran as an independent, and took a firm stand on only one point – opposition to Brown and the Toronto resolutions.[52] By Lambton standards, it was a polite, good-natured campaign. The candidates affirmed their respect and admiration for one another, and restricted their stronger statements to personalities outside the County. Alexander Mackenzie threw himself into a vigorous schedule of three meetings a day, in mid-morning, mid-afternoon and evening. He spoke in churches, schools, town halls, stopping houses, or simply out-of-doors on a wagon or hayrack. As he raced from place to place with his horses and buggy, Hope followed his opponent "for the purpose of keeping him straight".[53]

The nomination proceedings in front of the town hall attracted a sizeable crowd.[54] In plain, matter-of-fact language, the thirty-nine-year-old contractor told his neighbours that Canada's political system, like Britain's, was based on two strong parties. Except in an emergency, coalitions should be avoided, as they led to compromises and corruption. In the existing situation, political support had to be bought and hangers-on paid for their allegiance. Independents, such as his opponent, usually sided with the Government. The Administration, which had rejected representation by population and increased both taxes and public debt so rapidly, did not deserve Lambton's support, he argued.

At the close of the meeting, the crowd was divided; Mackenzie men on the right, Vidal men on the left. The two groups were about equal. With a few days left to campaign, both candidates charged back into the townships in an effort to upset the delicate balance. Their schedules crossed at Florence on the last Saturday afternoon.[55] Vidal was speaking from a wagon in the centre of the village when his opponent arrived. Mackenzie sat down and waited. The June sun was setting when Vidal finally concluded his address, and voices called for the Reform candidate. Vidal supporters complained that it was not a joint meeting, and refused the contractor an audience. The conciliatory tone vanished. In a storm of indignation, the Mackenzie Reformers trooped across to the school-house in the gathering darkness and held a meeting of their own. The County Treasurer's men were castigated with relish as enemies of fair play and as corruptionists; "Sandy" Mackenzie was lauded as the candidate who upheld the people's rights.

It was a close fight all the way. When the votes were counted, Alexander Mackenzie was declared elected by a majority of less than one hundred and fifty votes. Nevertheless, he had won, as the *Observer* gloated, over "the Tory, the Orange, the Catholic, and the loose-fish votes almost to a man!" The celebrations, and the victory bonfire down by the waterfront, lasted most of the night.[56]

One person who would have been proud and happy was not on hand to enjoy the celebration. Mary Fleming Mackenzie, the mother of the Mackenzie clan, died a few months too early to see her third son's victory over the disadvantages of his youth. Still, she had good reasons for satisfaction. All seven sons were at her bedside to hear her bid them goodbye, and they were all prosperous, upstanding, and Christian men. Their devotion to her had not flagged throughout the years; at sixty-six she had died content.

Elsewhere, the Reform cause had not prospered. Brown was defeated in Toronto, and Dorion in Lower Canada. Mowat had failed in his attempt to unseat John A. Macdonald in Kingston. William Lyon Mackenzie had declined to run and was approaching a near pauper's death in Toronto. The Reformers had succeeded in maintaining a majority of three seats in Upper Canada, but Lower Canada had voted for the Government again. The only solace for the Opposition was the imminent departure of Sir Edmund Head, the perpetrator of the "double shuffle", who, in their opinion, left the Colony "unwept, unhonoured and unsung".

CHAPTER 4

Deadlock

Fortunately, being a member of Parliament was not a full-time occupation. With the Civil War raging across the border, prosperity had returned and the construction business was booming. In addition to his contracting and real estate ventures, Mackenzie was importing slate from Lower Canada at, according to the advertisement in the *Observer*, "prices lower than they have ever been procured for".[1] He was supervising work on the new gaol; and the school board, the agricultural society, church, and other organizations were making heavy demands on his time.

As the new member, he could no longer remain behind the scenes. There were not only political speeches to deliver, but he was called upon to address every conceivable kind of social gathering. The St. Andrew's dinner in December 1861 was the first in a series extending over many years at which he had occasion to express his pride in his native land and extol the virtues of his fellow-Scots. At such times he was at his best. Relaxed and comfortable in the friendly surroundings, he revealed the warm, entertaining side of his nature generally reserved for family and intimate friends. Deft sallies of puckish humour leavened his messages and counter-balanced his inclination to dwell on man's position in the face of his destiny and his God. Soaring heights of idealism alternated with down-to-earth anecdotes of Burns' pitiful attempts to eke out an existence in a society that rejected him. Through it all ran a deep faith in Scotland and Scotsmen. Their patriotism, their proud attachment to civil and religious freedom, their high moral standards, their national system of education – these were the qualities, Mackenzie told his audiences, that Scotsmen in Canada had inherited, and had a duty to apply in their new land. Nor would he let them forget the great lesson of Robert

Burns: whatever his rank or fortune, "the man's the gowd for a' that".

Parliament was summoned by the new Governor General, Lord Monck, to meet in Quebec on March 20, 1862. Extra railway cars started from Sarnia and Windsor, and were made into a special train at Toronto to take the Parliamentarians to the old fortress city.[2] The General Manager of the Great Western Railway, C. J. Brydges, was aboard to see that they were kept happy. At Point Lévis, a mob of French-speaking canoemen waited with flag-bedecked barks to transport them across the river. The incoming tide swept the blocks of ice and snow upstream as the apprehensive law-makers stepped into the flat-bottomed vessels and the shouting, jostling "habitants" pushed off. Strong and agile, they cut through the lumps of snow and circumvented the cakes of ice that floated in the grey-black water. As the little armada approached, the grey Citadel glistened invitingly in the midday winter sun. It was nearly twenty years since Alexander Mackenzie had seen it for the first time as a youthful immigrant with sixteen shillings in his pocket. Then he had climbed the cliffs on foot; this time a sleigh and driver were waiting to take him to his hotel.

The absence of George Brown was a big disappointment to the new member for Lambton. The famous newspaperman had refused all the seats offered to him, and would not even come to the capital for fear of being accused of influencing the choice of a new leader in his place. A motley collection of Brownites, supporters of J. S. Macdonald, and "loose fish", the caucus finally decided that Michael Foley of Waterloo should act as leader. It was clear, however, that he had little prestige with the group. Foley was one of the men who had enraged Mackenzie by voting against Brown's resolution on federal union two years before. It was an inauspicious beginning.

The session was not yet a fortnight old when Alexander Mackenzie made his debut. He spoke in support of William McDougall's resolution for "securing to the population of Upper Canada their rightful share of the representation and their just influence in the Government".[3] The reputation of the sandy-haired Scot with the loose, navy-cut beard had preceded him. Many of his colleagues on both sides of the House had heard of the forthright contractor whose confidence in his own principles made him impervious to attack, but whose shafts were penetrating and deadly accurate. Except for the sharp, blue eyes and the determined set of his mouth, his external appearance hardly seemed to warrant such a description. His dark, formal suit hung awkwardly on a lean, muscular frame obviously more accustomed to the less cumbersome garments of a working man. The weather-beaten, angular features and hard, thick hands contrasted sharply with the stiff, white collars and cuffs from which they protruded, and with the paler, more delicate faces and hands of many of the other representatives of the people. He looked as much a stranger as John A. Macdonald, across the aisle, looked born to his position on the Ministerial benches.

Alexander Mackenzie had several attributes of a good Parliamentarian. Conscientious in checking every detail of his subject, and endowed with an exceptional memory, he presented his arguments in clear, concise form. His English was simple and accurate, and his voice, still marked with a decided "burr", carried well throughout the Chamber. His caustic humour was more effective in Parliament than at the banquet table, or even on the hustings. Lacking the wild gesticulations and dramatic presentation of many spell-binding orators, he was, in fact, well suited to Parliamentary debate. Above all, he gave the impression of having great inner strength, as if the world itself could collapse around him before he would be moved from his principles or his faith.

The new member's first speech was reasonable enough. He proved, with abundant statistics and references, that the western counties had a right to more than twice their present representation. He also conceded that it was understandable that the members of the existing Administration did not find it in their interest to grant it. Recurring to one of his favourite themes, the inherent evil of all coalitions, he complimented John A. Macdonald on the support he was receiving from the extreme Tories, and hoped it indicated a return to the two-party system. A government of "fossil Tories" was preferable to the existing combination.[4]

The *Globe* was pleased. "Mr. Mackenzie made a capital maiden effort, causing his hits to tell with great force", the Parliamentary correspondent reported. "Mr. Mackenzie is one of the ablest members of the House."[5] His "maiden effort" behind him, the member for Lambton plunged into a study of the current public works projects, which the *Globe* maintained were riddled with jobbery and corruption. He was well qualified to discuss the principal one: the Parliament Buildings at Ottawa. Nine hundred thousand dollars had been spent, a hundred thousand over his own bid, and there was scarcely more than a foundation to show for the money. In addition, the work had not been carried out by the original contractor, but a large part of it transferred arbitrarily to someone else. There were grounds to suspect conniving behind the scenes. In a harsh and thorough speech, Mackenzie asked for a select committee of investigation.[6] As Commissioner of Public Works, Georges-Etienne Cartier rose to defend the Government. Stung by the fledgling Parliamentarian's irony and censorious attitude, the Napoleon-like little Minister replied in kind. His brush-cut hair bristling, he cast aside the accusations as the lamentations of a disappointed bidder, and accused Mackenzie of having visited Ottawa disguised as a labourer in order to spy and gain information from the workers. No one commented that if he had been in Ottawa in coarse tweeds instead of dark worsted, it would hardly have been a disguise! Another Minister, Joseph Cauchon, who had strongly supported the successful bidder, suggested that Mackenzie was not a Scot for nothing; money seemed to be an important consideration to him. "Who told you I was a Scotchman?" interjected the novice Parliamentarian in his thick Highland brogue, to the general amusement. His origins were not his fault, he retorted; if he had been able to choose he would have been born in Quebec and brought up a Minister of the Crown.

Without waiting for the question of a committee on the new Parliament Buildings to be settled, he went on to attack another Tory "sacred cow", the Grand Trunk Railway, of which Cartier was the solicitor. Having declared war on the Ministry, he was going to make it a hard fight all the way.

Quebec was a cold, unfriendly, almost foreign place to most Upper Canadian Reformers. There was an English-speaking group in the old fortress city, but they were mostly Tories, and their one newspaper was a Tory organ. Unable to speak the language or even read the newspapers of the majority of the residents, they felt themselves on hostile territory, surrounded by strangers with nothing in mind but to exploit them and to impose their minority will. Unable to escape from the "nasty place", Mackenzie was pleased to have at least Archibald McKellar with whom to share his leisure hours. McKellar was excellent company. Always gay and optimistic, he shook his fellow-Scot out of his inclination to take the political situation too seriously, and brought out the sense of humour too often suppressed by family, business, and public cares. On one occasion, they were leaving the hotel for a Sunday morning stroll when they noticed another strait-laced Upper Canadian resident, Elijah Leonard, sitting in the bar-room, evidently waiting for someone. Mackenzie found a piece of paper, and writing, "What doest thou there Elijah?", sent it in with a messenger. A minute or so later, the victim appeared in the parlour with the air of a sinner caught in the act, and showed the paper to the two jokesters. Convinced that it was a supernatural message, he was never found in the bar-room again.[7]

Alexander Mackenzie had heard reports of John A. Macdonald's drinking habits, and while quite willing to believe them, he had no personal knowledge as evidence. As the session progressed, it became obvious that they were true.[8] The strain of keeping the Ministry together and mustering enough support to squeeze by divisions was telling more and more on the Attorney General. Often he seemed to have been drinking; sometimes he did not appear at all, and Cartier had to bear the burden of fending off the Opposition attacks. Macdonald, it was recounted, was drunk in his room. One Western member suggested a committee to investigate the long and frequent "illnesses", and determine if his health and habits were such as to enable him to carry on his duties.

Macdonald had cause for concern. As fast as he repaired a breach or added a recruit to his combination of supporters, it seemed to fall apart somewhere else. One of the urgent measures to be dealt with was a Militia Bill to strengthen Canada's frontier against the United States, the Americans having commenced to make menacing sounds against Britain as a result of alleged British sympathy to the south in the Civil War. After playing as long as possible the "waiting game" that won him the title of "Old Tomorrow", Macdonald pulled himself together and brought down a resolution to train thirty thousand Canadians at a cost of one million dollars. The Upper Canadians had deserted him a month earlier in his opposition to representation by population; now the Lower Canadians balked at his expensive defence plan. The bill was defeated on second reading. He resigned.

The Reformers were caught in an embarrassing situation. Brown was still away ill, and preparing to leave for a holiday in Scotland; Dorion was back at his law practice in Montreal. Foley's and Sicotte's leadership of Reformers and Rouges respectively was more titular than real. John Sandfield Macdonald still insisted on plotting his independent course; another group, including McDougall, McKellar, Mackenzie, and McGee, continued to look wistfully toward Toronto for signs of Brown's return. "Foley has now satisfied all men here of his utter incompetence", Mackenzie wrote to Brown when the crisis broke. "Dickson who was one of his firm friends at the first . . . told me (he) . . . was a *damned ignorant old wife* and Sicotte was a mean *narrow-minded* curse. A precious description of our Leaders!! but wonderfully near the truth."[9]

Passing over Foley, Lord Monck asked the more experienced John Sandfield Macdonald to form a government. To Mackenzie, the choice of Brown's rival looked like the sort of double dealing between Governor General and Tories that he suspected lay at the back of the "double shuffle" four years before, and he feared a scheme to bring Macdonald and Cartier back to power as soon as possible. Most of all, he was concerned about the representation question, but as a newcomer he hesitated to push himself forward and demand that its settlement should constitute the basis of any Reform administration. "I feel very much afraid that anxiety to . . . (keep the late Ministry out) and possibly a natural desire to get possession of power may induce our friends to yield that moral power which always belongs to the right side", he commented to the *Globe* publisher, "and that once lost, where will the end be?"[10]

Though just a "full private of recent standing", Alexander Mackenzie insisted that Brown should be kept informed of every stage of the negotiations to form a new Ministry. Everyone knew that its success would depend on his attitude. When the *Globe* publisher heard a rumour that it would not be formed on the "rep by pop" basis, he wired from Toronto to ask if the Reformers were "all made down there". Assurances were flashed back that there was no alternative to keep the "corruptionists" out. Within the caucus, Mackenzie proposed a resolution that, without agreeing to the abandonment of representation by population, they would support the new Administration in order to "secure the permanent removal from power of the late occupants of the Treasury Benches", and "to assist them at present in reforming the public departments and securing administrative justice to Upper Canada".[11] Someone else added a further phrase, "Reserving to ourselves, perfect liberty of action on the question of representation by population and separate schools." John Sandfield Macdonald urged them not to put the resolution on record as it would weaken his hand. Feeling the tone of the meeting already indicated approval of his suggestion, Mackenzie naïvely gave way. The caucus decided to give the Ministry a "fair and liberal trial".[12] "I think we should support any batch for the moment", Mackenzie advised his leader in Toronto.[13]

The Macdonald-Sicotte Administration included Michael Foley as Postmaster-General, William Howland as Minister of Finance, and William McDougall as Commissioner of Crown Lands. Dorion agreed to enter the Cabinet as Provincial Secretary, and D'Arcy McGee as President of the Council. Brown's stamp of approval was essential. Foley and another Minister rushed to Toronto with explanations. "The conclusion I have come to from all they have told me is that a greater set of jackasses . . . never got by accident into the government of any country," the *Globe* publisher scoffed in a letter to Holton in Montreal after one five-hour interview.[14] He was so concerned about the plan to abandon the federal union scheme and try again to make the double majority principle work that he toyed with the idea of taking to the country and stumping the constituencies against the new Ministers when they sought to be re-elected. He was confident that he could defeat most of them single-handed. However, both his concept of party unity and his personal plans made him hesitate. Still depressed and unwell, he was determined to spend a few months at "home" in Britain, and then devote himself to building up his business interests for a couple of years. To get into an intra-party fight would "knock everything on the head". Finally he decided to let the new Ministry go ahead, but to "hold them up to the mark under the stimulus of bit and spur", and to coerce them on the constitutional question on every occasion.[15] After a week of agonizing discussions, he had arrived at the same conclusion as Alexander Mackenzie.

If there was to be no "rep by pop", decided the new member for Lambton, then at least there should be a thorough examination of the public accounts, and a revelation of "past rascalities".[16] But in this, too, disillusionment awaited. He had expected that the change of ministry would be like tearing the lid from an overripe garbage can, and that putrid machinations would suddenly be exposed to the shocked senses of the public. However, nothing happened. The new Ministers adopted the estimates of their predecessors and proceeded to push them through the House as rapidly as possible. "I am still convinced we have to support the new men to keep the old men out," Mackenzie wrote to Toronto, "but I have seen some indications of collusion between John Sandfield and John A. . . . He is now actively engaged (I believe) in carrying out arrangements to cover over and whitewash the criminal conduct of the late Ministry. . . . 'Claw me and I'll claw you', 'If ye dinna touch me, I'll no touch you' is manifestly the motto."[17]

Armed with notes, newspaper clippings, and files, the ex-stonemason determined to ask some penetrating questions before he allowed the requests for public funds to pass. Another disappointment! Late one evening, an item to approve one hundred and eighty-thousand dollars already overpaid on the Ottawa project was brought forward; he tensed to take the floor after explanations had been given. "The moment the old

Jew [Benjamin] in the chair read the sum he roared 'carried'," Mackenzie related indignantly afterwards, "John A. and Sandfield & Co. cried out 'adjourn', the Speaker cried, 'carried' and in half an instant Speaker, Chairman, Mace, and all was out at the door and left us looking like idiots at one another."[18]

The irate Scot went over to the Premier and accused him of having arranged the "coup d'état", but the charge was denied. After the night's experiences, he determined to take a stronger stand. The following morning he went to see "J.S." again. In view of reports of collusion with the old Ministers, he said, he wanted an immediate answer whether a Commission would be set up to investigate the Ottawa project, and a promise that the names would be announced before the House rose. He himself had offered to serve, "without pay of course", but the Ministry evidently preferred someone with a more amenable disposition. The Premier suggested a list of names, and they finally agreed on three. Sandfield Macdonald promised to announce the Commission the following Monday.

In an aggressive mood, Mackenzie went right on to the railway legislation. He had learned that the Premier had adopted the Tory bill to fuse the Great Western and the Grand Trunk Railways; a measure, he felt, that was designed to put more railway contracts in Tory hands, and more profits in their pockets. Discovering that the Cabinet was threatening some of the "weak brethren" with resignation if it was not carried, he threatened the same unhappy men "to expose them thoroughly if they did".[19]

Mackenzie's loyalty to Brown was neither blind nor unquestioning; it was the allegiance of a strong party man for the leader he trusted. With the leader absent, he did not hesitate to determine his own course, but neither did he neglect to keep him informed. He made suggestions for *Globe* articles, and even criticized editorials when he disagreed. He objected to the *Globe*'s derisory references to McDougall's former annexationist sympathies; on the other hand, he warned the Government that if their press abused the "Brown party", "we should act in an unequally sharp manner".[20]

Shortly before the end of the session, he explained his position frankly in the House. "It was a choice," he said, "between the new men who asserted and believed they had a remedy and the old men who did not admit the existence of the evil."[21] Though he could not agree with their solution, he would support the Ministers until they had an opportunity to bring down their programme in the next session. It was not a comfortable position; Mackenzie returned home with misgivings. He had spoken out for a change in the system of representation; he had also voted for a Government that would oppose such a change if it were put forward by a private member. He had to find what consolation he could in the knowledge that the Reform Ministry did not, as John A. Macdonald had predicted, "crumble to pieces before the end of the session".[22]

In Sarnia, most of his neighbours had read his Parliamentary speeches as reproduced in the *Observer*, and they knew all about the Committee that Alex Mackenzie had obtained to investigate the Ottawa "scandal". Their obvious admiration at such an effective debut made it easier to explain his support of the new Administration. Everything went well until McDougall threw a bombshell into the political pot in June by declaring at a meeting in Woodstock that the Ministry had the "entire approval of the party in the course they adopted".[23] Mackenzie seized his pen and wrote a blistering denial for the *Globe*, recounting the caucus meeting and the blunt warning to the Government that they would meet Brownite opposition on the representation and school questions. When his indignation subsided, he decided to ask Brown's advice first, and to urge him to have a denial issued from a more senior member of the caucus. "Only one man . . . entirely approved of their course," he fumed, ". . . the unanimity was wonderful, although some of the new members had some soft spots in them."[24] The defeated leader was due to leave for his long-awaited holiday in a few days, and refused to become excited about the controversy. Canadians in general were sickening of the constant political struggle, and were not inclined to be diverted from making the most of the current economic boom engendered largely by the American Civil War. Mackenzie had to content himself with stating, whenever the occasion arose, that he had not compromised on the two basic issues of representation and education.

The Ottawa Commission began its hearings in August, and Alexander Mackenzie went down to testify.[25] He had spent a month examining the plans and the terrain of the new capital, he told the Commissioners, and he was convinced that his tenders had been reasonable if the standards set by the Government were to be met. The successful contractor had been utterly unable to keep within his estimated costs, and the result was shoddy workmanship. "A considerable portion of this work I call rather dressed rubble than pick-faced masonry," he declared. A mistake had been made in not insisting that the successful bidder submit a detailed statement of estimated costs as he himself had done. Mackenzie's testimony revealed that he had a thorough knowledge of his subject, and that he had been a well-qualified bidder. In his twenty years in Canada, he had learned his business well.

A small notice in the *Globe* in mid-August changed the Canadian political picture completely. From Scotland, Brown let it be known that he had decided to re-enter Parliament at the first opportunity.[26] The Clear Grits were to have their leader back again! Mackenzie's spirits soared. Bonnie old Scotland, what a marvellous land! Hardly had he set foot on her soil, than she poured new strength and courage into the worn, depressed Canadian politician! A little later, even more exciting news arrived. The forty-four-year-old bachelor was in love! His mind and heart freed for a short time from politics and business, he had succumbed to the charms of Anne Nelson, of the famous publishing family in Edinburgh. The wedding took place in November, and with it began one of the great love affairs in Canadian history. "I am a new man in mind and body and as happy as the day is long!" thrilled the groom, almost unable to believe his good fortune.[27]

The new feeling of peace and harmony extended to the political field as well. "Whenever the great interests of Canada are at risk we will forget our merely political partisanship and rally round the cause of our country. That, at least, will be my motto."[28] But there was another feature of the "new" Brown. He had always protested his indifference to parliamentary honours, and insisted that he preferred to exert his influence from an editorial desk. Anne had little interest in Canadian politics, and no desire to share her husband with such a demanding competitor. Notwithstanding the *Globe* announcement before the wedding, he returned to Canada determined to accomplish his mission through others rather than re-enter the Parliamentary arena himself. One of the men he could trust to do a full share in the front ranks was his fellow-Scot, the member for Lambton.

With Malcolm Cameron safely ensconced in the Upper Chamber, the harmony between Alexander Mackenzie and J. R. Gemmill was complete. The *Sarnia Observer* carried every speech he made, reported his activities, and sang his praises. The preliminary report of the Ottawa Commission was proclaimed as an example of the influence and ability of the fledgling Parliamentarian, and a justification of his course.[29] The fact that the Barrack Hill rock was harder and the terrain less level than the experts had judged, and the costs correspondingly higher for that reason as well as because of any waste and inefficiency, was passed over in silence.

When the 1863 session opened, it soon became evident that the Macdonald-Sicotte Government was more preoccupied with survival than reform. The vague reference to fairer representation in the Speech from the Throne, and the fact that Dorion had resigned a few weeks earlier, lowered the Ministry still further in the estimation of Brownites. On the other side of the Chamber, John A. Macdonald, also back from a successful rest-cure in Scotland, was prepared to upset the Ministry at the first opportunity and resume office himself. One of the Clear Grits, Matthew Cameron, placed the representation question squarely before the Legislature by proposing the same amendment to the Throne Speech that McDougall had moved as a private member the previous year. Alexander Mackenzie warned bluntly that his support of the Administration on general policy did not mean that he was prepared to "go it blind". Until a better plan was devised, he had no alternative but to vote for a change in representation. On such a change, he declared, depended his dream of seeing sectional strife ended and "Scotchmen, Englishmen, Irishmen, and Frenchmen joined together so as to become one great people – the inhabitants of a country extending from the shores of the Atlantic to the slopes of the Rocky Mountains".[30]

There was a new note of relaxed self-confidence in Mackenzie's voice, and a suggestion of broadmindedness that had been missing when he was merely a political organizer in a Western county. His speeches were still straightforward and forceful, but the sledge-hammer blows were replaced occasionally by sallies of dry humour and sarcastic overtones, so effective in Parliamentary debate. Chiding the Tory leader on his hasty departure from a by-election in Oxford after a single meeting a short time before, he suggested Macdonald's new motto should be, "I came, I saw, I skedaddled."[31] "Tell that to the Marines," he commented when Cartier denied a split between himself and John A.". The other members sat back in amazement at the audacity of the Westerner who dared to attack not only the past master of subtle wit and sarcasm, but also the vigorous, sharp-witted French Canadian. When he had finished, they burst into enthusiastic applause. The upstart was not to escape scot-free. A few days later, the *Globe* published extracts of the final report of the Ottawa Commission before it was tabled in the House. The Opposition learned with delight that the guilty party was the honourable member for Lambton. The Premier had shown him a copy of the report, and he in turn had shown it in confidence to the *Globe* correspondent in Quebec. The latter had used it for a "scoop". With a great display of wounded righteousness and abused propriety, John A. Macdonald castigated the Premier, Mackenzie, and the *Globe* with relish. Squirm and protest as he might, the newcomer had to take his medicine.[32]

Not long after the session began, George Brown broke one of the resolutions he had made to his wife. The supplications of Mackenzie and other friends were hard to resist, and the temptation of a vacant seat in Oxford County almost overwhelming. It was not his nature to sit on the sidelines while urgent problems remained unsolved; in March he was back in the Legislature.

The first serious split between Government supporters and Clear Grits occurred over Richard Scott's Bill to extend the separate school system in Upper Canada. Mackenzie moved the three months' hoist, a postponement designed to kill the Bill by putting off consideration until the session was over.[33] He opposed the Bill as injurious to the common school system, and likely to lower the general standard of education. As President of the Council, D'Arcy McGee appealed for Upper Canadian support, and precipitated a violent exchange with the outspoken Scot. The Bill was carried, but the vote divided the House clearly along sectional lines. Extension of the separate school system in Upper Canada was imposed by Lower Canadian votes; the double majority principle was dead.

When he judged the time ripe, John A. Macdonald proposed a motion of non-confidence.[34] The member for Lambton stuck to his position that he would support the Administration on all but the representation and school issues. In a two-hour speech, he threw back the Opposition leader's charge of inconsistency, and declared his "unalterable resolution to defend the country against the men who had so long mismanaged its affairs".[35] Despite the support of the Clear Grits and of Dorion, the Government was defeated.[36] With a sigh of relief, Sandfield Macdonald asked for a dissolution and went to the country.

It was one of Alexander Mackenzie's easiest elections. Ten days after the dissolution, he had received requisitions from so many townships that he had no doubt his efforts in Quebec had been satisfactory. As the campaign began, the Premier succeeded in enlarging the basis of his Ministry by bringing in Oliver Mowat from Upper Canada, and by replacing Sicotte and his friends in Lower Canada with Dorion, Letellier de St. Just, Luther Holton and Lucius Huntington. The new Cabinet Ministers were free to take whatever stand they chose on constitutional questions. Mackenzie had much more confidence in a Ministry containing Dorion, Mowat, and Holton, and had no hesitation in asking for re-election to support them. Although he would have preferred a purely Clear Grit Administration, he argued, it was a step in the right direction, and it would keep out of office the party that had burned the Parliament Buildings, insulted Lord Elgin, and perpetrated the "double shuffle". If elected, he promised, "every means which I can constitutionally take will be adopted to prevent such men ever again ruling the country".[37]

Nomination day was a politician's dream.[38] The June sun was bright and warm, and a soft breeze bathed the town in Lake Huron air. The atmosphere was more that of a huge family picnic than a political contest. The County warden made the nomination; the mayor seconded it. They were fortunate to have a tried and trusty representative, the audience was told, one of themselves, and not a lawyer or an outsider over whom they would have no control. The crowd cheered. The returning officer called for further nominations. Silence. The crowd cheered again. Alexander Mackenzie was in by acclamation.

The election did not solve anything. Upper Canada supported the Ministry, but Lower Canada opposed it. Brown was returned in South Oxford, and Hope Mackenzie, whose health had improved, had been victorious in North Oxford. In mid-August the law-makers made their way down the St. Lawrence to try once again to solve the Colony's problems. The air in the railway carriages was hot and foul, and the "shake-downs" in the parlour car, where Hope and Alexander tried to get a bit of rest during the two-day journey, gave its occupants the appearance of suffering from a severe attack of the palsy. A century later, the cars might have been popular as reducing machines.

The Cabinet shuffle had not gone smoothly. The ex-Ministers Sicotte, Foley, and McGee had gone into opposition, and the Government did not even have a "drinking majority".[39] Its supporters hardly dared leave the Chamber for fear it would be defeated before they got back. On one occasion, an enterprising member of the Opposition managed to lure two or three Reformers as far as Montmorency Falls. After showing them the sights, he led them through a series of taverns until they were well launched on a drinking bout, then slipped out and rushed back to the Legislature. As soon as he arrived, the Opposition called for a vote. The Ministry was thrown into consternation! Putting up one speaker after another, they fought desperately to keep the debate alive until the absentees could be found. Fortunately, the victims had discovered the trick and set out as fast as their unsteady legs could carry them for the city. They arrived footsore but sober in time to save the Ministry with the usual majority of one.[40]

With the air filled with charges, counter-charges, mud-slinging, and character assassination, little progress was made on constructive legislation. Brown's motion for a special committee to study the constitutional problem outside the glare of public debate did not even reach the floor of the House. Alexander Mackenzie worked hard at the details of government spending, attempting to squeeze every surplus dollar out of the estimates. Like most of the members, his temper grew short, and he attacked the Opposition as "the unfairest and most factious in Canadian history".[41] "My Administration did no wrong," protested Cartier, during one denunciation of the "corrupt old gang". "The honourable member is beyond redemption," retorted the Sarnia contractor with scarcely a pause in his attack. Somehow, the Macdonald-Dorion Government staggered through to the end of the session. In mid-October, the disgruntled and disillusioned members packed their suitcases and went home.

Both Mackenzies were glad to return to Sarnia. Hope had been sick most of the time he was in Quebec, and the frustration and tension had brought on an attack of the fever to which Alexander was subject ever since the early days in Kingston. Fortunately, there was no need for exceptional exertions. Malcolm Cameron had been named Queen's Printer, and was completely out of politics; the Tories were no challenge to their authority. The only ripple in the political pool was the election of Robert Mackenzie as mayor. It was hardly an interesting contest; the Mackenzie name was a guarantee of success.[42]

Brown succeeded in obtaining his Committee to study a federal system in the 1864 session. John A. Macdonald criticized the federal idea, and called for "a legislative union, in fact, in principle and in practice".[43] Cartier gave warning that he would accept nothing but equality between the two Canadas. Alexander Mackenzie spoke strongly in favour of the Committee, and expressed the hope that it would devise a system of giving justice, while at the same time removing friction and suspicion between the two parts of the Colony. With such varied opinions, it looked as if Brown was faced with an impossible task. When all the members were in the Committee room, he went to the door, locked it, and put the key in his pocket. "Gentlemen," he said, "now you must talk about this matter as you cannot leave this room without coming to see me."[44]

The representation question safely in Brown's hands, Mackenzie went back to the foot-slogging work of the Government Accounts and other Committees. Less interested in seeking publicity than most of his colleagues, he found the detailed work interesting and worth while. The Government knew that if he served on a committee, the work would be thoroughly done.

The strain of constant divisions and hairbreadth escapes took its toll on Ministerial nerves. After weeks of struggling for survival, the unpredictable Premier suddenly decided he was tired of it all. Too proud to court potential supporters, and increasingly sensitive to criticism, he resigned without waiting for an adverse vote. On March 30, John A. Macdonald was in control once again. "The old corruptionists are back," lamented the *Globe*.[45]

In a sense, the return of the "corruptionists" was a relief to Brown and Mackenzie. Quiescence and conciliation was a difficult role for both of them. With the Conservatives in power, they were free to stand on their own ground, and to strike out at their old enemies once more. Opposition was a task they knew well. Still playing his old game of building as broad a Ministry as possible, John A. Macdonald succeeded in bringing both D'Arcy McGee and Michael Foley into the Cabinet. This "betrayal", particularly by the former Parliamentary leader of the Reformers, thoroughly aroused the indignation of the Grits. John A. Macdonald and McGee had rollicked through Leeds constituency together the previous summer, campaigning against a newly appointed Minister.[46] Mackenzie and McKellar decided to return the compliment against Foley in Waterloo. They were both powerful teams. For Macdonald and McGee it had been one of the happiest binges in their lives; for Mackenzie and McKellar it was also a pleasant, though more sober, experience. They were both well informed men, and they knew how to put their messages across to the people. They enjoyed co-ordinating their attacks. "The opponent who found himself sandwiched between the two at a public meeting," recorded an eye-witness, "soon discovered he had got into a very tight place."[47] Mackenzie leavened his message to the electors with a dry Scotch humour, but it was McKellar who won their hearts. As much at home in Gaelic as in English, he was the very opposite of the popular image of the parsimonious, severe, Presbyterian Scot, and his humorous stories were as lethal as Mackenzie's sharper barbs. The two men complemented each other well; what McKellar lacked in weighty arguments and determination, he compensated with his popular personality. What Mackenzie lacked in personal magnetism, he supplied in hard facts and high principles.

One night during the contest, they found themselves at the same hotel as a group of Conservative campaigners. The latter were in a festive mood, and made merry until the wee hours of the morning. Despite the lack of sleep as a result of the revelry downstairs, Mackenzie rose as usual at 6 a.m. In the vacated main hall he found a large bundle of his opponents' propaganda. "Facts for the Irish Electors", "Black Record of the Grit Party", the headlines proclaimed. A freshly lit fire crackled in the big stove. The temptation was too great. "I remembered that it was one of the undoubted rights of belligerents to capture and destroy any of the enemy's munitions of war which fell in their way", he recounted to his partner later. "I determined, therefore, to exercise our belligerent rights as to confiscation, which I immediately proceeded to carry out by opening the big stove door and thrusting the whole bundle into the roaring flames. Then I went for a long and peaceful walk through the quiet little village and out into the green fields and woods adjoining until the hour for breakfast slowly came 'round."[48] Foley lost the election.

The 6 a.m. prankster was not the image in most people's minds of the member for Lambton. Many were inclined to believe the report in the Toronto *Leader* that he and the equally pugnacious Brown had quarrelled in the street, and that the *Globe* publisher had slapped his lieutenant's face.[49] Both men made vehement denials – a century later the denials had not yet completely nullified the report.

The new Ministry was not more stable than its three predecessors. Although Brown was absent in his Committee much of the time, Dorion and Mackenzie and other Grits kept up a constant attack in the House. On June 14, the *Globe* publisher reported that a majority of his Committee were "in favour of changes in the direction of a federal system, applied either to Canada alone, or to the whole British American provinces". He recommended further studies at the next session. Of the twenty members of the Committee, only three had opposed the conclusion he announced: John A. Macdonald, John S. Macdonald, and a solitary western Reformer.[50]

The same day, Dorion proposed a motion of censure concerning an advance of funds to the city of Montreal without legislative authority. Even John A. Macdonald had exhausted his ability to hold the Ministry together.[51] The motion carried. Four Ministries and two elections in three years had failed to provide stable, orderly government in Canada. The deadlock had come.

CHAPTER 5

The Confederation Scheme

What next? It seemed impossible that any combination of members could muster a majority. Even the wily John A. Macdonald could not turn the trick again. True, George Brown had not yet had a try, but he and his followers were opposed to broad coalitions or combinations, and it was unlikely that he could muster a majority on strictly Clear Grit lines. Brown himself was floating on a higher plane. Intense, tenacious, and an idealist by nature, he was completely absorbed in finding a federal solution to the continuing crisis. The collapse of the Ministry on the day he presented his report convinced him that a constitutional change was urgent. Why not utilize the crisis, he suggested to two Conservatives, as the members milled about the Legislature disconcertedly, "in settling forever the constitutional difficulties between Upper and Lower Canada"?[1] He was ready to co-operate "with the existing or any other Administration" for that purpose. The Conservatives could hardly believe their ears. Could this be the violent, uncompromising tyrant of the *Toronto Globe*, the arch-enemy of "popery" and Toryism?

John A. Macdonald had the Governor General's permission for dissolution in his hand when the news of Brown's suggestion arrived. Whatever happened, it seemed likely that the turn of the Grits had come, and once installed, they were likely to hold the reins of power for some time. Federation was suddenly no longer an abstract principle, but a tangible political reality. Macdonald leaped at the opportunity to find a real solution, and incidentally, to block the path of his opponents. On June 17, he and Galt called on the *Globe* publisher at the St. Louis Hotel.[2] When they left two hours later, the three men had agreed to work together for a solution on the basis of the Brown Committee report.

The House met at three o'clock. Macdonald confirmed that negotiations were going on between the two leaders with a view to forming a stronger government. Only extreme circumstances justified him in such a course, Brown stated when he confirmed the announcement. The House broke into cheers. The negotiations continued. The Grit leader wanted to set federation of the two Canadas as the primary goal, and to consider the union of all the British North American colonies as an ultimate objective. Caught by the vision of the larger scheme, Macdonald wanted to gamble for the top prize. He wanted also to bind his old rival firmly to whatever plan was adopted by having him enter the Cabinet. Fearing the charge of inconsistency with his past denunciation of coalitions, Brown preferred to remain on the outside.

By the morning of June 21, the Grit leader was in a position to call the caucus together and seek their approval. He told them that the genial elder statesman, Col. Taché, would head the Government, and that three Ministers would be Upper Canadian Reformers. Despite his protests, the Conservatives still insisted that he enter the Cabinet as one of the three. The single purpose of the Government would be to achieve a federal union of either all of British North America, or of the two sections of Canada. When the discussion was over, Hope Mackenzie made a motion approving the negotiations and the plan for a "federal union of the Canadas, with provision for its extension to the Maritime Provinces and the North-West Territory".[3] The caucus was still primarily concerned with solving the problems at home. The motion carried, with four abstentions. One of the abstainers, John Sandfield Macdonald, then moved that "the proposition for at least three members of the Opposition entering the Government be accepted". Alexander Mackenzie objected. He had observed with growing concern the concessions being made by his leader, and he feared that his desire for the success of a federal scheme would deliver him completely into the Tory leader's hands. Apart from his objection to coalitions on principle, he suspected that John A. Macdonald would try to exploit the pact with the Reformers for his own party purposes. He proposed an amendment to Sandfield Macdonald's motion, asking "that the proposition for three members entering the Cabinet be rejected, and that the proposition for the settlement of sectional difficulties receive an outside support". Like Hope's proposal, the suggestion bore evidence of previous consultation with the *Globe* publisher. Brown, Mowat, McKellar, and Hope supported him, but the amendment was lost eleven to twenty-six. Faced with this majority decision, Alexander Mackenzie supported another motion by Sandfield Macdonald that Brown should enter the Cabinet.

Brown shared wholeheartedly his lieutenant's reservations about accepting office. After the caucus meeting, he returned to the negotiating table and tried again to satisfy Macdonald with a promise of outside support. The pressure was too great. Governor General Monck, the Conservative Ministers, the Sandfield Macdonald Reformers, D'Arcy McGee – all pointed out that if he did not enter the Ministry the responsibility for failure would be laid at his feet. The next day, John A. Macdonald announced the "Great Coalition".[4] Its aim was very nearly identical to Hope's motion in caucus. At the next session, they would bring in a measure "for the purpose of removing the existing difficulties by introducing the federal principle into Canada, coupled with such provisions as will permit the Maritime Provinces and the North-West Territory to be incorporated into the same system of government". By sending representatives to the Lower Provinces and to England, they would endeavour to obtain assent "to such a measure as may enable all British North America to be united under a general legislature based on the federal principle".

When Macdonald had finished, Brown rose, his great frame and powerful voice unsteady from emotion. In a conciliatory tone, he traced the federal plan from the Reform and Rouge Conventions held in Toronto and Montreal respectively in 1859. After the negotiations in the Maritimes and London, he said, it would be possible to tell whether the larger or smaller scheme was more likely to carry. Whatever happened, he would leave the Government as soon as the federal cause could no longer be advanced. As he sat down, the pent-up emotion burst all bounds. Members broke into cheers, clapped their hands, and rushed across the floor to congratulate one another. One elderly little French member, it was reported, tore over to George Brown, climbed up on his huge frame, flung his arms round his neck, and "hung several seconds there suspended, to the visible consternation of Mr. Brown and to the infinite joy of all beholders".[5] Hope was born again.

Loud and lusty as it undoubtedly was, the enthusiasm was not unanimous. Some of Brown's closest friends failed to follow him in his new course. Antoine-Aimé Dorion and Luther Holton, colleagues in the short-lived Reform Cabinet of 1858, and men for whom he felt both admiration and friendship, remained aloof. Despite their confidence in Brown himself, they refused to accept the goal of a larger confederation, and had no choice but to remain in opposition. Apart from Brown, Alexander Mackenzie was the first Liberal – the term was becoming synonymous with Reformer – to speak in favour of Confederation.[6] He was ready to put aside even his repugnance for coalitions, he stated in his clear, methodical manner, for such a great objective. He had told the Macdonald-Sicotte Ministry that he would support even the Tories if they would undertake to settle the representation question, but he had not expected that he would be given an opportunity of redeeming that promise. He saw no need for scepticism. Even if the Government intended to deceive, he was sure that it could not stop the torrent it had released, and it would be swept aside if it tried. He could not conceive of such a monstrous fraud being perpetrated. While he preferred the settlement of Canadian problems before launching into the larger scheme, the latter was an end to be kept in view in order to consolidate British power on the continent, and it was right that Canada should take the initiative in working toward that goal. When one or other of the two plans was accomplished, he trusted that he and his friends who opposed the project would be united once more.

The session ended quickly. While the new Ministers prepared to meet the Maritimers at Charlottetown, Mackenzie toured his constituency, explaining why Brown had agreed to become President of the Council in a coalition with his old enemies, and had taken Mowat and McDougall with him into the Cabinet.[7] For years the "rep by pop" cry had been dinned into Upper Canadian ears; now it was necessary to assure them that this was not some enormous betrayal. He admitted that he would have preferred avoiding a coalition, and that he had hoped for something closer to a legislative union than the weak "joint authority" recommended at the 1859 Convention. But federation was worth the sacrifices if it allowed each section to keep its local laws and customs, and to control its own affairs. The meetings were a success. At the end of each one, a resolution was passed endorsing the federal plan. Even the editor of the new Tory weekly, the *Sarnia Canadian*, could find little to criticize in the conduct of the member for Lambton. There was one exception. The *Canadian* felt that the recent appointment of Robert Mackenzie as the local Indian agent was corruption of the worst kind!

The political excitement was too unsettling to return to the construction business; Alexander Mackenzie joined a group of Parliamentarians led by D'Arcy McGee in a tour of the Lower Provinces.[8] Most of them had never seen the Maritimes, and had no contact with the men who bore the same party labels and faced similar problems. They could not even shake hands with one another without leaving British soil. The travellers were taken by train through the United States to Portland, Maine, where a steamer was to meet them. Unfortunately, the long, stuffy train journey was followed by an equally lengthy wait in a drenching rain as the ship failed to appear. Tempers grew short, and some of the group gave up in disgust. Others cursed and grumbled when they discovered that the ship, when it did eventually arrive, had so little accommodation that they had to sleep on deck. The Irish humour of D'Arcy McGee was strained to the utmost as he struggled to keep up their morale, reminding the seasick passengers shivering in their rough blankets that if they did not have bed, they certainly had board! It was not an enthusiastic group of federalists that stepped on shore in Saint John, New Brunswick, the next morning.[9]

Public opinion in the Lower Provinces was alert to the possibilities of a smaller federation among themselves, but union with Canada evoked little enthusiasm. The Liberals seemed more inclined to oppose than welcome it. The eloquent, mastiff-like Joseph Howe, the most outstanding personality in Nova Scotia, spoke strongly against Confederation. To the Upper Canadians, he recalled their own fiery, unpredictable William Lyon Mackenzie, who had died a short time earlier. Unlike Mackenzie in his last years, Howe was obviously not alone in his stand. One thing was clear: a federal union with the Maritimes could only function properly if there was a direct rail connection from the Great Lakes to the Atlantic seaboard. On the way home, it was reported that the Northern United States ship on which they were travelling was being pursued by a Confederate vessel. The enemy never appeared, but it was painfully evident that Confederation, if it were achieved, would bring some major transportation problems in its wake.

Parliament re-assembled to debate Confederation in January, 1865. The Charlottetown Conference had been a success; and at the Quebec Conference that followed, a long series of resolutions had been drawn up for submission to the different Legislatures. On the way down to Quebec to discuss the Confederation Bill, Mackenzie declared his intention in Toronto to back the larger federal plan, and to push for the smaller federation if the Lower Provinces refused to join. He, too, had caught the vision of the greater scheme.

John A. Macdonald led off in the great debate with an able appeal to reason and conciliation. The different clauses, he stated, "had been agreed to by a system of natural compromise".[10] Everyone had been forced to make concessions; he had abandoned his preference for a legislative union in order to win the support of Lower Canada and the Maritimes. Brown rose to the occasion as well. "What we propose now," he intoned, "is but to lay the foundations of the structure . . . that will one day, we trust, extend from the Atlantic to the Pacific . . . and what we propose to do is to be done with the cordial sympathy and assistance of that great Power of which it is our happiness to form a part."[11]

The opposition to the scheme by Holton and Dorion was heart-breaking to men like Brown and Mackenzie, torn between their sense of duty on the one hand, and party and personal allegiances on the other. Holton's condemnation of Confederation as a "crude, immature, ill-considered scheme . . . which threatens to plunge the country into measureless debt, . . . into a period of calamities, a period of tribulation", cut as deeply as a personal attack. Dorion's principal concern was that the central Government was too strong, and would grow in strength until a legislative union resulted. Finding themselves in a minority, the French Canadians would be unable to defend their institutions and their heritage. He repeated his plea for "a real confederation, giving the largest powers to the local governments and merely a delegated authority to the general government".

The debate had been proceeding for over a fortnight when Alexander Mackenzie's turn came to speak.[12] To him fell the unpleasant task of replying to his friends and erstwhile allies. They underestimated the urgency of the appeal for reform in Upper Canada, he told the Rouge leader. When he arrived in the Legislature he had some misapprehensions too – misapprehensions about the attitude of Lower Canada – but he had found that he was wrong. French Canada's best guarantee of its rights was the knowledge that the British had agreed to respect their customs and religion, and it would be suicide for any political party to commit an injustice to them. When they refused to join the United States, they recognized that the British Crown was a safeguard to their "nationality". He, too, had made compromises. Like the Conservative leader, he had abandoned his hopes for a system closer to a legislative union, and plumped for the larger federal system in order to avoid the calamity of dissolving entirely the connection between the two Canadas. He had accepted a nominative Senate, although such a Chamber seemed a relic of feudal times. It was the best that could be done in view of the varied opinions at the conference table.

In addition to just and economic government, Mackenzie saw in Confederation an opportunity to forward his dream of Empire. Canada would be better able to defend herself. "It is not honourable, it is not manly," he protested, "for so powerful a colony as this to depend entirely on the Mother Country for protection." A canal up the Ottawa River to Georgian Bay could be built, giving "a great backbone to the country", and capable of carrying vessels of war as well as ships bearing products from "that magnificent country", the North West, that great potential source of strength and power. "Altogether," he summarized in a burst of eloquence, "I regard this scheme as a magnificent one, and I look forward to . . . being, before I die, a citizen of an immense empire built up on our part of the North American continent, where the folds of the British flag will float in triumph over a people possessing freedom, happiness, and prosperity equal to the people of any other nation on the earth."

As the debate proceeded, the split between supporters and opponents of the scheme widened rather than narrowed. Only John Sandfield Macdonald remained, in the words of D'Arcy McGee, "like the blank leaf between the Old and New Testaments, belonging neither to the one nor to the other".[13] When New Brunswick turned out the pro-Union Government in March, Dorion suggested a return to the original concept of a federation of the two Canadas. It was too late. Conservatives and Reformers alike were working toward a great, united Canada extending from sea to sea; they would not settle for less. "I look upon it as a scheme more national than federal in character . . . ," said Hope Mackenzie when his turn came. "I stand as an advocate of national unity." To him it offered "the prospect of building up a great nationality here and of handing down to our children institutions which our fathers have bought with their blood."[14]

As the flow of words continued into March, Macdonald and his colleagues began to worry lest the bitter resistance spread beyond the Chamber to the public mind. They decided to close off the debate by the only means at their disposal, by moving "that the main question be now put". After a final flurry, the opponents of Confederation were stifled; the Bill was carried ninety-one to thirty-three.[15]

The Confederation debate drew the Conservatives together and enhanced their leader's prestige; it was almost a lethal blow to the Liberal party. As their former opponents sat and watched, they castigated one another with reckless abandon. Sandfield Macdonald's dislike of Brown turned into open hostility, and Alexander Mackenzie was soon drawn into the fray in defence of his leader. Brown himself was too hypnotized by the great goal almost within their grasp; he left the defensive action to his friends. "Alexander Mackenzie is a little warm and speaks strongly," commented the *Quebec Mercury* after one exchange, "but is evidently a conscientious and honest man."[16]

* * * * *

While Brown, Macdonald, Galt, and Cartier sailed for England to plead the Confederation cause, Alexander and Hope Mackenzie explained the new scheme to their neighbours in western Canada. It was "rep by pop" and more, they repeated over and over; it was the promise of a great new future. As they defended the plan, the two men realized how much their own lives were tied up with that Canadian future. Hope had children of his own at last; the other brothers were all married, and the familiar Mackenzie traits – the straight, fine nose, the smallish, bright blue eyes, the strong chin, and the fair complexion – were to be found in nearly every group where the youth of Sarnia assembled.

At the end of the school year, Mary, not quite seventeen, but already a tall, handsome woman, graduated as a teacher and prepared to take her place in society. Like Canada, she, too, was growing up. Alex and "Jeannie" had no children of their own. It was hard for the forty-three-year-old Parliamentarian to realize that his only surviving child was almost an adult, that Helen had been gone thirteen years, and that he had laboured in Canada over half of his life. His daughter's graduation meant that they were nearly a generation removed from the Tummel Valley in Perthshire. She was a native Canadian; he, too, thought of Canada as his permanent home.

After Mary's graduation ceremony, Alexander Mackenzie and his friend Archibald McKellar set off on a combined holiday and business excursion to Lake Superior, the highway to the fabulous North West.[17] The leisurely pace of the freighter on which they travelled gave them an opportunity to visit the ports of call along the way, and to investigate the reports of vast mineral wealth on the rocky shore. At the western end of their journey, they climbed the craggy promontory of Thunder Cape and looked westward toward the sunset, beyond which lay the vast expanses of prairie dotted with buffalo herds and occasional clusters of Indian teepees. In their imagination they tried to picture the rich, fertile soil, the deep beds of coal, the great Saskatchewan River, and the towering mountains beyond. Soon it too would be a part of Canada, the Canada of which they had laid the foundations in Quebec.

They were in a relaxed and happy mood as they talked of the future, and drank in the strength and beauty of the vast unconquered region. They had bought a section of claims in the area below them, and could look about with a proprietary interest, dreaming dreams of advancing their own fortunes as the young country grew. "Archie" McKellar was pleasant company, and stimulated the humour of his companion. When he started down the steep cliff, Mackenzie remained behind. Unable to resist the opportunity of giving the great practical joker a scare, he rolled a boulder to the edge and sent it crashing down between the trees. Bouncing along, it veered from its original course and made straight for the jovial Scot. Hearing the terrified shouts from above, McKellar turned, and seeing the heavy missile hurtling down, threw himself behind a birch tree, hugging it with one arm for support. Seconds later, the boulder struck the tree with a sickening thud a foot or two above his arm, broke in two pieces, and continued down to the lake a thousand feet below. Charging down behind it, Alex, with tears in his eyes, prayed for his friend's forgiveness. McKellar escaped with a cut on the knee.[18]

In August they were back in Quebec. In the interval, Premier Taché had died and John A. Macdonald had made a bid to take control of the Government in name as well as in fact. Brown had blocked his path, and a still weaker figurehead, Sir Narcisse Belleau, was named instead. The anti-Unionist Government in New Brunswick was still holding out under Liberal Albert Smith, and the breach between Canadian Liberals was as serious as ever. Legislation was scarce, but a set of estimates had to be passed for the coming year. As long as the Coalition continued, Mackenzie had no alternative but to give it his support. That this meant voting for items he had opposed on previous occasions, such as the separate school grant, was painfully obvious. Holton did not fail to bring it to public attention. Recalling Holton's own votes when in the Sandfield Macdonald Administration, the member for Lambton replied in a volley of words that was described as an Australian boomerang, which, when shied at a target, sometimes returns to demolish its thrower.[19] Sandfield Macdonald felt the lash of the Scotsman's tongue frequently. Smarting at having to defend a Coalition which the former Premier himself had forced them into by his motions in caucus, Mackenzie replied savagely to the taunts from across the floor. He admitted the right, nay, even the duty, of every oppositionist to assume that the Ministry of the day had designs on the public purse and public liberties, he said, but the immediate task was to establish a strong national government. "That accomplished," – there was evident nostalgia in his voice – "parties will revert to their normal condition and the present anomalous state of affairs will cease."

The session closed in mid-September, and immediately the civil servants began moving their files and equipment to the new capital in Ottawa. The buildings were far from ready. When the Department of Agriculture steamed up the Ottawa River in three barges one late October day, the site beside the Rideau Canal still looked incongruously unworthy of its new appellation of Parliament Hill.[20] The squat, domeless, stone structure, and the untidy mass of building material surrounding it, were hardly a cheering sight for the travel-weary bureaucrats. The water in the river was so low that the barges had difficulty in reaching their destination below the cliff, and there was scarcely room to stack the boxes and crates into the space already covered by a roof. To the south, the rows and clusters of individual houses soon gave way to open fields, and seemed to offer precious little chance of finding decent accommodation. Only when they turned their backs on the overgrown lumber village, and gazed northward across the river to the endless miles of flaming autumn colours that faded to mauve and then to blue on the Gatineau skyline, did they take heart for their heavy task.

In addition to Confederation, other problems demanded attention. With the Civil War over, many Americans were threatening revenge on Britain for what they considered active sympathy with the Confederate cause. They resented the intercourse between London and the South, and claimed compensation for the damage done by the *Alabama*, a ship that had sunk several Northern vessels after having been built in Britain and sailed from an English port. Canada was reported to be full of Confederate sympathizers, and, indeed, one group of Southerners had launched an attack on St. Albans from Canadian soil. There was reckless talk of dealing with the Canadians once and for all, and reports of invasion preparations. In addition, the Fenian brotherhood, a group of Irishmen devoted to the liberation of their homeland, were collecting money and recruiting footloose veterans to "liberate" Canada as the first step in freeing their ancestral home.[21]

Under the pressure of public opinion, the United States Government decided to abrogate the Reciprocity Treaty of 1854. It was a subject in which the Liberals were deeply interested; free trade and reciprocity with the United States had long been cardinal points in their programme. George Brown had supported Hincks during the negotiations in 1853 and 1854, and he had almost been sent to Washington in 1863 by Sandfield Macdonald to forestall cancellation of the Treaty. He had an excellent knowledge of trade matters, and was well regarded in Washington because of his ardent support of the Anti-slavery Society during the Civil War. Above all, he was vitally interested in the subject. John A. Macdonald was not impressed by these qualifications. While Brown was on a tour of the Maritimes, he sent to Washington the protectionist-minded Alexander Galt, and William Howland, who had replaced Mowat in the Cabinet when the latter accepted a position on the Bench a few months earlier. Genuinely insulted, but relieved at the same time to have a suitable pretext to escape from the uncomfortable Coalition Ministry, Brown protested the proposals made by the two emissaries and resigned. Free at last, he rushed home to his wife and baby daughter.[22] Any further assistance needed to ensure the success of Confederation, he told his friends, could be given from outside.

Brown was back with Anne and Maddie in time for Christmas, but in his haste he had left one task undone: he had made no arrangements for a successor. Before leaving Quebec, he had consulted neither his Liberal colleagues nor the caucus about his decision. As long as McDougall and Howland remained, and a third Reformer could be found to accept a portfolio, the Government was still a coalition. In fact, he had walked out and left his old rival in charge of the Administration after giving him a fresh lease of political life by helping to achieve Confederation.

At John A. Macdonald's request, Howland telegraphed the leading Reformers in the West and asked them to meet him in Guelph at the earliest possible moment in order to discuss the choice of a successor. They met on Christmas day. Both Hope and Alexander Mackenzie attended the meeting; the latter was offered the post.[23]

It was a big decision. Alexander Mackenzie was vitally interested in the success of Confederation, and flattered by the offer. With only six years of formal education, it was higher than he had ever dared to aim. Just four years after entering Parliament, here was an invitation to be a member of the first Cabinet of the Dominion! At the same time, he agreed completely with his leader on all matters of public policy. If Brown felt compelled to resign, how could he possibly enter the Cabinet in his stead? Asking for time, he rushed to Toronto for consultations.

Brown refused to advise him, but he did explain that he had

differed with Galt over the form of a new trade agreement with the United States. The latter had favoured co-ordinated legislative action to a formal treaty, and had secured a Minute of Council in Brown's absence in the Maritimes, authorizing him to negotiate on that basis. Certainly, Mackenzie and Brown that Christmas evening also talked of the frustrations and iniquities of coalitions. Having spent the whole of Christmas day on the road, the ex-stonemason returned to Sarnia to make up his mind.

The call of principle and loyalty prevailed. The resignation of the President of the Council, he wrote to Howland on December 27, "was but the culminating act of a series of circumstances connected with the pending negotiations (in Washington) against which Mr. Brown protested as improper and seriously prejudicial to our interests as a Province".[24] His convictions made it impossible to defend the causes that had precipitated Brown's departure; he could not accept. The ageing and harmless Fergusson-Blair was named in his place; John A. Macdonald tightened still further his hold on the Administration.

"No man, however pure," William Lyon Mackenzie used to say, "can accept office without coming out as black as a baker would from a chimney-sweep's." The new system would change all that, Alexander Mackenzie told the ladies at the Strathroy Fruit Soirée as 1865 drew to an end; it would make possible economic, efficient, and upright administration.[25] It would be but the first step in building a strong, united nation. Such were the pious hopes of dozens of after-dinner orators throughout the land. In fact, the provinces were far from being strong or united; something more was needed than the Quebec "treaty" to weld them together. That catalyst was the Irish hatred of the British yoke. The Fenian threat emphasized the need for Canada to grow up in fact as well as in name, and for Canadians to stand on their own feet on their portion of the North American continent.

Having offered to give up much of the responsibility of government, the British authorities were not inclined to maintain large expenditures for military needs in British North America. "Canada leans on a broken reed if she supposes that in case of an invasion from America any considerable portion of the burden of her defence can be borne by this country," the London *Times* warned.[26] "If the colonists cannot, as a general rule, defend themselves against the Fenians, they can do nothing," commented Disraeli to his chief, Lord Derby. ". . . What is the use of these colonial deadweights which we do not govern?"[27]

Alexander Mackenzie agreed. It was not manly, he had told the Legislature during the Confederation debate, for so powerful a colony to depend entirely on the Mother Country for protection; Canada should at least pay a large portion of the expenses of Imperial troops on her soil.

As reports of Fenian preparations increased, Imperial troops and Canadian militiamen took up their positions along the border and waited. D-Day, it was believed, was to be St. Patrick's Day, the seventeenth of March. In the short time at their disposal, the Sarnians had not been able to form into an official regiment, but they took up their posts as the "Centre" Administrative Battalion, later to become the 27th Battalion (St. Clair Borderers).[28] The officers were chosen for their leadership in the community as much as for their military experience. Their commanding officer was a retired Imperial colonel, Fred Davis; one of the two majors was Alexander Mackenzie. They were a motley crew, with no uniforms, few weapons, and only a cursory knowledge of military discipline. Their strength lay mainly in their patriotism and morale.

It was a cold, dry spring in 1866. The militiamen patrolled the shore and the communication lines with the rest of the province, and drilled in the streets every evening. St. Patrick's Day passed, and March, then April, slipped away. The frequent frosts and the prospects of drought accentuated the tense, worried expressions on the faces of men, women and children alike. To maintain the spirits of both volunteers and local residents, a mammoth oyster dinner was organized in the Western Hotel. Despite the crisis, the young Reverend John Thompson was inducted into St. Andrew's Church where the Alexander Mackenzies often joined the rest of the clan for Sabbath worship, and the honourable member for Lambton took time off occasionally to make a speech.[29]

On May 27, the weather broke; warm air from the south forced its way north to meet the cold northern breezes; rain began to fall. Four days later the Fenians crossed the Niagara River.[30] The waiting was over! Faces smiled with relief. Troops from Hamilton and Toronto were despatched to the Niagara Peninsula; the Borderers redoubled their patrols. The St. Clair area remained quiet. By June 2, the fighting was over. "General" O'Neill's troops were driven back into the United States, and minor border crossings farther east were easily repelled. Nine Canadians, mostly University of Toronto students, lost their lives, but the Colony had defended itself almost unaided. Out of the brief struggle was born the tender infant of Canadian national pride.

In Sarnia, the exuberance was of short duration. The day of the victory over the Fenians, Hope Mackenzie died.[31] Never robust, the ex-mayor's health had been growing steadily worse. His gentle, open face bore the marks of constant suffering. During the Confederation debates, he had been ill most of the time. After the second session in 1865, he had consulted the best doctors in Montreal. Their verdict was unanimous: cancer. He was sent home to die. The funeral was the largest ever held in Sarnia.[32] In the blustering wind and rain, ladies lifted their long, dark skirts over the puddles in the streets as they crossed from one board sidewalk to another on the way to St. Andrew's Church. Stores were closed, and many windows draped in mourning. A large delegation from North Oxford came to pay a last tribute to their member of Parliament. At the head of the mourners, Alexander Mackenzie said farewell to the brother he had loved so well, and to whom he had always been willing to cede first place as long as his ailing body would carry him forward. In the harsh struggle of their youth, in their early days in Canada, in the fight for the rights of Upper Canadians, they had accomplished a great deal together. Nearby were Hope's widow and two small children. He would see that they were well cared for. He would carry on their common tasks, alone.

Two days after the funeral, the first and last Ottawa session of the Parliament of United Canada assembled. Though somewhat shorter, the journey was not more pleasant than to Quebec. The Montreal train took the passengers as far as Prescott, where they were transferred to the Ottawa cars some time around five in the morning. French-Canadian cabbies were waiting at the Sussex Street station in place of the Point Lévis canoemen, and whisked them into the centre of town. Most Parliamentarians preferred to stay at the Russell Hotel on Sparks and Elgin streets, just a few paces from the scene of their labours. Others, like Mackenzie, sought accommodation in boarding-houses, usually operated by the wives of civil servants anxious to augment their husbands' meagre earnings.

The members were not impressed with the new buildings. The Gothic architecture was an expensive concession to the whim of Sir Edmund Head, who, as Governor General, had made it the price of his signature of approval a few years earlier. The Committee rooms were small, complained Mackenzie, there were few private offices, the acoustics of the Chamber were poor, and the drainage was constructed with such ingenuity that "foul air at the mouth of the ducts merely performs a circuit and returns afterwards into the buildings.[33] All in all, it was "one of the greatest examples of magnitude without convenience ever seen on the face of the earth".

Little progress had been made with Confederation. The scheme had not yet been submitted to the British Parliament, and opposition to the plan was stiffening in the Maritimes and in Lower Canada. There were tales that Sir John A. Macdonald was drinking as much as ever, and had not been sober throughout the entire Fenian crisis.[34] Lord Monck was so concerned at the constant delays that he was threatening to apply for his recall to England.[35] George Brown and his supporters were equally impatient to end the truce between Grits and Tories. "The sooner the better," Mackenzie had told his friends before leaving Sarnia.[36]

Still smarting at being ignored in the reciprocity negotiations, Brown yearned to press to the attack. Galt and Howland had been unsuccessful in Washington, and were open to accusations of having gone to the United States cap in hand, and subjecting Canada to a rebuff. The temptation was irresistible. Before many weeks passed, the old party lines began to reappear. The Grit leader protested against the tariff changes, declaring that their introduction was a breach of the agreement that commercial policies were not to be altered until Confederation was achieved, and the Coalition dissolved. Mackenzie returned to his condemnation of sectarian grants, and warned the Ministry against attempting a gerrymander in redistributing the seats for the new House of Commons. The hostility between Brownites and McDougall and Howland broke into the open when the two Ministers announced their intention to remain in the Cabinet until Confederation was safely launched. "We have made up our minds to stand our ground and defend our position," McDougall proclaimed defiantly. ". . . I believe it is the duty of the Liberals to relieve the party and the country of the incubus, the terrorism and the domination exercised by Mr. Brown who is inserting a wedge to split the Liberal Party."[37]

Alexander Mackenzie replied to McDougall's attack, and widened his aim to sweep the whole Cabinet with his broadside.[38] Knowing Galt's and Howland's republican inclinations, he said, he had been worried that the two men might lead Canadians closer to the United States than they desired. Why had they not protested the statement by the American chairman of the joint discussions that "these are matters we will consider when you Canadian gentlemen come here as members of Congress from Canada"? He threw back the accusation that Brown was splitting the Liberal party, and declared that the

Liberal Ministers should have consulted the caucus and the people they represented before deciding to maintain the Coalition. He decried the tariff changes as a breach of the Coalition agreement, and regretted that the new era should be inaugurated with what he considered an "absurd and necessarily evil" protectionist policy.

In this atmosphere of disintegration and hostility, the provincial resolutions were passed, and the Parliament of United Canada fell silent for the last time. Its members boarded the Prescott train; the Ministers prepared for another trip to England to aid in the birth of its successor.

The British North America Bill passed through the Imperial Parliament easily; the principal objection was that the separation from the Mother Country was not complete enough.[39] Many Canadians thought otherwise; the plunge into the cold waters of semi-independence seemed suddenly a frightening experience. The first matter was to decide in a general election who would be the managers of the new Dominion. Two days after the third reading of the Bill in Westminster, the Lambton Reformers chose their candidate for the task. Only one name was considered – Alexander Mackenzie.[40]

Mackenzie was reluctant. With Confederation, most of the great reforms for which he had struggled were accomplished. Besides, political life was both exhausting and expensive. His brother Hope had died under the strain; the fatigue and tension often forced him to take to his bed with attacks of fever and dysentery. His contracting business had suffered, and he had spent far more money than his small stipend as a parliamentarian. After being the most prosperous of the seven brothers, he was on the way to becoming the poorest. While he laboured in Quebec or Ottawa, or toured the country arguing Reform policies, the others were progressing from tradesmen to prosperous business men. John had obtained a patent for a new plough, and distribution rights for all Canada. His shop was growing into a veritable little factory, and he had a chain of agents throughout the province. Leaving young Charles in charge, he had spent an entire summer renewing old acquaintances in Scotland. The contrast with Alexander's life was striking. He had given unselfishly of himself for several years, the latter reasoned; surely he had the right to return to his family and his business again.

As he sat at home debating the alternatives, a delegation from the Reform meeting arrived with the unanimous requisition. Their able, faithful, intelligent representative in the past, it read, he must continue in the new era just beginning. He was an enemy of coalitions and "no-party compromises; they agreed with him completely. The applause as he mounted the platform swept away all thoughts of an alternative course. The call to duty was written in every upturned face; he agreed to go on. He was sorry that he had not been able to honour the constituency by accepting a Cabinet post, he told them, but his political integrity was worth more to them – and to him – than such a distinction. As for the future, nothing in the new order of things would diminish his attachment to the British connection, and he would do everything in his power to perpetuate it. For the United States, Canada would always be a friendly neighbour, but Britain would always be "home". After his address, a local lawyer, Timothy Pardee, was chosen as his running mate in the Ontario provincial election, which was to be held simultaneously. When it was all over, the federal candidate went on to the Presbyterian Church to give a talk at the Sabbath School service. For him, politics and religion went hand in hand.

The day after the Lambton nomination, George Brown announced his determination not to take a seat in the Dominion Parliament. He was a "ministerial impossibility", he had said, and could not work as a member of a team. He felt, too, his principal purpose in entering Parliament was accomplished. Through the *Globe*, and in other ways, he could still give powerful support to the Reform cause. Above all, he would be free to spend more time with his wife and growing family. There were things more important than politics; Anne had just presented him with a son.

Brown once said that John A. Macdonald was an old cat always on the watch for mice.[41] By the end of May, it was obvious that he was up to his old tricks again. With the Governor General's command to form the first government of the Dominion, he was looking about for Cabinet colleagues who would assure him of broad, popular support.[42] To Brownites, it was just another clever manoeuvre to keep himself in power. Incensed at the refusal of McDougall and Howland to resign, the *Globe* publisher determined to read them out of the party. He called a convention for late June. The Reform Party would greet Confederation with purified ranks and a new set of goals.

Liberals from the Atlantic to the Pacific were present at the meeting in Toronto's Music Hall.[43] Edward Blake, brilliant son of the famous Reformer of Baldwin-Lafontaine days, was introducing the first resolution when McDougall and Howland appeared in response to Brown's invitation. Mingled cheers and boos arose as they made their way to the platform. "The atmosphere was so surcharged with passion and the fiery spirit of its great leader," wrote one partisan correspondent, "that deliberation was impossible".[44] Brown paced back and forth constantly on the stage, launching frequently into torrents of words, and swinging his huge arms in great sweeping gestures. The fifth resolution was the lethal one.[45] It condemned coalitions "for ordinary administrative purposes" as breeding-grounds of public immorality, waste, and corruption, and declared "the temporary alliance between the Reform and Conservative parties should now cease". Both Ministers replied. They could not abandon the new-born child, Confederation, they argued, until they were certain it could stand on its own feet. After all, the Liberals had a responsibility for it as long as they claimed a share in its paternity.

It was an able defence, but the jury was prejudiced against them. The next morning, Alexander Mackenzie replied.[46] It was because he feared just such a situation that he had tried to prevent the Reformers from entering the Cabinet in 1864, he stated. The lure of the Treasury benches had proven too great for the two men, and they were ready to serve still longer with Tories, who personified the very antithesis of Reform principles. The Reform party had been founded to fight their encroachments on the rights and privileges of the people, their policies of restriction, and their ecclesiastical despotism. No true Reformer or Liberal who believed in the equality of every man, and the abolition of all special privileges, could join such a company. He preferred to remain with men of principle like Dorion and the others who had honestly opposed Confederation, and who had made such sacrifices for their beliefs. Disciples of Brown he and McKellar might well be; the man did not exist whom he would more willingly follow as his leader or who deserved higher praise for his integrity and patriotism.

The audience listened in pleased astonishment, not having realized what a formidable politician the Sarnia contractor had become.[47] The anti-coalition resolution was sustained by all but three delegates. "The split in the Reform ranks seems to be permanent," chuckled the master Cabinet-maker in Ottawa.[48] There was a more heartening result for the Reformers. Stirred by the spirit of the Convention, and under heavy pressure from his followers, Brown decided to run as a candidate again.

* * * * *

Sarnia did full justice to the first Dominion Day.[49] With five hundred dollars to spend, the Committee arranged an impressive programme. Under a brilliant sun, a military band led a

CONFEDERATION!

THE MUCH-FATHERED YOUNGSTER.

[317]

From Bengough's *Caricature History of Canadian Politics*, Vol. I

parade through the principal streets. Immediately behind them came the town clerk in a two-horse carriage, bearing a copy of the Queen's proclamation. In a second carriage rode four young ladies dressed in white, representing the four provinces, Ontario, Quebec, New Brunswick, and Nova Scotia. Next were the civic officials of Sarnia and neighbouring Port Huron, the clergy, the veterans of 1812 and 1838, the Sarnia and Port Huron fire brigades, the Sabbath School children, and, finally, as many of the populace as could be induced to join.

Canada had achieved in one bloodless revolution, said Mackenzie when his turn came to speak, what it had taken the United States two great struggles to attain. The new system was a good one. British Columbia would be entering soon, and there was even room for the guests from across the St. Clair, if they cared to join! He was sure that the Canadian provinces would remain British; he was equally confident that they would remain friends with their fellow Anglo-Saxons across the border. It was nearly midnight when the guests from the United States took the ferry back to their side of the river. The reflections from the torchlight parade still shimmered on the water, and shadowy figures moved around the bonfires along the shore. The goals ahead were set by a local poet:

> "To win for Canada a name – a place
> Worthy the scion of a free-born race, –
> A name with freedom and with truth allied
> Spoken by all her sons with love and pride."[50]

CHAPTER 6

Her Majesty's Loyal Opposition

The Dominion of Canada was born in the midst of a rough election campaign. John A. Macdonald and his colleagues in the Liberal-Conservative Coalition appealed for a "fair trial" for the new creation: colony, nation, or whatever it might be called. On the provincial level, he had persuaded John Sandfield Macdonald to form a "Patent Combination" similar to his own so that they could "hunt in pairs".[1] Both Governments had one common trait: they were formed on anti-Grit lines.

At the Convention, Alexander Mackenzie had promised McDougall that he would carry the war into Africa, Africa being in this case the Minister's constituency of Lanark. He appeared at a Ministerialist meeting in Almonte and spoke for over an hour in rebuttal of McDougall's speech.[2] The latter referred to him disdainfully as Brown's henchman, and said it was time the *Globe* was abolished as the knout had been in Russia and slavery in the United States. He had never received pay from the *Globe* publisher, retorted the aggressive Scot, nor had he ever been indebted to him for his seat in Parliament! The following day, the Brownites held a meeting in Middleville, and McDougall appeared. The stormy debate continued.

McDougall followed his opponent right back to Lambton. Their first meeting in the western County was held in a Wyoming Township barn.[3] The Minister defended the Coalition; the local candidate attacked. The Minister assailed the opponents of Confederation in Quebec, and associated them with the Brownites; Mackenzie came to the defence of Dorion and Holton, reminding the audience that the two men had accepted Confederation and advised their friends to work for any changes within the framework of the new constitution. After the Clear Grits had left the meeting, the Coalitionists chose Alexander Vidal to oppose Mackenzie again. As soon as the choice was made, McDougall raced off to catch up with the ex-stonemason and rebut his arguments in Watford.

The joint meeting in Sarnia lasted until two o'clock in the morning. The excitement and controversy had brought on another attack of dysentery and played havoc with his disposition, but Mackenzie stuck to the platform and traded blow for blow until the end. His meeting at Fisher's schoolhouse in Plympton the following day nearly ended in disaster.[4] The building was so packed with rowdies that he had to abandon any attempt to outline his programme. When he and his travelling companion tried to leave, strong arms blocked their path. Some held the nervous horses' heads; some tried to upset the carriage; others tried to pull the two men down into the crowd. Mackenzie succeeded in getting aboard the vehicle but his friend was badly pummelled before he managed to clamber up behind. The rearing and plunging horses broke loose from their tormentors and dashed off at full gallop down the country lane with other carriages laden with opponents – "yelling and howling like savages", according to the *Observer* – in hot pursuit. A mile down the road, a barricade of rails had been erected over a culvert. The horses skidded to a stop, the rails were heaved aside, and the flight continued down the dusty trail. The horses were well suited to such a western campaign; in a few miles they had outdistanced their pursuers. Mackenzie continued on his schedule through the "swamps of Lambton".

In comparison, the rest of the campaign was quiet. It was reported that the ardent Reformer had to leave the Mooretown schoolhouse by the window after a violent exchange, but the report was denied.[5] Under the system of staggered elections, polling day in South Ontario, where Brown was running, arrived earlier than in Lambton. Mackenzie was still hard at work in the townships when he received the news on August 30 that his leader had been defeated. It was a severe blow. The Coalitionists redoubled their efforts in order to sweep his lieutenant from the political scene as well. "*You must take another constituency,*" Mackenzie scrawled on the corner of a counter between meetings, ". . . if you do not accept another the party will feel discouraged and broken."[6] Brown had burned his fingers for the last time. He refused categorically every offer of a seat.

With the tide running in favour of the Government, John Sandfield Macdonald arrived in Lambton to take part in the kill. At an outdoor meeting in Moore, the feeling ran so high that the crowd could not even agree on a chairman. After considerable bickering, the choice of candidates for the position was narrowed to two. With agreement still impossible, the Ontario Premier asked them both to get off the wagon and introduced himself.[7]

The McDougall-Mackenzie feud reached its zenith at Arkona schoolhouse. Bitter and enraged by the charge of want of principle, the Minister delivered one of his most violent attacks. Opposition to Her Majesty's Government at such a critical period was disloyalty to the Queen, he charged. "Did he (Maczenzie) want the new Dominion to crumble into its original atoms, and become a prey to the United States?" The Tories cheered. When Mackenzie rose to reply, his eyes flashed with anger, and his Gaelic accent was stronger than it had been in years. "Me disloyal?" he almost snarled. "Do I not wear the Queen's uniform? Have I not camped with my fellow-citizens on the border to repel the Fenian invaders who would trample underfoot the British flag? . . . Let me tell him to his face that he is mistaken. Loyalty to the Queen is a noble sentiment in which all true Liberals share, but loyalty to the Queen does not require a man to bow down to her manservant, her maidservant, or" – and here the fiery Scot turned to face his opponent – "her ass."[8]

The blow, reported a member of the audience, was as fierce as the stroke of a Lochaber axe; it ended the Minister's tour of the county. As he prepared to leave, the excited Mackenzie branded his departure as an act of cowardice, and then went on to attack the chairman for partisanship. When a prominent Grit tried to follow suit, the chairman punched him in the face. Pulling himself together, the Mackenzie supporter sent the chairman to the floor. McDougall completed his withdrawal, and Alexander Mackenzie finished his speech.[9]

The battle had gone on long enough. Mercifully, a violent thunder storm put an unceremonious end to the nomination proceedings. The citizens of Lambton had ample opportunity to make up their minds. On election day, they gave Mackenzie a comfortable majority of six hundred and eighty, and his provincial running mate a majority of a thousand. A huge bonfire of old oil barrels in the market square marked the triumph, and a torchlight parade and band led the way to the Belchamber Hotel, to hear the victors' addresses from the balcony. After a night's rest, Mackenzie rushed over to Bothwell to help his friend McKellar win his seat in the House of Commons. In this they failed.

The Canadian people gave John A. Macdonald the "fair trial" he requested. Every province but Nova Scotia elected a majority for the Coalition. With Brown and McKellar defeated, and

Mowat on the Bench, it was hard for Mackenzie to keep up his courage. There was one bright star on the horizon. Young Edward Blake, who had made such a good speech at the June Convention in Toronto, had been elected for the first time. "Excellent common sense, immense industry and good pluck," Brown had told Mackenzie in March. "Not much of a politician but anxious to learn and as sharp as a needle. He has a great opinion of you and I am persuaded you will be immense helps to each other."[10] Then, too, there were indications that Holton and Dorion would be back at his side after the disruption caused by the Confederation debates.[11] Fortunately, their friendship and esteem for one another had survived the political separation. And with luck there were the Liberals like Joseph Howe and Alfred Jones in Nova Scotia, and Albert Smith in New Brunswick, with whom a basis of co-operation might well be established.

George Brown refused to be budged again from his determination to keep out of public life. His wife longed for a visit to Scotland, and he had promised to take her. The boat was due to leave about three weeks before Parliament would assemble. He asked a few leading Liberals to come to Toronto before he sailed, for consultations. "I am fully convinced that the policy now is the quiescent one," he wrote to Mackenzie, "watching every movement and hitting in when a chance occurs. Give them the full length of their tether and they will soon quarrel."[12] It was easier advice for a man setting off on a holiday to give, than for an embattled warrior to accept. Before the ship weighed anchor, Mackenzie was telling his neighbours at a Reform dinner that despite the most corrupt election on record, during which eight thousand dollars of secret service money had been used by the Ministers, the Reformers had won a four thousand vote majority in Ontario. They would take up their positions on the Opposition benches and oppose the Tories – a Cabinet of Tories and "mongrels" was still a Tory Cabinet to him – and they would at least have none of the "indispositions" of some of the occupants of the Treasury benches with which to contend.[13]

The "Washington of the North" was in holiday attire when the Governor General drove onto Parliament Hill to open the first session of the Canadian Parliament in early November. Most of the twenty thousand inhabitants of the capital lined his path, hiding the unsightly evidence of continuing construction. "Your new nationality enters on its course backed by the moral support, the material aid and the most ardent good wishes of the Mother Country," read Lord Monck with a tremor in his voice.[14]

Under the glare of the three great pendant gaseliers, the two groups in the Commons Chamber eyed each other appraisingly across the narrow walk. On the Opposition front benches were the familiar faces of Mackenzie, Holton, and Dorion. Close behind them were the newcomer, Edward Blake, and the ex-Premier of New Brunswick, portly Albert Smith. Still looking a bit ill at ease in his statesman's clothes, Mackenzie sat bolt upright, only his sharp eyes in an otherwise impassive face revealing his eagerness to spring to the attack. Even with his beard more neatly trimmed and streaked with grey, he still seemed very much a representative of the rugged West. His appearance was a striking contrast with the olive complexion and delicately carved features of his seat-mate, Antoine-Aimé Dorion, whose relaxed, self-confident air appeared to reflect the best in Latin culture and intellectual capacity. Next to these two men of average stature, Luther Holton overflowed his seat as Brown had done in former years. His powerful frame seemed to contain a reserve of energy equal to any occasion, and the large well-shaped head was a treasure house of knowledge on public affairs. Edward Blake's appearance was unique. He was a thick-set, rather flabby-looking man with a broad boyish face and small oval glasses. An uneven fringe of beard extended downward from each ear along the line between chin and neck. Nothing betrayed his great ability as a lawyer, or his great potential as a Parliamentarian. The casual observer might have commented that in the absence of a leader, the Liberals had brought their encyclopaedia of universal knowledge into the House of Commons.

With the system of dual representation, which permitted members to hold both provincial and federal seats at the same time, many provincial legislators were present as well. They included the Premier of Quebec, Pierre Chauveau, Nova Scotia's Joseph Howe, and Sandfield Macdonald, who insisted that he was still a Reformer despite his numerous appearances on the same platform as the Dominion Premier during the election campaign. To add insult to injury he was allotted the seat of the Leader of the Opposition by the Government!

Alexander Mackenzie found the quiescence recommended by Brown a hard role to adopt. On the choice of a Speaker for the House of Commons, he wanted to put forward a candidate in whom he and his fellow-Oppositionists had confidence. Dorion told him that it was more statesmanlike to allow the Ministry to organize the House; besides, a weak choice such as the Premier had in mind would do more damage than they could possibly achieve by obstructing it. The straightforward Mackenzie retorted that he was willing to "sink the statesman for five minutes in that case."[15] His indignation at William McDougall had not diminished. The Minister of Public Works, in his "gilded dress", he commented with a vengeful eye across the aisle, reminded him of Byron's lines on George III's funeral:

> "It seemed the mockery of Hell to fold
> The rottenness of eighty [forty] years in gold."

The Liberals decided not to choose a new leader until they became a more homogeneous group. As Brown's most trusted lieutenant in Ontario, Mackenzie worked carefully but persistently to bring them all together. There were undoubtedly some capable men in the Opposition, but many of them had made pledges during the election to allow the Government a free hand at the outset. "I feel very much alone with you and McKellar out," the Sarnia contractor confided to his leader in Edinburgh, "but will continue – as I am here – to work in hope of better times coming soon . . . I hope Mrs. Brown and yourself . . . are now enjoying yourselves in Auld Scotia. I envy you . . ."[16]

Joseph Howe was carrying on a bitter fight against the terms under which his province had entered Confederation. The compensation for abandoning certain provincial sources of revenue he denounced as "eighty cents per head, the price of a Nova Scotian as well as a sheepskin".[17] His rival, Charles Tupper, defended the Government. Despite Howe's reluctance to be associated with his fellow-Liberals from the other provinces, Edward Blake came to his defence, throwing the weight of the Opposition behind the provincial cause. Like an expert surgeon at the operating table, his speech was a superbly able, but a cold, impersonal performance. His manner was "as devoid of warmth as is a flake of December snow and as devoid of magnetism as is a loaf of unleavened bread", commented one contemporary historian.[18] Nevertheless, the speech inspired great respect. It placed the thirty-four-year-old lawyer in the front ranks of the Opposition, and it placed the Liberal party in its historical position as the guardian of provincial rights.

The following day, Mackenzie followed with a strong attack on both the Ottawa and Toronto Coalitions, and called for a return to the old party divisions.[19] Without parties, he argued, there could never be an alternative to those in power, or a change of government. While leaving the door open for an alliance with Howe and the other Nova Scotia Liberals, he did not waver in his support of an expanding Dominion. The Roman Empire began to decline when it withdrew from its colonies, he warned. Britain, however, was not withdrawing; she was merely strengthening her Empire by granting so much freedom. With the Mother Country at their back, loyal Canadians would be able to defend their enormous portion of Her Majesty's domain, and relieve the Imperial Government of a considerable burden.

As in pre-Confederation days, the Ontario Reformers pressed for a new reciprocity treaty, efficiency and economy in government, and early annexation of the North West. Brown's dream of westward expansion had become his lieutenant's as well. He called for a settlement of the mining areas around the Great Lakes, and early communications with the North West to counter American designs on that area.[20] He had accepted a coalition in 1864 in order to avoid any possibility of absorption by the United States; he would work for a railway line to the West for the same reason.

In his North West policy, Mackenzie was in a minority. With the exception of McDougall, the Ministers were occupied with what they considered more immediate tasks, and most of the members were more concerned with adapting themselves to Confederation in their own provinces. The Opposition found their main source of unity rather in a common mistrust of the Administration. Maritimers felt that they had not received a fair deal; the Rouges feared for their racial, religious, and linguistic identity; the Clear Grits suspected Tories and Coalitionists *per se*. With such an attitude, they performed well their function of scrutinizing every action of the Ministry.

Parliament adjourned just in time for the members to reach home for Christmas. Before they reconvened in March, the Ontario Legislature met for the first time. The Reform Opposition was led by Archibald McKellar, with Blake, who had taken advantage of the system of dual representation, rapidly moving forward to the foremost place.

The winter recess was short, and duty soon called in Ottawa again. Brown having returned, Mackenzie spent the week-end at his home on the way down. Except for two adjournments to go to church on Sunday, the discussions with Brown, McKellar, and Blake continued until late Sunday night.[21] The *Globe* publisher's friends implored him to return to active politics, and offered him a choice of sure seats. He refused to be moved. "The thing is not to be thought of," he reassured his wife after the guests had gone.[22] Brown was not the only one under a petticoat régime. In Ottawa, Macdonald – Sir John since the achievement of Confederation – was married to the sister of his Deputy Minister in the Department of Justice. Though she had enjoyed the gay social rounds during their courtship, she decided the tone was too frivolous for a Premier. With subtle wiles, she discouraged Sunday politics, and gave up wine as an example to her husband to follow a more sober path. Depressed and discouraged, Macdonald yearned to be free of it all.[23]

With what comfort he could derive from listening to the advice of a man who urged others to do a job he himself refused, Mackenzie returned to the fray. The day the House opened for the 1868 session, he had an impressive list of questions ready.[24] Who was to replace the recently deceased Fergusson-Blair in the Ministry? What was being done about the route of the Intercolonial Railway to the Maritimes? the North West? Reciprocity? Tupper's mission to England to counter Nova Scotia's demands for better terms or secession? Few onlookers suspected he was still playing a quiescent game! "Lambton furnishes perhaps the most conspicuous representative on the floor," reported one newspaper.[25] "Always working faithfully and earnestly in his place . . . always watching the proceedings with the same intent guardianship of the interests of the party, always ready upon every subject on which he has something worth saying, and never to be tempted into idle words, presenting his telling argument with clear logical severity . . . inflexible as Fabricus, the sun shall be turned from its course before either cajolery or intimidation can deflect him from the line he has chosen."

Below the surface of the formal debates, there was plenty of evidence of cabal and intrigue. To bolster his prestige in Ontario, McDougall was struggling to obtain a Government decision in favour of the shortest possible rail route to the Maritimes. Georges-Etienne Cartier, the leading Quebec Minister, wanted the line to follow the St. Lawrence as far as possible, and then swing south to the Baie des Chaleurs and along northern New Brunswick, a much longer route that led through heavy forest and barren, rocky terrain. The Liberal Minister felt strongly enough to get in touch with his bitter campaign opponent of six months before, and try to use the Opposition to win his intra-Cabinet fight. He succeeded only in preparing his own exodus from the Ministry.[26]

Cartier himself was delving in a bit of intrigue with even more momentous possibilities. Annoyed at the award to Macdonald of a distinction higher than the one offered him, he had refused a title from the Queen. He went a step further; he wrote to George Brown, for whom he had developed a liking and respect during the months when they were working side by side for Confederation. "Cartier . . . sent me a letter suggesting a political alliance and my return to Parliament," Brown wrote to his wife on March 31.[27] "I replied that I could have nothing to do with Parliamentary life itself but that I would gladly support my party in an alliance with him on sound principles. He rejoined, urging me to come down to Ottawa and talk the matter over as he could not go to Toronto to see me without exciting some speculation." Rumours were widespread that the two men were preparing to "ditch" Sir John.

Brown consulted Mackenzie in Ottawa. Although he was generally considered the leader of the Ontario Reformers, the latter had to proceed cautiously. He, too, felt a strong personal sympathy for the energetic French Canadian, but his main concern was to rebuild the party on sound Liberal principles. Any split in the ranks would be harmful, and even tragic if the negotiations were revealed and then collapsed. His first reaction was that it was a good opportunity, and that Brown should come.[28] A few days later he was less certain, "I . . . feel . . . it possible that it might be a mistake, but I know your presence would have a most salutary effect on our own friends. You must judge from the tenor of Cartier's letter whether you could accomplish anything with him or not."[29] The urge of politics was strong, but other urges were stronger. Brown had promised his wife when he left her in Edinburgh earlier in the year that he would be back in the spring to fetch her and the babies. She would not be pleased if he broke his promise. He dropped the negotiations and sailed.

Nor was the master intriguer idle. When the Opposition protested the despatch of Charles Tupper, the political arch-enemy of Joseph Howe, to England to frustrate Howe's appeal for better terms, Macdonald admitted to Mackenzie that it was a bad mistake. "John A. told me after the House rose that Galt promised to go," the Grit leader wrote to Brown, "and relying on that promise he offered the mission to Tupper and when Galt refused to go he could not draw back his offer.[30] Rose, another Minister for whom Mackenzie had considerable sympathy, said it was an "unfortunate affair". Both Sir John and Rose remarked that Galt could not be trusted because of his drinking habits and his "chameleon character". Galt left town in a terrible huff. "So far good," commented Mackenzie dryly.

The Nova Scotia question was fraught with danger for the Oppositionists. Their enthusiasm for Howe's cause often led them to make strong anti-Union statements. Dorion and Mackenzie called the caucus together, and the latter bluntly warned that they risked splitting the party by such a course. Holton, still seeking to justify his course during the Confederation debate, and Huntington, who was a descendant of a distinguished New England family and had pro-American leanings, were the worst offenders. The Ontario leader told them they would have to cease "for they led the Nova Scotians to believe that the active sympathy of the Rouge party could be counted on as against the union and thus stimulated increased action on the part of the Anti's". "My impression is that we will not have any more of that sort of talk from them," he wrote to the *Globe* publisher after the caucus meeting.[31] As a compromise, it was agreed that Holton should demand a parliamentary committee to hear the grievances of the Nova Scotians. Mackenzie supported the motion in the House, and promised that he would work to rectify any genuine causes for complaint. At the same time, he objected to direct negotiations between a province and the Imperial Government. Holton's motion was defeated by the Government majority.

The Tupper mission provided D'Arcy McGee with the opportunity to make his last speech. The Premier and Mackenzie had wrangled ill-naturedly a good part of the evening before the eloquent Irishman took the floor. After defending Tupper, he went on to make a high-minded appeal for a more conciliatory attitude, and greater unity in face of the magnificent challenge awaiting Canadians. He paid tribute to "the moderate and large-minded, and truly national spirit" displayed by Mackenzie in "all these great questions affecting the carrying out and the maintenance and the welfare of the Union."[32] It was after one in the morning on a clear winter night when the popular McGee strolled down the walk to Wellington Street, and along Metcalfe to Sparks, where he said goodnight to a companion. As he put his key in the lock of the Sparks Street boarding-house door, he was shot in the back of the head and fell lifeless into the soft, fresh snow.

Canada was shocked. A strong opponent of Fenianism, McGee had received numerous threatening messages, but they had not been taken seriously. Although a relative newcomer, he was popular and accepted as an important part of the Canadian political scene. Before his health had failed in recent months, and Sir John had married, the capers of the two men had become legendary. On one occasion when they were both in the Cabinet, so one story went, the inebriated Premier had leaned affectionately on his friend's shoulder and said, "Look here McGee, two drunkards is too much for any government and one of us has to stop, so I suggest you quit."[33]

Alexander Mackenzie's affection for the Montreal member was just as sincere as Macdonald's. He had not forgotten that McGee had played nursemaid to his brother Hope during the first session in Quebec. He had long admired the Irishman's eloquence, and as fellow-Liberals they had fought side by side. Later, he had been a formidable opponent, but never ceased to be a friend. "It was my own lot for many years to work in political harmony with him," he told the House the day after the murder, "and it was my lot sometimes to oppose him. But through all the vicissitudes of political warfare we ever found him possess that generous disposition characteristic of the man and his country."[34] It was one of those occasions when onlookers could see through the mask of stoicism and propriety, and catch a glimpse of Mackenzie the man.

As a major in the Borderers, and an ardent Imperialist, the Grit spokesman took a particular interest in the Militia Bill designed to discourage and repel any further attacks from the south.[35] He called for a clearer definition of Canada's responsibility in defence, and argued that unless she participated in policy decisions, the Dominion could not be expected to contribute more than Canadians themselves felt reasonable. What was needed, he said, was a joint tribunal or board to decide expenditures. Instead of fortifying a few key areas, such as Montreal, Toronto and Kingston and leaving the rest of the border exposed, he suggested that Canada's twenty-five thousand militiamen, properly equipped, and backed by the eighty-thousand youths liable for military training, could handle any situation likely to arise. Such a system would also avoid the possibility of the military vote being turned into just another source of patronage and corruption as he felt the Intercolonial and other railways had become.

Parliament was a demanding mistress during the sessions, but fortunately the periods of respite still lasted nine or ten months a year. Alexander Mackenzie was back in Sarnia in time to don his uniform and take part in the eight days of compulsory drilling with his troops. On Canada's second birthday, he led them proudly down Front Street as part of the Dominion Day celebrations. Fresh rumours of Fenian activities lent a sense of urgency to their amateurish military efforts.

The cloak of leadership was shifting ineluctably from Brown's shoulders to his own. Invitations to address Liberal rallies poured in from all over Ontario, and when William Howland was named Lieutenant-Governor of Ontario, Mackenzie led the fight in which West York constituency was wrested from the Government.[36] The victory was encouraging for the Grits; it marked the Sarnia builder still more clearly as Brown's successor.

The session of 1869 was opened by the new Governor General,

Sir John Young. In the interval, Joseph Howe's resistance had been broken; Nova Scotia, in John A. Macdonald's words, took the shilling and enlisted.[37] Howe became President of the Council.

Government and Opposition were getting into their stride, and the bill of fare in the Throne Speech was an ample one. There were "better terms" for Nova Scotia, the purchase of most of the North-West Territories from the Hudson's Bay Company for a million and one-half dollars, and the possibility of Prince Edward Island's entrance into the union. Mackenzie was in excellent form.[38] He teased Cartier good-naturedly for having received in England a title not only equal but superior to that of the Premier's. As Canadian "Minister of War", he trusted that the "Honourable Baronet" had assured Emperor Napoleon and Chancellor Bismarck of the Dominion's pacific intentions when he was on the continent, so that Canadians could "sit down peacefully under our vine and fig tree, none daring to make us afraid". The amenities disposed of, he went on to attack the plan of expensive fortifications around the cities, condemned the long route of the Intercolonial Railway that had been adopted, and declared with evident relish that since two out of three Reform Ministers had left the Cabinet,* old-fashioned Toryism was obviously rampant again.

The return of Toryism was a favourite Reform theme. During the debate on an Opposition motion to abolish dual representation, one Reformer commented in mock sorrow on the numerous coffins being carried to the Tory cemetery as formerly able men were used and cast aside. The Cabinet was evidently a dangerous and infectious place, he scoffed, where men were stricken with weak knees, unsteady nerves, and an unnatural craving for the fleshpots of Egypt.[39] It was good humour, but the bid to break the hold of Ottawa on the provincial Administrations by abolishing dual representation was defeated. The Premier of Ontario would continue, in Mackenzie's words, to jump when his master in the Dominion capital pulled the strings.[40]

Opposition mockery increased when the remaining Reformer in the Cabinet, William McDougall, was named the first Lieutenant-Governor of the North-West Territories. Partisan politics aside, the choice was a logical one. Like Brown, he had urged the acquisition of the North West for many years, when the Conservatives were still scoffing at the idea as an impractical dream. While recognizing the importance of keeping the

*Fergusson-Blair died in late 1867 and neither he nor Howland were replaced by Reformers.

area from falling into United States' hands, Macdonald himself had written only four years earlier: "It seems to me the country is of no present value to Canada. We have unoccupied land enough to absorb the immigration for many years, and the opening up of the Saskatchewan would do to Canada what the Prairie lands of Illinois are doing now – drain away our youth and our strength."[41] Within the Cabinet, McDougall had continued the struggle, and eventually forced action on the North West as the price of agreeing to the longer route of the Intercolonial Railway to the Maritimes.[42] It was he and Cartier who had negotiated the transfer in London. The appointment of McDougall was a personal triumph. It was also a defeat. Tired of having to listen to a man who claimed to represent the Reform point of view, but who had long since been undercut by his own party, Sir John was sending the last Reformer in the Cabinet to the Tory cemetery.

Despite the bursts of temper and increasingly frequent exchanges of abuse, it was a worth-while session. Nova Scotia and the North West were absorbed into the Confederation, Prince Edward Island lurked near the entrance, and discussions were going on with Newfoundland. A few hours before the end, Mackenzie was sitting in the seat of Finance Minister John Rose discussing the business of the session when Holton asked for the opinion of that Minister on a subject being debated. The alert Scot leaped to his feet and said he was sure the matter would receive the full support of the Administration.[43] The flow of words ended on a jovial note.

Notwithstanding this attitude of aggressive confidence, it was a tired and discouraged politician who returned to Sarnia in time for the Dominion Day celebrations. The continuous strain was beginning to leave its mark. "The general disposition to go with the powers that be in all soil was never so strong as at present," Mackenzie confided disconsolately to Charles Black, a former Sarnian living in Montreal.[44] "It's very disgusting. I feel literally sick and wish with all my heart I was clear of an abominable life. My present intention is not to come back again though it is quite possible I may not be able to carry out this righteous intention." Certainly there was no truth, he assured his friend, in the "senseless malicious rumour" that he was to join the Government. He was determined to keep his hands clean at all costs.

Instead of freeing himself, Mackenzie was being bound ever tighter to a political career. Notwithstanding his refusals to accept the formal leadership, everyone looked upon him as occupying that position. "By consent of both friends and opponents," editorialized the *Sarnia Observer*, "it appears to be settled that in the next Government he must take a leading position. Perhaps but few Parliamentary leaders amongst us on either side have ever commanded more of the sincere respect . . . than does Alexander Mackenzie today."[45] They were soothing words, even to a man who was sick of it all. There was, however, the reverse side of the medal of political success. To his opponent, the *Toronto Telegraph*, Mackenzie was a "bully", a "jackass", a "foul-mouthed leader of a gang of itch-smitten picnickers", and "the ringleader of an unwashed scabby crowd."[46] The epithets were almost as high a recommendation as the eulogies of the faithful.

One of the Reformers least amenable to leadership was George Brown himself. He urged Mackenzie to assume the title, but he himself would neither lead nor be led. Still hoping to get him back into Parliament, Mackenzie offered the *Globe* publisher the candidacy in Lanark, where, it was rumoured, Malcolm Cameron was planning a political come-back. Brown reacted violently. He had no intention of being made the forlorn hope of the party, he retorted, and suffering further humiliation. One of the common traits of the two Scots was a biting testiness when aroused. "I think I need hardly say I would be the last man to subject you to any 'humiliation'," the answer came back.[47] "The (South) Ontario humiliation would not have happened if my opinion could have prevailed." As for the suggestion that Mackenzie should take the title of leader at once, "I would scorn to be the *manufactured* figurehead of the party." If he could not lead because he deserved to, he argued, the title would only make him as ridiculous as Foley had been in 1862.

Illness, fatigue, and a constant yearning for a quieter life did not make him lessen his pace. When Malcolm Cameron refused to fall into line, Mackenzie sent a man into the Lanark by-election and defeated him. The round of public speaking continued. At a picnic in Wentworth in late October, his speech was fiery enough to hold a huge crowd round him for several hours despite the damp and bone-chilling autumn air. A drunk interrupted his address. "You must be a Tory," said Mackenzie sarcastically, as if a drunk could be nothing else.[48] He was. The Reformers stood for British connection and the privileges of being British, the leading Reformer repeated over and over throughout the province; the Tories stood for maintaining themselves in power. The Premier had kicked McDougall and Howland upstairs into Lieutenant-Governorships; his latest move was to take into the Government a man who had been out of the country for fifteen years, a man who he had once said was "steeped to the lips in corruption", and make him Minister of Finance. That man was Sir Francis Hincks, whom Sir John was trying to promote as the real leader of the Reform party. It was a policy of divide and rule, seduce and rule.

Once launched, there was almost no limit to the belligerent Scotsman's oratorical audacity. "Canada's neighbours might like to swallow her up," he told his fellow-Scots at the St. Andrew's dinner in Sarnia, "but she could now give them a good case of indigestion if they tried."[49] There were three requisites of national greatness, he explained to an audience in Seaforth: unity, intelligence, and virtue. England had all three. That was why Britain was one of God's means of carrying on civilization, and why the British language was being used as a vehicle to civilize and christianize the whole earth. "The eloquent speech was listened to throughout with breathless enthusiasm," eulogized the *Goderich Signal*.[50]

Canada's civilizing crusade on Britain's behalf was running into trouble. When William McDougall arrived at the border of the North-West Territories after a long journey through the United States, he was told by the twenty-six-year-old Métis leader, Louis Riel, to keep out. As far as most of the Hudson's Bay officials and their Indian or half-breed customers were concerned, the expansionist dreams of Canada could only mean a restriction of their free and easy way of life. The handful of Canadians in Fort Garry were already making plans to take possession of the large tracts of land, and boasting that when the area was finally incorporated into the Dominion, they would be the rulers. Survey parties were staking out the new farms and roadways, heedless of the protests of the natives who claimed the rich soil as a legitimate heritage from their ancestors. The Hudson's Bay Company officials knew they could do little to halt the course of events. The Indians began to migrate farther west; the half-breeds called on the bright, young college graduate Louis Riel, a protégé of Archbishop Taché, to protect them from the invaders.

Unable to enter his intended domain, McDougall issued the proclamation announcing his appointment and the inclusion of the North West into Canada, and commanded the "insurgents" to surrender. What he did not know was that Sir John had not taken the necessary steps to make the proclamation valid. Hearing of the uprising, he had wired London to stop the money for the purchase of the huge area from being paid to the Hudson's Bay Company, and had asked the Colonial Office not to proceed with the transfer.[51] Until that was done, it was not Canadian soil, and McDougall's "proclamation" was meaningless. With sound intuition, Riel ignored the ex-Minister's statement, and the would-be Governor had no alternative but to return whence he came.

Events moved quickly. The Métis set up a provisional government, and placed the fifty-odd Canadians under surveillance. Some of them escaped and started preparations to overthrow Riel. Among those recaptured was a hot-headed young Orangeman from Northern Ireland, Thomas Scott. Swept off balance by the heady draught of power, and feverish with excitement, Riel and his friends decided to make an example of Scott as a warning to all who would defy their claim to authority. He was brought before a military tribunal, condemned as a rebel, and shot. A few days later, Archbishop Taché, recalled in great haste from Rome at Sir John's request, arrived with an amnesty promise from Ottawa providing the insurgents laid down their arms and accepted Canada's authority. The promise had been made before Scott's death. The Archbishop transmitted it regardless of the execution.

Spurred on by a wave of popular indignation across Canada, Alexander Mackenzie took the first opportunity in the 1870 session to denounce the Riel uprising as a revolt against British authority. When the news of Scott's death arrived, and Ontario demanded "an eye for an eye and a tooth for a tooth", he joined in the cries of "murder" and "treachery", insisting that British justice be enforced. Before the session was far advanced, McDougall had succeeded in being re-elected to Parliament. Huntington was absent, and the would-be Governor moved right into his seat beside Mackenzie on the Opposition front benches to join the attack. Mindful that the Government's future depended on maintaining its support in Quebec, Macdonald sought desperately for a peaceful solution. Donald Smith, Canadian vice-president of the Hudson's Bay Company, was asked to devise a settlement. Colonel de Salaberry and Reverend J. B. Thibault, a veteran missionary, were sent west as well. Riel, for his part, sent three delegates to Ottawa with his demands. Mackenzie and his followers denounced such intercourse with "traitors", and demanded immediate suppression of the uprising. Dorion and his Rouge colleagues hung back; Canada was moving toward another split along racial lines.

In addition to the vengeful McDougall, the Opposition was receiving support from two other powerful ex-Ministerialists. The Montreal financier, Alexander Galt, and the Kingston financier, Richard Cartwright, were both embittered at the treatment they had received at the hands of Macdonald, and were openly attacking him from the cross-benches as Independents. Though they refused to move directly into the Opposition ranks, they were impressive allies, and their revolt gave hope for the future.

Again and again the leading Reformer set forth the basic principles of his party: free trade, a low-cost economy, reciprocity, maintenance of the British connection, and Canadian control of purely Canadian affairs. He ridiculed the "national policy" of tariff protection as retrograde, futile, and injurious to Britain. One hundred and seventy-five thousand dollars, he commented ironically, was the tariff revenue estimated to bring the Americans to their knees, and make them accept the free exchange of goods with Canada.[52] In fact, most of that sum would come from Canadian pockets. The burden would be placed on the poorer Canadians, who were the largest consumers. The Government was like a certain Artemus Ward who was prepared to sacrifice one of his wife's relatives in order to win a war. National policy! he scoffed, national trash! The true Canadian policy was to buy as cheaply as possible, and get the best possible price for Canadian products. It was an effective attack. Under pressure from both without and within its ranks, the Ministry cancelled its new tariff on farm products, then reinstated it three hours later when control of the caucus had been regained. It was not an Opposition victory, but it was a sound accomplishment for a group outnumbered three to one.

Though rejecting a "national" tariff policy, Mackenzie was a vigorous advocate of a proud Canadian sentiment. There was no reason, he insisted, why Britons at home should pay taxes to maintain an army in such a powerful colony as Canada; Canadians should be able to look after themselves.[53] He felt some arrangement was necessary to co-ordinate the policies of the Empire so that they would help one another to maintain the Imperial strength on which they all depended. Imperial authority, however, did not mean subservience to Imperial dictation. A strong self-sufficient Canada was an asset and not a weakness in the Imperial chain. And Canada, he argued, should speak for herself in external relations wherever her interests alone were involved. The British authorities never understood Canada's position, and subordinated it to the British point of view. The states of Maine, Michigan, Minnesota, and Washington were all composed in part of areas that should have been included within Canadian borders. Canada should have the right to negotiate treaties, particularly in the commercial field, and then call on the British Government to express approval or disapproval.

The self-governing colonies would soon find it impossible, he warned, to conduct their intercourse with other nations entirely through the Colonial Office.

With the Conservatives anxious to sow doubts in the public mind about the loyalty of the Opposition, Canada's relationship to the Empire was a delicate political subject. When Huntington and Galt joined forces to demand a customs union with the United States, Mackenzie replied hotly to Macdonald's insinuations that his party leaned toward annexationism and republicanism.[54] He dissociated himself entirely from the motion, and came out flatly for connection in perpetuity with the Mother Country. It was far more disloyal, he countered, to adopt the United States' system of protection, and to abandon free trade "which has been so triumphantly vindicated in Great Britain and in many of her colonies, our own included". Living side by side with a powerful protectionist-minded nation, he quite conceived it would be necessary to depart occasionally from purely free trade practices, but it should never be done from a spirit of vengeance because of tariff barriers imposed against Canadian goods. On the other hand, he would continue to oppose the sort of interdependence between Canada and the United States implied in the proposal for reciprocal legislation, which would in fact mean that Canada would have to change her laws as legislation was altered in the United States. The Premier refused to take any action concerning Canadian-American relations except through the British Minister, Mackenzie complained, yet reciprocal legislation would create a greater degree of dictation by the United States than any treaty.

Even without the formal title, Alexander Mackenzie was an outstanding leader of the Opposition. He was both aggressive and tenacious. He suspected the worst in every Government action, and examined every detail to bare the misdeeds and unworthy motives he was certain lay at the bottom of every move. He presented alternatives that showed not only foresight but also a keen appreciation of public opinion. Their rejection with monotonous regularity by the House of Commons left no visible effect on his spirits. To one of the younger Liberals of the period, he recalled the story of another Scotsman who was asked on his death-bed if he would like to hear a few hymns to comfort him. "Hymns," snorted the dying man, "na, na, I want to argy*."[55] After two months of steady criticism, the exasperated Premier accused him of attacking every measure simply for the sake of opposition, and of setting himself up as a "watchtower on Zion".[56] Mackenzie shot back a denial that he had opposed

*Argue.

Alexander Mackenzie, about 1873

Hon. George Brown

every measure; he had given his approbation to one relating to cockfighting! "A Highlander," commented the *Sarnia Observer* approvingly, "does not know the word 'retreat'."[57]

The Red River crisis dominated the session of 1870. Canadians had not been so aroused since the Fenian raids in 1866. Indignation meetings were held in every part of Ontario, and hotly worded resolutions were dispatched to Ottawa, demanding firm action to restore order. In Sarnia, Robert Mackenzie seconded a motion condemning the "disloyal faction which has temporarily usurped the functions of government".[58] In the House of Commons, his brother insisted that two of the representatives from the North West, Father Ritchot and Richard Scott, should not be received by the Government because of their close connections with Riel, "while the representatives of the truly loyal settlers . . . were treated as outcasts and bastards." "There must be no squeamishness in this matter," he lectured the occupants of the Treasury benches.[59]

With the Opposition demanding an expeditionary force to quell the uprising, Riel holding out for the best possible terms, and Archbishop Taché pressing for the fulfilment of his promise of an amnesty, Macdonald "broke out" again.[60] Many expected he might do so once the nasty business was over, but he anticipated them and retired to his room with an ample supply of port. The Manitoba Bill, the Government's new approach to the problem, was due to be introduced the following Monday. On Friday, the Premier was seen staggering through the Russell Hotel. As the week-end passed, the same question was on every tongue: What about the Manitoba Bill and the Red River affair? As the three o'clock deadline approached, there was still no answer. Then, at the appointed time, Sir John appeared in his place. Pale and drawn, his voice weaker even than usual, he rose on schedule and began his delivery of the new Canadian child. As he proceeded, he gained strength and coherence, and it was soon abundantly evident that he was not only master of himself, but of the legislation as well. "A rum 'un to look at but a rare 'un to go," he loved to say about himself. The greatest Canadian politician had done it again.[61]

Mackenzie was not disposed to be generous. He castigated the Government for withholding the proclamation of the North-West Territories and the payment to the Hudson's Bay Company the previous fall. He attributed all subsequent troubles and tragedy to that action. He condemned the creation of a miniature province of hardly over one thousand square miles with a population of fifteen thousand, and endowing it with two Chambers, four federal members of Parliament and two senators. It reminded him, he scoffed, of some of the incidents in *Gulliver's Travels*. He called for wider suffrage and much greater extension of the limits of the province. Above all, he rejected the Premier's suggestion that the Government had no responsibility to deal with Scott's murderers as long as the proclamation had not been issued. Canada, he maintained, had a concurrent jurisdiction with the Hudson's Bay Company even before the sale was concluded.

The debate had proceeded for four days when the Premier collapsed. This time he was really ill, so ill that he could not be removed from his office. The doctors diagnosed a kidney stone. As he hovered on the verge of death, a hushed and subdued Parliament passed the Manitoba Bill. Leaving the proposal to create a Supreme Court and other legislation, they finished the estimates rapidly and went home. Sir John survived. About three weeks after the attack he was able to ask its cause. A gritty particle around which a growth had formed, the doctors explained. "Confound those Grits," he sighed with a trace of his old mischievous smile, "I knew they would be the death of me yet."[62]

Alexander Mackenzie's reputation was still growing. Such a rash of compliments accompanied his return to Sarnia that he would have been forgiven for wondering if it was he who had lain at death's door. Even Macdonald had confided to a friend that his leading opponent was the Hugh Miller of Canada, referring to another Scottish stonemason who had risen from humble origins to political prominence.[63] "No man in Canada has earned more loyally the right to . . . political gratitude," beamed the *Globe* proudly.[64]

Despite the high praise, all was not going well. Mackenzie's health was growing steadily worse, and his financial situation was causing him serious concern. Unlike Macdonald, he was not in debt, but his contracting business had practically disappeared, and his savings were dwindling rapidly. Whenever he was free from Parliament, he was kept busy organizing the party and preaching its gospel. Sometimes during the summer of 1870 he was so ill he could not do even that, and had to sit on the platform while others delivered the speeches. It was only the urgings of George Brown and other friends that kept him from giving up altogether. A group of Reformers in Ontario decided to raise ten thousand dollars to buy him a homestead so that he would have some security and a permanent home. He had no choice but to go on.

Mary was now able to accompany him on some of his political excursions during the summer months. She was an attractive and accomplished girl with a dignified bearing and the strong clear-cut features of all Mackenzies, in contrast to his wife, Jane, whose rounder face and shorter body gave the impression of rotundity. The picnics were a natural opportunity for father and daughter to be together and combine duty with pleasure. Mary mixed with the ladies, helped to prepare the lunch, and picked flowers in the fields, while the men-folk talked politics or went for a swim.[65] More reserved by nature, Jane preferred to remain at home and look after the household. One of the expeditions on which Mary could not accompany her father that summer was the visit to the U.S. Gunboat *Michigan* in Sarnia Harbour. Despite his temperance habits, Mackenzie praised the Captain's claret and bourbon, and expressed the appreciation of "those who desired it". He himself preferred to drink his toasts with the waters of the St. Clair.[66]

In July, the expeditionary force under General Wolseley passed through Sarnia on the way to put down Riel's provisional government, and clear the way for the Government of Manitoba. In the little western town they purchased a large quantity of hay from one of the Mackenzies. Political corruption, sneered the St. Catharines *Journal*; no doubt the Mackenzie influence in Ottawa was behind the deal.[67] The same month the Reform leader and a few political friends undertook a fact-finding tour of the Maritimes.[68] Despite Howe's entrance into the Cabinet, the Liberals in New Brunswick and Nova Scotia were gradually identifying themselves with their colleagues in opposition, and Mackenzie was being regarded more and more as their leader as well. He had established good working relations with Albert Smith in New Brunswick and Alfred Jones in Halifax. During the debate on the "better terms" for Nova Scotia, Mackenzie had been careful not to give the impression that he opposed the larger sums of money awarded to the Atlantic province, but explained that he wanted to "prevent any future tampering with the Union Act".[69] There was a moral certainty, he told Jones, that Quebec would soon run itself into trouble and try a raid on the federal Treasury, "which in her case would be far more serious . . . as it would be without any shadow of excuse."[70]

The Maritime trip was a successful and pleasant one. The visitors defended Confederation, and pleaded for patience in overcoming the troublesome "growing pains" of the initial stages. They met with members of the Annand Administration, the only truly Liberal Government in the Dominion, and worked to draw public support and the federal representatives to their side. Liberal chances looked excellent in New Brunswick, and on the return journey they received cheering news in the province of Quebec. "Public opinion has set in decidedly against Cartier," Mackenzie announced with delight after he arrived home.[71]

Shortly after his return, the Grit leader was struck down again by dysentery while camping out with the militia. It "very nearly carried me off", he told Jones as the year drew to a close.[72] With three sessions behind them, and the possibility of an election after the fourth, the Liberals could not afford to be ill. To keep his fall speaking schedule, he took large doses of opium. By Christmas he had succeeded in covering a good part of Ontario, and had chosen candidates in a number of constituencies.

CHAPTER 7

Dual Representation

Early in 1871 it became known that the British and Americans were about to make a major effort to settle some of the problems that had bedevilled relations between the two countries over the years. A Joint Commission was to be formed and Sir John A. Macdonald, his health restored, would be one of the British Commissioners. In addition to the exploitation of the Atlantic fisheries, they would discuss the American claims for the destruction by the *Alabama* during the Civil War, the navigation of the joint waterways, trade problems; and possibly the Canadian demand to be compensated for damage during the Fenian raids five years before.

It looked like a dull session in Ottawa. With the Premier away, there would be little important legislation, and a federal election would be postponed. However, a provincial contest in Ontario seemed a certainty. It would be the first big test for the Reformers since Confederation. Blake had replaced McKellar as provincial leader of the Opposition, and he and Mackenzie had stumped much of the province together. The federal Reform leader was determined to do his utmost to help oust the "Patent Combination", and install a truly Reform administration in Toronto.

The fourth session of the Ontario Legislature finished in mid-February, and John Sandfield Macdonald called an election for March. A week before he left for Ottawa, Mackenzie received a letter from political friends in Middlesex County asking if he would be their provincial candidate. At first the suggestion seemed out of the question. He was expending himself mercilessly already for the party cause, and he had certainly no time to spare for additional responsibilities. The help he had given to McKellar and Blake he had been able to combine with his federal duties. On the other hand, he, too, was anxious for a provincial victory. Blake's chances looked good, but every seat would count, and there was no doubt that he could win a seat which a lesser-known man could not take. But there was a moral question as well. As an outspoken opponent of the system of dual representation, could he accept a provincial seat without compromising his principles? Yet, he asked himself, what chance was there of getting that or any other law changed as long as the Liberals remained in opposition? He was very reluctant, he replied finally, and certainly would not contest West Middlesex unless the Liberals there could prove that he could win without taking off too much time while the Dominion Parliament was in session. His eager admirers did not wait; a few days later he received word that he had been nominated. He was just getting the work of the Opposition organized and was tense and edgy. "Now I admire chivalry – at a safe distance," the stormy Scot fumed in Ottawa, "but I have no idea of going up there merely to have a hard fight. I do not see how I can possibly leave here. Blake, I presume, must go west soon and we cannot both be away. The genius of Holton and Dorion with McDougall's utter want of tact and honesty would soon put the fat on the fire."[1]

Despite his protests, he went. It was a short, hot campaign. John Sandfield Macdonald displayed a curious combination of political probity and opportunism. On both counts he was blunt and even forthright. On the one hand, he introduced simultaneous elections throughout the province instead of staggering them as usual so that they could be exploited to the maximum advantage of the Government. He also gave effect to the great Reform cry for the trial of controverted elections by judges instead of by Government-dominated committees. At the same time, he used public contracts unashamedly to buy votes. "What the hell has Strathroy done for me?" he asked a delegation from that town who wanted a new building.[2] Just before the election he pushed through the Legislature a vote of one and one-half million dollars for railway projects, but refused to designate the projects or even the areas that were to receive public aid. "No doubt South Ontario would like to get some of that money," he told an audience there.[3] The implication was obvious. Hamiltonians were warned that if they had any "axes to grind", they had better support him. Yet through it all Sandfield Macdonald was an economical and progressive administrator, a frank, and – judged by political standards of the day – probably an honest man.

From the date Mackenzie accepted the nomination, there remained fifteen days to campaign. With the roads breaking under the spring thaw, wagon travel was impractical; he stuffed a few items of clothing and documents into saddlebags and galloped from place to place on horseback. Holding two meetings a day, he attacked the Macdonald clan in general and the "miserable, pettifogging, peddling practices" of the Ontario Administration in particular. He denounced the Ontario Ministry as the "mere creature of the Dominion Government", and claimed they, too, like their master in Ottawa, were only interested in remaining in office as long as possible. In a sense, it was an easy campaign. Completely on the offensive, and with no past record to encumber them, the Grits could carry the battle to the enemy. He stood for correct administration and parliamentary purity, Mackenzie told the electors; he and his fellow-campaigners were "clear grit in every sense of the word". What did it mean? called someone in Strathroy. "Clear Grit," he replied with an impatient flash of his steely, blue eyes, and an extra rasp of the Scottish brogue, "is pure sand without a particle of dirt in it."[4]

With the general swing against the Government, West Middlesex fell to the Grits. The voting was not yet over before Mackenzie changed out of his mud-clogged campaign togs and into his parliamentary clothes. When the local band arrived at his house in Sarnia to acclaim the victor, Jane told them that he was already on his way back to Ottawa.[5]

* * * * *

The Washington negotiations placed Sir John A. Macdonald in an embarrassing position. He knew that a treaty unfavourable to Canada would be a severe blow to his Government; he knew, too, that as the fifth member of the British delegation, he was expected to advise, but would have little influence on final decisions. In the House of Commons, he insisted that Britain had never sacrificed Canadian interests in pursuit of her own. Mackenzie stated flatly – and could prove – the contrary.[6]

Before he left for the American capital, Macdonald was reminded by the Opposition leader that the Canadians considered the Fenian claims as valid as the *Alabama* claims, and that they expected compensation from the United States. He also told the Premier that Canada's geographical position made it important to maintain control of the St. Lawrence waterway system. In view of the evident desire of the Americans to obtain navigation rights on the great river, this was a trump card that Canada must never let out of her hand. Finally, Mackenzie warned Sir John not to cede the exclusive right of Canadians to fisheries within three miles of their shore, including bays formed by headlands less than three miles apart. As Sir John set off on his mission, he took with him vivid memories of the stern and demanding Scot who would be expecting an exact accounting on his return.

In his chieftain's absence, Cartier introduced the resolutions admitting British Columbia with its ten thousand white residents into Confederation as the sixth province.[7] It was an historic step, linking the Dominion "from sea to sea", and constituted a formidable achievement for the Government. It would wipe out some of the memories of the bad stumble in incorporating the North West. In their eagerness to grasp the prize, the Ministry had offered handsome inducements. In fact, they had gone much farther than the British Columbia delegates themselves had demanded. Instead of a wagon road across the continent, they offered to build a railway line, even agreeing to begin it within two years and finish it within ten. "And the Railway, Credat Judaeus!" exclaimed one astonished delegate from the Pacific Coast, "is *guaranteed* without a reservation. Sir Georges Cartier says they will do that or 'burst'."[8]

The estimated cost of the railway, based on the line completed recently through the United States, was one hundred million dollars. By making grants of land to the company undertaking the construction, the cash outlay of the Dominion would be much reduced. But whatever the cost, the acting Premier told the House of Commons, there would be no additional taxation imposed on the country.[9]

The reassurance was designed in large part to quiet the fears of the sandy-haired Scot across the aisle who was so preoccupied with reducing Government spending and lowering both taxes and living costs. The attempt failed. Still outraged at the expense of the Intercolonial Railway, this appeared to him just another grandiose scheme to fill the pockets of Cartier and the other Ministers interested in railway operations, and to open up another vast field of patronage. All Canadians were in favour of the entrance of British Columbia, Mackenzie assured the House, but the terms were impossible of fulfilment. With practically no surveys in the whole area west of Lake Superior, the estimate of costs and the time limit were meaningless. It was irresponsible to commit the Canadian taxpayer to a contract based on mere speculation, which, with the best intentions in the world, could not be carried out. And it was unnecessary to do so, because such generous terms were not demanded. The abandonment of huge tracts of land to a commercial company was, in his opinion, equally unwise; it would place an excessive amount of the Dominion's patrimony in the hands of speculators. All in all, it was not the sort of arrangement he would enter into as a private contractor, and it was not one that he could approve on behalf of the Canadian people. Mackenzie proposed an amendment that "Canada should not be pledged to do more than proceed at once with the necessary survey, and, after the route is determined, to prosecute the work at as early a period as the state of its finances will justify."[10]

Finance Minister Hincks, the great conciliator of a generation before, tried to bring the opposing points of view closer together.[11] He agreed that no scheme should be adopted that would be ruinous to the Dominion, but pointed out the necessity of providing British Columbia with a clear indication of serious intentions. If unsurmountable difficulties arose, it was understood that changes would be necessary. That, said Mackenzie, was his point.[12] The conditions were impossible to fulfil, and the Government was asking Parliament for a statement of intention that he knew was unrealistic. It would be more honest to proceed with a less grandiose scheme. A narrow gauge railway, coupled with a steamer service on the lakes, could link Lake Superior to the Red River settlement quite easily. West of Fort Garry, a wagon road to the Rockies would be sufficient for some years to open the country to immigration. At the same time, work could be started on the Pacific coast to link British Columbia with the plains. The Grand Trunk, which passed through a well settled area, had never paid one per cent interest to its stockholders; it was impossible to believe that a line through twenty-five hundred miles of uncharted wilderness could be built as a paying enterprise. To him, the plan to pay ten thousand dollars a head to link the British Columbians with the Union was either insane recklessness or a painful lack of patriotism.

It was a losing fight, as Mackenzie well knew. Dorion and his Rouges followers stood by him, as did a few members from the Maritimes, but the Opposition bloc he was trying to build was not yet strong nor cohesive enough to stand such a test. "If the Nova Scotia members would go with us our amendment would be carried," he wrote to Brown a few days after the debate began, "but I believe they are resolved to go with the Government, all but Jones and Carmichael and Killam. They are without exception the meanest lot of plundering rascals ever known. Jones . . . is disgusted with his fellow-members."[13] Whatever might happen in the House of Commons under pressure of the Ministry, he was convinced that public opinion was strongly against the "monstrous scheme", and that it would never be carried out.

Had Mackenzie been able to follow events in the Tory caucus, he might have fought harder still. Hostility to the Government's proposal was so strong that many Conservatives were wavering. Seriously concerned, Cartier summoned the leader of the British Columbia delegation, J. W. Trutch, to a caucus meeting, and had him give assurances that the new province was not likely to insist on Canada's ruination to fulfil the terms of union. Had the assurances not been given, the British Columbian told his chief in Victoria, the measure would never have passed, and the Government would have been defeated.[14]

The Grit amendment was lost sixty-eight to eighty-five, a margin of only seventeen votes. Had only nine more members switched to his side, it would have carried. It was a substantial achievement after the usual defeats of two, three, or even five to one. In addition, an important concession was won. The Government proposed an additional resolution that the project should be "constructed and worked by private enterprise, and not by the Government, and that the public aid . . . should consist of such liberal grants of land and such subsidy in money, or other aid, not increasing the present rate of taxation".[15] The British Columbia delegates, who were following the debate from the spectators' gallery, offered no objections. The project carried, but the Opposition had shown themselves stronger than ever before. It was the worst fight since Confederation, one of the Ministers wrote to Sir John in the American capital.[16]

The 1871 session was over when the Washington Treaty was signed on May 8. Macdonald had fought hard and well, but he had been caught between the two great arms of the Anglo-Saxon pincer, and Canada had paid the price of patching up their past differences. The exclusive Canadian fisheries rights were abandoned for compensation to be settled at a later date. The St. Lawrence was to be open for all time to foreign vessels; Canada, for her part, received similar rights on three small rivers near the Alaskan border. The Fenian raids were not mentioned. On the other hand, the *Alabama* claims were to be settled. John A. Macdonald returned home an unhappy and discomfited man.[17]

"Macdonald must have (been) on a spree or else the English Com[ers] secured his compliance by some other means," the Grit chieftain commented to Jones.[18] On public platforms and in the press, the Liberals cried "betrayal".[19] Feeling public opinion swinging to their side, they took a strong stand on behalf of Canadian interests, even at the risk of incurring Imperial displeasure, and prepared for another all-out struggle at the next session of Parliament.

In addition to his regular attacks on the Macdonalds in Toronto and Ottawa, Mackenzie had undertaken still further responsibilities. In an attempt to bolster his sagging finances, he had joined with Brown, Blake, Postmaster-General Alexander Campbell, and several other prominent Canadians in founding the Isolated Risk Fire Insurance Company. Headquarters were established in Toronto; its President, unpaid, Alexander Mackenzie, M.P., M.P.P.[20]

Abandoning the contracting business, he tried to co-ordinate his three other functions. In addition to picking candidates for the approaching federal election, the Liberal leader prepared to topple the "Patent Combination" in Toronto, and whenever possible, worked to establish the new firm. "My impression is that by the exercise of great care and watchfulness over our agents that we can in time build up a good business," he confided in October to Alexander Campbell, whom he was anxious to enlist on his Board of Directors.[21] "We are just now considering the advisability of commencing business in Manitoba and New Brunswick. We have got a good beginning in Quebec."

One of the principal problems in securing federal candidates in Ontario was to make an effective appeal to the English-speaking Catholic vote. Rural Ontario was true enough to the Reform cause, but a large number of the Irish immigrants had become qualified to vote in recent years, and many remembered the old Brownite "no-popery" cry of earlier days. It was an embarrassing heritage that Reformers preferred to forget. Immediately following their 1867 Convention, a Catholic Reform Convention had been held in Toronto to draw a curtain over the past and make a fresh beginning. "From the days of O'Connell downwards," the Convention chairman had proclaimed, "Reform has been the Catholic ally."[22] One resolution condemned the Conservative party for its association with the Orange Society, a "secret politico-religious combination". The Catholic hierarchy was not impressed. The Archbishop sent a letter stating that most Catholics found their interest identified with the Conservative party.

As the 1872 election approached, the Grits determined to try again. Brown addressed an open letter to John O'Donohue, a prominent Catholic. In the days of Baldwin and Lafontaine, he recalled, the Protestant and Catholic Reformers had fought the battle of religious liberty side by side against the Tories. True, the Reformers had resisted the domination of the French

Catholics, but Confederation had settled that problem. Now the Protestants were in a majority in Ontario, and "it is the incumbent duty of the reform party . . . (to ensure) that a full share of parliamentary representation . . . should be awarded to the catholic minority."[23] As part of the same campaign, Senator William McMaster, an Irish immigrant, and also a director of the Isolated Risk Insurance Company, was delegated to entice the Archbishop from his strong anti-Liberal stand by an offer to run Catholic candidates in a certain number of constituencies.[24] It was a fact, the Archbishop conceded, that in the next Commons the Catholics could help the party that helped them. However, his suspiciousness remained; he needed to be convinced by deeds, not words. Simcoe was a good test case. If the Liberals chose a Protestant there, he would not ask the Catholics to change their votes, but if his candidate for the Liberal nomination was accepted, he would "urge the Catholics to go as one man for him".[25] It was not the sort of negotiation either side enjoyed. "Politics is a muddy sea to fish in," said His Grace.[26]

As the December session of the provincial Legislature approached, trouble developed from an unexpected source. With every day bringing him nearer to the Premiership, Edward Blake, the thirty-nine-year-old intellectual giant of the Reform party, was fairly frantic with apprehension. The top-ranking parliamentarian, the brilliant lawyer, the great Liberal hope, stood like a Colossus with the veteran politician, Sandfield Macdonald, at his feet, and he feared to reach out his hand to take the prize. "Take the leadership, I beg of you, as I did long ago," he wrote in panic to the ex-stonemason, "but if you will not, let us appoint a small committee. . . . I shall be at the command of yourself in the committee at all times. . . . For the work outside of the House I have long known myself to be utterly unfit, and I know now that I shall never be more fit for it."[27] He wanted not only to avoid the Premiership, but to get out of the Legislature entirely.

For a man who had put his toe in the provincial pond with great reluctance, the quicksand of responsibility was swallowing Mackenzie at an alarming rate. Already he had more burdens than any man, even one in the best of health, could bear for long. That Blake was in nearly every respect better qualified for the task of leadership, he was the first to admit; in fact, he was watching the progress of the younger man with personal interest, seeing in it the hope of relief from his own heavy load. The brilliant career prophesied for Blake by Brown and other Canadians might make it possible, he hoped, to return to a more normal life. He was willing to do his duty, but others had to do theirs as well. He stood firm and forced the young lawyer on.

The Ontario Legislature, which had been elected the previous spring, met in an atmosphere of tension and expectancy. Sandfield Macdonald proceeded as if he had received a clear mandate for a further five years, but Mackenzie was confident that he could not survive a fortnight. Eight seats were vacant due to charges of electoral corruption. The unpredictable Premier proposed that the eight members should take their places regardless, until the by-elections were held. It was an unprecedented suggestion. Blake and Mackenzie attacked. The provincial Opposition leader led off with a violent denunciation of the railway fund, and demanded full legislative control of its expenditure. Fighting for time, Macdonald persuaded a supporter to propose a sub-amendment to Blake's motion, postponing any debate of the railway fund until the by-elections had been held.[28] Mackenzie rose to join the fray. If the Premier considered the House complete enough to consider the address, he argued, it was complete enough to discuss the railway fund. The Opposition wanted a "fair stand-up fight", not trickery. Another Government supporter moved the adjournment of the debate. The Opposition objected. The Premier was forced to accept a vote at last. The Opposition won thirty-five to thirty-three.

The rest was a foregone conclusion. The sub-amendment was defeated by eight votes; Blake's motion carried by seven. Mackenzie followed with a motion of non-confidence in the Ministry, declaring the railway policy "fraught with danger to public liberty and constitutional government". The Administration, he said, was like the proverbial farmer's horse; it hadn't died, it hadn't been killed; it had just "gi'n out".[29] "A model of aggressive parliamentary warfare," proclaimed the *Globe* proudly the next day. The Government had perhaps "gi'n out", but it wouldn't lie down. Mackenzie's amendment carried, making the fourth defeat for the Ministry in a row, but still nothing happened. The Premier stuck to his place, and declared that no number of adverse votes could make him step down. The next day Blake tried again. His motion was met by a Government amendment to adjourn until the new year. The House refused by a vote of nearly two to one. The "axe-grinder"* was blocked at every turn. He gave up and resigned.

The new Administration was known as the Blake, or the Blake-Mackenzie, Ministry. Alexander Mackenzie had no in-

*An expression adopted by J. S. Macdonald's opponents after the latter told an audience in Hamilton that anyone who had any "axes to grind" had better support him.

tention or desire to make a career in provincial politics. He had run more or less against his own will, wanting only to add one more seat to the anti-Macdonald forces. With Sandfield Macdonald defeated, he had but one thought – to storm the other Macdonald fortress in Ottawa. Blake confessed later that his hardest task in forming the Government was to persuade his friend from Sarnia to join.[30] However, despite his fears and sensitivity, the young lawyer shared the Dominion Grit leader's capacity for stubborn insistence. In addition, he had the call of duty on his side. Five days before Christmas, Mackenzie stood before his old political ally, and more recently his bitter opponent, Lieutenant-Governor Howland, and took the oath of office as Treasurer of Ontario.[31] Beside him, being sworn in as one of his colleagues, was his old friend Archibald McKellar. Jane was chatting with a Presbyterian minister in her home when her husband's letter bearing the news arrived. As she read, a tear stole down her cheek. The minister asked if she had bad news. Unable to speak, she handed him the envelope. After announcing the news, Alexander looked back on their eighteen years together, and then asked her to pray for him that he "might be kept right amid the temptations and difficulties" of his responsible position.[32]

Sarnia was delighted. At last their local hero was a Minister! Many had been disappointed when he had refused to succeed Brown six years before. Some even wished the rumours that had spread periodically since then were true, and that he was going to enter Sir John A. Macdonald's Cabinet. Such reluctance to reap the rewards of his hard labours, to bring glory not only to himself but to his family and his constituency, was hard for them to understand. When he did accept a portfolio, they were told at Christmas time, it was only because he was able to take his principles with him into office. One of those principles was a harakiri sword for a provincial Minister; he was determined to see that dual representation was abolished as soon as possible.[33] A local poet borrowed the galloping metre of Cowper's "John Gilpin", and commemorated the victory in verse.

"Hurrah for Mackenzie the pride of the West!
Who has long fought the battle and conquered at last.
Long, long may he live his high office to hold,
For his sterling integrity has yet to be told.

'Tis an honour for Lambton to have such a man
Who never would yield to the Axe-grinder's clan,
Tho' many a time they have tried him hard,
He ne'er would accept of a traitor's reward."[34]

The new Ministers asked for re-election to carry out a broad programme. They proposed to put an end to the Ottawa-Toronto axis, restore parliamentary control of public expenditures, including the railway grants, extend the franchise, and inaugurate a vigorous immigration policy. It was an appealing set of goals; the voters returned them all by acclamation. By the time the session re-opened on January 17, 1872, Mackenzie was hard at work on his budget.

His pride wounded and his health failing, Sandfield Macdonald refused to lead the Opposition. The task fell to Matthew Cameron, another former member of the "Patent Combination". Cameron's main objective was to destroy the Clear Grit reputation for political purity. He accused the Ministers of having undercut their predecessors by luring away supporters with promises of favours, and of having abandoned their anti-Coalition doctrine by giving the former Independent Conservative, Richard Scott of Ottawa, a Cabinet portfolio. Blake denied the charges. Scott accepted the Liberal platform as announced years before, he replied; that made him a convert, not a continuing Conservative. There had been no compromises, no open questions, and there was therefore no coalition.[35]

One of the first Government measures was a resolution urging effectual steps to apprehend and punish the murderers of Thomas Scott in the Red River settlement. Riel and his principal colleagues had fled before the advancing troops of General Wolseley the previous year. Nothing could be less related to the Ontario Administration, but public opinion was still aroused, and the new Ministers wished to proclaim their sympathy with it. Riel was guilty not merely of high treason, they declared, he was guilty of murder. The resolution carried sixty-two to one.[36]

Alexander Mackenzie brought down his budget in early February.[37] It was a memorable occasion. His fellow-Scot, Sandfield Macdonald, had left the public Treasury fairly running over with a surplus of more than one hundred and seventy thousand dollars! In addition, the million and one-half dollars in the railway fund had not yet been allocated, and the new Cabinet was free to dispose of it as it liked. There would be money to educate the mute and blind children of poor families, began the new Treasurer. There would also be assistance to hospitals, workhouses, and poorhouses. To make teaching a regular profession, he proposed "entering the labour market and making the standing and remuneration of teachers more in accordance with the importance of their calling".

It was a "national development" budget. Expenditures on colonization roads and immigration were to be greatly increased. Special attention would be paid to the area along the Ottawa and French rivers, the natural route to Lake Superior and the North West. Railways in abundance were to be built into the northern part of the province. Immigrants to fill the new areas would be sought among the rural population of Britain and Ireland in order to ensure the best possible quality.

The call for action to bring justice to the North West was not forgotten. A vote of five thousand dollars would be asked, Mackenzie concluded, as a reward for the discovery and apprehension of the murderers of Thomas Scott. "Twenty-five thousand dollars, you ought to have said," interrupted the Leader of the Opposition. "I believe the result (of the vote) will be," intoned the Treasurer, "that the man who acted in this manner will either be apprehended and brought to justice or be compelled to hide from the light of day his coward face and his crime-stained hands."

The budget was an attractive package. It cost the Ontario taxpayer a mere two and one-half million dollars, and it left a still larger surplus for the new fiscal year. The other measures adopted during the six-week session were equally impressive. Control of the railway fund was placed under strict legislative control, members of the Legislature were prohibited from holding offices of emolument under the Crown, procedures for taking legal action against the Crown were simplified, aid to municipalities was increased, and assistance was granted to new settlers. One of the last of the long list was a measure to abolish dual representation, making Blake, Mackenzie, and several others ineligible to sit in both the House of Commons and the Ontario Legislature at the same time. It was to take effect at the beginning of the next session; before that time the two leading Liberals would have to decide which political field they would abandon.

For Alexander Mackenzie the choice was easy; he had chosen the federal field at the time of Confederation, and he had a position to fill in Ottawa. The excursion into provincial politics was merely temporary, and already his purpose was accomplished. At the same time, the brief period in office in Toronto was excellent training for things to come. It provided an insight into the complicated field of Government financing, and gave him a better understanding of provincial affairs. It also demonstrated that the task of guarding the public purse is a thankless one, and that political virtue is one of the most difficult types to preserve. "The merciless reproaches of the Hamilton people ... have wounded me deeply," Mackenzie wrote after his refusal to grant a request from that city had precipitated a violent reaction,[38] "the attribution of evil motives is new to me . . . but consciousness of having acted with the single purpose to do right enables me to bear it with some equanimity." His indifference to public office made it easier for him to accept abuse and to reject threats. "I accepted the position with reluctance and will resign it at the first opportunity," he told the same complainants. "If . . . (the) Reformers of Hamilton find this is sufficient excuse for turning Tories I wash my hands of all blame."

It was particularly important for a man who had cried "corruption" from the Opposition benches to be, like Caesar's wife, above suspicion. The fervent hope of his opponents was to be able to point the finger of outraged propriety as he had done so often, and cry "you too". The price of mining properties was high and a friend suggested that he could make a sizeable profit by disposing of his mining claims in the Thunder Bay area on Lake Superior. "Being a member of the Ontario Government, I cannot be concerned in any way with any one who has claims pending before the Government," the Treasurer wrote,[39] ". . . it being necessary for me to keep entirely clear from the remotest suspicion of being in any way directly or indirectly a participator in prospective advantages from transactions in which the Crown is interested in any way." The former immigrant had abandoned the freedom he had crossed an ocean to obtain, in order to assure it for his fellow-citizens.

CHAPTER 8

The Turning Tide

In Ottawa the pre-election session of 1872 was long and bitter. The three principal questions to be decided – the Washington Treaty, the Canadian Pacific Railway scheme, and the New Brunswick school question – were all controversial, and all pregnant with consequences for the future. There was no compromise; on every issue, sharp divisions between Government and Opposition occurred.

John A. Macdonald had waited the full legal limit of one year less a day between sessions before calling the members to Ottawa. Since his return from Washington, he had been trying to decide what approach to take to the Treaty that he had signed so unwillingly. One thing was clear: having placed his signature on the document, he could not dissociate himself from its terms. There was only one chance: to shift the debate onto the familiar ground of loyalty to the Mother Country. "It is therefore of very considerable importance," he wrote to a friend, "that Brown and the *Globe* should be committed irretrievably against the Treaty."[1] Both Brown and Mackenzie obliged; a month after the signing ceremony, they were denouncing it hotly.

The Canadian Pacific was just as big a headache for the Administration. In the year between sessions, Cartier and Macdonald had worked to find a suitable contractor to undertake the huge project. The two possibilities were the shipping magnate, Sir Hugh Allan and some of his American associates, and a Toronto group represented by Senator David MacPherson. Both men were personal friends of the Premier, but the Senator stood on closer terms. During the previous winter, he had collected a sixty-thousand-dollar "testimonial fund" to help his leader out from under his crushing load of debts.[2] Such an obligation was an additional complicating factor in an already complicated situation.

Two weeks after the session opened, Cartier introduced a Bill authorizing the Government to enter into an agreement for the construction of the railway. He repeated the assurance that there would be no increase in taxation, "not only . . . in spirit but to the letter".[3] The construction company was to receive thirty million dollars in cash and fifty million acres of land in alternate blocks twenty miles deep on either side of the line. The other blocks of land would be sold by the Government to recoup the high cash payment. The Bill also contained provisions for a branch line from the Red River settlement to the American border, and another from the main route across northern Ontario to a port on the eastern end of Lake Superior.

Alexander Mackenzie led off for the Opposition. He was as much as ever in favour of the entry of British Columbia into Confederation, he asserted, but the terms were so impossible of fulfilment that he could not believe the Government expected to meet them. The cash outlay requested was already five million dollars more than the figure quoted the previous year, and much more would be needed. A large portion of the route was so barren that most of the land grants would have to be made on the western prairies, he asserted, and as there were only between forty-five and sixty-five million acres of fertile soil there according to the scanty engineers' reports, little would be left for the immigrants. Settlement of the North West, one of the main purposes of a railway, would be thus defeated. It was a sound argument in view of the limited knowledge available to the Opposition. Mackenzie had no way of knowing that vastly more fertile soil was available, and that the Government had an assurance from the British Columbians that they would not insist on the rigid fulfilment of the terms.

The debate went on sporadically for about a month. By the time the final vote was reached, the Ministry was convinced that the Yellowhead Pass was the best route through the Rockies, but they still had only a "quasi-official" letter from Sir Hugh Allan as an offer to build.[4] As an alternative to the "impossible" terms, Mackenzie proposed once again making use of the extensive stretches of water along the route.[5] Lake Superior was an ideal waterway much of the year, he said, and there were further water stretches between Fort Garry and the Lakehead that could be utilized. Only connecting links of rail and some locks would be needed. From Fort Garry to the Rockies, a wagon road would suffice for the moment. Immediate construction of a link between the Northern Pacific Railway in the United States and Fort Garry would provide adequate transportation to the West until the prairies were more settled. It was not an imaginative continent-wide scheme, or one designed to please the British Columbia delegates, but it was realistic. Above all, the Opposition leader called for Parliamentary approval of all contracts, and specific sanction of any agreement with a chartering company.

A good number of the Government supporters, particularly those from Ontario, were inclined to agree that the undertaking was extravagant and perhaps even reckless. However, they were banking on the assurances of Cartier and Trutch that the bargain with British Columbia did not call on them to attempt the impossible. The Opposition alternative was voted down two to one.[6]

As Treasurer of the largest province, Mackenzie assumed the functions of financial critic in Ottawa. He denounced the "national policy" of high protective tariffs as detrimental to trade, and likely to precipitate another commercial depression. In a period of prosperity and surpluses, it was not an issue that could arouse public opinion. Much more potent politically was the New Brunswick school question. Despite bitter opposition from the Catholics, the provincial Administration had passed an Act removing rights that had been accorded at the time of Confederation. In the 1872 session, a private member proposed that Catholics be given the same rights in New Brunswick as Protestants in Quebec. The Liberals were carving out a place for themselves as the defenders of provincial rights, and could ill afford to propose or acquiesce in federal interference in a clearly provincial field. On the other hand, they were anxious to rehabilitate themselves in the eyes of the Catholic population, and had to make some positive gesture. The solution they hit upon revealed a new sense of strategy, and a broadness that had been lacking in earlier sessions. Though maintaining his personal preference for a non-secular system of education, Mackenzie stated that the greatest care should be taken to avoid interfering with local legislation, particularly where religion was concerned. It was only because there was some room for doubt about the validity of the New Brunswick legislation that he proposed that London be consulted "as to the right of the New Brunswick Legislature to make such changes in the School Law as to deprive the Roman Catholics of the privileges they enjoyed at the time of the Union".[7] It was a good solution; the master strategist across the floor could devise no better. It carried.

Notwithstanding the flow of words on other subjects, members knew that the big battle of the session would be the Washington Treaty. The Premier waited as long as he could before breaking his extended silence, but inevitably he had to take a stand in its defence. "I knew I would not get fair play," he began somewhat apprehensively. "Sir, a sense of duty prevailed."[8] If he had not accepted the Commissionership, he argued, England would have settled the questions without Canada's voice being heard. Once there, he could not jeopardize the Treaty. "An American statesman said to me, the rejection of the Treaty means war! Not war to-morrow or at any given period, but war whenever England happens to be engaged in other troubles and attacked from other sources . . . There was no humiliation . . . England would neither advise nor permit one of the faithful colonies to be degraded and cast down." The only weakness in the British stand, the Premier maintained, was that the Fenian claims were not put on the agenda. In compensation, Canada was to receive a cash grant of two and one-half million pounds from England. "Reject the Treaty," he concluded in a burst of oratory, "and you do not get reciprocity; reject the Treaty and you leave the fishermen of the Maritimes at the mercy of the Americans; reject the Treaty and you will have to call upon England to send her fleet to give both her moral and physical support although you will not adopt her policy; reject the Treaty and you will find that the bad feeling which formerly and until latterly existed in the United States against England will be transferred to Canada and the United States will say, and say justly, 'Here, when two great nations like England and the United States have settled all their differences and all their quarrels upon a perpetual basis, these happy results are to be frustrated and endangered by the Canadian people because they have not got the value of their fish for ten years'."[9]

It was an able speech. Most of the Opposition arguments had been foreseen and their rebuttal made in advance. This was not surprising; the Premier had used most of them in Washington himself. He was "greatly disappointed at the course taken by the British Commissioners", he had written to his colleague Charles Tupper from the American capital. "They seem to have only one thing in their minds – that is to go to England with a Treaty in their pockets – no matter at what cost to Canada."[10]

It was late in the evening when Alexander Mackenzie rose to reply.[11] In contrast to the subtle and dexterous Government leader, his words were reminiscent of his early life in the stone quarry. His austere appearance and his severe demeanour lent force to his denunciation of the concessions. The Premier of Canada had gone to Washington at the expense of the Canadian taxpayer, he asserted indignantly, and agreed to a policy so retrograde as to constitute a step in the decline of "that national spirit that is as essential to the well-being of a country as food is to the life and vitality of man". He cast aside the excuse that England stood alone and in danger because of United States designs. "Has it come to this, that the Premier of Canada has to make an appeal to the forbearance of Canadians because of the necessities of that great Empire of which we form a part? Are we to live as a portion of the British Empire? Is Britain herself to live merely by the sufferance of the United States, Russia and other nations? . . . I believe that England still holds supremacy over the nations of the world!" Nor would he accept the argument that Canada's refusal might lead to war with the United States. There was no danger of conflict arising from the current differences, Mackenzie insisted. The cession of the Atlantic fisheries and the St. Lawrence navigation rights had taken two strong weapons out of Canadian hands that would have been valuable in negotiating a new Reciprocity Treaty. He had no confidence in any British-American commission to fix compensation for the abandonment of the fisheries. "All know the loss this country has sustained through the ignorance or inability of those who were appointed by the English Government to negotiate our boundaries. . . . At Washington they [the Americans] wanted the St. Lawrence and got it and . . . they would set their hearts on something else within a year; they are constantly setting their hearts and their envious eyes on some portion of our territory and if gentlemen like the honourable gentlemen opposite are to be Commissioners, I fear they will obtain what they want." The "wretched consideration of money", instead of the Fenian claims, was to him a humiliating abandonment of Canada's honour. A rejection of the Treaty would "redound to the dignity and independence of Parliament, would prove our devotion to the true interests of the Empire and the honour of Canada, and would be a fearless assertion of our rights as a people and our dignity as British subjects."

It was a worthy reply, and proved once more that the Brownite and Mackenzie Grits were often more proudly British than many Britishers at home, more confidently imperialist than those who were entrusted with the destiny of the Empire.

Assertions of loyalty and accusations of disloyalty flowed profusely from both sides of the House. Tempers rose as the debate continued day after day, and far into the hours of darkness. Encouraged and invigorated by a worthy cause well led, the Liberals made an impressive onslaught; the Government back-benchers fought hard in defence of their embattled Premier. As the days passed, the Opposition speeches took on a more nationalistic tone. "I consider that my position as a Canadian representative demands of me that I give my first and best regards to the country I am most deeply interested in," stated Mackenzie in an attempt to stir the embryonic Canadian national consciousness.[12] The Empire did not ask Canada to accept the Treaty, and if it did, he would be inclined to discuss such great concessions before approving them. His words had no practical effect. The House was divided along party lines, and the Government majority was overwhelming. "I presume the Bill will be carried," the Opposition leader conceded on May 16, ". . . (but) I at least raised my voice against this national wrong and degradation."[13] He was right; the vote was again two to one.

In the dying days of Canada's first Parliament, the Liberals attempted to force a few reforms through the House. Blake introduced a Bill to provide elections in all constituencies the same day. Such an innovation, replied the Premier with renewed confidence, was contrary to British practice. "Un-British" as well, he declared, were motions to prevent Senators from obtaining remuneration from the Crown other than their sessional indemnities, and a suggestion by the Reformer, David Mills, for Senate reform. The proposal that controverted elections should be tried before judges, and steps taken to prevent corrupt practices, he denounced as "slander". An Opposition attempt to block the proposal for a distribution of seats based on the 1871 census, and to approach more closely the accepted rule of representation by population, was defeated like every other motion from the Speaker's left. "We have had a most triumphant session," wrote Macdonald as the members dispersed to their constituencies, "not having experienced a single check of any kind . . . I am going to the country with good hopes of success in Ontario."[14]

Alexander Mackenzie, too, was optimistic. "It will depend on Nova Scotia and New Brunswick," he told George Brown, and he saw grounds for hope of swinging the former behind the Liberal cause. Zealous Reformers in one constituency nominated Brown as their candidate, but he refused to descend again from his oracular pinnacle. Edward Blake was in a state of nervous prostration from the combined strain of the Ontario Premiership and the Ottawa session; he left almost immediately for a rest in England. In addition to directing the campaign, Mackenzie had to take charge of the provincial Administration as well.

Such a schedule made it impossible to extend his activities much beyond the borders of Ontario; he had to rely on fellow-Liberals such as Dorion and Holton in Quebec, Anglin and

Smith in New Brunswick, and Jones and Power in Nova Scotia. Nevertheless, the Liberals entered the campaign united as never before. The lack of a formal Dominion leader was more a matter of tactics than of any basic disagreement among members of the caucus. While the breach in Liberal ranks caused by Confederation, and the deeper and older split on religious lines, were fairly well healed in the minds of the leading party spokesmen, there were still divergences of view among Liberals in general that could be exploited by the Tories. The choice of a leader from any one province was certain to be embarrassing to candidates in the others. Without a Dominion leader, the campaign could be adapted to local conditions, and the process of consolidation and unification continued at a natural pace. But the most important reason that no party head was officially designated was the steadfast refusal of Alexander Mackenzie to assume the trappings of office in addition to its burdens.

With the Liberals more confident than at any time since the "double shuffle", and the Conservatives on the defensive over the Washington Treaty, the North West troubles, and the huge expenditures forecast in the British Columbia Act, the campaign was brisk. Macdonald arranged to have his own election in Kingston early in order to exploit the psychological effect of a smashing victory, and leave him free to deal with the marginal constituencies later in the summer. So confident was he of success that he did not even intend to include Kingston in his itinerary until he learned that the Liberals were determined to give him a fight on his own home ground.[15] To him this was just another minor annoyance at a time when he had a Dominion-wide campaign to supervise, and was trying desperately to get Sir Hugh Allan and Senator MacPherson to agree to amalgamate and build the Canadian Pacific Railway together. Sir Hugh was insisting on the presidency of the proposed company and a controlling share of the stock for himself and his friends; MacPherson was equally insistent that the presidency and vice-presidency be left an open question. The shipping magnate played his cards well; he agreed that the "friends of the Government will expect to be assisted with funds in the pending election".[16] Engaged in a desperate struggle to hold even his own constituency in Montreal, Georges-Etienne Cartier was pressing his leader hard to reach an agreement. At that juncture, nomination day arrived in Kingston. In his address, the Premier intimated that, far from being the Simon-pure Clear Grits they purported to be, his opponent and Alexander Mackenzie were both involved in an oil swindle in the West. The Liberal candidate retorted that Sir John was a liar, or words to that effect. His nerves strained by his many preoccupations, Macdonald slapped his opponent's face and grabbed for his throat. The platform guests intervened and stopped the fight.[17]

On August 1, the wheel of fortune seemed to take a turn in Sir John's favour. He won his own election by a small majority, and succeeded in giving Sir Hugh enough assurances to open his ample purse.[18] With renewed hope, he set off for the West, where Mackenzie was campaigning as if he intended to drive the Tories from the face of the earth.

Alexander Mackenzie was not enjoying clear sailing. In his own constituency, Alexander Vidal, now an open supporter of the Administration, was again in the field, and the Conservatives were working hard to unseat him. It was a dirty, mudslinging campaign.[19] In the oil-rich Petrolia area, the Grit leader was accused of having joined with his brothers to buy up one thousand barrels of oil shortly before a new tax was announced in the spring. He replied by offering to deposit one thousand dollars and allow an accountant to examine the records of his transactions, the money to be forfeited if any wrongdoing was found. The appointment of his brother as Superintendent of the local Indian Reserve was recalled, and to it was added, as an example of vicious patronage, the appointment of his friend Archibald Young to a position in a provincial asylum for the blind. His Thunder Bay mining claims, it was asserted, had been purchased after he became a provincial Minister, and he was accused of selling insurance to cover certain provincial buildings. The latter charge was true, admitted Mackenzie, and his share of the profits was one dollar and six cents, with the chance of a six dollar loss. Finally, he was accused of being too proud to ask favours of the Government for his constituency.

The paths of the two party leaders crossed in Sarnia itself.[20] The night before nomination day, the gunboat *Prince Edward* appeared in the St. Clair River with the Premier on board. He had come to deal with his principal tormentor on his own ground. He agreed to accept a nomination in Lambton County just long enough to make a speech, at the conclusion of which he would decline the honour. There were some things he wanted to tell the electors about this paragon of virtue, this uncompromising purist, this worshipper of the *Globe* dictator.

The crowd began arriving early in the market grounds. Some came by special train, some in buggies or wagons, others on horseback or on foot. When the Premier appeared, Mackenzie was already present, his face tanned a deep brown from the long hours of campaigning in the unusually hot August sun. In one respect, the roles were reversed. Though adept at speaking to crowds, Macdonald appeared to be in his true environment in Parliament, while Mackenzie remained obviously a representative of the world outside. In Sarnia, it was he who was at home among the farmers, oil drillers, and storekeepers, most of whom he knew personally. Criticize him as a stubborn Scot they might, but they did not doubt his word or his devotion to their interests. He was one of them, he had laboured side by side with them to build the West, he knew their problems, and he talked their language.

The meeting began amicably enough, with both men insisting that the other should have the "privilege" of speaking first. Macdonald won that initial skirmish and secured the second place so that he could rebut the arguments of his adversary. Mackenzie's role of host did not cause him to forget that he was engaged in an historic battle. Here was the man, he told his neighbours, who claimed the paternity of Confederation, but who in fact had accepted it only when compelled to do so. This was the man who agreed to a coalition, and then broke the agreement by trying to become Premier himself. He, too, had been invited into the spider's parlour, but Ministerial opinions of his eligibility had been revised since that time. This was the man who had rejected every attempt at parliamentary control of public spending, who had given British Columbia six members to represent ten thousand people while Lambton's thirty thousand had but one, who had been guilty of such duplicity in the North West, who had gone against his own convictions to choose the longer route for the Intercolonial Railway, and who had given an unconstitutional subsidy to Nova Scotia. As the list of charges was reeled off so bluntly before his very face, the Dominion Premier's expression changed from a pleasant smile to surprise, and from surprise to anger. Then there was the matter of buying votes with public buildings, the Clear Grit continued determinedly. "That's another falsehood," shouted Sir John, unable to restrain himself further. On the subject of falsehoods, Alexander Mackenzie replied, the Premier's statement at St. Thomas on the secret service fund fitted exactly into that category. More interruptions followed. "I was going to call him my honourable friend," Mackenzie said on almost slipping into parliamentary jargon, "but unless he retracts a statement he made on the Kingston hustings I cannot call him that." "I certainly won't retract it," retorted Macdonald, thoroughly aroused. "He says he won't retract it. I defy him to prove it. Until he does prove it I shall treat him as a slanderer."

In a battle of insults, the two men were well matched. Alexander Mackenzie was the hungriest aspirant for office he had ever known, said Sir John when his turn came, but he was more noted for grumbling than for constructive action. He was as bad tempered in Ottawa as he evidently was at home. The Ministry in Toronto of which he was a member was the most false, the most faithless, and the most corrupt that ever existed in Canada. In Ottawa a few years before, he had been the "touter" of a ring to rob the Indians by having some old claims of tavern keepers made valid. The Government had blocked the scheme, and Mackenzie had been so furious that he had crossed the floor and shaken his fist in the face of the Minister of National Revenue. "That's a lie," snapped the Liberal candidate. The Premier ignored the interjection. As chairman of the Printing Committee he had accepted a bribe from one company, Sir John raced on, he had organized a ring to raise the price of oil, he had some mysterious deal with the oil kings, and he had channelled land grants into the hands of some of his friends. Only when he had completed his full list of charges, did Macdonald decline the nomination and take his seat.

Not to be outdone, Mackenzie had taken the precaution of having a friend nominated so that a Liberal would be able to reply. The Conservatives did the same. Night was falling before the speeches were completed, and the head of the Government made his way back to the waiting ship. "It is the old story of hog shearing," commented the *Globe* in an editorial entitled, *Sir John at Lambton,* "much cry and little wool."[21] Mackenzie's confidence was not shaken. "Sir John, McDougall, and several others are making the most tremendous efforts to defeat me," he told Jones.[22] "I almost wish they could and thus relieve me but it won't happen this time . . . They may bring my majority to 500." The electors gave their decision the following week. In contrast to the Premier's majority of one hundred and thirty-one in Kingston, Alexander Mackenzie was re-elected with six hundred and thirty-five more votes than his opponent. It was another decisive victory for the Lambton Scot.

It was a tough campaign right to the end. The Conservatives made excellent use of a printers' strike at the *Globe,* and Brown's strike-breaking tactics, to alienate workers' votes. The Liberals might have a worker as their figurehead, they claimed, the real leader of the party was a tyrannical employer, and Macdonald was the true friend of the working man. Nevertheless, the Grits won a majority of the seats in Ontario, and a record number of twenty-eight in Quebec. The newest provinces of Manitoba and British Columbia returned full slates of Government supporters, and the Maritime members, though less identified with the ministerial and anti-ministerial groups, were largely Macdonald men as well. Among the casualties were both Cartier and Hincks, the unhappy William McDougall, and Mackenzie's good friend Alfred Jones. Sir John's majority was somewhere between ten and thirty.

Despite his fatigue, the Grit leader rushed straight up to Toronto at the end of the campaign to fulfil his duties as Acting Premier. He had fought hard to suppress a feeling of futility throughout the summer, and it had taken all his determination to continue the fight. "The news of your defeat reached me as I was about to address some thousands of people in Perth," he confided to Alfred Jones, "and I could hardly get through the task with credit."[23] He, too, wished for some respite from the continual battling and the bitter acrimony. "I can quite understand the 'sense of relief' you say you feel. I wish I had the same luxury. I never liked public life. I was driven into it by the local exigencies of the party and when the friends I am most attached to drop out of line either by retirement, defeat or death I feel a most depressing influence upon me."

The news from Blake was not more cheering. The mere sight of Canadian mail upset him, he wrote from London.[24] He, too, dreamed of retiring from public life. With no one else to do the work, Alexander Mackenzie had no choice but to carry on as long as his strength would allow. "I have only been 5 days at home for six months and my wife utters an occasional protest," he had remarked in May.[25]In the next six months, Jane saw him even less. During September, he laboured in Toronto, and continued his speech-making throughout Ontario; in October, he went to the Maritimes to discuss tactics at the next session.

The big question awaiting a solution was the leadership of the Ontario Administration. Both Blake and Mackenzie wanted to leave the provincial field. With a new session approaching, a decision was urgent. There seemed to be no suitable candidate among the other Cabinet colleagues. Archibald McKellar was popular, but he had stepped down from the leadership only a short time earlier because it was a task beyond his capacities. Among the other provincial Ministers, Peter Gow was not a strong man either, and Adam Crooks was still inexperienced. Richard Scott was only a recent convert to the Grit cause and could not lead. George Brown could have any position in the party he wished, but he refused them all. When Blake returned in mid-October, the search was still going on.

The right man was not far away. Since 1866 he had lived quietly round the corner from Osgoode Hall on Simcoe Street, and performed his duties as Vice-Chancellor in the judicial hierarchy with his usual care and assiduity. He was Oliver

Mowat, one of the Reform "Fathers of Confederation". The years of retirement from party strife had increased rather than diminished his prestige. On the morning of October 21, Brown and Blake called on him in the library of his Simcoe Street home and offered him the Premiership.[26]

The suggestion came as a complete surprise. To abandon the prestige of a high judicial position, the civilities of the legal profession, and the rich calm of a book-lined study, was far from his thoughts. He asked for time to consider. When Mackenzie returned in the afternoon from an engagement out of town, he followed up the attack. He spoke of their duty to Ontario, the dangers of allowing the Conservatives to take over again, and the importance of destroying forever the Ottawa-Toronto axis. It worked. Two days later Mowat accepted.

The Liberals were delighted. It was doubtless a master stroke. The Tory reaction was pleasingly violent. "Disgracing the ermine," they yelled in frustration.[27] Alexander Mackenzie's resignation as Treasurer was written out and dated October 14. On October 25 it was accepted. As he left the Council Chamber, another Sarnian, Thomas Pardee, his running mate in 1867, walked in to become the new Provincial Secretary.

With a lighter heart than in many months, the ex-stonemason returned to Sarnia and a more pleasant task. Reverend Thompson of St. Andrew's Church had asked him for Mary's hand in marriage. During the eight years that he had spent in the western parish, John Thompson had won the respect and affection of the Mackenzies, and they attended his services regularly after the small Baptist congregation was disbanded. He was undoubtedly an upright man, and Jane and Alexander were happy to welcome him as their son-in-law. As 1872 drew to a close, Mary exchanged the duties of a schoolmistress for those of a housewife.

CHAPTER 9

They Are Done For

The Liberals had failed to unseat their rivals in the election, but they had come close enough to taste blood. There were hopeful signs of reducing the narrow Government majority still further. For some reason that no one in central Canada seemed to understand, the British Columbians, who had given their full support to ministerial candidates in the summer, threw out the pro-Macdonald provincial Government before Christmas. In a by-election in Welland where the top men from both parties campaigned hotly, the Liberals carried the seat, albeit by a mere handful of votes. An air of mystery and intrigue surrounded the Pacific Railway project, and rumours were spreading that Senator MacPherson was being passed over in favour of Allan. If it were true, the Senator could be counted on to make life difficult for the Administration.

A letter from Edward Penny, editor of the *Montreal Herald*, on December 10, confirmed Mackenzie's suspicions.[1] He had information, he told the Grit leader, that Sir Hugh Allan had advanced one hundred and fifty thousand dollars to the Conservatives for electioneering purposes. The Tories were still up to their old tricks! Perhaps this was the chance to expose them once and for all! The Liberals girded for the attack.

With the election over and the possibility of power near at hand, everyone agreed that it was time to designate an official party leader. This time it was Mackenzie who took the initiative. The experience in Toronto had shown the importance of a clear understanding before the Premiership was offered to the party. Despite Blake's illness, Mackenzie was convinced that the young lawyer was the best man for the job, and that he should be made to accept his responsibility. Blake disagreed. Before the matter was even mooted, he told Mackenzie that the departure of his brother and another partner from the legal firm, and the return of Mowat to legal practice as a formidable rival, made it "absolutely necessary that I should devote myself almost exclusively to business for the next 3 or 4 years."[2] He did not even plan to attend the first session in Ottawa, except to "go down at the opening and do what I can in the first struggle".

Alexander Mackenzie was determined that Blake should not escape. He asked the Liberal members to meet him in Ottawa the day before the House opened. While Dorion explained the situation to the Quebec group, he told the English-speaking Liberals that a complete Dominion-wide organization under a single leader was needed, that he had acted in that capacity, but was "now resolved to retire from the position".[3] They should consider whether it would advance the general interests of the party more to have a leader from Quebec rather than from Ontario. With the delegation from Ontario the largest, it was likely that there would be more agreement on someone from that province, and in that case he thought that Blake should be chosen "as his splendid abilities and his standing in the country gave him many advantages, while his legal knowledge gave him additional power, placing him ahead of all the others in the House". Blake spoke next, and agreed on the necessity of choosing a leader, but insisted that if an Ontario man were chosen it must be Mackenzie, as he had laboured hard for five years and had been mainly responsible not only for the recent gains in the federal field, but for the provincial victory in 1871 as well. He himself would listen to no proposal to stand. After considerable discussion, a Committee was formed to decide on a name.

The Committee met three times. Dorion took the view that the Ontario members should choose the leader, and that the others should fall in behind him; that he personally would be glad to serve under Mackenzie, or would serve under Blake. Letellier preferred Blake; Holton preferred Dorion, with Blake as his second choice, and Mackenzie as a satisfactory third. Both Blake and Mackenzie insisted they would not accept. The first Committee meeting ended in an impasse, except for the decision that the leader must come from Ontario. On March 6, the day after the Speaker was chosen, and a few hours before the Speech from the Throne was to be heard, they tried again. Mackenzie was still determined to conscript Blake, and, if that was not successful, to see that Dorion was chosen. He was in for a surprise. At the end of a long and tough meeting, it was he and not Blake who was obliged to cede. By sheer hard work and dependability, the self-educated stonemason had risen to the top position in his party. And it had happened despite himself! At four o'clock, after the Speech from the Throne had been read, Dorion informed the caucus of the Committee's decision. Holton moved its adoption. The members concurred unanimously. "I am still afraid, indeed convinced that I made a mistake in accepting," the newly-crowned leader wrote to his predecessor George Brown, "but the way seemed closed up against retreat." "We'll see how matters go," he sighed resignedly, "and if everything does not go well I will endeavour to shake it off yet."[4] Illusion. The cloak of leadership is a boa-constrictor that tightens its grasp continually and releases its victim only when he is prostrate and broken from sickness, age, or defeat. Brown did not share the doubts of his former lieutenant. "We content ourselves with saying," the *Globe* commented, "that if a spotless character, a clear, vigorous intellect, incorruptible integrity, indomitable courage, great business capacity, knowledge of public affairs, and earnest devotion to Canada, can fit a man for the duties of the office, the selection of Mr. Mackenzie will prove a grand success."[5]

The Speech from the Throne was read by the new forty-seven-year-old Governor General, the Earl of Dufferin. A dapper landed Irish aristocrat, he had arrived the previous summer in the midst of the election campaign with an impressive array of servants, carriages, harness, linen, glassware – all the paraphernalia necessary to maintain a state of regal splendour on the outskirts of civilization. A Liberal at home, he had sat in the House of Lords for some years, and had served as both Under-Secretary of State for India, and Under-Secretary for War. His heart had been set on the Viceroyalty of India, and he had been somewhat disappointed at the Canadian appointment, but had soon adapted himself to the prospect of a term in North America. Elegant, rich, and highly cultured, he was determined to maintain the full measure of dignity and prestige of the Queen's representative in the primitive northern Colony. Canada was assured, said *The Times*, of a liberal dose of "blarney" from her new Governor General.[6]

A well-trained diplomat and politician, Dufferin's speeches were not the sort of "blarney" that shocked Canadian ears. Even before setting foot in the Dominion, he had a vision of her future surpassing that of most of her citizens. "It may be doubted whether the inhabitants of the Dominion themselves are as yet fully awake to the magnificent destiny in store for them," he told his fellow-Irishmen in a farewell address, "or have altogether realized the promise of their young and virile nationality. Like a virgin goddess in a primeval world, Canada walks in unconscious beauty among her golden woods and by

Ont. Dept. Travel & Publicity

Edward Blake with Mackenzie on his left

Jane Mackenzie and Mary Thompson

the margin of her trackless streams, catching but broken glances of her radiant majesty, as mirrored on their surface, and scarcely recks as yet the glories awaiting her in the Olympus of nations."[7] Not since that other Irishman, D'Arcy McGee, was shot down on Sparks Street shortly after Confederation, had the rather prosaic Canadians heard such eloquence. Dynamic and positive by nature, Lord Dufferin set out to lead the Dominion a step toward her destiny.

"I have caused a charter to be granted to a body of Canadian capitalists for the construction of the Pacific Railway," Dufferin read from the throne in the red and gold Senate Chamber. Mackenzie listened attentively. The statement did not agree with the report he had received a fortnight earlier that the agreement had been made with Sir Hugh Allan and some American capitalists. According to his information, the contract was granted to the Allan group in return for a three hundred thousand dollar contribution to the Tory election fund. The money had been paid during the campaign, and the negotiations with Senator MacPherson had been a mere blind.

Without documentary evidence, no charge could be made. He had no objection to American capital and American enterprise being used, Mackenzie told the House in the Throne Speech debate, but he feared that if the Americans who controlled the Northern Pacific also obtained control of the Canadian railway, the latter would become a mere feeder line.[8] The Premier was reassuring. It would be the duty and the pleasure of the Government to prove that they had omitted no protection which could be devised to keep the control of this great Canadian enterprise in Canadian hands. He hoped that there would be no need for foreign capital; British money would be more advantageous and would be another link with the Mother Country. To Mackenzie the statement was confusing. The bland statements of the Government leader were in direct contradiction to the persistent reports of American capital and election funds from the United States. The Opposition would have to wait for concrete evidence.

The first vote of the session came on one of a long series of charges of electoral corruption. Instead of the majority of at least twenty-five of which Macdonald had assured Dufferin, the Opposition was defeated by only sixteen votes. The Governor General reported to London that the Opposition was stronger, fiercer, and a good deal abler than during the last Parliament.[9] Five Nova Scotians had voted against the Government. If eight more of the uncommitted members had gone over to the Opposition, the vote would have been tied; one more would have toppled the Ministry. This was fairly close in a House where the members from the four smaller provinces were not firmly committed to any party, and there were rumblings of dissatisfaction among both Ontario and Quebec Government supporters. Both sides started an urgent canvass to win over every possible member before the vote on the second election case. By the time the House met on the following Monday, Mackenzie was convinced that he had at least eight more on his side. One of the Ministers began to reply to Blake's charges in the second case, and then suddenly announced that they would accept the motion annulling the election and allow a new contest. "There is little doubt we would have defeated them," wrote the disappointed Leader of the Opposition to Jones in Halifax.[10] "Of course they are damaged badly and unless your men go back on us we will certainly defeat them at an early day. . . . If you and Power had been here all would be right. You see how much one Election can influence a nation sometimes. However, we must not cry over spilled milk." The canvassing behind the scenes continued.

The Premier introduced a bill to hold all elections on the same day, but would not go as far as the adoption of the ballot system. Mackenzie congratulated him with cutting irony on his partial conversion, and warned him that he would continue to be driven until he recanted all the errors of his earlier years. There was no saying, he speculated, but that Sir John might even become a good Reformer in the end. If the Opposition could not upset the Cabinet, they could at least act as its political schoolmaster.[11]

After the charges of electoral corruption were disposed of, the session settled down to a steadier pace. In the corridors the rumours continued to circulate that the Opposition was preparing a sensational attack on the Pacific Railway scheme, but day after day passed and Mackenzie and his principal lieutenants remained as close-lipped as ever on that subject. In his role of financial critic, the member for Lambton referred to the railway plan, and the House tensed expectantly, but he soon went on to other subjects.

It was the second day in April before the bombshell was exploded. Lucius Huntington, the tall, handsome, silver-haired business man from Montreal, rose in his place next to the Opposition leader and read a resolution.[12] He could prove, it stated, that an agreement had been made between Sir Hugh Allan and a Mr. G. W. McMullen, acting for certain United States capitalists, whereby the latter agreed to furnish all the capital for the construction of the Canadian Pacific Railway, but that it should appear to be a purely Canadian company with Sir Hugh Allan at its head. The Government, the member for Montreal West went on, was aware of these negotiations, and agreed with Sir Hugh and his lawyer, J. J. Abbott, M.P., that the former should advance a large sum of money for the purpose of aiding the election of Ministers and their supporters in the general election. In compensation, he and his friends would receive the contract for the construction of the railway. Such funds from the United States capitalists were in fact advanced to the Ministers, Huntington asserted, and he therefore requested a committee to investigate the negotiations for the Canadian Pacific Railway contract.

When Huntington had finished reading the resolution, he sat down. All eyes turned toward the Premier. Macdonald sat mute and expressionless, as if in a temporary state of shock. Through his mind raced memories of his interviews with McMullen and Sir Hugh, and the figures of the money he and his colleagues had received during the campaign. How much did they know? he asked himself as he stared across the floor. Mackenzie's face was as rigid and unrevealing as his own. The seconds dragged on. The Premier tapped nervously with his pencil. Finally, the Speaker, with a questioning look in the direction of the Treasury benches, rose to his feet. A formal motion had been made and, comment or no comment, it had to be dealt with. "Is the House ready for the question?" he asked. "Question," came a spattering of nervous voices from the floor. The vote was taken. In the absence of any explanations, the members divided along party lines. The resolution was defeated by one hundred and seven to seventy-six.

The thirty-one-vote majority provided only temporary security for the Ministry. The rumours and questions were brought suddenly into the open, and members on all sides demanded an explanation of the Government's silence in the face of such a serious accusation by a leading Oppositionist. "We found great uneasiness among our friends. . . . It looked like stifling an enquiry," Macdonald wrote to his colleague Georges-Etienne Cartier, who was in London seeking in vain for a cure for his Bright's disease.[13] When the House met the next day, he announced that a five-man committee would be set up to consider the charges, and if necessary, a Royal Commission would be created "for the purpose of giving them additional power."[14]

The committee was to be composed of three Conservatives, plus Blake and Dorion. Why had the Prime Minister reversed his stand? Alexander Mackenzie demanded.[15] If Huntington's request for a committee was a want-of-confidence motion, was he not now moving one against himself? The Premier refused to be drawn out by the banter he usually loved. The Committee was satisfactory to the Opposition, but a Government-appointed Royal Commission, they feared, would be a mere tool in the hands of the Administration. Mackenzie demanded that the Committee be given permission to sit after the session ended, and to take evidence on oath. To meet the second part of the Opposition Leader's request, an Oaths Bill was rushed through the House.

In between discussions of the "railway scandal", the members tried to get on with current business, but all other subjects paled into insignificance. Even Mackenzie's motion condemning the cession of the navigation rights on the St. Lawrence in the Washington Treaty, and asserting "that the people of Canada should be consulted before the concession of any of her rights in the future," attracted little attention.[16] Like automatons, the majority voted it down. Charles Tupper, blindly loyal to his chief, surged forward to bolster the spirits of the Tories, and vented his scorn and indignation on the accusers. With Mackenzie he had a special score to settle. At a joint meeting in Strathroy, the pugnacious Scot had said he "would rather rule in hell than serve in heaven."[17] The burly Nova Scotian was not the sort of man to accept such insults lightly, and returned as good as he received.

When Macdonald saw the list of people Huntington desired to have called before the Committee as witnesses, he knew the situation was serious.[18] The Opposition obviously did know something after all. Uncertain which way to turn, he reverted to his familiar game of playing for time. The Government-dominated Committee tried to examine Huntington to find out how much knowledge he had in his possession, but the Montrealer made excuses not to appear before them. With Allan, Abbott, and Cartier all absent from Canada, the Premier then asked for an adjournment until July. The three Conservatives forced the request through the Committee. In the House, Sir John made a fervent disavowal of any misdoings.[19] He denied the charges "in toto", he told the Commons, and denounced the Huntington resolution as a "foul calumny". "Neither by word, deed or action, has the Government done anything which they could be ashamed of." "In God's name let them [the accused] have their trial," he almost shouted, "in God's name if they are guilty let them be punished, but in God's name let them have a fair trial."

The prayerful display of sincerity cheered his supporters, but it did not deter the Opposition Leader. It was evident that an arrangement, direct or indirect, had been made by Allan and others to secure the Pacific Railway contract, he insisted. Having reason to believe that such an arrangement existed, Huntington had a duty to bring the matter to the attention of the House, and there was no reason to delay examining the other witnesses. The appeal was in vain. The majority still sided with the Premier, and the postponement was granted.

In mid-May, Huntington attempted to raise the matter directly in the House, but the Speaker ruled that it was before the Committee, and a committee could not be circumvented.[20] Suppose, the Montrealer managed to say, the Government, in a corrupt bargain with the railway contractors, had received three hundred and sixty thousand dollars, and the letters to prove this were in the hands of a trustee of the Company? He asked that the Committee be reconvened to secure the papers. Macdonald acquiesced. Dorion demanded that the House be sitting in July when the Committee was hearing evidence in order to compel witnesses to attend, and in order to give members a chance to pass judgment on the findings. The thought of July in Ottawa was anathema to the back-benchers; the request was easily defeated. Nevertheless, one enthusiastic Liberal wrote home to his wife that night: "They are done for."[21]

The members were still struggling to get through the detailed work of the session when Sir John rose and announced that Sir Georges Cartier had died in London. He began to pay tribute to his popular colleague and long-time associate, but his voice broke, and he could not continue. Hector Langevin, the Minister of Public Works, completed the eulogy for the Government; Mackenzie, obviously shaken as well, spoke for the Opposition. He, too, had been fond of the high-spirited little French Canadian, and had admired his generous nature and administrative ability. He could not forget that Cartier had appreciated the fine qualities of George Brown, and had toyed with the idea of a Brown-Cartier alliance against Macdonald a few years before. On the other hand, he could not forget that Cartier was the Minister most directly implicated in the "Pacific scandal". "It was never my fortune to agree with him in his political views," he told the Commons diplomatically, "at the same time it was never my misfortune to have anything but the best personal relations with him."[22]

On May 23, the Premier had recovered his composure, and made the situation still more embarrassing. He moved not only that a public funeral should be held, but that a monument be constructed at public expense for the deceased Minister. The suggestion was tantamount to proclaiming Cartier a national hero, and placing his name above public controversy. Nothing in Macdonald's expression revealed this was his real intention.

Disagreeable as it was, Mackenzie had to object to the proposal as long as the investigation continued. The motion carried regardless.

Although Sir John was evidently drinking again, he played his hand well.[23] As the House was about to adjourn, he announced that a "pro-forma" meeting would be held in July to hear the results of the Committee's investigation.[24]

"A quorum will be present," said Holton.

"I will take care it is nothing else but pro-forma," replied the Premier.

The Government had gained a little time, which the Opposition, too, found useful. While Blake and Dorion concentrated on the investigation, Brown scribbled outraged denunciations of the Tories in his King Street editorial office, and Mackenzie raced from meeting to meeting condemning their "heinous" crime. He had always maintained that the Tories were corrupt and wicked by nature; the proof was coming to light at last!

The all-out political battle was interrupted briefly on July 1 to welcome Prince Edward Island as the seventh province in the Dominion family. On the following day, the "Huntington Committee" met for the first time in Montreal, the scene of the alleged crime. They were informed officially that they would not be able to take evidence on oath; the Oaths Bill had been disallowed in England.[25] This was as Macdonald had anticipated when the measure was passed. In fact, he and Dufferin had done their best to ensure disallowance. As an alternative, the Premier reverted blandly to his former proposal of a Royal Commission. The two Liberals in the Committee spurned the suggestion as "of evil consequences to create the precedent of a Government issuing a Commission of inquiry into matters of a charge against itself".[26] Balked once more, the Conservatives decided by a majority vote to postpone further meetings until Parliament met again on August 13.

Public interest had to be kept alive. The July 4 editions of the *Montreal Herald* and the *Toronto Globe* contained correspondence with Sir Hugh Allan and George McMullen, the American railway financier. Included was a telegram dated July 26, 1872 from the Prime Minister assuring Allan that the influence of the Government would be exercised to secure him the presidency of the Canadian Pacific.[27] But, the telegram stated, "the whole matter (ought) to be kept quiet until after the elections". A letter from Cartier to Allan, dated just four days later, stated that "the friends of the Government will expect to be assisted with funds during the pending elections, and any amount which you and your company may advance for that purpose will be recompensed. . . . A memorandum of requirements is below." The "requirements" included thirty-five thousand dollars for Sir John, fifty thousand dollars for Cartier himself, and five thousand for Langevin.

As July wore on, more revelations appeared. Later in the 1872 election, Cartier had asked for twenty thousand dollars more. Five days after the famous meeting in Sarnia, Macdonald had wired Allan's solicitor, J. J. Abbott: "Immediate. Private. I must have another ten thousand dollars; will be the last time of calling. Do not fail me." With such evidence before the public, Sir Hugh Allan decided to make a full statement. He admitted having advanced to the Conservatives during the 1872 campaign a total of three hundred and fifty thousand dollars. The month of July provided a further revelation. The incriminating documents had not been sold by the Americans to embarrass the Government when they met resistance to their participation in the railway scheme; they had been stolen by a discontented clerk in Abbott's office and turned over to the Opposition leaders in Montreal.

When time for the August meeting of Parliament arrived, the Government's position looked so serious that Lord Dufferin interrupted his summer sojourn in the Maritimes to return to the capital; in June, he had considered that a proxy would suffice. Even as late as July 21, he had written to his First Minister from Charlottetown: "Nothing can be more satisfactory than the way in which your own position and that of your colleagues remains unassailed in the midst of all these disreputable proceedings."[28] His Excellency's warm personal feelings for Macdonald were public knowledge. He found a striking resemblance to the British Prime Minister, Disraeli, . . . "if you could imagine Dizzy a 'blonde'. . ." and admired his polished manners and considerable culture.[29] His political adroitness struck a responsive chord. "My only regret is that I cannot have the pleasure of watching you 'handle the ribbons'," he had written enthusiastically after the 1872 election. "Everybody seems to agree that your management of the House is as neat a specimen of coaching as any one needs to witness."[30] The Macdonalds were frequent guests at Rideau Hall, and in May, Sir John had become the godfather of the Governor General's Canadian-born daughter. By nature an enthusiastic partisan, Dufferin accepted eagerly his chief adviser's word when the latter swore that every sixpence of the money raised by Allan among the American railwaymen had gone into Allan's own pockets, and that the charge of attempting to bribe Parliament was "a pretense and an absurdity".[31]

Despite his personal inclinations, Dufferin could not ignore completely the revelations and accusations of the Opposition. Ever suspicious of the successors of Metcalfe and Head, Brown and Mackenzie were issuing blunt warnings to the Governor General not to protect his advisers. "I can hardly believe he will dare venture," the Liberal leader told Brown the same day that Dufferin wrote to Macdonald so loyally from Charlottetown, "but if we judge from his conduct in asking the drunken debauchee to be Godfather for his child he can do a great deal."[32] His suspicions were increased when Dufferin refused to receive from Huntington a package containing copies of the incriminating documents on the grounds that he could only receive advice from his constitutional advisers.[33] With Brown leaving on one of his frequent trips to Britain, Mackenzie asked him to call on Prime Minister Gladstone, and the Colonial Minister, Lord Kimberley, and explain the Liberal view of the crisis.[34] "If the crown is made an instrument of oppression to shield criminal Ministers," he grumbled to Timothy Anglin after Brown's departure, "Colonial relations must be looked into."[35] The *Globe* publisher carried out his mission well. He delivered copies of the letters to Kimberley, and received assurances that the Imperial Government would adopt an attitude of strict neutrality, leaving the question to be decided entirely by the Governor General, his Ministers, and the Canadian Parliament.[36] "I cannot doubt that you are fully alive to the necessity of a thorough and immediate investigation into the astonishing charges against the Ministers," Kimberley wrote in a sobering letter to Dufferin on August 14.[37]

Sir John had said that there would be merely a "pro-forma" meeting on August 13; Alexander Mackenzie was determined that there should be a proper debate and a vote. He wrote letters asking the Liberals from the central provinces for a full attendance, and worked feverishly to bring doubtful members to his side.[38] The Independent Conservative, Richard Cartwright, was willing enough to upset his old leader, and Joseph Cauchon, another discontented Conservative from Quebec, had already promised to give him what support he could behind the scenes. A powerful newspaperman, Cauchon had edited *Le Canadien* for many years, and had been a Conservative Minister a decade before. In some respects, however, he was a doubtful ally. He had been charged with obtaining a contract in connection with the Beauport Asylum while a Minister, and exploiting it in someone else's name. He gave a convincing explanation to Mackenzie of his conduct, and referred to his patriotism in abandoning his previous stand to support Confederation. Anxious to muster every possible vote, the Grit Leader agreed to work with him. The situation in the Maritimes looked more and more favourable. Several New Brunswick members were openly espousing the Opposition cause. Nova Scotia's "grand old man", Joseph Howe, was dead, and the link he established between his followers and the Conservatives was gone. With Jones assisting in Halifax, Alexander Mackenzie was gradually swinging the "Bluenoses" to his group. "The ministerial party is doomed," he predicted confidently to Dorion on July 31.[39] Even if they succeeded in their plot on August 13, they could not escape another session.

As the members appeared in Ottawa, it was obvious that there was to be much more than a mere "pro-forma" meeting, and that the Opposition was likely to be in a majority. Macdonald had not bothered to ensure that enough of his supporters would be present to win a vote. Though Mackenzie's disdainful reference to debauchery was probably uncalled for, there was no doubt that the Premier was "unwell" again. During July he had disappeared from his Rivière du Loup summer home for several days, leaving his wife and friends searching frantically for him. After a rumour began circulating that he had committed suicide, he appeared in Lévis, opposite Quebec City, where he had been on an extended drinking bout.[40]

It was general knowledge that the Governor General had a brief speech ready in which he would announce the prorogation of Parliament and the formation of a Royal Commission. Shortly after noon on the "fatal 13th", Richard Cartwright led a delegation of members to ask Dufferin to stay his hand.[41] With them they had a petition containing ninety-two signatures in support of their request. His Excellency asked for an hour to consider the matter. Shortly before two, the petitioners reappeared, and he asked for thirty minutes more. As a matter of fact, it was already far too late. In late June, the Governor General had approved the idea of a Commission,[42] and in early August had signed the document creating it, although he had asked the Ministers to keep the fact a "profound secret".[43] At two-fifteen, three-quarters of an hour before the House was due to meet, he gave his reply. In view of the unanimous advice of his constitutional advisers, he had no alternative but to announce prorogation and appoint the Commission. At three o'clock the Liberals were in their seats and waiting to launch their attack. If they were to frustrate the Government's plan, they would have to act quickly between the time the Speaker entered the Chamber and called them to order, and the Gentleman Usher of the Black Rod arrived from the Senate, summoning them to hear the Governor General's message. As the minutes dragged by, all eyes switched nervously back and forth between the door and the clock. On the front bench of the Opposition, Alexander Mackenzie fingered his glasses nervously and gripped the papers in his hand. Across the floor, Sir John's seat was empty; as Prime Minister he had gone to welcome the Governor General at the entrance of the Parliament building.

Twenty past three. From his seat Mackenzie could see the Black Rod hovering outside the door of the Chamber.[44] It was another Tory plot! The Speaker was deliberately delaying his entrance until the Governor General was installed, and the Black Rod was ready to come in directly the doors were opened in order to cut off any discussion by the Commoners. At three twenty-five, the Speaker finally appeared. As soon as he mounted his dais, the Grit leader sprang to his feet. "I propose to address you, Sir, and the House, upon a question of privilege," he began hurriedly.[45] "In the present grave position of the country and the extraordinary circumstances under which we are called together, I feel it encumbent upon me to place this motion in your hands." The Speaker attempted to interrupt. "Privilege! privilege!" roared a chorus of Opposition voices. The House was not in session until the doors were opened, shouted the presiding officer above the din. He was right. In his eagerness, Mackenzie had forgotten part of the procedure! Afraid of losing his advantage, he stood by his desk while the Sergeant-at-Arms swung the heavy wooden portals aside, then rushed ahead with his motion. "Moved by Mr. Mackenzie, seconded by Mr. Holton: That this House during the present session ordered an inquiry by a committee of its own into certain grave charges in connection with the granting of the charter and contract for the construction of the Pacific Railway, which if true seriously affect the official honour and integrity of His Excellency's advisers and the privileges and the independence of Parliament. That the investigation thus ordered has not so far been proceeded with, owing to circumstances not anticipated when the inquiry was ordered, and that it is the imperative duty of this House at the earliest moment to take such steps as will secure a full Parliamentary inquiry; that constitutional usage requires that charges of corruption against Ministers of the Crown shall be investigated by Parliament, and that the assumption of that duty by any tribunal created by the Executive would be a flagrant violation of the principles of this House, and that this House will regard as highly reprehensible any person who may presume to advise His Excellency to prorogue Parliament before it should have an opportunity of taking action in the premises, inasmuch as such prorogation would render abortive all the steps taken up to the present time, would inflict an unprecedented indignity on Parliament and produce great dissatisfaction in the country . . ." As the Leader of the Opposition raced on, the three knocks of the Black Rod's mace resounded throughout the Chamber. Ministers and Government supporters looked up with relief and shouted the news that the messenger from the Senate had arrived. "Privilege! privilege!" chanted the Oppositionists. The Sergeant-at-Arms' voice was scarcely audible as he announced the news.

"No message shall interrupt me," roared Mackenzie. "I stand here representing a constituency in this province, and, I have reason to believe, the opinions of a very large number of people throughout the country. I propose to call the attention of the House to circumstances affecting the independence of Parliament." The Black Rod advanced to the Clerk's table in front of the Speaker, and shouted the summons to the Senate. Amid the cacophony of cries, his words were lost. "There is nothing in the circumstances which justifies His Excellency to prorogue Parliament for the purpose of protecting an accused Ministry," insisted the clear Scottish voice, "and I propose to proceed with the discussion of this matter to which our attention has been called on previous occasions. I have placed this motion in your hands because I have heard it is the intention to prorogue this House." The Black Rod bowed and retreated with all the dignity he could preserve in such a chaotic setting. The Speaker stepped down from his dais and followed as quickly as possible. Some thirty-five Government supporters followed suit; the others remained adamantly in their places.

Continuing in his role of a John Hampden defending the rights of the people against the Crown and the court clique, Alexander Mackenzie led his supporters into the Railway Committee Room off the central hall for a protest meeting.[46] "For the safety of the people the independence of Parliament must be upheld," he told them. To turn Parliament out of doors on the advice of an Administration advising upon matters affecting its own position was an act altogether unknown in British history. Public opinion was behind them, and "it now becomes us to do nothing which will detract from our position and at the same time to obtain the opinion of the country as will convince His Excellency that he has been grievously misinformed." Blake, Huntington, and Dorion followed with equally heated denunciations of the day's events. After supper, the protest meeting continued. Joseph Cauchon cast off his reservations about appearing openly as an ally of the Grits, and proposed a resolution condemning prorogation as "a gross violation of the privileges and independence of Parliament and the rights of the people". It carried amid loud cheers. Another resolution declared that the House of Commons should, "at the first opportunity at which it is allowed to meet . . . take the matter into its own hands and prosecute the inquiry." The torrent of outraged virtue concluded an hour and a half before midnight with three cheers for the Queen, and three cheers for the Opposition.

The following day, the Royal Commission, composed of three judges, was appointed. To clarify his position and counter the accusations of partisanship, Dufferin sent for Alexander Mackenzie and explained again that as a constitutional Governor he had no alternative but to accept the advice of his Ministers. Nevertheless, the feeling remained in Mackenzie's mind that His Excellency was in sympathy, if not in league, with the Tories. With the goal of upsetting his life-long opponents so near at hand, Mackenzie set off for the Maritimes to enlist the support of as many as possible of the members who did not attend the August meeting. He appeared in Prince Edward Island in the midst of an election campaign to choose the first six members of Parliament. The Liberals there were led by David Laird, a former Premier, and seemed in a good position to win every seat, but the representatives of a new province often voted with the party that brought them into Confederation. On the Island he saw several candidates, had full explanations with them, and called on a "ponderous political personage called Bishop McIntyre who has 40,000 of the 90,000 on the Island in his flock".[47] Close on Mackenzie's heels, Charles Tupper crossed the Northumberland Straits to draw them to the Government side. The news in New Brunswick and Nova Scotia was equally encouraging for the Liberals. "I saw many of the public men in the Maritime Provinces and can safely say that there is a very healthy feeling prevailing there," he reported back to Ontario.[48]

Elsewhere in Canada, the competition for parliamentary supporters was just as intense. The colourful new Liberal Premier of British Columbia and federal member, Amor De Cosmos, had hardly crossed into western Ontario before he was besieged by representatives of the two parties. Edward Blake and James Edgar met him at the railway station at London; Alexander Campbell was with him when he left Toronto for the capital. The Opposition grew increasingly optimistic. Several Conservatives were ready to co-operate "to establish any honest government in place of the present one", Richard Cartwright assured the Liberal leader, "unless indeed you proclaimed your intention of running the machine on strict party lines in which case you would place them in an awkward predicament."[49] Mackenzie was too near his goal to argue. That was no obstacle, he reassured the Independent Conservative eagerly. "I have only adopted party organization as a means to an end . . . nothing would give me greater pleasure than to cooperate with others calling themselves conservatives to ensure success and give these gentlemen all my assistance at an election afterwards."[50] It was a compromise with his earlier views of adhering to strict party lines and Grit principles, but in the rush of events everything seemed secondary to throwing the "corruptionists" out of office.

The situation looked so favourable that Blake was already worrying about having to accept office again. "For your own information . . . my determination is fixed not to go in," he wrote to Cartwright. "If there were (which there are not) reasons making my presence in a new administration of vital consequence I would only come in as one of the council without office."[51] With his temperament and qualifications, he was trying to convince himself, he would be more useful outside a Liberal Government than within.

The focal point of political interest became the Commission hearings in Montreal. John A. Macdonald decided not only to testify, but to examine witnesses himself on behalf of the Government. Lucius Huntington refused to appear, protesting that he could not recognize any tribunal set up to do a task belonging to Parliament. George McMullen, the Chicago financier accused of supplying the campaign funds, also refused. Nevertheless, the Commission established the fact that the Ministers had asked for help from Sir Hugh Allan, and had received three hundred and fifty thousand dollars through him while he was endeavouring to secure the Pacific Railway contract. Before the investigation ended, news arrived in Canada that Sir Hugh was unable to finance the scheme after all, and the charter was surrendered. Responsible, in part at least, for the failure, was *The Times* of London, which adopted an attitude of shocked distaste at the revelations, and discouraged the London moneylenders from dealing with men like Allan and Macdonald.

Lord Dufferin clung hard to his confidence in the integrity of his First Minister. "I congratulate you with all my heart on the favourable result of the investigation so far," he wrote on September 12. "As I said to you in very early days I am convinced that you will come out entirely exonerated from the atrocious charges."[52] Ten days later he was less confident. "Try and find out from Sir John how much money he really owns to," he asked his secretary from Quebec.[53] Both English public opinion and the Colonial Office were evidently disturbed at the testimony before the Commission. Suppressing his personal sentiments, the Governor General was obliged to face the fact that something was wrong. "A greater amount of lying and baseness could not be well crammed into a smaller compass," he complained unhappily to Lord Kimberley as he despatched the first portion of the evidence.[54] But what else could be expected in such a primeval society? "Every day I am becoming more and more sensible of the inconvenience of conducting the Government of this enormous Territory with such poor and scanty administrative materials. It is having to handle a full rigged ship with the crew of a schooner."[55] If Macdonald and his colleagues were corrupt, he was convinced that the Opposition, who had been attacking him so bitterly with accusations of partisanship and threats of dire consequences, was every bit as bad. Only when the evidence was complete, and the Royal Commission report delivered, did he admit his doubts. Writing as "a warm and sincere friend" he told the Premier that "forced by most anxious study of the evidence . . . I shall be bound to sacrifice my personal inclinations to what may become my duty to Sovereign and this country."[56] Even then he continued to hope that, somehow, Sir John would redeem his personal reputation.

Parliament re-assembled on October 23 in an atmosphere of tenseness and expectation. "The evidence obtained under the Commission deserves careful consideration," stated the Throne Speech noncommittally. "The report will be laid before Parliament and it will be for you then to determine whether it can be of any assistance to you." The members seized the copies of the evidence and began preparing feverishly for the debate the following Monday.

Alexander Mackenzie launched the attack at once.[57] The huge pile of references on the desk before him, and his methodical approach, revealed long hours of preparation during the weekend. This was but the last stage in the Government's decline, he began quietly and firmly, as he set out to reconstruct the events of the "scandal"; the inevitable end was at hand. The Premier had testified that he had asked Cartier to see Allan about funds for the 1872 election campaign, as Sir Hugh "was interested in all the enterprises which the Government had been forwarding". Allan had met with Cartier and Abbott, and then had written in a private letter: "I think the game I have been playing is now likely to be attended with success." On August 6, 1872, in the midst of the election campaign, he had reported to his American associates, "I have already paid over $200,000 and

"PROGRESSING FAVORABLY."

MISS CANADA (ANXIOUSLY).—"DOCTORS, HOW DO YOU FIND THE POOR DEAR PREMIER?"
DR. B—N (FOR THE M.D.'S).—"MADAM, WE'VE JUST HAD A CONSULTATION; THE SYMPTOMS ARE HOPELESS. WE BELIEVE HE CAN'T SURVIVE OCTOBER!"

From Bengough's *Caricature History of Canadian Politics*, Vol. I

will have at least $100,000 more to pay. I must soon know what our New York friends are going to do." The next day it was done. "Yesterday we signed an agreement by which, for certain monetary considerations they agreed to give our Company the contract." Nevertheless, the Premier had stated during the campaign that he had received no money for the elections.

After dealing with the evidence, the Opposition Leader went on to the events of August 13. Such devious proceedings were an insult to Parliament, he declared, and had caused the complete failure of the parliamentary system. The members should express their views on the Commission evidence, and also on

HON. A. MCK——E: *I wouldna strike ye when ye're down, but I'll just cap ye ower wi' your big sins.*

RT. HON. SIR J. A. M——D: *Just you wait a bit. I'm not extinguished yet.*

Canadian Illustrated News: February 7, 1874

the continuance of such practices. Seconded by Thomas Coffin, one of the recent converts from Nova Scotia, he moved that ". . . his Excellency's advisers have invited the severest censure of this House."

To counter each of the points in the carefully documented speech was impossible. As Sir John sat silent, his faithful lieutenant, Dr. Tupper, who did not appear to be directly implicated in the "scandal", rose to defend the Ministry. What he lacked in facts, he made up easily in bombast and bluster. Of course, the Opposition Leader knew all about corruption, he roared defiantly; he had relied on it so often in the past. He was an expert on unworthy actions as well. "The honourable gentleman went throughout the length and breadth of this country issuing every disloyal statement toward Great Britain . . . he is an enemy to Canada and unworthy of the position of being the leader of public sentiment . . . is it not undignified . . . to make a charge calculated to leave a stain not only upon the Government but upon the country itself (?) . . . an injury has been inflicted upon the fair name of Canada." To know Sir John's character was enough evidence that the charge was utterly false and baseless, shouted the burly Nova Scotian; it should not be heeded, coming from annexationists and men who considered Confederation a failure.

Thus the great debate was launched. Unsuccessful in having a hidden observation post built into one of the galleries, Lord Dufferin sent his wife to attend the sittings and report in detail. An ardent admirer of Macdonald, her descriptions buoyed his hopes for the survival of the likeable Premier. However, Macdonald, so brilliant a strategist on many occasions in the past, was awash in a sea of indecision. Uncertain which way to turn, he played his "waiting game" again. In this instance, waiting was poor tactics. As he sat glumly in his seat in Parliament, or pondered the situation drunkenly in his East Block office, his support gradually disintegrated around him. "Matters here are in a dreadful state," the Governor General lamented in a letter to England on November 2.[58] "Had the Government taken a division on the 2nd or 3rd night of the Debate after a good rattling speech from Sir John, I really think they would have won by a decent majority. . . . Every day fresh defections are taking place in his ranks – in fact his friends have thrown in the sponge. He himself is very unwell. You know what that means."

It was not merely the charm of his First Minister that made Dufferin forget the course of events. As a result of the constant lecturing and scolding in the *Globe*, he had developed a strong antipathy for George Brown and the Reformers in general, and had convinced himself that the low political morals indicated in the Pacific scandal were a common trait of all Canadian politicians. "Had there really been on the side of the Opposition an honest set of men capable of forming a strong Government," he wrote to Kimberley, "I might perhaps have been tempted to have forced the situation . . . but it did not seem to me desirable to run any risk for the sake of making Mackenzie Prime Minister. Though I like him personally he is a poor creature and under the thumb of George Brown. Blake is by far the best man of the two but they tell me he could not command a personal following and that George Brown prefers a puppet like Mackenzie as head of the party to a more independent man like Blake."[59]

With October past and November beginning, the silence of the Premier became more and more difficult to explain. The other Ministers put up speaker after speaker to reply as best they could to the Opposition barrages, but mainly to gain time until their chief decided what to do. The campaign in the corridors and hotel rooms to line up votes went on. As the second week of the debate drew to a close, Macdonald told Dufferin that he was waiting until Blake spoke, as he imagined that the Toronto lawyer had "some document of a fatally compromising character" with which to deliver the *coup de grâce* of the Government.[60] If Blake spoke last, the effect might be irreparable. The Governor General was alarmed at the admission, "suggestive as it was of many interpretations".

It was November 3 before Sir John broke his silence. He had been visibly under the influence of alcohol all day, and in an encounter with Blake on a minor matter he had blundered badly.[61] Three hours later he rose, pale, haggard, and looking as though a puff of wind would knock him down. He began slowly, uncertainly, and almost inaudibly, then gathered strength and confidence. The empty glass on his desk was removed frequently by the page boys and replaced with full ones, leaving the hushed members to guess if the colourless liquid was water or a stronger beverage.*[62] Whatever the source of his energy and courage, it was a magnificent speech, well worthy of the veteran politician. Lady Dufferin and her friends were electrified with admiration and hope.[63] When he sat down after five hours, there were smiles on the faces of the Government supporters again.

Blake rose immediately to reply. He spoke a few minutes and then adjourned the debate until the following afternoon. The members went home after two in the morning with the memory of Sir John's masterful performance vividly in their minds; Lady Dufferin rushed back to Rideau Hall to waken her husband and tell him excitedly of the great spectacle she had witnessed.

When he continued the next day, it soon became evident that Blake had no "fatally compromising" document, but he had a powerful case and he presented it superbly well. Gloom spread once more to the faces on the Speaker's right, and the Oppositionists brightened visibly as he proceeded. "I believe that this night or tomorrow will be the end of wholesale corrup-

*Hon. Peter Mitchell, one of Macdonald's colleagues, recounted later that the Premier had arranged with three different persons to send in glasses of gin instead of the usual water.

tion in the public life of this country," he concluded as darkness fell again on Parliament Hill. ". . . Let us by our vote, regretfully it may be, give the perpetrators their just reward."[64]

Though Alexander Mackenzie was confident that he could win the vote, there were two important persons who had not declared themselves – David Laird of Prince Edward Island, and Donald Smith, the big red-bearded Hudson's Bay Company executive who represented Selkirk constituency in Manitoba. Each man controlled several votes. Though Smith had begun his career with a thirty-year stay in an isolated Labrador trading post, he was fast becoming a notable financier, and wielded considerable influence. In a desperate bid for votes, some of the Ministers had persuaded the Premier to talk to him, but when he was ushered into the office he had found Sir John in a belligerently drunken mood, and had been cursed out instead of being coaxed and cajoled as he expected.[65] He left as uncommitted as he entered. Another attempt to bolster the Government's defences was even more disastrous. The *Globe* of November 4 contained a statement by one member declaring that he had been offered five thousand dollars for his vote.[66] When the matter was brought up in the House, the Premier could only ask for time to study the documents containing the charge.

With Macdonald's and Blake's speeches delivered, there was no reason to delay the decision. On the 4th, Laird announced that he would vote with the Opposition, thus automatically committing over half of his colleagues from Prince Edward Island to do the same. Later in the day, Donald Smith made his long-awaited statement. For most of his speech neither side was certain which way he would go. Only at the very end did he declare that he could not conscientiously vote confidence in the Government. The Opposition broke into cheers.

There was still no sign of a formal vote when the House adjourned at one-thirty in the morning. Alexander Mackenzie turned the situation over in his mind as he walked down to his Albert Street room in the crisp, clear November night. He knew that the Administration could only be saved by some sharp act on Macdonald's part, but he could not think what even the resourceful "John A." could do to stop the course of events. When the chief Opposition whip, James Edgar, turned up at Mackenzie's boarding-house at three in the morning after a night-cap with some comrades, his leader was still awake. Edgar sat down on the edge of the bed, and the two men speculated on what the dawn would bring.[67] Both felt the hour of decision was at hand.

Mackenzie was up early as usual on November 5. He was still worried about collusion between Sir John and Lord Dufferin. "The incoming administration must take some steps to define their position and that of Parliament," he grumbled of His Excellency in an early morning note to Brown. "With a man of so little prudence and so much vanity there is no safety without laying down the line over which he must not pass. Parliament is at present in the humour to assert its privileges and teach him a lesson."[68] He was still trying to imagine what loophole the Tory chieftain might discover when Dufferin's messenger arrived.

CHAPTER 10

The New Broom

When Alexander Mackenzie walked into the Governor General's East Block office that early November afternoon, he still feared he might be stepping into a trap. Macdonald's long interview with His Excellency just before the Liberal leader was summoned by Lieutenant-Colonel Fletcher suggested the possibility of a plot much more than the cursory formalities of a resignation. The presence of the partisan Lady Dufferin, seated in her carriage near the entrance, increased his apprehension.[1]

The two men were comparative strangers to one another. Dufferin knew little of Mackenzie's past, and still less of his personality and capacities. The friend of Tennyson, Browning, Dickens, and most of the titled families of Britain, he showed the aristocrat's disdain for self-made men. The Liberal leader's knowledge of Her Majesty's representative was scarcely more extensive. They had met on formal occasions, and he had been summoned to the office before, but neither had shown the warmer, more intimate side of his character. Earlier in the year, he had pleaded with His Excellency to commute the death sentence of a Sarnia woman convicted of murdering her drunken husband, but the request had been refused. During the fall he had written a strong letter, protesting the suggestion that some of the signatures on the petition submitted in August were not valid. Just a few days before, he had been enraged when the Governor General sent down to Parliament copies of despatches on the Pacific Scandal that he considered biased, and designed, not only to whitewash the Conservative Administration, but to alter the course of the debate. He had vowed to protest such proceedings in vigorous terms.[2]

To Mackenzie's surprise, the visit was very cordial. Not only did Dufferin ask him to form a new administration, but he offered an immediate dissolution of Parliament. "Tainted as it must be" with Allan's money, he asserted, the existing House could not be respected. Laying a careful defence of his own past conduct, he told the Grit chieftain that his accession to office was much more honourable than if it had occurred on August 13. "Now I said," Dufferin reported to Kimberley later, "you become Prime Minister of your native [*sic*] country not through any unfair advantage nor by the vote of a packed house, nor through the premature condemnation of men who have been given no opportunity of making their defence, nor in consequence of any violent act of intervention on my part, but because your opponents after every chance has been given them have been condemned by a full Parliament of Canada."[3] Mackenzie accepted the expressions of confidence and the offers of help to make the new Administration "agreeable and successful". In the congenial atmosphere, he abandoned his intention of bringing up the matter of the objectionable despatches, and contented himself with saying that he intended to discuss the subject at some future time.

Edward Blake was waiting when the Premier-designate left the East Block, and they walked together to a secluded room to discuss the new Ministry. He had told the Governor General Blake was the one who should be forming the Ministry, related the diffident Scot.[4] Not so, replied the brilliant lawyer; he could not even take a part. The scene was reminiscent of the formation of the Ontario Administration in reverse. Blake was adamant. When his own urging failed, Mackenzie resorted to other means. He organized a petition of the Reform members to pressure him into accepting the Cabinet post. "I want you to send him a strong telegram as soon as you can after getting this," he wrote to George Brown in time for the night train to Toronto.[5] "I don't see how I can get along without him. Pressure alone can now make him come in and I fear even that will fail." Only when confronted with one hundred and four signatures from the Liberal caucus, did Edward Blake agree to enter, and then only as President of Council without any departmental responsibility, and for a short period of time.

A greater surprise was the attitude of Luther Holton. On two occasions, in 1858 and 1863, he had been Finance Minister, but had never brought down a budget. Instead of seizing eagerly the opportunity to return to the Finance Ministry as Mackenzie expected, he pleaded "personal reasons", and declined to accept any post whatsoever. Alexander Mackenzie was annoyed. "He probably was conscious that he did not have a brilliant Finance Minister in him," he commented sarcastically to Brown.[6] The Department of Finance was the one that the Premier-designate himself preferred. He had been the principal financial critic of the Opposition since Confederation, and was well qualified for the task. However, he had also been the principal critic of the Department of Public Works, and there was no one to whom he felt he could confide the important portfolio. A Public Works Minister had to be able to resist the terrible pressure of friends and enemies alike for favours, to direct such gigantic projects as the Intercolonial and Canadian Pacific Railways, and to supervise the extension of the canal system. To be absolutely certain of honesty and efficiency, he determined to keep it for himself. Richard Cartwright, who had bolted the Conservative party when Hincks was named Finance Minister, now accepted gladly the opportunity to show his ability in the financial field.

At least the choice of a French-speaking lieutenant was easy. Antoine-Aimé Dorion was the undisputed leader of the Quebec Liberals, and a close personal friend whose integrity and reputation were above suspicion. He was recognized as one of the outstanding legal minds in the Dominion, and his constructive attitude since Confederation had proven his loyalty and patriotism. Earlier in the year, Alexander Mackenzie had suggested his name as party leader; had he accepted, he himself would have been forming the Government. Mackenzie offered him the Department of Justice that had been directed since Confederation by Sir John A. Macdonald. He accepted, and brought with him into the Cabinet from French Canada, Luc Letellier de St. Just as Minister of Agriculture, and Télesphore Fournier as Minister of Inland Revenue. From Ontario, Mackenzie chose Donald A. Macdonald of Cornwall, brother of Sandfield Macdonald, as Postmaster General, Senator David Christie, one of the original Clear Grits, as Secretary of State, and the Irish Catholic, Richard Scott, a former colleague in the Ontario Cabinet, as Minister without portfolio. The Prince Edward Islanders received their reward with David Laird's appointment as Minister of the Interior. The Nova Scotians were represented by two recent converts, Thomas Coffin and William Ross, named respectively Receiver General and Minister of Militia and Defence. Neither was an outstanding man, but Alfred Jones, the strongest man in the Nova Scotia Liberal ranks, was playing the role of the reluctant hero as well. A prosperous business man, he, too, preferred to remain outside the Cabinet. New Brunswick was more fortunate. The ex-Premier, Albert Smith, became Minister of Marine and Fisheries, and Isaac Burpee, a Saint John merchant, Minister of Customs.

To the public, and indeed to most of the Liberal caucus, the ex-stonemason seemed to go about his task with calm assurance and methodical determination. "It was *so* characteristic of him," one member reported. ". . . He appeared no more uplifted than if he had been going out to an ordinary day's work. No word of exultation escaped his lips; he was in fact more subdued and reticent than usual."[7] Appearances were deceptive; it was not Mackenzie's nature to display his personal feelings. In fact, he was thoroughly upset, particularly by the refusal of Blake and Holton to join the Administration, and even considered giving up the mandate entirely. "Although few cabinets were ever built so rapidly I was sick, sick, before it was done; really ill in fact," he confessed to Alfred Jones.[8]

There were some gaps in the list that Alexander Mackenzie brought to His Excellency after two days of Cabinet building. British Columbia and Manitoba had no representatives because of his desire to keep the number of Ministers as low as possible; and the Irish, despite pressure and threats, had failed to have a man of their choice named to a Cabinet position. "I have a great mind to tell them to go to Jericho," the Premier-elect wrote indignantly to Brown after failing to convince them that Richard Scott, notwithstanding his name, was a member of a distinguished Catholic family.[9] After Holton's refusal, he had hesitated between Huntington and the Independent Conservative, Alexander Galt, and finally left one portfolio open to see if the latter could be enticed into the Cabinet.[10] Furthermore, some of the men were untried. Mistakes would have to be rectified as they were discovered.

Mackenzie asked Lord Dufferin to prorogue Parliament at once and send the other members home so that he and his future colleagues could be sworn in and get on with their new jobs. His Excellency demurred.[11] Why the great hurry? he wanted to know. It was after lunch on Friday, and there was no time to make the necessary arrangements so that the ceremony could be carried out with due pomp and circumstance. Why not wait until Monday? The reason was not easy to explain. Through Mackenzie's mind ran the scenes of 1858, when Brown and his Cabinet had been sworn in before prorogation, and had been defeated later in the day. Any delay in sending the members home would give Sir John the chance to repeat the "double shuffle" or devise some other manoeuvre. A motion for adjournment on Monday night might give Macdonald the opportunity for some disastrous amendment, he suggested. You do not seem inclined to trust those people any more than they were to trust you on August 13, Dufferin teased. The Liberal leader laughed grimly and acquiesced. While the Ministers were being sworn in, Luther Holton announced their names to the House of Commons. At least one member who aspired to ministerial rank, it was reported, wept a tear of disappointment.[12]

Thus the great challenge began. Most of the Ministers had no experience whatsoever in public administration. Some hardly knew the way to their new offices. Their departments were filled with civil servants whom they had long suspected to be the willing tools of the Tories, and, most likely, spies who would report every useful bit of information to them. Not knowing where to begin, they took the easy solution of disappearing to their constituencies to be re-elected, leaving the new Prime Minister to set the ship in motion.

The Conservative Ministers had used their power to the last. When Sir John resigned, he announced that the Minister of Finance, Leonard Tilley, had been appointed Lieutenant-Governor of New Brunswick; John Crawford, M.P., Lieutenant-Governor of Ontario; Hugh Macdonald, President of the Council, a judge of the Nova Scotia Supreme Court; and Thomas Ferguson, M.P., Collector of Customs in Collingwood, Ontario.[13] In addition, Mackenzie soon learned, one hundred minor appointments had been made in the last week the Tories were in office and several hundred during the summer and fall. The fact that the senior appointments bore Dufferin's signature deepened his distrust of the Governor General. Many Liberals cried for immediate cancellation of the lot, and Mackenzie's first inclination was to agree. His Excellency protested that the appointments had been made for several days before the old Government resigned, even though they were only announced at the last minute. He urged Mackenzie to let them stand. The latter gave in, and contented himself with cancelling only those lesser appointments that had not been formally completed when the Conservatives left office.

With only his year in the provincial Administration to guide him, Alexander Mackenzie moved into the Public Works office in the West Block and attacked the huge pile of decisions awaiting him. During the months of crisis the work of the different departments had been badly neglected from lack of ministerial direction, and leading civil servants were anxious for overdue policy decisions. Most of the officials were new to him, and it was impossible to judge at the outset which were responsible public servants, and which were poor appointments made to satisfy a certain section of the country, win a few votes, or repay political services. Under the existing system, practically all had been chosen because of their political affiliation, and it was generally accepted that the Civil Service was hostile to the new régime. "I have a horde of spies round me in the office who will carry to late Ministers all they can see or hear," the new Premier complained to his friend Charles Black in Montreal.[14] He had not even a secretary to help with routine correspondence. "As letters come in bushels I have to answer them as fast as I can drive the pen." One mail delivery contained so many letters that it took him three hours to read through them and extract the most important from the pile. "Difficulties crowd around of all sorts and brain and temper will be alike tried," he warned. "However, I will 'put a stout heart to a stai brae'."

Above all, Mackenzie was determined that it should be an honest Administration. He was sickened to note that many of the "bushels" of letters contained just the sort of requests for partisan favours that he had criticized for so many years. To grant them would be to remove the very reason for a Liberal Administration. Government purchases would be arranged by open contract, he replied to one eager Liberal. "Every opportunity will be given to the company you refer to, to tender for the same. In every case of course the lowest tender will be accepted unless there should be some special circumstance making that undesirable in the public interest."[15] Forcing aside his conviction that even his own office staff was a "horde of spies", he refused to dismiss civil servants simply in order to replace them with the ever growing list of "friends". "I am no believer in a retaliatory policy," he insisted. ". . . Every officer will receive ample protection – except where his power is used to oppress those under him. My object will be . . . justice for all, let the consequences be what they may."[16] In the dazzling new era of honest government, some remnants of the old system could not be abolished. Appointments in the different constituencies were still to be made by the members of Parliament supporting the Government, or by the defeated candidates in the case of Opposition constituencies. Since the beginning of Canadian political history, it was assumed that the local member was in the best position to choose local employees, and that appointments in the capital were made by the Cabinet. Even these Mackenzie tried to avoid. "Unless they are in my own Department I have nothing to do with vacancies," he told one supplicant.[17]

There was one series of political appointments he did wish to make. In 1867, the Senate had been composed of approximately an equal number of members from each party. The thirty-one appointments made by Sir John since that time had weighted the Upper Chamber heavily in favour of the Conservatives. With all the vacancies filled by the outgoing Ministry, Alex-

MISS CANADA'S SCHOOL (DEDICATED TO THE NEW PREMIER).
MISS CANADA (TO THE BOY AT THE HEAD)—"NOW, ALEXANDER, BE VERY CAREFUL, OR I'LL PUT YOU WHERE JOHN IS!"

From Bengough's *Caricature History of Canadian Politics*, Vol. I

ander Mackenzie decided to use the constitutional provision authorizing the appointment of six additional Senators in certain exceptional circumstances.[18] Even half that number, he told Lord Dufferin, would give him an opportunity to restore some equilibrium, and to provide the sort of leadership he himself planned to give in the Commons. Permission for such a step had to be obtained from Her Majesty – in other words, the approval of the Colonial Office had to be requested through the Governor General.

Both Dufferin and Mackenzie were eager to establish a good working relationship, and to disprove the frequent reports of strong differences between them. His Excellency informed the Colonial Office that he had a "great personal liking" for his new First Minister,[19] and asked for changes in a recent despatch to show his course during the crisis in the most favourable light.[20] Lord Kimberley was anxious to assist his former colleague to establish good terms with the new Ministers. Throughout the summer and autumn, he had been uneasy about the enthusiastic support that Dufferin was giving to Sir John, and had tried to warn him away from becoming implicated in the struggle. "In *this* country such a conduct would undoubtedly ruin any Government," he had commented in early October.[21]

"On the whole my judgment would be somewhat more unfavourable to your Ministers than yours is," he had written again during the final debate.[22] It was with a great sense of relief that he had learned the dénouement of the unsavoury story. "The account you give in your letter of the sixth [of November] of your late First Minister takes one's breath almost away. He should have lived in the good old times of the two-bottle men when one of the duties of the Secretary of the Treasury is said to have been to hold his hat on occasion for the convenience of the First Lord when 'clearing himself' for his speech. . . . I should have thought it a great misfortune for Canada if the late Ministers had remained in office . . . I felt a little apprehension lest you were making *too* good a defence for the Commission . . . (which) might perhaps expose you to possible attack as identifying yourself with your late Minister's action."[23]

Lady Dufferin found adaptation to the new political climate more difficult. She was fond of the gallant and witty Conservative leader, and enjoyed the company of the wealthy and influential men that frequented Ottawa during his régime. The severe parsimonious Scot did not seem likely to enhance the pleasure of her stay in the "small town with incongruously beautiful buildings crowning its insignificance" and its dreadful roads.[24] However, she was not a vindictive or a bigoted woman. After sitting beside the new Premier at a Rideau Hall dinner, she confessed in her diary that she liked him and found him "very straightforward and nice".[25] But she could not switch her allegiance so quickly. "I am trying to become a Grit," she told her mother, "but I can't quite manage it. It takes as much time as the outside edge backwards."

After a fortnight of hard labour, Mackenzie forced himself away from his desk long enough to appear at his nomination in Sarnia. In Toronto, he stopped for a discussion with George Brown. In the loneliness of his new exalted position, the *Globe* publisher was one man in whom he could confide, and whose judgment he could trust. "Let me know what you think of the Canadian Pacific and other problems," he wrote in announcing his arrival.[26] In earlier years, the great newspaperman had led, and Alexander Mackenzie had been content to follow. Now the roles were reversed; it was Brown's turn to provide the loyal support. This he was ready and willing to do, but an important question remained to be answered: could they simply reverse the roles, or would the Premier really be, as the Tories were already proclaiming, a mere puppet of the *Globe* "dictator"? Mackenzie had no such fears; he wanted all the advice and assistance that he could get from the man he respected and loved above all others outside his family. And Brown, for his part, had no intention of trying to run the Government from Toronto. He could hardly wait for attacks upon the new Premier before springing to his defence. In response to comments that the new Government leader was a mere ex-labourer, a "horny-handed son of toil", the *Globe* affirmed that "there is not one of Mr. Mackenzie's detractors who is half so familiar as he is with the masterpieces of English literature, or anything like so well acquainted with the politics of the present or the past, whether reference be had to those of Canada or the world".[27]

The train journey home was a veritable victory parade. In Toronto and London, the ex-stonemason was fêted as a conquering hero; at small stations, crowds shouted their congratulations and pressed forward to shake his hand. As the train puffed farther and farther into the west, the enthusiasm grew, and the engineer tried in vain to keep to his schedule. The somewhat sombre Scot reacted well to the acclaim; shouting his thanks and his appreciation, his face relaxed into a happy smile.

The Sarnia crowd was the biggest of all. Nearly every resident felt a personal interest in the victory of his local member. As the train rattled to a halt, a band struck up a victory air, hats and kerchiefs waved, and strong lungs cried out a welcome to the new head of the Government. Mackenzie was led in a luxurious carriage to the Belchamber Hotel, and escorted onto the balcony from which it was customary to address the populace. As the "noble vindicator of public morality", the Sarnians were told by the mayor, Alexander Mackenzie would end forever the possibility of such acts as had blotted the history of the Dominion in the recent past.[28] The ex-stonemason replied briefly, and escaped as soon as he could. He had a more urgent purpose in mind. During the Pacific crisis, he had again been obliged to spend entire months without seeing his family. Mary was expecting a baby early in the new year and he had hardly seen her and John since their wedding. He wanted to spend a few precious hours with them before rushing back to the capital. A Sabbath day lay between him and his nomination; with months and years of loneliness in Ottawa ahead of him, he wished to enjoy it at home.

Wet snow was falling as the fifty-one-year-old Premier mounted the familiar hustings near the court-house to ask once again for the confidence of his neighbours. Already they seemed to observe a new note of dignity and authority in his bearing. The old pugnaciousness appeared to have given way to a calm self-confidence. Even Malcolm Cameron, who was one of the platform guests, shook his hand warmly and was evidently impressed!

A few years ago, said the nominator, Alexander Mackenzie had piloted a Bill through Parliament, ensuring easier egress from public buildings. Sir John had found recently that it was useful legislation! The Tories scoffed that the Premier was a mere hard-handed artisan who did not know how to bow to the ladies, or wear a cut-away with grace. He could bow to the people; that was the important thing. The yeomanry of Canada had no objection to the cut of his coat or his undistinguished accent.

He was not the leader of the Dominion because of personal ambition, the candidate told his neighbours. He had gone from duty to duty, ever hoping to retire and live among them again, but never succeeding in that wish. With the opportunity available at last to apply Reform principles in the Dominion, he could not turn back. The new Administration would ensure the independence of Parliament from control by the executive, alter the electoral laws, and resist the greedy contractors that filled the corridors of the Parliament Buildings. They would draw up a new Canadian Pacific Railway policy, instead of the "insane act of the (old) Administration". It would be a workable and responsible plan, and not "a bargain made to be broken". Above all, it would be a pure Reform Administration. The former Conservatives in the Cabinet had accepted the age-old Reform objectives; there had been no compromise of principle, and there was, therefore, no coalition as the Conservatives were asserting.

There was no Opposition candidate. When the Premier had completed his address, he was declared elected. The crowds gave three lusty cheers for the Queen, three for their victorious neighbour, and three for the new Administration; then they sloshed off through the melting snow. "That will be a bright page in the history of Canada," Brown wired from Toronto, "that tells that the first Reform Minister of this great Dominion was the noblest 'working man' in the land."[29]

Scarcely were the speeches and cheering over before Alexander Mackenzie set out for the capital, where duty called. All his colleagues were elected by acclamation except Richard Cartwright, with whom Sir John thought to settle a score, but he, too, was returned by his constituents on voting day. George Brown set forth the goals of the Liberal Administration in an editorial on November 28.[30] "The Liberal party . . . can be traced from one generation to another as that of thought – of restless inquiry and eager anxiety to make war against what is thought to be untrue, and to change or modify what is recognized as unreasonable though ancient, and what is unjust, though venerable with age. . . . When the arrangements even of Liberalism have stiffened into dead formalities, and red tape again takes the place of honest work, then Liberalism will again find its work in striking at such abuses . . . while it proclaims more resolutely than ever that rest is rust, and that social and individual progress is the law at once of life and health, a law which neither nation nor individual can forget or ignore but at their peril."

It was difficult to think of lofty principles as long as his desk was stacked with paper. Fortunately, Mackenzie had found a secretary, an ex-newspaperman named William Buckingham, who had been secretary to Michael Foley a decade before. By the following Sunday, they had put in a full week of fourteen-hour days, and had made some progress in cleaning up the arrears of public business. "I devote an hour this peaceful beautiful Sabbath morning to the pleasant duty [of letter writing]," he wrote to Mary from his office before going to church on December 1.[31] "Today the great army of contractors and office seekers are shut out and the very office has a Sabbath look. The view from my window, and from my desk, takes in the whole upper Town with the Falls and the first reach of the Ottawa. The sun is to-day bright as an autumn day and not a breath of wind disturbs the repose that seems to rest on all natural and artificial objects. All seems more than usual indicative of a 'day of rest' being understood to be present by both men and nature. It makes me long for rest from the incessant vexations of the seething cauldron of public political life. It makes me also look forward with a joyful expectancy to that glorious rest prepared by our heavenly Father for his people when the cares of this life are done."

It was the office seekers with their bundles of letters, and, more often than not, a "very limited stock of knowledge or acquirements", who made his days most difficult. However, he reported to his daughter, he had hit on a method of getting rid of about three-fourths of them. "I give one interview as a specimen. A farmer's son from Ontario presented himself with the usual letters. I could not shake him off. At last I said in desperation – Well, are you ready for your examination? He started, asking, have I to be examined? Yes. In what? In writing, spelling, composition, mensuration, Algebra, Geometry, and all the other technical mathematical phrases I could think of at short notice. The effect was magical – he gathered up his papers and left instantly. I have since constantly applied the same blister, but in one case the fellow was willing even to go the length of Latin and Greek. I found he was an impecunious Oxford graduate. I now intend to instruct my Secretary to conduct the preliminary examinations by putting a series of questions and only to admit those who can pass that ordeal to the 'presence chamber'. If I must be subjected to this torment I mean to take all the comfort out of it I can."

Deputations, he found, were more difficult to handle, and less easy to turn away. They ranged from representatives of provincial Governments to "the honourable society of charwomen". "I have only a dim recollection of what it was all about," he related to Mary concerning the latter, "as they concluded, after some orderly preliminary skirmishing, that their object would be best obtained by all speaking at once. You recollect Kennedy's description of the Highlanders' ecstasy at having Seventeen pipers in one room playing different tunes, at least if you don't I did yesterday. Who can wonder at the Turks' idea of Women's destiny? I shall only see one at a time after this."

Alexander Mackenzie's sense of humour, and the feeling of having God on his side, were precious assets for the great task he was beginning. The blunt irreverence for accepted political practices with which he applied his policy of scrupulous honesty was a more doubtful qualification for a Government leader. There was truth in the assertion that Macdonald could say "no" with more success than Mackenzie could say "yes".

Some appointments brought real satisfaction to the new Premier. A few days after the first vacancy occurred, and without waiting for news from London regarding the additional appointments, he submitted George Brown's name for a Senate seat. After the *Globe* publisher's tirades against Lord Dufferin during the summer and autumn, Mackenzie feared the recommendation might not be well received. To his surprise, His Excellency appeared very pleased, and congratulated the Ministry on "so much being done to redeem the Senate from contempt".[32] Had the Conservatives not filled the Lieutenant-Governorship of Ontario before leaving office, Brown would have been offered that position, but a Senatorship suited his purpose even better. He could remain a political partisan, and have a convenient platform in the capital whenever he felt inclined to air his political views there. While remaining relatively independent of the Administration, he could support it with a strong editorial policy, and still have time to pursue his many business interests.

Unwilling to leave his desk for more than a few hours, Alexander Mackenzie's only trip outside of Ottawa during the Christmas season was a quick run down to Montreal to speak at a banquet in honour of Lucius Huntington, the man who had precipitated the Pacific Railway crisis. Though he was not the principal guest of honour, the reception given the new head of the Government was almost overwhelming. Unaccustomed to being a celebrity, the rousing welcome nearly swept him off his feet. "I served, Mr. Chairman," he told the enthusiastic audience diffidently when his turn came to speak, "in a Government under Mr. Blake; I served as a private in the ranks under Mr. Dorion and under Mr. Holton, and if they are now in the position of serving under me, I can only say that I am almost ashamed of having followers of such rank and ability; and I shall be delighted at any time to reverse the position and serve under my previous leaders."[33] His listeners soon discovered that such modesty was not to be interpreted as a sign of softness. His mind was quite clear about the principles and practices for which his Administration stood, and "right or wrong we are going to abide by them; and if Parliament and the country condemn them, then we shall ever hold ourselves ready to retire, and let some Administration whose assertions are made in accord with the majority of the people, take our places." They would be guided by one principle above all others – not to undertake any project for mere public effect, but only for the public good. "We are told, Sir, that we have no experience," he said, referring to a reported comment by the Chairman that there were no titled men in the Liberal ranks. "The fact is that the sort of title bearers we have amongst us, and the way in which those titles have been used, has rather disgusted the people of this country with that sort of thing altogether." He agreed with a versifier in his home town:

"A Queen can mak' a Kingston knight
A Ravenscraig* for a' that,
But men like Blake's aboon her might,
Gude faith she mauna fa that."

It was not enough to speak vaguely of principles and policies; it was necessary to draw them up in precise terms and present them to the public with a request for a clear mandate to put them into practice. Mackenzie was anxious to go to the polls almost immediately, but some of the Ministers hung back and suggested that a short session should be held first to draw up a new election act. The "dissolutionists" preferred to take a

*Sir Hugh Allan's palatial Montreal residence.

chance with the old Act, rather than give Sir John an opportunity to manoeuvre in the old Parliament. It was a convincing argument. "We mean to have an Election immediately," Mackenzie wrote secretly to Alfred Jones two days after Christmas.[34]

One of the most urgent matters was to draw up a new Pacific Railway policy. It was becoming increasingly obvious that the arrangement negotiated by Cartier was completely unrealistic. More than two years had passed since the entry of British Columbia into Confederation. Instead of a beginning on the project being made within that time, as Cartier so generously offered, the survey work was hardly more than well begun. The chief engineer, Sandford Fleming, had decided on the Yellowhead route past Jasper House, and had hiked much of the distance on foot to inspect it, but the survey parties had done little work west of Fort Garry. To quiet the complaints from Victoria, Sir John had passed an Order in Council during the Pacific crisis, designating Esquimalt as the terminus of the railway; actual construction, however, was still far in the future.[35] To make matters worse, the economic depression that had struck the United States a few months earlier was beginning to make its influence felt in Canada almost simultaneously with the change of Government; funds for public projects were likely to be sharply reduced. With Sir Hugh Allan's failure to finance his project, matters were about where they had been three years before.

In drawing up a new Pacific Railway policy, it was important to secure the agreement of the British Columbians. Mackenzie determined to send an emissary to tell them frankly that the original terms were, as he had always affirmed, impossible to carry out, and to try to obtain their agreement to the alternative he had put forward in 1871. Having failed to draw Alexander Galt into the Cabinet, he tried to enlist him for the mission.[36] Galt had refused to run as a candidate in the 1872 election, and was more interested in his financial career than in politics. "I believe your policy on the Pacific R.R. would have presented no difficulty in the way of my accepting the trust," he replied on January 2, 1874. "But unfortunately my own personal engagements seem on reflection quite to preclude my acting."[37] A week later, Casimir Gzowski, a Polish immigrant who had become a prominent railway builder, refused the mission in turn. As a personal friend of John A. Macdonald, he did not want to be too closely identified with the new régime.[38]

In contrast to the eagerness of "hangers-on", reluctance for public office seemed almost a national trait with the capable men of the period. A letter from Edward Blake in Toronto was more disappointing still. He was determined to leave the Ministry almost as soon as he had entered. "During the election I am 'yours to command'," he wrote at the beginning of 1874, "for it might be inconvenient that there should be any announcement pending the contest, but that over, and your majority secured, I must go."[39] During the years in Opposition it was a familiar pattern for men of ability to prefer to devote their time to more remunerative and pleasant pursuits; Mackenzie had not expected the same attitude when the Liberals were given the opportunity they had sought for so long to govern the country. "I am almost afraid to open your letters," he replied to his reluctant colleague, "they are so full of what sounds like evil tidings. . . . Your retirement we need not discuss now. The discussion only further damps one's feelings and unfits us for work."[40] Like Sir John, he was learning already to play for time.

The quietly confident and efficient Minister of Justice, Antoine-Aimé Dorion, reported that all was ready in Quebec; the Maritimes were ready too. The election writs were issued on January 7. Even without a new electoral law, it was possible to give practical effect to one reform. All constituencies, it was announced, would vote on the same day. After the election, an act would be passed to make the change permanent. In the first session, there would be further reforms, including the trial of controverted elections before judges, strong measures to suppress bribery and corruption, vote by ballot, extension of the franchise, and abolition of the real estate qualification for members.[41] A Supreme Court would be created, a stricter insolvency law passed, the canal system developed to encourage shipping, and the militia system revised. Negotiations would be carried on with British Columbia to relax the "impossible terms of union", and to make a new agreement to build the railway line "with such speed and under such arrangements as the resources of the country will permit without too largely increasing the burden of taxation on the people". In the meantime, Government policy would be to utilize the "enormous stretches of magnificent water communication" between Georgian Bay and the Rockies, "thus avoiding for the present the construction of about 1300 miles of railway, estimated to cost from sixty to eighty millions of dollars." The branch line from Fort Garry to the United States border would be pressed forward, and another line commenced between the south shore of Lake Nipissing and the mouth of the French River on Georgian Bay. These "great works" would be part of an extensive immigration and development programme. Finally, the Liberals would follow an "honest, vigorous, just, and economical policy" in the general administration of the Dominion designed to respect provincial rights but at the same time to "remove sectional jealousies and effect a genuine consolidation of the Union".

Although it did not seem likely to be a stiff contest, the Premier campaigned hard, not even taking time to appear in Sarnia for his own nomination, or to return to Ottawa to witness Lucius Huntington being sworn into the Cabinet as President of the Council.* The Tories were forecasting a strict free trade policy that would flood the Dominion with cheap American products. Mackenzie replied that, "while he was a free trader in principle", the fifteen per cent tariff might have to be increased to meet commitments inherited from the Tories. It was an unpalatable statement to make at election time, but there were good grounds for believing in its accuracy.[42] Trade was falling rapidly, and Cartwright was faced with a half-million-dollar deficit in a twenty-three-million-dollar budget. Tilley's forecast of higher taxes had been no idle threat, even before the recession appeared on the horizon. "Cartwright . . . is likely . . . to be tried by hard times and a tight money market," wrote a former Conservative Cabinet Minister.[43]

It was an easy victory. Ontario, which had given the Grits a clear majority in 1872, supported them more solidly than ever before. Quebec, too, elected a record number of Liberals, and the Maritime provinces voted almost uniformly for the Administration. From the moment the first returns reached Mackenzie in Toronto on his way back to Ottawa, he had no doubts about the final result. "What a slaughter," he wrote to Jones in congratulating him on his election in Halifax.[44] "The old corruptionists are fairly stupefied by our success." There was only one cloud in a perfect day. Edward Blake's letter of resignation was dated 7 o'clock on election morning.[45]

When the Premier arrived back in Ottawa in the late afternoon of January 31, a messenger was waiting to ask him to go immediately to Government House.[46] Lord Dufferin was anxious to make good his promise to give his new advisers the same co-operation and confidence he had shown their predecessors. Adjusting quickly to the new situation, he had decided that "however narrow and inexperienced Mackenzie may be, I imagine he is a thoroughly upright, well-principled, and well-meaning man."[47] It was a step in the right direction after his early condemnation of all Canadian politicians as dishonourable and corrupt. The Premier stayed to dinner, and the two

*Senator Richard Scott became Secretary of State. Senator David Christie retired from the Cabinet. *See* Appendix.

men talked out the evening by the huge fireplace at Rideau Hall. When Mackenzie returned home late at night, he discovered that he had missed a public reception in his honour. However, he went to bed with the comforting knowledge that he would have an eighty-seat majority in a House of two hundred and six, and that the Queen's representative wished him well. And from Sarnia came the happy news that he was a grandfather. Mary had given birth to a daughter.

CHAPTER 11

Rest is Rust

The new Ministers allowed themselves six weeks to prepare for their first session. Alexander Mackenzie found a house on Kent Street, not far from St. Andrew's Church and near enough to the West Block to be able to walk back and forth, and set to work. The most urgent problem awaiting solution was the Pacific Railway. During the summer of 1873, British Columbia had protested to Macdonald that the first part of the agreement, a beginning of the line within two years, had been broken.[1] Engaged in the life and death struggle of his Administration, Sir John had not bothered to reply. Judging from his past utterances over the years, British Columbians were convinced that Mackenzie was an implacable enemy of the "bargain". After the Sarnia speech in November, a crowd had invaded the Legislative Buildings in Victoria to protest any revision in the terms of union. Macdonald added fuel to the fire. The speech was "a breach of a solemn contract entered into with British Columbia and the Imperial Government . . . ," he proclaimed during the election.[2] "For this breach of faith British Columbia has a right to secede, for this was one of the conditions of Confederation." If the Liberals did not give up their "hermaphrodite" system, they would have to give up the British connection and the endorsement of England, "as Britain would not tolerate such a dishonour". After failing to engage either Galt or Gzowski for the Victoria mission, the Premier had dropped the search until after the election. In early February, he tried again. This time his choice fell on James Edgar, the former Liberal whip who somehow had failed to be re-elected in the January contest. The subject was not completely foreign to the thirty-two-year-old lawyer; he had taken part in discussions with Amor De Cosmos when the latter had attempted to persuade the Liberals to advocate still better terms, including a cash grant instead of a financial guarantee for the Esquimalt drydock. At that time, Mackenzie had been non-committal. In the interim, De Cosmos had been defeated as Premier because of the attitude of his fellow Liberals in the new Administration in Ottawa.

Edgar's instructions were implicit and precise.[3] He was to tell the new Premier, George Walkem, that in proposing an extension of the ten-year limit, the Dominion Government was acting on the advice of its engineers that the 1871 terms were impossible of fulfilment, and that an attempt to carry them out would only lead to useless expense and financial disorder. The five-hundred-mile Intercolonial Railway in the Maritimes had been under construction for nearly ten years and was not yet completed; the Pacific Railway route was nearly five times as long. Under the circumstances, it was only honest to state that the 1881 deadline was illusory. At the same time, Mackenzie's letter to Edgar ran, a concession deserved a concession. Despite Macdonald's Order in Council, the terms of union only referred to a railway to the Pacific seaboard. A co-operative attitude on the part of British Columbians, and Vancouver Islanders, in particular, would encourage the Canadian Government to give a more liberal interpretation to the meaning of the word "sea-board", and consider a line to Esquimalt, the harbour on which Victoria was situated. The new Administration had already shown its positive attitude toward the Province by increasing its assistance for the Esquimalt graving dock, and by offering to advance in cash the interest on the remainder of the debt with which British Columbia had entered Confederation. If Ottawa did not feel bound strictly by the terms of union and was prepared to go beyond them, Victoria should be willing to do the same. By circulating on the mainland and the Island, Edgar was to assess public opinion and suggest to Mackenzie a compromise arrangement. Any proposals he received should be carefully noted, but he should not make any definite commitments unless he received specific instructions.

Armed with letters of introduction, five hundred dollars in public funds, and Mackenzie's good wishes for "great success as our first plenipotentiary", Edgar set off in late February.[4] Dufferin was so optimistic that he considered it a topic of "no very great importance".[5] "Under the most favourable circum-stances ten years was too short a period for the accomplishment of so vast a project . . . ," he reported to London. "I hope . . . in a few weeks to report that the dispute has been amicably arrang-ed. In the meantime I have written to the Lieutenant-Governor directing him to do his best to keep the pretensions of his people within reasonable bounds." The Lieutenant-Governor was Joseph Trutch, the man who had prevented a revolt in the Conservative caucus in 1870 by giving assurances that Ottawa would not be held to the letter of the agreement.

Simultaneously with his search for a settlement of the Pacific Railway problem, Alexander Mackenzie was preparing a still more extensive set of negotiations. Before Christmas, one of the Governor General's guests had been Henry Rothery, Registrar of the British Admiralty Court, who was in North America to prepare the arbitration of the outstanding Canadian fishery claims. During his conversations with the new Ministers, reciprocity with the United States, one of the old perennials of Liberal platforms, was inevitably mooted.

A few days before the elections, Rothery reported from Washington that the American authorities were interested in avoiding a direct payment of fisheries compensation by sinking the question in the larger issue of a new trade arrangement.[6] The Ministers were delighted. Canadian prosperity during the Civil War had lessened the effects of cancellation of the 1854 Reciprocity Treaty, the Premier explained to the Governor General, but an economic crisis would show the seriousness of the loss. There would be opposition from protectionist and anti-British elements in the United States, but his conversations with the United States Consul and American business men had led him to agree with Rothery's findings. He suggested that George Brown, the greatest Canadian proponent of reciprocity, be sent to Washington to assess the situation.

Frustrated in his desire to play a part in earlier trade negotiations with the United States, Brown accepted eagerly. As an ardent supporter of the North and an active member of the Anti-Slavery Society during the Civil War, he had many friends and acquaintances in Washington, including President Grant himself. The elections were scarcely over before he took the train to the American capital. There was every reason to believe the Government was prepared to discuss the substitution of a satisfactory reciprocity treaty for a cash fisheries compensation, he reported enthusiastically a few days later. Impatient as ever, he felt time was of the essence as any ministerial changes in Washington might alter the situation. He urged Mackenzie to have the Imperial Government cable their representative, Sir Edward Thornton, instructing him to begin negotiations at once. "It really looks as if you might be enabled to announce in the Speech from the Throne the prospect of a renewal of the Treaty!" wrote the *Globe* publisher enthusiastically.[7]

In addition to asking the Governor General to wire London

to authorize negotiations, the Premier made a further request: George Brown should be a full-fledged member of the British team.[8] As recently as the previous year, he had moved a resolution urging Canadian representation whenever Canadian interests were involved, but the suggestion had been defeated by the Conservatives. Now he had an opportunity to put the principle into practice himself. Brown had raised the subject with Thornton and Rothery in Washington, but they had "snubbed it on the spot."[9] Their superiors were more understanding.

About the time of the Canadian elections, Dufferin's old Prime Minister, William Gladstone, was defeated, and with him departed the Earl of Kimberley. Canada's role in the reciprocity negotiations was one of the first matters submitted for the Earl of Carnarvon's attention when he became Secretary of State for Colonial affairs in the new Disraeli Cabinet. The incoming Secretary was only forty-three years old, but had helped to pilot the Confederation Bill through the Imperial Parliament when a member of an earlier Ministry. In contrast to Kimberley, he was an enthusiastic Imperialist, and despite political differences, a personal friend of the Canadian Governor General. A prey to indecision at times, he was affectionately referred to by Disraeli as "Twitters".[10]

A long conversation with Mackenzie had persuaded Lord Dufferin that the request for a Canadian plenipotentiary was not unreasonable. "Considering how prone public opinion in the Dominion is to accuse English diplomacy of sacrificing Canadian interests", he wrote to Carnarvon on February 26, "I am inclined to think it would be both an assistance and a safeguard that Representatives of the Canadian Government should share whatever responsibilities are incurred."[11] If the negotiations fell through, the Canadians would be partly responsible, and in any event, "the Imperial Government would only be where it was under the Washington Treaty". Carnarvon agreed. "We sh'ld not initiate it," he advised Dufferin, ". . . we sh'ld give our good offices, for it amounts to this, at the express desire of Canada so that it sh'ld never be a matter of reproach to us."[12] At the same time, he felt that there was more chance of success if the United States did not feel the British had their hearts set on an agreement. He would have preferred a delegate from the Dominion who had the confidence of both political parties, but Dufferin assured him that such a Canadian did not exist. Brown was not a bad choice, the Governor General replied reassuringly, he knew the subject well, and he was "thoroughly British and anti-Yankee".[13] Instructions were sent to Thornton to open negotiations "tho' of course cautiously".[14]

On March 11, Alexander Mackenzie sent a long memorandum to Rideau Hall outlining the Canadian view.[15] Despite the abandonment of the St. Lawrence navigation rights during the previous Washington negotiations, he felt that Canada's bargaining position was not a weak one. There was no intention or desire of suggesting any changes which might affect injuriously British or Imperial interests. At the same time, it was hoped to go much farther than the "free list" of goods set out in the 1854 Treaty. Regardless of the negotiations, the Government planned to deepen and extend its canal system. In the circumstances, they would be prepared to offer to enlarge the canals and to cede the freedom of navigation on them that the Americans were so anxious to obtain. In return, they should be able to obtain certain trade advantages, and "by skilful negotiation", freedom of navigation on American canals. Canada would be prepared to extend the 1854 free list to include lumber and other wood products, agricultural machinery, salt, mineral oil, bricks, plaster and manufactured articles "not produced in or imported from England to this continent". "It is all but impossible to frame a proposal . . . from which we would not move," Mackenzie concluded. "I therefore cannot present any precise proposition." By the time Parliament met, Senator Brown was negotiating in Washington as a British plenipotentiary on an equal basis with Sir Edward Thornton, and Albert Smith, the Minister of Fisheries, was in the background as a semi-official accredited agent.

A major problem inherited by the new Administration was the effective control of the vast North West. The Blackfoot and the Crees were at war and scalping one another at an alarming rate.[16] With practically no law officers west of Manitoba, murderers and thieves moved about with impunity. American traders had erected forts the size of Hudson's Bay posts, and were trading liquor and rifles for buffalo skins. The value placed on the skins was so low that the Indians were fast destroying their principal food supply to obtain the devastating firearms and "firewater". One group of Americans became involved in a dispute with natives in the Cypress Hills and slaughtered some thirty men, women, and children in order to teach the others a lesson. Lieutenant-Governor Morris of Manitoba, who was also responsible for the North West, appealed for some law enforcement body. With the Imperial troops withdrawn from everywhere in Canada but Esquimalt and Halifax, and the militia unprepared for such a task, it was decided to form a special unit of three hundred horsemen along the lines of the Irish Constabulary in Britain. Civilians in uniform, they would be an *élite* troop of highly trained men, at least five feet ten inches in height, and in exceptional physical condition. Colonel George French, an artillery officer, was to be in charge of the unit and lead it into the North West. Scouts would precede them to assure the Indians that they were coming as friends and not as enemies. When the Liberals assumed office in Ottawa, one hundred and fifty men were under training in Kingston. Throughout the winter, they filled their complement and prepared to march in early spring.

Another worrisome problem west of the Great Lakes was the Riel affair, on which both Mackenzie and Blake had taken such an uncompromising stand in the Ontario Legislature. Tension between French- and English-speaking Canadians in the tiny prairie province had not subsided since the Red River uprising. Clashes were frequent. In 1872, the Speaker of the Legislature was tarred and feathered, and during the 1872 election, one man was shot. In the same election, Louis Riel was a candidate in Provencher constituency in absentia, but he was persuaded to withdraw after Cartier was defeated in Montreal. In return for assuring the veteran Minister a seat in Parliament in his place, his friends hoped that the amnesty would be proclaimed at last. Unfortunately for him, Riel had not succeeded in extracting a written promise from Sir John. The Conservative Government fell without any action having been taken.

When the Liberals arrived in power, Archbishop Taché was one of their first visitors. Denouncing Macdonald bitterly for not granting the amnesty as agreed when he was summoned back from Rome, Taché demanded that the new Ministry accord it forthwith. Realizing the force of public opinion behind him in French Canada, the Quebec Ministers were anxious to meet the Archbishop's request. For Mackenzie and the other Ministers from Ontario it was not easy to reverse completely their earlier position, particularly with English Canada still demanding the rebel leader's blood. Archbishop Taché had to be satisfied with a private assurance from Letellier that "I think (or I hope) that we shall be able to give the amnesty to our Lower Canadian friends as a New Year's gift."[17] When the election was declared, Dorion asked the Lieutenant-Governor of Manitoba to urge Archbishop Taché to prevent Riel from running again.[18] Once bitten, twice shy. The Archbishop demanded a written promise of amnesty. It could not be provided. Dorion had to content himself with stating that the French-speaking members were "de tout coeur" in favour of an amnesty, and that if, as claimed by Riel's friends, it was proven that it had been promised by Sir John and the former Governor General,

"I can nearly give the assurance that the amnesty will be requested of the Imperial Government."[19] It was not enough. Louis Riel was elected in Provencher again.

The situation was further complicated by the discovery and arrest in Manitoba of Riel's former Adjutant General in the provisional government, Ambroise Lepine. He was jailed by the Manitoba Government, and charged as an accomplice in the murder of Thomas Scott. It was evident to everyone that whatever sentence Lepine was given, Riel could not receive less. A heavy sentence would make an amnesty for one or both of them difficult, if not impossible. There was another consideration. If Riel appeared in Parliament, Mackenzie might find himself in the embarrassing position of qualifying for the five thousand dollar reward that he had offered as Treasurer of Ontario! "My present Government is no less non-plussed by those difficulties than was Macdonald," Dufferin commented.[20] "They cannot afford to quarrel with their French supporters, while on the other hand they don't like to offend the Orangemen of Ontario and they would give anything to get quit of all responsibility in the matter."

* * * * *

Despite the continual interruptions by office seekers, and the burdens of the Department of Public Works, Mackenzie was ready with an impressive list of legislation when the Third Parliament of Canada met on March 26, 1874. He was waiting just inside the entrance in his new Windsor uniform as the Governor General drove up the hill through the fresh fall of snow. The Tories noted a dark cloud over the city, and remarked that the Windsor uniform did not hang naturally on the new Premier.[21] To the Liberals it was a perfect day, and the suit a perfect fit.

The first day, as usual, was spent on ritual. The Governor General asked the Commoners who was to speak for them. When told that they had no one, they were instructed to return to their own Chamber to choose a Speaker. Alexander Mackenzie made his way to the other end of the building to take his seat for the first time on the right of the Speaker's chair. Opposite him, in his old place, was Sir John, looking older and greyer, but concealing the wounds of recent months under a cloak of good-natured indifference. Macdonald's desire to resign from the Tory leadership was public knowledge, but no successor was available. Cartier was dead, Langevin defeated, and Tilley promoted into political obscurity. Of his former leading comrades in war, only the loyal Tupper remained, and he was not considered equal to the task. Among the sea of new faces which filled the Government side of the House, and overflowed to box in the Opposition on the Speaker's left, were two veterans, Alfred Jones and Malcolm Cameron, both back after a period of absence. The "Coon", now a portly and lovable old man, was ready to give his full support to his adversary of pioneering years. The Premier proposed Timothy Anglin of New Brunswick as Speaker. Sir John probed gently to discover why the name of Holton, who was still outside the Cabinet, was not put forward. He was not enlightened. Anglin was chosen unanimously, and the House adjourned.

Even the Opposition admitted that the weather was fine the next day.[22] A myriad of tiny snow crystals flashed and sparkled in the morning sun as the Premier mounted Parliament Hill. The air was crisp and invigorating, and the grounds looked as clean as the new page of Canadian history about to be written.

As if to give the lie to the Tory prediction of an era of frugality and dullness under the Liberals, the Throne Speech ceremony was the most brilliant that Canadians had ever seen. Lady Dufferin led the parade of female elegance in a gown of lavender satin, with a large bouquet of imported flowers in her arm.[23] In a slow, distinct voice, only a trifle too high for such a dignified occasion, His Excellency read the Speech prepared for him by Alexander Mackenzie, who was sitting nearby. There would be legislation concerning election laws, the militia, insolvency, and the establishment of a Supreme Court. The transcontinental railway project would be considered. Canal and harbour improvements were being prosecuted vigorously, and a Canadian Commissioner was taking part in the Washington negotiations. Steps would have to be taken to meet the current budgetary deficit. "I trust," the message concluded, "that your deliberations may be directed by wisdom and aided by Divine Providence."

Beneath the stiff formality, an undercurrent of excitement was spreading rapidly throughout the building. Louis Riel was in town![24] Accompanied by another French-speaking member, he had appeared in the clerk's office, signed the roll, taken the oath, and was ready to occupy his place in the House! Yet he was wanted on a charge of murder in Manitoba, and a warrant for his arrest had been quickly sworn out in Ottawa. Constables were on his trail. Would he really dare to enter the Commons Chamber? The question was on everyone's lips. Throughout the weekend, rumours of his presence continued to circulate. The local constables committed several regrettable mistakes of identity, and arrested some innocent men, but the Métis rebel remained free. On Monday, the faces of the darker-skinned new members were scanned closely, and compared with primitive photos of Riel. Three o'clock came and went. He did not appear.

Thomas Moss, a clever young Toronto lawyer who belonged to the "Canada First" movement, a group of progressive and liberal-minded Canadian nationalists, moved the adoption of the Throne Speech. As the seconder, Mackenzie had chosen another bright young newcomer, the thirty-three-year-old member for Drummond-Arthabaska, Wilfrid Laurier. Laurier's clean-shaven face, very exceptional in the sea of flowing beards and moustaches, drew attention to his sensitive features. Together with his long, slight frame, his fine hands, and warm kindly eyes, they gave an impression of refined gentility that contrasted with the sturdy appearance of many representatives of the people. When he spoke, any impression of weakness was immediately allayed. With three years' experience in the Quebec Legislature behind him, he was at home in the House of Commons from the beginning. His English still rudimentary, he extolled the virtues of the Empire in eloquent French, explaining that Quebec Liberalism traced its origins more to the English than to the French revolutionary school. The hostile *Toronto Mail* reported that he concluded his maiden speech "with a brilliant peroration and resumed his seat amid applause".[25]

The Opposition leader refused to be impressed with the Throne Speech. It was just some more of that old "Brown stuff", that appeared in the *Globe*, said Sir John. His only precise objection was the proposal to introduce the secret ballot.[26] When a man voted, he felt that he should be responsible for that vote, and not be able to conceal it from the world. Still somewhat uncomfortable in his new role of Government leader, Mackenzie tried to maintain the same moderate tone. He was inclined to agree about the ballot, he confessed, but it had become necessary in order to protect the employees of large companies from undue pressure on election day. Only when he refuted Sir John's claims to paternity of some of the proposed measures, did a trace of the old fighting spirit appear. Anything the Tory leader had done, he scoffed, was forced on him by the Liberals.

Riel kept the Dominion waiting. It was common knowledge that several Quebec members were in touch with him, and seeking a way to get him into the House without being arrested. The *Montreal Gazette* carried a report of a meeting in Hull organized by the St. Jean Baptiste Society at which, it claimed, an escort of three thousand men was suggested, with a plan to take the Parliament Buildings by storm if their petition to seat Riel was rejected. Riel's former secretary was present, and with him a man who was placed in a seat upstairs, from where he could see and hear all that transpired. "This man," the *Gazette* stated, "is supposed to have been Riel in disguise."[27]

With no arrest to satisfy Protestant passions, Mackenzie Bowell, a leading Orangeman in the Conservative ranks, moved that the Attorney General of Manitoba, H. G. Clarke, appear at the Bar of the House, and give proof of Riel's record.[28] As Minister of Justice, Dorion consented. Clarke was ready and willing. He had sworn to take the fugitive member, and had travelled from Winnipeg to capture him. He gave his evidence cheerfully.[29] Bowell followed the testimony with a motion that Riel "do attend in his place tomorrow at three o'clock p.m." The motion carried with embarrassed silence on the Treasury benches. Still Riel did not appear. A second motion along similar lines a few days later was equally barren of results. A Committee was struck to study the Red River uprising. Bowell refused to be satisfied. He made a formal motion for expulsion.

Alexander Mackenzie had no alternative but to speak to the motion. Much as he might wish the whole thorny problem off the face of the earth, he could not retreat altogether from his earlier position. The honourable member for Provencher was a fugitive from justice and should be tried for the charge against him, he maintained.[30] He could not agree that Scott's death was a political execution; to him it was an offence against humanity, justice, and law. The people of the North West had lost control of their passions and had committed an unjustifiable act; it was up to the courts to decide its gravity. At the same time, the House of Commons Committee could establish whether or not an amnesty had in fact been granted, and, with that assistance, the Government could decide if it covered Riel at the time of the crime.

Both Liberals and Conservatives split badly on the motion for expulsion. Mackenzie and Blake voted for it; Dorion, Fournier, Cauchon, and Laurier against. Macdonald was conveniently absent from the House. When it carried on racial lines, a French-speaking Conservative moved that a complete amnesty should be granted. The French-speaking Liberals joined in defeating the proposal. Riel was back where he started before the election. He remained as elusive as ever.

The House had been sitting only a fortnight when Cartwright brought down his first budget.[31] In contrast to Mackenzie's provincial budget two years before, it was hardly a cheering report. The receipts were falling rapidly, and obligations were increasing. Based on Tilley's taxation rates, the Government was heading for a million dollar deficit. Despite every effort to curtail spending, the Prime Minister needed an additional four hundred thousand dollars for Public Works projects. To raise a record twenty-four and one-half million dollars, customs duties would have to be raised from fifteen to seventeen and a half per cent. As far as possible, the burden would be placed on luxury items. Honourable members would have to be self-denying for a while, the Finance Minister lectured the backbenchers. The depression had arrived.

The Tories were jubilant. Nothing could change public opinion as fast as a spate of hard times. As financial critic for the Opposition, Charles Tupper set out to place the blame for the economic recession squarely at the feet of the Government. Liberal times were hard times, he said in effect, and Liberal Administrations weak, wasteful, and even corrupt. The attack brought the Premier to his feet in a vigorous denial that the depression had only started after he and his colleagues had assumed office. Whatever the facts, the important political result was that the Grits were on the defensive.

By early May, Mackenzie was ready to present his new railway plan to Parliament. The Edgar mission had failed. After a long series of discussions with Premier Walkem, Lieutenant-Governor Trutch, and others, the Toronto lawyer had obtained permission from Ottawa to state that the Dominion Government would be prepared to build a railway from Esquimalt to Nanaimo on Vancouver Island at once, pursue the surveys as vigorously as possible, erect a transcontinental telegraph line, and spend a minimum of a million and a half dollars a year within the Province on the railway.[32] Committed to a policy of "the bond and nothing but the bond", Walkem was not in a position to accept a compromise.[33] Embarrassed for want of a reply, he suddenly asked Edgar for his "official authority for appearing in the role of an agent contracting for the Dominion of Canada".[34] In Ottawa, Mackenzie assured the House of Commons that the proposals were made on behalf of the Ministry. Walkem refused to accept the assurance. Indignant at such a "disingenious course", the Canadian Premier recalled his spokesman.

After the rebuff in Victoria, Mackenzie determined to put forward his own plan. Early in the session, Parliament passed a resolution inspired by the Ministry that the line should be assisted by the Treasury, but without "increasing the present rate of taxation". The Premier's proposal was based on three premises.[35] The original scheme arranged with Allan had failed

PACIFIC PASTIMES; OR THE HARD "ROAD TO TRAVEL."

From Bengough's *Caricature History of Canadian Politics*, Vol. I

completely, the House of Commons had agreed in 1870 that the project should not require increased taxation, and, the previous Government having failed to keep its agreement, their successors were honour bound to devise a new approach. He repeated his offer to build the Esquimalt-Nanaimo railway in return for a relaxation of the ten-year limit. The rest of the plan was essentially the same as he had outlined at Sarnia the previous November. The "water stretches" would be used between Ontario and the Rockies wherever possible, and the survey parties would press on to find a route from the Yellowhead Pass in the Rockies, through the Cascades, to the Pacific. Connecting links with Georgian Bay and the United States line south of Fort Garry would be pushed forward vigorously. As there was no time to submit contracts to Parliament before the end of the session, the Georgian Bay line would be started during the summer, and a statement of costs submitted later. With that exception, where the costs would be higher because of the difficult terrain, the Government would call for bids on the basis of ten thousand dollars and twenty thousand acres of land per mile. Control of two-thirds of the land thus ceded would be retained in order to ensure its proper exploitation.

Coupled with the plan was a vote of seven hundred thousand dollars to help British Columbia with local projects, and the offer of a new arrangement on the Esquimalt dock. It was a carefully prepared and reasonable package, but it was not the original bargain. With De Cosmos in Ottawa trying to outshine Walkem in Victoria as a defender of British Columbia's interests, and the Conservatives anxious to stigmatize the Government as betrayers of the terms of the union, a compromise solution was impossible. Mackenzie's plan received a cold reception.

On the whole, it was a very productive session. Over one hundred pieces of legislation were passed in less than two months. A new military college was authorized, a Hansard record of debates approved, and nearly the full list of election reforms called for by the Liberals over the years was enacted. Left over until the next session were the Supreme Court Bill, and any legislation arising from the reciprocity negotiations in Washington, Brown and Thornton not having reached an agreement with the United States. "It was much easier than we had anticipated," Mackenzie wrote to Brown in Washington.[36] "The Opposition is practically dead. Hardly a rag is left ... They don't show fight on anything ... Only fancy every cent concurred in last night of the whole $24,000,000 at one sitting!" It had never happened while he was in the Opposition.

The Premier was proud of the social tone of the new Liberal era as well.[37] In the face of Conservative predictions of a dull social season, he and his colleagues entertained generously. The Mackenzies adopted a policy of ignoring party lines; Conservatives were as frequent guests as Liberals at their regular dinner parties. Despite his personal views on drinking, the Premier's table was well supplied with champagne, wines, and other spirits. With careful coaching, Jane adapted well to her new role of leading lady. She received graciously and easily, and danced the modern steps at the Governor General's ball and other functions. The formal functions and the dignity of office did not make the Mackenzies forget that they were Westerners, and that the West had a proud tradition of hospitality of its own. Their home was always open to friends who cared to drop in for a chat or a meal.

The Ministry suffered one heavy blow during the session, but it was a blow administered by the Premier himself. The Chief Justiceship of Quebec had become vacant, and had to be filled before the Easter legal term. There was general agreement that the man best qualified to fill the position was the Minister of Justice, Antoine-Aimé Dorion. His Quebec friends suggested that he should at least be offered the post and have an opportunity of refusing it, as he had done on a previous occasion. Shortly before the deadline, Mackenzie called his colleague into his office and made the offer.[38] The suggestion that he should take the opportunity to retire from active politics came as a complete surprise to the Rouge leader. He could not leave the Government when important work such as the Supreme Court Bill was in preparation, he protested. In a burst of friendship and generosity, the Premier told him that he must consider the matter from a personal point of view and no other; he had given his best to the country for so long, and deserved the best that the country could offer in return. If he preferred to be the first Chief Justice of the Supreme Court of Canada, that position would be available to him. He was to give his answer the following day. "I . . . said . . . that . . . while the separation would be a painful one to myself," Mackenzie wrote to Blake that evening, "it would be still more painful to me in after years to know that I would be blamed for doing him a personal wrong by not acting properly when I had the power."[39] The Minister of Justice was still undecided when he returned. He would not consider leaving until Mackenzie assured him that he could get on without him. With a heavy heart, the Government leader insisted that the public business was not the primary consideration, and that he should give in to his own personal inclinations and those of his family. The veteran Rouge leader accepted. For the Liberal Administration, it was an irreparable loss.

The Premier could understand well the call of private life. The success of the Government during its first session did not diminish his own desire to be free of the burdens of office. "I see the *Gazette* says you are to take my place," he wrote to Blake during the negotiations with Dorion.[40] "I wish to heaven it were true." With the departure of his principal lieutenant in Quebec, "a new series of difficulties stare me in the face. Who succeeds? . . . Please let me know what you think." Blake ignored the comment on the *Gazette* report, but was willing to advise on the Cabinet reconstruction.[41] Fournier or Smith, he suggested, could take over the Justice portfolio, and Félix Geoffrion of Montreal, generally recognized as the ablest French Canadian in the Liberal caucus, but unfortunately not a lawyer, could be brought into the Cabinet. Both Nova Scotia Ministers should be replaced, and one of the seats given to Holton. Above all, the Premier should give up the Department of Public Works, or the general administration of the affairs of the Dominion would suffer. As President of the Council or Receiver General, he would still have time to keep a watchful eye on the key spending department.

Dorion agreed. In a parting message, he urged Mackenzie to try to bring Blake, Jones, and Holton into the Cabinet, and to abandon the Public Works portfolio before he injured his health seriously. The Premier was willing to try again. He called Holton to Ottawa and offered him a Cabinet seat; he also asked him to take advantage of his intimacy with Blake to persuade the latter to re-enter the Government. Despite an "almost invincible repugnance to entering office under any circumstances", Holton agreed that public men had obligations they could not avoid.[42] "If my judgment were convinced that the sacrifice of feeling and inclination had become necessary I should feel bound to make it." In the end, he asked for a postponement until his daughter, who was expecting a baby later in the year, and was in delicate health, was out of danger. The Montrealer's appeal to Blake had a note of frantic urgency. "The universal sentiment of the party and of the members of the Administration is that your acceptance of office is the one thing needful to ensure the efficiency and the stability of the Govt. I go farther and say for myself that I regard it as imperatively necessary if the position is to be saved."[43] Why "imperatively necessary"? The Administration was functioning well enough, and there was no threat from outside. The only danger was a split within the ranks of the Liberals themselves. Edward Blake not only refused to lead; he also refused to be led. Since his departure from the Cabinet he had moved farther and farther from his former colleagues. Attracted by his unquestioned ability, many younger men gathered around him, forming a Blake wing within the party. In Toronto, one liberal thinker watched the development with keen anticipation. He was Goldwin Smith, a former Oxford don who had found his way to Canada after several years of lecturing in the United States. Married to a rich Toronto widow, Goldwin Smith soon began to carve himself a place in Canadian society as a political journalist. There was one great problem: a colossus already stood astride the field of liberal journalism in Canada, and his former lieutenant was the leader of the Liberal party. Inevitably, Smith and Brown soon became bitter opponents. In April, 1874, the *Nation*, an erudite liberal weekly, appeared in Toronto under the guidance of the ex-professor.

A brilliant intellectual and a clever polemicist, Goldwin Smith had no pretension to political leadership. Nor among the members of the Canada First movement whose views coincided largely with his own was there an obvious leader. They had begun as a group of nationalist-minded Liberals in 1870, devoted to restoring order in the North West. Encouraged by the success of a lecture by one of their number entitled "Canada First, Our New Nationality", they broadened their programme and decided to form a national society. In January 1874, the Canada National Association was born.[44] Its platform was a good Reform document. It called for maintenance of the British connection, but a stronger Canadian voice in its trade relations, a system of income franchise, the secret ballot, compulsory voting, representation of minorities, vastly increased immigration, encouragement of native industries, income taxes, Dominion officers in charge of an improved militia, reorganization of the Senate, and pure and economic administration of the Dominion's affairs. In Parliament, Thomas Moss, who moved the first Liberal Speech from the Throne, was a Canada First member, and David Mills, an expert in legal theory whom Sir John A. Macdonald dubbed the "philosopher of Bothwell", had obvious sympathies with the group. All of them, including Goldwin Smith, looked to Blake as their natural leader.[45]

With such a large group of Liberal intellectuals dissociating themselves from the party leadership, there were some grounds for Luther Holton's foreboding concerning the Government's future. The Conservatives exploited the situation adroitly with flat assertions that Brown was the real leader of the Liberal Administration, and Mackenzie a mere pawn in his hands. The younger men found the heavy-handed editorial policy of the *Globe* as stultifying as the painstaking, even cautious attitude of the Premier. Their unquestioning loyalty to the Empire ran directly counter to the Canada First dream of young nationhood. George Brown did nothing to avoid the breach. "A number of young men, and a few others, who, though no longer young, are still abundantly juvenile, have lately come before the public as the founders of a new political party, the prophets of a new political millennium," he scoffed editorially when the Canada National Association was formed.[46] "Let these sucking politicians . . . go to school and study the alphabet of politics . . . while their beards are grown."

Lord Dufferin was no more happy about the new movement than Mackenzie or Brown. He had vivid memories of a similar revolt against the Liberal Administration of which he had been a member at home when Goldwin Smith was still teaching at Oxford. "Goldwin Smith seems inclined to do as much mischief as he can in precipitating the 'Independence' cry," he wrote to Carnarvon during Mackenzie's first session as Premier.[47] "He lives at Toronto surrounded by a little knot of young men to whom he lays down the Law, and whom he seeks to inspire with eminently wrong-headed ideas." Though the Canada Firsters claimed to be a "movement" and not a political party, the situation was dangerous for the Mackenzie Administration. To strengthen the Cabinet and forestall an open split, it was obviously desirable to bring Blake back into the Government. Blake, however, refused to be moved. "I write . . . to say," he informed Mackenzie, "that after careful consideration I have been unable to change the conclusion to which I had previously come as to office . . . I have expressed to Holton the gratification which I was sure his accession to the Government would cause to our friends."[48] When the negotiations were over, the Prime Minister was as much alone and overburdened as before. He made Fournier Minister of Justice, brought in Geoffrion as Minister of Revenue, and went back to work.

CHAPTER 12

Midsummer Toil and Trouble

In Washington, Brown and Thornton were pursuing zealously their negotiations with the Secretary of State, Hamilton Fish.[1] The canny old American statesman was playing his cards well, but his changeable attitude and elusive manner increased the antipathy of the British team for the United States diplomats. The British delegation were having their own internal problems. At the beginning, Brown had lingered in Toronto arranging his private business and had not appeared in time for the first meeting with Fish. Without him, it was nearly impossible to start the discussions. His tardiness pointed out the delicate situation in which they found themselves. Thornton was the nominal leader, but Brown was the essential part of the team. To the British statesman, the Canadian was a presumptuous intruder; he complained to Dufferin of the tardy arrival. The Governor General, in turn, delivered a severe lecture to Mackenzie. Swept away by his indignation at the breach of diplomatic etiquette, he denounced Brown as "absurdly arrogant", and the *Globe* as "scurrilous", warned the Premier that the new Senator was likely to prove a source of weakness to the Administration, and told him that he must obtain "faithful and implicit obedience" from him. It was a tall order; no one had ever accomplished it before![2]

When the Canadian Minister of Fisheries went down to the American capital during the session to lend a hand with the negotiations, he found Brown in complete charge. Henry Rothery, who had awakened hopes for a new Reciprocity Treaty during his visit to Ottawa before Christmas, was pouting at being shoved aside. Sir Edward Thornton was treating his fellow plenipotentiary with diplomatic restraint. Albert Smith soon found that as long as Brown was present, even a Minister of the Crown dared not interfere. A telegram from the Premier in Ottawa, obviously inspired by the *Globe* publisher, pointed out that the Minister of Fisheries had no right to overrule the plenipotentiaries, and that any directives from the Government must originate in Ottawa. Smith returned to Canada. "I regret exceedingly that he should have given you so much trouble," Mackenzie wrote to Brown in Washington.[3] "He was so anxious to go that I found we would have him in ill humour unless he was sent and I had work enough and trouble enough without having him complaining. . . . My impression was that he merely wished to be there to share the glory and would be content to keep quiet." Not even a Cabinet colleague could come between the two friends.

At the outset, British and Americans manoeuvred non-committally for position. More patient and cunning, Fish soon succeeded in persuading the British team to draw up a definite proposal. Brown retired to a secluded part of the British Legation and went to work. Coded telegrams flashed back and forth between Washington and Ottawa's West Block as the memorandum was prepared. In three weeks the Canadian Senator was back in Fish's office. "An impartial examination of the commercial relations between the United States and the British North American Provinces for the last fifty years," he read to the Secretary of State, "cannot fail to establish, we venture to think, beyond all doubt, that the traffic between them has been exceedingly valuable to both countries, but that the United States have, from first to last, reaped the largest advantage from it."[4] The abrogation of the Treaty of 1854, he went on, was more harmful to them than to Canada, and a new agreement would be decidedly to their advantage. His proposals followed closely Mackenzie's memorandum to Lord Dufferin earlier in the year. The free list would be increased, the coasting trade of each country opened to the vessels of the other, and the fishery rights granted to the Americans under the Treaty of Washington would be maintained. Lake Michigan would be open to Canadian ships.

Fish listened politely, but avoided giving his personal reaction to the proposals. The bargaining began. For weeks he played with the British negotiators, sometimes throwing cold water on the whole idea of a new trade agreement, sometimes letting them believe it was just a step away. In Ottawa and Washington, Canadian hopes rose and fell according to the face he presented. The experience was exasperating to the direct and independent Mackenzie and Brown. "I don't like Fish's manner in the interviews," the Premier complained impatiently in early May.[5] "It looks as if he considered us a sort of political beggars looking with longing eyes to him for the crumbs the Republic might drop to us." The awkwardness of the situation was increased by the knowledge that the Opposition were predicting the failure of the negotiations, and watching carefully for signs to confirm their prediction. "I am afraid our Tories have been working underhand against us . . . ," Mackenzie commented bitterly.[6] "I am quite convinced that they are devilish enough to use their utmost efforts to injure us by hurting your mission. I sincerely hope you will be able to accomplish all you desire not only for the thing itself but to balk these fellows."

The biggest stumbling-block was the Canadian insistence that British goods should not be discriminated against. Only a threat to break off negotiations forced Fish to accept this as one of the fixed conditions of the British-Canadian relationship. In a show-down meeting on May 25, he finally agreed to consider a draft treaty based on the Brown memorandum, but omitting any mention of the coasting trade, and limiting the list of Canadian manufactures. The draft would be sent to the Senate by the President before signature as was done with the Washington Treaty. "What do you say?" Brown asked the Canadian Government leader excitedly. "Shall we accept his proposition? Thornton and I perfectly agree that we ought. Possibly Fish still pursues his humbugging game, but there is no indication of that."[7] Ottawa wired assent, and the drafting began.

At the same time that he was carrying on the negotiations with the State Department, the *Globe* publisher was working furiously to enlist support for his cause among Congressmen and senior officials. When agreement seemed almost certain, the American Minister brought up the question of the canals again. Hope faded once more. By the end of June, the discussions had reached such a critical stage that Brown rushed up to Ottawa to discuss the items on the free list.[8] In a few days he was back in Fish's office again. With the Canadians and Americans in agreement, only British approval was needed before the President could send the draft to the Senate. The session in Washington was drawing to a close, and time was of the essence. Another road-block appeared. Lord Derby, the Foreign Minister, insisted on seeing the entire draft before giving any opinion! More delay! The complete text was telegraphed across the Atlantic.[9] Brown and Thornton waited nervously in Washington, and Mackenzie in Ottawa, as the days passed and Fish made continual references to further concessions. The American Secretary of State played his cards well to the end. While the British delegation waited for the reply from London, he suggested free navigation of the Gut of Canso, deeper canals on the St. Lawrence, removal of salt from the free list, and exclusion of Lake Michigan from the agreement. "Make best bargain you can," Alexander Mackenzie wired on June 12, just five days before Congress was due to adjourn.[10] "Malt all right and so will salt be if I can manage that old beggar," Brown replied the following day.[11]

On June 13, Lord Derby was "graciously pleased" to approve the draft.[12] The British delegates rushed to Fish's office. "Would you believe it," the Canadian reported to his chief, "he was at his old tricks nearly as bad as ever. 'The difficulties were immense. The Senate would certainly throw the draft treaty out.' In short, there was no hope unless we made new concessions now suggested for the first time." The grinding-down process began again. Thornton's nerves were wearing even shorter than the others. He was unwell, and had booked passage to return to England for a rest. Anxious for a decision, he persuaded Brown to tell Fish flatly that unless the draft treaty was signed and sent to the Senate the following week, the negotiations would automatically end, and the fisheries arbitration would proceed. The bluff worked. "Draft treaty goes to Senate tomorrow morning with message from the President recommending it to their favourable consideration," Brown wired to Ottawa jubilantly on June 17.[13] The end of the session had been postponed a few precious days; there was still time.

The Fish-Brown Treaty, as it was being called already, was far from a gift package for Canada. The tariff concessions implied a loss of three million dollars in revenue each year, the fisheries rights were ceded for the twenty-one years it was to run, and extensive works were to be carried out on the canal system. The Liberals were confident that the loss in revenue would be more than compensated over the years by the increase in trade, and that the treaty would mark the beginning of a new era of co-operation and prosperity on the North American continent. It would be the first great accomplishment of the new régime.

President Grant congratulated George Brown on having negotiated the treaty, and referred to it in enthusiastic terms.[14] His enthusiasm was not reflected in the message with which he accompanied the draft to the Senate. "I am of the opinion that a proper treaty for such purposes would result beneficially for the United States . . .," he told the United States Senate, "but whether it makes all the concessions which could justly be required of Great Britain, or whether it calls for more concessions from the United States than we should yield, I am not prepared to say."[15] No American signature appeared on the proposed treaty; it was submitted as a British suggestion, and Congress was asked merely to advise whether it would give "its constitutional concurrence to the conclusion of a treaty with Great Britain." Far from a request backed by the prestige of the White House, it was an invitation to begin the discussions all over again in the full glare of public debate. In the sweltering June weather, the Senators had no appetite for an additional large item on their legislative agenda. Their departure from the capital already delayed, the members of the Foreign Relations Committee postponed the subject until the following year without even introducing it to the main body. The Canadian Senator was helpless to intervene; he, too, rushed home to his family. "Whether we obtain the Treaty or not," the Premier wrote to Mrs. Brown, "we have gained this great advantage that the Yankees know now the Canadians are able to do their negotiating effectively, and that the days of English poltroonery and blundering is [*sic*] over on this continent. . . . After this we will at least be respected and can respect ourselves."[16]

As if the heavy load of problems and the exasperations of the first summer in Ottawa were not enough, the Mackenzies lost their home by fire in early June. The flames spread with such speed that furniture, personal treasures such as Mackenzie's letters to his wife over the years, even their clothing, were destroyed, and they were fortunate to escape with their lives. But these were private considerations, and there were public matters demanding immediate attention. They rented a house just west of Parliament Hill between Wellington Street and the river, not five minutes' walk from the West Block.* From his new balcony, the Premier could see the massive Government buildings that dominated the fast-growing town, and in front of him he could watch the sun setting behind the Gatineau Hills. The lot extended to the river, and on warm June evenings he could hear the frogs croaking at the water's edge. "Cliffside", as the owner called it, even had a small tank in which he could bathe if he had the time. With a minimum of delay, he moved in and went back to work.

The British Columbia pot was boiling dangerously hot. After the rupture of negotiations with the British Columbia Government in May, and his unilateral announcement of the future Pacific Railway policy, Mackenzie had withdrawn the proposals made by James Edgar. At the end of June, Premier Walkem appeared in Ottawa en route to London, where he intended to protest the non-fulfilment of the terms of union. Mackenzie's

*On the present site of the Supreme Court building.

indignation at the treatment accorded Edgar had not subsided. He was still further disturbed by the suggestion contained in a telegram from Lord Carnarvon that it might be advisable for the Colonial Office to intervene in the dispute.[17] The implication that the Dominion Government could not manage its own affairs was, in his opinion, an additional insult. The Governor General's patronizing attitude often seemed to indicate a similar viewpoint. Dufferin's close scrutiny of every detail of the Administration, his picayune criticism of the wording of despatches, his confidential correspondence with Carnarvon in London and Thornton in Washington that his advisers were not permitted to see, all these had nourished the flame of resentment against Imperial dictation. The proposal of Imperial arbitration between himself and the devious British Columbia Premier was the final insult. Mackenzie replied bluntly that he could not think of any point on which the Imperial Government could act.[18]

As was to be expected, the talks between the two Premiers did not go well. "He asked me, after a little conversation, what we proposed to do," Mackenzie reported to a British Columbia member on July 10.[19] "I replied that I did not intend to make any proposals of any sort and if he had any to make I would listen to them, but he said, 'Surely you have something to say.' I said, no, not a word. You have chosen to set aside our proposals on a merely technical objection and you can now do exactly what you like and we will do what we think is right. He took offence at my using the term technical as applied to their act but soon regained his good humour. He asked me if I thought it was a statesmanlike course to say nothing. I said probably not but we made no pretensions to statesmanship we were plain business men and meant what we said."

The British Columbian protested his desire to come to an understanding, and thus avoid the trip to England. He finally agreed to place the position of his Government in writing, and retired to Russell House to prepare a statement. The fact was that Walkem, too, was in a delicate position. Having ridden into power on an anti-Ottawa slogan, he could not afford to compromise. Any retreat from the terms of union would be fatal to his Administration. Even the indignation of the belligerent Grit leader was preferable to that. "Your letter is no proposal," came the irate reply from the West Block a few hours after he submitted his statement, "it is just a criticism of Edgar's, which I don't admit. I didn't invite an expression of opinion on Dominion policy, you said you would make a written proposition. On Monday July 13 you called on me to say you proposed leaving for England but would be glad not to go, if we would start construction on the island. I said that was already proposed through Edgar and declined. You said no one in British Columbia was so insane as to think the line could be done by 1881 and they would be satisfied if diligence were shown. I will still listen to a proposition from British Columbia but I have none to make."[20] The door was closed. Walkem sailed.

Meanwhile, Lord Dufferin had become keenly interested in the Colonial Minister's offer of arbitration. Despite repeated statements to the contrary, both he and Carnarvon still felt that the Mother Country had a direct interest in the Dominion's affairs. In this instance, they agreed with the British Columbians that the Imperial Government, as a party to the contract by which the Pacific province entered Confederation, was directly concerned.[21] This view was directly opposed to Mackenzie's goal of establishing the complete control of Canadians over their own affairs.

One factor operated in Dufferin's and Carnarvon's favour. The Canadian Premier was not willing to pursue his campaign for Canadian administrative autonomy to the point of suggesting a loosening of the bonds of Empire. Wrong and misguided as Downing Street might be, he could never be disloyal. "It would be ungracious to refuse Lord Carnarvon's offer of mediation," Mackenzie conceded in response to the Governor General's cajolery, "but I think it was made in the belief that we differed in the interpretation of some point that a third party could decide".[22] The only possible complaint so far, he argued, was that the line was not begun within two years. Sir John had expressed the opinion in a telegram to a member from Cariboo, British Columbia, that the terms were kept by prosecution of the survey. "Now whether that was the case or not I will not say. But suppose we leave that point to Lord Carnarvon and he decides more was required by the terms. What then? We *could not* comply, and it would be just an opinion against the Dominion Government . . . I am quite willing to leave to His Lordship to say if we have exercised all diligence in doing all that could reasonably have been asked, but compliance in new conditions would be difficult. It must be remembered that public opinion is exasperated on this question. Even Dr. Tupper who is responsible for the bargain in the first instance announced that my plan would ruin the country if persisted in . . . The present House would defeat any proposal from Lord Carnarvon to finish the line in 1881."

It was not merely a question of finances. Construction could not begin until the line was chosen, and it was impossible to use more surveyors than were already employed in determining the best route. "If I had all the wealth of India I couldn't go faster," the embattled Premier assured a British Columbia Senator.[23] Nevertheless, Carnarvon's will and Dufferin's powers of persuasion were not easy to withstand, and in the end the Canadian Government agreed to let the Colonial Secretary decide whether they were failing, or had failed, to meet their engagement so far as circumstances permitted. Their acquiescence was based on the conviction that their case was unassailable, that Dufferin agreed it was reasonable, and that Carnarvon's study could only lead to the same conclusion.

The Governor General supported his advisers in a private letter to the Colonial Secretary. He argued that Mackenzie's alternative plan was "fair and reasonable", and "as much as could fairly be granted, with due consideration to the interests of the country at large. . . ." British Columbia, he urged, "should not hold Canada to the literal fulfilment of what at the time seems to have been acknowledged by all parties to have been a physically impossible undertaking".[24] Carnarvon accepted Dufferin's apologies for the sharpness of Mackenzie's initial reaction as "stone chippings of the workshop . . . which attest an early stage of literary culture," and proceeded to his self-appointed task.[25] With a gnawing feeling of uneasiness, the Canadian Premier turned to other problems.

* * * * *

Alexander Mackenzie was lonely during that summer of 1874. After arranging the new house, Jane went off to the seashore with friends, leaving him alone in the capital. When the long day's work was over, time lay heavily on his hands. His eyes exhausted from the long hours of studying public documents, he had to put all work aside and fill the empty hours as best he could. He whiled away the evenings with lengthy letters to his absent wife. He thought of advertising to find her, he chided her affectionately for not writing, "as 'a disconcerted husband would be glad to hear tidings of his wife who left Ottawa on the morning of the 4th and has not since been heard of. Her age about – . Skin fair, hair mixed, teeth good and nearly new, small fat docile disposition and $30 in her pocket.' Do you think that would reach you? I saw the Sergeant last night. He told me he was going down to-day and I asked him if he saw you not to mention that I was crying when he came in. Mr. Buckingham and I use up a handkerchief daily. I think of using a towell [*sic*] after this for economical reasons. If you stay away long it may come to a sheet . . ."[26] "The question is where are you?" he wrote again the same week.[27] "I presume you are vindicating your title to the Baptist profession by immersing well and thus at once sticking to your principles and laying in a stock of health for the winter. A horrible thought just strikes me, however, that if you should now suddenly grow fat (and) become the 'Grosse Femme' of the family!! To be sure we could sing in our misery; As she grew fat he grew thin, Ha, Ha, the wooing o't. Sandy fluched and Sandy prayed, but she grew big as Ailsa Craig – No doubt the compensatory laws of nature are very admirable and it may be satisfactory to know that we keep up the weight between us but I would rather carry my share of it."

Mackenzie longed to escape the summer heat and join his wife in strolls along the seashore, where, he told her, he always felt the comfort of God's immediate presence. He dreamed of crossing the Atlantic and showing Jane the Scottish hills, but this too was out of the question; he was duty bound to his desk. The constant attacks of his opponents did not lighten his task. "I see some Tory papers say I am eaten up with ambition," he wrote to Jane on his first Sunday alone.[28] "I think I know myself and can honestly say I am not. I am ambitious to succeed in governing the country well and without any reproach but beyond that my ambition is of very humble kind . . . I think I have ambition enough, however, to strengthen me to fight in, I hope, a manly way the base herd of hireling scribes who would for political gain write away a man's character, and courage to back up that ambition." Beyond that he hoped only for the peace and quiet of the ordinary citizen.

August provided one opportunity to get out of Ottawa that Mackenzie could not refuse. Lord Dufferin was touring Ontario and asked him to join the party for their visit to Lambton. Despite their occasional disagreements, the Governor General was becoming more and more impressed with his chief adviser. While he referred scornfully to most Canadian politicians as liars, he wrote of Mackenzie as "pure as crystal, and as true as steel with lots of common sense". "If only he had a little more talent to give him 'initiative' and 'ascendancy' he would make a capital Minister."[29] They met in Windsor and boarded the steamer *Steinhoff*, which carried them up the Detroit and St. Clair rivers along the route of the Premier's first voyage to his western home. As they hove into sight of Sarnia on a bright summer afternoon, they could distinguish the steeple of John Thompson's church, the docks built by Malcolm Cameron almost two score years before, and the blackened railway station on the water's edge. Six steamers were waiting to escort them into the harbour, and a gunboat fired a royal salute. Even the Port Huron ferry was freshly scrubbed and bedecked with flags for the occasion. On the wharf, the Premier's former comrades in arms, the 27th Militia Battalion, stood stiffly at attention in bright clean uniforms that contrasted sharply with the motley dress worn during the Fenian raids. One of the members of the reception committee who welcomed them ashore was his brother Charles. It was a memorable homecoming.[30]

Alexander Mackenzie introduced the Queen's representative to his neighbours. Dufferin was in fine oratorical form. In addition to being replete with corn and flowing with oil, he declared, the Sarnia area sent to Parliament the man who presided over the councils of the nation. They could be proud of the intellectual achievement and the outstanding qualities that had raised their member to his high position. Sarnians relaxed and basked in their pride of their bounteous area, their loyalty to the Empire, and their illustrious citizen. The respite was brief. Cartwright was in England raising a loan, and most of the other Ministers were at home; Mackenzie abandoned the Viceregal party as soon as possible and rushed back to the Capital.

When he first began his investigations, Lord Carnarvon had been impressed with the position of the Dominion Government in the Pacific Railway dispute, and declared it "by no means unreasonable".[31] However, George Walkem arrived shortly afterwards and succeeded in changing his view. To test the reaction in Ottawa, the Colonial Minister sent out a trial set of terms in late August, suggesting that the Vancouver Island railway should be built, surveys speeded up, the minimum expenditure in the Province increased to two million dollars per year, and the wagon road and telegraph line abandoned since the provincial Premier considered them useless.[32]

Tired and irritated from overwork, Alexander Mackenzie reacted violently. In suggesting that more be done, he felt that Lord Carnarvon was implying it was not true that the Dominion was doing its best to meet the terms of union. He had assurances from the chief engineer that it would be impossible to put another theodolite into the field, and that money was being wasted because efficiency was being sacrificed for the sake of speed. The criticism he was receiving from Edward Blake and other Liberals for going so far in the suggestions transmitted by James Edgar made him even more sensitive to such an inference. In addition, he was receiving reports that only a handful of the three thousand voters in British Columbia were behind the agitation, and that most of the residents felt the Canadian position was fair and reasonable. To further complicate the situation, the engineers reported that the Cascade Range, situated between the Rocky Mountains and the sea, was much more difficult to penetrate than had been anticipated, and the Bute Inlet route, which had been favoured because it led directly to a point opposite Nanaimo, was almost impossible. Exploration had to be commenced along the Fraser River farther south to find an alternative. To make a premature choice meant risking a catastrophic waste of money.

The constant care and annoyances had their inevitable effect. Whereas Sir John used to "break out", Mackenzie's stomach revolted, and he was forced to take to his bed with a severe internal inflammation. It was a very sick man who wrote the hot reply to Carnarvon's "trial terms".[33] Dufferin apologized for the roughness of the language, but stood by his chief adviser. The final set of "Carnarvon terms" was a carefully drawn compromise.[34] The Esquimalt-Nanaimo Railway was to be begun at once. The survey parties should be pushed with the utmost vigour, and the wagon road and telegraph line, which Mackenzie insisted were necessary in any case, constructed immediately. A minimum of two million dollars should be spent within the province after the surveys were completed. The deadline for the completion of the line would be extended nine years until 1890. Having pronounced his verdict, Lord Carnarvon warned the two parties to the dispute that he would brook no refusals. "If they were to demur now through fear of political opposition from Blake or other opponents," he wrote to Dufferin of the Canadian Ministers, "they would without improving their position or credit make it almost impossible for me to place any confidence in dealing with them."[35] The Canadian Government subordinated its reason to its loyalty and accepted. As Dufferin predicted, Walkem hurried back to British Columbia "across the bridge of gold we have built for him."[36] A crisis had been avoided, but the Governor General had discovered that "a Colonial Government is a kittle team to drive".[37]

While Alexander Mackenzie was struggling to recover his strength in order to return to work, a surprising letter arrived from Edward Blake. "In your letter of 20 May referring to a statement in the *M^l^ Gazette* that you were about to retain the Public Works and I was to become first minister," wrote the Toronto lawyer, "you told me that you wished to heaven it were true. To this I did not respond because I thought the difficulties in the way of my entering the Government were insuperable. The pressure on me from various influential quarters since that time has been so great, and has within even the last few days so much increased, . . . that I have been led to reconsider the matter, and have been brought reluctantly to the conclusion that it might be my duty under certain circumstances to face my difficulties and overcome my personal reluctance to office. . . . If you . . . do in truth prefer to retain the great department which you hold, an office which you alone can adequately fill, but the tenure of which is not compatible with that of the first ministership, I will add up myself to the effort of so arranging my professional and personal affairs as to enable me to . . . meet your views. But on the other hand, if what you wrote me was but the result of some temporary feeling, or if your mind has since changed, and you prefer to remain first minister, I shall rejoice to know that I can . . . retain my present position."[38]

The implication was clear; he would accept the Premiership or nothing. What was behind the new attitude, Mackenzie wondered. What had induced Blake to reach out his hand for an office from which he had recoiled so frantically less than two years before? Who were the "various influential quarters" desirous of changing the head of the Government? The Canada First group? The many favour-seekers he had turned away empty-handed? Holton? Jones? or even some of his Cabinet colleagues? By a strange coincidence, a day or two before the letter arrived, a New Brunswick paper that supported the Administration had announced that just such a change would be carried out.

Still weak and tired from his bout of dysentery, the Premier had decided to spend a few days repairing and altering the new house. As he worked with his hands again for the first time in several years, he had time to think. Did he really want to make way for his former colleague? Was it just a minor revolt, or was he losing control of a large number of his followers? The thought of a cabal against him stung his Scottish pride, and stirred his pugnacious character. Blake was impatient. He had exposed himself to a rebuff and a rude shock to his own tender pride; he waited with growing apprehension for a reply. After eleven days, he could restrain himself no longer. "Considering that the question I raised was as to your own feelings," he wrote on September 17,[39] "I think I may reasonably draw from a silence so long continued the inference that these are adverse to the change, and as I said in my note this conclusion ends the matter for me. I leave town for Peterboro circuit in an hour, once more thank goodness free."

Mackenzie was jolted into action. He had needed time to think over the whole position carefully, he replied the following day. "In the words you quote I expressed my feelings fully."[40] In the spring he had attempted to get both Blake and Holton into the

Cabinet and had even arranged for two Ministers to retire in order to make room for them. When the changes had not materialized, he had told his Cabinet there would be no change for the present. He confessed that the implication of a plot within the Cabinet also disturbed him. "I foresaw that to at once carry out the programme laid down for me [*sic!*] would subject me to humiliation if I remained in the Gov't, and while willing enough to leave the Government I saw that this involved leaving the House also. This I would not hesitate a moment to do so far as I am personally concerned, but I had to consider the general effect on the party and to give some thought to personal friends. . . . The matter causes me much anxiety and I am as yet unable to see my way to the right conclusion. . . . I propose if possible to go to Toronto on Tuesday and hope to see you."

It had happened; Blake's fingers had been slapped by the equally proud Prime Minister. Much as he desired to bring him into the Cabinet, it was clear that Mackenzie would not abandon the leadership of the Government. Blake had only one thought: to withdraw as quickly as possible and lick his imagined wounds. "It is abundantly plain that the proposed arrangement is absolutely out of the question," he replied tersely on September 24.[41] "My aim was to meet your views, and it is I trust needless for me to say that I could not for a moment contemplate anything which might in your judgment incur your humiliation in, or your retirement from the Government. I beg you will not add to your other cares which are quite heavy enough by devoting a moment's further thought to the matter."

Nine days later the most able man in the Liberal party declared his independence of the Administration. At a Liberal rally in Aurora on October 3, 1874, Blake surprised the other platform guests, including Premier Mowat and Archibald McKellar, as well as the large picnic audience, by casting doubts on the reciprocity negotiations, and criticizing the Government's conciliatory attitude towards British Columbia.[42] The Pacific province, he declared, was, after all, only a useless "sea of mountains". He dissociated himself from the Edgar proposals and warned against attempts "to entangle the country further . . . If the Columbians were to say – 'You must go on . . . according to the terms or take the alternative of releasing us from the Confederation' – I would – take the alternative! I believe that is the view of the people of this country, and it may as well be plainly stated, because such a plain statement is the very thing which will prevent the British Columbians from making such extravagant demands."

Having unburdened himself of his pent-up indignation

against the Pacific province, he went on to more speculative subjects. The Empire should be organized on a federal basis, he felt. As long as Canadians did not accept their responsibilities, they could not claim the rights and privileges of free-born Britons. "How long is this talk . . . of the desirability, aye, of the necessity of fostering a national spirit among the people of Canada, to be mere talk? It is impossible to foster a national spirit unless you have national interests to attend to . . . The time will come . . . when we shall realize that we are four millions of Britons who are not free. . . . Tomorrow, by the policy of England . . . this country might be plunged into the horrors of a war." Canada's system of government was superior to that of either Britain or the United States, the tense and earnest lawyer continued, but reforms were still needed. The Senate should be made fully elective, and at least some Senators chosen by the provincial legislatures for a fixed term to ensure representation of the provinces as the British North America Act intended. A still more stringent electoral law was needed, including compulsory voting. Minorities should be assured of representation in Parliament.

The Aurora speech broke like a thunderbolt on the political scene. The *Globe* maintained a stunned silence for two or three days, then grumbled that it preferred to "Canada first", or "Heligoland first", or "Norfolk Island first"* "the grand old British race first and all who love their Sovereign, and all who swear by the Old Flag, as first and last and midst as well."[43] The *Nation,* on the other hand, hailed it jubilantly as a display of "courage at once rare and heroic", and forecast an early breakup of the old parties. "There has long been a section of the Reform party that was dissatisfied with its practical Conservatism; and that section is in complete sympathy with Mr. Blake."[44]

As far as Alexander Mackenzie was concerned, it was just another annoyance imposed by the unpredictable genius of the party. He and Brown found consolation in belittling its significance in letters to one another. There was not much new, he wrote to the *Globe* publisher on October 8, most of the subjects having been discussed in public before. However, the elaborate reference to them at a time when the Government had so many problems to contend with was "neither wise nor friendly, though it may not be so meant".[45]

Try as he might to minimize the incident, Mackenzie could not avoid recognizing that it was related to a movement to oust him from the Premiership. His analysis of the causes of the

*A small island in the Pacific Ocean.

revolt was less penetrating. Ever conscious of his guardianship of the public purse, he attributed it to the fact that "the public interest forces me to stand between them and some cherished but improper object".[46] That the idealists of the party feared he was settling down to a conservative, unimaginative, penny-pinching reign, he could not admit. At the same time, he could not bring himself to believe that Blake could be a party to an open revolt. Erratic he might be, but Mackenzie had "perfect confidence" in his honour, he told George Brown.[47] "Another year will enable the Gov't to fit into grooves of their own and get rid of the many embarrassments of the present position so that there would be less chance of encountering any malcontents in our own ranks." Reforms were still needed, he conceded, but there was no use discussing them in public until a concrete proposal had been formulated. A change in the Senate was inevitable, but would only be possible when the balance between Liberal and Conservative members was restored. "We can take our time to consider what is best," he concluded, taking a leaf out of Sir John's book. Both Brown and Dufferin supported the Premier, the former assuring him that the "old intelligent Reformers" were indignant, and that Blake and Goldwin Smith had been harmed by the incident.[48] The Governor General, who had a growing antipathy for Blake, was convinced that he had "gone in with Goldwin Smith for independence".[49] Mackenzie disagreed. "Well," his Excellency replied, "it either meant that or opposition to you, or it was mere buncombe. And he is not the man for the latter article."

With Blake, the Premier was surprisingly patient and conciliatory. "I congratulate you on your speech even if it is 'disturbing'," he wrote as a sort of postscript to a letter on other subjects on October 13.[50] "I am unable to see how we can maintain secret voting and have compulsory voting as a man may put a blank in the box; I have not however discussed the matter in my own mind much."

The *Globe* prolonged the incident with a series of articles rebutting the Aurora speech. Although he refused to enter the public debate, Mackenzie defended Brown's right to do so. "It seems to me a little unreasonable to ask the *Globe* to forbear discussing what Mr. Blake discussed," he replied to one of Blake's friends, John Cameron of London, who objected to the series. ". . . The truth is that there was no necessity for the speech and unnecessary speeches generally do harm."[51] His defence of Brown drew from him a few comments on the Aurora speech. Since the Liberals had delegated the franchise to the provincial Legislatures, it was impossible to change it. It was impossible to have both secret and compulsory voting, and the idea of Imperial federation was a "chimera". Representation of minorities was also impossible in practice. It took considerable self-restraint, he told Cameron, to resist making a speech himself, "to pursue the crude theories to their legitimate conclusion".

There was an interesting by-product of the Aurora incident. Stung by the suggestion on the part of Tories, Goldwin Smith, and even Blake supporters, that he was a mere tool of George Brown, the Premier declared to Cameron that "no man has had so much to do with him as me and I always found him reasonable and had my say as often as he. Since the formation of the Gov't I have never received a single letter from him asking for or pushing any favour or opinion upon me. He has been of all politicians, of all men, the most considerate . . . I am aware he is a man of strong will and decisive character (and Canada has reaped the benefit of that trait) . . . it [the *Globe*] is usually right, always actuated by high principle." It was an eloquent statement of loyal friendship; it was also a warning to the Blake wing that nothing could separate the two Scots.

Fortunately, the public were not vitally interested in abstract principles, and the storm soon subsided. Alexander Mackenzie returned to his lonely task. There was a suggestion of resignation in his attitude, but with it a quiet confidence that had been absent a year before. It was a pleasant fall. When he appeared at Rideau Hall with his bulging briefcase in the late afternoons of November, he often found the Governor General playing tennis in his shirt-sleeves. As the sun sank slowly out of sight across the Ottawa River, he relaxed on a bench beside the court and watched the balls speed back and forth until His Excellency was ready to return to more serious matters.

* * * * *

The details of the Public Works Department were as demanding as ever, and the struggle to maintain his high standards of integrity for the Administration was unceasing. Under the new and stricter electoral law, numerous Liberals as well as Conservatives were being brought before judges on charges of corrupt electoral practices. With the Opposition seeking constantly for an opportunity to cry "You too!" to the accusations of Tory scandals, it was like dancing on a maze of billiard balls. If one slipped out of place – if one culpable act was discovered – a general disaster was likely to result.

The Maritimers were particularly insistent in their demands

for partisan favours. He had appointed Charles Brydges, the former Managing Director of the Great Western and Grand Trunk Railways, as General Superintendent of Government Railways, and given him instructions to put the Intercolonial and Prince Edward Island lines on a sound financial basis. Brydges was to choose friends of the Government if they were qualified, but was told distinctly that "good men must be got at all hazards".[52] Even Alfred Jones flew into a pet when his political friends were not given the jobs they asked for, and Brydges soon became one of the most hated men in the Maritimes. "It is impossible to fill the Railway offices on political grounds; they must have experience," Mackenzie argued with the member for Halifax, "and if we cannot get experienced men among our friends we must take them elsewhere just as you would do in a private company or in your own office. . . . Don't ask me to do a thing you would not freely do in my place." Still, he conceded philosophically after his initial indignation had subsided, "I know you are under pressure and suppose I can expect to have it dished out to me in turn."[53] Speaker Anglin escaped less easily; he was scolded in no uncertain terms for trying to force inexperienced men on the railway management.

Even his colleagues felt the lash of the Premier's tongue when they failed to meet his standards. The Minister of Justice, Télesphore Fournier, was involved in a drunken brawl in a tavern. The Opposition press reported the incident with glee. "What is being discussed in the newspapers" was very painful to him, harmful to the party, and a disservice to the liberal cause, the stern Scot lectured.[54] "At first I felt that I should be bound to ask you to send in your resignation . . . (but) my personal respect for you revolted at my doing anything to injure you." However, he added that "I do not think it can be allowed to happen again." Then there was Lucius Huntington who had maintained his business connections in Montreal, and who was being accused of financial transactions too closely related to the Government's operations. Such insinuations were commonplace, and were directed at many of the Ministers, including the Premier himself, but were never substantiated. In Huntington's case, they had an unexpected result. He had intended to retire from the Cabinet in order to try to put together a new railway syndicate with George Stephen, Senator Foster, and other financial tycoons, with a view to building the Pacific Railway.[55] Holton, whose ardour for Blake was cooling rapidly since the Aurora speech, had agreed to come into the Ministry at long last in his place. However, when the *Montreal Gazette* accused Huntington of unethical business transactions, Holton adopted the attitude that a change at that time would lend weight to the charge, and give the appearance of "unloading" the author of the Pacific scandal. His entrance into the Government was postponed again.

Another colleague, William Ross, of Cape Breton, was retired before the year's end to the post of Collector of Customs in Halifax. He was a disappointment from the beginning. Indiscreet and boastful, and of dubious political morality, he cared much for the trappings of office and nothing for administrative responsibility. Nevertheless, the task of getting him to resign had been trying as he did not want to give up the prestige and the seven-thousand-dollar salary for a position at less than half that sum. Finally, in exasperation, Mackenzie told him that he had to have "brains and hands that could work".[56] "How such a gobemouche was ever named by his fellows as a cabinet minister is a mystery," the Premier grumbled to Jones. "He has neither Education, commonsense good manners or a spark of Manliness."[57] William Vail, the Provincial Secretary in Nova Scotia, succeeded the unhappy Cape Bretoner as Minister of Militia and Defence.

All the other problems during the fall of 1874 were secondary compared to the storm brewing in the West, and threatening to spread to every corner of the Dominion. The Riel affair was coming to a head. After his election was annulled by Parliament, the half-breed rebel was immediately chosen again by his loyal neighbours in the ensuing by-election. Riel himself was seen occasionally moving in and out of bishops' residences in Quebec; Joseph Cauchon was introduced to him on Durham Terrace in the old French capital. "I suppose when he dies he will be canonized," Mackenzie commented sarcastically on learning who was hiding him.[58]

Still feeling betrayed by Macdonald, Archbishop Taché continued to demand the amnesty he had promised the provisional government during the Red River uprising. Led by their Bishops, the Catholics of Canada flocked to his support, shoaling letters and petitions on the Liberal Administration. The evidence of the Special Committee of the House of Commons showed that they had sound arguments on which to base their case. If an Archbishop's word was worth anything, there was no doubt that Sir John had promised the amnesty. Archbishop Taché testified before the Committee that he had told the ex-Premier when he was on the way from Rome to Fort Garry in 1870: "There have been acts committed which are blameworthy, and there may be others before my arrival there. May I promise them an amnesty?" Sir John had answered, according to the Archbishop's statement, "Yes, you may promise it to them."[59]

In addition, Père Ritchot had returned from Ottawa convinced that he had received a promise of immunity, but he, too, had failed to get the promise in writing.[60] The Ministers had said that it would be an insult to Her Majesty to have to give a written guarantee. Also brought to light was a letter from Sir Georges-Etienne Cartier to the Archbishop, dated July 5, 1870, while General Wolseley's troops were on the way West to restore order, stating that "Her Majesty has already, by the proclamation of the 6th December last, which She caused to be issued by Sir John [the Governor General] so to speak promised an amnesty."[61] The same Minister had agreed that Riel and his friends should be treated as at least a *de facto* government until General Wolseley's troops arrived. "Let Mr. Riel continue to maintain order and govern the country as he has done up to the present moment," Cartier told Father Ritchot; the amnesty would be there before the new Lieutenant-Governor arrived.[62]

In December 1871, Sir John Macdonald had asked Archbishop Taché to persuade Riel to leave the country until the strong feeling against him had subsided. "If you can succeed in keeping him out of the way for a while," Macdonald had written, "I will make his case mine."[63] To encourage him and Ambroise Lepine to disappear, the head of the Canadian Government had caused five thousand dollars to be paid through Lieutenant-Governor Archibald and Donald Smith to the Catholic prelate. It was the following year that Sir John, asked about Riel's whereabouts, declared, "God knows, I wish I could catch him. He is safe, thanks to Mr. Blake, with full opportunity, if he so desires, to plot and plan, in order to destroy the peace and prosperity of that great and growing country."[64]

When Cartier asked the Archbishop, in 1872, to induce Riel to resign the Provencher seat in his favour, the implication was clear that the act would be compensated by action on the amnesty question. Taché had wired Sir John for a specific promise, but the latter had replied guardedly that "Sir George will do all he can to meet the wishes of the parties; this statement should be satisfactory."[65] In the same year, Riel had suddenly reappeared in Fort Garry at the head of a small troop of armed men, and offered his assistance to Lieutenant-Governor Archibald. This act was in keeping with his oft-repeated statements of loyalty to the British flag, and his protests that he wanted only to protect the rights of the "habitants" against the Canadians. Archibald had accepted the offer of assistance, and promised him immunity "pour la circonstance actuelle".[66] He assured him that his co-operation would be "very welcome", and entitled him to "most favourable consideration". When the danger was over, he sent a formal letter of approval for the patriotic action.

Though he doubted the veracity of both Archbishop Taché and Abbé Ritchot, even Lord Dufferin had to agree that "in the face of these circumstances we cannot but feel that Riel is a man whom the Government of Canada cannot hang and one need scarcely be surprised if his French sympathizers who have always regarded him as a hero and patriot would consider his one crime, or rather his 'error of judgment', as they would term it, as having been practically condoned by the authorities."[67] To Catholics, the heart of the matter was less Riel's guilt or innocence than the honour of Archbishop Taché, who had made a promise that had not been fulfilled, and whose word was being doubted by many Protestants. Alexander Mackenzie and his colleagues were willing enough to accept the evidence and lay the blame at Sir John A. Macdonald's feet, but a ghost from their own past was haunting them: their outspoken statements and the offer of a reward in the Ontario Legislature. They suggested that the most convenient solution would be for the Queen to proclaim the amnesty without advice from them, and accompany it with the removal of political rights.

Lord Carnarvon was anxious to dispose of the "difficult and delicate" question, but he had his own political position to consider. Public opinion in England was aroused as well, and he knew that if he did not have a distinct request for an amnesty from the Canadian Government, "the blame will be very conveniently laid on my shoulders".[68] He could expect little understanding from his own people, who saw only that a British subject had been killed, and that those responsible were not yet punished. "I doubt whether ¼ of the English reading public is aware that there is a French population in Canada," he told Lord Dufferin.[69]

While the trans-Atlantic negotiations were proceeding, a jury in Manitoba, including several half-breeds, surprised the worried politicians by finding Ambroise Lepine guilty of the murder of Thomas Scott, and sentencing him to death.[70] This meant by direct implication that Riel was liable to the same sentence if brought to trial; Catholic Canada cried in one voice for the complete amnesty of both. The French-speaking Cabinet Ministers told Mackenzie flatly that they would have to resign unless the death sentence was commuted, and reduced to at least some minor penalty such as banishment with loss of civil rights.

Lord Dufferin was caught between the two sets of political

considerations. "This is the most thorny business I ever have had to deal with," he complained, "thanks to the imbecility of almost everyone who has hitherto meddled with it."[71] Nevertheless, he acted with courage and wisdom. To "satisfy the conflicting exigencies of the case" he requested permission from London to dispense with both instructions from home and from his own advisers, and to proclaim the amnesty on his own authority.[72] The politicians on both sides of the Atlantic were happy to agree. There was one further complication. Amnesty would not be welcome among the vengeance-hungry Ontario populace. A provincial election was called for January 1875, and Oliver Mowat was worried that the Leader of the Opposition, a prominent Orangeman, would succeed in turning public indignation against his Administration, the successor of the Blake-Mackenzie Government. Dufferin agreed to defer his statement until the provincial contest was over. Lieutenant-Governor Morris of Manitoba was warned not to allow the death sentence of Lepine to be carried out if the course of justice outpaced the evolution of political events.[73] Alexander Mackenzie sighed with relief, and prepared to withstand the criticism of hiding behind the Royal prerogative. He could take satisfaction in the knowledge that while Sir John would attack him, he could not but admire the adroit solution that had been devised.

The year was drawing to an end. Shortly before Christmas the Mackenzies went down to Montreal for a few days of relaxation as guests of the Holtons. While the ladies shopped, the men talked of the events of the past months and made plans for the future. Considering that politics is largely a matter of compromise, and that there are seldom definite or final solutions over a short period of time to any problems, the Administration had got on pretty well. The boat had been rocked on a few occasions, but it had never been in danger of capsizing. They could look to the future with confidence and hope. Had they been able to read the Governor General's confidential report to Lord Carnarvon, the two men would have been still more encouraged. "From a general point of view they [the Ministers] may be regarded not only as a strong, but a very strong Government. Sir John Macdonald and his party are entirely routed and nobody expects them to rally during the present Parliament. Sir John himself has just been unseated for bribery at Kingston, and he has narrowly escaped from personal disqualification. This following his other misfortunes has still further diminished his prestige, nor among the adherents still faithful to him, is there a man of sufficient ability to re-organize the oppo-

THE MASON AND THE OVERSEER

OVERSEER (Lord Dufferin): *A very good job, Mac, and you will be kept on: though a few of these stones may perhaps be condemned by the Boss.*

Canadian Illustrated News: April 17, 1875

sition. On the other hand all the government candidates recently unseated under the new Bribery Act, are re-elected; the Conservative ex-Speaker has been defeated; and with the exception of Blake's speech, no sinister occurrence has compromised the prospects of the Administration. Even Blake's speech though indicative at the time of an inclination to secession on the part of one of the ablest members of the Grit party, has been so much disapproved of by his friends, that it has rather increased than otherwise Mackenzie's personal ascendancy, as showing that however inferior he may be in education and brilliancy, – his sober common sense is likely to prove a safer guide than the talent of the other. Even though the Reciprocity Treaty seems likely to fail through the hostility of Fish and the U.S. Government, its initiation will not have brought any discredit upon Ministers, as it was becoming every day more apparent that the country heartily approved of it."[74] It was a satisfying verdict of a fruitful year's labour.

CHAPTER 13

Steady On

The Government was prepared for its second session. The Ministers had their legislation ready, they understood the work of their departments, and they had the comforting knowledge that the Prime Minister was in complete charge of the Dominion's affairs. In Ontario, the Mowat Administration was re-elected by a comfortable majority in mid-January 1875. In Quebec, the Protestant Huguenot, Henri Joly de Lotbinière, who had begun his parliamentary career with Mackenzie in 1862, was the Leader of the Opposition, and the Liberals there were hopeful of upsetting the Conservatives. Premier Walkem of British Columbia had passed through Ottawa on his return from England in a much more conciliatory mood than during his previous visit.

The main fly in the ointment was the reciprocity treaty. Despite an increase in Democratic representation in the partial elections of November, the United States Government was succumbing to the cries of the protectionists, who feared free competition with the low-cost Canadian economy. With the financial depression still worsening, Canadian and English manufacturers, too, were apprehensive of competition from outside their borders. Canadian Boards of Trade expressed their concern with free trade arrangements. George Brown spent part of December in Washington endeavouring to tie up support for the treaty. He met little open hostility but general apathy; most Americans agreed it was almost useless to try to push the project through Congress in 1875.[1] Hamilton Fish took advantage of the situation to demand a few more concessions from the British negotiators. Thornton and Brown stood firm. Again the treaty did not even reach the floor of the Senate; it was turned back by the Committee to which it had been submitted the previous June. Arrangements for proceeding with the fisheries arbitration under the terms of the Washington Treaty were resumed.

The Speech from the Throne was less ambitious than in 1874. Reference was made to the success of the North West Mounted Police, who had wintered in the Territory and were establishing law and order there. Legislation was forecast to re-organize the administration of the vast area. Gratifying progress was reported on the Pacific Railway. The Supreme Court was announced for the fourth time. "Meagre fare", commented the Leader of the Opposition somewhat indifferently.[2] The quality of the dishes made up for the lack of quantity, replied the Premier with matching good humour.

Foremost on everyone's mind was a matter alluded to only vaguely in the Throne Speech: settlement of the Riel affair. Mackenzie was prepared. He placed a motion on the Order Paper calling for an amnesty for "all persons concerned in the North West troubles . . . saving only L. Riel, A. D. Lepine, and W. B. O'Donohue", the latter an American citizen in Riel's entourage who had identified himself with the Fenians in 1872. Riel and Lepine were to receive the amnesty, conditional on five years' banishment from Canada.

The Government leader's speech on the Red River uprising and its subsequent reverberations was a carefully prepared statement designed to provide an honourable solution to an ignoble heritage from the Tory Administration.[3] Without changing his stand that the murder of Thomas Scott was cruel and unnecessary, he argued that the commitments made by Macdonald and Cartier left no alternative but to grant the amnesty, subject to temporary banishment. It was a good speech – so good that the Orangist Mackenzie Bowell labelled it "the malignant ingenuity of a subtle mind".[4] Sir John denied that the record showed the Crown was pledged to an amnesty. Edward Blake followed him with the same sort of detailed review of evidence that had proven so fatal to the Conservative leader during the Pacific scandal debate in 1873. It was just as effective. Mackenzie's motion carried one hundred and twenty-six to fifty, with Sir John in opposition. A few days later Dufferin, acting "according to his independent judgment, and on his own personal responsibility", commuted Lepine's sentence to two years' imprisonment.[5] Riel was again expelled from the House of Commons. "The fact is that in these matters we can be too logical," Carnarvon told the House of Lords.[6] Logic or subterfuge, the Red River crisis was over at last.

The financial situation lent itself less to clever strategy. Even with a harvest of two million dollars from the tax increase,

Cartwright had to announce a deficit of several hundred thousand dollars.[7] This sum would have been doubled if the Premier, ignoring increasing obligations, had not cut the spending of his department to six hundred thousand dollars below the last Conservative budget. The English loan had brought seventeen and one-half million dollars into Canada, but ten had been used to pay the maturing public debt. In the throes of the economic crisis, the Government was keeping expenditures at a minimum until fairer weather appeared on the horizon. The Minister of Finance budgeted for a "reasonable surplus" in 1875-6, provided the rate of revenue was maintained.

In view of the hue and cry in British Columbia, and the "Carnarvon terms", one item was difficult to reduce. Alexander Mackenzie asked for a vote of over six million dollars, one quarter of the total budget, for the Pacific Railway project.[8] The utilization of the water communications was a temporary measure, he assured the House, until a continuous railway could be built. The Government was confident it could keep its obligations to British Columbia as amended, but it would continue to proceed with caution in view of the heavy burden on the Dominion's finances. In two years, he predicted, it would be possible to move from the head of Lake Superior to Winnipeg in four or five days. West of Winnipeg the line was already marked out, and the roadbed to the United States was graded. A decision on the route through the mountains was expected soon. In the east, work was in progress to extend the line to Ottawa and Montreal. Taking advantage of the economic slump in Britain, two and a half million dollars' worth of steel rails had been purchased at a bargain price of fifty-four dollars a ton.

On behalf of the Opposition, Dr. Tupper criticized the expenditures on the branch lines from Manitoba to the United States, and from the Lake Nipissing area to Lake Superior, suggesting they were dictated by political considerations.[9] The available funds, he contended, should be spent in laying an all-rail main line, "with a due regard for economy". The members were not impressed, and the Government's policy was strongly upheld. More serious was the open opposition from Edward Blake. He attacked the "improvident and reckless promise made on behalf of this country of building a line on Vancouver Island", and regretted that the Government, without consulting Parliament, "felt it necessary to yield to the extent to which they did yield to the request of Lord Carnarvon".[10] Albeit "regretfully", the prominent Reformer appeared to be widening the rift with his former colleagues on the one hand, and with the Imperial authorities on the other. In January, he had joined with Goldwin Smith, Thomas Moss, and David Mills in founding a new newspaper in Toronto in direct opposition to the *Globe*, and given it the significant title, *The Liberal*.[11] Some things were not clear. If Blake had views so closely in keeping with those of Goldwin Smith and the members of his new "National Club", and with the Canada First movement, political observers asked, why did he not adopt the *Nation* as his propaganda arm? The paradox was one of the enigmas of Edward Blake.

Discussion of the Pacific Railway did not stop there. In the purchase of the steel rails, the Conservatives thought they had discovered a scandal to tarnish the Liberal escutcheon. It was reported that Charles Mackenzie was associated with a firm that had handled part of the purchase. "With the taint of oil well scandals and silver 'rings' yet about his skirts", sneered the *Toronto Mail*, "the Premier has surely not yielded to the temptation of enriching another relative."[12] Alexander Mackenzie reacted in one of those violent outbursts that inspired Macdonald to treat a milder Scottish Liberal as "Mackenzie and water".[13] He had gone to great lengths to avoid just such accusations. In the case of the steel rails, he had overridden the advice of his engineers that it was more important to get good steel than to accept the lowest tender, and that in a "stiffening market" advertisements by the Canadian Government for such a large purchase would have the effect of forcing the price upward. He had given specific instructions to advertise for tenders, to "relieve us from any charge of favouritism such as would probably be made by simply giving an order."[14]

In Parliament he denied again the charges of collusion with the oil and mining industries, and declared that no relative of his had been employed "in connection with any Government work, or anything approaching a Government work".[15] Since he had been in the Public Works Department he had never even opened a tender for a contract; all were opened by the principal officer of the Department, a Macdonald appointee. The lowest tender was invariably accepted as soon as security was furnished by the contractor; if the latter were unable to do so for some legitimate reason, the officers passed on to the next in line. Mackenzie himself saw the tenders only after the officers had established the list according to price, and the list was adhered to. If any members believed there were grounds for suspicion, they could ask for a committee and could make a full investigation. The outburst of righteous indignation quelled the attackers for the moment.

Three days later the *Mail* was on the offensive again, this time with a charge of "Burpeeism".[16] The Minister of Customs, Isaac Burpee, was accused of selling some Crown lands in New Brunswick to his brother, and the Premier was suspected of having intervened to arrange the sale. Burpee denounced the charge as "false and slanderous", and maintained that the highest price offered for the land had been accepted. With or without foundation, such frequent and repeated charges sowed doubts in the public mind. A bit of the mud was bound to stick if enough was thrown.

Occasionally, the ghosts of Mackenzie's narrow Upper Canadian past returned to haunt him. One such instance was the agitation over the New Brunswick school legislation. By the provincial Act passed in 1871, support of the separate schools from the provincial Treasury was withdrawn, thus removing one of the conditions existing at the time of Confederation. When the matter was raised during the Tory régime, Mackenzie had suggested that London be consulted about the validity of the change. The Imperial Privy Council declared that education was a provincial responsibility, and that there was no case for disallowance. The problem was thrown back into the lap of the new Administration in Ottawa.

In 1875, a New Brunswick member introduced a resolution in the House of Commons to amend the British North America Act, and to restore the rights existing in the first years after Confederation.[17] With the racial and religious split over the Riel affair still a recent memory, Alexander Mackenzie was anxious to avoid dividing the Canadian people once more. However, in his desire to conciliate the large Catholic population, he seemed to contradict his earlier opposition to separate schools, as well as his defence of provincial rights. He believed in the secular system, the Premier admitted candidly when the resolution was brought forward for discussion, and he had fought for that system in the old Parliament. "I hoped to be able – young and inexperienced as I then was – to establish a system to which all would ultimately yield their assent."[18] However, he had found that a large proportion of the population clung to the opposing view, and it had been "impracticable in operation and impossible in political contingencies." As a result, he had supported the entire Confederation project, including the maintenance of separate schools. To attempt to remove a privilege granted at that time, and precipitate wide-spread agitation, was unwise. "If any personal act of mine, if anything I could do would assist to relieve those who believe they are living under a grievance in the Province of New Brunswick," he assured the House of Commons, "that act would be gladly undertaken and zealously performed; but I have no right – the House has no right – to interfere with the legislation of a Province." If the Parliament of Canada were competent to set aside a portion of the British North America Act for such a just cause, it could do it in other instances that might be still more serious. He could only express the view that the majority in New Brunswick would find it in their interest to remove the cause of discontent themselves. Mackenzie concluded his statement with an amendment that a change in the British North America Act would be "fraught with danger to the autonomy of the Provinces".

It was not a solution, but it was a recognition that there are seldom final solutions in politics. Above all, the speech revealed the great progress of the Prime Minister from a narrow parochial politician to a Dominion-wide statesman. His amendment was accepted, and with it another one praying the Queen to use her influence with the Legislature of New Brunswick to remove the grounds for discontent.

The long-awaited Supreme Court Bill was presented by Télesphore Fournier midway through the session. While no mention was made of appeals to the Judicial Committee of the Privy Council in Westminster, the Minister of Justice stated that he himself wished "to see the practice put an end to altogether".[19] Aemilius Irving of Hamilton, a Government supporter, introduced an amendment to abolish the right of appeal "saving any right which Her Majesty may be graciously pleased to exercise by virtue of Her Royal Prerogative". The Government accepted the suggestion.

Until the amendment was introduced, the Bill seemed likely to have an easy passage. When he sensed the strong sympathy among Government supporters for the proposed change, Sir John leaped to the attack, condemning it as a step in the direction of "severance of the Dominion from the Mother Country". Mackenzie replied that recourse to the Privy Council was already restricted to cases involving over four thousand dollars, and practically speaking, to those persons or companies wealthy enough to afford it. As long as the right to petition the Queen was maintained, he argued, there was no severance of relations with Britain.[20] Nevertheless, it was a further step in the direction of Canadian control of Canadian affairs. Had the Blake wing of the Liberal party and the French-speaking element had their way, the appeals to London would have been abolished altogether. Mackenzie was too loyal to the Empire for such a step. Mollified by the Premier's explanation, Macdonald agreed that the head of the Government was as strongly in favour of maintaining the "connection" as anyone in Canada. It was one of the safeguards of the link with Britain, he told the House, to have such an honourable gentleman as Premier of the country.[21] The Bill passed as amended. Lord Dufferin hesitated briefly over the appeal clause, then signed, and it was sped across the Atlantic for Imperial consent.

Alexander Mackenzie continued to give a good deal of attention to the development of the North West. A Commission was established to decide the border between Ontario and Manitoba, with a view to assuring administrative control of the vast uncharted area between the two Provinces. A vigorous policy of signing treaties with the Indians was adopted on the grounds that peaceful agreements, however costly, were still cheaper than an Indian war. The North West Mounted Police continued their work of establishing respect and confidence among the natives, and driving out the American traders. When Colonel French failed to maintain the high standard of discipline and efficiency of the corps, he was replaced by Colonel Macleod. During the 1875 session, Mackenzie introduced a bill to create a separate government for the vast area between Manitoba and British Columbia.[22] Included were provisions for a popular legislature, schools, and a municipal system. Above all, he wanted to ensure an efficient system of justice. In recent years, some one hundred and fifty persons had been killed, and not one assailant brought to trial. Murderers and thieves walked about in broad daylight. With the immediate prospect of large construction crews entering the territory, followed shortly by waves of immigrants, an efficient administration was urgent. It was too important a task for the Lieutenant-Governor of Manitoba to continue to perform as an adjunct to his normal functions.

Reform-minded as he was, Mackenzie refused to be stampeded into action by more impatient Liberals. As in the previous session, David Mills, an intimate friend of Blake, asked for consideration of a change in the manner of choosing Senators.[23] The Premier agreed that the present system of nominating Senators was unsatisfactory, and welcomed a committee study of the problem. The Ministry would not shirk its duty, he promised, if a satisfactory alternative could be devised.

The running battle to control patronage in the Civil Service never ceased. As the depression deepened and work became scarcer, the pressure became almost intolerable. "Friends (?) expect to be benefitted by offices they are unfit for," Mackenzie fumed in a letter to a fellow Liberal, "by contracts they are not entitled to, by advances they have not earned. Enemies ally themselves with friends and push the friends to the front. Some dig trenches at a distance and approach in regular siege form. A weak Minister would ruin the party in a month and the country very soon."[24] He slept on his arms day and night to keep the record of the Government clean. Even such a dear friend as Archibald Young, his comrade in many a political battle, and Hope's father-in-law, left his office empty-handed.[25] Civil servants should keep out of politics, Mackenzie insisted in the House, and politics be kept out of the Civil Service. "When there is a change of administration new ministers are to give every public servant in the Departments their confidence and their support, and no Minister is justified in removing a public servant, especially one who has performed a large amount of service and occupied a high position in the Department unless he is satisfied himself the public interests absolutely demand such a removal . . . I have endeavoured . . . to give every officer, whether I have always agreed with him politically or his mode of management, fair play and nothing more."[26] A more efficient method of selecting good and efficient officers, such as by competitive examination, was being considered. The fight for honesty and efficiency in the Administration would continue.

* * * * *

The session closed on a sour note. In keeping with his acceptance of the Carnarvon terms, Alexander Mackenzie introduced a Bill for the construction of the Esquimalt-Nanaimo railway.[27] Edward Blake opposed it. The legislation passed the House of Commons successfully enough, but ran into difficulties in the Senate. Although the Conservative leader had voted for it in the Commons, the Senate Opposition leader, Alexander Campbell, led a violent attack to block it. With the Upper Chamber heavily loaded in his favour, it was a serious threat. Would the Tory Senators follow their party leader or their Senate leader? Would the Grit Senators follow Mackenzie or Blake? The vote was close. With two Liberal appointees voting with Campbell, the Bill was defeated by two votes. The Pacific Railway crisis was on again.

The party split was obviously serious.[28] Jones and several other influential Liberals had already started a fresh movement to bring the two leading men together again. Blake remained adamant. He had offered to serve under Holton, or to take the lead himself, he told Jones, but Mackenzie had refused.[29] The only alternative he would consider was to leave Parliament altogether. Holton tried in turn. The Toronto lawyer complained that he could not accept the Government's railway policy, and should not have to answer for it. In addition, he felt the Premier was not firm enough with Downing Street. "He may wish to quarrel with the Imperial Government, in which case he will not have his way in my day," Mackenzie muttered to Brown. "I have ascertained that there is overwhelming preponderance of opinion against him in the House."[30]

With several Ministers anxious to have Blake in the Cabinet, negotiations could not stop there. Even though Lord Dufferin was anxious to support him in the struggle for power, Mackenzie decided to take the initiative. He had been hoping, he wrote to Blake, as the session drew to an end, that Jones' proposal to reconstruct the Cabinet with Holton as Minister of Public Works, Blake as a prominent colleague, and himself in a minor post in addition to the Prime Ministership, would be accepted.[31] Before he left Ottawa for the summer, would the Toronto lawyer meet him and discuss the whole matter? The meeting took place the following day, and lasted for three hours. In the end, Blake agreed to return to Toronto and consult his wife and friends. Mackenzie then called in Holton to discuss the Cabinet shuffle. The latter was hesitating again. His daughter had nearly died in childbirth, and was still ill. He asked for more time.[32]

The Premier's patience broke. He was anxious to get away from Ottawa for a few weeks, and had booked passage for himself and Jane to visit England and Scotland during the summer. Everyone and everything seemed bound to frustrate the realization of this precious dream. Whether he and Blake came in or not, Mackenzie told the big Montreal business man, he was putting himself right by giving them every opportunity. If they did not accept, he would "put off my coat and drive the machine myself if it should cost me my life".[33]

Shortly after Blake's arrival in Toronto, the defeat of the Esquimalt-Nanaimo Railway Bill was announced. If the Government accepted the vote as the verdict of Parliament, his principal objection to its policy was removed. What was the policy now regarding the terms of union? he wrote back to Ottawa.[34] The door was still open. Three days later Mackenzie arrived in Toronto to continue the negotiations. The strain and fatigue were beginning to tell; he had to take to his bed in the afternoon with an attack of fever. At six o'clock the following morning he penned a note to Blake before taking the train to keep another series of appointments. "I can only say . . . that I am bound in honour to do what we engaged to do," he wrote after apologizing for not seeing him because of the attack of fever, "unless we can make some other arrangement with the Columbians, and that I am quite willing to try."[35] Blake still

refused to budge. Exasperated, Mackenzie offered hir
Chief Justiceship of the new Supreme Court, and an o
tunity to emulate his father's brilliant judicial career. N
was not prepared to retire from politics either.[36] The negotiations dragged to a halt.

Desperate to settle the matter one way or another, Mackenzie suppressed his pride and wrote a private letter to George Walkem.[37] Cargoes of rails were being shipped to British Columbia, and the surveys for the Island Railway were ordered, he told the British Columbia Premier, but the construction could not be proceeded with in 1875 because of the Senate vote. Although he was still anxious to carry out "the letter and the spirit of the proposals made", the Conservatives had blocked their path. In the circumstances, could Walkem put forward "informally and confidentially . . . any suggestions which may lead to some other arrangement to which the assent of Parliament may be obtained"?

Settlement of the party rift could not wait the several weeks necessary to receive a reply. The Liberals were planning a testimonial dinner for the Prime Minister, and it would be awkward if Blake decided to shun the affair. The talking and correspondence were resumed. By the end of April, a whole month after the first meeting between the two men, Blake had accepted the idea of serving under Mackenzie again.[38] There was a price attached: abandonment of the Carnarvon terms, or at least of the Esquimalt-Nanaimo Railway. He suggested continuing the Pacific Railway project with the general aim in mind of spending two million dollars a year in British Columbia and completing the line by 1890, subject to the condition that taxation should not be increased for that purpose. As compensation for the Island Railway, the Pacific province would receive eight hundred thousand dollars for local public works projects, whether connected with the Railway or not. "Should we fail to get the assent of Columbia to such a plan," Blake concluded, "we can proceed to execute it in good faith, and time will solve the difficulty."

It was a tough decision. Blake was probably right when he argued that public opinion in the largest provinces was on his side. But was that a reason to repudiate the Carnarvon terms, and provoke the wrath of the Imperial authorities? For four days the Premier tortured himself in an attempt to find a solution that would safeguard both the political future and the honour of the Government. Somehow, he had to tame the brilliant but erratic genius of the party and harness him to the Administration. "I come . . . to the general conclusion that we can find a ground of common agreement", he wrote briefly on May 5.[39] Then he stuffed his heavy file on the controversy in his despatch case and hurried down to Montreal for a talk with Luther Holton. Holton was definite. The former President of the Council should be brought back as nearly as possible on his own terms.[40] After all, his conditions were not so very far from the Carnarvon terms, and the stipulation not to increase taxation was already approved by Parliament. He himself would accept a Cabinet post as part of the new arrangement later in the year. The Premier gave in.

The three men met in Ottawa on May 18. Fournier, it was agreed, would be made one of the judges of the new Supreme Court, and Blake would succeed him as Minister of Justice. The Government would try to reach an agreement with British Columbia to pay a cash subsidy instead of building the Vancouver Island Railway, and would spend at least two million dollars a year with a view to completing the main line by 1890, if that were possible without an increase in taxation. If Victoria or London objected, they would carry out these aims regardless.[41]

Lord Dufferin was not in Ottawa to receive the news. After a three-year "exile" from home, he had sailed for Britain a few days earlier. Before he left, he told his First Minister he would not blame him if he took Blake into the Ministry, but hoped the necessity would not arise, as he feared the Torontonian would act the traitor as much inside as out.[42] Mackenzie would have an opportunity of explaining the situation to him and to Lord Carnarvon shortly; there was still time for his own holiday at "home".

The next days were frantically busy. While Jane packed, Alexander Mackenzie plunged into the backlog of work that had piled up while his mind was on the delicate negotiations. Some appointments had to be made. The Lieutenant-Governorship of Ontario was vacant again, and he had an opportunity at last to offer it to George Brown.[43]

During the winter he had tried to obtain a title for the *Globe* publisher as a reward for his services in Washington, but Dufferin and Carnarvon had been reluctant and succeeded in putting him off. His Excellency reminded the Premier of his own slighting remarks about titles at the Huntington banquet in December 1873, and asked for an assurance that Brown would accept such an honour. Mackenzie was not in a position to give the assurance; the matter had to be postponed. The Lieutenant-Governorship was a prize that he could offer without consultation with London. Though flattered by the offer, the great newspaperman declined. He had authority and prestige enough to satisfy his vanity, and the position would only restrict his independence. Seated at his editorial desk and scribbling furiously with a stubby pencil, or speaking in the red and gold Senate Chamber, he wielded more power than as a representative of the Crown.

The Premier was not disappointed; he had no desire to lose the active support of his dear friend, though gratitude for past services had compelled him to make the offer. He also considered Archibald McKellar, but the star of his old fellow-campaigner appeared to be waning.[44] His career as a provincial Minister had not been a success, and Mowat was anxious to replace him by a man less vulnerable to opposition attack. With regret, Mackenzie concluded that he had neither the prestige nor the qualifications for the Lieutenant-Governorship. There was a third possibility. If Blake was to enter the Cabinet, some Minister from Ontario must leave. Cartwright was indispensable; Scott was in the Senate. That left only Donald Macdonald, the Postmaster General. He accepted.*

During the same busy week, Mackenzie succeeded, despite Carnarvon's resistance, in having a Canadian named as the British representative on the three-man Fisheries Commission that was to decide the compensation by the United States under the Washington Treaty. His choice fell on Alexander Galt, the former Minister of Finance who had bolted the Conservative Government because of a disagreement with Sir John.[45] Galt was an experienced negotiator, and agreed to serve. "I have arranged everything as far as possible," the Premier wrote hurriedly to Blake on May 20, ". . . I will probably write you from Montreal or Quebec. Meantime I wish you goodbye."[46] His dream was coming true. He was to see the heather-clad hills of Scotland again, and to show Jane the land of his birth.

* * * * *

The thirty years had brought many changes. Instead of the motley collection of reading material he had brought on board in 1842, the former immigrant's baggage bulged with documents on subjects he wanted to discuss in London. There were other differences as well. He no longer needed to seek out a quiet corner on deck to do his reading; and his place at meal times was at the Captain's table rather than in the immigrants' galley. The weather smiled on them; except for a brief scare in

*Blake was made Minister of Justice. Fournier accepted the Postmaster Generalship until the Supreme Court was created.

the iceberg area off Newfoundland, they made the crossing without incident.

High on his list of matters to be discussed with Lord Carnarvon and the other Imperial Ministers was the awarding of titles to Canadians. While he was personally indifferent to them, Mackenzie recognized their importance within the Imperial structure, including the self-governing Dominion. In particular, the refusal of his recommendation of George Brown still rankled. In his view, Brown was not only the most loyal of British subjects, but the man most deserving to be considered as the founding father of Confederation. Lord Dufferin, who met Mackenzie in London, suggested that in the absence of an established aristocracy, some men of letters and science should be considered. That might well be, countered the Canadian Premier, but first of all Brown's case had to be dealt with.[47] Lord Carnarvon agreed to consider the matter further.

The British law officers were worried about the Irving amendment to the Supreme Court Act concerning appeals to the Privy Council. The Lord Chancellor felt it was a threat to the Imperial connection, and was considering disallowance. Although a mere layman in matters of law, Mackenzie plunged into the discussions, protesting the loyalty of Canada and Canadians to the Empire, and denying any desire to sever the links with the Mother Country. This loyalty did not prevent him from remarking that the Dominion had lawyers as able as those in England, and that they were perfectly satisfied with the legislation.[48] He did not drop the subject until he had extracted an understanding that the Act would be allowed to stand, and that any changes the Imperial law officers felt to be essential could be made after it was in force.[49]

One of the principal objectives of Alexander Mackenzie's trip was to negotiate the purchase of the remaining Hudson's Bay Company lands in the North West. The first wave of the Mennonite settlers that he had arranged to bring from Russia had arrived, and a brisk campaign was afoot in rural Britain to bring out experienced farmers. To assure orderly colonization, he wanted all the land to be in the hands of the new North West Territories Government. Like Brown before him, he objected to a large commercial company controlling such a large proportion of the soil on which Canada's future depended. Donald Smith had broached the subject to the Right Honourable George Goschen, Chairman of the Executive Committee of the Hudson's Bay Company, but the latter had refused to indicate the price he considered reasonable and just. On his arrival in London, the Canadian Premier tried again.[50] Both he and Goschen proved to be canny traders. It was only after several interviews that the Hudson's Bay Company official threw out the figure of six hundred thousand pounds as a trial balloon, this sum not to include the land around the posts, or compensation for damage during the Red River uprising. Mackenzie immediately wired Ottawa to ask if his colleagues would consider paying five hundred and fifty thousand.

The telegram arrived at the worst possible moment.[51] The financial crisis was entering a critical phase. Two important banks had just failed, and more were on the verge of closing their doors. The lumber industry was at a complete standstill, and the farmers still weeks away from their harvest. Cartwright had moved to Montreal to supervise the situation, and to help the banks keep in business by loans of bonds if the need arose. He advised the Premier strongly to avoid making any further financial committments.

It was an awkward situation. Goschen had called a meeting of his Committee to discuss the Canadian counter-proposal. On Dominion Day, Mackenzie shut himself up in his room in the Westminster Hotel, and drafted a letter to the Company.[52] It, too, would benefit from the progress being planned in the North West, he argued. If it did not sell, friction between the settlers and such a large corporate owner was certain to arise. The Dominion Government would ask Parliament to exchange five hundred and fifty thousand pounds of its four per cent bonds for all the land, exclusive of the property in the town of Winnipeg and a reasonable acreage around each trading post. The Red River claims would be cancelled. Surely, he told himself, the Minister of Finance could manage such an excellent bargain.

The news from Canada continued to be bad. Another bank had closed, and the decline in revenues appeared likely to continue. A shipment of rails had arrived, and there was no money to pay for them. In London, the Premier had made another disagreeable discovery. The agents for the loan raised in the previous year had purchased one million pounds of the three and a half million pound loan themselves, and the Bank of Montreal had taken half a million, to encourage other investors to buy. The bonds would have to be re-sold. Alexander Mackenzie was shocked. "It will injure Cartwright very much and the Government as a whole," he wrote to Blake. "The truth must be told, however. I have no faith in pretention of any sort."[53]

In general, the talks with the members of the Imperial Government were satisfactory. He discussed the proposed fishery negotiations with Prime Minister Disraeli, Foreign Minister Derby, and Lord Carnarvon. "I told them frankly we were all but ruined from first to last by English diplomacy and treaty making and we would have no more of it at any price," he reported back to Blake. Disraeli agreed that the Washington Treaty was "the most abominable thing in our history", and was quite happy to let the Canadian Commissioner take charge of the fishery question.[54] The Imperial Ministers showed sympathetic understanding of the Esquimalt-Nanaimo Railway predicament, and Lord Dufferin confirmed that the Government had shown good faith until the adverse vote in the Senate blocked their course.[55] Notwithstanding the general courtesy and friendliness, the Canadian found disappointingly little of the fiery Imperialism that burned in his own breast. Affairs outside of the British Isles appeared to be of little interest to the British people. "I have listened a lot," he told Dufferin after a fortnight of discussions, "and I conclude that Canada is more British than Britain."[56]

The stratification of British society was in direct contradiction to his democratic views, and strengthened his inclination to oppose the general practice of awarding titles in the Dominion. The dukes were social tyrants, he reported, and the knights mostly flunkies. At a luncheon in Windsor Castle, a Duchess complained to him that it was "a very trying thing now to deal with society. There are so many people forced upon you whom you don't want to see, people who have no position."[57] The ex-stonemason did not enlighten her on his antecedents. He was shocked at the opportunity open to demagogues to exploit the abusive class system. "My opinion (is) that there will be a conflict of some kind ere long between two extremes of society," he forecast in a letter to Canada.[58] Unbeknownst to him, Karl Marx was in the same city, hard at work on *Das Kapital*.

After a formal visit to the Queen and the Prime Minister, the Mackenzies left the Imperial capital for a brief respite in Paris. "I . . . don't intend to leave my address behind me," he wrote to Jones in Halifax,[59] "letters and telegrams can go to the D—l or further." It was their first visit outside of the English-speaking world, and they felt strange and awed in foreign surroundings. As a builder, Mackenzie was particularly interested in the different styles of architecture; as a politician, he paid a visit to the National Assembly in Versailles and observed a debate. As a statesman, he spent a large part of his time in a hotel room answering the correspondence that pursued him in spite of his attempts to elude it.

The visit to Scotland, which was to be the holiday portion of the summer trip, was becoming filled rapidly with engagements. Every town and village where he had lived wanted to fête the returning hero; hopes of a quiet rest among his old surroundings began to fade. Back in London on the way north, Mackenzie worked frantically to finish the official business before the precious days all slipped away. His schedule was so tight that he had no time to prepare a speech for a dinner in his honour, and barely managed to scribble a few notes on a piece of paper during the meal. Speaking from the heart, he delivered a message of loyalty to Crown and Empire, of confidence in the future of Canada "within her own separate and individual orbit", but within the Imperial framework.[60] The age of hostility between citizens of the United States and Canada was over, he assured his audience, and the two English-speaking peoples would continue to build side by side in peace and friendship. To Englishmen beginning to stir themselves out of a deep scepticism of the Empire's future, the words of the Canadian Prime Minister were heartening. Lord Dufferin and Lord Carnarvon were pleased.

The speeches in Scotland contained the same mixture of emerging Canadian nationalism and devotion to the Empire.[61] In Mackenzie's mind there was no contradiction between the two sentiments; each enhanced rather than detracted from the other. One day, "perhaps not in my lifetime but in the life of my immediate successors", he told the burghers of Dundee, Canada would surpass England not only in territory but in population and in political grandeur.[62] Then Canada would be able to do her share in the work of "evangelization – speaking both in a Christian and commercial sense – for, sir, it is the mission of the Anglo-Saxon race to carry the power of Anglo-Saxon civilization over every country in the world." At times the strains of Canadian nationalism sounded even stronger than the Imperial fervour. In addition to transplanting British freedom, the Dominion had a "spirit of toleration of class to class, and creed to creed", an equality between citizens which made it difficult to accept the social system in the Mother Country. In Canada, there existed neither established church, nor differences of class, nor other artificial barriers. The province of Ontario, where he lived, had a vast system of public education, and a university in Toronto that made available to Canadians "of every creed or class or circumstance" the highest possible education at the smallest price that could be named anywhere in the world.

In addition to freedom and equality, Canada was a land of opportunity. She had coal fields as large as the entire British Isles, other resources of nearly every description, and she would soon have a railway that would put her in direct contact with the markets of the Far East. It was a land where men worked hard for what they received. He, too, had felled trees and braved the harsh winters in early years. He had not found exactly what he had expected when he left Scotland, but what he had found made him decide to make it his permanent home. Above all, Canada afforded him an opportunity to live according to his personal convictions. "I have always held those political opinions which point to the universal brotherhood of man, no matter in what rank of life he may have taken his origin," Alexander Mackenzie told a group of workers in Dundee.[63] "I have believed, sir, and I now believe, in the extinction of all class legislation, and of all legislation that tends to promote any body of men or any class of men from the mere fact of their belonging to a class of higher position . . . in the community. . . . In our great colonies . . . we take the ground simply and completely that every man stands equal in the eye of the law, and every man has the same opportunity by exercise of the talent with which God has blessed him to rise in the world, in the confidence of his fellow-citizens, the one quite as much as the other." It was a simple but noble statement of Liberal faith. It explained in a few words his sympathy for the Chartists as a lad, his search for a new life in Canada, his struggle against the Family Compact, and against the coalitions and combinations of all kinds that tended to perpetuate privilege and caste. It was the basis of his life.

The presentations and ovations were almost overwhelming. On the train from Dundee to Perth, Mackenzie sought out an empty compartment in order to enjoy a few precious minutes of solitude. In vain. He was soon joined by a bustling, middle-aged lady who eyed him from head to foot and tried to engage him in conversation.[64] Was he a Colonial? Yes, he was. From Canada? Aye. Did he know there was to be a great celebration for the Canadian Prime Minister in Perth that day? He knew that as well. Had he ever met Mr. Mackenzie? Oh! yes, he had seen him. What was he really like? "Is he a grand-looking man, and does he deserve all the flattering reputation which the Scottish newspapers give him for ability and stern integrity in all he does?" "I have always had my doubts about that," came the straightforward reply. The arrival in Perth halted the interrogation. Alexander Mackenzie helped the lady to alight, and moved toward the welcoming committee awaiting him.

After receiving the freedom of Dundee and Perth, the Canadian Premier moved up the valley to Dunkeld, his last home in Scotland. George Brown, also holidaying in the Highlands, was on hand to witness the triumphant return of the former Perthshire youth. A classmate who had shared the hard benches and stern discipline of the old school at Moulin seconded the address of welcome. The next day, a ceremony was held in a huge tent erected in a meadow near the house in Logierait where he had been born. The sturdy two-storey structure erected by his father's own hands was bedecked with flags. Looking around him, Mackenzie could see the familiar scenes of his youth: the wee village bracketed by the Tay and Tummel rivers, the church and churchyard where his father and grandparents were buried along with many other relatives, the fields where he had tilled the soil and herded the flocks, the Pass of Killiekrankie, and the peaks that faded into the distance. He was home at last. And yet, was it truly home, or just a place from which he had begun his travels? He would never forget his birthplace, he told the audience with emotion, but the years had changed his allegiance. He was still a loyal Scot, but Canada would continue to claim his "first attention".[65]

The real holidays arrived in late July. For ten days, the Mackenzies rested in Pitlochry, wandered about the area, and visited friends of the Premier's youth. Invitations continued to arrive in alarming numbers; all but two were refused. He agreed to return to Irvine where he had met Helen, and to speak in Greenock from where he had sailed in 1842.

The Scottish climate worked its renowned restorative wonders. The Canadian Tories would have smiled to hear the Grit leader tell an audience near Sir John's birthplace that "one can only hold the position of Prime Minister of Canada so long as the national interests are fairly administered, as I have no doubt they will always be, whatever political party is in power."[66] Such political magnanimity was scarcely Canadian!

Having begun the discussions to sell the Hudson's Bay Company lands, Sir George Goschen was pressing for an agreement. However, the news from Canada was still unfavourable, and on July 23, Richard Scott wrote that the Cabinet felt the purchase would not be popular and should be postponed.[67] Mackenzie disagreed; he was still anxious to complete the deal if a real bargain could be arranged. Back in London, he decided to have one more try.[68] Half a million pounds cash or five hundred and fifty thousand in bonds, subject to approval in Canada, he offered the day before their ship was due to sail for Quebec. Goschen accepted "subject to minor modifications".[69] There was still time! Torn between his desire to accomplish a diplomatic coup, and his uneasiness over the reaction in Ottawa, Alexander Mackenzie waited nervously in his hotel while the Company officials drew up the proposal in formal terms. Disappointment again! The draft contained sections to which he could not agree.[70] Packing it in his travelling case, he resigned himself to continuing the negotiations by mail after he had consulted his colleagues, and sailed.

CHAPTER 14

Hold the Line

He returned to Canada determined to develop Canada's character of "manly independence", Alexander Mackenzie told the crowd that welcomed him at the Ottawa railway station, and to administer her affairs in a manner becoming a great people which formed such an important part of the British Confederation.[1] He could see no contradiction between that spirit and a loyal attachment to the Empire, and he was gratified to find that the scepticism in Britain about the future of the connection had practically disappeared.

There was a huge pile of work waiting in the West Block office. Most urgent of all was the financial situation. Instead of a small surplus, Canada was heading for a deficit of two or three million dollars. Cartwright had made excuses not to pay British Columbia a two hundred and fifty thousand dollar instalment on a grant to the Province for public works projects. It was evident that he was in league with Blake in trying to force the Province to relinquish the Esquimalt-Nanaimo project.[2]

A quick glance at the public accounts was enough to convince the Premier that the Finance Minister would have to return to London for another loan. The Government would have to tighten its belt still further; the cries of anguish from the Reform politicians would increase, but would have to be resisted. Spending for recovery was still an unknown economic theory; the word went out to hold the line. Even the project so dear to Mackenzie's heart for the purchase of the Hudson's Bay Company lands would have to be postponed.

The Fisheries arbitration had not yet begun because London and Washington could not agree on the third member of the Commission. The head of the Canadian Government suggested that perhaps the time had come to have recourse to the provision in the Washington Treaty empowering the Austrian

Lord Dufferin in fancy dress

Wilfrid Laurier

Ambassador to the United States to make the appointment in case of disagreement. Another arbitration was no further advanced – Ontario's western border was still undefined. Mackenzie and Mowat agreed to ask Sir Edward Thornton to serve as the third member of that Commission along with two Canadian judges. But before the sittings began, he intended to obtain general agreement with the Ontario Premier on the line the border should follow.

As Minister of Justice Blake was ready with the appointments to the Supreme Court. Since Dorion preferred to stay in Quebec, Chief Justice Richards of Ontario was to become the first head of the highest court of appeal in the Dominion. The swearing-in ceremony was prepared when a telegram arrived from Lord Carnarvon, asking for an official legal opinion on the controversial appeal clause. Certain that he had laid all doubts at rest before he left London, Mackenzie was annoyed. The Minister of Justice reacted still more violently, and threatened to resign if the Act were disallowed.[3] Lord Dufferin was still in England and could not be consulted; the Administrator, General O'Haly was in Saint John. Ignoring the established procedure of sending messages through the Queen's representative, the Premier wired back that delay was impossible as the Order in Council was passed and all arrangements had been made. "Administrator in New Brunswick . . .", the message concluded, "I earnestly ask message to be sent him if not already sent."[4] The Minister of Colonies gave way. Any changes in the Act could be made later without invalidating it, he conceded.[5] Lord Dufferin returned just in time to preside at the inaugural banquet on October 8.

Still full of energy, Alexander Mackenzie dashed down to Toronto to attend the wedding of the daughter of the new Lieutenant-Governor of Ontario, took time to advise Brown on the construction of his palatial new residence on the outskirts of the Queen City, and popped in at Kingston to examine the progress on the new military college. "Do you know the thickness of this wall?" he asked one of the soldiers as they passed a martello tower. "No, sir," came the embarrassed reply. "I do, it is five feet ten inches," said Mackenzie with obvious satisfaction. "I built it myself."[6]

The work of administration was simple and straightforward enough; it was the continual petty annoyances that bothered the Government leader. The Maritimers were still pursuing their campaign to remove Brydges from his railway post. Quebec Liberals were annoyed because one of the judges of the new Supreme Court was a former political opponent. The requests for favours increased as the hard times reduced Mackenzie's ability to satisfy them. The effects of the summer were rapidly dissipated, and the old bluntness returned. One manufacturer reinforced his plea for a railway branch line with a reference to his previous support of the Liberal party. Until that moment, Mackenzie had listened with careful attention. At the suggestion of political considerations, the business man reported later, "the Premier of Canada stood up, and placing his hands behind his back said, 'Sir, the Government declines to entertain your proposition', and without another word turned his back upon me and left the room."[7] On the other hand, he replied to a friend enquiring about reduced railway fares for church ministers, that special rates could not be made available but that he would gladly pay the fare in question out of his own pocket.

Mackenzie's ironic sense of humour did not leave him entirely. The West Block was still only partially built, and it was his responsibility as Minister of Public Works to complete it. When he drew up the plans, he placed his office under the tower that was to be erected on the western side. As a builder, he knew that a corner of the rectangular tower could be constructed to accommodate a circular staircase leading to the exterior. Without passing through the ante-chamber filled with eager supplicants for office and favours, he could escape down such a stairway and be home in less than five minutes, leaving his tormentors to wait in vain. He approved the specifications in pleased anticipation.

Despite the Prime Minister's constant efforts to maintain the reputation of the Liberal régime for honesty and integrity, the Opposition's insinuations and accusations continued. On September 24, the Conservative weekly, the *West Durham News*, published extracts from a private and confidential letter written just before the 1872 election by George Brown to Senator John Simpson, head of the Ontario Bank.[8] In it Brown complained that the Liberals were having a hard struggle against the "enormous sums" of the Tory candidates, and had expended their campaign funds. "A big push has to be made on Saturday and Monday . . . if we are not to succumb to the cash of the Government . . . there are but half a dozen people who can come down handsomely and we have done all we possibly can do and we have to ask a few outsiders to help us. Will you be one?" The letter certainly appeared to compromise the Grits. Moreover, trumpeted the *News*, proof existed that the Liberals spent during the 1872 campaign "more than twice the amount of what Sir John took from Sir Hugh", and that Mackenzie had a one-million-dollar fund for the 1874 campaign.

It was a thrust at the very vitals of the Mackenzie Administration. The Premier had campaigned throughout his entire public life for public purity; he had been elected to office by a people filled with shocked disgust at the misdemeanours of his predecessor. If the charges were proven, his career would be destroyed in a single blow. The accusations were made on Friday; the *Globe* carried Brown's reply the following Monday.[9] Though neither he nor Simpson had any such letter in their possession, he had "some recollection of writing some such letter about the time mentioned to three, or possibly four, political friends". There had been a Liberal election fund, Brown admitted, but it had been used for "legal and proper expenses" and "the entire amount so raised and so expended was $3,700 – or the trumpery sum of $45. to each of the 82 constituencies, had they all participated in it". There had been no other fund to his knowledge, and had there been, he thought he would have known of it.

It was a satisfactory explanation to those who wished to accept one; to political opponents it disproved nothing. Two days later, the *Mail* added fuel to the fire by publishing a letter from Senator Simpson, soliciting support in the 1874 campaign.[10] The Senator asked his friends to support the Liberal Government in order to redeem the name of the Dominion, and because the men in charge were his "personal and esteemed friends". That was proper enough, but more followed. He would be able, through them, he stated, "to get justice for our party in appointments and otherwise", and "our bank and other Ontario banks (and through them the country) will have the use of the Government surplus until required." The *Official Gazette* showed that the new Finance Minister had some one hundred and eighty thousand dollars on deposit with the Ontario Bank at that time. By January 1875, the sum had risen to over a million.

What did it mean? Were the Grits as bad as the Tories? people asked, and were the Premier's stern features a mere mask to hide another series of raids on the public purse? Whatever explanations were offered, some doubts remained. As the housemaid explained lamely to her mistress when she found herself in difficulties, the Liberals could only protest that theirs was just a small baby compared to the other one. The Conservatives began to stir throughout the Dominion.

In Quebec, too, the Liberals were in an embarrassing posture. Many of them were members of the Institut Canadien at Montreal, an intellectual society nourished by liberal ideas from France.[11] Outraged at their criticism of clerical domination in the province, the Ultramontane Bishop Bourget had excommunicated all members of the Institut who refused to resign. One who would not submit was a certain Joseph Guibord. Shortly afterwards, Guibord fell mortally ill, and despite a deathbed plea, he was refused absolution. Under the circumstances, he could not be buried in a Catholic cemetery.

Several of the more fiery members of the Institut sprang to his defence and the Guibord case became a *cause célèbre*, not only in the courts, but in the struggle between Rouges and Bleus, as Liberals and Conservatives were popularly called in Quebec. After five years of legal procedures, the Imperial Privy Council handed down a decision ordering burial on Catholic ground. In late 1875, the jubilant friends of Guibord arranged a huge funeral procession from the Protestant cemetery, where the remains had been kept in the interim, to a Catholic burial site. They found the entrance blocked by a large and decidedly hostile crowd. Bitter and disappointed, the mourners had no alternative but to return with their charge. The municipal and provincial authorities having refused to intervene, they appealed to the Dominion Government. Incensed by such defiance of the law, Dufferin raged that it was time for a firm hand, and that the incident proved the necessity for an efficient national police force in Canada along the lines of the Irish Constabulary. In vain, Blake and Mackenzie protested that the municipal authorities were responsible for law and order, and that Ottawa had the right to call out troops only if there was a real danger of war, invasion, or insurrection.[12] If deaths occurred, they would be liable to prosecution for murder. The Governor General retorted that it was no time to argue over jurisdictions.[13] His advisers stood firm. In addition to the legal aspects of the question, they argued, the despatch of troops would be political suicide in French Canada, and would turn Quebec sentiment against the Crown. On the other hand, the fact remained that as long as the Guibord affair continued, the Conservatives had a wedge to drive between the Catholics and the Liberal Administration.

In October, Alexander Mackenzie escaped from the capital long enough to make a brief visit to Sarnia. Having climbed from the very bottom of the political ladder, he realized the importance of solid constituency support, and knew that the political graveyard is filled with brilliant careers cut short because men became too busy with the affairs of State to attend to the affairs of individual voters. Lambton had hardly seen its member since he took charge of the Dominion's affairs two years before; it was time to report and ensure its support again.

In a sense, the trip to Sarnia marked a new beginning. Two

years earlier, as a novice Premier, he had outlined the goals of his Administration. Most of these, he told the familiar faces in the Court House, had been accomplished.[14] Canada had her new election laws, her Supreme Court, her Military College, her North West Territories Government, and her North West Mounted Police. The Riel case had been settled in a way satisfactory to all who really had the interests of the country at heart. The Administration was being run honestly, Canada had asserted her rights to manage her own affairs, and the Grit policies of free trade and expanded immigration were in force. Not all the Government's projects had been brought to completion but "not one . . . has been left to rust or die out", and any mistakes had been "honestly taken". The time had come to restate Liberal principles and to set new goals.

Of all the achievements, Alexander Mackenzie was most proud of Canada's growing stature in the world. Never again, he told his neighbours, would any British statesman think of interfering in treaty negotiations where Canada's interests alone were concerned. Canada had "passed the bounds of an ordinary Colony of Great Britain, we have assumed the proportions of a nation". Her policy would be to do her own work in the international as well as in the national field, "but to be the foremost, and I hope the strongest Colonial ally that Great Britain can possibly have".

As in the United States, there were domestic problems of real moment to be faced. The hard times had led to cries of protection from Canadian manufacturers. It was a nefarious system, he warned, "which simply means . . . some other portion of the community will pay for protecting the particular manufacturers against all comers from the outside". Neither absolute free trade nor absolute protection were applicable in Canada, though he would inaugurate the former if the circumstances permitted as "a free inter-exchange of thought, information, and commodities is the true means of enriching a country or making a country great, while the system of protection as it exists in the United States is altogether evil". The economic crisis was caused by over-production, and tariff barriers would not remove the stagnation in trade or lower the prices in order to set the economy in motion again. To speak of protection of agricultural products, which Canada exported rather than imported, was more ridiculous still.

Another major problem was the railway to the Pacific. The Government desired an all-Canadian route as rapidly as possible in order to open up and populate the fertile plains of the West, Mackenzie argued. But "it would be the height of madness to emperil our credit in the English market and increase the taxation of this country, and make it dear for the emigrant to come to or the workman to live in". If the 1890 Pacific Railway deadline could be met, it would be done, but at least there would be a transportation system as far as the Rockies by that time. As in other fields, the policy adopted would be cautious and responsible.

Though he made but a passing reference to it in his address, a recent incident rankled the righteous Scot deeply. William McDougall, who had resumed his alliance with Sir John, was reported as stating at a public meeting that "there is a ring in Sarnia more scandalous than Sir Hugh Allan's railway affair".[15] The real purchasers of the large quantity of rails for the Pacific Railway, he claimed, were the Premier's brothers, who had made sixty thousand dollars on the transaction. The big transaction had been made, not to take advantage of a bargain price, but to enable them to make the huge profit.

The accusation aroused Alexander Mackenzie's sensitivities for several reasons. He resented the fact that his political career had exposed his brothers to such continual slander. Rather than assist them, his participation in public affairs had prevented them from taking advantage of any number of profitable business opportunities from fear of just such accusations of corruption. Coming from someone who knew him and his family so well, the charges were still harder to bear. It was a delicate subject for the Premier for another reason: an error of judgment had been committed in the steel rail purchase. Though most of the rails were not likely to be needed for a year or two, the engineers had urged that the bargain price was the least they could ever expect to pay.[16] In fact, prices continued to fall, and much cheaper rates could have been obtained. Then, too, it was a fact that one of his brothers, Charles, had been associated with the firm, Cooper, Fairman and Company of Montreal, which had arranged part of the purchase. However, fearing just the sort of accusation that had been made, Charles had resigned shortly after the decision to tender was taken. His resignation was submitted in December 1874. The first Directors' meeting at which it could be accepted was held in the spring of 1875. In between, the contracts were awarded.

While in Sarnia, Alexander Mackenzie sat down with his brother Charles and prepared a formal statement to be printed in the *Globe*.[17] The charge was a "deliberate falsehood", it began. The steel rails were obtained by open competition, the lowest tenders being accepted in all cases. "No brother or relation of mine has any interest, direct or indirect, near or remote, in any of these contracts, or ever received, or has any claim to a cent of profit from any of these contracts or ever received or has any claim to a cent of profit from one or any of them." Categorical as it was, nothing could deter the Conservatives from exploiting the situation. Using it, Brown's "big push" letter, and the protection cry, they succeeded in carrying the by-election in Toronto West that had been made necessary by the appointment of Thomas Moss to the Bench a short time before. The tide was beginning to turn.

* * * * *

The problems seemed to grow constantly in size and quantity. Both the Grand Trunk and Great Western Railways were in serious financial condition, and their Directors wanted the Government to take them over.[18] With the Intercolonial running a heavy deficit – as he had predicted when the route was chosen – Mackenzie had only one desire: to turn over all publicly-owned lines to private enterprise as soon as possible. To add to his worries, a Cabinet shuffle was becoming essential again. Félix Geoffrion, whom he had hoped to make a veritable successor of Dorion, was ill with a brain ailment, and completely incapacitated. With Fournier gone, Letellier was the only active French-speaking member in the Administration. The Quebec members were arguing bitterly about a suitable successor. In addition, Manitoba was calling for emergency assistance in the face of drought and a grasshopper plague, and British Columbia's Premier was still maintaining a stubborn silence with regard to Ottawa's request for suggestions of a new compromise on the Pacific Railway.

The constant strain of heavy work, the Railway, Tory attacks, and the frustrations of being unable to find solutions to so many problems, were beginning to take their toll. By late 1875, the store of good humour and health that Mackenzie had built up while in Britain had vanished. The attacks of the old stomach ailment were becoming more severe; each one left him weaker and more dispirited than the last. Desperate to find some way of stopping the sickening pain and the sapping of his physical resources, he rushed to New York in October for expert medical advice. "Poor Mack," Brown commented sympathetically from the comfort and luxury of his seat on the political side-lines,[19] "I fear the world is going very sadly with him. . . . He is a good fellow." The American doctors had no solution either. It was part of the price of maintaining such a ruthless pace. Mackenzie set his chin more firmly and went on.

Ignoring his personal welfare, the Premier went directly from New York to the Maritimes. In Saint John, he spoke at a banquet with J. G. Blaine, a former Speaker of the United States House of Representatives.[20] Canada's neighbours had a great destiny before them, Mackenzie told the other guests meaningfully, but it was not in the form of territorial expansion. Their aim should be to work with the British Empire in spreading civilization throughout the world. "If I have an ambition," the ex-stonemason declared in an outburst of crusading fervour, "it has been to have my country play a part in the liberation of nations from the fetters which ignorance and bad government have imposed upon them; and while desirous always to see peace on earth and good-will towards men prevail, I know that these blessings can sometimes only be maintained at the cannon's mouth."

The Maritimes tour went well. Instead of the parsimonious, narrow-minded Scot many expected, the Premier proved himself to be a congenial and understanding person, as well as an inspired leader. Liberal hopes rose as he moved from centre to centre. On the return trip, he agreed to stop in Rimouski and make his first address to a completely French-speaking audience.[21] Encouraged by the enthusiastic reception accorded him, he was in fine form, and extolled the accomplishments of the great French Canadians of the past. He himself had served gladly under one, he said, and the time might well come when another would be his leader. The open-mindedness of the Quebec people was illustrated by the fact that Robert Baldwin had been given a seat in Rimouski when defeated in Upper Canada, and the first Jew to sit in a legislature within the Empire had represented a constituency in Lower Canada. Time and reason, he hoped, would cause the "feeling of liberality . . . to expand and extend, so that the narrow prejudices of class and creed may be made to fall back before the liberal views, thoughts and aspirations which must ever guide and direct the councils of a great and enlightened people." Alexander Mackenzie had come a long way from the days when he wrote violent "anti-popery" and "rep by pop" diatribes in the *Lambton Shield.*

In Quebec City, the Premier stopped for consultations about the Cabinet vacancy. His personal choice was Henri Joly, Leader of the Opposition in the provincial Legislature, but he recognized, as did Joly himself, that a Catholic was required.[22] A second possibility was Joseph Cauchon, still waiting on the sidelines to be rewarded for abandoning Sir John. Despite his chequered and rather questionable past, the ebullient little newspaperman had two arguments in his favour.[23] First, he was from Quebec City, and the new Minister was to represent that area. More important still, he boasted excellent relations with the clergy. With the Guibord affair still unsettled, and Macdonald's former lieutenant, Hector Langevin, brother of one of the Bishops, a candidate in the Charlevoix by-election, it was a factor that could not be ignored.

The third possible Cabinet Minister was Wilfrid Laurier. It was generally assumed that the gracious and reasonable young lawyer was Cabinet material. Unfortunately, he, too, had certain drawbacks. He was not from the Quebec City area, and even if he were, many of his fellow-members from Quebec resented his rapid ascendancy to public prominence. He was also closely identified in the public mind with the radical liberalism that the Bishops denounced.

Joly recommended Laurier without hesitation. Brown warned against Cauchon; and, though he had not met him, favoured "the young vigorous, popular and eloquent man of the present moment – Laurier, I think is his name."[24] A fresh new name was more in keeping with the spirit of the Government, the *Globe* publisher pointed out, and he had no antecedents to fetter his action. "Laurier is a rising young fellow," Holton agreed, but Cauchon had more "Parliamentary vigour and experience".[25]

On balance, more French-speaking members seemed to prefer the older man. Two other arguments carried weight with the Premier. A friend in the Catholic court was needed desperately, and by accepting Cauchon's services during the Pacific crisis and since, a promotion had been clearly implied if not actually expressed. In addition, Laurier could be brought in later if Geoffrion resigned and a new Minister had to be appointed from the Montreal area. After weeks of hesitation, the Premier invited the veteran newspaperman to Ottawa, listened carefully to his explanations of the accusations against him, and finally offered him the Presidency of the Council. "I have no doubt (he) will justify the appointment," Mackenzie wrote to Archibald Young with a note of forced optimism.[26]

The English Cabinet seat for Quebec still caused concern. During the summer Holton had tried, at Cartwright's instigation, to persuade Sir Alexander Galt to run against the Conservative candidate in the Montreal West by-election.[27] Had he done so and been victorious, it would have been logical to offer him the Cabinet post. He had declined, however. On returning to Canada, Mackenzie acceded to Huntington's request for a department to administer, and transferred him from the Presidency of the Council to the Postmaster Generalship. In the meantime, Holton's reluctance to accept office was decreasing.[28]

His daughter had died in October, and he assumed that his appointment to replace Huntington was a matter of course. But the author of the Pacific scandal was enjoying his new functions and had no desire to leave. Within the Cabinet, the ardour of Blake and Cartwright for Holton had cooled, and they were happy with the status quo. The burly Montrealer had waited too long. When balked, he, too, proved to be hyper-sensitive. In a flurry of rage, he accused the Premier and half of the Cabinet of plotting against him. With peace only recently restored between Liberal factions in Ontario, the same unhappy divisions were beginning to appear in Quebec.

The stirring in the Tory ranks was a call to battle for Alexander Mackenzie. Casting aside his usual reluctance to participate in by-elections, he accepted an invitation to address a banquet in Montreal in support of Thomas Workman, the Liberal standard-bearer. It was a fighting speech.[29] The Conservative utterances, he declared, reminded him of a poem:

> "The Prince of Cambays' daily food
> Is asp and basilisk and toad;
> Which gives to him so strong a breath,
> He nightly stinks a queen to death."

He lashed out at his opponents for their personal attacks on himself, Blake, Dorion, and other leading Liberals. If such were the tactics of gentlemen, as they purported to be, then thank God he was not one! The Tories had accused him of everything, including bringing into Canada the Colorado potato bug. Well, he was still convinced that the people preferred the bug to Sir John. The terms of union with British Columbia, the route of the Intercolonial, the New Brunswick school question, the steel rails accusations, the Washington Treaty, the "big push" letter – the Premier attacked on every front. It was a splendid performance, recalling the devastating broadsides of his Opposition days. There was one difference. In late 1875 he was on the defensive, a dangerous posture for a politician.

The Montreal speech had one adverse effect: it roused Sir John A. Macdonald to reply.[30] For two years, the Conservative leader had been a forlorn figure on Parliament Hill, his mind more on retirement and oblivion than re-conquest of his old glory. Leaving the task of criticizing the Administration largely to the dynamic and irrepressible Dr. Tupper, he had seemed almost a memory out of the past – a past his fellow Conservatives often preferred to forget. Then, with his fine political sense, the old Tory chieftain noted the change. The Toronto victory confirmed the trend. Nine days after Mackenzie's address, Sir John followed him to Montreal and spoke for the "party of which, for the present at least, I may be considered the leader". The initial response was heartening, and he warmed to his task. The Premier's speeches were usually as "dry as a limeburner's shoe", he joked; it was strange that when he burst into poetry he should quote "that rakehelly old cavalier Sam Butler" to leaven his message. The poem indicated the sort of answers given in Parliament to Opposition questions. "We tell him, 'Your Pacific policy is wrong.' He answers, 'You are an asp.' We tell him, 'The tariff is a mistake.' 'You are a basilisk.' We say to him, 'How about the steel rails?' 'You are a toad.'... I suppose the honourable gentleman calls this what we in Scotland call 'wut'." The audience was amused. Rising to the occasion, Macdonald delivered a magnificent address in his best tradition. Humour, sincerity, ridicule, indignation, patriotism, and even pathos – all were applied with a masterly hand. The speech ended with a rousing accusation that Liberal talk of independence was "veiled treason", and a fervent declaration: "a British subject I was born and a British subject I hope to die". It was not an original utterance; Baldwin had used it over thirty years before. It was not the less effective for that; "John A." had begun his come-back.

* * * * *

In the same city, the earthly remains of Joseph Guibord found at last their final resting-place. Balked in their first attempt, his friends formed a guard of honour of over a thousand men, and on November 16 they marched again to the Catholic cemetery. No resistance was offered. To make certain the wanderings were over, they covered the coffin with cement and iron. "There reposes a rebel," wrote the Bishop of Montreal in closing the incident, "who was buried by the force of arms."[31]

Guibord was disposed of, but his memory would not die. The Catholic clergy intensified their campaign against Catholic liberalism, and political liberalism was included automatically in the same denunciations. The sky was "bleu", hell was "rouge", replied the curés when told that there was no distinction; it was as simple as that. A new political party, the Parti National, attracted many young Liberals anxious to escape the opprobrium of their name.[32]

Into this delicate situation strode the new Postmaster General, Lucius Huntington. A friend of Radolfe Laflamme, a fiery Rouge Parliamentarian, member of the Institut, and counsel for the Guibord family during their long and painful struggle, he was alarmed by the acquiescence of the English-speaking population before the threat to civil liberties in Quebec. In a speech in Argenteuil in December 1875, he lashed out at the Catholic clergy for their interference in public affairs, and called for a real separation of church and state.[33] Reports of the Minister's remarks spread quickly along the lower St. Lawrence, where Bishop Langevin's brother was campaigning for election in Charlevoix. The curés referred to them as proof of the Godlessness of the Rouges, and threatened the parishioners with dire consequences if they refused to vote Conservative.[34] The Archbishop demanded an explanation from Cauchon of what he considered a revolutionary, anti-Catholic and anti-French-Canadian statement.[35] Above all, he was concerned with Huntington's declaration that his views were shared by the whole Liberal party, and that he would resign if that were not so. "Have not Catholic members of the party a duty to fulfil in the circumstances?" the church leader asked meaningfully.

Having vaunted his influence with the clergy, Joseph Cauchon was in a difficult position. He appealed for "prudence and a wise moderation" to avoid the danger of French Canada being crushed.[36] The Archbishop was not in a moderate mood, and replied hotly that acquiescence meant consent.[37] The ingratiating little Minister hastened to assure him that he would take a strong stand in Ottawa.[38] Writing to Mackenzie, however, the President of the Council minimized the difficulty.[39] Most of the hierarchy opposed Langevin in Charlevoix, he reported, and the campaign was going well despite the activity of local priests and postmasters. One hundred and twenty priests had assured him of their support at a university dinner. "You know my views, that it is better to have them with you than against you." In Argenteuil the Liberal candidate was sure to be elected "if I succeed in stopping these obnoxious priests". The Premier was less sanguine. "The news from Charlevoix . . . is good if correct," he commented to Brown early in 1876.[40] "I fear Huntington's speech has done us harm with the priests . . . the speech was all correct in principle but I fear we are not strong enough with the English in Quebec hostile to us to carry that principle into effect." To complicate matters still further, Luther Holton, campaigning openly for a Cabinet position now, was demanding a public repudiation by the Government of the man blocking his way through the Privy Council door.[41]

As a palliative, Alexander Mackenzie sent a conciliatory letter through Cauchon to the Archbishop, assuring him that the Postmaster General had spoken only for himself and not on behalf of the Cabinet, and that he had intended his remarks to apply only to extremist elements in Quebec. At the same time, he sent a similar message through the Catholic Lieutenant-Governor of Ontario, Donald Macdonald, to Archbishop Lynch in Toronto. The Archbishop of Quebec indicated his approval of the gesture; his Ontario counterpart addressed a public reply through the press, assuring the Premier that priests in his archdiocese were strictly forbidden to make political harangues from the pulpit or threaten spiritual disability for voting with any party.[42] Ontario priests were warned that it was very imprudent to become political partisans. Mackenzie took advantage of the exchange to reiterate his view that religion had no place in the political arena, and that the Government's policy was "the separation of Church and State, the amplest recognition of civil as well as religious liberty, and the accordance of impartial justice and equal rights to every individual, irrespective of his religious creed or his political faith".[43] The attempt to reach a basis of understanding was worthy, but barren of political results. Both Charlevoix and Argenteuil fell to the enemy. In Ontario, a by-election in Renfrew was lost as well.

Another bout of illness in January while the legislation and estimates were in preparation determined Mackenzie to remain in Ottawa throughout the session. All his strength was needed for the task at hand. British Columbia had answered his request for a suggestion of a new compromise with an appeal to Lord Carnarvon to enforce fulfilment of the terms associated with his name. The appeal was accompanied by a violent denunciation of the Dominion Government. The Canadian Premier's first reaction was to ask the Supreme Court to decide if there had been a violation of the agreement as Walkem suggested. Dufferin counselled moderation. This was just another instance requiring skill and statesmanship to keep the Empire together, he soothed; it was a task for Britain rather than for the new judicial body.[44] After their previous experience with British statesmen, the idea did not appeal to the Canadian Ministers. They refused to consider it. "My impression is that we will simply go on the even tenor of our way," the Premier confided to George Brown on January 18, "begin as soon as we can, and go as fast as we can, and let them whistle."[45]

The core of opposition to British interference was Edward Blake. He was annoyed by the stiffening resistance of Lord Cairns and the British legal officers to the appeal clause in the Supreme Court Act. After having reported to Blake on his return from England that he had convinced them to let the clause stand, Mackenzie felt his honour at stake and was as adamant as his Minister of Justice in insisting that Canada's views should be accepted.[46] Carnarvon suggested that the only solution was for Blake to discuss the matter in London. The Canadians agreed, but made it clear that they would not accept an adverse decision. "He [Blake] seems to me to have a morbid hatred of the legal authority of England," Dufferin wrote to Downing Street, "engendered probably by the frequency with which it has overruled his own opinions and decisions in respect of points of Constitutional Law."[47] On both sides of the Atlantic, lawyers prepared for a tough struggle when the Canadian session of Parliament was over.

Another exasperating negotiation with London concerned Brown's title. The *Globe* publisher had been aware of the possibility of such an award for over a year, and his name had been submitted by Dufferin along with those of Chief Justice Richards and Chief Justice Dorion in September 1875. A few days later, the "big push" letter had appeared, and the Governor General began to have doubts about awarding a title to someone accused of a scandal that looked, "if proven", as momentous as the Pacific Railway affair. After the latter incident, the British Government had made it clear that Sir John should not appear in England expecting to be sworn in to the Imperial Privy Council to which he had been appointed some time before, and that he had no right to use the designation "Right Honourable".

His Excellency asked Mackenzie to tell him "frankly and candidly", and without allowing any "private or political connection with Mr. Brown to bias your judgment", whether or not there was any foundation for the charges.[48] Irritated by the counsel of frankness and objectivity, the Premier replied sharply that he had declared in 1873 that the election fund was three or four thousand dollars, too small a sum to imply improper practices.[49] He himself had not seen the letter to Simpson, but he understood it was sent to half a dozen friends. Apparently the banker had not replied, and he was not aware that he had ever contributed to an election fund. Such requests for funds were perfectly legal. He himself had nothing to hide, and he did not think that Brown had either. Lord Dufferin was reassured, but he still hesitated. Mackenzie finally agreed to a further postponement of the title.

The constant reminders of Canadian subjection to British authority were annoying. There seemed to be no clear dividing line between Imperial and Dominion jurisdiction, and Dufferin was inclined to intervene in the most minute details of Government business. With a team composed of a dynamic and Im-

perialist-minded Governor General, and a stubbornly
nomy-minded Dominion First Minister, there was a cons
danger of a clash. When Dufferin spoke of "my Ministers", he left the impression that he felt himself truly in charge of the Administration; when Mackenzie made policy statements, he left no doubt that he and no other was in command. It was largely the Premier's unswerving loyalty to Queen and Empire that enabled them to work together without constant disagreements.

* * * * *

The Speech from the Throne was not a cheerful document to prepare. The great international depression had struck Canada with full force, and trade was in a slump. Further reductions in expenditure were necessary. The Government was investigating the possibility of commercial expansion in the West Indies, but no favourable results could be reported.

Holton sprang to his feet at the first opportunity in the 1876 session to demand a statement on Huntington's Argenteuil speech.[50] Alexander Mackenzie replied calmly that he had not known of the speech in advance and, disapproving of anything that tended to bring religion into a political discussion, he regretted "the remarks of my honourable friend, and the tone and interpretation given to them by many". He did not accept the charge that an attack on the Catholic church was intended. But, Holton insisted, did the Premier approve or disapprove of the contents of the speech? Mackenzie maintained a stubborn silence. They were his own views, Huntington stated when his turn came; he was speaking as a Lower Canadian and not as a Minister. "I spoke . . . of the dread I have of the Ultramontanes, and I asked them [the electors] to give to the Liberals their aid. . . . I repeat that the true course of the British population in Quebec to-day is to ally themselves with the Liberals in the effort to maintain free institutions." The Liberal Administration slipped a bit farther in Quebec; Luther Holton's chances of entering the Ministry died.

The Opposition had never been so alert. What was the railway policy now that Blake was in the Ministry? they wanted to know. What about the Aurora speech? Was not Cauchon's appointment a contradiction of the Premier's policy of opposing coalitions? Was "Cauchon Rouge" a new colour in the political spectrum? It worked. Mackenzie took the bait and began the session in a bad temper. It was a new role for the honourable member for Cumberland (Dr. Tupper), he retorted, to come out as the champion of morality.[51] No one held office except as a representative of the great Liberal party, and he held the same view of the "viciousness" of coalitions as when he refused to become a member of one with Sir John. As for the Pacific Railway policy, any Government action had to be preceded by a money Bill; that would afford an opportunity to discuss the subject.

From the beginning, it promised to be a hot session. Hector Langevin countered Cauchon's accusations of electoral corruption by asserting that he would prove the President of the Council had used Government pressure in the Charlevoix contest. David Mills called for a committee to enquire into the causes of the financial depression. The Ministry accepted his motion; they too were at a loss to explain the recurring economic crises that wreaked such havoc in the whole western world.

The first important debate took place on the budget.[52] For some weeks reports had been circulating that the Government would have a deficit of two or three million dollars, and that some changes in the Dominion's housekeeping would be needed. Tupper had called vaguely for a "national policy", the *Nation* showed protectionist sympathies, and George Stephen, the Montreal financier, urged a "patriotic fiscal policy" to meet the crisis. Within the Liberal caucus, protectionist sentiment was growing rapidly; some Government supporters from urban centres had felt obliged to pledge themselves to higher tariffs against American competitors. The Maritime members, led by Alfred Jones, pressed for continuance of the greatest possible degree of free trade. A fortnight before the session began, the Cabinet were still toying with a further two and a half per cent increase in customs duties, combined with ruthless application of the paring knife on the new set of estimates. Any such changes would be a mere provisional arrangement due to the abnormal state of trade, Alexander Mackenzie assured the Governor General; the policy of the Government would still be to adhere to the principle of free trade "as closely as the circumstances of the Country will permit".[53]

When the Finance Minister began his budget address on February 25, the tariff policy was still a well-kept secret. Corridor gossip had it that Dr. Tupper, the Opposition financial critic, had one speech ready to rebut a protectionist budget, and one to demand protection. By ruthless trimming, the deficit had been reduced to less than one million dollars, Cartwright began, but Canada had not yet begun to move out of the commercial crisis, "great and almost unparalleled in severity". Alternatives had been considered. A great deal of distress existed, and the

Government wanted to relieve it if possible. However, a higher tariff was merely a "tax (on) nineteen-twentieths of the population for the sake of one-twentieth", and would risk "inflicting very great and permanent injury on the whole population of Canada". He would not propose "a servile plagiarism of the blunders which the United States have committed". The Government would reduce the budget by two and a half million dollars, and continue to hold the line.

Dr. Tupper rose to his feet a protectionist. On the Liberal back-benches, scattered scowls of dissatisfaction were plainly visible. The Premier, however, was delighted to see the Tories committed to such an anti-British policy, "a relic of a barbarous age". After the sitting, he joshed Tupper good-naturedly on his dilemma, and secured an admission that the Nova Scotian was prepared to take the opposite line of attack if the tariff had been raised.[54]

Sir John was still wary of the protectionist cry, and spoke of a "moderate" tariff wall, "not to retain the water altogether . . . but . . . allow a certain amount of the steam to percolate over".[55] He moved a rather insipid resolution calling for a "readjustment" of the tariff to "alleviate the stagnation of business . . . (and) afford encouragement and protection to struggling manufacturers and industries as well as the agricultural interests of the country". Sixty-four members voted for the resolution, one hundred sixteen against. "You will be glad to hear that in a severe tariff debate the Free Trade principles of the Gov't were sustained by a majority of 55," Lord Dufferin reported to London.[56] He did not mention that several Liberals had voted against the Ministry.

Encouraged by the first signs of a crack in the Liberal front, the Opposition pressed the attack. The campaign to cast doubts on the virtue of the Mackenzie régime was intensified, and every possible accusation was aired.[57] Special groups proved a source of increasing embarrassment. The Irish Catholics were demanding that the case of William O'Donohue, the only Red River rebel not included in the amnesty, should be reconsidered. The Government voted down the request for an enquiry. There was dissatisfaction among Protestants as well. Outraged church-goers condemned the Government for allowing railways, canals and other public utilities to function on Sunday.[58] Stern Baptist Mackenzie had to admit that he shared their view, but that he found it difficult to stop all forms of public transportation from Saturday midnight until Monday. One member suggested that it was just as shocking for Members of Parliament to return to the "Hill" on the Sabbath. "Where would we spend Sunday?" a voice interjected. "In church, of course," boomed a strong Irish brogue in reply. The Temperance Societies were urging the Government to bring in some anti-liquor legislation, and reminding them that they had not acted on the study of United States legislation carried out in 1874. Mackenzie was not at all certain that public opinion was ready for such a step, and besides, the five millions of revenue from the "wets" were very welcome during the economic crisis!

The Pacific Railway remained a burning issue. The British Columbia Legislature petitioned the Queen to "cause the Dominion Government to be immediately moved to carry out the terms of the said [Carnarvon] settlement".[59] Ottawa rejected the attack upon its honour and good faith, "so gross that they must decline to discuss it", and accused the Walkem Administration of seeking only to obtain as great an expenditure as possible within the province rather than securing the completion of the railway.[60] "It remains only," Mackenzie stated bluntly in reply to the rejection of his offer of seven hundred fifty thousand dollars as compensation for delays, "to endeavour to construct the Pacific Railway as rapidly as the resources of the country will permit." They were back where they had been two years before.

On a motion by Amor De Cosmos calling for fulfilment of the Carnarvon terms, the House debated for over a week.[61] Mackenzie stood his ground. The rails that had arrived in Victoria for the Island railway would be used on the mainland, he reported, and three million dollars would be spent on the project in the coming year. Dr. Tupper tried to exploit the situation by accusing the Government of bad faith in not ensuring the passage of the Esquimalt-Nanaimo Bill in the Senate. He denounced the attempt to build the Pacific Railway as a public project, and called for construction by private enterprise. It was a solution that Mackenzie himself yearned for, but as long as the hard times continued it was a forlorn hope. As the debate drew to a close, George Ross, a close supporter of the Administration, moved that the railway should be built "as the resources of the country will permit without increasing the existing rate of taxation".[62] It was a neat manoeuvre to force the members to declare themselves for or against increased spending. The Tories retreated. The motion carried one hundred fifty-nine to ten. Frustrated at the overwhelming opinion against him, De Cosmos fairly screamed the threat of separation across the floor.

The Mills Committee brought forth no panacea for the financial depression.[63] After listening to a cascade of protectionist propaganda from manufacturing interests, they concluded that "a national policy founded on the greatest freedom of trade which the public credit will permit is the most advantageous to this country". The United States and other countries that practiced protection were suffering as much as Canada. The American capitalists sought to use the floor of Congress as an arena to raise their own rate of income above the general level by taxing the rest of the community, and consumers were forced to suffer privations as a result. They could not recommend such a system for Canada. The report was a ringing defence of the Government's stand; the Ministers stiffened in defence of their principles.

By the time the last vote of the session was taken, nerves were taut and tempers short on both sides of the Chamber. It was the most ill-humoured session since the Pacific scandal, "the kind of warfare that would disgrace a Hottentot Legislature", grumbled Mackenzie.[64] "The rascals have all gone," he wrote to Mary on Good Friday with obvious relief, "having gathered up their dead and wounded. I am also engaged in repairing damages."[65] On the whole he was not dissatisfied with the two months' work. Sir John had not been as formidable as he might have been, and there was no one of comparable ability on the Opposition benches. Thomas Hodgins, an Ontario Liberal, assured him that he had proven himself, "truly a 'masterful man' over the best of your opponents", and reported that even the *Mail* editor admitted he was the ablest man in the Liberal party.[66] Mackenzie himself was convinced that he had been in complete control all the way.

CHAPTER 15

Tempest over the Pacific

The 1876 session over, Edward Blake prepared to beard the British legal lions in their den. Alexander Mackenzie resigned himself to another lonely siege in the capital. Lord Dufferin was afire with a plan of his own. Under the guise of an official visit to British Columbia, he wanted to take a personal hand in settling the Pacific Railway dispute. It was a challenge of proportions that attracted him, and one for which he felt himself well qualified. After the wide publicity given to the issue in England, a successful intervention would redound to his credit at home, and he was already thinking in terms of his next assignment, with a hopeful eye on India.

Determined to stand firm on his British Columbia policy, the Premier was unenthusiastic. Only after weeks of pressure during the latter part of the session did he agree reluctantly to a purely formal visit. Lord Dufferin needed no more encouragement. He dashed off a private letter to Lord Carnarvon, asking him to approve the project, and authorize him to communicate with the Government of British Columbia on his behalf. "I think if I were to appear upon the scene in the double capacity of your delegate, and also as representative of the Dominion, I might manage to make an amicable arrangement about the Nanaimo Railway and perhaps all other matters."[1] The Colonial Minister was delighted. The petition from the British Columbia Legislature lay unanswered in his office, and *The Times* and *Pall Mall* were vocal in their support of the petitioners. The question was in danger of becoming a political issue in Westminster itself. He agreed heartily with the proposed trip, and expressed his hope that further concessions would lead to a new compromise.[2]

Pleased with his initial success, the Governor General showed the message to Mackenzie. The Premier reacted violently.[3]

Further concessions! Evidently London did not understand the Canadian position. The Pacific Railway policy had already been stated in Parliament; it could not be changed. His heart set on his "mission", Dufferin insisted. He had already chosen the members of his entourage, and planned his entrance into Esquimalt harbour on the deck of a Royal Navy warship. Even if public opinion was behind the Government, and the original scheme foolish and ill-advised, he argued, something had to be done to release the tense situation.[4]

As requested by Downing Street, the Cabinet stated their view of the British Columbia petition. "The arrangements proposed in 1874 having been found impossible of execution," ran the Minute of Council, "and British Columbia having declined to entertain the subsequent proposals made to her, and insisting still upon the performance of what has been found impossible, it only remains for the Government to make such arrangements for the construction of the Pacific Railway as the resources of the country will permit without increasing the existing rates of taxation."[5] His Excellency was annoyed; a series of difficult interviews between him and his chief adviser followed. He cast aside Mackenzie's protestations that every nerve was being strained to build the line, and suggested that, by "cooking the Public Accounts", the appearance of requiring additional taxes could easily be created. The insinuation of bad faith cut deeply into the Premier's Scottish pride, and he replied with warmth. Dufferin followed up the attack by suggesting that Mackenzie was not strong enough to control his Cabinet, and was being forced into a false position by Blake and Cartwright. Whether or not he could withstand the arguments of his colleagues, it was quite evident that he could withstand the arguments of the Crown. He stuck to his position that British Columbia would accept the Dominion proposals, "unless they received such a reply from Her Majesty's Government as might induce them to persevere in unreasonable demands".[6]

Carnarvon and Dufferin were far ahead of the Canadian Premier. In early May, a despatch arrived in Ottawa for communication to the Government of British Columbia, instructing the Governor General to proceed to the Pacific province. The wording was a shock to the Canadian Ministers. "I should of course have great difficulty in believing that a government which only a year ago had undertaken specific obligations could contemplate any departure from, much less any amendment of them," declared the Colonial Minister.[7] "The understanding was of a tripartite character and I cannot, of course suppose that the Canadian government could consider itself absolved from any engagement into which it had entered with British Columbia – except . . . after . . . communication with me." "I shall be very much guided . . . by conclusions to which you may be led after personal communication with the Provincial Government." There was no need to discuss whether the Vancouver Island line was part of the main railway, Lord Carnarvon argued, as Canada had promised to build it.

If such a document were sent, Mackenzie protested, it would constitute a complete repudiation of the Canadian position. He urged that it be withdrawn as holding out false hopes, and protested the implication that the Governor General was to collect evidence for a further arbitration. "I am surprised beyond measure that Lord Carnarvon treats the question merely as a bargain and its execution merely as a matter of willingness or unwillingness on our part," he complained.[8] "It is evident he does not appreciate the efforts we have made, the risks we have run in going counter to public opinion as far as we have, that he ignores the position of the Conservative opposition." As Blake would be in London in two weeks, he suggested that the whole subject could be discussed with the Colonial Minister at first hand. In the meantime, if Lord Carnarvon really wanted to be helpful he could tell British Columbia that Ottawa had done everything in its power, and would be urged to continue to do so.

Ignoring completely his constitutional position, Lord Dufferin pursued the struggle with his advisers. He gave them, in his own words, "a very disagreeable and stormy time", but they refused to retreat.[9] Sickening of the very name of the Colonial Minister, Mackenzie asked in exasperation, "After all, who is Lord Carnarvon?"[10] He had "written his fingers off," the Governor General insisted, in explaining the difficulties of their position in London.[11] He was "quite convinced that British Columbia has no earthly cause of complaint against you in regard of any of your acts, nor indeed as far as I can see as regards your speeches". Indeed, he was so certain of the merits of Ottawa's stand that he felt he could induce the Provincial Government to listen to reason if he made the trip; he only wanted the Dominion to come out of the whole business with credit and a clear conscience.

Mackenzie's impatience with London was increasing rapidly. Lord Carnarvon's letter reflected a suitable attitude for dealing with Crown colonies and small dependencies, he replied, but not with the Dominion.[12] In 1874, they had yielded to his request to accept arbitration against their better judgment, and it had been a mistake. The Carnarvon terms had not been carried out because the same Imperial Minister had refused to grant a request to increase the number of Liberals in the Senate. Now he wished to adjudicate again, knowing full well that he had no power to enforce a decision. The Government was going ahead at a breakneck pace that was irreconcilable with business principles in order to demonstrate their good faith, and the general interest of the country was being neglected because of "this bargain and these unreasonable people". If Lord Carnarvon wanted to help, he could point out "the real state of the case . . . and doubtless have much effect in stopping a senseless agitation."

Bluff and bluster having failed, Dufferin suddenly changed tactics. "After five and twenty years experience of public life I can say without flattery that I never met anyone with whom I felt I could talk more frankly and unreservedly with the perfect conviction of the crystal sincerity of their character and intentions than yourself," he wrote his First Minister on May 22.[13] He was convinced more than ever that the Imperial authorities should not "fidget or fuss" with the affairs of Canada, and that it should be taken for granted that the Dominion Government were the best judges of what suited Canada's interest. His own temperament would resent being made "the instrument of anything that might be called Imperial dictation"; as a good Whig, he had always sided with the Colonies in their efforts to obtain constitutional freedom. He had "strongly condemned the original appeal of British Columbia to England", and had told Lord Carnarvon that he gave too much comfort to Walkem. Because of this advice "he [Carnarvon] wishes me to be the instrument by which . . . his modified appreciation of their claims is to be communicated . . . I am . . . commissioned to preach reason and sense to the British Columbia Government on behalf of yourself and Canada, and he supplements my mission by an open commission to preach reason and sense on his own behalf as well."

The tone of His Excellency's private report to the Secretary of State for the Colonies four days later was a striking contrast. "Were their intentions as honest as we could wish them," he commented disparagingly, "they would not, of course feel so acutely as they have done . . . but I fear we are dealing with very loose fish. . . . I very much doubt whether eventually you will not have to deal with this subject with a high hand, if British Columbia is to obtain anything like justice."[14] In the meantime, he explained, he had adopted a more amiable attitude in order to avoid a really serious collision with his advisers, and had accepted completely the revisions to Lord Carnarvon's despatch suggested by them.

What was behind the Governor General's treacherous attitude to his advisers? Was it purely the fear of an open clash? Did he become concerned suddenly for his own career as an Imperial officer if he became personally involved in the problems of the "colonists"? By coincidence, a letter from Lord Carnarvon had arrived at that critical juncture, announcing that the Queen had awarded him the Grand Cross of St. Michael and St. George.[15] It was an indication that he was making progress in the direction of his real ambition, the Viceroyalty of India. The British Columbia dispute paled in comparison. What was more, Lord Lytton, the incumbent of the coveted position, was ill, and reports of his recall were being circulated. Was Lord Dufferin already framing in his mind the letter he wrote from his summer home a few weeks later, requesting that his transfer to India be considered if a new nomination became necessary?[16] Whatever his motives, the crisis was suddenly dissipated for the moment. Lord Carnarvon accepted the Canadian modifications to his despatch, and the Dominion leaders agreed to the "progress" to the Pacific province. Dufferin was given no powers of negotiation or investigation; the British Columbians were to be exhorted to reason and understanding.

* * * * *

A year or two earlier the wrangling might have broken Mackenzie's health and spirits. In his third year as Premier, he took it in his stride. When Blake left for England, and Lord Dufferin for a fishing trip on the lower St. Lawrence prior to his Western adventure, the Premier turned to the summer's work. During the spring, a young niece and her friend had come to stay with them, and brightened the large empty house overlooking the Ottawa River. He found pleasure in watching the robins hopping on the lawn, and listening to the bull frogs down by the water's edge.[17] Then the young people left, and soon after them Jane followed to spend the summer in Sarnia, away from the suffocating heat of the capital. There was a new attraction in the little Western town – Mary had given birth to a son. While the rest of the family billed and cooed over the new arrival, Grandfather Mackenzie was left alone with the affairs of state. "I . . . mean to get a 'Dust Sieve' for my head, a musketo [*sic*] net and a cooler for the whole corpus and so fight Heat, Dust and Insects," he wrote Charlie Black in Montreal.[18] "Can't you come up for a few days? I can turn you into the yard to smoke as it is just cleaned. You can spit in the tank as we have no use for it now and you can sit on the Upper Verandah and see the trains pass."

Running the Dominion seemed to be a continual series of headaches, and precious few consolations. The New York State officials refused to allow Canadian bottoms to use their canals on the same terms as American boats circulating in Canada. As a result, the lucrative lumber-carrying trade was being lost to the Dominion. Canadian protests had to be channelled through London and Washington to reach a destination a few miles away; in the process they were diluted and distorted almost beyond recognition, and were invariably ineffective. The attempt to have a Canadian Agent General assist in promoting Canadian affairs in London failed. Mackenzie had appointed to the position Edward Jenkins, son of a Canadian church minister, a McGill graduate, and a member of the Imperial Parliament for the constituency of Dundee. Shortly after Jenkins' appointment, his party had fallen from power in Britain, leaving him on the Opposition benches with a semi-diplomatic funcion to perform with his adversaries. Quite apart from his boastful and indiscreet nature, it was an impossible situation. His declarations as Canada's representative were often closely intermixed with attacks on the Conservatives in Westminster. The appointment was cancelled in early 1876, and Sir John Rose, the former Conservative Finance Minister in Ottawa who had joined a London banking firm, and with whom the Premier was on excellent terms, agreed to represent the Dominion whenever necessary as "Financial Commissioner".[19]

With most of the Ministers absent, a host of troublesome details landed on the Premier's desk. Holton was annoyed because Laflamme and not he was making appointments on the Beauharnois Canal. Jones was unhappy because non-Liberals were receiving contracts in Nova Scotia. The citizens of Rimouski were indignant because a local member had recommended a man who had never been aboard a steamer to operate the mail ship. Lord Dufferin was certain there must be a position in the Civil Service for his son's tutor, who was "conversant with books".[20] Even the Archbishop of Canterbury had a friend he wished to place on the Government payroll!

With a new stoicism, Alexander Mackenzie laboured on, crossing over Wellington Street three times a day to eat at the Rideau Club, and returning home to sleep when his sore eyes forced him to abandon work after dark. He was very comfortable, he assured his wife, "that is as comfortable as a man can be when the cause for his happiness is absent".[21] In mid-June, he had a quick run down to Quebec and stayed with the Dufferins in the Citadel. Looking out from the old fortress at the scene of his arrival as an immigrant lad with sixteen shillings in his pocket, he could not suppress a surge of pride. Little did he dream the day he had persuaded the British soldier to show him the ramparts that he would one day be master of the whole country. "I wonder at my own audacity and perseverance," he confided to his wife.[22] The scene evoked sadder memories, memories of those who had fallen along the way, and particularly of Hope, with whom he had shared so much. At fifty-four, and so heavily burdened with responsibility, he had a feeling that he was entitled to be the next to go, to be quit of the cares and worries that left him no rest on earth. When the time came, he reflected, he would "care as little for post-mortem eulogies as I care for ante-mortem censures".

The sadness was transitory. He and Dufferin had to address a banquet, and one ambitious Liberal had placed a carriage at his disposal so that he could tour the city. A French-speaking lady paid him such attentions, Mackenzie reported with amusement to Jane, that "I imagined I had more personal attractions than you or I supposed, and I feared the danger of being among appreciative ladies in your absence."[23] However, when she managed to arrange a "tête-à-tête", his illusions were quickly dissipated. She wanted a "senatorship for her Papa, a judgeship for her sister's husband!! and a Cabinet office for her husband!!!" He concluded that there was no need for uneasiness about his "personal attractions".

There were by-election contests in North Ontario, South Ontario, and Wellington South constituencies during the summer. Hoping to keep to his desk as much as possible, Alexander Mackenzie delegated Lucius Huntington to speak for the Government, but the genial eloquence of the Postmaster General proved no match for Charles Tupper, and he was soundly trounced at a meeting in Oshawa. At the urging of friends, the Premier decided to take a hand himself. The encounter took place in Whitby.[24] Hands behind his back, Mackenzie led off with a quiet orderly defence of the Administration, replete with facts and figures, but relatively devoid of oratorical flourish. The "great stretcher" was in splendid form. Sensing victory at hand, he charged into his task, matching the violence of his denunciations with the vigour of his gesticulations. "He held the Government responsible," recounted a member of the audience in later years, "for drought and blight, for excessive heat and extreme cold, for the blasted corn and the barren fig tree." As the tirade continued, Tory hopes rose, and Grit spirits fell in inverse proportion. By the time he finished, the Liberal cause seemed hopeless.

Alexander Mackenzie had the right to a fifteen-minute rebuttal. "As the last word fell from Dr. Tupper's lips," the same witness wrote, "he sprang to the front of the platform. He stood, stern and unsmiling, while the long cheering for the Conservative spokesman died away. Then with swift, impetuous sentences he fell upon Dr. Tupper. He wasted not a word or a moment. He struck blow after blow with such direct force that the whole structure which Dr. Tupper had reared with such superb assurance and confidence seemed to fall column by column into ruin. I have heard many speeches since that day, but nothing so trenchant and destructive . . . Conservatives around me who never had and never would cast a vote for a Liberal candidate rose to their feet and cheered with delight over the performance. That I have seen once only."

The indignation of the pugnacious Scot was not simulated. Tupper had followed his leader's example of claiming that patronage was more rife than ever in the Public Works Department. "Let any Conservative try to get a contract," Sir John had told a Cooksville audience shortly before, "let any Conservative apply for an office and they would not get it."[25] Mackenzie had noted the statement and prepared "a crushing nailer" to deal with the charge.[26] He never opened tenders, he told the Whitby audience; they were opened by "upright members of the Civil Service, men whom I honour for the impartial discharge of their duties – men who command public confidence." They were not tools of his; he had not appointed them. Let them be called before any committee and be asked if there was any manipulation of contracts, he challenged, as he repudiated the charges "with the utmost scorn that it is possible to manifest".[27]

Good as the performance in Whitby undoubtedly was, it was not good enough. All three constituencies were lost. A week after the polling, the Liberals met in Convention in Toronto to lick their wounds and analyse the defeat. The protectionist cry was obviously having some effect, even among the farmers. "It would almost serve them right to give the blockheads what they ask," growled Cartwright.[28] The Irish Catholics, still annoyed at not having one of their number in the Cabinet, had opposed the Government. In vain, the Liberals had vaunted the origins of Richard Scott, the Secretary of State; his name was about as Irish as the Premier's brogue. With the whiskey vote already against him, Mackenzie had lost the temperance vote as well by not acting on their plea for prohibitionist legislation. Then, too, the Grits had neglected their organization during the years in power. There was nothing in the three constituencies resembling the disciplined corps of men that had assured victory in Lambton County in former years. In less than three years, they had forgotten that they were not only statesmen and administrators, but politicians too. Finally, the people of Canada were weary and bored by the hard times, and protested in the most effective way they could. Alexander Mackenzie returned to Ottawa, realizing that he would have to get out of the capital more frequently and carry the fight to the enemy.

* * * * *

Edward Blake got on much better in London than either he or the British had expected. Briefed by Dufferin that he was hypersensitive, anti-British, and unstable, and advised to "allow the fighting to be done for you by your gladiators", Carnarvon was prepared for the worst.[29] Instead, he found the Canadian Minister of Justice amiable, reasonable, and highly intelligent. The dire warnings served at least to assure the Canadian a courteous and attentive reception! Blake argued that an increased expenditure on the Pacific Railway was an impossibility because the Dominion had reached the limit of productive taxation. Higher customs taxes, the major source of revenue, would yield a decreased income as trade would be stifled. Canada would lose the advantages of a low-cost economy, and Britain would find more foreign products entering Canada in competition with her own. Since Canada was doing all she could, it was useless to talk about the "terms" or compensation.

Lord Carnarvon listened well and seemed impressed. Blake felt that he had made good progress. He went on to his discussions with Lord Cairns and the legal experts. Mackenzie had predicted that, with Blake's great "mental power", Cairns' "shallow mem^dum" on the Supreme Court Act would be "torn to pieces".[30] Considering that the Chancellor had been "dead against the Act", the result was an agreeable surprise.[31] Far from being a weak constitutional lawyer as Dufferin had intimated, the Canadian's arguments were carefully prepared, exhaustive, and well presented. However, he, too, had begun to have some doubts about Clause 47, which abolished the appeals to the Privy Council, and then contradicted itself by preserving the Queen's prerogative to grant such appeals. In the end, the two men agreed that the clause was inoperative in practice, and was best ignored.[32] The entire Supreme Court Act was allowed to stand.

Though he did not win his arguments completely in every case, the trip to England was on the whole a victory for the Canadian lawyer.[33] He drew up a draft extradition act, made arrangements for a Maritime court on the Great Lakes, urged that the commutation of death sentences was within Canadian

THE "QUEER COINCIDENCE."

G. B.—"I WONDER WHY THIS UNSAVORY TRAMP DISNA FOLLOW YON OTHER PAIRTY, BUT ALWAYS CLINGS TO OOR HEELS."

[89]

From Bengough's *Caricature History of Canadian Politics*, Vol. II

jurisdiction and not the prerogative of the Governor General, and discussed the disallowance of provincial legislation, the Governor General's commission and instructions, and a whole series of other legal matters. But even with such considerable achievements, he continued to share Mackenzie's view of British aristocracy and officialdom. "Our whole relations to the Home Authorities are such as to render the negotiations intolerable to me," he wrote back to Canada.[34] "With every desire to oblige and to do what is right according to their lights *they have no light.*" Averse to new situations and unfamiliar faces, and sensitive lest he show up badly, he fretted between interviews and fumed at delays. By August, he was almost ill from exasperation. At the earliest possible hour, he boarded a ship and left for home. Mackenzie had looked forward to the return of his powerful colleague to share the burden of work after a long and lonely summer. The Minister of Justice arrived in a state of near collapse, and retired to Toronto for a rest.

Lord Dufferin had hoped that the Imperial authorities would "infuse a more generous spirit" into Blake's mind concerning the Canadian Pacific Railway. If they could manage that, he was confident that he could overcome the objections of the Premier, and still extract some conciliatory message to take on his "mission". It was evident that while he had changed his tactics, he had not changed the objectives of his voyage.[35]

Mackenzie refused to budge. After two months of coercion, the Governor General had to reconcile himself to accepting the despatch that had been modified by the Canadians in May. Nevertheless, the Premier watched the train leave the station with foreboding. "We are in for it now," the Grit leader commented as the Viceregal party set off.[36] Richard Scott was more optimistic. "He has been so thoroughly disciplined as to what *he must not say* that I trust there will be no mishaps."[37] As they made their way across the American prairies, Dufferin received one more bit of advice from his worried First Minister. Every effort should be made to discourage any talk of separation from the Dominion, as it "would be looked upon as a process of disintegration" and exploited elsewhere. "I would rather act the Tyrant a little than consent. National interests must subordinate local interests even if the latter should seem about right."[38] That, then, was Lord Dufferin's mission: to help hold the Dominion together as an important part of the British Empire.

The Tories were developing a new political tactic. They organized a series of picnics across Ontario, and began resuscitating their "old chieftain" in the public mind. Political picnics were not new in 1876; the novelty lay in the fact that the audiences were not subjected to endless harangues, but were actually entertained. Sir John Macdonald rated high as an entertainer. Whatever their opinions of him, all Canadians knew of the veteran parliamentarian; his deeds and misdeeds were legend. They flocked to see and hear him. "How are you boys?" he would call out with a carefree wave and a twinkle in his eye. He described protection by telling them it was like the comment of the drunken squaw: "a little too much was just enough". He talked the language of the people, and he diverted them from the stern righteousness of the Scottish régime in Ottawa.[39] It was like a fresh sea breeze after a torrid, windless afternoon. They loved it, and they loved the genial old man who understood them so well.

The Liberals decided to stage some picnics as well. Mackenzie, Mowat, Cartwright, and Huntington did not try to compete with the drollery or wit of their old opponent, or the bumptiousness of the tireless Tupper, but they outlined the Liberal record and defined their principles. At Clinton, the Dominion Prime Minister warmed to his task sufficiently to declare, as in former days, that "the heart of the average Tory is deceitful above all things and desperately 'wecked' ".[40] He repeated over and over his conviction that protection was a "monster", "the essence of injustice", "the acme of human selfishness". The revenue of the country was beginning to improve, he told his audiences, and the end of the depression was in sight.

The result of the Liberal counter-offensive was encouraging; they won the next three by-elections. Alexander Mackenzie was still a formidable man on the platform. Nonetheless, it was evident that he had merely snatched victory from defeat. Public opinion was wavering, and many were swinging to the Tory side. Few battles were ever won from a defensive position, and the Government was on the defensive.

One of the first things that Edward Blake did on his return to Ottawa was to submit his resignation again.[41] The *Globe* complained that the Government was commuting too many death sentences, and some Ministers echoed similar sentiments in a Cabinet meeting. Feeling personally assailed, the excitable Torontonian declared that he could not deal with such a serious matter in the face of adverse criticism. He had intended to review the situation after the next session, he told the Premier, but the new circumstances compelled him to resign at once.

At a time when the Ministry was fighting desperately to keep from losing still more ground, the letter of resignation came as a bombshell. "I need not say how much your letter has distressed me," Mackenzie replied immediately.[42] "I feel pained that your over-sensitiveness should force you into what I cannot help considering wrong ground." The financial depression and the difficulties in Quebec made the Government vulnerable; further problems would be implied and others enhanced "if the strongest man retires". Casting pride aside, Alexander Mackenzie pleaded openly. "Indeed I do not see how we could get on. Let me beg of you to consider your letter as not written, and let me know if there is anything else than that question you refer to which causes you any annoyance. . . . There may be changes which you think should be made. I think I need hardly say to you that I am ready to discuss anything with you with a view to meet your wishes."

It was a pathetic plea; it was also a courageous and even patriotic letter for the proud Highlander to write. Blake was mollified by the cry of desperation. He had no changes to suggest and nothing caused him annoyance, he answered in a letter that betrayed how deeply upset he was. There was a danger that a life would be taken that should be spared, and the responsibility would lie on his shoulders. He, too, fell into pathos. "I should be glad if it were possible for me to continue my poor efforts to assist you . . . I have . . . lost . . . what little strength I ever had in the country, I shall lose the rest by my retirement. I shall make no effort to regain it; and the ranks of the party will supply you with another and more fortunate Minister."[43]

Blake was obviously in a profound nervous depression, and looking regretfully at the bridges he had burned behind him. He had given up his chance of leading the Canada First movement; his newspaper, the *Liberal*, had died, and its editor was on the staff of the *Globe*; and he had abandoned the opportunity to be the first Chief Justice of the Supreme Court of Canada. If his career in Ottawa ended badly, he could return to his lucrative law practice, but, his frequent affirmations to the contrary, a lucrative law practice did not appear to be his sole heart's desire.

The next morning the Premier, supported closely by Smith and Cartwright, followed up the attack. There was no reason for such drastic action, they repeated over and over in a multitude of arguments; he was essential to the future of the Government. As the day wore on, the resistance of the unhappy Minister weakened, and he finally gave in. "Though I continue of the opinion that I am placed in a false position . . ." he wrote on September 26, "I yield my own views and authorize you not to proceed further in the matter of my resignation."[44] He was "truly sorry" to have caused his colleagues such trouble.

Saved again! The greatest crisis to date had lasted only thirty-six hours, and only a few of the Ministers had been aware of it. Even George Brown knew nothing, although he might have suspected some unusual motivation from a letter he received from the Premier about the editorial on commutations. "Christ 'interfered' with the sentence of Heaven as expressed in the Mosaic law in sparing the woman", Mackenzie told the *Globe* publisher bluntly. "You would have stoned her to death."[45]

Another leading Liberal unknowingly chose the wrong moment to harass the Government leader. There was a great feeling of dissatisfaction and despondency among Quebec Liberals,

Oliver Mowat

Sir Richard Cartwright

wrote the discomfitted Holton during the crisis.[46] In an election not fifteen would be returned. All asked, "Can Mr. Mackenzie be aware of the position of matters here?" As he had never asked for office [*sic*!], Holton said, he could speak plainly. There was a "machinery of intrigue" against him in Montreal, and the situation was so serious that "something must be done . . . to regain public confidence . . . or we perish ignobly and under your Leadership".

The Premier reacted strongly.[47] There was no "machinery of intrigue" that he was aware of, and he was "as loyal to you as you have ever been to me". The comments on the state of the party were "very painful", and recalled the first mistake they had made. In fairness to him and the party, Holton and Blake should have joined the Ministry at the beginning, and he had very nearly thrown up his commission to form a government when they refused. Now they were in difficulties, and "I might under the circumstances claim the sympathy and get the advice of friends instead of the cold intimation that under my leadership the party will 'perish ignobly'." He never sought the leadership and did not hold it for personal reasons. "If I am to continue to lead it [the party] I want and need all your kindest and plainest suggestions and those of others . . . If on the other hand my leadership is considered a failure I need not assure you how gladly I will relieve myself of a burden of care the terrible weight of which presses me to earth." The most effective part of the letter was its conclusion. "Whatever may be your view of my mere political action I shall ever be your sincere friend A. Mackenzie." It worked. Luther Holton beat a hasty retreat into a more sympathetic and friendly tone. He merely wanted to be helpful, he assured his leader, and to warn him of Blake's ambitions.[48]

The Government leader was the first to admit that some changes were necessary, and he had been preparing them throughout the summer and autumn. In August, he had written to Patrick Power in Halifax, offering him a Cabinet seat in place of Thomas Coffin.[49] Power was not only a stronger man than the Receiver General; he was also an Irish Catholic. The difficulty was that he, too, was a reluctant statesman who fled the honour and labours of public office. In Quebec, the Cauchon appointment proved to have been a mistake. The chequered past of the President of the Council was a political liability that the Liberals could not afford to assume, and even members who had urged his appointment a year before were now crying for his removal. However, the ever-confident newspaperman had achieved one political coup of no mean proportion. He had succeeded in having a letter written from the Vatican to the Archbishop, warning Canadian priests against engaging in political activity. The Archbishop had transmitted the warning, and reminded them that the church could not protect them if their utterances involved them in lawsuits. As the Riel affair and the New Brunswick school question were not matters of dogma or of morals, they were told not to press their views too far. It was a solid accomplishment for Joseph Cauchon; it merited at least a stay of sentence and a more diplomatic exit than the Premier had in mind.

Félix Geoffrion would have to go as well. For a year he had been unable to look after the work of his Department. Though he looked as robust and cheerful as ever, he leaned heavily on his chief, questioning him about the simplest details, and forgetting the answers before he reached his own office.[50] It was a tragic state for a man picked to succeed the capable Antoine-Aimé Dorion. The most suitable successor to Geoffrion appeared to be the fiery Rouge lawyer, Radolfe Laflamme. Unfortunately, there were disadvantages in his appointment as well. He had been legal counsel for the Guibord family, and was a leading member of the Institut Canadien. Holton was campaigning actively to prevent his appointment. In addition, he had purchased some land near the Lachine Canal, and re-sold it to the Government. The Opposition were implying that he had used confidential information from Ottawa to fill his own pockets.

Another man whose exit was in preparation was David Laird of Prince Edward Island. Laird was not an inefficient Minister, but the Department of Interior, which was responsible for the entire North West, needed exceptionally strong and imaginative leadership and, if possible, a minister with legal training. It was a post that presented sufficient challenge to attract a good man into the Cabinet. The man with the necessary qualities was available; he was Blake's friend, David Mills. On the other hand, Mackenzie was considering the possibility of handing Mills his own Department, and relieving himself at last of the terrible administrative burden it entailed. Whatever portfolio he accepted, the legal expert was needed in the Ministry.

It was not an easy shuffle to arrange. Power refused categorically to join the Administration. Mills preferred to associate himself with the development of the North West rather than the thankless task of issuing and refusing public contracts and solving the mammoth railway problems. Quebec Liberals were horrified at the thought of elevating Cauchon to political limbo by making him Lieutenant-Governor of "la belle province". Holton fought hard against the appointment of both Laflamme and Mills, and insisted that a new Minister of Public Works was essential. Mackenzie agreed. For his own part, he was still anxious to have Holton in the Cabinet, but the Montreal business man had alienated too many other Ministers, and there was no portfolio available. "I would have as Premier to deal with many matters which are in this Dep't though I had ten P.W. Ministers," Mackenzie urged sharply.[51] "My real trouble has been the result of sectional representation forcing upon (me) men of so inferior calibre as to be utterly useless. . . . Offering Mills a seat . . . you may think . . . may in a certain way affect myself prejudicially some day . . . but then troublesome people are safer in harness than cantering alongside your carriage kicking up their heels and frightening the team." The same political truth might well have been applied to the recipient of the letter.

Despite the problems, several changes were made. David Laird overcame his reluctance to leave Ottawa, and set off through the United States to become the first Lieutenant-Governor of the North West Territories. David Mills became Canada's second Minister of the Interior. The vacant Lieutenant-Governorship of Quebec was filled by Luc Letellier de St. Just, the Minister of Agriculture, who was recently widowed, and anxious to have more time to care for his eleven children. Charles Pelletier, the member for Kamouraska, took both his Senate seat and Cabinet portfolio. Holton's objections notwithstanding, Radolfe Laflamme succeeded Geoffrion as Minister of Internal Revenue. Cauchon remained in the Cabinet until a convenient opportunity was found to dispose of him. The Premier continued as Minister of Public Works. As part of the shoring-up process, Cartwright left for London to raise the third loan in as many years.

* * * * *

In early October, Lord Dufferin arrived in Toronto from his western trip and sat down to write his report while putting in a period of residence in the Queen City. He was in excellent health and spirits, and his great capacity for enthusiasm had forced aside all thoughts of abandoning his Canadian post. Lord Carnarvon had intimated that the Indian position was not likely to become available for some time; His Excellency decided to succeed where he was.[52]

Victoria had given the Viceregal party a rousing welcome, but the overtones were ominous. Banners proclaiming loyalty to the Empire were interspersed with messages such as "Confederation without Confederation", "Our railway iron rusts", "Welcome to our sea of mountains". One was particularly blunt: "Carnarvon or Separation". Learning of it before he left the ship, Dufferin suggested that one letter be changed to make the sign read "Carnarvon or Reparation", but the suggestion was declined.[53] He finally determined to avoid an incident by detouring the street bearing the offensive message. A well-trained diplomat, he soothed ruffled feelings the following day by driving under the arch while on a shopping expedition, and bowing to the authors of the slogan.

The problem could not be ignored out of existence. A large deputation appeared at his official residence to demand separation if the Carnarvon terms were not fulfilled. The agile Queen's representative sidestepped the embarrassing interview by declaring that he could not receive complimentary messages without the advice of his Ministers, and that they should petition the Crown "in the usual manner". Nevertheless, he received twenty-five of the dissatisfied men in private audience under his "own roof" the following day, and took copious notes of their complaints.[54]

Vitally interested in the Pacific crisis, the Governor General was unable to maintain a detached attitude for long. After a few days, he was listening to complaints from nine in the morning until seven in the evening, and seeking eagerly for a new solution to the quarrel. At first, his findings seemed to coincide with those of his Ministers. His secretary reported to Mackenzie that His Excellency "finds very great difficulty in keeping his temper with these foolish people."[55] Writing during a tour up the Fraser River on September 6, Dufferin told Carnarvon that there were no serious obstacles to a settlement, and no serious discontent with Canada, "except among the inhabitants of Victoria, and this has solely been generated by their disappointment about the Nanaimo and Esquimalt Railway".[56] Having investigated that project, he considered his First Minister "most culpable in having offered to build it", and condemned the expenditure of a million dollars on it as absurd.

Back in the "nest of hornets" after three weeks on the mainland, the Governor General appeared to suffer a mental lapse.[57] Ignoring the long and bitter discussions in Ottawa the previous spring, he started thinking in terms of a new Imperial intervention. He was aghast, he informed the Colonial Minister, at the inexcusable blunders of his Ministers, and planned to place the whole problem before him "in such a way as will enable you to frame whatever decision you may think the conditions of the problem require". In a telegram to Ottawa, Dufferin asked Mac-

BRITISH COLUMBIA IN A PET

UNCLE ALEC: *Don't frown so, my dear, you'll have your railway bye-and-bye.*

MISS B. COLUMBIA: *I want it* now. *You promised I should have it, and if I don't, I'll complain to Ma.*

Canadian Illustrated News: September 9, 1876

kenzie for approval to suggest a conference in London to work out a new agreement. The Canadian Prime Minister rejected the request as firmly as he dared.[58]

Victorians were as convinced of the legitimacy of their grievances as Ottawa was convinced that they were unreasonable. As an impartial judge, and more particularly, as the Queen's representative, they fully expected Lord Dufferin to express a verdict in their favour. They waited impatiently for a statement that would justify their stand, and point the way to a solution. The Governor General broke his long public silence on the controversial issue in a two-hour oration one morning in mid-September.[59] After the usual portion of "blarney", he told his listeners that he had no message from Ottawa or London, and that he had come merely to assure them that the Government and their fellow-Canadians were one with them "in heart, thought and feelings". Then, having dashed their hopes, he proceeded to discuss the Pacific Railway project in detail. He would rather cut off his right hand, he declared fervently, than utter a single word on the subject that he did not know to be an absolute truth. Canada had failed to fulfil the terms of union, but there was no wilful breach of faith; the conditions had been impossible to carry out. The Carnarvon terms had been accepted, and due diligence had been shown, but the Senate had rejected the Esquimalt-Nanaimo Bill. Some said the Canadian Premier had surreptitiously arranged that. "Had Mr. Mackenzie dealt so treacherously by Lord Carnarvon, by the representative of his sovereign in this country, or by you, he would have been guilty of a most atrocious act. . . . I pledge my own honour on this point . . . had I thought him guilty of it either he would have ceased to be Prime Minister, or I should have left the country." The very opposite was the fact; Mackenzie had protested "with more warmth than he has ever used" against the decision that had prevented him from making further Senate appointments, thus causing the Bill's defeat. It was wrong to say he could have prevented the "mischance"; Senators could not be dealt with as if they were a "regiment of soldiers. . . . A Senator is equally independent of the Crown, the Minister or the people."

Some people affirm that the Premier should have resigned, the Governor General proceeded. Well, he would not have accepted the resignation. Some said he should have introduced the Bill again. Canada at large had shown unmistakeably its approval of the Senate vote, and it would have no chance of being passed. There seemed to be an impression that, after the Senate defeat, Mackenzie cynically refused to take any further action in the matter. "Had my Government done so they would have exposed themselves to the severest reprehension, and such conduct would have been both faithless to you and disrespectful to Lord Carnarvon." On the contrary, he had offered a "very considerable grant of money", and every other item of the Carnarvon terms was in the process of fulfilment. The surveys were being completed "at enormous expense", the fifty millions of land and the thirty millions of money were ready, the terminus was practically decided, and tenders would be called for "almost immediately".

What did all this mean, in effect? Dufferin asked. The province would have three quarters of a million dollars in compensation, and a railway line to a mainland port. But when trade across the Pacific began to expand, a better harbour would be needed, and "of course, the Nanaimo Railway springs into existence of its own accord and you will be in possession both of your money compensation and of the thing for which it was paid". What was the alternative? The secessionists in Victoria would never succeed in persuading the mainland, or even their fellow-Islanders to leave Confederation. But supposing Vancouver Island did leave? The railway would go on, but New Westminster would become the flourishing terminal city. Esquimalt would remain a naval harbour, and Vancouver Island "would be ruled as Jamaica, Malta, Gibraltar, Heligoland and Ascencion are ruled, through the instrumentality of some naval or other officer. Nanaimo would be the principal town on the Island and Victoria would lapse for many a year into the condition of a village . . . God forbid that any such prophecy should be realized."

The Viceregal visit, and the peroration concluding it, had some salutary effects. The *Colonist* received such an injection of courage that it dared to come out openly in favour of the Mackenzie Administration. De Cosmos' newspaper sulked in semi-disgrace, and the "Carnarvon Club" was thrown into turmoil. Open to the charge of disloyalty if they disagreed with the Queen's representative, the Victorians subsided into a begrudging silence.

Lord Dufferin was pleased with his achievement, but it was only the first part of his plan. Having dampened the hopes in British Columbia, and made the residents of the Pacific province more amenable to reason, he still wanted to arrange a three-way conference, and through it a final settlement. One of the principal aims of his speech had been to re-establish the reputation of the Dominion, and of Mackenzie, for good faith, he informed Carnarvon in a private communication from Toronto, "though . . . there were many parts of the Canadian Government's conduct which did not bear handling".[60] In spite of his passionate defence of his Ministers, he was afraid the Colonial Office would "have to put very strong pressure upon Mackenzie to get him to do what is just and right".[61] It would have to be done, however, without the appearance of coercion, which would lead to agitation against London, "the never-failing resort of politicians in this country when they have got into a scrape".

The Governor General was prepared to go to considerable lengths to impose his will on Ottawa. Mackenzie should, in fact, have offered to resign when the Esquimalt-Nanaimo Bill was defeated, he told Carnarvon, but at that time there was no alternative to the Liberals. Since then "Mackenzie's many blunders, and above all the degree to which his party is implicated in electioneering malpractices, and the Big Push Letter are really I believe producing a reaction against the Grits. Still the tide is very far from having swung completely round, though it may have done sufficiently so to enable me to command the situation when Parliament meets."[62] One factor made him hesitate. While Sir John might succeed in solving the British Columbia crisis, his protectionist policy "would prove very distasteful in England". As he launched on the next stage of his plan, Lord Dufferin had apparently forgotten not only the views of his Ministers and his own constitutional position, but the fact that the Liberal party was the historic defender of responsible government in Canada against Governor Generals and Imperial authorities alike.

* * * * *

Having read the Victoria speech carefully, Alexander Mackenzie was optimistic when he arrived in Toronto to meet His Excellency on October 8. His hopes were soon dashed; the speech bore little relationship to Dufferin's real views. The Governor General even complained of the Liberal press quoting his praise of his First Minister to bolster the Government's prestige. The discussions were resumed with as much heat as the previous spring. More confident and aggressive with his trip behind him, Dufferin said that the Canadian people should have an opportunity to give their opinion on the question of secession – if it came to that. "He [Mackenzie] snorted, and put up his back . . . ," Dufferin recorded later, "and said that if an appeal was made to the Canadian people tomorrow they would vote British Columbia out of the Union with the greatest enthusiasm, for which statement I am afraid there is considerable foundation."[63]

The moment of anger passed, and in the evening the Premier assured His Excellency that he was "quite ready to sacrifice his powers and everything else for the preservation of the Union".[64] He returned to the Capital a troubled and unhappy man. All his efforts had been in vain. The Pacific Railway was like a monster that had suddenly sprung to life again, and was threatening to destroy them all. On the one side stood the demanding Pacific province, backed by the Governor General, and perhaps by the Colonial Office. On the other side, he faced a further million-dollar deficit, a wave of popular resentment against the Railway, and Edward Blake, whose resignation hung constantly over his head like a Damocles' sword. Back in Ottawa, a letter from Alfred Jones placed the views of the anti-Railway group plainly before him. "I have always been under the impression that you were personally more anxious to push that work than were the members of the party as a whole, and knowing how strong the feeling against it is in the Maritime Provinces and looking to the future when you may have to rely mainly on us . . . I hope you will be firm and let the B.C.'s know that we are not going to ruin the whole Dominion for their benefit!"[65]

Go and see Lord Carnarvon when you are in England, Mackenzie requested Cartwright; he should know that the Government had gone in advance of public opinion already.[66] Tell him that if the Opposition had maintained its attitude in favour of the line, the hand of the Administration would have been strengthened, but the Opposition leaders had stated at the last session that they never felt bound to do more than offer a company thirty million dollars and fifty million acres. If that failed, stated the Conservatives, the Dominion was absolved of all responsibility. On top of that, Dr. Tupper had declared, "there was no necessity whatever for loading the public Exchequer and burthening the revenues of this country with the expenditures required for this work".[67]

Caught on the defensive by the Victoria speech, and by public opinion in central and eastern Canada, Sir John declared in Simcoe in October that violation of the ten-year limit did not mean breaking the spirit of the terms of union with British Columbia. "If the government did fairly and honestly apply themselves to perform the work as speedily as possible they did in spirit perform their contract."[68] This coincided with a statement by former Lieutenant-Governor Trutch to a Parliamentary Committee the previous year that "if they had said twelve or eighteen years that time would have been accepted with equal readiness as all that was understood was that the line should be built as soon as possible".[69] Mackenzie was encouraged. Even *The Times* realized, apparently, that the Liberal Government had done its very best; no one could do more. "I am all but resolved not to move another peg to satisfy them," Alexander Mackenzie wrote to his brother Charles just before Dufferin was due back in Ottawa, "and practically to tell them they may go to Jericho. . . . I think at present I shall not budge an inch."[70]

His Excellency found Mackenzie's attitude "not satisfactory".[71] After some preliminary skirmishing, the Premier escaped for a quick visit to the Universal Exhibition in Philadelphia, and Blake became the target of the Irish charm and persuasive powers. To Dufferin's surprise, the Minister of Justice seemed less rigid in his attitude, and did not exclude the possibility of a new set of "Carnarvon terms".[72] Encouraged, he drew up a plan to have Parliament vote two and a quarter million dollars for a narrow-gauge railway from the Upper Fraser to Kamloops Lake in order to open the interior of British Columbia, an additional three quarters of a million for the Island, and a further "solatium", the entire cost of the Esquimalt Dry Dock, for Victoria. When Mackenzie arrived back in the capital he found the Governor General anxious to obtain his approval for a delegate to go to England to meet with Lord Carnarvon and a British Columbia representative for a settlement along those lines.[73] "Rest assured that I am fighting your battle tooth and nail . . . ," His Excellency wrote to the new Premier of British Columbia, Andrew Elliott, on November 8, "and I think I already see daylight."[74] Then, with commendable caution, he added, "Do not let it be known that I have written to you and burn this letter."

The clash came on Thursday, November 16.[75] Lord Dufferin summoned the Prime Minister to Rideau Hall to hear what his advisers planned to do. Alexander Mackenzie stated that he and his colleagues were agreed that there was "nothing more to be done on our part". The Vancouver Island Bill having been defeated and the compensation refused, the Government had determined "to proceed with the construction of the Railway as fast as the resources of the country will permit". The Governor General reacted violently. The wording of the compensation offer had been a trap, he argued vehemently, Mills was taken into the Cabinet during his absence with the knowledge that he was a declared enemy of the Railway, and Lord Carnarvon, whose honour was involved, was being ill used.

Mackenzie bristled in turn. Lord Carnarvon should not have pressed his interference on others; in a "great country" like Canada, it was not well for Colonial Secretaries to be too ready in interfering with questions that had no bearing on Imperial interests. Warming to the counter-attack, he denied that Lord Dufferin's honour was at stake as the Ministers were responsible for the acts of the Government, and he had nothing to do with the whole question except as a constitutional Governor. The Cabinet had to answer to the people of Canada and to no one else. If any mistake had been made, it was in allowing anything to be said or done "beyond the strict line of constitutional action", and he would never consent to another arbitration by the Colonial Minister. He was willing, however, to retire and let Lord Dufferin "find someone else who might suit his views better to conduct the government".

The Governor General protested that he had no such desire. When the excitement had subsided, Mackenzie repeated the offer. "My dear Mackenzie," Dufferin replied, "you know I want nothing of the kind . . . and if it were otherwise then I could not help myself." He again pressed the Premier to consider sending a delegate to London, but to no avail. The interview ended with His Excellency expressing the hope that the warmth he had shown would not be taken badly, and with Mackenzie giving appropriate reassurances. The round was a tie.

The following day the negotiations were continued at a safer distance. From his study in Rideau Hall, Lord Dufferin wrote that he was "not at all satisfied with our interview", and thought the Premier had shown "a less conciliatory mood than I had hoped".[76] Alexander Mackenzie protested – also in writing – that he did not feel unconciliatory, that he was "extremely desirous to settle this dispute in a way that can be justified to the world. . . . I have strained my influence, the resources of the country, and the permanent influence of the political party I lead with this in view and having done this so far in vain I confess I sometimes feel my indignation rise a little when I see in England and Columbia reflections on my personal honour and the political integrity of my administration."[77]

Late Saturday afternoon, the contestants met again. Working furiously in the interim, Dufferin had prepared a voluminous despatch for the Colonial Office, and had asked Mackenzie and Blake to come up to Rideau Hall and indicate any inaccuracies. After reading it through, the Premier was asked if he had any changes to suggest. He replied that such a document should not be sent to the Colonial Office at all. The battle was joined once more. "I had a most stormy interview Saturday night with Blake and Mackenzie, and nearly came to blows," the Governor General reported to Lord Carnarvon on Monday.[78]

The Minister of Justice, according to Mackenzie's version of the incident, pointed out that it had been decided in the spring that the visit to British Columbia was strictly a "progress" as Governor General, and that he had not, and could not have, any mission from the Dominion Government or any ambassadorial function.[79] In the circumstances, the only legitimate portion of the paper was his private report to Lord Carnarvon of what information he had gleaned on the trip. A "long and painful" discussion of the different Minutes of Council followed, with Dufferin characterizing the passages concerning an increase in taxation and compensation as "deceitful and most disgraceful".

"They intimated . . . ," His Excellency wrote in his subsequent report, "that they intended the phrase [concerning compensation] 'delays which may occur' to cover all delays however indefinite or posterior to the commencement of construction. This is pretty much what the B.C. petition accuses them of doing. At this announcement I confess I completely lost my temper and told them both in very harsh language what I thought of their principle of interpreting public documents. Mackenzie was simply pitiable, and Blake was upon the point of crying, as he very readily does when he is excited."[80]

"I again told him that in my judgment the Minutes of Council would only bear one meaning," the Premier recorded afterwards, "that we surely did not intend to build the Railway for nothing, the something required was therefore such time as was required, and that there was no dispute in 1874 as to what that was. I told him that we had so far rigidly observed the Carnarvon terms, all except the building of the Railway from Nanaimo to Esquimalt, that every person must have known that particular item required the assent of Parliament, that the assent could not be forced from the Senate, and having failed, we had at once proposed as a substitute a money payment which we agreed to propose to Parliament if they assented. His Lordship then said that we had (not) tried to carry the Senate, that the management of it by members of the Gov't in the Senate was miserable & disgraceful, and that we had not organized a proper whip, and that a member recently named by us had voted against. I replied that he was mistaken, that we had made a vigorous canvass and that I knew of nothing that could have been done from first to last that we had not done."[81]

"Though we went on arguing for some time afterwards," wrote Dufferin, "I could not extract from them more than these two admissions. 1st That if you [Carnarvon] dealt with the Esquimalt and Nanaimo Railway equivalent question at all, you could not help facing their interpretation of the nature of their obligations, as displayed in their Orders in Council. 2ndly That if you could not acquiesce in their views, it might be better for you to postpone action altogether for the present. I then tried to get from them at least a qualified assurance that they would agree if the situation gets more critical to a conference between delegates from the two governments in London, but all that Blake would say was that he would not shut his mind to the suggestion. On this we parted . . ."[82]

Alexander Mackenzie's narration of the same scene is more vivid.[83] "After a lengthy discussion chiefly with Mr. Blake in which His Ex'cy reverted over and over again to the same topics, he turned to me and in a very excited tone said,'I call upon you to answer this question. I have a right to call upon you as Prime Minister to answer me now, and I insist upon an answer. I call upon you to tell me distinctly what you meant by "compensation for delays" in your Minute referring to the Island Railway'. I replied that I had no objection to answer any question properly put, but that he had no right in a verbal discussion to demand an answer in such a manner. I said that if he desired any information to write down what he wanted and I would of course furnish it. He then admitted that I was right. I told him that I thought the Minute and content in the other papers was quite clear as to the compensation.

"His Lordship after this scene spoke more calmly, and I embraced the opportunity to tell (him) that Lord Carnarvon and he must remember that Canada was not a Crown Colony (or a colony at all in the ordinary acceptation of the term) that 4,000,000 of people with a government responsible to the people only could not and would not be dealt with as small communities had been sometimes dealt with; that we were capable of managing our own affairs and the country would insist on doing it and that no government could survive who would attempt even at the insistence of a Colonial Secretary to trifle with Parliamentary decisions.

"His Lordship said he admitted that. In a few minutes he asked me if we took the ground that the construction of the Island Railway, or the substituted payment was a general compensation. I said it was. He at once sprang to his feet and in a very violent tone said; 'Well, after that there is no use having any further discussion. I feel ashamed of it.' Mr. Blake and I at once took our hats and moved towards the door, when he stopped us and said, 'Don't let us quarrell [*sic*] about it! Sit down again and let us discuss it quietly and don't mind what has happened'. We accordingly sat down, but nothing further of any moment occurred, and very soon he remarked that it was probably useless to discuss the matter further then. To this we assented. He then shook hands with both of us and said to me, 'I hope Mackenzie you won't mind what has happened tonight. I was too hasty but meant no ill.' I replied, 'It is all between ourselves', and the interview terminated."

Whatever the adjectives applied to him, the Premier had stood firm. Devotion to the Crown and Empire had not caused him to submit to the dictation of Her Majesty's representative. The tradition of British freedom was maintained.

The next day was Sunday, the day of rest and prayer. Lord Dufferin spent part of it trying to repair the breach in his relations with his advisers.[84] "We had certainly a very stormy meeting . . . ," he wrote to his Prime Minister, "but . . . whatever may have passed has not left the shadow of an unfriendly reminiscence on my mind." His one-hundred-and-eighty-page "laborious composition" had been designed to assist rather than embarrass the Government, he insisted, and he had intended to conclude with a recommendation that the answer to the British Columbia petition be postponed. Nevertheless, he was still convinced of the necessity for a conference in London. One point still rankled. "You said last night you are not a Crown Colony, which is true, but neither are you a Republic. If you were, you would find a President, imposed upon you by the popular vote, a much more troublesome master than ever I am likely to be. But within the walls of the Privy Council I have as much right to contend for my opinion as any of my Ministers, and in matters of moment they must not expect me to accept their advice merely because they give it, but they must approve it to my understanding and conscience . . ."

The Sabbath brought peace to neither side. Early the next week, Blake tried his hand at putting a solution on paper. Lord Carnarvon's intervention in 1874 was a "one-shot" affair, he wrote Lord Dufferin;[85] the question of deciding the new attitude of the Dominion Government was up to the Ministers themselves. A Governor General had a right to ask for explanations, and he could accept or refuse them. However, if he refused, his advisers were faced with the alternative of abandoning their proposals or their places. Once a decision was taken to adopt a certain course, they had a right to expect the Governor General to support them, or at least not to oppose them in that matter. While he was free to advise the Imperial authorities as he chose, he spoke as Governor General only with the advice of his Ministers. In the present situation, if he and Lord Carnarvon could not state that the refusal of the cash compensation placed the situation back where it was before the latter first intervened, then it was better to have no statement at all.

Dufferin was still not beaten. He framed his "Minute" of the British Columbia controversy with a view to forcing his Ministers into a "definite declaration of their intentions", and "in the hopes of showing them what a disingenious course they were pursuing".[86] "They will find it a very hard nut to crack," he commented to his chief in London. In the meantime, the Governor General made a "private" recommendation to Carnarvon.[87] The Colonial Minister could simply state that any discussion of the compensation should be postponed until the results of the Dominion Government's efforts to float the main line were known. He could say that the surveys had been prosecuted with the utmost despatch, but it would take time for the potential contractors to study the reports and have recommendations made to them by their engineers. In view of the inadequacies of the Bute Inlet route, further time was needed, and it was evident that no serious beginning could be expected in 1877. There were some advantages for Victoria in accepting a delay, he reasoned. Whereas complaints made in 1876 might be cavilled at as querulous and premature, the delay of a single summer would enable British Columbia to come into court with a much stronger case.

It was a possible solution. When the anxious Secretary of State received the suggestions, he ordered them to be transposed at once into the first person, as if they had emanated from him, and they became the official British attitude. The rest of Dufferin's "private" letter was less statesmanlike. In eighteen months, Dufferin explained, the Canadian Government would probably be weaker, the Opposition more formidable, and, consequently, the Crown stronger. If his present advisers continued to be obstinate, and British Columbia demanded separation, "a change of Ministry and a dissolution, or at least a strong hint at such an alternative" might be in order. He had told the former Lieutenant-Governor of British Columbia, Joseph Trutch, "what a battle I was waging with my Ministers on behalf of his Province", and counselled calm for the present in order to avoid "playing into the hands of the enemies of the Province". In a year or eighteen months, His Excellency confided to Trutch, the grievances would be no longer hypothetical and "it might be necessary for us to take off the gloves".[88] At the present time, the Conservatives were gaining, but "the pear is very far from being ripe". It was a dangerous diplomatic manoeuvre, hardly creditable for a representative of the stern and righteous Queen Victoria. She would not have been pleased. One slip, and a brilliant career would be plunged into the abyss of disgrace.

Notwithstanding the firmness of his stand, Alexander Mackenzie continued the search for a solution. "Though I retain my opinions . . . I have yet some hope of being able to find ground on which we can agree", he wrote the Governor General a week after their memorable Saturday evening.[89] As soon as Cartwright returned, he would call a full meeting of Council to discuss the subject. Lord Dufferin turned his attention to the rest of the Cabinet, particularly those from the Maritimes. "Of one thing rest assured," he told the Minister of Fisheries, "I am *quite* convinced that it would be a misfortune for the country if anything occurred to upset my present Ministers. As far as my personal comfort is concerned . . . I am most anxious that they should retain power at *least* until I leave the country."[90]

The year 1876 was drawing to a close. On December 15, two days after Cartwright's return from England with his third loan, Alexander Mackenzie communicated his final reply to Rideau Hall.[91] If he could not have the favourable statement from Lord Carnarvon that he felt was called for, a fixed delay was preferable to an unfavourable one. He was sure that the idea of a conference would not be well received in Canada, and he was "the reverse of sanguine" of its results. However, his earnest desire to reach an agreement led him to waive his objections, "unless contrary to my expectation some unforeseen circumstance should render it inadmissable", and to agree to a meeting if His Lordship thought it advisable at that time.

It was done. The Ministry and the Crown were together again. Dufferin was as radiant as Mackenzie was full of foreboding. "I am in hopes that now I shall not have to trouble you again on the B.C. difficulty as long as I am in Canada," he wrote jubilantly to London.[92] In addition, he felt he had managed to maintain a workable relationship with his advisers. "Notwithstanding the little bourrasque I described to you, – Blake, Mackenzie and I are on the best of terms. In fact they feel – at all events Mackenzie does – that it has been in his own interests I have been fighting, and that I am thoroughly friendly to him and his Government."[93] If true, it was a diplomatic achievement indeed!

Riding the crest of his triumph, His Excellency wrote a "private" letter to the Premier of British Columbia. If the Dominion Government did not make a bona fide commencement on the railway in the province by the spring of 1878, there would be a London conference to discuss not only compensation for the Island railway, but "every other subject of difference between yourselves and us . . . With the conference sitting in the colonial office so to speak, the Secretary of State would actually prove a very powerful assistant in getting justice done to you. . . ."[94] He was still everybody's friend.

CHAPTER 16

"Protection is a Monster"[1]

The British Columbia dispute had forced other matters into the background. A multitude of decisions had to be taken before another session of Parliament was upon them. Bone-tired and alarmingly thin, Alexander Mackenzie gave in to the urgings of his family and agreed to a brief Christmas respite in Sarnia before the labours of 1877 began. His first grandson was nearly of walking age, and they had not yet met.

The Premier returned to Ottawa four days before year's end in a violent snowstorm. He arrived none too soon. The next day a strike of railroad workers cut the service in the Belleville area. Disgruntled by increasing lay-offs on the Grand Trunk line, the men fought back as best they could. As the trains arrived in the lakeshore town, the crews stepped out, leaving men, women and children stranded in the blinding snow. Strike-breakers were mishandled; angry mobs of unemployed wandered over the tracks.

The General Manager of the Grand Trunk, James Hickson, had asked the men to take a cut in wages to help to save the Company from bankruptcy. Supported by the headquarters of their union in Cincinnati, Ohio, they refused. Convinced that the strike order emanated from the same foreign source, Hickson wired Ottawa for "immediate aid to be given to civil authorities at Belleville where mob law prevails".[2] The sympathy of the working-man Prime Minister was more with the railway than with the men. A rugged free enterpriser who believed that wages and employment must be determined by the law of supply and demand, he could not condone uneconomic conditions that decreased efficiency. He himself was straining every nerve to reduce government expenditures, and cutting staff wherever possible. Included in his list of economies was a plan to reduce the salaries of Ministers, and to cut the indemnities of Members of Parliament from one thousand to eight hundred dollars per session, although he knew there were "a good many mercenary devils among our followers" who would object.[3]

Fortunately, Mackenzie was not called upon to comment on the merits of the strike, and merely replied to Hickson that the provincial authorities, and through them the municipalities, were responsible for law and order; the federal government had no authority to intervene except in a national emergency.[4] He urged Mowat to force the municipalities to do their duty. George Brown was less restrained. The *Globe* denounced the violence of the strikers, the abandonment of the passengers in such inclement weather, and the foreign intervention in Canada's economic life.

The strike spread rapidly, and in four or five days the entire line from Montreal to Sarnia was paralysed. Hickson continued to bombard Ottawa with telegrams, urging that troops be called out. The Premier flashed back the same answer over and over again that the strike could not be considered an insurrection, and that he would be open to a charge of murder if he ordered the troops to intervene and lives were lost. The municipalities had the right to ask for troops, but they hesitated to do so in face of the wrath of the strikers. Helpless and exasperated, the railway Manager gave in. "After the receipt of your telegraphic message . . . there was no other course . . . but to . . . compromise with the mutinous men", he cabled sulkily to Ottawa on January 3.[5] Mackenzie could only express his regret. "I trust it will not be necessary for the Company to make any arrangements at all with persons who have acted so badly," he replied.[6] It was an unfortunate incident for the Liberals. The influential railway Manager was annoyed, and Brown had made it quite clear that his sympathy – and by implication the sympathy of his friends in Ottawa – was not with the workers.

Following the Cabinet shuffle, all the Ministers had been re-elected, but Laird's seat in Prince Edward Island was taken by a former Conservative Premier, James Pope. Alexander Mackenzie had hoped to have as candidate the incumbent Premier, Louis Davies, but the Islanders felt his candidacy would split the Province along religious lines and even advised the Dominion Premier himself to stay away, lest he lose them more votes than he could win.[7] They lost the seat, and with it the chance to regain their Cabinet representation in Ottawa.

An uneasy peace reigned in Quebec. Cauchon was still the "bête noire" of many Liberals, and the Holton faction were encouraging the attacks on Huntington and Laflamme. In Quebec

City, Henri Taschereau, member of one of the most prominent French-Canadian families, was upset because he had not been made a minister. After the experience with Fournier, the Premier would take no chances with a man who, it was reported, liked to drink.[8] As long as he was unable to entice Henri Joly away from the Quebec Legislature, the man Mackenzie wanted most of all in the Cabinet was Wilfrid Laurier. "Nothing would have given me greater pleasure than to have had you now as my colleague," he told the young lawyer early in 1877.[9] "Circumstances which I cannot control, and the necessity of considering the representation of localities in your Province have led to the choice of Pelletier." Laurier was not eager to seize the prize. "From that moment my quietness and happiness will be gone," he confided to a friend. "It will be a war with the clergy, a war every day, every moment . . . I shall be denounced as anti-Christ. You may laugh at that, but it is no laughing matter to me."[10] The fact was that the Liberals were caught in another squeeze. In Ontario, they were being denounced by the Orangemen as subservient to the Catholic bishops, in Quebec as Godless revolutionaries like their namesakes in Europe. "I shall pursue the course already taken on principle," Mackenzie commented doggedly, "and trust that my intentions will be vindicated by action and the result will be beneficial to Canada."[11]

The number of requests for favours that had to be heard and, in most cases, refused, seemed limitless. The Ministry was becoming known as a band of miserly Scots who could not even be generous with someone else's money. Highlanders were in such bad odour, the Premier commented, that he no longer dared appoint one, even when he was the best qualified for a position.[12] The line-up in his ante-chamber was as long as ever. "People are now getting so particular that it seems to be unsatisfactory to tell them that their claims will be '*taken into consideration*' ", Mackenzie remarked ruefully to Thomas Moss in mid-January.[13] "Very unreasonable is it not? They all '*want to know*' and I don't want to tell. My stock of civil phrases (never too large) has nearly failed. One fellow had the impudence to tell me the other day that he had heard that before but it didn't do him any good, after I had made him one of my prettiest speeches. . . . I was mad enough some twelve months ago to order all extra work to be given to needy ladies. I have been compelled to hold a daily levee ever since to that class not all of whom have much personal attractions to soften the interview and they are not content with a look at Buckingham's face, though a handsomer man than me. But about your client, well, we will do the best we can. . . ." Around him the sound of hammers and saws continued as the new section of the West Block neared completion. He watched the progress with a deep personal interest. Soon he would be installed in the tower, and the secret stairway would enable him to foil his tormentors.

There was so little that could be said in the 1877 Throne Speech. Blake's Extradition Bill was still not approved in London. The Ontario-Manitoba border was still undecided. The third member of the Fisheries Commission had not yet been named. Some Americans were beginning to discuss reciprocity again, but Mackenzie was not interested in anything less than a concrete proposal from the top echelon in Washington. The depression continued. "Lenten fare", commented Sir John with some justification, after listening to the brief message.[14]

The Pacific Railway remained a hot issue. The public had not been told of the agreement for a conference in 1878 if the line was not begun by that time; they knew only that Lord Carnarvon wished to delay his reply to the petition until the surveys were completed and tenders called. Convinced that he represented the total indignation of the province, Amor De Cosmos warned that "the days and weeks were few" before separation would be demanded, unless the Carnarvon terms were fulfilled.[15] The absence of any mention of the Esquimalt-Nanaimo Railway in the Speech from the Throne, he stated, was ample grounds for the "divorce".

When in difficulty, counter-attack. In the second week of debate, an article in the *Globe* charged misuse of the Secret Service Fund while Macdonald was still in office. In the last session before the 1872 elections, the former Premier had asked Parliament for a seventy-five thousand dollar increase in the Fund. The Liberals had insisted that a record be kept of the expenditures and that a Confidential Committee, composed of three Government supporters and two members of the Opposition, be set up to inspect the expenditures once a year. Sir John had agreed, providing the new arrangement did not apply to the past. Two years after he left office, the Conservative leader had returned twenty-five thousand dollars to the federal Treasury on Mackenzie's insistence, but had kept six thousand six hundred dollers to pay outstanding claims. Why the long delay since he left office? the *Globe* wanted to know, and on what authority could a man disburse public funds two years after leaving office?

He had discussed the matter with the Government leader, Sir John A. Macdonald informed the House, and Mackenzie had insisted that a proper entry be made in the record of public expenditures.[16] The Tory chieftain had maintained that this was not necessary according to British precedent, as the operations of a Special Service Fund were disclosed to a committee in England, but the Secret Service Fund expenditure was never revealed, and the balance was taken along by the retiring Ministers and used for "their own party purposes in opposition". Sir John agreed to appear before the Public Accounts Committee, but would not reveal the names of the recipients of the six thousand six hundred dollars. There was little doubt in anyone's mind that it was a refund to whomever had advanced the money to whisk Riel and Lepine out of the country several years earlier. He was asked to return it to the Treasury.

Another ghost in Sir John's closet had been disinterred the previous summer. The Northern Railway Company, operating in northern Ontario with a large loan from the Dominion Government, was found to have contributed heavily to an eighty-thousand-dollar testimonial fund for the Tory leader, to have paid over five thousand dollars of the expenses of the Company President when he was a Conservative candidate, and to have disbursed other items entered in the accounts as "Parliamentary expenses, etc."[17]

Mackenzie had set up a Royal Commission to examine the books of the Company, and named Oliver Mowat as legal counsel. The manager of the Company, an honorary aide-de-camp to the Governor General, played for time by acting ill, then announced suddenly that the loan to Ottawa had been repaid. The Commission's grounds for the investigation evaporated. Nevertheless, the Grits had succeeded in reminding the public of Tory practices in the past.

Early in the session, tragedy struck the Mackenzie family. John Mackenzie, fourth of the immigrant brothers, had been ill for some time, and the Premier had received regular bulletins about his health. On Saturday, February 17, a telegram arrived advising that his condition was serious. The Liberal leader dropped everything and dashed for the railway station. On the way, he rushed into the East Block and up to Blake's office on the second floor to tell his colleague of his departure. Afraid of breaking under the emotional strain if he engaged in a conversation, he seized a piece of paper on the desk of Blake's secretary and scribbled a hurried note. "My brother has had a relapse and is fast sinking. I must leave. Let someone see Buckingham about my office work. I leave everything in good order. If estimates are on, ample information is classified in my desk."[18]

It was too late. Another telegram overtook him in Kingston, announcing John's death. "I had a melancholy home-coming," Alexander Mackenzie wrote to the Minister of Justice on Monday, "my brothers and I have always lived in such complete

WHAT INVESTIGATION REVEALED.

From Bengough's *Caricature History of Canadian Politics*, Vol. I

harmony carrying our boy[hood] days with us to the close of our life that I cannot tell you the grief one's death causes the others. I could not master my feelings enough to speak to you on Saturday and even now I seem to have passed through a horrid dream . . . He died peacefully having been able to bid all the family goodbye but myself. Up to the last half hour he kept asking if Alex had not come . . . John's wife . . . is so completely broken down that no tear moists her eye and I dread the results unless nature comes to her relief by allowing grief its natural flow."[19]

The number of stones in the family plot in Lakeview cemetery was growing. His mother, two brothers, his first wife Helen, Hope's first wife, two babies of his own – the Mackenzie blood was becoming intermixed with the Canadian soil. They had succeeded well in their land of adoption. John left behind him over one hundred thousand dollars, a tidy sum for a former artisan, and much more than he would have earned at home in Perthshire. Only Alexander was a poor man; he was giving his life to his country.

The brief absence from Ottawa prevented the Premier from hearing Speaker Anglin announce an innovation in Parliamentary procedure. Henceforth, prayers would be said at the beginning of each sitting. A few years earlier, Mackenzie had been responsible for introducing the Hansard record; the second permanent mark that the stern God-fearing Baptist would leave on the Canadian Parliament was the daily request for Divine guidance in doing the nation's business.

The daily prayers had no visibly moderating effect on the tone of the debates. When Mackenzie arrived back in Ottawa, Cartwright was engaged in a bitter defence of his budget. The Finance Minister had announced a deficit for the previous year of nearly two million dollars. Despite slashed expenditures in every possible field, he was forced to increase taxes on tea, coffee, malt, beer, cigars, steel tubing, and other goods. Seven years of Tory prosperity were followed by three years of Liberal distress, boomed Charles Tupper. That was the long heralded "reform". He scoffed at Cartwright's argument that the Government was "like a fiy on the wheel", and had no control over economic swings; a Conservative "national" policy was the answer.

The Premier plunged into the debate, condemning the "tirade of abuse" of "party claquers".[20] Protection, he replied savagely, was comparable to "a person who had got a box on one ear and turned round desiring a corresponding one on the other ear". Dr. Tupper wanted to cure a sore on one side of the patient by putting a blister on the other. The Tory policy of increasing customs taxes would dry up revenues by stifling trade, and "as you must have revenue from somewhere you will have to get it by direct taxation". "Direct taxation": that was the spectre written into the Canadian constitution that made politicians and taxpayers alike tremble in apprehension.

The wily Opposition leader was more cautious than his burly lieutenant. He called for a "readjustment" of the tariff to "benefit and foster the agricultural, mining and manufacturing interests of the Dominion".[21] Mackenzie was disappointed. "The honourable member for Kingston has not . . . ventured very far upon the ice . . .", he teased. "I always sympathize deeply with any gentleman who is pledged from party consideration to advocate a policy he has no faith in." Sir John refused to be tied to the "monster" of protection. "You need not think that I am going to get into that hole," he commented outside the Chamber.[22]

The debate was hot, and grew hotter as the days passed. The Premier kept the House sitting late into the night in an effort to bring the issue to a vote. It was three o'clock in a morning of the fourth week before the "ayes" and "nays" were counted. Sir John's amendment was defeated by seventy to one hundred and nineteen. It was a comfortable majority, but it revealed a rift in the Liberal ranks.

We are overjoyed at the complete defeat of our opponents, Laurier wrote to Quebec on March 31.[23] Simultaneously came the good news that the Liberals had held Kamouraska constituency, vacated shortly before by Senator Charles Pelletier, and that Hector Langevin had been unseated for corrupt electoral practices in Charlevoix. It was a day of triumph, but not without a price; after the vote, Alexander Mackenzie took to his bed. For the first time, he was forced to miss the daily sittings of the House of Commons because of his health. Far more than the long hours of labour, the constant vilification and petty annoyances were grinding down his health. A few days after his return from John's funeral, the Tory *Sarnia Canadian* repeated the steel rail charges. No denials, no exposition of the facts, no challenge to request an investigation seemed to still the attacks. "I am quite willing that every transaction in my Department, everything in it shall be subjected to a strict scrutiny by a committee of one and that one the honourable member for Kingston," he challenged.[24] It was no use; the accusations continued unabated. Suppressing his distaste for the whole dirty business, he decided to "nail a Tory paper" for libel, in an effort to stop the campaign of abuse. "The truth is that I have had many a bitter quarrel with our own supporters because I would not go an inch out of my way to give them a contract . . .", Mackenzie wrote to his brother Charles in March, "I imagined in short that my conduct was not only beyond reproach but that I was open to the charge of leaning backwards . . . I am particularly concerned that my brothers should be attacked and abused as they are on my account. This and my natural disinclination to deal in personal attack or insinuation almost sickens me of public life."[25]

The Premier's illness revealed a basic weakness in the Liberal Administration. With all the Cabinet changes, he had still not been able to develop a strong team of Ministers, and to delegate to them their full share of the burdens. Like a motherless brood, Parliament seemed unable to get through even routine matters in his absence. Blake gave the impression that he was hanging back, as if he were reluctant to associate himself too closely with the policies of the embattled Administration. Had he known what was passing through his colleague's mind, Mackenzie would have been still more upset. Discouraged about his own future and that of the Government, the prodigy of the party was contemplating submitting his resignation again.

Most of the other Ministers seemed weak and ineffective to the weary Premier. Huntington was no fighter and his prudence had not increased since the Argenteuil affair, he complained to his brother. "Smith is lazy, Burpee knows his own business, nothing more. Vail I cannot let loose. Coffin has neither talent, tongue or sense. Mills and Cartwright are always willing and effective, Cauchon no use. Scott is not always near me and he often blunders in the Senate in spite of all my posting of him daily. You will see I have my own troubles, still I don't lose heart very often."[26] There was just cause!

At the earliest possible moment, the Grit leader dragged himself back to the Chamber. He was beginning to resemble an automaton, producing legislation and policy statements at a prodigious rate, answering barrages of questions, and blocking attacks from across the floor. Worst of all, he was forced to say "no" on nearly every subject that arose. No, he was not ready to bring in prohibition legislation; no, he would not prevent all transportation from operating on Sundays; no, he would not admit that his dead brother John had used improper influence in obtaining the contract to sell hay to the Mounted Police!

There seemed to be no end to the cries of "scandal". Speaker Anglin, it was discovered, was a shareholder in a firm that had done some printing for one of the Government departments, and had jeopardized his seat in Parliament. Alexander Mackenzie tried to protect him until the session was over so that he could continue his duties. In Goderich, on Lake Huron, the lowest bidder had not received a harbour contract, and the record showed that the successful tenderer was a constituent of Edward Blake. The Minister of Justice had written a letter to the Premier. "David Moore, of Walkerton," it read, "asks me to inform you that he is about to tender for the Goderich works, and I do so accordingly. I told my friend Moore that an introduction was unnecessary, as you would let the works fairly, without respect to persons."[27] It was a simple enough letter on the surface. Opposition members read between the lines the sinister machinations of political intrigue. The Prime Minister read into the record the recommendation of the chief engineer that the lowest bidder be passed over because he, himself, on reflection, did not feel he would be able to perform the work. The Tories were not impressed. The fact was, Sir John insisted, that twenty thousand dollars had been thrown away to give the contract to Blake's constituent.

No session was complete without a wrangle over the Pacific

Railway.[28] Contractors in London and Canada were studying the engineering data, Mackenzie reported, but no offers had yet been made to the Government. He asked for another million and a half dollars to proceed with the project. The Opposition delivered a scatter-gun attack on a host of details, but were careful not to commit themselves to a specific alternative. Their amendment read simply that "this House cannot approve of the course pursued by the Government with respect to the Canadian Pacific Railway". Tired but undaunted, the Liberal leader heaped scorn on his attackers in a two and a half hour rebuttal. "Usually a motion of want of confidence is a somewhat solemn or grand matter," he began severely, "but . . . we have had them for breakfast, dinner and supper lately. . . . This is a general aggregation of all the particular charges, just in the same way that boarding-house people, who, having used the joint of meat warm, serve it up as cold hash the next day . . . Three years ago it would have been a matter of surprise . . . if the honourable gentleman or any of his colleagues would have uttered the word Canadian Pacific Railway unless they were forced to it in a court of justice . . ."[29] No counter arguments could stop the debate. Only when the Opposition had run its full course in the early hours of April 25, was the vote taken. The Government won an easy victory. Five days later, the members went home.

* * * * *

It had been a hard session. Blake had collapsed completely before the end, and Mackenzie, commented Dufferin, looked "like a washed-out rag, and limp enough to hang upon a clothes line".[30] Near the end, the sittings had gone on frequently until two, three, or even four o'clock in the morning. Except for his trip to Sarnia, and his brief illness, the Premier had invariably been in his seat until the last, and at his desk in the West Block at nine in the morning. It was reported that on occasion he stayed up all night in his residence preparing the work for the next day. Friends and opponents alike generally agreed that no Government leader had ever worked harder or more conscientiously, but they all wondered how long he could stand the gruelling pace.

Alexander Mackenzie himself was not dissatisfied. On the whole he was convinced that the Government had more than held its ground, and that the Tories had been hurt most in the mud-spattering contest. The only serious matter for the Liberals was the Anglin case, and they had succeeded in proving that it was an administrative matter in which no ministerial

AFTER THE FALL OF THE CURTAIN

THE TIRED LEADING MAN: *How glad I am that it's over. Thank goodness I won't have to come on again for another nine months.*

Canadian Illustrated News: May 5, 1877

decision had been involved. The Speaker would have to resign, but he would be re-elected and could be chosen as presiding officer again in 1878. "Wishing that your scalp may long be spared", the Grit chieftain concluded his report on the session cheerfully when he wrote to David Laird in the North West.[31]

The Governor General was less optimistic about the Conservative chances than on his return from the Pacific coast. Sir John was leading a more sober life and his health was greatly improved, but Lord Dufferin did not feel they had gained as much ground as they had expected. "I feel less certain than ever about the future," he wrote to Lord Carnarvon.[32] The fact was that he was having doubts about the desirability of a change.

The new charges against the Conservative leader had recalled the distasteful events of the Pacific scandal, and had made him appreciate the virtues, albeit rather exasperating on occasion, of his First Minister. With a creditable effort on both sides, they had succeeded in re-establishing a satisfactory working relationship, and had even agreed on an official report of the trip to British Columbia. Victoria had accepted the delay, though declining to comment on the question of compensation for the Island railway. During the session, His Excellency had refrained from interfering in administrative matters, and left his advisers free to get on with their work. Pleased at having survived the British Columbia crisis, and absorbed in the lavish entertainments at which he and Lady Dufferin were so expert, he surprised the Colonial Office by offering to accept an extension of his term in Canada![33] The gesture was not entirely a compliment to the Dominion; he was timing his reappearance in London to coincide with the availability of the Indian post.

The rush of politicians' sheepskin trunks to the station had hardly begun before Mackenzie was embarked on his summer programme of work. "Remember, economy is our role for the general election," he reminded Laflamme on April 28.[34] "Pray give your attention at once to lopping off all useless officers at Toronto and elsewhere," he instructed the Minister of Customs, "without any regard to your bowels of compassion for disreputable or useless Tory office holders. These people deserve no compassion and we want to come within the estimates between now and the election."[35] "All the season's business should be arranged while the session is fresh in our memory," he urged Charles Pelletier.[36] Officially the campaign was still a year away; for the Premier it had already begun.

The plan for a counter-attack received a rude shock before it was fairly launched. Blake resigned again. There was no doubt about his illness this time. Behind the robust façade, the strain of responsibility and controversy was wearing away at his delicate nervous system. Proud of his intellectual capacity, he feared the sort of damage to his brain that had brought his famous father to an early grave. The news deflated the Premier's courage and optimism in a trice. "Barely out of a severe session I had hoped for some peace of mind and bodily rest," he replied to the unwelcome news.[37] "Your letter is worse than all. I begin to feel I cannot sustain the struggle of leading the party. Is it not possible for you to reconsider?" He pleaded again for time.

Joseph Cauchon had been warned that he would have to leave the Cabinet, and had agreed to take the Lieutenant-Governorship of Manitoba when it became available in the fall. Mackenzie searched for a way to make the Presidency of the Council available still earlier so that Blake could remain in the Ministry without the burdens of an administrative department. With Chief Justice Richards in poor health, the top position in the Supreme Court was about to become available again, but if the Minister of Justice retired to the Bench his name would be lost to the party in the approaching contest. The Liberals were not even sure that they could win his seat in a by-election.

In the midst of the doubt and perplexity, a pleasant surprise arrived for both Mackenzie and Blake: Carnarvon enquired in mid-May if they would allow their names to be added to the Queen's birthday list to be made Knights Commander of St. Michael and St. George! Lord Dufferin being absent in New York, the message was transmitted by his secretary. Notwithstanding their previously expressed opinions on class distinctions, it was a strong temptation for the two men. They were devoted subjects of the Queen, and the offer from Her Majesty was nearly a command. In addition, they had the usual quantity of natural pride in having their efforts recognized. But, were loyalty and pride a strong enough combination to outweigh their Liberal belief in the equality of all citizens? "I will not conceal the natural desire I had to accept the honour so generously offered," the Premier confessed to the Governor General after heart-searching reflection, but he could not see his way clear to accept.[38] "I think Imperial titles can only be worn with dignity by such persons as the principal Judges of our higher Courts whose official position is such as to remove them from many of the social obligations of Society, or by persons who have not only a position in a public sense but whose private fortune would justify them in assuming a higher status than what generally prevails in Canada." He was in neither category, but he had recommended three men – Dorion, Richards, and Brown – who were.

Why did he refuse? Was it merely his poor financial position? Was his inherent respect for British aristocracy so great that, despite his derogatory remarks, he felt an ex-stonemason had no place in such company? Was he determined that his name should not pass before that of George Brown? Was he more proud of his title of British freeman, or too sensitive to expose himself to ridicule for contradicting his past utterances? Perhaps the *Parliamentary Companion* contained the answer. "As a Liberal," it stated, in that year 1877, the Premier believed in "the universal brotherhood of man, no matter in what rank of life he may have taken his origin, . . . the extinction of all class legislation . . . , that every man is equal in the eye of the law."[39] Such a philosophy was hardly compatible with the title of Sir Alexander, or the abbreviation "Bart." after his name.

Without consultation between them, Edward Blake declined the honour as well. "However suitable . . . in the societies of the old world they are not very congenial to this country," the ailing Minister wrote the Governor General.[40] He, too, was not inclined to "these trappings" of outer distinction.[41] Dufferin accepted the refusals gracefully. "I am quite charmed with your letter . . . ," he replied to his First Minister. "It is written in the very best taste, and is full of modest dignity, and good sense, and I have no doubt that Lord Carnarvon will duly appreciate the simple, straightforward nobility of thought which breathes in every line."[42] It was a nobility that required no formal label.

The matter of titles did not rest there. A few days later the Governor General mentioned casually that the Imperial Government planned to confer a C.M.G. on Sandford Fleming, the chief engineer of the Pacific Railway. A fellow-Scot from neighbouring Fifeshire, Fleming's long service undoubtedly warranted recognition, and he would wear the dignity well. The alarming thing was that London did not deem it necessary to consult the Canadian Government before making an award to a Canadian public servant. Mackenzie's fighting spirit was aroused. "I have . . . a strong conviction that a practice which may be convenient in small colonies is wholly unsuitable in Canada . . . ," he wrote to Rideau Hall.[43] "I yield to no one in my anxiety to maintain the power and prestige of Britain on this continent, but I am satisfied this can best be done – I might say can only be done – by Canadians. It is quite impossible that an English Minister can understand Canadian affairs so well as to undertake without Canadian advice to act in such cases. . . ." Canada was a difficult country to govern, he argued. There were no classes, but there were considerations of race and religion that could not be understood from the other side of the Atlantic.

The Colonial Minister replied that he would be "happy to give a most careful consideration to any opinion or suggestion that may proceed from one whom I respect so much as Mr. McKenzie [*sic*]".[44] Though he would not agree that the recommendations for honours should only emanate from Canada, the embryo of that principle was born.

Blake's fretting made at least a partial Cabinet shuffle essential. It was impossible to remove Cauchon at once because Bishop Conroy of Ireland was in Canada as a Papal envoy to investigate the dissension among the faithful in Quebec, and the ex-newspaperman was preparing a long statement of the

Government's argument. He was needed to defend the Liberal case. In addition, Blake refused to serve as a pretext for dropping the unpopular Minister from the Cabinet. In mid-June, Cauchon was made Minister of Inland Revenue, Blake became President of the Council once more, and Laflamme, Minister of Justice. Laflamme's appointment was Blake's recommendation; Holton and his friends were ignored again. Cauchon would be removed completely in September, Mackenzie wrote to Wilfrid Laurier, and a Cabinet place would be available for him at last.

Bishop Conroy's arrival created a sizeable stir on the political scene. Lieutenant-Governor Letellier and Joseph Cauchon heaped attention on him in Quebec City. In Ottawa, he was received by the Governor General, and he and the Premier exchanged visits. "Laflamme has suddenly become very pious," Mackenzie commented dryly to Letellier, on June 17.[45] "Pelletier declares he never could endure Red Republicanism. Huntington is to attend the confessional and recant his Argenteuil speech or declare he never made it, he is not quite certain which statement to make. Cauchon is radiant . . . Scott thinks we are all Catholics and he is so happy. I don't like to contradict him. The poor protestants in the Cabinet are, of course, out in the cold."

Laurier was not idle. With the day of heavy responsibility approaching, he determined to place the position of the Quebec Liberals clearly before the Canadian people. An invitation to speak to the Quebec Canadian Club provided the opportunity; he set to work early in June to prepare his remarks. Alexander Mackenzie was pessimistic. It might be better to wait until Father Conroy was gone, he wrote to his future colleague in response to a request for advice on the proposed address. "I have no faith in clerical dignitaries being favourable to liberal opinion in itself."[46] As the day approached, Laurier, too, became apprehensive, and confessed to the Premier that he felt "at times sorry of having gone into it". However, the date was set, and the speech was ready. Promising to "make it a point to be prudent", and not say anything "impeachable", he went ahead.[47]

Political liberalism was not Catholic liberalism, he told the two thousand French-speaking Canadians who crowded into the hall built for about half that number, nor was Canadian Liberalism to be identified with the revolutionary and Godless form in Europe. Canadian Liberals traced their ancestry to England, "the classic land of liberty". "I am a Liberal," the tall handsome lawyer proclaimed.[48] "I am one of those who think that everywhere, in human things, there are abuses to be remedied, new horizons to be opened up, and new forces to be developed. . . ." Such a declaration had nothing to do with religion; it simply identified him with those who were by nature forward-looking, instead of those who were content with the present. Certainly the fact that the Liberals were popularly known as the "Rouges", and the Conservatives as the "Bleus", bore no analogy to the fact that "le ciel est bleu, l'enfer est rouge", as the curés were wont to declare. Sir Georges-Etienne Cartier, with his love of English institutions, would not approve of his party modelling itself after the reactionary groups in France, Laurier argued. To use the Catholic faith as the basis for a political organization was disrespectful, and could only give rise to its counterpart, a Protestant party. Under such conditions, Canada could easily be thrown into a religious war. The Liberals wanted all citizens to enjoy British freedom to the full, and had no desire to restrict the clergy. "In the name of what principle should the friends of liberty seek to deny to the priest the right to have and express political opinions . . .?" However, that right ceased, as did all rights, at the point where it interfered with the rights of others, and the electors' independence was a right that the Liberals were bound to defend. There was no country under the sun in which the Catholic Church was freer or more privileged, the eloquent young politician concluded. "Why then should you, by claiming rights incompatible with our state of society, expose this country to agitations of which it is impossible to foresee the consequences?" Whether or not they agreed, the audience listened with rapt attention and respect. In those two brief hours of 1877, the thirty-six-year-old Laurier soared to prominence as a national figure.

A counter-attack against the Tories could not be carried out uniquely in Ottawa. Working at a feverish pace that put him back in bed for a few days in early June, Alexander Mackenzie struggled to clear his desk so that he could take the Liberal case directly to the people. There was need. Senator Macpherson, the Tory financier who had turned against Sir John when he was by-passed on the Pacific Railway contract in 1873, was now turning on the Grits for similar reasons four years later. He published a pamphlet containing a complete list of charges, innuendo, and slander against the Mackenzie régime.[49]

From early June, the weather was frustratingly hot in the capital. The MacGregor Lake area, north of the Ottawa River, was one huge forest fire, and dense smoke covered the town, making eyes smart and throats burn. To the Government leader, it was just one more source of irritation. The third loan was dwindling fast, and Cartwright was urging that the work on the Pacific Railway be stopped completely until revenues began to rise again. Anxious to get their hands on any available funds, the Cabinet approved of the nomination of Maurice Delfossé, the Belgian Ambassador to the United States, as the third member of the Fisheries Commission, despite fears that he had been "squared" by the Americans.[50]

In Prince Edward Island, the Protestant-dominated Liberal Government was trying to force a system of secular education on the Catholics. "You are free to legislate oppression within the framework of the Constitution Act," Mackenzie wrote to Premier Davies, "but . . . you may depend upon it that this question has got to be settled by some compromise by one party or the other. . . . The New Brunswick Government have made a certain amount of concession . . ."[51] "Take it easy," wrote Jones from Halifax, "even you can't stand such a pace for long."

On June 27, Mackenzie joined the picnic parade in Kingston.[52] The role of attacker suited him well. Though pale and desperately thin, he lashed out at his tormentors in his best fighting tradition. Between the bitter denunciations of his opponents, the homely anecdotes and dry humour were still evident. In Forest, a few miles up the Lake Huron shore from Sarnia, he told the audience of fellow Highlanders that the Tories reminded him of a Scot who was asked on his deathbed to forgive his enemies.[53] "Well, if there's nae help for it, I maun e'en dae it," he finally agreed, "but" – turning to his son – "deil tak ye, Tonald, if *ye* forgie them." At Newmarket, they reminded him of a horse thief who had just been acquitted, and was asked after the trial by his lawyer if he really did steal the horse. "Well, I thought until I heard you address the jury that I did," came the reply, "but now I must say I have my doubts about it." The Tories seemed to have convinced themselves that Sir Hugh Allan and the Pacific scandal never existed.

The list of facts and figures seemed inexhaustible; even the jokes lasted the course. An old lady in Hamilton, he told one "splendid demonstration", shook her head in sorrow that Mr. Mackenzie should do such terrible things as he was accused by the Conservatives of doing. After telling her the charges were untrue, a Liberal sympathizer asked, "What would you say if the Conservatives did such bad things?" "Ah," she replied, "there is a great difference, for you know Sir John doesn't pretend to be a Christian, and Mr. Mackenzie does." Let them fire their worst charges at us, the Premier shouted defiantly in Wellington, the Liberals, unlike Davy Crockett's famous raccoon, would not "come down". Despite the difficult times, he would not let Liberals forget the principles for which they stood. "We are no Liberal party if we say that we have done all that can he done," he told a crowd in Colborne on July 9, "for reform will never cease as long as this world is peopled by sinners, and controlled, as it sometimes is, by sordid motives."[54] "Everything looks well," he reported on his arrival back in Ottawa the following day.

Work was piled high again at the office. Lord Dufferin wanted to make a "progress" to the North West, and extensive preparations for his large entourage were required. George Brown's title had run into another pitfall.[55] Senator Simpson had brought a libel action against the newspaper, *The Durham News*, in connection with the "big push" letter, and one judge, a former Conservative politician, had referred to the famous letter as having been "written with a corrupt intent, to interfere with the freedom of elections". In a *Globe* editorial, Brown replied in kind. Still fearful of any connection with a Canadian "scandal", London dropped the publisher's name from the honours list again.

A letter from the member for Brantford was interesting. One of his constituents, a Professor Bell, was promoting the use of a "speaking telephone" invented by his son Alexander.[56] To set off the publicity campaign, he wanted to install a line between Rideau Hall and the Premier's office. There was already an alphabet telegraph service between them, but the delicate machine was usually out of order. At twenty dollars per annum, Alexander Mackenzie decided that the Government could afford the new apparatus.

More serious, the Orangemen were preparing a "walk" through the streets of Montreal on July 12, and wanted military protection. As in the Guibord and Brockville incidents, the Premier replied that it was a municipal responsibility. The French-Canadian mayor of Montreal had no inclination to protect the militant Protestants whose aim was to flaunt the pride in their race and religion in Catholic faces. The "walk" took place, but fighting broke out, and one Orangeman, Thomas Hackett, was killed. "The real murderer of poor Hackett is Alexander Mackenzie," cried one newspaper, "because he refused him the protection to which every British subject is entitled."[57] With Catholics accusing him of aiding the Orangemen, the Liberal leader was caught between two fires again.

On August 1, the pre-campaign electioneering was resumed. Declining a private railway car for fear of accusations of accepting favours, the Premier, his wife, and daughter Mary set off on a tour of the Maritimes. They spent the first Sabbath in Summerside, the second in Halifax. In between, the speeches, receptions, and interviews followed one another with merciless rapidity. The fisheries negotiations appeared to be going well in Halifax. Galt and Smith were working together smoothly, and they had confidence in Delfossé. In Digby, the news was less cheering. The Minister of Militia, William Vail, had run afoul of the election act; he, too, had a share in a publishing company doing government printing! Mackenzie urged him to resign at once and stand for re-election, but he resisted such a "suicidal decision".[58] "It occurred to me that you need a Government Commissioner at the Paris Universal Exhibition," the discouraged Minister of Militia sighed after a discussion lasting several hours, "maybe you had better send me there for the winter." The Liberal chieftain returned to Ottawa as careworn as before.

There was friction again with London over Canada's claim to deal with her own affairs. Some eight thousand United States Indians, led by Chief Sitting Bull, had crossed into the North West in the foothills area to escape being imprisoned on a reserve. The Canadian Indians saw with alarm this horde of hungry people who wished to share their fast-dwindling buffalo herds. Colonel McLeod and his handful of redcoats would be powerless to intervene if a large-scale clash occurred. A further danger was that Sitting Bull would use Canadian soil as a base for an attack on his hated enemies, the United States troops, and would even succeed in recruiting Canadian natives into his ranks for the struggle. With Dufferin absent, and time of the essence, Alexander Mackenzie had despatched David Mills to Washington to work out a joint solution to the problem.[59]

Mills had been very successful – and proper. He had explained his mission to Francis Plunkett, the chargé d'affaires at the British Legation, and they had gone together on some of the visits to the American authorities. The Canadian saw the President and several Cabinet Ministers and was assured that someone would be despatched to the West to persuade the Indian chief to move back across the border. Pleased with the success of his first diplomatic mission, the Minister of the Interior returned to Ottawa, and prepared to leave for the North West himself. Much to his surprise, the amiable and helpful Plunkett protested to London the breach of protocol in dealing directly with the Americans.

On receipt of a remonstrance from Downing Street, Lord Dufferin agreed that it was a "very pernicious precedent" and could not be allowed to pass unchallenged.[60] Alexander Mackenzie replied that there had been no time to follow the circuitous route of getting in touch with His Excellency in the North West, asking him to communicate with London, and explaining the whole situation in terms sufficiently explicit to enable a British diplomat in Washington to persuade the Americans to take prompt and effective action.[61] The Governor General confided to Carnarvon that "the diplomatic relations of Canada with the Yankees is one of the tender spots in the relations of the Dominion with the Mother Country".[62] Canadians had reached a point where it was necessary to "menager" constantly their "amour propre", or "a great deal of bitterness and ill-will might be generated".[63] The Canadian Ministers made excuses for the breach of established procedure, but they were highly pleased with themselves for having created the precedent, and with having negotiated directly with a foreign power for the first time.

The Halifax fishery negotiations indicated still more clearly the anomalous situation that was developing. Seeing the tide swinging against them, the Americans again suggested sinking the fishery discussion in the larger question of a general trade agreement. Mackenzie had always felt that agreements between British and Americans were reached at Canadian expense; now the British suddenly became alarmed that their interests might suffer if the North Americans were to discuss their mutual interests directly. Lord Carnarvon and Lord Derby, the Foreign Minister, reminded Dufferin that "the Imperial not less than the Colonial side of the Question" must be kept in view.[64] He counselled the Governor General to avoid direct communications with the United States Secretary of State.[65]

Britain could instruct the Queen's representative, but she could no longer prevent the direct contact between Canadians and Americans. Though they were well surrounded by British advisers, Alexander Galt and Albert Smith were in constant communication with their neighbours on Canadian soil. Under other circumstances, the situation might have been fraught with danger for the Empire. However, in response to United States "feelers", Mackenzie made it plain that there would be no discussion of reciprocity without Imperial sanction. On the other hand, he told Galt, "you will understand still better that there shall be no discussion by the Imperial diplomatists without our sanction.[66] He instructed the Canadian negotiator to go ahead and get the award, as the Dominion needed the money badly. Besides, a favourable settlement "will justify me in insisting that we know our neighbours and our own business better than any Englishman". Both Dufferin and Carnarvon agreed that it was fortunate that the Dominion was in Mackenzie's hands.[67]

September 3, 1877, was a historic day in Canada. A telephone box and a wooden hand telephone had been installed in the Premier's office, and a similar set of equipment in the Governor General's study at Rideau Hall. With His Excellency still absent in the North West, Buckingham went up to the Viceregal residence. When all was ready, he tapped the diaphragm of the box; the clear Gaelic accents of his employer filled the room. It worked! "When conversation is carried on in the ordinary tone and the words are clearly enunciated intercourse can be kept up with as much ease as if the two individuals were in the same room," boasted the sales propaganda at the Ottawa Exhibition that fall.[68] It was somewhat of an exaggeration. Nevertheless, the reporter covering the event was justified in telling his readers that "the trial was marked with eminent success".[69] The telephone had arrived in Canada.

* * * * *

The Liberals held a second series of picnics in the autumn.[70] The Conservatives had been active, and there was no dearth of charges to refute. Sir John had stated that the Mackenzies had gone on an overseas holiday in 1875 at Government expense; the Premier replied that neither he nor Jane had spent a dollar of public money. The Tory leader was still trying to identify the Grits with annexationism and anti-British sentiments; they denied the charges at every occasion. The rallies were well attended. At Simcoe, fifteen to eighteen thousand people cheered as a twenty-four-horse team brought Alexander Mackenzie from the station to the picnic grounds at the head of a mile-long procession. "Sandy's at the Helm", "Welcome Nature's Nobleman", "He Rose from the Foundation to the Keystone", proclaimed the banners.[71] The Reform bandwagon appeared to be rolling again.

After such a hard summer's work, the Premier found it more difficult to maintain an impression of vigour and enthusiasm during a two, three, or even four hour address. The cool harvest air cut mercilessly into his thin body, and the dust irritated his throat and lungs. At a Saturday meeting in Aylmer, he had to summon all his courage to keep from betraying his weariness, and he yearned for the tranquillity of the Sabbath the following day. The fifty-mile ride to London behind a team of horses following the meeting was pure agony; he was a very sick man when he crawled gratefully into his hotel room in the middle of the night.

On Sunday afternoon, it was evident that their leader could

not continue, and Huntington, Mowat, and Cartwright went on without him.[72] He caught up with them two days later at Port Elgin. Pale, alarmingly thin, his beard a colourless grey with only traces of red near the roots, he wanted to be on hand for the final rally. Only when the tour was over did he turn his face toward Ottawa. On his arrival in the capital, he went to bed. The doctor did not let him get out of bed for a week, and kept him, he wrote to Mary, on a diet of "Quinine, sulphate of iron, and other medical abominations unnameable".[73] But there was no release from the crushing task he had undertaken. The faithful Buckingham fended off visitors valiantly and postponed decisions, but many urgent problems still had to be brought to the Premier's bedside. At the earliest possible moment, Mackenzie climbed painfully up to his office on Parliament Hill.

"I did not wish to trouble you while you were ill . . . ," a letter from Toronto ran a few days later, "[but] I do not find myself improving in health or ability to work . . . and thus I see nothing for it but to retire."[74] Blake was determined to leave public life entirely. Once again, it was an awkward moment for a change. Laurier had been sworn in as Minister of Inland Revenue at last, and was campaigning for re-election. Cauchon was grumbling openly about being sent into exile in Manitoba. His sentiments towards the tiny Western province were reciprocated.[75] Even the French-speaking element felt that they were being used as a political waste-basket, and the Orangemen were threatening to tar and feather him on his arrival. There were troubles enough; Blake's departure could hurt the Administration sufficiently to jeopardize Laurier's election. Again, Alexander Mackenzie was obliged to beg for time.

In Quebec, Laurier's speech had found favour with many moderate-thinking people, and Bishop Conroy's visit had resulted already in a grudging admission by the Bishops that no political party was condemned by Rome. However, the "ultramontane" or extremist elements resented the achievement, and stiffened in a sullen resistance to the Liberals. In particular, they resented the forced retirement of the seventy-seven-year-old Ultramontane Bishop Bourget of Montreal, and adopted him as a martyr to their cause. The Drummond-Arthabaska by-election became the focal point of the politico-religious struggle.

The new Minister began his campaign confidently, but soon realized that he was faced with stiff opposition. Another Ultramontane Bishop, Monseigneur Laflèche, was clearly against him, and the curés were active for the "Bleu" cause. The Conservative candidate was a wealthy business man, known to be on good terms with the Bishop. Sir John exploited the situation

M. CAUCHON DISPOSED OF.

Grip: October 13, 1877

adroitly. Unable to speak French, he toured the province in the company of Langevin and the "Bleu" member, Louis Masson. Gazing nostalgically into space, he evoked memories of his many political battles by the side of the great Georges-Etienne Cartier against the Liberals. The saddest day of his life, declared the old man, his voice filled with emotion, was when he saw Sir Georges lowered into his grave. "Gentlemen, I promise solemnly, if God grants me longer life, to avenge the memory of that great man, any time and any place, wherever I go, wherever I can make myself heard."[76] It was just the right note; the audience loved it. No one seemed to notice that Cartier was not under attack, and that Laurier traced his own political ancestry, in part at least, to the Napoleon of Quebec.

It was a tough fight. "Mr. Laurier wants to make the priests marry," cried an Ultramontane paper, "he calls them men with withered hearts. . . . He qualifies the Holy Father as a tyrant. . . . He has in him the principles of Robespierre and Gambetta."[77] The habitants were under heavy pressure. "You tell me that if I vote for a Liberal, I shall be damned," one told his priest, "I cannot vote for Mr. Bourbeau for you tell me that if I do not follow my conscience, I shall be damned; I cannot vote for neither, for you tell me that if I do not vote at all, I shall be damned. Since I must be damned anyway, I'll be damned for doing what I like. I am going to vote for Mr. Laurier."[78] On nomination day, Wilfrid Laurier was still confident of a majority of three hundred – if there were no bribery.[79] Dorion wrote to Mackenzie with tongue in cheek, that "if I was mixing with politics as I sometimes did heretofore, I would compliment you on your recent movements as regards Lower Canada".[80] Then the tide turned. The manager of the local railway was disgruntled because the Liberals had appointed him to the Senate. In the last weekend of the campaign, he brought in a trainload of "Bleu" supporters and set them to work canvassing one part of the constituency that Laurier had neglected.[81] When the ballots were counted on October 27, the Minister was defeated by twenty-nine votes.

It was the most violent election in many a year, the discomfited Laurier wrote to his chief in Ottawa. One of his men had been killed, the basest appeal had been made to religious prejudices, and votes had been bought, "as in the good old times".[82] His health was worn down by the campaign, but he would have to run again. Mackenzie wired him to demand a recount, and told him that seats in Montreal and Quebec were available for another try. Charles Pelletier reported that Laurier could run in Quebec Centre, but eight thousand dollars would be needed to carry the seat. The Premier reacted violently to the suggestion of spending such huge sums. "Think of a Minister's friends deliberately contributing money!" he snorted.[83] "The thing would be a disgrace." Above all, contractors must not be asked to contribute. He would help defray legitimate expenses from his own pocket; good organization would have to do the rest. "Let not the word 'discouragement' be mentioned," he directed. "Let the difficulty be bravely met and resolutely overcome. Let no one show a lack of moral courage." The Minister of Agriculture protested in vain that no bribery was intended, but that Quebec politics were conducted differently than in Ontario.

Laurier realized the gravity of the situation. "I am the last card of the party in this province," he told the Dominion leader.[84] "If I am kept down the party is well nigh gone down completely." There was no use trying to win a seat in the Montreal area; the protectionist cry had swept the city, and the leading Liberals were bickering constantly over the debris of their organization. Mackenzie summoned Huntington and Laflamme to Ottawa for discussions. "I was so anxious about Laurier and the necessity for organization and vigorous action that I slept none all night and was here at 8.30," the Premier wrote from his office on November 5.[85] "They managed to come at 11 and then their whole story was what Holton did or said." Holton was as bad. "His attitude has done mischief in Quebec and must be stopped," the Government leader grumbled, "even if he is driven to take his choice of being a close friend or an open enemy."[86] He resolved to go down and take a hand in straightening out matters himself.

Three days in Montreal confirmed the impression that Laurier had been defeated because his organization was weak. Mackenzie preached co-operation in order to build a strong corps of workers in every constituency. Holton complained that Laflamme alienated people by promising favours that he could not produce. The Premier excused it as part of a natural desire to please everyone, but in an interview with the Minister he told him frankly that he would have to avoid making commitments he could not keep. Before the Montreal discussions were over, the factions agreed to join in a dinner at which the Grit chieftain appealed again for unity and action.[87]

There were some hopeful signs. The Tory *Montreal Star* paid tribute to the visitor's "undoubted courage of his opinions and the ability to announce them with effect", and declared him to be a distinguished Canadian statesman.[88] From Quebec came news that Quebec East was available for Laurier's second try, and that he was confident of a majority of one thousand.[89] On the other hand, Blake sent letters from his doctors supporting his plea that he must retire from office at once. Mackenzie put the letters aside and waited for the news from "la belle province".

All Canada was watching the contest in the old fortress city. The Government was "too scrupulous", complained Pelletier impatiently.[90] There were so many jobless men who would vote

Liberal if a few extra public works were undertaken, and they were given employment. The Conservative provincial Government was hiring those who would vote "Bleu" in Quebec City, and giving the dyed-in-the-wool "Rouges" jobs so far outside the city that they couldn't possibly turn up to vote on election day. The Liberals must do the same, entreated the Minister of Agriculture, as the populace only laughed at Ottawa's "too strict economy" and "our friends (are) displeased". Mackenzie was adamant. The Government had undertaken all the work it could afford in Quebec.[91] A six-hundred-dollar contribution to the campaign fund was the limit of the Ministers' assistance.*

The virtuous Scot made one important compromise to avoid a disaster. In September, the Cabinet had passed an Order in Council granting an amnesty to William O'Donohue, the last of the Red River rebels. On November 22 Lord Carnarvon's assent arrived. Salving his conscience by pointing out that the Order in Council pre-dated both of Laurier's by-election contests, Mackenzie authorized the candidate to state that the Official Gazette of the following Saturday would put O'Donohue "on the same footing as the others".[92] The message arrived a few days before polling began.[93] At the same time, he insisted to Pelletier and Laurier that the result would depend entirely on organization. "Get the men out early and have a committee in every polling district and a sub-committee in every street," he wrote nervously. "I am thus urgent as the news is generally good. I fear there is something wrong." Laurier reported that the amnesty "movement" had "a most satisfactory result".[94] Perhaps Father Conroy helped as well. In a timely address in Montreal, he advised a crowd to heed the pastoral letter of the Bishops in which they had reluctantly admitted that political liberalism and Catholic liberalism were not the same thing. "Do not be induced to follow . . . those who from an excess of religious or political zeal attempt to apply condemnations against persons or parties that have never been pronounced," he counselled.[95]

The day after Mackenzie's apprehension-filled letter was despatched, his luck seemed to change. From Halifax came a telegram that Canada had been awarded five and one-half million dollars by the Fisheries Commission! Nearly twenty per cent of the total federal budget! It was a welcome windfall. "As I cannot find you by the telephone," the Premier scribbled excitedly to Lord Dufferin, "I write a note to say we got five million. . . ."[96] Then, in early November, Quebec East gave Laurier a majority of three hundred votes. The Liberals had won a round at last. The fight would go on.

*Eight hundred dollars were sent eventually by the Ministers, and one thousand eight hundred by Montreal Liberals.[92]

CHAPTER 17

Fear Not, Favour Not

The last session was approaching. On its outcome would depend very largely the fate of the Liberal Administration, and the verdict of their hard labours. And more than ever before, the Grit leader had to face it alone.

Blake was gone. After every argument had been used and every delaying tactic applied, he left in January. It was a sad parting. The eulogistic editorial that Mackenzie inspired in the *Globe* in December had been partly a desperate last card to retain a valuable colleague, and partly a tribute from a sincere admirer.[1] On the rough road they had travelled together, a bond of solidarity and understanding approaching affection had grown. "I cannot tell you how much it saddened me," the Premier replied to the letter of resignation of January 18, 1878. "Although I knew the present separation had become inevitable the actual accomplishment I had instinctively kept out of view."[2] There was no formal goodbye. By the time the letter was delivered, Edward Blake was on his way to Toronto. He was so upset that he could not control his emotions sufficiently to say farewell to his colleagues.[3]

To fill the great void, Alexander Mackenzie tried to persuade Oliver Mowat to come to Ottawa. The Ontario Premier was as indispensable on the provincial scene as Mackenzie in the Dominion capital. No successor was in sight; he could not leave without placing his Government in jeopardy. In Nova Scotia, William Vail's defeat in a by-election finally forced Alfred Jones to overcome his reluctance to hold office and take the militia portfolio. Vail's estimate of his chances proved accurate; his reaction to defeat was less praiseworthy. "Wipe out the secret ballot before the general election," he urged Mackenzie; it only favoured duplicity on the part of the electors.[4] "And take all proposed spending in the Digby area out of the estimates"; the people must learn that they could not profit by defeating a Minister. The strait-laced Scot was indignant as such an attitude; it was the very thing he had entered public life to combat. "All's well that ends well," he sighed with relief when Vail was gone and Jones installed in his place.[5]

The Pacific Railway. The words would be carved on his tombstone, or at least written into the coroner's report as one of the principal causes of his death. It had ruined his health and his temper, damaged his reputation, and almost brought him to blows with the Queen's representative. It was important to choose a route and present a reasonable report before the election. The difficulty was that Sandford Fleming, the Chief Engineer, was on an extended leave of absence in England, and his subordinates could not agree on the most suitable line through the mountains. In contrast to most of the engineers, the Acting Chief, Marcus Smith, opposed the Yellowhead Pass route because of the large "sterile stretch" between the Prairies and the coast.[6] His argument was based on a trip he had taken from the narrows of Lake Manitoba to Edmonton, and on to the Pacific. He reported far more fertile soil to the north than had been suspected, with grass and pea-vine so dense and high that horses had difficulty in breaking through. In Edmonton, two surveyors told him that they had gone north to Fort Assiniboine, crossed the Swan Hills, and found themselves in another vast and fertile plain leading directly up to the Rockies. Conversation with Indians indicated that a railway across the mountains at that point would be easier to construct than farther south. Smith preferred a northern route across the Prairies, skirting the northern edge of the Swan Hills, and emerging at Bute Inlet on the Pacific.

Alexander Mackenzie had long been tempted by a northern route that would be less difficult to build, and give more direct access to Asian markets. He had even sent engineers to investigate the Pine River Pass to see if a line to the coast could be built at some point above Vancouver Island. He was less inclined, however, to agree with Marcus Smith's choice of Bute Inlet. Strangely enough, the only British officer who favoured it was Admiral DeHorsey, the naval commander in Esquimalt. This may have been due to his friendships in Victoria, and his aspirations to see "his" harbour become the railway terminus.

If Parliament could look at the whole scheme in a national, and not a provincial sense, the northern route was probably more favourable, the Premier informed His Excellency, but the necessary surveys would entail further delays.[7] A choice was essential for the session. The alternatives, therefore, were the Bute and Burrard Inlet routes. The former was undoubtedly more expensive, and fifty miles longer. The Burrard route followed the Fraser River, and passed through the rich farming district inland from New Westminster that had so impressed Lord Dufferin in 1875. A temporary boat service could be organized as far up the river as Yale, he reasoned, and the railway line between Yale and Kamloops started immediately. Thus, the interior of British Columbia would be opened up in a very short time. There were two objections: the Burrard route lay much nearer the United States border, and residents of Victoria would not be pleased. The first consideration carried little weight with Mackenzie; he had accustomed himself to the second. He chose Burrard.

The Governor General was delighted. Two additional years of surveys had led to the conclusion at which he himself had arrived in 1875. "I do not think that up to this point there has been any bad faith shown by Mackenzie," he reported to Lord Carnarvon.[8] Marcus Smith, on the other hand, was outraged and sulked in his office, listening hopefully to the speculation that the Grits might be defeated in a few months. To add insult to injury, the Premier had not only drastically reduced his staff; he had also moved him into the old office of the Minister of Public Works when the new space in the tower was completed at year's end. Smith found it totally inadequate for his needs.[9]

Some apprehensive Liberals urged that the 1878 session be postponed as long as possible on the theory that the Opposition would talk until Easter, regardless of when they began. Although he, too, was becoming increasingly nervous and uneasy, Alexander Mackenzie was determined to carry on as usual; the date was set at February 7. The first hurdle was to get Timothy Anglin back in the Speaker's Chair. His re-election in Gloucester had been an easy matter, but the Opposition were known to be planning to block his return as presiding officer. The strong-headed Grit was determined that they should have no such satisfaction. As soon as the Clerk had read the list of new members, Mackenzie was on his feet, proposing Anglin as Speaker.[10] Impossible, protested Sir John in a long and carefully documented argument replete with British precedents; he was not even a member as he had not been introduced to the Speaker since his election. The Premier was ready. British precedents did not apply, he replied, as the oath of office was given to new members by the Speaker in the Chamber at Westminster, whereas in Canada the oath was given beforehand by the Clerk, and that had been done in this instance. Consequently, the introduction to the Speaker was a mere formality in the Dominion. One Conservative member protested that there could not be a vote without a Speaker. Mackenzie was ready for that argument too. The highest British authority agreed that on exceptional occasions the Clerk could conduct a vote. The vote was taken. Anglin was installed by one hundred and sixteen to fifty-three.

It was a heartening beginning for the Grits. Their leader was amused. "The debate, begun by Sir John, with the air of one of the chivalrous knights pictured in Ivanhoe, came to an ignominious end . . . ," he wrote to Mary during the debate the following day. "Every child . . . laughed at them . . . Lady Macdonald in the gallery, like the Queen of day, stamped her foot and exclaimed 'Did ever any person see such tactics!!' "[11]

The tone of the 1878 Throne Speech was confident. Increasing revenues and an abundant harvest gave hope that the commercial depression was passing; pressing public works would be carried out without increasing taxes; a decision on the Pacific Railway would be announced soon. The Liberals presented their strongest front line. Instead of following the usual practice of allowing new members to "flesh their maiden swords" by moving the Throne Speech debate, two veterans were assigned the task of putting up a vigorous defence of the Administration.

Scenting victory at hand, the Tories attacked eagerly. In a few brief hours, all semblance of restraint and cordiality vanished; the debate became sharp and even ugly. Alfred Jones was accused of having said some years earlier that he would cheer if the British flag were lowered over Nova Scotia. Such accusations, the Premier retorted hotly, were hardly appropriate from men like the Conservative leader, who associated with men who burned the Parliament Buildings in Montreal, raised a black flag to insult the Governor General and pelted him with rotten eggs, and talked of driving the French Canadians into the sea. Restraint was cast to the winds; it was promising to be a hot session.

When George Brown arrived in Ottawa at the beginning of the session, he moved right into "Cliffside" as the guest of the Prime Minister. In every moment that they could spare from the business of Parliament, they turned the residence into a party headquarters for the purpose of planning campaign strategy. Mackenzie had hoped that Blake and Edgar would take charge of the contest in Ontario, but the illness of the former threw much of the responsibility back on his own shoulders. James Patullo, Secretary of the Reform Association of Ontario, agreed to spend most of his time finding candidates and setting up constituency organizations. Recalling his own experiences as Reform Secretary twenty years earlier, Mackenzie felt that a good organization was of infinitely more importance than public meetings.[12] Already, he had conducted a personal survey of the situation in each constituency, and written letters urging prominent men to run as Government candidates. Throughout the session, he continued to direct operations from his office and his home, with his former leader acting as his faithful lieutenant.

Richard Cartwright's budget was hardly a pre-election document. The 1876-7 deficit, he announced, was a million and a half dollars. Sounds of delight rose from Opposition benches at the announcement. "Do honourable gentlemen consider it a subject of merriment, a subject of rejoicing?" snarled the harassed Finance Minister.[13] There was to be no change in policy. The revenue tariff would be maintained and expenses curtailed; increasing prosperity would wipe out the deficit in the current year. To Liberal members and candidates, the announcement had a discouraging and ominous sound. After four years of defending a diet of sparsity they had hoped for a few sweeter morsels to take home to the electorate.

The field of vision and hope was left entirely to the Opposition. Sir John did not miss the opportunities available to him. He called for a "National Policy" that would "benefit and foster the agricultural, mining and other interests of the Dominion".[14] It was all rather vague, but the Tory leader had erected a marvellously convenient umbrella designed to attract protectionists, nationalists, former Canada Firsters, Goldwin Smith – in fact, practically everyone dissatisfied with the status quo. And the status quo, as Laurier had commented, was deadly dull.

The main political eruption of the season was precipitated, not in Ottawa, but in Quebec. Lieutenant-Governor Letellier was having difficulties with his advisers.[15] His predecessor, Adolphe Caron, had been too full of years and gout to worry about administrative details, and the Ministers had lost the habit of going through the formal procedures required by the constitution. His approval of Government decisions had been taken for granted, and his signature affixed as a matter of course. Suspicious of his former adversaries' every move, Letellier objected to being ignored, and reacted sharply when his prerogatives were not respected. In November of 1877, he protested to Premier de Boucherville that proclamations were issued in his name which he had never signed. Other instances followed. The tension between the two men grew rapidly. On one occasion, the Lieutenant-Governor objected to a proposal substituting executive for judicial authority in matters relating to the Quebec, Montreal, Ottawa, and Occidental Railway. The Ministry announced it regardless. Business taxes were imposed without notifying him. Proclamations for Thanksgiving Day and the opening of Parliament were issued over his signature without prior consultation. Exasperated, Letellier threw caution aside, dismissed the Conservatives and asked Henri Joly, the Leader of the Opposition, to form a Government.

Alexander Mackenzie's first reaction was that his former colleague had committed a serious blunder. "My own feelings are so strong against any exercise of arbitrary power that I doubt the wisdom or justice of the dismissal," he confided to James Edgar, "but I give no opinion to anyone. They undoubtedly handled the Govr shamefully. Fancy their calling Parliament together without consulting or informing the Governor!"[16] It was political quicksand for the Grits. "We have always as Liberals fought against this," he told Pelletier, and they must not be forced into the position of defending it.[17] Besides, "the elevation of our friends [in Quebec] with a wrong principle to defend would be a very doubtful advantage." To Letellier he sent only one piece of advice – dissolve the Legislature and let the people decide. The advice was accepted.

On the provincial level Liberal fortunes in French Canada had been improving steadily, and many felt that Joly, even with the political drawback of a Protestant heritage, was not far from the Premiership when the crisis broke. Alexander Mackenzie hoped fervently for his success. He congratulated his old friend on forming a Cabinet and on the election prospects, and offered his assistance. "I know, of course, that you would not ask any more than I would do, any improper thing to be done; but it may often happen that the public interest may be as well served by a course acceptable to our political friends as otherwise, in which case we can of course meet their views."[18]

It was April before the subject was debated in the House of Commons. In his major effort of the session, Sir John condemned the dismissal as "unwise and subversive", and called on the Prime Minister to defend "those great principles" of his Liberal predecessors, or be condemned as a reactionary.[19] Mackenzie flung off the alternatives with scorn. The honourable gentleman was hardly in a position to lecture the Liberals on responsible government, he scoffed; they had fought a long time against him and his friends in order to establish it in Canada. The Opposition motion was an attack on the autonomy of the province, and called for an unwarranted use of the powers of the House to condemn an act committed in the provincial field. The Government would not interfere in any way in the controversy, and it asked all lovers of responsible government to defeat the motion as "contrary to the very principles on which government is based, as injurious in its results and reflecting on the character of the people to whom it is to apply". In brief, both party leaders wanted to establish themselves as the defenders of the same cherished principles. Each threw his best orators into the fray. Laurier spoke for the Government, Langevin and Masson for the Opposition. Anxious to reach a decision and get on with other business, Mackenzie kept the House sitting well into the night, and on one occasion until after six in the morning. With the election campaign in Quebec in full swing, the Conservatives kept the debate going as long as possible. They read books aloud, told stories, and when spirits rose, sang songs. On one occasion, suddenly noticing Lady Dufferin in the gallery after midnight, both sides rose and joined in "God Save the Queen". The Countess fled in embarrassment. "We have had like Jones and the Parrot 'a deuce of a time'," the Premier wrote after the all-night sitting.[20] ". . . John A. got very drunk early last evening, and early this morning they had to get him stowed away somewhere. McDougall of Three Rivers is also very drunk and kept the floor off and on for nearly two hours uttering utter nonsense and just able to stand. Campbell of Cape Breton was in a shocking state. He got on the floor in front of the Speaker with his hat on and a stick in his hand which he flourished round his head, daring the Govt. or any member to fight him, yelling at the highest pitch of his voice. Plumb, Caron, and others were also drunk but did not so seriously expose themselves. . . . I am glad to say that not one person on our side tasted any liquor." There were other versions. Macdonald protested that he had been tired and gone to sleep on a bench. One Tory newspaper commented that things had come to a pretty state when "men like Premier Mackenzie have stiff pulls of whiskey set upon their desk under the guise of coffee. . . ."[21]

The talent for high jinks exhausted, the decision came on April 13. The Ministry won by thirty-three votes. "Some people expected me to defend you," Mackenzie wrote to Letellier after the debate.[22] "I considered it to be the right course to take the ground that we had no business to interfere . . . [and] was able to rebuke those who assailed you." There was a note of warning in the letter. "Liberals are always necessarily jealous of the arbitrary use of power. What is done by a friendly Governor to-day may be done by an unfriendly Governor to-morrow!"

The strain was beginning to tell on Mackenzie as well as on Sir John. He had less control of his temper, and was frequently baited into reckless replies. When the Opposition Leader refused his challenge to make a specific charge of corruption that could be investigated, he said that Macdonald had "too little manliness to make a charge".[23] He condemned the protectionist policy of the Tories as a political expedient. "All interests cannot be protected because there would then be no person left to do the protecting," he argued vehemently.[24] "Protection means in its principle and essence a gross injustice to some classes of the community." After one violent outburst a courageous Government supporter sent him a piece of paper with the message in large letters: "A pint of molasses will catch more flies than a hogshead of vinegar."[25] In his seat on the front bench, the Premier snapped his jaw in anger, tore the paper into fragments, and threw it on the floor.

The heat generated in debate extended beyond the Chamber. One British Columbia member appeared with a black eye that he had received while trying to continue a debate in the corridor. Yet, somehow, a great deal of work was accomplished. The Government repented and relaxed its election law, permitting members of Parliament to own stock in companies having public contracts. A Bill was introduced abolishing the useless Cabinet post of Receiver General and creating a second legal portfolio, a Solicitor Generalship, in order to divide the heavy burden of the Minister of Justice. At London's request, Mills brought in a resolution declaring that the northern reaches of Canada included "the entire continent to the Arctic Ocean, and all the Islands in the same, westward to the 141st Meridian West of Greenwich".[26] The claim of sovereignty was staked out as a warning to Canada's neighbours to the south as well as to those across the Pole.

At long last Mackenzie gave Canada some temperance legislation. Known as the Scott Act in honour of the man who introduced it in the Senate, it was far from the sort of Bill that the Premier would have introduced twenty or thirty years before. But then, the Premier was no longer the same person. He had grown in knowledge and in comprehension, and many of his narrower conceptions had faded with the years. He could appreciate civilized drinking, and served fine wines and liquors in his home. It was against excessive drinking that he protested, and even then, his respect for human liberty made him reluctant to use force in curbing it unless an overwhelming majority of the population demanded such a step.[27] As a result, the Temperance Bill was a milk-and-water compromise. If twenty-five per cent of the electorate of a municipality petitioned the Governor in Council, a vote was to be taken. If over fifty per cent of the voters favoured prohibition, it would be proclaimed in ninety days. If, after three years, twenty-five per cent petitioned for a repeal, the ban would be lifted. The proposal precipitated a hot debate. Speaker Anglin descended from his dais and denounced it as "pernicious" and "tyrannical". Arthur Bunster of Vancouver said that the dangerous people in society were not the drinkers but the "scheming, cold-blooded, cold-water and cold-hearted . . . persons". The Leader of the Opposition maintained a discreet silence. The Bill was passed.

The last big debate of the Third Parliament was on the Pacific Railway.[28] As Minister of Public Works, Mackenzie explained that forty-seven thousand miles had been examined, and twelve thousand miles surveyed. The resulting decision was that the line would go through the narrows of Lake Manitoba, pass Jasper House, follow the Yellowhead route, and descend the Fraser Valley to Burrard Inlet. The population of Manitoba wanted the line to pass through Winnipeg instead of twenty-eight miles to the north, but that was not the most direct route, and would not place the line in the heart of the fertile growing land. Vancouver Islanders, too, would be disappointed, but that was a normal state of affairs. "A delusion and a snare," denounced Amor De Cosmos, "a Machiavellian effort to deceive the people of British Columbia."[29] Other members from the Pacific province followed his lead. The Opposition cavilled, carped, and tore at every aspect of the proposal. Mackenzie stood his ground. When the railway estimates were passed on May 9, he had not given an inch.

The last words of the session of 1878 were harsh and bitter.[30] Just before the Black Rod arrived to summon the Commoners for the final Throne Speech, Donald Smith rose. He wished to deny the charge by Dr. Tupper that he had deserted the former Government for pecuniary reasons, and had profited financially from the Liberal régime. Tupper objected to waiting until the last moment before raising the matter. "A more cowardly thing I have never seen ventured on in this House," he roared across the floor, his face flushed with rage. Smith threw back the charge and tried to continue. "That fellow Smith is the greatest liar I ever met," came the excited voice of Sir John A. Macdonald. Amid the tumult, the Black Rod entered, and the Speaker led the way out of the Chamber. The disputants did not follow. "I could lick him quicker than hell could scorch a feather," the Tory leader threatened as he moved across the aisle. Other members intervened before he could try.

It was over. The only harmonious moment during the long struggle had occurred when the Premier proposed a resolution of thanks to the retiring Governor General.[31] He had been a most popular and effective representative of the Sovereign, everyone agreed, and would be universally missed. The sentiment was mutual. Far from having endured six years of barren exile as he had anticipated, Dufferin had found the work worth while, and even his wife thought of their departure with a heavy heart. "I was particularly touched at the pleasant way in which you alluded to our personal relations", His Excellency wrote to Mackenzie after the resolution passed the House.[32] "For my part I can say that I have derived nothing but unalloyed pleasure from them. The better I have become acquainted with you, the more I have learned to respect the honor and the straightforward integrity of your character, and the unmistakeable desire to do your duty faithfully by the Queen, the Empire and the Dominion." Even allowing for a certain amount of "blarney", there was evidently both sympathy and respect in the message.

* * * * *

"I got released on Friday from the worst session I was ever in as private or officer . . . ," Alexander Mackenzie wrote to his brother Charles on May 12.[33] "I was at last for the first time completely used up but no one knew it. I don't think I could have possibly sat for another week. . . . For all that I felt all through the session was successful for us, and I am sure Macdonald is too good a judge not to feel the same."

It was not just the end of a session; it was the end of the Liberal mandate, the end of five years of Liberal rule. Despite the hazards and roadblocks, they had completed the course, and he was still at the helm. The internal rivalries had subsided, and there was no challenge to his authority. With Blake ill, Dorion retired, and Mowat fully occupied in Toronto, there was no alternative to his leadership either inside or outside the Cabinet. "For many reasons I would be glad to stop there," the Premier confided to his brother, "but I must try again. There is no escape from it. There is no dispute about the leadership in any quarter, consequently there is no way out, however anxious I might be." Fatigue and jaded nerves curbed neither his courage nor his confidence. Absorbed in his work, and confident that he had justice and reason on his side, he seemed completely deaf to the boastful predictions of his opponents, and even the pessimism of many associates. "The election will be a keenly contested one.

We will probably lose some seats and gain some but I think we will be very nearly as strong as we are now . . . 5 or 6 will probably be the outside difference." Like most active politicians, he was the last to know how he really rated with the public.

The big question was the date. Although he had contemplated as recently as January delaying the contest until late 1878 or even early 1879, he now preferred getting it over in June. The Maritimers agreed.[34] Quebec, however, was far from ready, and several Ontario constituencies needed more time. Joly had won exactly the same number of seats as his adversaries in the provincial contest, and was apprehensive of entering his first session with such a delicate balance while the federal election was on. A reaction against the federal Liberals could snuff out his chances in Quebec City. He favoured delay. Blake joined in counselling a fall contest.

There were other considerations. The British Empire, including Canada, was on the verge of war with Russia. Added to that, the Fenians were reported to be preparing another attack for early summer. It was no time for those in charge of the Dominion's affairs to be electioneering. Mackenzie was "oppressed as with a nightmare" at the thought of a postponement, but he decided to wait until fall.[35]

Long before assuming the Prime Ministership, the Grit leader had insisted that the Dominion should be responsible for Imperial defences in North America. With war seeming almost certain, and only a handful of British troops at Halifax and Esquimalt, London asked him to translate his assertions into action. Mackenzie replied that Canada was willing and anxious to do her duty. She could look after the land defences, but she would need the assistance of the Imperial Navy on the coasts.[36] While Canada would call out the local artillery force on the Pacific coast and rush guns to defend Esquimalt, it would be next to impossible to assume the defence of all British Columbia, with its small population and enormous coastline just across the ocean from Siberia. The Canadian militia was small in number and troops and would have to move either through the United States, or over the unfinished "water stretches" and across the Prairies and mountains on Indian trails. "It would be far cheaper to let the Russians destroy everything," Lord Dufferin reported to the Colonial Office on behalf of his Ministers.[37] There was no indication of political motivation in the suggestion!

To demonstrate their good faith, the Canadians despatched their chief artillery officer to Victoria. Political realities were not ignored. The Governor General dropped a hint that it would be a happy circumstance if the Imperial authorities decided to build the long-awaited Esquimalt graving dock as a defence measure.[38] With public opinion in Canada so hostile to British Columbia, he argued, "fearful opposition" would be aroused at the enormous expense involved in defending "an admiralty dock-yard and a village of shanties, for Victoria is little more".[39] Construction of the dock would ease the burden and eliminate one barrier to Canadian unity.

This ardent supporter of his constitutional advisers was the new Dufferin that had been revealed in the early months of 1878. In January, Lord Carnarvon had resigned from the Imperial Cabinet on a disagreement unrelated to Canada. For four years, the two "old boys" from Eton and Oxford, secure in the confidence of their intellectual, financial, and genealogical superiority, had tried to shape the destiny of the Dominion according to their vision of Empire. Now the team was dissolved. The future plans of the eloquent Irishman were thrown into turmoil. Carnarvon's successor, Sir Michael Hicks-Beach, was a relatively unknown quantity, except that he was a former political opponent. Any future appointment would clearly depend on Dufferin's record of accomplishment in Canada, and not on any friendly connections at the seat of power. His Excellency suddenly became the very model of a constitutional governor.

"Nothing could have been more satisfactory than Mr. Mackenzie's language," His Excellency reported to the new Colonial Minister on May 27.[40] Canada would do whatever could be done in Esquimalt and elsewhere. It had been impossible to improve the militia service during the depression, but the Premier would certainly do so in 1879. Immediate steps were being taken to erect cannon around the Atlantic ports, and gunboats were being organized on the Great Lakes and St. Lawrence. The new attitude of the Governor General made Mackenzie's task much more pleasant. The crisis spurred their common loyalty to Queen and Empire; their differences disappeared in a noble purpose greater than themselves. "We will not ask the Imperial Government for anything," the Premier told His Excellency proudly, "as we think Canada should have and does have pride enough to be above shirking her duty in providing for the defence of her own coasts. We are part of the Empire and will bear our share of the burden as well as we share in its glories."[41] Even in such a critical hour, Mackenzie's confidence in Canada's identity as a self-governing unit within the Empire was evident. If North American security allowed, Dominion troops could be sent to other theatres of war, he offered, but they should be formed into Canadian units and maintain their separate identity.[42]

Ever since his early days when he laboured on the Kingston fortifications, Alexander Mackenzie had been interested in Canadian defence strategy. As a young parliamentarian, he had been a keen critic of Cartier's militia policy, and he was proud of having founded the first military school in the Dominion. In 1874 he had hired a British General to re-organize Canada's forces, and he had plans to train non-commissioned officers. William Ross, William Vail, and Alfred Jones had all borne the title of Minister of Militia, but it was the Premier who was in command. During the 1878 crisis, he supervised every detail with the same thorough care with which he watched over the Public Works and a myriad of other items of government business.

In January, the Fenians had forty-nine thousand dollars to use for transporting men and arms to the Canadian border, he told his brother Charles who was in charge of the defences on the St. Clair, and they had secret lodges in Montreal and Toronto.[43] Arms were abundant. If the Russians decided to give them financial aid, the situation would be serious. Three Czarist officers, reported a spy from New Hampshire, had distributed money preparatory to an attack on Montreal.[44] In Berlin, representatives of the Great Powers were meeting to try to avoid war. Canada tensed and waited. "I have requested the Imperial authorities to trust us with very early intelligence of a possible rupture," Mackenzie wrote to Sir John Rose on May 17.[45]

The only explosion came from neither Russians nor Fenians, but from hungry Canadians. In early June, a riot broke out in Quebec City. The pattern was similar to the Belleville disturbances. Unable to feed their families on wages of fifty cents a day, some labourers went on strike. Others preferred even that pittance to nothing, and continued to work. A mob of unemployed attacked the strike-breakers. The local police were powerless to maintain order. Letellier and Joly panicked, read the Riot Act, and called for troops. Eight hundred men were despatched from Montreal. Alexander Mackenzie was fairly beside himself with concern.[46] The Communist infiltration from the United States was responsible for the disturbance, he believed, and that was no reason to call out such large numbers of troops. Above all, he wanted no Imperial troops from the Halifax garrison to be involved.

There was bloodshed. When the mob refused the order to disperse, the soldiers fired. One man fell mortally wounded; the others took to their heels. There were no casualties among the troops. "Captain Short got a crack on the head but it is thick," the Governor General was informed by the Commanding Officer.[47] The crisis evaporated. After the event, Mackenzie concluded that the Colonel in charge had acted with forbearance and prudence, and had even waited a dangerously long time before firing on the rioters.[48] By a happy circumstance, the sole casualty was a Protestant, and perhaps a "Communist". There was not even a popular martyr.

* * * * *

The Liberal campaign was to be launched at Lindsay on May 28. The Grit chieftain was struggling desperately to regain his strength sufficiently to inject the necessary fighting spirit into his followers. "My heart is affecting me so much as to cause great weakness and loss of sleep," he complained a few days before the meeting.[49] His poor health sometimes depressed his spirits as well. Was it possible that Sir John's boastful predictions were justified? Could it be that some of the pessimism around him was well founded? He could not believe it. "I do not doubt that I have the country at my back," he commented to Charlie Black in a grudging admission that there was room for doubt, "but even if I should fail to carry the country with me, I know 1st that I have no reproach in my conscience as to public affairs, and 2nd that I have established a mode of conducting the public business that no coming government, however bad, can wholly destroy. . . . I shall leave the Govt when the time comes, and public life when my time comes, . . . poorer than when I commenced and with the knowledge that no improper act can be laid to my charge."[50]

His chief lieutenants, Cartwright and Laurier, were on hand for the Lindsay meeting. There were no promises; the Grits were running on their record. Honesty, integrity and economy were the watchwords of their campaign. "We have reason to congratulate ourselves," Mackenzie told the crowd in the Lindsay drill shed, "that . . . we have managed to carry through almost every measure of importance which we promised at the commencement of our career".[51] The motto for the future: more of the same. Making his first appearance outside Quebec, Laurier justified completely his chief's confidence in him, and made one of his stirring appeals for national unity that marked his career in later years.

In Toronto the following day, Jane held a "drawing-room", and the Premier laid the Liberal case before a "Workingman's Demonstration".[52] With the extension of the franchise, the working population had soared to a prominent political position. Sir John was campaigning effectively as "a workingman's friend", and attacking the Liberals for the unsympathetic attitude displayed toward labour by the *Globe*. Alexander Mackenzie campaigned as a workingman himself.

It was surprising to him, the ex-stonemason told his audience, that any workingman who "knew his history" could be a Conservative. The Tories were the same men who had oppressed them over the years, and the "demon of protection" was but the last stage in that oppression. The repeal of the Corn Laws had demonstrated the evil of such a policy. The protectionists wanted not only a tax to meet the expenses of running the Dominion, but another to put in their own pockets. Such a system could only result in beggary and serfdom. "What does it matter to you workingmen whether you are in subjection to some tyrant who doles out to you what he pleases in wages, or whether you are under the tyranny of laws which prevent you buying where you please and selling where you like?" Sir John's proposal to put a duty on foreign breadstuffs was the equivalent of taxing "the very bread which the poor man eats, the coal he burns, the oil he consumes". Such a narrow "Canada for Canadians" policy was like saying that Robinson Crusoe kept the Island of Juan Fernandez for himself. "The very idea of protection is embodied in Robinson Crusoe building his own house," Mackenzie declared, "and with a knife made out of bone whittling a weed out of which he made cloth with needles of bone [and] stitching it into articles of clothing . . . undoubtedly Robinson Crusoe was the leader of the Protectionist party on the Island of Juan Fernandez at that time. Let any of our protectionist friends . . . go and live as Mr. Robinson did and thus practice what they so adroitly teach. I believe not only in Canada for the Canadians, but the United States, South America, the West Indies and our share of the European and Australasian trade." The right policy for Canada was to remain "on all fours" with the Empire in its great work of wiping out all tyranny and evil, both political and economic, that would destroy the progress of the past half-century.

It was the Liberals who gave the workers of Canada their opportunities, the Premier insisted, who made it possible that "the humblest son of the humblest working man may find his way to the position which I now occupy". Would that have been possible in the old days of the Family Compact? The Tories believed, like James I, in their divine right to rule, and to dole out to the workers what they decided was right and fair. That was not good enough for Canadians. Canada had a system that made it possible to create a class of workingmen "without its equal in any country in the world". It was of little importance to him personally if he were defeated or sustained, but it was of vast importance to the industrial interests that they should not be "murdered", and that the workers should not be "ruined".

Election propaganda aside, it was an able statement of British *laissez-faire* philosophy from the workingman's point of view. It was the statement of a man who believed sincerely in that system, and who had the courage to stand up for what he believed.

A day later Mackenzie spoke to his neighbours in Sarnia, under banners proclaiming "Honour to Whom Honour is Due", "Fear not, Favour not", "Uprightness in Government".[53] He had spent a third of a century in Canada, he told them, one-half of it as their representative. If they wished, he would carry on a while longer. There was some heckling. It was a phenomenon he had not encountered at home for some time. Not to be compared to the battles of former days, it was an indication of changing times.

The visit to Lambton was just long enough to remind him how lonesome and self-sacrificing his life had become. His grand-daughter Helen was big enough to sit on his knee and sing him Scottish songs, and to read a letter – if he had time to write her one. His grandson was growing rapidly. Mary was no longer young. He longed for a more peaceful existence surrounded by family and friends, instead of the gruelling pace that was driving him to his grave. And yet, unable to call a halt, he was campaigning hard for another sentence.

The first run through Ontario lasted a fortnight. Day after day, the weary party leader summoned up the strength to maintain a battle pose and strike out at his opponents. Each night he crawled thankfully into his room to rest. Though the results seemed encouraging, he could not stand the pace for long. "I must have a little rest or break down," he confided to a friend.[54]

The Mackenzies arrived back in Ottawa in time for an event that loyal friends had long been planning: June 17 was their silver wedding anniversary. They decided to celebrate by inviting a few friends to spend the evening in their Ottawa home. Much to the surprise of both of them, presents and greetings arrived from every direction, and well-wishers took the house by storm. It should have been a gay event, but the exhausted Premier reacted adversely. To the general surprise, he declared that he could not accept such presents as long as he was in public office. "My evening's enjoyment is . . . utterly destroyed by the sending of presents," he complained to one donor, ". . . I never felt so mortified in my life. It looks as if we had got the little evening party up on purpose,"[55] Jane had to re-wrap all the gifts and return them to their owners.

As far as he could judge, all was going well. Sir John seemed to be in difficulties in Kingston, and the Reform meetings were well attended. The war scare had suddenly evaporated; Britain and Russia had decided to come to terms. "I am off for the north side of the Lower St. Lawrence . . . ," Mackenzie announced almost gaily to Brown on June 18, "where no office seekers can live, where no telegraph penetrates and where a mail seldom reaches."[56] It would be the first holiday since the trip to Scotland in 1875.

Temperatures in the low forties and fifties, and the refreshing sea air, were soothing to a feverish body and mind. But there was no real rest from responsibility. Before the end of the month Alexander Mackenzie was back in the stifling Ottawa heat again. "I have cast off all dignity, and work all day long in my shirt sleeves. But I hope the Tory papers won't hear of conduct in every way so shocking."[57] He was pretty well decided on a mid-September election, preceded by a vigorous speaking-tour after the haying season. In the meantime, he was still Prime Minister, and public business required attention.

Montreal was simmering again. Frustrated the previous summer, the Orangemen were determined to prove that they could hold a "walk" in the bilingual city. The Catholics, including the French-speaking mayor, were equally determined that they could not. In reply to their request for protection, Mackenzie urged abandonment of the plan.[58] Troops would be available, he told the mayor, but he hoped that the municipal authorities would assert their authority and that military force would not be required.[59] To the railways he sent an urgent message suggesting that the trains be stopped outside the city on July 11 and 12, and that all passengers be disarmed.[60] Lord Dufferin reverted to his favourite theme that Canada needed a national police force similar to the Irish Constabulary. Sir Michael Hicks-Beach agreed that it was time Canadians learned to look after themselves in such instances. On learning of the approaching crisis, his first concern was to make certain that Canadians accepted their responsibility. "Don't allow Imperial troops to be used," he warned the Governor General, until "such a lesson had been given to both Govt and people that they would not forget the necessity of taking care of themselves . . . (and) only on the urgent written request of your Ministers."[61] As the critical hour approached, the Canadian Premier was forced to admit that there were disadvantages in not having a national police force to deal with such emergencies.[62] When the North West Mounted Police were available, they would find other duties waiting.

The day dawned clear. The Orangemen having refused to cancel the parade, General Selby-Smyth had established field headquarters in an office building in the centre of town, and three thousand troops were ready for action. The critical question was when to intervene. Telegrams flew back and forth between Ottawa, Montreal, and Quebec, where Dufferin was in residence.[63] At eleven o'clock, the crowd of Irish and French Catholics was so large that Selby-Smyth decided to occupy a part of Place d'Armes and Victoria Square. The marching troops added to the tension. All eyes were turned in the direction of the hall where the Orangemen were assembled. Suddenly, at eleven thirty, the mayor acted. A large squad of special constables swooped down the street, arrested a group of Orange leaders, and whisked them away before the others realized what had happened. Other policemen formed up round the building. "We are blockaded in our Hall by special constables who are as bad as the mob outside," came an anguished telegram from the District Orange leader.[64] Mackenzie did not move. The crowd milled restlessly along St. James Street, waiting for the "walkers" to appear.

Time dragged on. By six o'clock, the Orangemen had not only decided to abandon their parade, but were frightened to leave their meeting-place. Gradually the disappointed crowd began to disintegrate. After nightfall, dark shadows slipped quietly into the streets; the "walkers" went home. Another tragedy had been averted. On the other hand, many an Orangeman swore vengeance on the Liberal régime.

Downing Street was pleased with the Canadian Premier's cool-headedness in the crisis, and complimented him on his efficiency and loyalty. Dufferin approved the commendations. "Mackenzie is shrewd, sensible, public-spirited, and thoroughly loyal to Great Britain," he replied to Hicks-Beach, "but . . . very obstinate, and in my dealings with him I have made it a rule never [*sic*!] to press a point so persistently as to provoke him into 'putting his foot down' for when once he has committed himself to a direct negative it becomes almost impossible to move him. It is better when one has approached the verge of ultimate resistance, to acquiesce for the moment in a temporary compromise and to recur to the charge at some more favourable opportunity."[65] It was a wiser and more respectful Governor General who wrote those words than the man who tried to settle the British Columbia crisis over his Ministers' heads.

In most respects the Dominion's business was going on as usual. The Yale-Kamloops section of the Canadian Pacific Railway was surveyed, and tenders were invited. George Walkem, back in office as Premier, was threatening an injunction to prevent the rails destined for the Esquimalt-Nanaimo line being shipped to the mainland, and a further threat of secession was passed by the Legislature in Victoria. Dufferin was no longer attempting to ingratiate himself with both sides at the same time. Walkem was "a clever little intriguer and nothing he says is to be depended upon," he informed Sir Michael,[66] and the politicians of Victoria were "of the calibre of suburban vestrymen and resort to the most violent language and methods on the smallest provocation."[67] He advised a letter to British Columbia stating flatly in terms, "as will present the reiteration of such compositions", that Mackenzie's proposed action was a fair substitute for the Carnarvon terms. "Even if it falls short of the terms of the original bargain . . . that bargain was so improvident . . . that its absolute fulfilment would be hopeless." That much the Dominion Premier had won. What had been lost beyond recuperation was the Liberal vote in British Columbia.

On the Prairies, the Pembina line from Winnipeg to the United States was almost completed; the first locomotive, the *Countess of Dufferin*, had arrived, and trains would be operating in the fall. The telegraph line was completed to the mountains, and the section between Lake Superior and Winnipeg was going ahead steadily. All this cost money. With little concrete evidence of returning prosperity, the public purse was nearly empty again. Cartwright could not very well leave for England to raise a fourth loan just before an election. There was one possible solution: the fisheries award. The Americans were not obliged to pay the five and a half millions for a year, but perhaps they could be persuaded to loosen their purse strings a bit earlier. "What are the chances," Alexander Mackenzie enquired through Dufferin of Sir Edward Thornton in Washington, "of putting our fingers on this 'Yankee Gold'?"[68] A few short weeks before the election it was already too late; the reputation for Scottish parsimony would cling to them to the end.

Quebec seemed as torn with problems as ever. Laurier was labouring valiantly to organize the eastern portion of the province, but the Huntington and Holton factions appeared more interested in perpetuating their feud than in working together. Holton was threatening not to run unless he was made a Minister, and demanded that both Huntington and Laflamme be removed. Huntington felt secure in the knowledge that the English-speaking Liberals preferred him to his rival. Laflamme's position was more precarious. His indiscretions had not ceased after the warning given to him the previous year; Mackenzie determined to let him go.[69] Then, after a very painful scene with the Minister of Justice, he discovered that the health of his proposed successor, Louis Jetté, was not strong enough to enable him to accept the office. With a sigh of resignation, the Premier gave up. In one of the most hostile areas in Canada, where at least two Liberal members of Parliament had climbed on the protectionist bandwagon, they would just have to struggle through.

In August, the Premier and the Finance Minister set off on a tour of the Maritimes. In general, the situation looked favourable. New Brunswick Liberals were optimistic despite the return of Leonard Tilley to the political scene after a term as Lieutenant-Governor. Jones and Patrick Power were both running in Halifax, and the crowds were so enthusiastic in Prince Edward Island that there seemed to be little bad feeling over the absence of a Cabinet Minister from the Island. Mackenzie and Cartwright decided that the main battle ground was rural Ontario. They rushed back to the capital, cleared their desks, and threw themselves into the fight.

The Conservatives were in full voice and vigour. Senator Macpherson's pamphlet was in every hand, and the Liberal "jobs", "scandals", and "rings" on every Tory lip. The *Mail* denounced the "four years of incompetence", the "corruption and jobbery", the "incapacity", "extravagance", and "what looks like tampering with the unclean thing – calculated disloyalty and conspired treason".[70] Respect for personalities had vanished. "It has long been suspected how pigeon the liver of the Prime Minister is . . . ,"[71] sneered the Tory newspaper, "he could doubtless superintend the construction of a public work with credit, but he is manifestly incapable of projecting and initiating great public undertakings successfully."[72]

A year or two earlier, Sir John had been wary of protection. With the National Policy vision stirring the public imagination, he altered his view. "Yes, Protection has done so much for us. I must do something for Protection," he conceded with delightful irony to Goldwin Smith.[73] To Liberals who doubted the wonders of the National Policy, he had an easy answer: "Give us the chance and we will show you!"

On nomination day Alexander Mackenzie was in Sarnia as usual.[74] His opponent was a young lawyer, John A. Mackenzie, a striking combination of names in the age of the two "Macs". For the Premier it was just another meeting in the harrowing schedule. He rebutted the usual tales, put forth the usual arguments, and went on. As far as he could tell, the defences were holding firm. Yet, there were ominous signs; the Tories were just as confident. "Why, I cannot understand," he remarked, "my meetings are everywhere successful – could hardly be more so."[75]

The "fatal 17th" of September was a bright clear day in Ottawa. The crisp autumn air put an extra flush of colour in people's cheeks, and an extra spring in their step. From the Premier's office, the Chaudière Falls could be seen glistening in the sun; beyond, the green foliage was gradually being transformed into russet and gold; and still further away, the blue-green hills were shading to purple and mauve. The talking was over; the ballots were distributed; Canadians were about to cast their first secret votes in a general election. Throughout the country, party workers had been out since dawn bringing voters to the polls; on Parliament Hill, the civil servants went about their work in an atmosphere of nervous expectancy. Having returned to the capital the previous afternoon, Alexander Mackenzie waited with confidence.

The early news was good. The Maritimes seemed to be holding firm. In Ontario, Sir John was beaten. Then, as the telegrams continued to arrive, the turn in the tide appeared. The Conservatives were making gains in Quebec and Ontario. From Nova Scotia came word that Jones, Power, and Coffin were down. The rural areas were voting for protection! As the evening wore on, the reports worsened. Cartwright was defeated in Lennox, and Blake, who had been absent on a health cure in England all summer, was beaten in South Bruce. Toronto was swept completely by the Tories. Hamilton, Montreal, London, and even Ottawa itself – all voted for Sir John. In Lambton, the Premier was elected by a narrow margin of one hundred and forty-six votes. Even without the verdict of Manitoba and British Columbia – and their allegiance was clearly not with the Grits – the result was obvious. The Liberals were beaten by the same huge majority as they had won over the Conservatives in 1874. The Canadians had preferred Conservative optimism to Liberal caution, the "Kingston Knight's" warm humanity to the ex-stonemason's rigid – though heavily assailed – integrity; they preferred Macdonald drunk to Mackenzie sober.

* * * * *

It was not easy for Mackenzie to grasp. He had been so certain of victory. True, there had been problems, but then there were always problems – problems without final solutions except the working of time. And he had met the problems squarely and honestly. They had accomplished a great deal. Canada had an efficient set of election laws, a Supreme Court, a Military College, an improved militia system, and a Temperance Act. The New Brunswick school dispute had been settled, the North West troubles laid to rest, and there was a separate Government between Manitoba and the Rockies. The Intercolonial Railway had been completed, the canal system extended, and the Pacific Railway pushed forward as quickly as possible. Canada had won the right to exert a preponderant role in her own external affairs. Above all, the country had been run honestly for four years, and a system of efficient administration established for the future. And all this had been accomplished during one of the worst economic crises in human history. True, there had been accusations of maladministration and cries of scandal, but he had "nailed" them as quickly as they appeared, and explained the real facts to the people. Was it the "National Policy" cry? Surely Canadians were not so gullible as to fall for that? He had told them over and over what utter humbug it was. One thing was certain: the Tory propaganda had been effective, and by postponing the election until the autumn he had played into their hands.

The protectionist fallacy had taken deeper root than the Liberals thought, especially with the farming population, Mackenzie wrote to the Governor General four days after the débâcle. "I have nothing to regret in looking back at my course. Even had I known of the tendency of the public mind I would not for the sake of office yield up my convictions on that or on any other subject. I tried to keep Canada in line with England and in harmony with enlightened modern thought on commercial subjects, and I have failed, as better men have failed before me. . . . I now propose to get my colleagues here as soon as possible to finish up what business we have on hand, after which I propose to wait upon Your Excellency at Quebec to tender you my resignation."[76]

With the moment of final parting at hand, the Premier realized that on the rough and even stormy road they had travelled together, he had developed an affection for the exuberant Irish nobleman. Whatever their differences and disagreements, a bond of respect and understanding had grown between them. "I have to express my deep gratitude to you for your unvarying kindness to me," he concluded, "and the constant anxiety shown to aid me in every way in carrying on the Government. This I shall never forget. I will only say for myself that I have endeavoured to do what is right in the interests of the Crown and the people, and I can now look back with the personal pleasure which a clear conscience, political and personal, necessarily gives."

Lord Dufferin was no less surprised at the election results

than his First Minister. Of course, he had hedged his bet by dropping a jocular remark to Sir John when they met during the summer to have his carpet bag ready,[77] and he had given a thumb-nail sketch of both men to the Marquess of Lorne, who was to succeed him. Mackenzie had come out better in the comparison; he had only been labelled a semi-educated and rather bad-tempered man, while Macdonald's political morality, the retiring Governor General commented, made it necessary "to keep a little more on the qui vive than with Mackenzie".[78] His Excellency soon recovered from the election news, and adjusted himself to the new circumstances. There were some advantages in the change, he told Hicks-Beach on September 20. "Sir John is undoubtedly the ablest politician in the country – in fact the only man I have yet met who is entitled to be called a Statesman. Though Mackenzie and the leading men of the existing Government were honest and well-meaning, they were frightfully narrow, uneducated and deficient in constructive talent. They were not even very good Administrators."[79]

While preparing for the new scene on the Dominion stage, Lord Dufferin did not neglect to draw the curtains gracefully on the last. "No consideration need preclude me from assuring you," he wrote to the ex-stonemason in a "private" letter, "that in my opinion, neither in England nor in Canada has any public servant of the Crown administered the affairs of the nation with a stricter integrity, with a purer patriotism, with a more indefatigable industry, or nobler aspirations than yourself, and though the chances of war have gone against you at the polls, you have the satisfaction of knowing that your single-minded simplicity of purpose, firmness, and upright conduct have won for you alike the respect and goodwill of friends and foes".[80] Sincere or not, they were comforting words in a trying hour.

The time for reflection and post-mortems would come. The immediate task was to finish the chapter as it had been written. "It is our duty to make an honourable retreat from office," Mackenzie told one Senator, who wanted to arrange just one contract before the end.[81] Opinion was far from unanimous that the Liberals should resign. Holton, Joly, and even Brown thought they should hang on, call Parliament, and force the Conservatives to state their policy. It was tempting to make Sir John "produce his policy" of "enriching all by Act of Parliament", but there were more practical considerations.[82] The Government's coffers were empty, and someone had to find some money. Since the Conservatives would in all likelihood take power regardless of the tactics employed, it was better for them to get on with it at once.

There was another reason. Alexander Mackenzie had decided

to relinquish the party leadership. He had given his time, his ability, his health, almost his life, for the Liberal party. Recriminations and blame would soon follow defeat. Well, he would not tolerate insults. As soon as he had found seats for Blake and Cartwright, he would step down. "Seriously, the Reform party if it wants to succeed must seek another leader," he commented to James Edgar.[83] "The suitable man must have graduated as a horse thief or at least have distinguished himself as having chiseled a municipality or robbed a Railway company. As I am bound to acknowledge my incapacity for such work I mean to resign."

The spate of "midsummer madness" had cut more deeply into the sensitive Scottish pride than most people knew. As the days passed, the full significance of his rejection by the people burned into his soul, turning his ironic humour into a bitterness that he had not known before. "Is it not a woeful commentary on the intelligence of the people to have to state that the Government was defeated because it refused to levy more taxes and make commodities dearer? . . . Well, we will as the *World* says, contemplate with interest the spectacle of a nation lifting itself by the bootstraps out of the mud and increasing its wealth by changing its money from one pocket to the other."[84]

Suddenly he was a stranger in the Prime Minister's seat. The faces in the corridor were no longer those of his loyal helpers, but men and women waiting expectantly for the arrival of their new employer. He felt like an impostor in another man's home. Already there were callers demanding positions and favours that had been promised as rewards for defeating the Grits. Mackenzie was anxious to be done and away.

There were piles of letters expressing regret at the election results and gratitude for his service. There were insults too. Most disappointing, there were hordes of "cormorants" from the Liberal ranks, demanding again at the last minute the favours he had refused to give during five long years. "We have resolved to make no more appointments," he repeated over and over.[85] Some of the requests were difficult to withstand. "Do not forget that you promised to give me a city in the North West," wrote Lord Dufferin from the Citadel.[86] He had been thinking it over, Cartwright told him, and he thought Brown should have the offer of an honour, that as retiring Premier, Mackenzie should have an Imperial Privy Councillorship, and that he himself, in order to provide "the strongest possible evidence that they [Downing Street] were in complete sympathy with us on the trade question," a K.C.M.G. "In ordinary circumstances I . . . would most likely have declined it if offered but . . ."[87]

A few appointments were made that he was sure he could defend as essential to the public service. Many more were left for the incoming Administration. On the night of October 8, Alexander Mackenzie closed his office and went home to write his final letter as Premier of Canada. It seemed incredible that the whole battle for sound trade principles had to be fought over again, he told Lord Dufferin. "Any action which will to any extent assimilate the commercial system of Canada to that of the United States, will to that extent weaken the ties which bind her to the Empire, and which it was the aim of my administration to strengthen and perpetuate."[88] It was ground he could not adopt. He would return to his place in the Opposition. He was thin as a slate, his health was permanently impaired, he was thousands of dollars poorer than in 1873, but he was still a man of principle.

"I assure you I felt a very bitter pang in shaking you by the hand yesterday . . . ," Lord Dufferin wrote from Montreal the day after they parted for the last time.[89] "I have such a sincere personal esteem for you, that it felt like parting from one of my oldest friends." One chapter ended, and the next began the same day. Sir John was in Montreal to be sworn into office. "On personal grounds," beamed the Governor General as the old Tory chieftain was ushered in, the warmest wish of his heart was gratified.[90] The Mackenzie era was at an end.

CHAPTER 18

The Shades of Opposition

"What are you about? and what are all our friends doing?"[1] "How are you getting on? Write me a long letter (very plain) and give me the news."[2] Huntington in Montreal, and Jones in Halifax, read the familiar handwriting of the ex-Premier with pleasure. It was the first communication from Mackenzie in several weeks; in fact, almost since he moved to Toronto after the defeat. Hardly anyone knew his new address, and, anyway, there was so little to say to a defeated leader.

It had not been an easy time. After the "fatal 17th", the Grit leader had been so anxious to be gone from Ottawa that he had but one thought in mind – to go home to Lambton and forget politics and public service forever. "I entered public life with reluctance," he told Lord Dufferin as the retiring Governor prepared to sail for Britain. "I quit it (for so I consider the recent election to require) without regret, content in the belief that the historian will associate my name with the enunciation of sound principles if nothing more."[3] George Brown and many others disagreed.[4] With the Canadians worshipping false gods, and the administration once more in the hands of the "corruptionists", there was more need than ever before of crusading zeal. "It would be a profound mistake personally, financially and politically to go back to Sarnia," the *Globe* publisher had argued shortly after the election.[5] He urged Mackenzie to come and stay with him for a few days while they talked things over and examined the alternatives. Though he had tried to be relieved of the position in 1875, Mackenzie was still President of the Isolated Risk Insurance Company, even if he had not been near the office in five years. And he had already received an offer of another directorship in the Queen City.[6]

Brown's magnificent home was an ideal retreat after the last harrowing months in office, and a perfect centre of operations to plan the future. On only one point was the *Globe* publisher adamant: he would not listen to talk of resigning the leadership. Earlier in the year, Mackenzie, himself, had admitted that there was no competition for the post. The thing to do was not to sit down and mope, insisted Brown, but to reorganize and launch a counter-attack. John A. Macdonald had moved to Toronto in 1876 and begun again; the Reformer could do the same. With his construction business gone, and his major interests more national than parochial, the Grit leader was forced to agree.

The Mackenzies found a house on the corner of Wellington and Windsor streets, not far from the lake front and the railway station. House-hunting proved to be a disagreeable experience.[7] They could no longer afford as fine a home as they had been obliged to maintain in Ottawa, and the less expensive dwellings seemed shabby and inadequate. As soon as they appeared in a doorway, they were recognized. If the price of the building was not raised automatically, they had at least to pay the price of an awkward conversation about the recent defeat. After a few attempts, they developed a tactic of examining a prospective purchase from the outside with the air of casual passers-by, and then letting Jane go in and poke round in the rooms and closets and kitchen and ask the necessary questions, while the ex-Premier took a walk around the block. When they finally made a choice, it was more to end the odious ordeal than because they were completely satisfied. With a sigh of resignation, they signed the bill of sale, then went over to the Jarvis Street Baptist Church and applied for admission to that congregation.

The Ottawa house was rented only and created no problem. His old rival, Dr. Tupper, not only took over the Public Works portfolio and the new office in the West Block tower, but offered to purchase "Cliffside" as well. It was like rubbing salt in a fresh wound to be obliged to cede their very parlour and bedroom, but political and financial realities left no alternative. They offered to leave their furniture – for the right price. Jane's maid was less resigned. She refused to let Mrs. Tupper go into the clothes closets during her tour of inspection, and gave notice that she had no intention of remaining to serve a Tory master and mistress.[8] It was a heart-warming touch in a cold, bleak tale.

Installing themselves in the new house was at least a distraction. Working with his hands was one way the ex-stonemason had been able to relax in Ottawa, even if it only meant sewing on his own buttons in Jane's absence. It was a positive activity, and it gave him time to think. The bits and pieces of the Liberal party had to be picked up, sorted out, and placed in a semblance of order so that the task of reconstruction could begin. The situation was bad but it was not desperate. Thirty-four of the seats that had been won by the Tories in Ontario were carried by less than one hundred and fifty votes.[9] The Liberal popular vote had fallen only 4.4 per cent, from 52.2 per cent to 47.8 per cent, and was still above the Conservative level of 1874. Less than one person in twenty had changed his allegiance. In addition, Mowat was still firmly in control of provincial affairs, and was confident that he could win an election the following spring. The Ontario Liberal organizer reported that the protection cry was the main cause of defeat. By the spring of 1879, the people would realize that they had reached for a lifebelt in the economic tempest and found themselves with a millstone around their necks.

The Liberal party was not only penniless, but the Ontario Association was five thousand dollars in debt. It was decided to take over Goldwin Smith's defunct National Club, and turn it into a Liberal headquarters. Alexander Mackenzie headed the list of donors who gave a thousand dollars each to get it off to a proper start. "We hope to get $30 to 40 thousand," he wrote to his former secretary, William Buckingham.[10] Poor Buckingham, he was one of the first victims of the new Tory régime. So completely loyal and devoted to his chief that he had nearly broken under the strain of office, there was no place for him in the new order of things in Ottawa. Like his former chief, he, too, was forced to pack his belongings, close his home, and leave.

The battle would be fought largely on the economic front, and strong men would be needed to counter the arguments of the Government. The Liberal member for Centre Huron was persuaded to resign his seat and give Richard Cartwright an opportunity to return to Parliament. The by-election contest was brisk, but despite the traditional tendency of voters to climb aboard the Government bandwagon in the first months after a general election, the former Finance Minister was returned with an increased majority. The Grits were encouraged. The people were beginning to see through the "political quackery". A farmer in the Toronto market-place told Mackenzie that "prices were low and trade bad on and before September 17 but they have since gone to Hell".[11] The Tory promise of an extra twenty-five cents per bushel for wheat, fifteen cents for barley, and ten cents for oats and corn was beginning to look like a politician's mirage.

"Up to today I have been up to my eyes getting my house in a habitable condition and am now going for my correspondence," the former Premier told Huntington on December 9.[12] ". . . I am also going to try to organize the party afresh. . . ." "We must not be discouraged but prepare for the inevitable reaction which is already showing itself in Ontario," he wrote to Pelletier in Quebec.[13] With a note of warmth and a trace of the old determination, Mackenzie was acting like a party leader once again. Talk of resignation was receding rapidly. He expressed aggrieved surprise to Holton that some people considered the leadership to be on the auction block. "I intended when we meet in Ottawa to give an opportunity of electing another person if the party desired but I have a lively feeling of indignation at all caballing. . . . I shall not commit myself to anything."[14] It was true, he admitted, that some Blake-wing Liberal papers were encouraging rumours of a change of leadership, but he had seen Blake twice since the latter's return to Canada, and neither had mentioned the election. The former Minister of Justice had looked well, was evidently rebuilding his law practice, and had contributed a thousand dollars to the Reform Club fund.

Christmas, 1878, was the most pleasant in years for the Mackenzies. They spent a full week in the Cromwell Street home in Sarnia, relaxing with John and Mary and the children, and exchanging visits with the other members of the clan. They were happy days, days he had dreamed of spending during the long, hard years in Ottawa. And yet, they were not enough. The call of public duty was part of his very nature, and there was work to be done. On New Year's Eve, he was back in Toronto to discuss strategy with Blake. There were reports that the sensitivities of the temperamental lawyer had been wounded again when a seat was procured for Cartwright and none for him. There was no slight intended, Mackenzie assured his former colleague, safe seats were difficult to find, and Cartwright's knowledge of financial matters was essential in the new Parliament. Freedom from office did not bring freedom from the delicate task of conciliating the members of the Liberal team.[15]

In January, he was so busy that he forgot his own fifty-seventh birthday. The daughter of a life-long friend sent a pair of suspenders and reminded him of the occasion. "Thank you for your contribution toward 'bracing me up for coming duties'," he replied jocularly,[16] ". . . Rideau Hall sends me an invitation with the words 'full dress'. I shall grace my Windsor uniform with the new braces, when I can say that the unseen is perhaps better than the seen." There was a good portion of bluff in the cheerful attitude. Actually, he was dreading the return to the capital. "I shall feel very dejected . . . ," he confessed privately, "Not so much at being on the Opposition benches, as at the loss of so many old Ontario friends."[17]

On the last Sunday evening before Parliament opened, he stayed home from church, writing letters and thinking about the future. "I have no idea what the session will bring . . . or what line we may adopt," he told Mary, "but my impression is that *our* policy will be to allow them to shape *their* policy without much comment until they are committed fully but we will probably point out the nature and extent of election pledges."[18] Evenings, like the one they had spent recently, listening to a Toronto lady read to a circle of friends, were in many respects more appealing.

Canada's Fourth Parliament was opened with a brilliant display of pomp and pageantry. The Dominion was still slightly overwhelmed to have as the new Governor General a son-in-law of the great Queen Victoria, or rather, to have one of her daughters in residence at Rideau Hall. As the royal carriage mounted Parliament Hill on a sunny afternoon in February, the crowds craned their necks for a closer look at Princess Louise. His Excellency the Marquess of Lorne was of secondary interest.

The Throne Speech announced "the strictest economy", and a "readjustment" of the tariff to combat the continuing depression. The fisheries award, which would have been so convenient a few months earlier, had been paid. The Government would press forward with the Pacific Railway, to meet "the reasonable expectations" of British Columbia. Re-installed on the Treasury benches, the Conservatives looked confident. Sir John was both Prime Minister and Minister of the Interior. Evidently, he, too, had found it impossible to follow the practice advocated by both Mackenzie and himself in opposition of leaving the First Minister free from departmental responsibility. Samuel Tilley was back as Minister of Finance, Hector Langevin was Postmaster General, Mackenzie Bowell was Minister of Customs. Still outside the Cabinet were several arch-protectionists such as Dalton McCarthy, J. H. Cameron and Hector Cameron, whose views were apparently too extreme for Sir John.

Alexander Mackenzie looked perfectly at home in his old role of Opposition leader. Still erect and alert, and with his forelock and beard grey from years of responsibility, he had an appearance of dignity and authority that was lacking a decade before. One aspect of his appearance was unchanged: he still looked across at his adversaries with the sharp, penetrating eyes of the guardian of public virtue.

He teased Sir John for proposing a new name as Speaker.[19] What had happened to his earlier view that the same person should be kept on from one Parliament to another? Why did he not again propose Timothy Anglin, who had been re-elected by acclamation by his constituents? What did the "reasonable expectations" of British Columbia mean? As the Premier himself had commented annually for the past five years, the Throne Speech was "meagre fare".

The first weeks were spent in preliminary skirmishing, with the Opposition waiting for the famous National Policy to be unveiled. "We are weary waiting for Tilley and his budget," the Grit leader wrote to his daughter on March 11.[20] "It is now said he is sick but I understand he has only sore eyes . . . The truth is, as an Irishman said, 'he has the Devil's own job on hand', and his sickness is largely of the mental type. Were he an honest politician and not a mere political hack I would sympathize with him, for the work of reconciling a legion of conflicting interests all demanding to be enriched at someone's expense must be an immense task for the ablest man and the most suave character the country could produce, far more to a man not above mediocrity." Mackenzie was particularly bitter toward the new Finance Minister. Less than a year earlier, he had considered extending his term as Lieutenant-Governor of New Brunswick, only to discover that Tilley was planning to return to active politics as an outspoken critic of the Liberal Administration. The ex-Premier regretted such a generous non-partisan attitude, and resented the man who was its intended object.

There were pleasanter aspects of the Ottawa scene. Learning of the Grit leader's ability with "broom and stane", Lord Lorne challenged Mackenzie to a curling match. The game was given wide publicity and attracted considerable interest. After a three-hour contest, His Excellency emerged the victor by a narrow margin. "Gilmour and I played carelessly at first, not wishing to beat him badly," the vanquished Scot explained ruefully to his daughter, "but he got the start of me all at once by two chance shots that gave him 6 points and we were fairly beaten 12 to 15. I am going down again on Saturday and will retrieve our losses."[21]

The Governor General was agreeable company, but it was the Princess who won his heart. She told him that her mother had visited Dunkeld, and that it was the most beautiful place she had ever seen. Both she and the Queen loved the Highlands and the Highlanders dearly, and she tried to speak her rather shaky Gaelic whenever possible. The Viceregal couple felt as much at home in Ottawa as in Argyllshire, because "we meet so many

Scotchmen".[22] It was quite a compliment from a couple bearing the title of Duke and Duchess of Argyll.

The Conservative candidates in Quebec had made it clear that Lieutenant-Governor Letellier would be deposed as soon as they were in power. As the session proceeded, they increased their pressure on Sir John to remove "the Grizly [*sic*] Bear which Mackenzie has sent to adorn the park of Spencer Wood".[23] "Old Tomorrow" played for time as he sought a way to satisfy his supporters. In March, two Conservative members introduced an amendment condemning the *coup d'état* of the Lieutenant-Governor as "unwise and subversive".[24] It looked suspiciously like an attempt to test Parliamentary opinion without committing the Minister in advance. With a display of his old pugnacity, Alexander Mackenzie derided the Cabinet for not having the courage to take the matter into their own hands. "There was never anything more dangerous brought into the Federal Legislature than this attempt to interfere with the autonomy of the Provinces . . . ," he declared. "If there is one province that more particularly requires the shield of the constitutional authority to be thrown around it, it is the Province of Quebec." Hecklers interrupted. "A good case does not require so much shouting," the Scot retorted in a withering burst of indignation that restored silence on the Government back benches. "I would . . . vote against any interference with provincial action," he went on, "unless indeed the Government were prepared and brought down reasons to show that the action was unconstitutional, wholly improper, beyond his powers, that his continuance in office was a danger, a public menace to the security of the community. . . . Our federal system is a fraud if this Parliament is to constantly exercise surveillance over the actions of the local legislatures and local Governors."

It was, doubtless, solid ground, ground consistent with the traditional Liberal stand that the wishes of any one province should not be overridden by the combined votes of the others. Mackenzie had recommended a provincial election to obtain the view of the Quebec population on the crisis. The people of Quebec had upheld Letellier's action, albeit by a narrow majority. Respect for provincial rights demanded acceptance of the *status quo*. Sir John A. Macdonald, who had always favoured a stronger central Government, and a closer eye on the provinces, disagreed. Goading him into action was the Quebec section of his caucus, which had vowed to destroy the Lieutenant-Governor. The debate ended with a vote along party lines. Letellier was condemned one hundred and thirty-six to fifty-one.

The budget was a valiant attempt to reconcile political and economic realities, but it was far from an announcement of the Canadian millennium so blandly promised.[25] Even with a new three-million-pound loan on the London market, the fisheries award, and considerable tariff increases, the end of the budgetary deficits was not in sight. The tariffs that had been raised from fifteen to seventeen and a half per cent by the Liberals in 1874, and that they had nearly raised to twenty per cent in 1876, were now increased to that figure. To satisfy particular sectors of the economy, some rates were raised to thirty or forty per cent. Tilley estimated a ten per cent increase in revenues as a result of the tax changes. It was not enough to balance the budget. The Tories, too, were forced to keep spending to a minimum and wait for the end of the depression.

"So the elephant has come a most unshapely animal laden with Rings and covered with excrescences," scoffed the Opposition leader, ". . . (and) already . . . some of the manufacturers find their toes trod upon by the indulgences bestowed on others."[26] Opposing a protectionist-minded Administration, Mackenzie slipped easily into the doctrinaire free trade position of his early years. "What gave rise to the Communistic movement in Pittsburgh and the great manufacturing centres of Pennsylvania?" he asked.[27] "Was it not that the protectionists had reduced the people to beggary; that their employees had been ruined by it; . . . that they thought, as a mob thoughtlessly will sometimes, that the only remedy was an equal distribution of property? . . . no Government can be held responsible for the depressions which will occur in commercial affairs. . . . at a time when employment is scarce and money not plentiful, is it not desirable to make everything as cheap as possible to the poorer classes? . . . The protection introduced will in my opinion have the effect of degrading the working classes, building up the fortunes of a few manufacturers, and in the course of a few years, ruining even those manufacturers, after they have accomplished the ruin of the working classes." Such a return to class distinctions and social injustice, he argued, was "contrary to the beneficence of the Maker of the world", and to "all just laws, human and divine". Moreover, a protectionist policy was open disloyalty to the Empire. "I believe that the cause of human freedom depends much, in the darker places of the world, upon the unity of the great British family. . . . For this reason I believe that it is exceedingly important that this great colony of Britain should maintain the same system of commercial legislation that Britain enjoys . . . (and) which is so consonant with all our ideas of human freedom and progression." It was no use. The Canadian people had voted for protection, and the Conservative majority were committed to it. Mackenzie's amendment did not have a chance.

Concealing well his feeling of discouragement, the Liberal leader scrutinized every item of legislation with the same careful attention he had given to public matters as Prime Minister. The new Ministers soon learned that he often knew their work better than they knew it themselves. With his prodigious memory for facts and figures, he seldom lost a dispute over a point of information, and embarrassed the Cabinet frequently. "I acknowledge that I am not, like my honourable friend, infallible," Macdonald commented testily after one exchange.[28] "Of course not," the Grit chieftain flashed back, "but the honourable gentleman would be if he were to accept my declarations always."

There was undoubtedly some satisfaction in seeing the critics of earlier years struggle with the same old problems, and in holding them rigidly to their former declarations. The Pacific Railway was as big a headache for Tupper as it had been for him. The "enfant terrible", Amor De Cosmos, introduced a motion for "the peaceful separation of British Columbia", and declared that "the people of British Columbia has as little faith in one side as they had in the other".[29] Although he failed to find a seconder for his motion, the agitation in the Pacific Province was evidently widespread and serious. The amusing aspect of this secessionist movement was that the Prime Minister, following his defeat in Kingston, had secured a seat in Victoria. The day before the May 1 deadline set by the secessionists for acceptance of their terms, Mackenzie observed that Sir John was absent from the Chamber. He presumed, he said drily, that the honourable gentleman was packing, preparatory to moving out of the Confederation the following day.[30] At the same time, he maintained his position that the complaints from British Columbia were groundless.

Dr. Tupper took a moderate line on the Pacific Railway problem. "I am free to confess," he said with unusual humility, "that when the Administration of my honourable friend [Sir John] first inaugurated this policy . . . it was apparently much easier of accomplishment than it has since proved to be . . . (and) that the late Government . . . (did) direct their efforts with the sincere and anxious desire, as far as the position of the country admitted, to carry out the obligations undertaken."[31] Such words a few years earlier would have made it possible to avoid an ugly chapter in Canadian history. The Government asked for six million dollars to carry on with construction of the line, but did not specify where the money was to be spent. They asked for authority to build one hundred and twenty-five miles of railway in British Columbia, but admitted "we do not know where". They cancelled the choice of the Burrard Inlet route, and ordered further surveys of the Bute and Pine River routes. No mention was made of the Esquimalt-Nanaimo road. Finally, the route across the Prairies was changed to run through Winnipeg and south of Lake Manitoba as the majority of Manitobans desired.

The new Pacific Railway policy left the Government vulnerable to attack, and Mackenzie did not fail to take advantage of the situation. Dr. Tupper's statement was a tacit avowal that the original time limit was illusory and misleading, he charged. It was also a direct contradiction of repeated Conservative statements when they were in opposition that all monies should be voted for specific projects, and all contracts approved in advance. The Grit leader scoffed at the suggestion that British financiers could be enticed to take a financial interest in the line despite the fact that discriminatory tariffs had been raised against them. He warned the Ministry that he would oppose extra taxation to build the railway as a public project.

The Opposition onslaught was serious enough to call the Government leader into the fray. "It may be," Sir John conceded as the session drew to an end, "that in the far distant future we will have an opportunity of looking down upon the House from a very impartial standpoint and see the position of the parties reversed, but I repeat, it will not be in my time."[32] "I will merely remark," Mackenzie retorted, "that the honourable gentleman does not mean he would look downward. He will look upward." "I always look up to my honourable friend," Macdonald replied with even humour.

The fate of Letellier was not decided during the session. Following the private motion of censure, Sir John advised the Governor General that the Lieutenant-Governor's usefulness was gone, and that he should be removed from office. The Imperial Government refused to act without a firmer request from Canada, such as a formal resolution of Parliament. Alexander Mackenzie had blocked that course of action by his statement that it would be an infringement of provincial rights. In a private letter, he also suggested that Premier Joly send a representative to England to plead Letellier's case if federal Ministers went to argue their own.[33] To remove a Lieutenant-Governor because a vote of Parliament declared his "usefulness" gone, the Liberal leader declared, was centralization, a violation of the federal contract, and wanton interference with the province. Hesitant, the Government let the session end without a decision.

They had been three hard months of work, but the Opposition had done its duty. Mackenzie's record of attendance was as good as ever, and his interest unflagging. Despite the overwhelming odds, there had been some grounds for satisfaction. In one committee he had fought so hard against a Marine Telegraph Bill that it had been defeated. He directed an attack on another Bill in the Senate, and secured its defeat by a vote of thirty-two to thirty. A Bill dealing with the Northern Railway Company was withdrawn after he argued that it entailed a breach of faith with the English creditors. They were all fairly unimportant measures, but the achievement was heartening for the Liberals. "We have this powerful government beaten in the attempt to secure a monopoly for the Anglo-American Cable Company . . . ," Alexander Mackenzie wrote to Jane.[34] "The fate of these Bills shew what a small but resolute body of men can accomplish."

Above all, they had been three lonesome months. Brown was seldom in the capital, and Holton was often in Montreal with his ailing wife. Most people were more interested in the members of the new Ministry, who were courted as assiduously – and often by the same persons – as the Liberals a short time before. With Jane in Toronto, and only a small room several blocks south of the Parliament Buildings, Mackenzie lived for his work, taking time only occasionally for a walk to Hull or a visit with friends. By May, he was weary and anxious to have the talking cease, "to enable us sooner to see our wives and sweethearts".[35] He let the last items of legislation pass with little comment, and rushed home as early as possible to Toronto.

* * * * *

The spring of 1879 brought one satisfying achievement. In 1877, he had arranged titles for Chief Justices Dorion and Richards, and in 1878, Albert Smith had received a title for his part in the Halifax fishery negotiations. By dint of long conversations with the Marquess of Lorne, he now succeeded in obtaining honours for several other prominent Liberals.[36] Though he was still unwilling to let his own name be submitted, he persuaded the Governor General to recommend Brown, Cartwright, and William Howland, the former Lieutenant-Governor of Ontario. Once again, he presented the details of Brown's past, including his agitation for federal union, his select committee in 1864, his suggestion of a coalition to achieve Confederation, and his efforts to obtain a new reciprocity treaty. The *Globe* publisher was the originator of the Confederation scheme, he insisted, and yet he was the only one of the leading Fathers of Confederation who had not yet received an honour.

Less than three weeks after Mackenzie's exhaustive memorandum to Lorne, Brown received a message to present himself at Montreal on Victoria Day and be officially named a Knight Commander of the Order of St. Michael and St. George. His name was already printed in the *Official Gazette*; only the ceremony remained. George Brown went to Montreal, but he declined the title. Why? Had he, too, preached the Liberal doctrine of social equality so long that he could not accept without contradicting his previous utterances? Did he refuse because he could not accept a lesser honour than the one borne by Sir John? "Under appropriate circumstances he might, and no doubt would, have accepted a title of honour," wrote Mackenzie three years later.[37] Whatever the reason, he had received the offer at last, and he had chosen, like his former lieutenant, to remain a commoner of his own free will. Cartwright and Howland had fewer scruples; they accepted without hesitation.

At fifty-seven, in uncertain health, and with a party to lead, there were few opportunities to supplement the meagre indemnity that Mackenzie received as a member of Parliament. The Isolated Risk Insurance Company had not earned much money during his years in Ottawa, but he set to work to rebuild and expand its operations. In another field, British investors were frequently in need of expert advice on investment prospects in Canada. It was a task for which he was well qualified, and he was soon busy as an economic consultant for some Scottish financial interests. Between politics and business, there was little time for idle reflection. And it was better so. Few realized how deep was the wound of September 17, or how much bitterness and resentment he nourished beneath a calm exterior. "We already know that all things are ordered well and for the best by our Heavenly Father, who cannot commit any mistake," he wrote to the daughter of a deceased friend, and yet, "I sometimes think when such as he departs, that their lot is better than that of those who remain here to battle with the selfishness, coldness, and injustice of the world."[38] In a world of sin and sinners, death was salvation, and a welcome end to suffering and evil.

In the political field, there was no doubt in Alexander Mackenzie's mind who were the sinners: the authors and proponents of the National Policy. When Mowat called an election in the early summer of 1879, the Tory leaders swept into Ontario, intent on driving the Liberals from office in the provincial as well as the federal field. Mackenzie threw himself into the fight with a frenzied determination to frustrate them in their goal. Mowat was returned with a majority of thirty in a Legislature of eighty-eight members. The Grits were jubilant. In addition to the Ontario contest, the Liberals won three provincial by-elections in Quebec. "No ministry in my time ever passed through such a succession of humiliating defeats," Mackenzie wrote to Henri Joly.[39] Jones reported that Tupper could not easily carry a single county in Nova Scotia, and New Brunswick and Prince Edward Island Liberals claimed a similar shift in public opinion there. With time, the situation was bound to change.

Mackenzie's moral indignation was aroused as well against the Colonial Office and the Governor General because of their attitude in the Letellier case. Joly had gone to England himself, and had been told by Hicks-Beach that it was a purely Canadian matter in which Britain could not become involved. Moreover, he stated, if the Canadian Government ordained that Lieutenant-Governors should wear blue neckties, and they wore white, it was within the Government's competence to dismiss them for disobedience. "The fellow did not or would not appear to have the least idea of what was due to constitutional principles, usage or propriety," the Grit leader commented acidly.[40] Evidently it was an instance in which he would have welcomed British interference in Dominion affairs, or at least a declaration in support of provincial rights.

With such a *carte blanche* from London, the Conservatives wasted no time. In late July of 1879, Macdonald and three colleagues appeared in Quebec. With them was Théodore Robitaille, the Member of Parliament for Bonaventure. They issued two decrees: one dismissing Letellier, the other appointing Robitaille in his place. Mackenzie was so indignant that he refused until the last moment to attend the Governor General's ball in Toronto shortly afterward, and he complained of the favourable coverage given to the event by the *Globe*. "The *Globe* goes too far in praising everything," he wrote to his former secretary.[41] "The Ball was got up for 1200 people as the minimum number. It was attended by about 530 some of them being deadheads. The floor was not one-third covered. The waltzing pair had space to wheel six feet of tail without touching one another."

If the *Globe* could not escape his censure, then nothing could avoid his scathing tongue. The British Liberals annoyed him with "their intense ignorance of the colonies and want of appreciation of our position".[42] When Galt agreed to go to Spain and France to negotiate commercial treaties, he accused him of binding himself to Sir John's chariot wheel. "This after all his loud professions of his hostility to him from 1868 to 1878 Sept. 17!!!"[43] The frustration and gnawing rancour hit him in his weakest spot, and he was forced to take to his bed with a new attack of the old stomach ailment.

While he was recuperating, a piece of spectacular news broke upon the political scene. Blake announced his decision to return to politics. In appraising the causes of the defeat, Blake-wing Liberals were not slow to point out that the brilliant lawyer was not a member of the Government in 1878. For those who sought a scapegoat, it was easy to direct criticisms at the rigid, uncompromising, and increasingly uncommunicative ex-stonemason. Certainly Mackenzie had alienated many a fellow-Liberal, and turned away many a potential convert by his strict adherence to principle. It had been a mistake, some argued, not to pay at least lip service to public opinion as Sir John had done, and make a gesture in the direction of protection. In the valley of defeat, they felt it would take more than rejected principles to restore party fortunes. As usual in such circumstances, the disappointed party members began to look around for a new Moses to lead them out of the wilderness, a man of breadth and vision and prestige. Such a man, said many, was Edward Blake. He was elected by acclamation in Durham West.

The months passed quickly, and soon it was time to return to Ottawa. It was "a simple duty which must be discharged", the Leader of the Opposition confided to Mary in late January, 1880.[44] "I would much rather not go though I find the average opinion to be that I am longing for a scrimmage with the powers that be."

There were some differences in the House of Commons. In addition to Edward Blake's victory, the Grits had won a by-election in Lanark, and felt the tide was turning in their favour. Instead of one lone knight – Sir John – as during the Liberal régime, there were a full half-dozen members entitled to be addressed as both "gallant" and "honourable". In addition to Albert Smith, Cartwright, Tilley, Tupper and Langevin had all been knighted. The era of Toryism seemed truly to have arrived.

"I have no luck, I'll pass again," said a caricature of Mackenzie in the Montreal journal, *Le Vrai Canard,* that winter.[45]

"You should," replied Macdonald, "look at this hand of cards. Four aces again."

Luck seemed indeed to be breaking for the sixty-five-year-old Premier. The harvest had been abundant, and there were numerous indications of returning prosperity. The Intercolonial Railway was almost self-supporting, and the Burrard Inlet route had been chosen again for the Pacific Railway. Suppressing a growing feeling of despondency, the Opposition leader put on an aggressive front. "Lenten fare," he scoffed at the

Throne Speech, as Sir John had done not many years before.[46] He attacked a new restriction limiting immigration to persons with twenty dollars in their pockets. Many thousands of successful Canadians would never have qualified for entrance if such economic discrimination had been imposed earlier, he argued. He might have mentioned that he himself would not have been eligible in 1842.

Unwilling to accept the assurances that the depression was over, the Grit leader insisted that he could see more evidence of distress than when he resigned. In his view, the wealth of the Dominion was flowing into the hands of the monopolists, and their profits were being paid for by the masses of the population. The only true answer was a low-cost economy and an extension of foreign trade, not a bellicose attitude to Canada's most lucrative market, the United States. He saw indications that the Tories were showing their true colours again. They were spending the taxpayers' money with reckless abandon on the Pacific Railway. Senator Macpherson had been lured into the Cabinet and "neutralized", as Sir John had done with so many foes in the past. Combinations, compromises, and financial irresponsibility, warned Mackenzie, were becoming the pattern of Canadian public life again.

There was a serious omission in the Opposition leader's stand. He divided his time between sharp criticism of the Ministry and an equally virulent defence of his own Administration, but there were few references to the very essence of his party – reform. Even during the harrowing days of 1877 and 1878, he had not forgotten that the Liberal party was worthy of its name only as long as it was striving continually to reform abuses and devise new ways of improving the lot of Canadians. Now the Conservatives were keeping him in a defensive posture by continual references to September 17, 1878. There was no ignominy connected with that defeat, he retorted again in the budget debate.[47] "We were not accused of any public crime or dishonourable conduct. We fought the battle, whether right or wrong, upon a straight line, and upon principle. . . . We were defeated; but I am satisfied that . . . at this moment if the country had to pronounce again upon the subject it would pronounce in our favour." Mowat's victory, fought directly on the merits and demerits of the National Policy, he asserted, was a clear indication that the people had begun to realize their mistake.

As the session crawled into the second month, the tug of war over revised tariff schedules continued. The Liberals cried discrimination and economic class distinction, and predicted national ruin. With one eye on the economic horizon for signs of reviving trade, the Conservatives spoke confidently of a new era of prosperity as soon as their policies took effect. Alexander Mackenzie pursued his path with dogged determination, but he was drawing more and more into himself. Only a few intimate friends were able to penetrate the cold impersonal shell that he threw about him. He did not even call the caucus together in 1880 to give the members an opportunity to express their views and air their grievances. Jane begged to be allowed to come to Ottawa to keep him company, and friends in the capital urged him to abandon his room and live with them, but he made excuses for not doing so.[48] And yet, he was desperately lonely. "It is pleasant to count the days now few until I see you again," he wrote to his "dearest Jeannie" on March 2.[49] "I think I am just as keen and enthusiastic as I was 27 years ago to see you and be with you. Then I liked you for what I believed you was [*sic*]. Now I love you for what I know you are. . . . I always feel backward in language of a demonstrative character and will only say now what I always think that I have the best of wives. God bless her."

His health had not improved with the release from office. At a dinner party given by the Speaker, another member got drunk and took his coat, hat, umbrella and overshoes by mistake, leaving the Opposition leader to walk home through the wet snow in his thin shoes and formal dress. The next day he was in bed with an attack of dysentery.[50]

When Alexander Mackenzie walked up to Parliament Hill on the morning of March 15, he was not turning over in his mind, as usual, the questions he would ask the Government after prayers. A heavy burden lay on his heart; Luther Holton was dead. Though five years older than his leader, he had always looked the very picture of robust health and exuberant energy. Since their defeat, the old friendship between the two men had been completely re-established, unmarred by past disagreements over public matters. It was a relationship that Mackenzie cherished second only to his friendship for Brown. Holton had been perfectly well until the last moment, then was stricken in his hotel room with violent stomach pains, and died before the doctor arrived. "Poor fellow," the Grit chieftain wrote to his wife, "he was so solicitous about my own health . . . and always trying to arrange some little plan to relieve me of some work. . . . Every morning came his enquiry, 'How are you to-day, Mackenzie?' "[51] The midnight procession to place the body on the Montreal train was a sad affair.

As Prime Minister, Sir John A. Macdonald rose at the opening of the House to pay an eloquent tribute to one of his most formidable opponents. His face pale but set with determination, the Leader of the Opposition stood up slowly when his turn came to follow suit. He remained for a moment with head bowed. "I look upon his death at this moment, as it would be at any time," Mackenzie began hesitantly, "as a national calamity."[52] He paused again, summoning the strength to continue. "I feel myself utterly unable to say . . ." Nothing more could be forced past the huge lump in his throat. With a convulsive shudder of his whole frame, he gave up the attempt and subsided into his seat. It was the first time that he had ever broken down in public. His faithful lieutenant, Wilfrid Laurier, completed the tribute.

Just ten days later, tragedy struck again.[53] In the *Globe* headquarters in Toronto, a man who had been discharged for drinking and neglect of his duties appeared in George Brown's office and demanded a testimony of character. The publisher refused, and tried to send him along to the appropriate department head. An argument ensued; the ex-employee drew a pistol, and before Brown could wrest it from him, it was discharged into his thigh. The huge newspaperman had little difficulty in overpowering his assailant, and made light of the wound. He was persuaded to return home and to receive medical attention, but assured his friends that he would be back at his desk in a few days.

As usual, he was over-optimistic. The days passed, and the anticipated recovery from what was, after all, a fairly simple flesh wound, did not materialize. After a fortnight, Mackenzie was almost frantic with anxiety. One evening the news was so discouraging that the entire House of Commons seemed to him saddened and listless. The next brought better news. "The writer well remembers the feeling of unalloyed pleasure which was expressed in all faces by the reassuring messages," he reported later.[54] "Thank God for all His goodness is what naturally rises to my lips," he wrote joyfully to Mrs. Brown.[55] The hopes were soon dashed; gangrene had set in, and the steady, relentless ebbing of the great body's resources began again. The inevitable end was at hand. Thirty years of close co-operation and understanding were drawing to a close. Seldom had two men of such strong convictions and outspoken natures agreed so well. They had been drawn together in pioneering days by similar principles. An identity of views had grown into mutual respect, respect into friendship, and friendship into love. With George Brown's death, a part of Alexander Mackenzie himself would die.

As Brown lay dying in Toronto, rumours were spreading of

serious differences within the Liberal caucus in Ottawa. Since Blake's election, the Conservative newspapers had not ceased to speculate about a change in the Grit leadership, and the Blake wing of the party did nothing to discourage the reports. Younger members of the caucus, who still burned with zeal for political power and an opportunity to leave their mark in Canadian history, were becoming more and more restless under such rigid and sterile leadership. Mackenzie not only presented few precise alternative policies, but he took few of his fellow-Liberals into his confidence, and disdained to cultivate the personal loyalty of his followers. To those who were anxious to return to power at almost any price, who were ready to cater to the protectionists, or even align themselves more closely with the United States, as Canadians are sometimes wont to do in hours of discouragement, the stern, unbending Scot was an obstacle in their path.

There are two versions of what happened. The conspiracy had been going on since the defeat, Alexander Mackenzie told the Premier of Prince Edward Island.[56] Some Liberals complained that while he was zealous and devoted to his duty, he was too unyielding on trade policies. They were right; he would not compromise on that. After Blake's return, he began to feel that he was being pushed aside. Lonesome, hurt, and bitter, with Holton dead and Brown dying, he decided to give up. "I believed I could, with the support of all my old colleagues but one, have secured a majority in the caucus," he told Premier Davies, "but I did not believe Mr. Blake would submit. I consulted no one until I made up (my) own mind what to do. If I called a meeting I must denounce the course which had been taken. I would then have a rupture. I resolved to simply announce to the House my retirement and let the party call a meeting which I would not attend." He called his former colleagues together – with the exception of Blake, who was no longer a Minister in September 1878, and Mills, whom he suspected of engineering the attempt to overthrow him – and announced his decision to resign. Scott alone, he told Davies, approved his course; the others insisted that "they could restore order". "I was, however, so satisfied that my plan was the only one to avoid a break-up that I could not yield and they . . . ultimately consented."

Wilfrid Laurier's biographer has a different version of the incident.[57] Mounting opposition to the increasingly lonely and austere leader resulted in the chairman of the caucus, Joseph Rymal, calling a meeting of the Liberal members on his own initiative, O. D. Skelton relates. A resolution was passed, asking Mackenzie to "consider the question of the leadership", and five former colleagues were delegated to put the matter to him. "Pelletier," the Grit leader said to the first to enter the room, "is not this simply a conspiracy of Mills and Rymal to put Blake in?" "No, Mr. Mackenzie," Pelletier stammered, "we thought that in the state of your health . . ." "There is nothing the matter with my health. It is all a conspiracy of a few men." There was a long and painful silence, then Laurier spoke out. "As a sincere friend of yours, Mr. Mackenzie, I must tell you that is not so; there is a general movement. We have been defeated; you have been defeated; it is only human nature that a defeated army should seek another general. There is not a man who has not high regard for your services, but there is a general feeling . . ." "Very well," Mackenzie broke in, "if that is so I shall very soon cease to lead the Liberal party."

It is not impossible that both versions contain a large degree of truth. That the righteous Scot may have given a biased account of the tragic meeting only reveals more vividly the depth of his wound. Whatever happened, he spent most of that day of April 27, 1880, in the Commons Chamber as usual, criticizing details of legislation, asking questions, and following the debate as if nothing untoward was about to happen. As the Speaker moved to adjourn the sitting at two in the morning, he rose. "I desire to say a word or two with regard to my personal relations," he stated in a flat, matter-of-fact tone.[58] "I yesterday determined to withdraw from the position as Leader of the Opposition and from this time forth I will speak and act for no person but myself." He sat down. The sparsely filled Chamber was silent as the stunned members took in the full significance of the statement. Sir John stood up a bit uncertainly. "Of course we on this side of the House have nothing to say to such a decision," he replied in a conversational tone, "but all I can say is that I hope the honourable gentleman who takes the place of the honourable member for Lambton and his party will display the same ability, earnestness and zeal for what he thinks and believes to be for the good of the country as has been displayed by my honourable friend who has just taken his seat."

The next day, Mackenzie was back in his seat at the usual hour, giving the same careful attention as before to the business before the House. To the onlooker, he appeared as unaffected as if nothing of consequence had occurred. On a measure to establish a High Commissionership in London, he attacked the restrictions placed on the occupant of such a position, and insisted that it would reduce him to the role of a servile lackey, to be consulted or ignored according to the whim of the officials in Downing Street. We established the principle that the Canadian view must prevail in Canadian affairs, he reminded the Commoners.[59]

Though he was unwilling to risk serious injury to the party by fighting back against those who sought to oust him from the leadership, Mackenzie refused to attend the caucus that chose Edward Blake as his successor. The resolution of thanks from the members was transmitted in writing. "We express in the warmest and most emphatic manner our high appreciation of the eminent services rendered the Liberal Party by one who both as private member and leader of the party has always evinced the most constant loyalty and disinterested self sacrifice in the propagation and defence of Liberal principles."[60]

Eleven days after the resignation, George Brown was dead. As Mackenzie and Sir Antoine-Aimé Dorion led the funeral procession through the streets of Toronto, they were burying much more than a fallen comrade. They were drawing the curtain on an era of the Liberal party, and an important chapter of Canadian history.

CHAPTER 19

"O Take Me Home"[1]

The press and public men of the Dominion were loud in their praise of the retiring leader; his own thoughts were for another. "Mr. Brown's death is indeed to me a great loss in a personal and political sense," he wrote to Charlie Black in Montreal after his arrival back in Toronto.[2] "An intimacy of thirty years made me love him as a brother. . . . Our friendship was an unselfish one. He was a man of true greatness of soul; impulsive, almost rash now and then, but his impulses were dictated by great intelligence, honest purpose and a noble generosity. We did not always agree but we never quarrelled. He was said to control my Government; so scrupulous was he about not influencing me that he never wrote me on public affairs unless I addressed him on some special case. . . . His place will not be filled in this generation."

The deaths of Brown and Holton, his own retirement, and the knowledge that their life-long opponents were becoming more securely ensconced in power every day as prosperity returned – all gave cause for doubt and perplexity. "It is hard to submit . . . ," he confided to a Protestant minister, "but God has His own wise purposes to fulfil and we must."[3] Above all, he regretted that the *Globe* publisher had died such a misunderstood and often maligned man. The true story of his life needed to be told in order to render to him the justice that was due. What more useful purpose for a true friend than to assure that justice? Alexander Mackenzie resolved to shut off distasteful memories of the last days in Ottawa, and to write the first study of George Brown.

The flood of expressions of loyalty and support was so great that the retired leader wondered if he had not made a mistake in resigning, and if he should not have challenged and beaten the cabal against him. Some discontented Tories even suggested that he form a new party with their support.[4] However, he had long ago discounted the attractions of power, and the gratitude of men in general. His time could be spent more profitably in being true to one who was true to him.

He had another project as well. A large Scottish firm had extensive timber reserves in Ontario, Quebec, and the United States. It wanted him to advise on the erection of mills, and the exploitation of the rich berths.[5] Mackenzie sent survey parties into the woods, visited many of the prospective mill sites in northern Ontario, toured the Georgian Bay area in a steamer tug, and acted generally as Canadian representative of the firm. With the insurance business, the Brown biography, and the consulting work, he was soon as busy and as keen as ever.

He had been writing so much "that my arm is often sore and my mind sick of letter writing", he complained almost happily in mid-June.[6] He had left Ottawa as thin and weak as in 1878; the new interests and the outdoor life restored his appetite, put a trace of the old spring in his step, and fresh colour in his cheeks. In the fall, a plea for assistance was erroneously addressed to him as the head of the Dominion Government. "It is doubtless from some man driven frantic by the 'National Policy'," he wrote to Sir John in re-directing it, "and he goes to the proper quarter for relief."[7] A trace of the old combativeness and cutting irony was returning.

The Government called the members to Ottawa before Christmas to approve a new contract for the Canadian Pacific Railway. A year earlier, Mackenzie would have looked forward eagerly to giving the Tories a difficult time; now he almost resented the interruption from his other occupations. "My engagements have been so constant and urgent the past months that I have had no time to devote to Mr. Brown's life," he told his son-in-law, ". . . I may do something on it at Ottawa as it is not my intention to do much serious work in the House. Indeed, I do not feel physically able to take any great load on my shoulders."[8] The stay in Ottawa would at least afford an opportunity to consult his doctors there, and to ask them why he was not able to recover his former strength, or free himself from the recurring attacks of dysentery.

The atmosphere on Parliament Hill was so upsetting that Alexander Mackenzie was put on a diet of "more medicine than food".[9] "Dr. Wright says I was suffering from malarial poisoning of long standing, but that otherwise I am healthy," he reported after the examination. Malarial poisoning – it was an unhappy relic of that happy summer with Helen on the banks of the St. Lawrence. He had been twenty-three, she twenty. She had died of the fever they had both contracted; he was to carry the germs for the rest of his life.

It was frustrating because, once in Ottawa, he felt stirring within him the old urge to "pitch into the Tories". In addition, Sir John Rose wanted to know if he would be available for employment outside Canada, providing a satisfactory climate and position were offered, and inquired what salary he would accept.[10] Such a possibility was out of the question as long as he was in such uncertain health. Fortified with quinine from a new series of treatments, he determined to have a try at attacking the Government in the new year. "I have observed, Sir, that during my enforced silence some of my opponents . . . ventured the opinion that I was afraid to meet the redoubtable warriors on the other side of the House," he lectured the occupants of the Treasury benches.[11] "I think that after twenty sessions of Parliament in which I never failed to have the courage of my convictions . . . it might have been taken for granted that whatever happened I should at least not be afraid to meet my opponents in debate. There is one thing, Sir, I admit I am afraid of, that is, I am always afraid – I have never had the courage – to misrepresent the opinions of my opponents or misquote their speeches." Friends beamed with pleasure to see evidence of the old battle spirit again. Opponents stirred uneasily to see who was to be the target of the sharp tongue. It was that "iniquitous measure", the Pacific Railway scheme, and its author, Sir Charles Tupper.

It was a hard-hitting and effective speech in which he refused to see any merit in the new plan, and clung more tenaciously than ever to his own alternative. However, it put the aging Grit back in bed. The doctors told him that his "vital organs" were sound enough, but that he had overtaxed his strength for years, and his body could no longer stand the strains he imposed upon it.[12] In his weakened condition, he was a natural prey to colds, fevers, and other ailments that came along. Finding it an effort even to walk through the Parliament Buildings, Mackenzie resolved to take better care of himself. He missed the remainder of the Pacific Railway debate, which resulted in a new deadline of 1891 for completion of the line, and he missed the budget debate as well.

Semi-idleness was impossible as long as he remained in the capital. By mid-February, he was asking the occasional question again, and by March he was harassing the Ministers almost as much as ever. "I congratulate the honourable gentleman on the vigour with which he is able to administer these rebukes," Sir John remarked after the Minister of Justice had received a particularly sharp volley. "Long may it be so."[13] If his physical resources were limited, Mackenzie's faith was undiminished by the trials and suffering, and he maintained his complete confidence that all was ordained by a benevolent Power. One spring night after the day's sitting had ended, he took his friend Louis Davies, the former Premier of Prince Edward Island, by the arm and led him to the cliff overlooking the Ottawa River. They stood bare-headed, gazing out across the dark forms of the Gatineau Hills at the countless stars in the blue-black sky. After a long silence, Mackenzie gestured upwards, and said in an awe-filled tone: "And yet they say there is no God."[14] Everything else might be disintegrating around him; nothing and no one could rob him of his most precious possession. Over all were the everlasting arms.

Concerned over his loss of twenty-two pounds in weight during the winter, Alexander Mackenzie's doctors continued to urge a slower pace, and suggested a complete change of environment to escape Canadian politics. He was like the ox that D'Arcy McGee used to tell about, the ex-Premier conceded, he had "kind o' gi'en out".[15] He and Jane decided to take a trip to Europe and visit the Highlands they had dreamed of roaming together when the heavy responsibilities of public life were over. In 1875, there had been so little time to relax and enjoy themselves; now they would have all the freedom and privileges of private citizens.

They could have gone as Sir Alexander and Lady Jane had they wished. In 1881, Lord Lorne made the second offer of a title in three years.[16] A large private fortune was not necessary, His Excellency argued, and it was not right that there should be such an unequal distribution of titles between the two parties. "It is because I know it w'd be universally approved that I ask you to let me forward my request to Her Majesty that you become my brother in Knighthood." The coaxing was of no avail. "The only distinction I feel to be consistent with my position would be an appointment as a Privy Councillor," Mackenzie replied, "that being rather an official designation than a title, and only an extension of the Colonial title held by the Canadian Ministers and ex-Ministers. I am not however pressing or even asking for the bestowal of that honour."[17]

The ocean crossing took a mere eight days and a half. Jane and their travelling companions, the Mowats, were ill most of the time, but Mackenzie was able to report back to Canada proudly that he did not miss a meal on account of seasickness. In London, they watched a debate in the British House of Commons, but soon became bored and went on to pleasanter distractions. They were shocked to see how much one of their political idols, William Gladstone, had aged; it was another sign of the advancing years.

After three days in the Imperial capital, the Mackenzies went on to Paris. "I am out all the time, and have a red sunburnt face and freckled hands," the Canadian politician wrote happily from the French capital.[18] "... I am much stronger than when I left.... I walk all I can, then ride mostly on top of the omnibuses. I vary my pleasure now and then by a row with a cabman and once with a café keeper at St. Germain. My French vocabulary is neither large nor select but what is available I freely used ... When utterly perplexed I sometimes try Gaelic, especially as I can freely swear in the original." From the French metropolis, their path led to Switzerland, and from Switzerland to Germany and on to Belgium. Interlaken was like Dunkeld, Alexander Mackenzie told his brother Robert, except the hills were five times as high and the lake three miles across.[19] Furka Pass reminded him of Killiekrankie "multiplied fifty times". In Cologne, they were amused to find themselves in the "city of smells".[20] In general, they were no different from other tourists. The languages, the forms of transportation, the geography, the crops, the architecture – everything attracted the ex-stonemason's attention. They made exciting new discoveries of life in foreign lands, worried about accommodation and exchange rates, and got into the usual difficulties of strangers in an unfamiliar setting.

Interesting as it was, a European tour was not their primary goal. As soon as it was completed, they rushed back to London and on to the land of the heather. There was no doubt about it: for the immigrant from Perthshire, Scotland was still the greatest country in the world. "No city we have seen will for a moment compare with Edinburgh for natural beauty, special and general architecture, wide streets or places of resort for the people," he wrote enthusiastically to Charles from Arthur's Seat.[21] "Little wonder that they called it the 'Magnificent Queen of cities'." After leaving Edinburgh, the Mackenzies installed themselves in a little hotel in Dunkeld and roamed the Perthshire countryside with all the carefree abandon of a young couple on a honeymoon. "The highest civilization with the wildest natural beauty," Alexander boasted proudly of his ancestral home. "... We have traversed every hill and driven on every possible road. It is curious that I don't feel so tired climbing high hills as walking on the level."[22] Apparently it depended on the geographical location of the hills and the levels.

Even the old sense of humour returned. One day they drove

several miles to call on the mother of a Canadian friend. The old lady kept a bric-à-brac shop in an ancient stone and sod building so low that Mackenzie could hardly stand without touching the ceiling. To avoid imposing themselves on a person in such modest circumstances, he and Jane lunched in the village before making their call. Nevertheless, the hospitable old shopkeeper insisted that they eat again. "I longed to be able to ask her, like Horne Tooke, to give us feed in money," the discomfited guest wrote later, ". . . but necessity knows no law so we ate and drank and slacked a button or two. We then thought of escaping but the whiskey was yet to come. This assault I manfully resisted until it occurred to me that Davis Pain-Killer might not be found and some internal remedy would be needed so I yielded once more and swallowed the whiskey. It is said that bottling claret you must not let the cork touch the claret and you must have more than ¼″ between the cork and claret. If I had been corked after leaving Mrs. Crerar's the only trouble would be to get the ¼″ . . . When I visit anyone again in this region I shan't take any breakfast; indeed I am not sure but what I shall imitate Bill Smith and fast for two days before to save the expense of calling a doctor."[23]

Despite the old lady's whiskey and the double meals, Scotland was a tonic to the sick man's body. By mid-August, he had regained the twenty pounds and was within eleven of his maximum weight.[24] Avoiding public appearances as much as possible, he climbed mountains, visited Loch Lomond, John O' Groats, Drysburgh Abbey, and many other places he had not seen before. However, with his health so largely restored, his thoughts turned automatically towards "home", and that was unquestionably the place where he had spent his entire adult life. Scotland was the land of his birth, but Canada was part of him, and he was part of it. As the holiday drew to a close, he and Jane became impatient to return to their Wellington Street house in Toronto, to worship at the Jarvis Street church, to see their friends, their relatives, and especially their grandchildren. They wanted to know about, and even to worry about, Canadian affairs. So anxious were they to be back that they ignored invitations in both Montreal and Ottawa, and rushed straight through to Toronto in early September.

* * * * *

During his absence in that summer of 1881, the railway syndicate formed by Sir George Stephen to build the Canadian Pacific Railway had put Mackenzie's name on the Board of Trustees created to supervise the use made of the land grants obtained by the company. The honorarium accompanying the position was two thousand dollars a year, a tidy sum for a man approaching his sixtieth birthday in uncertain health and without financial reserves. "Morally and legally I have a perfect right to act, but is it expedient?" he asked himself when he learned of the appointment.[25] "Will it not be suspected that I will be influenced perhaps in my judgment; will it not injure my personal influence and possibly the party?" Argue with himself as he might, he could not bring himself to accept. "I would not for all the thousands that could be offered place myself in an equivocal position in which it would be possible to impugn my integrity, or in which the party would be injured," he told William Buckingham. The syndicate was disappointed as they had hoped to make it the first in a series of prestige appointments designed to neutralize opposition to their plans. They tried to persuade the retired Grit leader to let his name stand for the moment, and then resign when the Board was complete. He refused; there were things more important than money, even to a parsimonious Scot.

His health much improved, Alexander Mackenzie was anxious to get to work again. Business matters awaited his attention, and the Brown biography was scarcely begun. The old call of politics, too, was stirring within him again. With another election approaching, he had decided to contest a constituency in York County where he lived, instead of attempting to represent Lambton and his old neighbours whom he now saw but seldom. Two weeks after his return from abroad, he made his first speech as the prospective candidate for York East. The meeting was disappointing. Canada had not only recovered from the depression, but was launched on another boom; the electors were not waiting with bated breath to rectify the error of '78. "The York meeting was a failure yesterday," Mackenzie admitted, ". . . The farmers are not yet in a mood to care about meetings. Wheat at $1.34 indisposes them to grumble and swear at John A. Between good harvests here for three years and the very bad ones in England the rascals have had the devil's own luck."[26]

The burst of energy did not last long. With the arrival of cold weather, he was back in bed again. This time there was an additional complaint, even more disturbing than the stomach cramps and the loss of weight. There was a tightness in his throat that made it difficult to speak. Was he losing his voice? What a terrible fate for a politician! Was this some punishment for the years of castigating his opponents with such destructive sharpness? Surely he had not put this God-given talent to such poor use that he deserved to lose it while the Macdonalds and Tuppers and Blakes brayed on? It was a frightening prospect. "I hope time will bring it back to full power," the worried politician wrote to Charlie Black. "In the meantime it is rather ackward [*sic*] to have my tongue tied."[27]

When the session of 1882 began, Alexander Mackenzie was in his Commons seat, and looking much improved in health. Even his voice seemed to have returned to a large extent. The Throne Speech was clearly a pre-election document, with boastful proclamations of abundant prosperity, plentiful harvests, and remunerative prices. There was obviously a plan for a concerted attack on the Leader of the Opposition as well. Tupper, Bowell, and other Conservatives had been delving into Blake's past, and uncovering every past vote or declaration that could be used against him. Forgetting his own deep grievances, Mackenzie sprang to the defence of his seat-mate. With fire in his eyes, and his grey beard jutting defiantly, he rose to hurl back the torrent of abuse. But when he began to speak, he realized that his voice was no longer equal to the task. After a few sentences, the tightness in his throat returned and he was forced to sink back into his seat. His opponents thundered on unanswered.

Refusing to admit defeat, the pugnacious Scot changed tactics. He sat quietly, consciously relaxing his throat muscles and giving them an opportunity to gain strength. His eyes and ears as alert as ever, he followed every second of the debate. Then, when he felt that he could utter a few words, he rose to his feet and expressed in a series of short, concise sentences the view or argument that he would normally have developed in a longer speech. The interjections were always brief, and his voice was not strong, but his fellow-Commoners learned to listen with respect. He was still precise, clear, and accurate, and his words went directly to the heart of the matter every time. It was more than could be said of most of the more vocal members.

Mackenzie was still well enough to fill the role of acting Leader of the Opposition when Blake went to Toronto in late February to be at the bedside of his ailing sister. The ex-Premier enjoyed the responsibility and the confidence shown him by his successor, and he was gratified to be able to play even the role of the trusted lieutenant. Old intra-party animosities and bitterness seemed secondary to the new battle with his diminishing health. He transmitted Blake's wishes, and presided over the shadow Cabinet that divided the work among the

Opposition members. "I fear I must give up all hope of speaking for any length on any subject," he sighed in a letter to Blake. "I will, however, try to attend to Public Works matters."[28]

As the session progressed, Mackenzie's strength increased somewhat, and he determined to make an all-out effort in the budget debate.[29] He began to speak slowly, his voice in a conversational key, each word following in neat order like a stonemason building a structure that must stand the test of time. At sixty, he was less interested in breaking new ground than in keeping straight the record of the past, and countering the misstatements from across the floor. He touched on all the old arguments again – maintenance of the link with the Mother Country, autonomy in purely Canadian matters, the evil of imposing high taxes and protecting vested interests. He reminded the House that George Brown had been one of the first public men to urge incorporation of the North West into Canada. He refused to admit that the current prosperity was in any way related to an economic policy of shifting money from one pocket to another by Government action. Protection was a mere relic of barbarism, he insisted, and the economic swings were still beyond the comprehension of economists and legislators alike.

His voice held up amazingly well. From the evils of protection, he went on to consolidate the Liberal claim to a true Canadian national policy within the Empire. "It is quite evident that this country cannot go on to submit to negotiations – on this continent at all events – being conducted by people who know nothing whatever of the country . . ." The tightness in his throat was increasing, and he had to struggle hard to force out the words. Tilley rose and suggested that he might prefer to continue the following day, but he rejected the offer with an impatient gesture. The Liberals were accused of being hostile to the manufacturing interests, he stated. "It is an absurd charge! Why should they be? Are not many of us interested in manufactures? Have not many of us friends who are manufacturers? I believe that the policy of the honourable gentlemen opposite has worked injuriously to manufacturers . . ." He was opposed to any policy that was discriminatory or created classes in Canada. "We hold that no class of persons or occupations should have anything more than a fair opportunity to develop their energies and their productions to the utmost extent that can be done consistent with the welfare and interests of others." It was the end of the speech. No further words would come. With a despairing shrug, he resumed his seat. He had not even the strength to indicate if he wished to continue at a later time. Looking across to the clock above the entrance, he noted that it was approaching eleven o'clock. He had spoken for an hour.

He did not try to repeat the feat again soon. By carefully harbouring his precious resources, he was able to criticize the estimates of his former department, now divided into two in order to ease the burden. Frequently, he launched into a heated outburst, only to find silence imposed upon him after a few words. It was the late night sittings that fatigued him most. He soon found that by leaving the Parliament Buildings early in the evening and isolating himself in his room, he could increase his output the following day. Maximum results in the Chamber were becoming a fixation; for the rest of the session he put aside all other activities, including supervision of the North American Life Insurance Company, the successor of the Isolated Risk Insurance Company, and concentrated on making himself heard on Parliament Hill. On Blake's motion to enable Canada to make her own commercial treaties, subject to subsequent British approval, he spoke for a full half-hour. "We now have perfect liberty of action in legislation," he told the House. ". . . Why should we not have the same freedom in negotiating business with other countries? . . . I for one give my cordial support to anything that will extend our liberty of action and make us entirely equal in all respects to other legislatures and the Ministers of the Mother Country itself.[30] The Government defeated the suggestion.

The great gerrymander brought forth his strongest outburst of indignation. Following the 1881 census, Sir John A. Macdonald was faced with the problem of creating several new constituencies, and he decided to take the opportunity, as he put it, to "hive the Grits".[31] Ignoring municipal and county borders, he rearranged the constituencies in a brazen attempt to give his candidates every possible advantage in the election. Reform-minded Lambton was divided; Mackenzie's new constituency was gerrymandered, or "John-A-mandered", as well. "A masterpiece of political trickery," fumed the former Grit leader.[32] Hours of protest and some fifty amendments were of no avail; the Conservative backbenchers stood solidly behind their chieftain in the attempt to perpetuate themselves in power.

The session ended in May, and the campaign began at once. Alexander Mackenzie made his first speech in Malvern two days after the dissolution. It was his tenth campaign, he told the huge crowd, and he had never been defeated.[33] Encouraged by the reception accorded him, and by his capacity to make himself heard, he began a thorough canvass. It was a wet spring, and he was often drenched as he stood on the platform or rode from meeting to meeting. On May 27, he met his opponent on a platform in Yorkville, and gave both an hour-long speech and a short rebuttal.[34] On May 30 he spoke in Weston, on June 3 in Cardwell. Noticing that he was becoming so tense and nervous that he could no longer sleep at night, Jane tried to persuade him to slow down. In vain. In the forenoon of June 6, he was calling on a voter in Markham Township when he was taken ill.[35] A doctor was summoned, and he was pronounced to be suffering from his old complaint of stomach inflammation. But there was more. In addition to his throat, which refused completely to function, his left arm and side were stiff and numb. He had suffered a stroke.

The Tory press reported him dead, but the Grit papers minimized his illness. Daily reports were issued by his doctors, and vivid descriptions were given of the setting between Richmond Hill and Unionville where he lay. "A white house prettily situated on a green knoll, and surrounded by an orchard," reported the *Globe*. On June 11, he was able to speak a bit again. The doctor told him that his tongue looked better, but that a few days before it had been "remarkable". That was what the Tories always said, he managed to reply.[36] The comment was reported joyfully as an indication that the danger period was over. As he was moved carefully back to his Toronto home and Jane's tender care, the Liberals in East York sprang into action to assure his election. Scoffing at recurring reports that he was dead or dying, they scoured the constituency with the same vigour that he had shown on Brown's behalf thirty years before.[37] On June 20, he was elected with a majority of one hundred and eight votes.

"The noblest Roman of them all," proclaimed the *Hamilton Spectator* in announcing the victory.[38] Unfortunately, it was one of the rare causes for jubilation in the Liberal ranks. The Conservatives were given another lease of power from the Canadian people. The election results seemed to highlight the victory in East York. Grits and Tories alike expressed satisfaction that Mackenzie would be back in Parliament.[39] "Your truth, honour and patriotism cannot be denied," wrote one admirer, "and your almost matchless knowledge, experience, and ability are among the recognized treasures of the nation."[40] Disappointed Liberals recalled that Mackenzie would never have campaigned as Blake had done on a hedging acceptance of protection, nor left doubts in the public mind concerning his loyalty to the Empire. The 1882 election seemed to obscure the ignominy of 1878. It raised the former party leader to the role of a respected elder statesman.

By the end of June, Alexander Mackenzie could sit up and

work on the Brown manuscript, and by mid-July he was able to move about and carry on a quiet conversation. On July 24, he and Jane undertook an excursion to visit friends in Hamilton. When they arrived home, a surprise awaited them. Two prominent Montreal Liberals had called in their absence to present them with a cheque for four thousand dollars collected among political friends in Quebec![41] An expression of gratitude for past services to the party, it was intended to be used for "a few months' tour on the other side of the Atlantic or such place as would suit you best". What should he do? he asked himself as he held the piece of paper in his hand. Should he return it by the first post? Should he decline this gesture of kindness and friendship as he had declined the silver wedding presents and other offerings? Would he still be open to criticism now that he was a mere private member? After a week of agonizing reflection, he decided to accept. "I did not want to compromise my independence or humble myself," he told the donors, but coming from such friends he thought he could "properly comply with their desire and kindly wishes".[42] Once the door was opened a trifle, the flood of kindness continued. He discovered that the York East Liberals had paid his five hundred dollars election expenses.[43] And a delegation arrived from Sarnia with another cheque for five thousand five hundred dollars.[44] Quite apart from the usefulness of the money, it was a handsome indication that so many years of devotion to duty were appreciated.

It was too late in the season to go as far as Scotland, but Mackenzie decided to take his son-in-law, who was also in need of a holiday, for a quiet rest on the Maine seashore. Complaining of having to walk "with the steps of a decrepid [*sic*] old man though in spirit I feel young yet," he and Thompson roamed along the coast and let the sea breezes drive the fine salty spray against their tired bodies.[45] "I have been recalling the events of the last 50 years," he wrote to Jane in Toronto, "and have come to the conclusion I might and should have done more work than I accomplished. I see wasted opportunities which cannot be recalled; and carelessness of personal welfare which now bears fruit in an enfeebled physical system. How precious is the knowledge of a sure and certain resurrection of the glorified body through the redemption wrought in and by our Lord and Saviour Jesus Christ free from all seeds of decay and disease. And after all, what matters a few more years here when such prospects are in store."[46] The greatest victory lay still ahead.

He refused to give up. By carefully gauging his physical resources on his return to Toronto, he managed to visit the insurance office regularly, and to complete the book on George Brown.

"The writer regrets that this duty [of recording Brown's accomplishments] did not fall into more competent hands," he wrote in the preface before sending it to the printer that fall, "and that a more graphic picture should not be presented of one who was so deservedly popular, and who gave so much of his life and strength, as a journalist and politician, to combatting public wrongs, and establishing a new constitution embodying just principles of government."[47] The task had taken much longer than he had anticipated, but it was done at last. He had paid a final tribute to his dearest friend, and had taken the first step in assuring him his rightful place in Canadian history.

When the 1883 session began, Mackenzie was again in his place on the Opposition front benches. The prosperity was continuing, said the Governor General. One thousand miles of railway track had been laid between Lake Superior and the Saskatchewan River, and construction crews were moving steadily toward the Rockies. Charles Hibbert Tupper, the son of Sir Charles, moved the acceptance of the Throne Speech. It was another indication that Mackenzie and his opponents were growing old.

For a sick man, the ex-Premier did well during the session. His mind was as alert and keen as ever, and he worked hard on the Government reports and other documents that reveal the real functioning of an administration. Visitors seldom saw him idle. He could listen to the debate, and carry on his own research at his Commons desk simultaneously. When he rose to say a few words, the moment was carefully chosen, and he was seldom, if ever, proven wrong. Ministers still had cause for concern when they saw him pulling himself laboriously to his feet. The tone had softened, but the message was still the same. Carrying on the crusade for freedom, equality, and honesty, he opposed the delegation of parliamentary responsibility to commissions, and government intervention in fields of private enterprise. A *laissez-faire* Liberal, he insisted that the Government should allow the economic machine to operate with a minimum of rules and regulations.

Mackenzie still believed in the inherent wickedness of all Tories, and delighted in pointing to acts such as the gerrymander to substantiate his accusations. His attacks on protectionism, and his defence of the Imperial connection, continued whenever his failing body allowed. He would maintain the struggle to vindicate his principles, he warned the Ministry, "no matter how long it may take to succeed".[48] He refused to believe that the National Policy and the prosperous times were related in any way, and would not be convinced that additional taxation could produce additional wealth. "That policy cannot be just which does an injustice to the humblest individual of the commonwealth," he protested. ". . . I for one will never agree to consent to endorse it while I have a voice to lift in the Legislature or out of it." The flashes of indignation and humour showed that beneath the calm exterior, the fires burned brightly still.

* * * * *

When Parliament prorogued on May 25, the Mackenzies and Thompsons were already across the Atlantic. "My voice is so much better that I now think the summer holiday will restore it to its old strength," he wrote hopefully to Buckingham.[49] He could not give up. The ladies wanted to see Italy so the tour was started there. Of all the cities, he was most impressed by Milan with its "rich handsome streets", and the white marble cathedral, like "poetry in stone".[50] They were thrilled to see oranges and lemons growing on the trees, to be delivered to their hotel in a gondola in Venice, and to study the exquisite architecture and paintings in Florence. "I am not sorry I came to Italy," Mackenzie wrote to his brother Charles, "as I have seen much that could not be known without a visit."[51]

In London, he delivered a short address to the Empire Club. Lord Dufferin, who was in the capital prior to realizing at last his dream of becoming Viceroy of India after a period in the frigid Russian capital, declared it "full of weight, good sense, force and effect."[52] The days in London were pleasant, but the old politician's heart gave an extra beat of pleasure when he crossed the Scottish border once again. "Auld Reekie, despite the whiskey, is still 'Queen of Cities'," he declared.[53] The continental cities had their charm, "but to my mind 'Fair Edina' for natural beauty and for artistic excellence, bears the palm."[54] There he was in the very heart of the civilization to which he belonged. Greyfriars churchyard reminded him of the struggle against the religious despots who once ruled Scotland. The Grassmarket recalled the men who preferred to lose their lives rather than abandon their religious beliefs. The Princess Street gardens, he remembered, was once a bog where the "cultured infidel" David Hume had become stuck, and been forced by an old woman to repeat the Lord's Prayer before she helped him out. Up on Castle Rock, he saw the window from which the boy king James VI was lowered to the ground, and found himself wishing that the rope had broken "so as to have saved the nation the long years of misery it had to suffer at the hands of one fool and two rascals, each called a British Sovereign".

"Scotland's sons have much to be proud of in their struggle for independence and popular rights," he commented proudly.

Edinburgh had one shrine that he visited with reverence – the home and grave of John Knox. "Scotland, aye, the world, owes more to John Knox than to any other man," he wrote fervently after visiting the historic site. "He educated Scotland for the home of freedom.... He was a statesman of the broadest type. . . . Luther was a great man – so was Calvin; but neither had the liberality of thought nor the practical ability of John Knox." Even the souvenirs of Mary, Queen of Scots, gave the aging Perthshireman cause for reflection. "Was she a bad woman? is the question that comes up for answer when looking on her frank, full eyes and lovely face. I fear she was not pure either as a sovereign or as a woman, but she was in a wretched school. . . . I confess to a lingering feeling of sympathy which makes me blame others more than her."

The trip outside of Canada gave a boost to Mackenzie's health, but the throat muscles still rebelled. During the 1884 session of Parliament, he had to restrict himself to sporadic interventions whenever he could restrain himself no longer. The winter was severe, and the snow in Ottawa of record depth; he limited his activity to the daily walk between his hotel and office, and lengthened his weekend visits to Toronto. "The honourable and distinguished member for York East", a junior member called him; he was becoming venerable with age.[55] Visitors pointed out the slight, erect, grey-bearded figure to one another from the galleries. When he rose to speak, the other members leaned forward to catch the words that came so painfully from the stiff throat.

There were so many things he yearned to say. His "water stretches" plan for the Pacific Railway was still being held up to ridicule, and the inaccuracies concerning his Administration shocked and upset him.[56] The Canadian Pacific Railway was in financial trouble. Galt was being replaced as High Commissioner in London by Tupper because of his independent views. "I regret to say that . . . we have a depression at the present time," confessed Tilley in his budget address.[57] So many issues, so many openings, but he had no voice! His mind leaped, his body throbbed, his tongue was ready, but his throat refused to obey. Near the end of the session, he managed to lash out in a series of short sentences at the "scandalous misstatements" concerning his North West policy. "I can only hope that some day we will meet at Philippi," he wheezed at his old opponent, Dr. Tupper, "where I shall endeavour to give him what he deserves."[58]

Alexander Mackenzie finished the session no better nor worse than he began. Encouraged at having at least halted the deterioration, he was toying with the idea of accomplishing another long-standing dream. For over thirty years, he had spoken from public platforms and in Parliament of the great North West. Canada's future, the future of the Empire itself, he had said frequently, were linked with the great fertile plains, the immense coal fields, and the rich timber resources there. As Minister of Public Works, he had studied so many maps and reports that he knew the area by heart. Yet he had never been west of Lake Superior. Now Van Horne and Stephen of the Canadian Pacific syndicate were urging him to go. "There is not a man in Canada to-day I am so anxious should see that country," George Stephen wrote.[59] Blake's negative attitude and his determination to prove that the West was, in fact, a "sea of mountains" interspersed with alkali deserts and inhabited by enormous grasshoppers, were destroying public confidence at a time when the whole project hung in the balance.

Could he stand the trip? His health was really improved, Mackenzie tried to convince himself; he had a good appetite and slept six to seven hours a night, quite enough for a man of his age and more than he had allowed himself as Prime Minister. But there was a certain "nervous trepidation", a constant tingling of the whole nervous system, that made him uneasy. For the first time in his life, he hung back, almost afraid to go on. "I am . . . easily tired (and there I suppose 62 comes in)," he told Mary, "and I rather shrink from undertaking labour mental or physical (and there I fear, laziness comes in)."[60]

Still, idleness did not become him. He read almost constantly – Thomas Carlyle, Sandford Fleming's book, *England and Canada*, Huntington's novel – anything and everything from which he felt he had something to learn. He even contemplated writing another volume himself, "A Chapter of Canadian History". "If I do it will be a bomb shell in more than one sore spot," he confided to his daughter, "but I rather shrink from taking so decisive a step in disintegrating the liberal party, as my own friends would suffer with those who deserve to feel some pain."[61] Some of the rancour for the events of 1880 still remained, and beneath the enforced silence his indignation still simmered at the partial abandonment by some Liberals of the principles that marked his political career. "How I wish I had my voice restored," he moaned. "There never was a finer opportunity for a public man and it is being wasted by child's play, as was last session." The trip to Europe the previous summer had done some good; perhaps the trip to the West would do even more. He accepted Stephen's offer. "If my western tour brings relief I will strike out on my return," he promised himself.[62]

The North West was all and more than he expected.[63] The depth of the vast stretches of fertile soil, the size of the farms, the growing towns, and above all, the towering Rocky Mountains, made him forget the harsh reality of advancing years. He had pioneered in the West when that term applied to western Ontario; he was swept up by the familiar challenge and the rugged beauty of life on the Canadian frontier. Looking out of the railway carriage as they crossed the prairies, he saw stands of wheat, oats and barley taller than himself. They visited farms with wheat-fields of over one thousand acres, and saw herds of over a hundred horses. Twenty-five reapers were employed on a single farm to bring in the bounteous harvest. By the time he reached Medicine Hat, and had a look at the rich coal seams, he was ready to declare that the wealth of the North West "was perfectly incomprehensible to anyone".[64]

The first sight of the Rockies was unforgettable. "We sighted the mountains first about 130 miles from the entrance to the pass," he reported enthusiastically to Mary, "and at dusk reached the magnificent portal. We saw the beautiful Bow River and its splendid scenery for over 100 miles. Nothing could be finer than its perfectly-planned terraces and carefully-formed escarpments, finished as by a gigantic gardener."[65] They continued past Banff and up to the Kicking Horse Pass where construction of the railway line was still under way. "The road winds and twists, striving to avoid the river; in vain . . . The growth of spruce and tamarind is so dense that . . . but one or two glimpses of the white maddened streams are to be had. . . . From the place called the entrance of the Pass . . . the immense ranges of hills stand like a prodigious army, presenting arms and welcoming the visitor into the sublime vestibule. . . . Some . . . seem to have been built by tremendous agencies, and show a castellated appearance very like a monster ruin."

In Calgary, he and Jane – she hardly left his side now – attended a meeting organized to protest acts of the North West Territories Administration, and to demand self-government.[66] It was a cry that struck a responsive chord in the old politician's heart; these pioneers were fighting the same battle, and against the same reactionary crowd – Sir John A. Macdonald and his fellow-Tories – as he had done in his early years in Canada. He took careful notes, assured the westerners of his support, and promised to speak out on their behalf in Ottawa. In Manitoba, on his return journey, Donald Smith turned over to them his palatial residence of "Silver Heights" on the outskirts of Winnipeg, and they were invited to a whole series of excursions and public functions. He had read a lot about the West, he told a luncheon meeting in Stonewall, but this visit showed him that half the story had not yet been told. Toronto was the centre of the Canadian population at the moment, but there were those living who would see the centre of population as far west as Winnipeg.[67]

On September 2, he spoke to a capacity crowd in the Winnipeg Opera House, where he was introduced as Canada's "sterling statesman".[68] His voice was fading noticeably from the constant strain, and he had great difficulty in making himself heard. He may have been wrong in some of his past actions, he confessed, but he still felt that the more northerly railway route through Manitoba would have opened up more of the Prairies, and that Winnipeg would have been still more prosperous as a result. The West was undoubtedly the finest part of the entire continent, and it was important to plan its development carefully and wisely. Canada had all the elements of greatness, and Canadians were right in hoping to become a large nation and "expecting to exercise our influence in promoting the civilization and prosperity of the nations". In this way they would be helping to carry out the destiny of the British race to extend its influence to all portions of the universe. He himself would continue to do what he could in the struggle to uphold the principles in which he believed.

Yes, there was so much to do. There was only one cloud in the pleasant western sky. In Qu' Appelle a Dr. Edwards examined his health. There was no doubt about it, the physician told Jane, the former Prime Minister had done permanent damage to his health by the constant strain of public life.[69] His nervous system was irreparably impaired.

* * * * *

Back in Toronto, Alexander Mackenzie sent a message of congratulations to Stephen and Van Horne on their accomplishments in the West.[70] The public statement indicated an open breach with Blake's Canadian Pacific policy, and even with the line adopted by the *Globe*. On the other hand, he was still foursquare with the views expounded by George Brown over the years, and he still stood up for his former leader's dream of a rich and populous British nation extending from ocean to ocean. And as George Stephen commented, he did not do any political harm to his own principles either.[71]

As he arrived from the West, Oliver Mowat also was returning to Toronto from a major victory in England. The Ontario Boundary award arranged by him and Mackenzie in 1878 had not been accepted by the Conservative Government, and they had refused to ratify it. Through two election campaigns and in countless other ways, Sir John had tried to destroy the "little tyrant", who dared to trade blow for blow with him. The boundary dispute was finally submitted to the Imperial Privy Council, and Mowat's view was upheld. In September of 1884, a mammoth victory demonstration, attended by fifty thousand people, was held in Toronto, and Alexander Mackenzie was asked to preside. "Determined, systematic efforts have been put forth by the federal Government, practically to abrogate the Constitution of this country," he declared with all the force and vehemence that he could muster, "and we owe it to Mr. Mowat and his Cabinet that those efforts have been successfully resisted. . . . Long may he live, and may provincial rights always be defended with equal ability."[72] He received a tremendous ovation. Blake followed with a fervent hope that his former chief would recover his health, and "once more give heart and hope to his friends, and strike terror and dismay into his enemies".

No one hoped for a cure more than Mackenzie himself. Fairly seething with partisan political passion, he set off for New York to see if some American doctor did not have an answer. A celebrated nerve and brain specialist put him through a series of tests, and diagnosed the case as an enlargement of one of the blood vessels on the brain, with consequent pressure on a nerve.[73] He seemed to have little new to offer – the same ice treatment on the back of the head at bedtime, mineral water night and morning, some drug three times a day, plenty of walking, and absolutely no strain on the nervous system. How could a Liberal politician follow such a régime when the Tories were in power, and there were so many vital issues at stake? He could not even resist a partisan interest in the election campaign under way in New York, and found himself studying the tactics and issues with keen interest. Politics was an integral part of his life.

If he could not make himself heard in the Chamber, he could still carry on his research and take part in the serious work done in the committees. No Committee on Privileges and Election, or Railways, Canals and Telegraph Lines, or Public Accounts, or Banking and Commerce was complete without him. With his extensive knowledge of the details of the different departments, he was able to act as a sort of self-appointed auditor general and watch over a large portion of the Dominion administration. If his voice prevented him from using the information he unearthed, there was always a fellow-Liberal anxious to reap the benefit of the careful research.

During the 1885 session, his Ottawa physician put him on a new series of treatments called the "Massauge" system, which Mackenzie told his daughter, "may be described as rubbing and exercising *all* the muscles and joints combined with simple applications and medicated baths. . . . It is rather hard to see the connection between the soles of the feet and calves of the legs and a difficulty in the throat."[74] Anything was worth trying.

The old fighting spirit could still be stung into action occasionally. Derisive references to the "water stretches" were a sure way of making the bright eyes flash and a trace of colour return to the pallid face. "The honourable gentleman who could be so wanting in intelligence as to suppose that possible," he growled hoarsely when a Conservative accused him of having started the Lake Superior-Winnipeg line in the middle instead of at both ends, "would very likely be wanting in the honesty and fair play which would have prevented him from making the statement he did. . . ."[75] "Parliament is to be turned into a gathering for the convenience of honourable gentlemen and to pass their measures," he grumbled when he failed to obtain information he was seeking, "instead of being the grand inquest of the nation for the transaction of public business."[76]

Whenever the West was mentioned, Alexander Mackenzie's interest was particularly keen. The Frog Lake massacre and the second Riel rebellion were of vital concern to him, and recalled the difficult decision of 1874 when he decided to go against his earlier declarations and demand an amnesty for the half-breed rebel. That compromise, too, he now felt, had been a mistake. And yet he had only sufficient voice to ask about the welfare of the refugees from the tragic incident.[77] When the time came, he voted silently for Riel's death. He did find the strength to strike a blow on behalf of the people he had met in Calgary. They would not be denied self-government, he warned the Ministry. "The people are determined that no attempt to keep the power out of their hands will succeed, and efforts will only be repelled by improper means."[78] If the dissatisfaction revealed among the natives by the Riel uprising was not to be repeated among the whites, the Westerners must be given the rights of free British men and women.

The Opposition gave the Government, in Macdonald's own words, "the most harassing and disagreeable session I have witnessed in forty years".[79] Even with the various treatments, Mackenzie could only keep up with his correspondence, labour away quietly in his office or at his Commons desk, and make the occasional interjection. "My complaint, stripped of all technical disguises," he wrote Charlie Black in a hand less steady than in former years, "is partial paralysis of the left arm, throat, and some little in the leg or thigh. I have no pain – only a feeling of tiredness and want of power. I do everything usually done with my left arm, but it is slow work, as the muscles do not obey the mind without much coaxing. . . . I have done all I could for effecting a cure, but without success. . . . For some years I drew on my reserve strength until it was used up, and now the treasure is gone."[80] That was the bitter truth, and there was no use attempting to avoid it any longer; he would never be well again.

Mackenzie missed much of the session of 1886. He and Jane had bought a new house on Wellesley Street, between Yonge Street and the Legislative Buildings. It was a quieter area, out of the reach of boat horns and train whistles, and the traffic of downtown Toronto. It was just a few steps from the university, with its lovely grounds, contiguous to Queen's Park. The Jarvis Street Baptist Church was within walking distance on a fine day. Here, between the Legislature, the non-secular university which had been one of his first political goals, and the church, they made their last home.

Unable to espouse any great public causes, the old Grit decided to take one more trip to Scotland. Yes, "politics is very low", he agreed with Charlie Black shortly before he sailed. "Like priests, like people."[81] "As Jeremiah exclaimed under a similar set of circumstances – 'The people will have it so'. Unfortunately I am totally unable to speak, or I would try and contrast my way and theirs of carrying on the Gov't of the country. I am hanging on to my seat (only able to vote) in the hope that I may recover. Of that there is little hope, I fear, at my age." His greatest satisfaction was in receiving assurances that people approved of the course that he had taken while he was still able to fight.

Even the Tummel valley could no longer work its restorative wonders on the tired body. By leaning on Jane's arm, he was able to walk as much as two or three miles in a full day, but he no longer dared to climb among the heather or stray away from the beaten paths. Britain was having another election, and he was pleased to see Scotland stand loyally behind the Grand Old Man, William Gladstone. England, however, turned her back on him, and he went down to defeat.[82]

Canada, too, was on the verge of another election. Alexander Mackenzie returned home in the fall and agreed to let his name stand again in East York, although he could utter scarcely a word on his own behalf. Edward Blake entered the constituency and made an eloquent appeal for his former leader. "I have found him the truest and most faithful of friends and colleagues," said Blake with evident emotion, ". . . I know of no man of equal diligence, of equal sacrifice, of greater integrity, of a nicer sense of public and private virtue, no man more sternly devoted to the cause which he in his conscience believed to be right."[83] The brief words that the old man was able to utter in accepting his nomination reminded Blake of Tennyson's lines in which Ulysses, also an old man, calls his comrades to one more great adventure.

"Though much is taken much abides,
And though we are not now that strength
Which in old days moved earth and heaven,
That which we are, we are
One equal temper of heroic hearts
Made weak by time and fate, but strong in will
To strive, to seek, to find, and not to yield!"

Even Sir John, looking still older and more grizzled than he, but in better health, now agreed that Mackenzie was an honest man and had always acted according to his best judgment. York East was proud of its "stainless statesman". He was returned in early 1887 by one hundred and sixty votes.

The 1887 election was another defeat for the Grits. Blake collapsed again, and Cartwright and Laurier had to bear the burden of leadership during the first session of the new Parliament. Mackenzie attended faithfully, but his interjections were becoming ever shorter and less frequent. More detached from the great public debates, a trace of the old sense of humour was evident at times. "After taking all our money he now proposes to take our purses," he managed to say when Sir Charles Tupper, back in Canada as Minister of Finance, announced a tax on pocket-books and purses.[84] "Does this include the collar of the K.C.M.G.?" he asked when the tax on collars was raised. "I am happy to tell my honourable friend from East York that if he had complied with the desire of Her Majesty to decorate him he would have gleaned that there was no charge on the collar of a K.C.M.G.," the portly old Nova Scotian replied genially. It was too late to be angry with one another any more.

The last spike had been driven in the Canadian Pacific Railway by Donald Smith, now Sir Donald, Lord Strathcona. Mackenzie longed for another look at the mountains and considered a trip to Banff, but his courage failed him. He wanted to see the new canal at Sault Ste. Marie that had been part of his "water stretches" plan. The Tories had belittled it, but they had built it nevertheless. But even Lake Superior was a long way off. The journey between Ottawa and Toronto was all that he could stand.

At the end of the 1887 session, the forty-five-year-old Wilfrid Laurier was chosen as the new leader of the Liberal party. Sir Richard Cartwright, who had disapproved of Blake's attempts to court the manufacturers by compromising on the Liberal free trade policy, put pressure on the new party chieftain to come out for commercial union with the United States. The suggestion was a shocking one to Alexander Mackenzie who had always insisted on a Canadian commercial policy in line with Britain. "I regard 'commercial union' as put by its advocates as impracticable," he wrote to Cartwright in a painfully shaky hand. ". . . I know from private correspondence that a large number of the Union advocates are firmly persuaded that a commercial union would be a sure step toward annexation and *therefore* favour it. . . . We complain of protection and propose to bind ourselves to a more extreme system. We are to raise a barrier against English trade and so commence a downgrade political life. My feelings revolt at the proposal."[85]

But what was the use of having an opinion? The *Globe* and the *Mail* were both for the new policy, and he had scarcely any voice or writing ability left to combat it. And yet, by an almost superhuman effort, he could still strike the occasional blow. During the 1888 session, David Mills suggested that the British authorities should be consulted on some aspect of the new fishery negotiations. "I object to any such invitation," the old Grit interrupted in a feeble but indignant voice. "We need not ask Lord Salisbury to interfere in Canadian affairs. I say to the Finance Minister that we ought not to invite Lord Salisbury or any other statesman to interfere more than what is absolutely necessary. I entirely object to it."[86] The hushed Chamber listened with astonishment, hoping it was an indication of a miraculous recovery. The members waited in vain. Nothing more came. Mackenzie sank back into his chair.

A month later, he tried to insist that Canada should have a voice in the negotiations to free some Canadian fishing-vessels seized by Russia in the Bering Straits. "Her Majesty's Government alone . . . can negotiate," replied Tupper.[87] The Tories had still learned nothing, and he had not the voice left to remind them once again that Canada must look after its own affairs.

For the Mackenzies, the highlight of 1888 occurred in Sarnia and not in Ottawa or Toronto. Nearly forty years old, and with

Helen and Alex nearly grown, Mary was pregnant again! The worried grandfather fussed over her health. "A change is essential," he wrote from the House of Commons. "If Toronto is not suitable then go to Megantic or Halifax and I will pay the fare."[88] It was a boy, and he was named Robert. "We duly rec[d] John's telegram informing us that 'a man child was born into the World', and I now attempt writing as many words as will enable me to congratulate you both on the happy event."[89] A dozen lines was all the faltering hands could manage. It was one of the last letters he was able to pen.

The end was drawing irrevocably nearer; it was impossible to halt the steady encroachment on his strength. During the session of 1889, he managed twenty brief interjections. In 1890, there were six; in 1891, one. White-haired, pale, and silent, he still sat erect in his place, but only the bright eyes revealed the close attention he was paying to the debate. In 1891, he uttered his last words in the House of Commons. The Liberals were attacking the expense of maintaining a Canadian officer in Paris. The appointee had been made a senator by the member for East York, retorted the Conservatives. The old man stirred. "I repent it," came the soft but firm reply from the long-silent lips.[90] The members started in semi-disbelief. All eyes turned in his direction. There was nothing more. The Hansard record was complete.

Still another election was approaching, and the Liberals of East York wanted him to be their standard bearer once again. Even if he could not speak, he could still vote in their name. It was with a touch of pride that he informed them that he had been absent from the House of Commons only three days during the past two years. The National Policy was a failure, he managed to tell a small group of constituents who called upon him at home; high taxes, the enormous increase in the public debt, and the recurring depressions were proof of the folly of 1878.[91] He had taken great pains at that time to show that the Government could not create wealth, but that they may distribute it wisely or unwisely. Thousands of Reform votes were lost in 1878 because they thought he was wrong in his free trade policy. "Surely it is not too much to ask that they should fall into line again, and carry with them a large number of hitherto Conservative voters." His political faith was still unshaken; he was a Clear Grit to the end.

Though unable to make a single appearance in his constituency, the message of Mackenzie was not unheard. Oliver Mowat, the owlish seventy-year-old Ontario Premier whom the Conservatives had not been able to vanquish in nearly twenty years, addressed a public letter to him which was circulated throughout the country.[92] "My dear and honoured friend," it ran, "you and I are among the oldest Canadian Liberals in public life. Throughout our time, and for long before, the principles of the Liberal party have been British connexion, special interest in all that concerns the masses of the people, justice to all classes, creeds and nationalities, pure and economical government, a revenue tariff, and the freest trade with our neighbours that is practicable and consistent with our position as a self-governing people forming part of the British Empire. Underlying all these has always been the principle of 'Canada First'. We perceive, and we are glad to know and believe, that in order to be for Canada first it was necessary to be for British connexion also. The two things are not incompatible. On the contrary, they are bound up together." The "so-called national policy", the McKinley tariff, and other unfriendly devices to prevent normal intercourse between the United States and Canada, were injurious to both countries, Mowat argued on behalf of both himself and Mackenzie. "As a remedy for existing evils, the Liberals in Parliament (including yourself) adopted as a plank of the Liberal platform, unrestricted reciprocity of trade in the products, natural and manufactured, of Canada and the United States." The letter was a carefully aimed blow at the proponents of commercial union, and an appeal for unrestricted reciprocity. It worked. The commercial union cause soon waned. Mute and helpless, Alexander Mackenzie had still been able to play some part in keeping the Liberals in line with their historic principles.

The grand old man of the Liberal party squeezed through the 1891 election with his narrowest majority of seventeen votes. When the session opened, he was at his place in the Commons as usual, with Jane near at hand to help him to and from their Ottawa lodgings. Across the aisle, Sir John was still in the Premier's seat, but looking more frail and wrinkled than ever at seventy-six. "You'll never die, John A.," the crowds had called to him during the last campaign. He seemed to believe it himself. "I tell my friends, I tell my foes," he lectured his fellow-Commoners as the work began once again, "J'y suis, j'y reste."[93] A little over a month later, he was dead. In the same week, another famous figure disappeared. Sir Antoine-Aimé Dorion, whom Mackenzie had admired and loved next to Brown himself, passed away as well. And to neither friend nor foe in political battles extending over half a century did he have the strength to pay a last tribute of respect.

Senator J. J. Abbott, the Montreal lawyer from whose office

the incriminating Pacific scandal documents had been stolen in 1873, succeeded Sir John. Laurier was finding his feet as Leader of the Opposition, and striking out manfully at their adversaries. Blake was gone;* Sir Richard Cartwright was old and crotchety and deafer than ever, but still dangerous when aroused. Félix Geoffrion still held his seat, and David Mills and James Edgar were among Laurier's leading lieutenants. Richard Scott was still Liberal Leader in the Senate, and near him were Charles Pelletier and ex-Premier Louis Davies. Even his old rival, Alexander Vidal, was there as a Tory nominee. In Toronto, Charles Mackenzie represented Sarnia in the provincial Legislature. Even if his own usefulness was about at an end, the work would go on.

On January 28, 1892, the Mackenzie family gathered in the Wellesley Street home to observe the old statesman's seventieth birthday.[94] He was cheerful and relaxed, and his brief, whispered conversation revealed the old humour and sharp intellect that marked his character. He had few regrets, but he was ready to admit that postponing the 1878 election from spring to fall had been a terrible mistake. Now it was too late to worry about even that. He whiled away the hours of leisure by reading, playing whist, and enjoying friends who came to tea.

Five days after the birthday party, he was leaving the house as usual to visit his insurance office when he slipped and fell. He was carried back into the house, but he never rose again. From late January until the winds of April announced the first signs of spring, Jane, Mary, his brother Charles, and other members of the family maintained the bedside vigil. On Easter morning, April 17, he slipped into unconsciousness. "O take me home," they heard him pray.[95] Shortly afterwards, he died.

* * * * *

"It was a beautiful morning to die on," said the two nuns from St. Joseph's Convent across the street when they came over in the bright warm sunshine to pay their respects.[96] In Ottawa, the Parliamentarians met briefly on the following Tuesday to express their tribute, and then adjourned. Premier Abbott recalled his "straightforward, laborious, and careful management of the country", his "unfailing industry", and "the extraordinary amount of knowledge which he displayed".[97] He had won for himself "the almost universal respect of the entire Dominion of Canada without the slightest distinction or difference as to party", said the Government leader. "Honesty of pur-

*to the United Kingdom Parliament.

pose was the leading one [of his characteristics]," said Richard Scott. "... Possibly his political career might have carried with it long years of office; but he was one of those men who refused to sacrifice principle to policy."[98] "He strove for the right as he saw the right," said Wilfrid Laurier, whose career Mackenzie had launched. "And it is indeed a matter of history that ... he could have ... perhaps continued to enjoy power if he had consented to deviate ever so little from those principles of political economy which alone he held to be true. But on this occasion his stern character again asserted itself. ... He united many qualities seldom found together, and which combined made him one of the truest and strongest characters to be met in Canadian history."[99]

The Jarvis Street church was packed with friends and admirers who came for the funeral ceremony. The Honourable John Thompson, Government Leader in the House of Commons, led the delegation of Ministers and Government supporters. Laurier, Mills, Blake, Mowat, Cartwright, Anglin, McKellar, Scott, Donald Smith – they and many more familiar faces were present. "Oh, how Alexander Mackenzie loved Canada!" intoned the Baptist minister. "And if he could speak to us today with lips unsealed, it would be to urge us to fidelity in all that would tend to develop her resources and hence her glory. ... Thou grand old veteran of thy country's liberties, farewell!"[100]

A special train transported the body, still accompanied by the faithful Jane, on its final journey west. On the Sarnia platform, Robert Mackenzie, who was too advanced in age to go to Toronto, led the delegation of mourners. Six pairs of healthy hands – the hands of the sons of James and John and Charles – took the heavy casket from the carriage. In the half-light of early evening, the long cortège moved slowly up Front Street to Charles's residence on Christina Street.

The next morning the crowd overflowed St. Andrew's Church, the lot on which it stood, and the street beyond. Reverend Professor Gregg, the first church minister that the young stonemason had met on his arrival in Canada half a century before, delivered the sermon. In death, as in life, he associated the name of Alexander Mackenzie with that of the other great Scottish Grit, George Brown.[101] "Both were natives of Scotland, both were heirs of noble memories, memories of noble men, who nobly lived, who nobly suffered, and who nobly died in the cause of religious liberty. Both were gifted by nature with singular mental abilities. The two fought side by side for the right. Both had high aims and high ambitions, high moral aims, and I do not hesitate to add, high religious and Christian principles.

. . . The name of Alexander Mackenzie, I have no hesitation in affirming, is a stainless name. . . . He was sustained in his career by an unflinching faith in the ever-ruling Providence of God."

The procession of some hundred carriages spread out for over a mile as the body was moved along the black-draped streets and past the rows of Union Jacks at half-mast on the way to Lakeview cemetery. On a small elevated plain, his place was ready. Near it were the graves of his first wife, Helen, his mother, his infant son and daughter, his brothers Hope, John, James, and Adam. Fifty years earlier he had led the family to the New World. Here they had lived, here they had left their mark, and here they were finding their final resting-place. As the body was lowered into the grave, the clouds broke, and the spring sun smiled down comfortingly upon the mourning crowd.

"Famed for honesty and ability"; "His services to the country and personal integrity acknowledged by all", proclaimed the *Mail,* his bitterest opponent in former years.[102] *Grip,* the prickly conscience of Canada, said it in verse:

> "His amplest service to the land was this –
> Beyond, above the tasks he undertook,
> And those he finished – be not one forgot!
> He gave the world an answer in his life
> To that smug lie of this degenerate age –
> 'An honest Politician cannot be'."[103]

REFERENCES

CHAPTER 1

In the Forests of the Far West

1 W. Buckingham and G. W. Ross: *The Honourable Alexander Mackenzie,* p. 33ff.
2 *Mackenzie-Thompson Papers.* Personal record kept by A. Mackenzie Sr.
3 Ibid.
4 Ibid.
5 W. Buckingham and G. W. Ross, op. cit., p. 45.
6 Ibid., p. 50.
7 *Emigration and Colonization.* Letter to the Duke of Wellington by John Crawford, Esq., London, 1842. Pamphlet No. 1881, Public Archives of Canada.
8 *Address on Emigration and Colonization,* by Hon. R. B. Sullivan, Toronto, 1847. Toronto Public Library.
9 *General Instructions to Emigrants.* Pamphlet No. 1859. Public Archives of Canada.
10 *Montreal Gazette,* May 16, 1842.
11 W. Buckingham and G. W. Ross, op. cit., p. 57.
12 *The Emigrant to North America,* p. 62. Pamphlet No. 1948. Public Archives of Canada.
13 *Mackenzie-Thompson Papers.* Mackenzie to his wife, June 17, 1876.
14 *Mackenzie-Thompson Papers.* Mackenzie to his brother Robert, June 7, 1842.
15 Ibid.
16 Ibid.
17 Ibid.
18 Ibid.
19 *Toronto Examiner,* May 28, 1842.
20 *Mackenzie Papers,* p. 2567. Statement by Alexander Mackenzie.
21 Donald Creighton: *The Young Politician,* p. 84.
22 W. Buckingham and G. W. Ross, op. cit., pp. 94-8.
23 Ibid., p. 96.
24 Ibid., p. 96.
25 *The Emigrant to North America,* p. 64. Pamphlet No. 1948. Public Archives of Canada.
26 W. Buckingham and G. W. Ross, op. cit., pp. 99-100.
27 Ibid., p. 100.
28 Ibid., p. 100.
29 *Proceedings at the First General Meeting of the Reform Association of Canada;* Toronto, March 25, 1844. Pamphlet No. 1961. Public Archives of Canada.
30 W. Buckingham and G. W. Ross, op. cit., pp. 104-5.
31 Ibid., p. 102.

32 Ibid., p. 103.
33 W. H. Smith: *Canada, Past and Present.* Published by Thomas MacLean, 1852.
34 W. Buckingham and G. W. Ross, op. cit., pp. 104-5.

CHAPTER 2

"Heelanders" on the St. Clair

1 *Mackenzie-Thompson Papers.* Receipt for payment by A. Vidal.
2 W. Buckingham and G. W. Ross, op. cit., p. 103.
3 *The Banner.* Feb. 23, 1844.
4 Minutes of Proceedings of the Second Convention of Delegates of the British American League; Kingston, 1849. Pamphlet No. 2160. Public Archives of Canada.
5 J. M. S. Careless: *Brown of the Globe,* pp. 109-11.
6 *Globe Weekly.* April 4, 1850.
7 Alexander Mackenzie: *Life and Speeches of Hon. George Brown,* pp. 36-7. Toronto, 1882. Brown to Mackenzie, Sept. 13, 1851.
8 *Brown Papers,* p. 17. Mackenzie to Brown (no date), 1851.
9 *Mackenzie Papers,* p. 22. Brown to Mackenzie, Oct. 23, 1851.
10 Ibid., p. 23. Brown to Mackenzie, Nov. 7, 1851.
11 Jas. Young: *Public Men and Public Life*; Toronto, 1912. Vol. I, p. 55.
12 *Globe,* Dec. 6, 1871.
13 W. Buckingham and G. W. Ross, op. cit., p. 106.
14 *Lambton Shield.* Sarnia Public Library, Sarnia, Ontario.
15 *Globe,* Sept. 2, 1852
16 W. Buckingham and G. W. Ross, op. cit., p. 110. Brown to Mackenzie, Aug. 23, 1852.
17 *Mackenzie Papers,* p. 1. Brown to Mackenzie, Sept. 4, 1852.
18 Ibid., Brown to Mackenzie, Sept. 4, 1852.
19 Ibid.
20 W. Buckingham and G. W. Ross, op. cit., p. 116.
21 *Brown Papers,* p. 147. Mackenzie to Brown, June 19, 1853.
22 Ibid., p. 157. Mackenzie to Brown, July 28, 1853.
23 W. Buckingham and G. W. Ross, op. cit., p. 126.
24 Sarnia *Observer,* Nov. 16, 1853. Public Archives of Canada.
25 *Mackenzie-Thompson Papers.* Extract from Lambton *Shield.*
26 Ibid.
27 *Brown Papers,* p. 195. Mackenzie to Brown, Jan. 2, 1854.
28 *Mackenzie-Thompson Papers.* Brown to Mackenzie, April 18, 1854.
29 Sarnia *Observer,* April 27, 1854.
30 *Mackenzie-Thompson Papers.* Lambton *Shield.*
31 *Brown Papers,* p. 202. Mackenzie to Brown, May 1, 1854.
32 Ibid., p. 202.
33 *Mackenzie-Thompson Papers.* Lambton *Shield.*
34 Sarnia *Observer,* May 11, 1854.
35 W. Buckingham and G. W. Ross, op. cit., p. 120.
36 *Mackenzie-Thompson Papers.* W. L. Mackenzie to A. Mackenzie, June 23, 1854.
37 *Brown Papers,* p. 206. Mackenzie to Brown, June 28, 1854.
38 Sarnia *Observer,* July 20, 1854.

CHAPTER 3

Reform Secretary

1 *W. L. Mackenzie-Lindsey Papers.* Mackenzie to W. L. Mackenzie, Feb. 27, 1856.
2 Ibid., June 9, 1856.
3 *Brown Papers*, p. 265. Circular from S. Gordon Brown and Wm. McDougall, Dec. 15, 1856.
4 J. M. S. Careless, op. cit., p. 233ff.
5 *Brown Papers*, p. 268. Mackenzie to Brown, Dec. 18, 1856.
6 Sarnia *Observer*, Jan. 22, 1857.
7 *W. L. Mackenzie-Lindsey Papers.* Mackenzie to W. L. Mackenzie, Jan. 22, 1857.
8 R. Rumilly: *Histoire de la Province de Québec.* Vol. I, p. 10.
9 Sarnia *Observer*, Oct. 15, 1857. Letter to the Editor.
10 Ibid., Oct. 8, 1857.
11 *Mackenzie Papers*, p. 25. Brown to Mackenzie, Nov. 25, 1857.
12 Sarnia *Observer*, Dec. 3, 1857.
13 Ibid.
14 *Mackenzie Papers*, p. 25. Brown to Mackenzie, Nov. 25, 1857.
15 Sarnia *Observer*, Dec. 3, 1857.
16 W. Buckingham and G. W. Ross, op. cit., p. 124.
17 Sarnia *Observer*, Dec. 10, 1857.
18 Ibid., Dec. 24, 1857.
19 Ibid., Dec. 31, 1857.
20 Donald Creighton, op. cit., p. 261.
21 Debates. July 28, 1858. (Prior to 1870 the record of debates in the Library of Parliament consists of newspaper reports from the leading newspapers of the period.)
22 A. Mackenzie, op. cit., pp. 60-1.
23 Donald Creighton, op. cit., p. 267.
24 A. Mackenzie, op. cit., pp. 62-8.
J. M. S. Careless, op. cit., p. 265ff.
25 *Globe*, Aug. 5, 1858.
26 A. Mackenzie, op. cit., pp. 64-8.
27 *Mackenzie Papers*, p. 39. Brown to Holton, Sept. 17, 1858.
28 Sarnia *Observer*, Dec. 9, 1858.
29 Ibid., Dec. 30, 1858.
30 Ibid., Jan. 13, 1858.
31 Ibid., Dec. 2, 1858.
32 Ibid., July 29, 1859.
33 Ibid., May 6, 1859.
34 *Mackenzie-Thompson Papers.* Report in Sarnia *Observer* (no date).
35 A. Mackenzie, op. cit., p. 196. Brown to Holton, July 8, 1859.
36 Sarnia *Observer*, Oct. 28, 1859.
37 Sarnia *Observer*, Nov. 18, 1859.
38 J. M. S. Careless, op. cit., p. 320.
39 *Brown Papers*, p. 519. Mackenzie to Brown, April 13, 1860.
40 Sarnia *Observer*, June 15, 1860.
41 Ibid., June 29, 1860.

42 Ibid.
43 *Mackenzie-Thompson Papers.* Interview with James Stewart contained in newspaper report, 1892.
44 Documents relating to the Construction of the Parliamentary and Departmental Buildings at Ottawa, 1862-63. Compiled by F. P. Rubridge. Public Archives of Canada.
Tenders for Parliament Buildings, Records of Dept. of Public Works. Public Archives of Canada.
45 Sarnia *Observer*, Nov. 16, 1860.
46 W. Buckingham and G. W. Ross, op. cit., p. 125. Brown to Mackenzie.
47 Sarnia *Observer*, Dec. 28, 1860.
48 Donald Creighton, op. cit., p. 310.
49 Sarnia *Observer*, June 14, 1861.
50 Ibid.
51 Ibid., June 21, 1861.
52 Ibid., June 28, 1861.
53 Ibid.
54 Ibid., July 5, 1861.
55 Ibid., July 12, 1861.
56 Ibid.

CHAPTER 4

Deadlock

1 Sarnia *Observer*, July 12, 1861.
2 *Globe,* March 24, 1862.
3 Sarnia *Observer*, April 4, 1862. Report of Debate of March 27, 1862.
4 Ibid., April 11, 1862.
5 *Globe*, March 31, 1862.
6 Debates, May 8, 1862.
7 *Mackenzie-Thompson Papers.* Newspaper clipping of story recounted at Mackenzie's death.
8 Donald Creighton, op. cit., pp. 331-2.
9 *Brown Papers*, p. 666. Mackenzie to Brown, May 22, 1862.
10 Ibid.
11 Ibid., p. 723, June 23, 1862.
12 Ibid., p. 670. Mowat to Brown, May 23, 1862.
13 Ibid., p. 669. Mackenzie to Brown, May 22, 1862.
14 *Mackenzie Papers*, p. 63. Brown to Holton, May 29, 1862.
15 Ibid., p. 69. Brown to Holton, June 2, 1862.
16 Brown Papers, p. 671. Mowat to Brown, May 23, 1862.
17 Ibid., p. 711. Mackenzie to Brown, May 31, 1862.
18 Ibid.
19 Ibid.
20 Ibid.
21 Debates, May 27, 1862.
22 *Macdonald Papers*, Additional Volume I. Macdonald to Amsden, July 30, 1862.
23 *Brown Papers*, p. 723. Mackenzie to Brown, June 23, 1862.
24 Ibid.
25 Documents relating to the Construction of the Parliamentary and Departmental Buildings at Ottawa, 1862-3, Public Archives of Canada.
26 Sarnia *Observer*, Aug. 8, 1862.

27 *Mackenzie Papers*, p. 78. Brown to Holton, Jan. 5, 1863.
28 *Globe*, Dec. 27, 1862.
29 Documents relating to the Construction of the Parliamentary and Departmental Buildings at Ottawa, 1862-3. Public Archives of Canada.
30 Debates, Feb. 20, 1863.
31 Ibid.
32 Ibid., Feb. 27, 1863.
33 Ibid., March 5, 1863.
34 Donald Creighton, op. cit., p. 341.
35 Debates, May 6, 1863.
36 Ibid., May 8, 1863.
37 Sarnia *Observer*, May 22, 1863. A. Mackenzie's address to the Electors.
38 Ibid., June 5, 1863.
39 Ibid., Aug. 28, 1863.
40 Jas. Young, op. cit., Vol. I, p. 197.
41 Debates, Oct. 8, 1863.
42 Sarnia *Observer*, Dec. 25, 1863.
43 *Globe*, March 15, 1864.
44 J. Phelan: *The Ardent Exile*, p. 215.
45 *Globe*, March 31, 1864.
46 Donald Creighton, op. cit., pp. 345-6.
47 Jas. Young, op. cit., Vol. I, p. 202ff.
48 Ibid.
49 Sarnia *Observer*, June 3, 1864. Report of Debate, May 25, 1864.
50 W. Buckingham and G. W. Ross, op. cit., pp. 162-3.
51 Sarnia *Observer*, June 17, 1864. Report of Debate, June 14, 1864.

CHAPTER 5

The Confederation Scheme

1 Debates, June 22, 1864. Statement by John A. Macdonald to Legislative Assembly.
2 Donald Creighton, op. cit., pp. 355-6.
A. Mackenzie, op. cit., pp. 86-94.
3 A. Mackenzie, op. cit., pp. 92-4.
4 Debates, June 22, 1864.
5 Chester Martin: *Foundations of Canadian Nationhood*, p. 314.
6 Sarnia *Observer*, June 8, 1864. Debate of June 22, 1864.
7 Ibid., July 15, 1864.
8 Ibid., Aug. 12, 1864.
9 J. Phelan, op. cit., pp. 221-4.
10 Confederation Debates, Feb. 6, 1865.
11 Ibid., Feb. 8. 1865.
12 Ibid., Feb. 20, 1865.
13 I. Skelton: *Life and Times of D'Arcy McGee*, p. 321.
14 Confederation Debates, March 6, 1865.
15 Ibid., March 19, 1865.
16 Quoted in Sarnia *Observer*, March 31, 1865.
17 Sarnia *Observer*, Aug. 4, 1865.
18 *Mackenzie-Thompson Papers*. Newspaper account on Mackenzie's death, 1892.

19 Parliamentary Debate on Educational Grants, Sept. 7, 1865.
20 Sarnia *Observer*, Oct. 27, 1865.
21 C. P. Stacey: "Fenianism and the Tide of National Feeling in Canada"; *Canadian Historical Review*, 1931.
22 A. Mackenzie, op. cit., pp. 103-6.
23 Sarnia *Observer*, Dec. 29, 1865.
24 W. Buckingham and G. W. Ross, op. cit., pp. 201-3.
25 Sarnia *Observer*, Jan. 12, 1866. Report of address delivered Dec. 29, 1865.
26 Quoted in *Globe*, Oct. 1, 1864.
27 Sept. 30, 1866. Quoted in C. P. Stacey: "British Military Policy in Canada"; *Canadian Historical Review*, 1934, p. 26.
28 Canadian Militia Records, Public Archives of Canada.
29 Sarnia *Observer*, April 27, 1865.
30 A. S. Hamilton: *The Fenian Invasion*. 1886.
31 Sarnia *Observer*, June 8, 1866.
32 Ibid.
33 Ibid., June 29, 1866. Report of Debate of June 14, 1866.
34 Donald Creighton, op. cit., pp. 448-9.
35 Chester Martin, op. cit., p. 321.
36 Sarnia *Observer*, May 4, 1866.
37 W. Buckingham and G. W. Ross, op. cit., p. 205.
38 Sarnia *Observer*, July 20, 1866. Report of Debate of July 11, 1876.
39 British Parliamentary Debates, Third Session, Vol. 185, p. 1184.
40 Sarnia *Observer*, March 8, 1867.
41 J. Phelan, op. cit., p. 212.
42 Donald Creighton, op. cit., pp. 470-4.
43 Sarnia *Observer*, July 5, 1867.
44 G. W. Ross: *Getting into Parliament and After*, p. 20.
45 Sarnia *Observer*, July 5, 1867.
46 Ibid., July 12, 1867.
47 Jas. Young, op. cit., Vol. I, p. 319.
48 Donald Creighton, op. cit., p. 471.
49 Sarnia *Observer*, July 5, 1867.
50 Ibid., July 12. 1867.

CHAPTER 6

Her Majesty's Loyal Opposition

1 John Saywell: *The Office of the Lieutenant-Governor*, p. 110.
2 Sarnia *Observer*, July 19, 1867.
3 Ibid., Aug. 9, 1867.
4 Ibid., Aug. 23, 1867.
5 Ibid., Aug. 30, 1867.
6 *Mackenzie Papers*, p. 138. Mackenzie to Brown, Aug. 28, 1867.
7 Sarnia *Observer*, Sept. 13, 1867.
8 G. W. Ross, op. cit., pp. 27-8.
9 Sarnia *Observer*, Sept. 13, 1867.
10 *Mackenzie Papers*, p. 116. Brown to Mackenzie, March 12, 1867.
11 A. Mackenzie, op. cit., pp. 210-12.
12 *Mackenzie Papers*, p. 140. Brown to Mackenzie, Oct. 3, 1867.

13 Sarnia *Observer*, Oct. 18, 1867.
14 Jas. Young, op. cit., Vol. II, pp. 36-7.
15 *Mackenzie Papers*, p. 144. Mackenzie to Brown, Nov. 8, 1867.
16 Ibid.
17 Jas. Young, op. cit., Vol. II, p. 41.
18 J. C. Dent: *The Last Forty Years*, Vol. II, pp. 480-1.
19 Sarnia *Observer*, Nov. 22, 1867. Report of speech of Nov. 12, 1867.
20 Ibid., Dec. 13, 1867. Report of speech of Dec. 5, 1867.
21 *Brown Papers*, p. 1689. Brown to Anne, March 8, 1868.
22 Ibid., p. 1697. Brown to Anne, March 12, 1867.
23 Donald Creighton: *The Old Chieftain*, pp. 7-12.
24 Sarnia *Observer*, March 20, 1868. Report of proceedings in Parliament, March 12, 1868.
25 United Service Gazette report. Reproduced in Sarnia *Observer*, May 1, 1868.
26 *Brown Papers*, p. 1703. Mackenzie to Brown, March 16, 1868.
Ibid., p. 1707. Mackenzie to Brown, March 19, 1868.
27 Ibid., p. 1710. Brown to Anne, March 19, 1868.
28 Ibid., p. 1714. Mackenzie to Brown, March 21, 1868.
29 Ibid., p. 1726. Mackenzie to Brown, March 23, 1868.
30 Ibid., p. 1707. Mackenzie to Brown, March 19, 1868.
31 Ibid., p. 1707, Mackenzie to Brown, March 19, 1868.
32 I. Skelton, op. cit., p. 538.
33 E. B. Biggar: *Anecdotal Life of Sir John Macdonald*. Montreal, 1891, p. 193.
34 W. Buckingham and G. W. Ross, op. cit., pp. 240-1.
35 Sarnia *Observer*, May 8, 1868. Report of Debate of April 23, 1868.
36 Sarnia *Observer*, Aug. 6, 1868.
37 *Macdonald Papers*. Letterbook 12, p. 429. Macdonald to Davis, Jan. 15, 1869.
38 Sarnia *Observer*, April 30, 1869. Report of Debate of April 16, 1869.
39 Debates, April 28, 1869. Remarks by Jos. Rymal, M.P.
40 Ibid.
41 R. M. Hamilton: *Canadian Quotations*, p. 241. Macdonald to Sir Edward Watkins, March 27, 1865.
42 *Reform Government in the Dominion*. Toronto, 1878, p. 5.
43 Sarnia *Observer*, July 1, 1869. Report of Debate of June 21, 1869.
44 *Mackenzie Papers*, p. 151. Mackenzie to Chas. Black, May 10, 1869.
45 Sarnia *Observer*, July 9, 1869.
46 Ibid., Oct. 22, 1869.
47 *Brown Papers*, p. 1787. Mackenzie to Brown, Aug. 21, 1869.
48 Sarnia *Observer*, Oct. 29, 1869.
49 Sarnia *Observer*, Dec. 3, 1869.
50 Ibid., Dec. 10, 1869.
51 Donald Creighton: *The Old Chieftain*, pp. 42-8.
52 Debates, April 27, 1870. Report of Ottawa *Times*. Library of Parliament, p. 1226ff.
53 Ibid., May 2, 1870, p. 1287ff.
54 Ibid., March 21, 1870, p. 603ff.
55 G. W. Ross, op. cit., p. 31.
56 Debates, April 1, 1870, p. 829ff.
57 Sarnia *Observer*, April 29, 1870.
58 Ibid., April 15, 1870.
59 Debates, April 6, 1870, p. 900ff.

60 Donald Creighton: *The Old Chieftain*, pp. 67-8.
61 Debates, May 2, 1870, p. 1287ff.
62 Sir James A. Grant: *Recollections*, p. 9. Typewritten copy in Library of Parliament.
63 Ibid., p. 9. Hugh Miller (1802-56), a self-educated Scot, became widely known as a geologist, writer, and newspaperman. An "old Whig", he played a leading role in Britain in the struggle for a system of national education, extension of the franchise, and freedom of worship.
64 Sarnia *Observer*, Sept. 30, 1870.
65 Ibid., July 22, 1870.
66 Ibid., Aug. 12, 1870.
67 Ibid., July 1, 1870.
68 Ibid., July 22, 1870.
69 Annual Report, 1952, Public Archives of Nova Scotia. (Hereafter referred to as Jones Papers.) Mackenzie to Jones, March 3, 1870.
70 Ibid., Mackenzie to Jones, March 3, 1870.
71 Ibid., Dec. 3, 1870.
72 Ibid.

CHAPTER 7

Dual Representation

1 Mackenzie Papers, p. 176. Mackenzie to Brown, Feb. 27, 1871.
2 G. W. Ross, op. cit., p. 33.
3 W. Buckingham and G. W. Ross, op. cit., p. 292.
4 G. W. Ross, op. cit., p. 33.
5 Sarnia *Observer*, March 24, 1871.
6 Debates, Feb. 16, 1871, p. 18ff.
Ibid., Feb. 24, 1871, pp. 111-13.
7 Ibid., March 28, 1871, p. 660ff.
8 Margaret Ormsby: *British Columbia; A History*, pp. 247-9.
9 H. Innis: *History of the Canadian Pacific Railway*, p. 75.
10 Debates, March 28, 1871, p. 674.
11 Ibid., March 30, 1871, p. 720ff.
12 Ibid., March 31, 1871, p. 744ff.
13 *Brown Papers*, p. 1828. Mackenzie to Brown, March 30, 1871.
14 Margaret Ormsby, op. cit., p. 249.
15 H. Innis, op. cit., p. 75.
16 *Macdonald Papers*, Vol. 252. Alexander Morris to Macdonald, April 1, 1871.
17 Donald Creighton: *The Old Chieftain*, p. 100ff.
18 *Jones Papers*. Mackenzie to Jones, May 21, 1871.
19 Sarnia *Observer*, June 9, 16, 23, 1871.
20 Ibid., July 4, 1871.
21 *Campbell Papers*, Ontario Public Archives. Mackenzie to Campbell, Oct. 11, 1871.
22 *Globe Weekly*, July 19, 1871.
23 *Globe*, March 9, 1871.
24 *Mackenzie Papers*, p. 196. Senator McMaster to Mackenzie, Dec. 9, 1871.
25 Ibid., p. 198. Vicar General J. Janot to Senator McMaster, Dec. 11, 1871.

26 Ibid.
27 Ibid., p. 202. Blake to Mackenzie, Dec. —, 1871.
28 Sarnia *Observer*, Dec. 15, 1871. Report of Debate of Dec. 12, 1871.
29 Ibid., Dec. 22, 1871.
30 Edward Blake Election Campaign Speech, Wingham, Ont. Pamphlets Section, Public Archives of Canada.
31 Sarnia *Observer*, Dec. 22, 1871.
32 W. Buckingham and G. W. Ross, op. cit., p. 458.
33 Sarnia *Observer*, Jan. 12, 1872.
34 Sarnia *Observer*, Jan. 26, 1872.
35 Ibid., Jan. 5, 1872.
36 Ibid., Jan. 26, 1872.
37 *Mackenzie-Thompson Papers*. Budget Address of Hon. A. Mackenzie.
38 *Mackenzie Letterbooks*, Vol. I, pp. 15-18.
39 *Mackenzie Papers*, p. 219. Mackenzie to Henry C. Lloyd, Jan. 12, 1872.

CHAPTER 8

The Turning Tide

1 J. Pope: *Correspondence of Sir John A. Macdonald*, p. 45. Macdonald to Alexander Morris, April 21, 1871.
2 *Macdonald Papers*, Vol. 539. Macpherson to Macdonald, Feb. 21, 1872. Ibid., Vol. 543. Trust Deed, March 27, 1872.
3 Debates, April 26, 1872, p. 172.
4 Ibid., April 16, 1872, p. 37.
5 Ibid., May, 7, 1872, p. 416.
Ibid., May 28, 1872, pp. 874-5.
6 Ibid., June 1, 1872, p. 925.
7 Ibid., May 31, 1872, p. 908.
8 Ibid., May 3, 1872, p. 305.
9 Ibid., May 3, 1872, p. 342.
10 R. M. Hamilton, op. cit., p. 60. Macdonald to Tupper, April 1, 1871.
11 Debates, May 3, 1872, pp. 345-54.
12 Ibid., May 16, 1872, p. 634.
13 Ibid., May 16, 1872, p. 638.
14 *Macdonald Papers*, Vol. 520. Macdonald to Sir John Rose, June 18, 1872.
15 Donald Creighton: *The Old Chieftain*, p. 136.
16 Ibid., p. 139.
17 Sarnia *Observer*, Aug. 2, 1872.
18 Donald Creighton: *The Old Chieftain*, pp. 139-40.
19 Sarnia *Observer*, July 26, Aug. 2, Aug. 9, Aug. 16, Aug. 23, 1872.
20 Ibid., Aug. 23, 1872.
21 *Globe*, Aug. 23, 1872.
22 *Jones Papers*, Mackenzie to Jones, Aug. 26, 1872.
23 Ibid.
24 *Mackenzie Papers*, p. 242. Blake to Mackenzie, Sept. 12, 1872.
25 Ibid., p. 231. Mackenzie to C. R. Black, May 25, 1872.
26 C. Biggar: *Sir Oliver Mowat*, Vol. I, pp. 152-3.
27 E.g. Toronto *Mail*.

CHAPTER 9

They Are Done For

1 *Brown Papers*, p. 1928. E. Penny to Mackenzie, Dec. 10, 1872.
2 *Blake Papers*. Film M2414, No. 4. Blake to Mackenzie, Dec. 7, 1872.
3 W. Buckingham and G. W. Ross, op. cit., pp. 329-31.
Brown Papers, p. 1938. Mackenzie to Brown, March 5, 1873.
4 Ibid., p. 1942. Mackenzie to Brown, March 7, 1873.
5 *Globe*, March 10, 1873.
6 R. A. McEachern: *Canadian Discussion of the Imperial Relationship*. M.A. Thesis, University of Toronto, 1933, Vol. I, p. 49.
7 W. Leggo: *History of the Administration of the Earl of Dufferin in Canada*, p. 31.
8 Debates, March 11, 1873. Ottawa *Times* and Toronto *Mail* reports, Library of Parliament.
9 *Dufferin Papers*, Film No. 1143, p. 40. Dufferin to "Cyril". March 11, 1873.
10 *Jones Papers*. Mackenzie to Jones, March 11, 1873.
11 Debates, March 21, 1873.
12 Ibid., April 2, 1873.
13 *Macdonald Papers*, Vol. 202. Macdonald to Cartier, April 10, 1873.
14 Debates, April 3, 1873.
15 Ibid., April 8, 1873.
16 Ibid., May 5, 1873.
17 Ibid., April 24, 1873.
18 Donald Creighton: *The Old Chieftain*, pp. 155-6.
19 Debates, May 6, 1873.
20 Ibid., May 15, 1873.
21 *Edgar Papers*. Edgar to his wife, May 16, 1873.
22 Debates, May 20, 1873.
23 Donald Creighton: *The Old Chieftain*, pp. 158-9.
24 Debates, May 23, 1873.
25 Donald Creighton: *The Old Chieftain*, p. 159.
Dufferin Papers, Film No. 1152, p. 23. Dufferin to Macdonald, May 31, 1873. "I have telegraphed as you have suggested to hasten the disallowance of the Oaths Bill . . ."
26 W. Buckingham and G. W. Ross, op. cit., p. 338.
27 Jas. Young, op. cit., Vol. II, p. 134ff.
28 *Dufferin Papers*, Film No. 1148, Vol. I, p. 75. Dufferin to Macdonald, July 21, 1873.
29 Ibid., Film No. 1152, Dufferin to the Duchess of Argyll, July 31, 1872.
30 *Macdonald Papers*, Vol. 78, p. 228. Dufferin to Macdonald, March 6, 1873.
31 *Dufferin Papers*, Film. No. 1148, p. 40. Dufferin to Kimberley, Feb. 21, 1873.
32 *Brown Papers*, p. 1949. Mackenzie to Brown, July 21, 1873.
33 *Dufferin Papers*, Film No. 1143, p. 67. Dufferin to Huntington, Aug. 3, 1873.
34 *Brown Papers*, p. 1949. Mackenzie to Brown, July 21, 1873.
35 *Mackenzie Letterbooks*, Vol. I, p. 87. Mackenzie to Anglin, Aug. 1, 1873.

36 *Dufferin Papers*, Film No. 1141. Kimberley to Dufferin, Aug. 9, 1873. *Mackenzie Papers*, p. 266. Brown to Mackenzie, Aug. 9, 1873.
37 *Dufferin Papers*, Film No. 1141, Kimberley to Dufferin, Aug. 14, 1873.
38 *Mackenzie Letterbooks*, Vol. I, p. 63, e.g. July 11, 1873.
39 *Jones Papers*. Mackenzie to Jones, July 31, 1873.
40 Donald Creighton: *The Old Chieftain*, pp. 164-5.
41 W. Leggo, op. cit., pp. 162-4. Despatch of Dufferin to Kimberley, Aug. 15, 1873.
42 *Dufferin Papers*, Film No. 1143, Dufferin to Macdonald, June 28, 1873.
43 Ibid., p. 69. Dufferin to Langevin, Aug. 3, 1873.
44 Jas. Young, op. cit., Vol. II, p. 146.
45 Debates, Aug. 14, 1873. Ottawa *Times* and Toronto *Mail* reports.
46 Ibid., Aug. 14, 1873.
47 *Cartwright Papers*. Mackenzie to Cartwright, Sept. 4, 1873.
48 Ibid.
49 *Cartwright Papers*. Cartwright to Mackenzie, Aug. 23, 1873.
50 Ibid., Mackenzie to Cartwright, Sept. 4, 1873.
51 Ibid., Blake to Cartwright, Aug. 23, 1873.
52 *Dufferin Papers*, Film No. 1148, p. 26. Dufferin to Macdonald, Sept. 12, 1873.
53 Ibid., Film No. 1148, Vol. I, p. 2. Dufferin to Fletcher, Sept. 20, 1873.
54 Ibid., Film No. 1139, p. 1. Dufferin to Kimberley, Sept. 26, 1873.
55 Ibid., Film No. 1148, Vol. I, p. 12. Dufferin to Thornton, Sept. 25, 1873.
56 Ibid., Film No. 1143, p. 130. Dufferin to Macdonald, Oct. 19, 1873.
57 Debates, Oct. 27, 1873.
58 *Dufferin Papers*, Film. No. 1148, Vol. I, p. 74. Dufferin to Herbert, Nov. 2, 1873.
59 Ibid., Film No. 1139, p. 44. Dufferin to Kimberley, Oct. 10, 1873.
60 Ibid., p. 180. Dufferin to Kimberley, Nov. 6, 1873.
61 Ibid., pp. 188-90. Dufferin to Kimberley, Nov. 1873.
62 Letter from Hon. Peter Mitchell to A. F. Gault, Oct. 7, 1893. (In possession of Professor A. L. Burt, University of Chicago.)
63 *Dufferin Papers*, Film No. 1139, p. 188. Dufferin to Kimberley, Nov. 6, 1873.
64 Debates, Nov. 4, 1873.
65 Letter from Hon. Peter Mitchell to A. F. Gault, op. cit., Oct. 7, 1893.
66 *Globe*, Nov. 4, 1873.
67 *Edgar Papers*. Edgar to his wife, Nov. 5, 1873.
68 *Brown Papers*, p. 1974. Mackenzie to Brown, Nov. 5, 1873.

CHAPTER 10

The New Broom

1 Lady Harriet Dufferin: *My Canadian Journal*, p. 122.
2 *Brown Papers*, p. 1974. Mackenzie to Brown, Nov. 5, 1873.
3 *Dufferin Papers*, Film No. 1129, p. 198. Dufferin to Kimberley, Nov. 6, 1873.
4 *Blake Papers*, Film No. M241, No. 17. Mackenzie to Blake, Sept. 18, 1874.

Ibid., Film No. M241, No. 19. Mackenzie to Blake, Oct. 13, 1874.
5 *Brown Papers*, p. 1976. Mackenzie to Brown, Nov. 5, 1873.
6 Ibid., p. 1978. Mackenzie to Brown, Nov. 13, 1873.
7 Jas. Young, op. cit., p. 167.
8. *Jones Papers*. Mackenzie to Jones, Nov. 10, 1873.
9 *Brown Papers*, p. 1978. Mackenzie to Brown, Nov. 13, 1873.
10 *Dufferin Papers*, Film No. 1139, p. 230. Dufferin to Kimberley, Nov. 20, 1873.
11 Ibid., Film No. 1139, p. 200. Dufferin to Kimberley, Nov. 13, 1873.
12 Jas. Young, op. cit., Vol. II, p. 167.
13 Debates, Nov. 5, 1873.
14 *Mackenzie Papers*, p. 284. Mackenzie to C. R. Black, Nov. 10, 1873.
15 *Mackenzie Letterbooks*, Vol. III, p. 28. Mackenzie to Lewis Ross, Nov. 14, 1873.
16 Ibid., Vol. III, p. 44. Mackenzie to Patrick Power, Nov. 18, 1873.
17 Ibid., Vol. III, p. 83. Mackenzie to Wm. McLeod, Nov. 29, 1873.
18 Ibid., Vol. I, pp. 103-6. Memorandum to Lord Dufferin on Senate appointments.
19 *Dufferin Papers*, Film No. 1139, p. 198. Dufferin to Kimberley, Nov. 6, 1873.
20 Ibid., Film No. 1139, p. 206, Dufferin to Kimberley, Nov. 13, 1873.
Ibid., Film No. 1148, p. 68. Dufferin to Herbert, Nov. 2, 1873.
21 Ibid., Film No. 1141. Kimberley to Dufferin, Oct. 8, 1873.
22 Ibid., Film No. 1141. Kimberley to Dufferin, Oct. 29, 1873.
23 Ibid., Film No. 1141. Kimberley to Dufferin, Nov. 20, 1873.
24 Lady Harriet Dufferin, op. cit., p. 44, Nov. 2, 1872.
25 Ibid., p. 123, Nov. 15, 1873.
26 *Brown Papers*, p. 1978. Mackenzie to Brown, Nov. 13, 1873.
27 *Globe*, Nov. 11, 1873.
28 Sarnia *Observer*, Nov. 25, 1873.
29 *Mackenzie Papers*, p. 282. Brown to Chas. Taylor, Chairman, Reform Banquet, Sarnia, Nov. 24, 1873.
30 *Globe*, Nov. 28, 1873.
31 *Mackenzie Papers*, p. 286. Mackenzie to Mary Thompson, Dec. 1, 1873.
32 *Brown Papers*, p. 1984. Mackenzie to Brown, Dec. 22, 1873.
33 *Globe*, Dec. 25, 1873.
34 *Jones Papers*. Mackenzie to Jones, Dec. 27, 1873.
35 Government of Canada Order in Council, June 7, 1873.
36 *Mackenzie Letterbooks*, Vol. III, p. 263. Mackenzie to Galt, Dec. 25, 1873.
37 O. D. Skelton: *Life and Times of Sir A. T. Galt*, p. 468. Letter of Galt to Mackenzie, Jan. 2, 1874.
38 *Gzowski Papers*. Blake to Col. Casimir Gzowski, Jan. 4, 1874.
Ibid., Gzowski to Blake, Jan. 9, 1874.
39 *Mackenzie Papers*, p. 294. Blake to Mackenzie, Jan. 3, 1874.
40 *Blake Papers*, Film No. M241, No. 8, Mackenzie to Blake, Jan. 4, 1874.
44 *Jones Papers*. Mackenzie to Jones, Feb. 5, 1874.
42 Donald Creighton: *The Old Chieftain*, p. 182.
43 O. D. Skelton, op. cit., p. 467. Letter of Hon. Alexander Campbell to Galt, Dec. 25, 1873.
44 *Jones Papers*. Mackenzie to Jones, Feb. 5, 1874.
45 *Mackenzie Papers*, p. 298. Blake to Mackenzie, Jan. 29, 1874.
46 *Dufferin Papers*, Film No. 1142, p. 24. Dufferin to Mackenzie, Jan. 31, 1874.
47 Ibid., Film No. 1139, p. 226. Dufferin to Kimberley, Nov. 20, 1873.

CHAPTER 11

Rest Is Rust

1 W. Leggo, op. cit., pp. 326-7.
2 Jas. Young, op. cit., Vol. II, p. 183.
3 *Edgar Papers.* Mackenzie to Edgar, Feb. 19, 1874.
Ibid., Mackenzie to Edgar, Feb. 21, 1874.
4 Ibid., Mackenzie to Edgar, Feb. 19, 1874.
Ibid., Mackenzie to Edgar, Feb. 21, 1874.
5 De Kiewiet and Underhill. *Dufferin-Carnarvon Correspondence,* pp. 3-4.
Dufferin to Carnarvon, Feb. 26, 1874.
6 *Dufferin Papers,* Film No. 1139. Rothery to Dufferin, Jan. 27, 1874.
Ibid., Film No. 1142, Rothery to Dufferin, Jan. 21, 1874.
7 *Mackenzie Papers,* p. 309. Brown to Mackenzie, Feb. 10, 1874.
8 R. E. Campbell: *George Brown's Attempted Reciprocity Treaty of 1874.*
University of Toronto Thesis, 1936, p. 61ff.
Mackenzie Letterbooks, Vol. III, p. 405ff. Memorandum by Prime Minister, March 9, 1874.
De Kiewiet and Underhill, op. cit., pp. 1-2. Dufferin to Carnarvon, Feb. 26, 1874.
9 Ibid., p. 9. Dufferin to Carnarvon, March 16, 1874.
10 Ibid., p. xxiii.
11 Ibid., p. 3. Dufferin to Carnarvon, Feb. 26, 1874.
12 Ibid., p. 5. Carnarvon to Dufferin, Feb. 26, 1874.
13 Ibid., p. 8. Dufferin to Carnarvon, March 13, 1874.
14 De Kiewiet and Underhill, op. cit., p. 5. Carnarvon to Dufferin, Feb. 26, 1874.
15 *Dufferin Papers,* Film No. 1153, Mackenzie to Dufferin, March 11, 1874.
16 *Morris Papers.* Letters from Lieutenant-Governor A. Morris to Mackenzie and to the Minister of the Interior, Oct. 15, Dec. 4, Dec. 26, 1873.
17 Testimony of Msgr. Taché before Special Committee on the North West, 1874. *House of Commons Journals,* 1874, Vol. III, Appendix 6, p. 62.
18 Parliamentary Debates, Feb. 11, 1875. Speech by Mackenzie Bowell.
19 R. Rumilly, op. cit., Vol. I, pp. 252-3.
20 Dufferin Papers, Film No. 1139, p. 218. Dufferin to Kimberley, Nov. 20, 1873.
21 Toronto *Mail,* March 26, 1874.
22 Ibid., March 27, 1874.
23 Ibid.
24 Jas. Young, op. cit., Vol. II, p. 187ff.
25 Toronto *Mail,* March 30, 1874.
26 Parliamentary Debates, March 30, 1874.
27 Montreal *Gazette,* April 8, 1874.
28 Parliamentary Debates, March 30, 1874.
29 Ibid., March 31, 1874.
30 Ibid., April 15, 1874.
31 Ibid., April 14, 1874.
32 W. Leggo, op. cit., pp. 338-40.
33 Jas. Young, op. cit., Vol. II, p. 199.
34 W. Leggo, op. cit., p. 340.

35 Toronto *Mail*, May 12, 1874.
36 *Mackenzie Papers*, p. 363. Mackenzie to Brown, May 6, 1874.
37 Ibid.
38 *Dufferin Papers*, Film No. 1143, p. 19. Mackenzie to Dufferin, "Saturday", May, 1874.
39 *Blake Papers*, Film No. M241, No. 10. Mackenzie to Blake, May 29, 1874.
40 Ibid., Film No. M241, No. 9. Mackenzie to Blake, May 28, 1874.
41 Ibid., Film No. M241, No. 10. Blake to Mackenzie, May 29, 1874.
42 Ibid., Film No. M239, No. 3. Holton to Blake, June 14, 1874.
43 *Blake Papers*, Film No. M239, No. 3. Holton to Blake, June 14, 1874.
44 Col. George T. Denison: *The Struggle for Imperial Unity*, p. 58.
45 Canada First: *A Memorial of the Late Wm. A. Foster, Q.C.*, 1890.
46 *Globe*, Jan. 9, 1874.
47 De Kiewiet and Underhill, op. cit., p. 36. Dufferin to Carnarvon, April 25, 1874.
48 *Mackenzie Papers*, p. 576. Blake to Mackenzie, June 18, 1874.

CHAPTER 12

Midsummer Toil and Trouble

1 R. E. Campbell, op. cit., p. 61ff.
2 *Dufferin Papers*, Film No. 1142, p. 86. Dufferin to Mackenzie, March 30, 1874.
3 *Mackenzie Papers*, p. 334. Mackenzie to Brown, April 15, 1874.
4 Imperial Blue Books, Command 1060, 1874; North America No. 4. Public Archives of Canada.
5 *Mackenzie Papers*, p. 364. Mackenzie to Brown, May 6, 1874.
6 Ibid., p. 367. Mackenzie to Brown, May 8, 1874.
7 Ibid., p. 394. Brown to Mackenzie, May 25, 1874.
8 Ibid., p. 456. Brown to Mackenzie, May 30, 1874.
9 Ibid., p. 520. Brown to Mackenzie, June, 9, 1874.
10 Ibid., p. 537. Mackenzie to Brown, June 12, 1874.
11 Ibid., p. 538. Brown to Mackenzie, June 12, 1874.
12 A. Mackenzie, op. cit., p. 215. Brown to a relative (presumably Gordon Brown), June 12, 1874.
13 *Mackenzie Papers*, p. 572. Brown to Mackenzie, June 17, 1874.
14 Ibid., p. 574. Brown to Mackenzie, June 18, 1874.
15 R. E. Campbell, op. cit., p. 115.
16 *Brown Papers*, p. 2150. Mackenzie to Mrs. Brown, June 29, 1874.
17 De Kiewiet and Underhill, op. cit., p. 47. Carnarvon to Dufferin, June 17, 1874.
18 *Dufferin Papers*, Film No. 1144, p. 26. Mackenzie to Dufferin, July 2, 1874.
19 *Mackenzie Letterbooks*, Vol. I, p. 168ff. Mackenzie to F. J. Roscoe, M.P., July 10, 1874.
20 Ibid., Vol. III, p. 524ff., Mackenzie to Walkem, July 15, 1874.
21 *Dufferin Papers*, Film No. 1142, p. 170. Dufferin to Mackenzie, July 13, 1874.
Ibid., Film No. 1142, p. 178. Dufferin to Mackenzie, July 16, 1874.
22 *Mackenzie Letterbooks*, Vol. I, p. 172ff. Mackenzie to Dufferin, July 13, 1874.

23 Ibid., Vol. II, p. 684ff. Mackenzie to Senator W. S. Macdonald, Oct. 14, 1874.
24 De Kiewiet and Underhill, op. cit., p. 55. Dufferin to Carnarvon, July 17, 1874.
25 Ibid., p. 57. Carnarvon to Dufferin, July 23, 1874.
26 *Mackenzie-Thompson Papers*. Mackenzie to his wife, Aug. 10, 1874.
27 Ibid., Mackenzie to his wife, Aug. 9, 1874.
28 Ibid.
29 *Dufferin Papers*, Film No. 1152, p. 74. Dufferin to Thornton, April 14, 1874.
30 Sarnia *Observer*, Aug. 20, 1874.
31 De Kiewiet and Underhill, op. cit., p. 60. Carnarvon to Dufferin, July 30, 1874.
32 W. Leggo, op. cit., pp. 348-51. Despatch from Carnarvon to Dufferin, Aug. 16, 1874.
33 *Dufferin Papers*, Film No. 1144, p. 48. Mackenzie to Dufferin, Sept. 3, 1874.
34 W. Leggo, op. cit., pp. 368-70. Despatch from Carnarvon, Nov. 17, 1874.
35 De Kiewiet and Underhill, op. cit., p. 105. Carnarvon to Dufferin, Nov. 18, 1874.
36 Ibid., p. 72. Dufferin to Carnarvon, Sept. 17, 1874.
37 Ibid., p. 126. Dufferin to Carnarvon, Dec. 21, 1874.
38 *Blake Papers*, Film No. M241, No. 14. Blake to Mackenzie, Sept. 6, 1874.
39 Ibid., Film No. M241, No. 16. Blake to Mackenzie, Sept. 17, 1874.
40 Ibid., Film No. M241, No. 17. Mackenzie to Blake, Sept. 18, 1874.
41 Ibid., Film No. M241, No. 18. Blake to Mackenzie, Sept. 24, 1874.
42 Edward Blake: *A National Sentiment*. Ottawa, 1874. Pamphlet No. 3946, Public Archives of Canada.
43 *Globe*, Oct. 7, 1874.
44 *Nation*, Oct. 8, 1874.
45 *Mackenzie Papers*, p. 640. Mackenzie to Brown, Oct. 8, 1874.
46 Ibid.
47 Ibid.
48 Ibid., p. 652. Brown to Mackenzie, Oct. 18, 1874.
49 Ibid., p. 651. Mackenzie to Brown, Oct. 19, 1874.
50 *Blake Papers*, Film No. M241, No. 19. Mackenzie to Blake, Oct. 13, 1874.
51 *Mackenzie Letterbooks*, Vol. III, p. 722. Mackenzie to J. Cameron, Oct. 18, 1874.
52 *Jones Papers*. Mackenzie to Jones, Nov. 18, 1874.
53 Ibid.
54 *Mackenzie Letterbooks*, Vol. I, pp. 243-4. Mackenzie to Fournier, Dec. 7, 1874.
55 *Mackenzie Papers*, p. 703ff. George Stephen to Huntington, Dec. 14, 1874.
56 *Blake Papers*, Film No. M241, No. 17. Mackenzie to Blake, Sept. 18, 1874.
57 *Jones Papers*. Mackenzie to Jones, Nov. 27, 1874.
58 *Mackenzie Letterbooks*, Vol. I, p. 248. Mackenzie to Lt.-Gov. A. Morris, Dec. 11, 1874.
59 House of Commons *Journals*, 1874; Appendix 6, p. 18.
60 Ibid., pp. 39-40; p. 70.
61 Ibid., p. 38.
62 Ibid., p. 77.
G. F. G. Stanley: *The Birth of Western Canada*, London, 1936.

A. S. Morton: *History of Western Canada*, to 1870-71. Toronto.
Parliamentary Debates, Feb. 11, 1875. Speech by Hon. A. Mackenzie.
63 On Dec. 7, 1871. House of Commons *Journals*, 1874, Appendix 6, p. 54.
Testimony of Archbishop Taché.
64 Quoted by Edward Blake in Parliamentary Debates, Feb. 12, 1875.
Statement by Sir John Macdonald at Peterboro, Ont., July, 1872.
65 Sept. 12, 1872. House of Commons *Journals*, 1874, Appendix 6, p. 59.
66 De Kiewiet and Underhill, op. cit., p. 90. Dufferin to Carnarvon, Oct. 12, 1874.
67 Ibid.
68 Ibid., p. 102. Carnarvon to Dufferin, Nov. 12, 1874.
69 Ibid., p. 113. Carnarvon to Dufferin, Dec. 3, 1874.
70 Ibid., pp. 96-7. Dufferin to Carnarvon, Dec. 6, 1874.
Ibid., pp. 99-100. Telegram, Dufferin to Carnarvon, Nov. 12, 1874.
71 Ibid., p. 113. Dufferin to Carnarvon, Dec. 4, 1874.
72 W. Leggo, op. cit., p. 321. Dufferin to Carnarvon, Jan. 18, 1875.
73 *Dufferin Papers*, Film No. 1148, p. 89. Dufferin to Lt.-Gov. A. Morris, Dec. 15, 1874.
74 De Kiewiet and Underhill, op. cit., pp. 115-16. Dufferin to Carnarvon, Dec. 8, 1874.

CHAPTER 13

Steady On

1 *Brown Papers*. Brown to Anne, Dec. 16, 1874.
Mackenzie Letterbooks, Vol. IV, p. 78. Mackenzie to J. H. Fairbank, Dec. 16, 1874.
2 Parliamentary Debates, Feb. 5, 1875.
3 Ibid., Feb. 11, 1875.
4 Ibid.
5 W. Leggo, op. cit., p. 320. Letter from H. C. Fletcher to Minister of Justice, Jan. 15, 1875.
6 Ibid., p. 325.
7 Parliamentary Debates, Feb. 16, 1875. Budget Address.
8 Ibid., p. 503ff, March 5, 1875.
9 Ibid., p. 513ff, p. 696.
10 Ibid., p. 540ff.
11 J. Willison: *Reminiscences, Political and Personal*, p. 79.
12 Parliamentary Debates, p. 664, March 12, 1875.
13 G. W. Ross, op. cit., p. 180.
14 *Mackenzie Letterbooks*, Vol. I, p. 216. Mackenzie to C. J. Brydges, Sept. 17, 1874.
Mackenzie Papers, p. 623. C. J. Brydges to Mackenzie, Sept. 18, 1874.
15 G. W. Ross, op. cit., p. 180.
16 Parliamentary Debates, p. 700. March 15, 1875.
17 Ibid., p. 580. March 8, 1875.
18 Ibid., p. 609ff. March 10, 1875.
19 Frank Mackinnon: "The Supreme Court of Canada", *Canadian Historical Review*, 1946, p. 258.
Parliamentary Debates, Feb. 23, 1875.

Frank Underhill: "Edward Blake, The Supreme Court Act, and the Appeal to the Privy Council", 1875-6, *Canadian Historical Review*, 1938, p. 245ff.
20 Parliamentary Debates, March 30, 1875, p. 979ff.
21 Ibid., p. 980.
22 Ibid., p. 635ff, March 11, 1875.
23 Ibid., March 1, 1875.
24 R. M. Hamilton, op. cit., p. 162. Mackenzie to Thos. Hodgins, April 27, 1875.
25 *Mackenzie Letterbooks*, Vol. IV, p. 309. Mackenzie to A. Young, April 19, 1875.
26 Parliamentary Debates, Feb. 25, 1875.
27 Ibid., March 19, 1875.
28 *Brown Papers*, p. 2268. Brown to Anne, March 22, 1875.
29 *Mackenzie Papers*, p. 749. Blake to Jones, March 20, 1875.
Mackenzie Letterbooks, Vol. I, p. 265. Blake to Jones, March 20, 1875.
30 Ibid., Vol. I, p. 261. Mackenzie to Brown, March 23, 1875.
31 *Blake Papers*, Film No. M241, No. 291. Mackenzie to Blake, "Saturday morning".
Mackenzie Papers, p. 749ff. Correspondence between Holton, Jones, and Blake.
32 *Mackenzie Letterbooks*, Vol. I, p. 269. Mackenzie to Jones, April 8, 1875.
33 Ibid.
34 *Blake Papers*, Film No. M241, No. 24. Blake to Mackenzie, April 8, 1875.
35 Ibid., Film No. M241, No. 25. Mackenzie to Blake, April 12, 1875.
36 Ibid., Film No. M241, No. 27. Blake to Mackenzie, April 22, 1875.
Ibid., Blake to Mackenzie, May 6, 1875.
37 Ibid., Film No. M241, No. 26. Mackenzie to Walkem, April 20, 1875.
38 Ibid., Film No. M241, No. 29. Blake to Mackenzie, April 30, 1875.
39 Ibid., Film No. M241, No. 30. Mackenzie to Blake, May 5, 1875.
40 *Mackenzie Papers*, p. 811. Holton to Mackenzie, May 12, 1875.
41 *Blake Papers*, Film No. M241, No. 36. Blake to Mackenzie, May 18, 1875.
42 *Mackenzie Papers*, p. 814. Mackenzie to Brown, May 13, 1875.
43 Ibid.
44 Ibid.
45 O. D. Skelton, op. cit., pp. 498-9.
46 *Blake Papers*, Film No. M241, No. 37. Mackenzie to Blake, May 26, 1875.
47 *Dufferin Papers*, Film No. 1143, p. 79. Mackenzie to Dufferin, Aug. 3, 1875.
48 *Blake Papers*, Film No. M241, No. 39. Mackenzie to Blake, June 30, 1875.
49 *Mackenzie Letterbooks*, Vol. I, p. 341. Mackenzie to Lieut.-Gen. Haly, Oct. 1, 1875.
50 *Mackenzie Papers*, p. 872, p. 882, p. 884, p. 887, p. 898, etc. Correspondence between Mackenzie and Rt. Hon. George Goschen, in June, July, and Aug. 1875.
51 *Mackenzie Papers*, p. 876. Scott to Mackenzie, June 25, 1875.
Ibid., p. 880. Cartwright to Mackenzie, June 25, 1875.
52 Ibid., p. 887ff. Mackenzie to Goschen, July 1, 1875.
53 *Blake Papers*, Film No. M241, No. 40. Mackenzie to Blake, July 21, 1875.
54 O. D. Skelton, op. cit., pp. 502-3. Letter from Mackenzie to Galt, July 15, 1875.
55 *Blake Papers*, Film No. M241, No. 40. Mackenzie to Blake, July 21, 1875.

56 *Dufferin Papers,* Film No. 1144, p. 75. Mackenzie to Dufferin, June 25, 1875.
57 *Blake Papers,* Film No. M241, No. 39. Mackenzie to Blake, June 30, 1875.
58 Ibid.
59 *Jones Papers.* Mackenzie to Jones, July 1, 1875.
60 Jas. Young, op. cit., p. 217. Expression used by Lord Dufferin at a Canadian Club banquet in London, England.
61 *Speeches of the Hon. A. Mackenzie during his recent visit to Scotland,* Toronto, 1876.
62 Ibid., p. 21.
63 Ibid., p. 43.
64 Jas. Young, op. cit., Vol. II, p. 218ff.
65 *Speeches of the Hon. A. Mackenzie,* etc., op. cit., p. 98.
66 Ibid., p. 105.
67 *Mackenzie Papers,* p. 930. Scott to Mackenzie, July 26, 1875.
68 *Mackenzie Papers,* p. 949. Mackenzie to Goschen, Aug. 18, 1875.
69 Ibid., p. 954. Goschen to Mackenzie, Aug. 18, 1875.
70 Ibid., p. 957. Mackenzie to Goschen, Aug. 18, 1875.

CHAPTER 14

Hold the Line

1 *Speeches of the Hon. A. Mackenzie,* op. cit., pp. 132-5.
2 *Blake Papers,* Film No. M239, No. 9. Cartwright to Blake, July 26, 1875. Ibid., Film No. M239, No. 10. Cartwright to Blake, Aug. 7, 1875.
3 Ibid., Film No. M241, No. 53. Blake to Mackenzie, Sept. 25, 1875.
4 *Mackenzie Letterbooks,* Vol. IV, p. 624. Mackenzie to Carnarvon, Sept. 27, 1875.
5 Ibid., Vol. IV, p. 634. Carnarvon to Mackenzie, Oct. 1, 1875.
6 Recounted in Royal Military College *Review,* Kingston, 1957.
7 *Mackenzie-Thompson Papers.* Newspaper account at Mackenzie's death in 1892.
8 West Durham *News,* Sept. 24, 1875. Copy in *Dufferin Papers,* Film No. 1152, included with memorandum of "Big Push" letter.
9 *Globe,* Sept. 27, 1875.
10 Toronto *Mail,* Sept. 29, 1875.
11 R. Rumilly, op. cit., Vol. I, p. 130ff.
12 *Dufferin Papers,* Film No. 1143, p. 82. Mackenzie to Dufferin, Oct. 27, 1875.
13 De Kiewiet and Underhill, op. cit., p. 159. Dufferin to Carnarvon, Oct. 29, 1875.
14 *Speeches of the Hon. A. Mackenzie,* op. cit., p. 137ff.
15 *Mackenzie Letterbooks,* Vol. IV, p. 636. W. Buckingham to David Mills, Oct. 2, 1875.
16 Ibid., Vol. I, p. 356. Mackenzie to Thos. Workman, Oct. 15. 1875.
17 *Globe,* Oct. 15, 1875.
18 *Mackenzie Letterbooks,* Vol. I, p. 392. Mackenzie to Dufferin, Jan. 6, 1875.
19 *Brown Papers,* p. 2357. Brown to Anne, Oct. 21, 1875.
20 *Speeches of the Hon. A. Mackenzie,* op. cit., p. 174ff.
21 Ibid., p. 190ff.
22 *Mackenzie Letterbooks,* Vol. I, p. 368. Mackenzie to Joly, Oct. 26, 1875.

23 Ibid., Vol. II, p. 155. Mackenzie to Jas. Young, Dec. 7, 1875.
24 *Mackenzie Papers*, p. 1046. Brown to Mackenzie, Nov. 13, 1875.
25 Ibid., p. 1011. Holton to Mackenzie, Oct. 19, 1875.
26 *Mackenzie Letterbooks*, Vol. I, p. 157. Mackenzie to Jas. Young, Dec. 7, 1875.
27 *Mackenzie Papers*, p. 963. Galt to Holton, Sept. 1, 1875.
28 *Mackenzie Letterbooks*, Vol. I, pp. 396-410. Mackenzie to Holton, Jan. 16, 17, and Feb. 9, 1875.
29 *Speeches of the Hon. A. Mackenzie*, op. cit., p. 197ff.
30 Montreal *Gazette*, Nov. 26, 1875.
31 Mason Wade: *The French Canadians*, p. 349.
32 R. Rumilly, op. cit., Vol. I, p. 169ff.
33 Mason Wade, op. cit., p. 361.
34 *Blake Papers*, Film No. M244. Statements by residents of Charlevoix, Feb. 1, 1876.
35 *Mackenzie Papers*, p. 1094. Archbishop Taschereau to Cauchon, Jan. 6, 1876.
36 Ibid., p. 1096. Cauchon to Archbishop Taschereau, Jan. 8, 1876.
37 Ibid., p. 1098. Archbishop Taschereau to Cauchon, Jan. 10, 1876.
38 Ibid., p. 1101. Cauchon to Archbishop Taschereau, Jan. 11, 1876.
39 Ibid., p. 1113. Cauchon to Mackenzie, Jan. 7, 1876.
40 Ibid., p. 1115. Mackenzie to Brown, Jan. 17, 1876.
41 Ibid., p. 1125. Mackenzie to Brown, Jan. 22, 1876.
Ibid., p. 1131. Holton to Mackenzie, Jan. 28, 1876.
Ibid., p. 1152. Holton to Mackenzie, Feb. 6, 1876.
42 *Mackenzie Letterbooks*, Vol. V, p. 338. Archbishop Lynch to Mackenzie, Jan. 20, 1876.
43 Ibid., Vol. V, p. 357. Mackenzie to Archbishop Lynch, Jan. 26, 1876.
44 *Dufferin Papers*, Film No. 1142. Dufferin to Mackenzie, Jan. 4, 1876.
45 *Mackenzie Papers*, p. 1116. Mackenzie to Brown, Jan. 17, 1876.
46 *Blake Papers*, Film No. M241, Nos. 72 and 73. Mackenzie to Blake, Nov. 9 and 10, 1876.
47 De Kiewiet and Underhill, op. cit., p. 162. Dufferin to Carnarvon, Nov. 11, 1876.
48 *Dufferin Papers*, Film No. 1142. Dufferin to Mackenzie, Nov. 22, 1875.
49 *Mackenzie Papers*, Vol. I, p. 373. Mackenzie to Dufferin, Nov. 22, 1875.
50 Parliamentary Debates, Feb. 11, 1876.
51 Ibid., p. 61.
52 Ibid., Feb. 25, 1876.
53 De Kiewiet and Underhill, op. cit., pp. 193-4. Mackenzie to Dufferin, Feb. 15, 1876.
Ibid., Vol. I, p. 176. Mackenzie to F. Davies, July 14, 1876.
54 Jas. Young, op. cit., Vol. II, pp. 234-7.
55 Parliamentary Debates, March 7, 1876, p. 491ff.
56 De Kiewiet and Underhill, op. cit., p. 197. Dufferin to Carnarvon, March 10, 1876.
57 Parliamentary Debates, March 27, 1876.
58 *Mackenzie Letterbooks*, Vol. II, p. 573. Mackenzie to Rev. J. W. Manning, July 21, 1874. Ibid., Vol. I, p. 176. Mackenzie to F. Davies, July 14, 1874.
59 W. Leggo, op. cit., p. 411.
60 Ibid., pp. 418-19.
61 Parliamentary Debates, March 28, 1876.
62 Ibid., April 7, 1876.

63 House of Commons *Journals*, 1876, p. 19ff.
64 Parliamentary Debates, April 1, 1876.
65 *Mackenzie Papers*, p. 1195. Mackenzie to Mary Thompson, April 14, 1876.
66 Ibid., p. 1203. Thos. Hodgins to Mackenzie, April 21, 1876.

CHAPTER 15

Tempest Over the Pacific

1 De Kiewiet and Underhill, op. cit., p. 205. Dufferin to Carnarvon, March 31, 1876.
2 Ibid., p. 207. Carnarvon to Dufferin, April 4, 1876.
3 *Dufferin Papers*, Film No. 1144, Mackenzie to Dufferin, May 1, 1876.
4 Ibid., Film No. 1142. Dufferin to Mackenzie, May 19, 20, 22, 1876.
5 W. Leggo, op. cit., pp. 419-20.
6 *Mackenzie Letterbooks*, Vol. II, p. 437. Mackenzie to Dufferin, May 1, 1876.
7 Ibid., Vol. I, p. 454. Mackenzie to Dufferin, May 17, 1876.
8 Ibid.
9 De Kiewiet and Underhill, op. cit., p. 231. Dufferin to Carnarvon, May 18, 1876.
10 *Dufferin Papers*, Film No. 1142. Dufferin to Mackenzie, May 22, 1876.
11 Ibid., Film No. 1142. May 19, 1876.
12 *Mackenzie Letterbooks*, Vol. I, pp. 461-73. Mackenzie to Dufferin, May 20, 1876.
13 *Dufferin Papers*, Film No. 1142. Dufferin to Mackenzie, May 22, 1876.
14 De Kiewiet and Underhill, op. cit., pp. 231-33. Dufferin to Carnarvon, May 26, 1876.
15 Ibid., p. 226. Carnarvon to Dufferin, May 8, 1876.
16 *Dufferin Papers*, Film No. 1142. Carnarvon to Dufferin, Aug. 15, 1876.
17 *Mackenzie Papers*, p. 1211. Mackenzie to Mary Thompson, April 29, 1876.
18 Ibid., p. 1238. Mackenzie to C. R. Black, May 28, 1876.
19 D. Farr: *The Colonial Office and Canada*, p. 257.
20 *Mackenzie Papers*, p. 1260. Dufferin to Mackenzie, June 14, 1876.
21 *Mackenzie-Thompson Papers*. Mackenzie to his wife, June 9, 1876.
22 Ibid., Mackenzie to his wife, June 17, 1876.
23 Ibid., Mackenzie to his wife, June 25, 1876.
24 J. Willison, op. cit., p. 32ff.
25 *Mackenzie Papers*, p. 1276. London *Advertiser* article.
26 Ibid., p. 1277. Mackenzie to W. Buckingham, July 5, 1876.
27 Ibid., p. 1276. London *Advertiser* article.
28 *Blake Papers*, Film No. M239, No. 20. Cartwright to Blake, July 6, 1876.
29 De Kiewiet and Underhill, op. cit., p. 242. Dufferin to Carnarvon, June 1, 1876.
30 D. Farr, op. cit., p. 145.
31 *Mackenzie Letterbooks*, Vol. I, p. 487. Mackenzie to Mills (no date), 1876.
32 F. Underhill, op. cit., p. 245ff.
33 *Blake Papers*, Film No. M239. Memorandum by Blake while in London.

34 De Kiewiet and Underhill, op. cit., p. 256. Blake to Mackenzie (no date).
35 Ibid., p. 233ff. Dufferin to Carnarvon, June 1, 1876.
36 *Blake Papers,* Film No. M241, No. 147. Mackenzie to Blake, July 28, 1876.
37 Ibid., Film No. M242, No. 24. Scott to Blake, Aug. 4, 1876.
38 *Dufferin Papers,* Film No. 1144. Mackenzie to Dufferin, Aug. 5, 1876.
39 Jas. Young, op. cit., Vol. II, p. 248.
40 J. Willison, op. cit., p. 35.
41 *Mackenzie Papers,* p. 1348. Blake to Mackenzie, Sept. 25, 1876.
42 Ibid., p. 1354. Mackenzie to Blake, Sept. 25, 1876.
43 Ibid., p. 1346. Blake to Mackenzie, Sept. 25, 1876.
44 Ibid., p. 1358. Blake to Mackenzie, Sept. 26, 1876.
45 *Mackenzie Letterbooks,* Vol. I, p. 632. Mackenzie to Brown, Sept. 26, 1876.
46 *Mackenzie Papers,* p. 1356. Holton to Mackenzie, Sept. 26, 1876.
47 *Mackenzie Letterbooks,* Vol. I, p. 636. Mackenzie to Holton, Sept. 26, 1876.
48 *Mackenzie Papers,* p. 1366. Holton to Mackenzie, Sept. 28, 1876.
49 *Mackenzie Letterbooks,* Vol. I, p. 594. Mackenzie to Power, Aug. 24, 1876.
50 Ibid., Vol. I, p. 687. Mackenzie to Dorion, Oct. 13, 1876.
51 Ibid., Vol. I, p. 689. Mackenzie to Holton, Oct. 14. 1876.
52 *Dufferin Papers,* Film No. 1142. Carnarvon to Dufferin, Aug. 15, 1876.
53 De Kiewiet and Underhill, op. cit., p. 270. Dufferin to Carnarvon, Oct. 8, 1876.
54 Ibid., p. 271. Dufferin to Carnarvon, Oct. 8, 1876.
55 *Mackenzie Papers,* p. 1328. Littleton to Mackenzie, Aug. 21, 1876.
56 De Kiewiet and Underhill, op. cit., pp. 258-9. Dufferin to Carnarvon, Sept. 6, 1876.
57 Ibid., p. 259. Dufferin to Carnarvon, Sept. 14, 1876.
58 *Dufferin Papers,* Film No. 1143. Mackenzie to Dufferin, Sept. 25, 1876.
59 W. Leggo, op. cit., p. 455ff.
60 De Kiewiet and Underhill, op. cit., p. 278. Dufferin to Carnarvon, Oct. 8, 1876.
61 Ibid.
62 Ibid., p. 279. Dufferin to Carnarvon, Oct. 8, 1876.
63 Ibid., pp. 282-3. Dufferin to Carnarvon, Oct. 9, 1876.
64 Ibid., p. 283.
65 *Mackenzie Papers,* p. 1382. Jones to Mackenzie, Oct. 10, 1876.
66 *Mackenzie Letterbooks,* Vol. I, p. 673. Mackenzie to Cartwright, Oct. 11, 1876.
Ibid., Vol. I, p. 730. Mackenzie to Cartwright, Oct. 20, 1876.
67 Ibid., Vol. I, p. 673. Mackenzie to Cartwright, Oct. 11, 1876.
68 Ibid., Vol. I, p. 673. Mackenzie to Cartwright, Oct. 20, 1876.
69 *Sessional Papers,* 1875. No. 191, p. 25.
70 *Mackenzie Papers,* p. 141. Mackenzie to Chas. Mackenzie, Oct. 20, 1876.
71 De Kiewiet and Underhill, op. cit., p. 292. Dufferin to Carnarvon, Oct. 26, 1876.
72 Ibid., pp. 294-300. Dufferin to Carnarvon, Nov. 2, 1876.
73 Ibid., pp. 302-6. Dufferin to Carnarvon, Nov. 4, 1876.
74 *Dufferin Papers,* Film No. 1148, p. 186. Dufferin to Premier Elliott, Nov. 8, 1876.

75 *Mackenzie Letterbooks*, Vol. I, p. 779ff. Memorandum by Alexander Mackenzie of conversation with Lord Dufferin, Nov. 16 and 18, 1876.
76 *Mackenzie Papers*, p. 1348. Dufferin to Mackenzie, Nov. 17, 1876.
77 *Dufferin Papers*, Film No. 1144. Mackenzie to Dufferin, Nov. 17, 1876.
78 De Kiewiet and Underhill, op. cit., p. 309. Dufferin to Carnarvon, Nov. 20, 1876.
79 *Mackenzie Letterbooks*, Vol. I, p. 779ff. Memorandum by Alexander Mackenzie of conversation with Lord Dufferin, Nov. 16 and 18, 1876.
80 De Kiewiet and Underhill, op. cit., p. 310. Dufferin to Carnarvon, Nov. 23, 1876.
81 *Mackenzie Letterbooks*, Vol. I, p. 779ff. Memorandum by Alexander Mackenzie of conversation with Lord Dufferin, Nov. 16 and 18, 1876.
82 De Kiewiet and Underhill, op. cit., p. 310. Dufferin to Carnarvon, Nov. 20, 1876.
83 *Mackenzie Letterbooks*, Vol. I, p. 779ff. Memorandum by Alexander Mackenzie of conversation with Lord Dufferin, Nov. 16 and 18, 1876.
84 Ibid., Vol. I, p. 823ff. Dufferin to Mackenzie, Nov. 19, 1876.
85 *Blake Papers,* Film No. M238, No. 98. Blake to Dufferin, Nov. 22, 1876.
86 De Kiewiet and Underhill, op. cit., pp. 310-15. Dufferin to Carnarvon, Nov. 23, 1876.
87 Ibid.
88 Ibid.
89 Ibid., pp. 319-20. Mackenzie to Dufferin, Nov. 25, 1876.
90 *Dufferin Papers,* Film No. 1148, p. 195. Dufferin to A. J. Smith, Dec. 9, 1876.
91 De Kiewiet and Underhill, op. cit., pp. 325-8. Mackenzie to Dufferin, Dec. 15, 1876.
92 Ibid., p. 325. Dufferin to Carnarvon, Dec. 14, 1876.
93 Ibid., p. 329. Dufferin to Carnarvon, Dec. 28, 1876.
94 *Dufferin Papers*, Film No. 1148, p. 196. Dufferin to Premier Elliott, Jan. 6, 1876.

CHAPTER 16

"Protection is a Monster"

1 Jas. Young, op. cit., Vol. II, p. 250. Letter from Mackenzie to Young, July 21, 1876.
2 *Mackenzie Letterbooks*, Vol. VI, p. 89. Hickson to Mackenzie, Dec. 30, 1876.
3 Ibid., Vol. VI, p. 65. Memorandum by Alexander Mackenzie.
4 Ibid., Vol. VII, pp. 89 and 96. Mackenzie to Hickson, Dec. 30, 1876.
5 Ibid., Vol. VII, p. 102. Hickson to Mackenzie, Jan. 3, 1877.
6 *Mackenzie Papers*, p. 1492. Mackenzie to Hickson, Jan. 7, 1877.
7 Ibid., p. 1386. Hon. L. H. Davies to Mackenzie, Oct. 13, 1876.
8 Ibid., p. 1506. Mackenzie to Brown, Jan. 19, 1877.
9 *Mackenzie Letterbooks*, Vol. VII, p. 59. Mackenzie to Laurier, Jan. 23, 1877.
10 Mason Wade, op. cit., p. 361.
11 *Mackenzie Letterbooks*, Vol. VII, p. 37. Mackenzie to Rev. Kelroy, Jan. 8, 1877.
12 Ibid., Vol. I, p. 706. Mackenzie to M. C. Cameron, Oct. 17, 1876.

13 Ibid., Vol. VII, p. 47. Mackenzie to Justice Thomas Moss, Jan. 18, 1877.
14 Parliamentary Debates, p. 14, Feb. 9, 1877.
15 Ibid., p. 20, Feb. 9, 1877.
16 Ibid., p. 44ff, Feb. 15, 1877.
17 *Mackenzie Letterbooks* (Separate Volume at end of Letterbooks). Report of Royal Commission on Northern Railway Company.
18 *Blake Papers*, Film No. M241, No. 279. Mackenzie to Blake, Feb. 17, 1877.
19 Ibid., Film No. M241, No. 280. Mackenzie to Blake, Feb. 19, 1877.
20 Parliamentary Debates, p. 170ff. Feb. 20, 1877.
21 Ibid., p. 401ff. March 1, 1877.
22 Jas. Young, op. cit., Vol. II, p. 307.
23 L. Pacaud: *Sir Wilfrid Laurier*, p. 23. Laurier to Pacaud, March 31, 1877.
24 Parliamentary Debates, p. 208, Feb. 22, 1877.
25 *Mackenzie Papers*, p. 1548. Mackenzie to Chas. Mackenzie, March 4, 1877.
26 Ibid.
27 Parliamentary Debates, p. 1542ff, April 17, 1877.
28 Ibid., April 20-3, 1877.
29 Ibid., p. 1711ff, April 23, 1877.
30 De Kiewiet and Underhill, op. cit., p. 350. Dufferin to Carnarvon, May 3, 1877.
31 *Mackenzie Letterbooks*, Vol. VII, p. 128. Mackenzie to Laird, May 14, 1877.
32 De Kiewiet and Underhill, op. cit., p. 350. Dufferin to Carnarvon, April 27, 1877.
33 Ibid., p. 349. Carnarvon to Dufferin, April 25, 1877.
34 *Mackenzie Letterbooks*, Vol. VII, p. 119. Mackenzie to Laflamme, April 28, 1877.
35 Ibid., Vol. VII, p. 118. Mackenzie to Burpee, April 28, 1877.
36 Ibid., Vol. VII, p. 121. Mackenzie to Pelletier, April 28, 1877.
37 Ibid., Vol. VII, p. 124. Mackenzie to Blake, April 30, 1877.
38 Ibid., Vol. VII, p. 140. Mackenzie to Dufferin, May 17, 1877.
39 *Canadian Parliamentary Companion*, pp. 168-9, 1877.
40 *Blake Papers*, Film No. M239, No. 125. Blake to Dufferin, May 17, 1877.
41 *Mackenzie Papers*, p. 1595. Blake to Mackenzie, May 21, 1877.
42 Ibid., p. 1597. Dufferin to Mackenzie, May 23, 1877.
43 De Kiewiet and Underhill, op. cit., pp. 355-6. Mackenzie to Dufferin, May 28, 1877.
44 Ibid., pp. 364-6. Carnarvon to Dufferin, Aug. 28, 1877.
45 *Mackenzie Letterbooks*, Vol. VII, p. 157. Mackenzie to Letellier, June 7, 1877.
46 Ibid., Vol. VII, p. 178. Mackenzie to Laurier, June 21, 1877.
47 *Mackenzie Papers*, p. 1637. Laurier to Mackenzie, June 22, 1877.
48 Mason Wade, op. cit., pp. 362-7.
49 *Senator MacPherson to his Former Electors*, 1877. Pamphlet Section, Public Archives of Canada.
50 De Kiewiet and Underhill, op. cit., p. 334. Dufferin to Carnarvon, Feb. 15, 1877.
51 *Mackenzie Letterbooks*, Vol. VI, p. 535. Mackenzie to Hon. L. H. Davies, June 12, 1877.
52 *Reform Government in the Dominion*, p. 2ff.
53 Ibid., p. 14ff.

54 *Mackenzie-Thompson Papers.* Address by Rev. F. Wallace: Alexander Mackenzie, A Study for Young Men.
55 De Kiewiet and Underhill, op. cit., p. 358. Dufferin to Carnarvon, July 20, 1877.
A. Mackenzie, op. cit., pp. 128-34.
56 *Mackenzie Letterbooks,* Vol. VIII, p. 70. W. Buckingham to W. Patterson, M.P., Brantford, Ont., July 17, 1877.
57 London *Herald.* Quoted in Sarnia *Observer,* July 22, 1877.
Mackenzie Letterbooks, Vol. VII, p. 197. Mackenzie to Holton, July 23, 1877.
58 *Mackenzie Papers,* p. 1659. Vail to Mackenzie, July 18, 1877.
Ibid., p. 1678. Vail to Mackenzie, Aug. 16, 1877.
59 *Dufferin Papers,* Film No. 1144, p. 136. Mackenzie to Dufferin, Aug. 23, 1877.
60 De Kiewiet and Underhill, p. 362. Dufferin to Carnarvon, Aug. 25, 1877.
61 *Dufferin Papers,* Film No. 1144, p. 140. Mackenzie to Dufferin, Sept. 3, 1877.
62 De Kiewiet and Underhill, op. cit., p. 367. Dufferin to Carnarvon, Oct. 1, 1877.
63 Ibid., pp. 369-70. Dufferin to Carnarvon, Oct. 9, 1877.
64 Ibid., p. 364. Minute, Carnarvon to Herbert.
65 Ibid., p. 368. Carnarvon to Dufferin, Oct. 1, 1877.
66 *Mackenzie Letterbooks,* Vol. VII, p. 244. Mackenzie to Galt, Oct. 2, 1877.
67 De Kiewiet and Underhill, op. cit., p. 371. Dufferin to Carnarvon, Oct. 15, 1877.
Ibid., pp. 367-8. Carnarvon to Dufferin, Oct. 1, 1877.
68 Bell Telephone Archives, Montreal.
69 Sarnia *Observer,* Sept. 14, 1877.
70 *Reform Government in the Dominion,* p. 121.
71 Sarnia *Observer,* Sept. 21, 1877.
72 Ibid., Sept. 28, 1877.
73 *Mackenzie Papers,* p. 1706. Mackenzie to Mary Thompson, Oct. 9, 1877.
74 Ibid., p. 1704. Blake to Mackenzie, Oct. 6, 1877.
75 *Mills Papers.* Mills to Mackenzie, Nov. 11, 1877.
76 R. Rumilly, op. cit., Vol. II, pp. 86-7.
77 *Union des Cantons de l'Est.* Quoted in Sarnia *Observer,* Nov. 2, 1877.
78 Mason Wade, op. cit., p. 369.
79 *Mackenzie Papers,* p. 1712. Laurier to Mackenzie, Oct. 22, 1877.
80 Ibid., p. 1710. Dorion to Mackenzie, Oct. 15, 1877.
81 *Mackenzie Papers,* p. 1713. Laurier to Mackenzie, Oct. 29, 1877.
82 *Mackenzie Papers,* p. 1713. Laurier to Mackenzie, Oct. 29, 1877.
83 *Mackenzie Letterbooks,* Vol. VII, p. 292. Mackenzie to Pelletier, Nov. 1, 1877.
84 *Mackenzie Papers,* p. 1721. Laurier to Mackenzie, Nov. 1, 1877.
85 *Mackenzie Letterbooks,* Vol. VII, p. 305. Mackenzie to Cartwright, Nov. 5, 1877.
86 Ibid., Vol. VII, p. 283. Mackenzie to J. Cameron, Oct. 31, 1877.
87 *Mackenzie Letterbooks,* Vol. VII, p. 310. Mackenzie to A. J. Smith, Nov. 10, 1877.
88 Montreal *Star.* Quoted in Sarnia *Observer,* Nov. 16, 1877.
89 *Mackenzie Papers,* p. 1744. Laurier to Mackenzie, Nov. 9, 1877.
90 Ibid., p. 1756. Pelletier to Mackenzie, Nov. 17, 1877.
Ibid., p. 1766. Pelletier to Mackenzie, Nov. 23, 1877.

91 *Mackenzie Letterbooks*, Vol. VII, p. 334. Mackenzie to Pelletier, Nov. 21, 1877.
92 Ibid., Vol. VII, p. 364. Mackenzie to Thos. Hodgins, Nov. 30, 1877.
93 Ibid., Vol. VII, p. 336. Mackenzie to Laurier, Nov. 22, 1877.
94 *Mackenzie Papers*, p. 1770. Laurier to Mackenzie, Nov. 23. 1877.
95 R. Rumilly, op. cit., Vol. II, p. 104.
96 *Dufferin Papers*, Film No. 1144, p. 184. Mackenzie to Dufferin (no date).

CHAPTER 17

Fear Not, Favour Not

1 *Mackenzie Letterbooks*, Vol. VII, p. 343. Mackenzie to Brown, Nov. 24, 1877.
2 *Blake Papers*, Film No. M241, No. 269. Mackenzie to Blake, Jan. 18, 1878.
3 *Mackenzie Papers*, p. 1834. Blake to Mackenzie, Jan. 17, 1878.
4 Ibid., p. 1845. Vail to Mackenzie, Jan. 18, 1878.
Ibid., p. 1857. Vail to Mackenzie, Feb. 5, 1878.
5 Ibid., p. 1853. Mackenzie to Robert Mackenzie, Jan. 31, 1878.
6 See Marcus Smith *Papers*, Letters to Sandford Fleming, Public Archives of Canada.
7 *Mackenzie Letterbooks*, Vol. VII, p. 380ff. Mackenzie to Dufferin, Dec. 6, 1877.
8 De Kiewiet and Underhill, op. cit., pp. 386-8. Dufferin to Carnarvon, Dec. 7, 1877.
9 Marcus Smith *Papers*. Correspondence with Sandford Fleming.
10 Parliamentary Debates, Feb. 7, 1878.
11 *Mackenzie Papers*, p. 1859. Mackenzie to Mary Thompson, Feb. 12, 1878.
12 *Mackenzie Letterbooks*, Vol. I, p. 51. Mackenzie to G. T. Smith, Whitby, Ont., June 14, 1873.
13 Parliamentary Debates, p. 427ff. Feb. 22, 1878.
14 Parliamentary Debates, p. 854, March 7, 1878.
15 P. B. Casgrain. *Letellier de St-Just et son Temps*. 1885.
16 *Edgar Papers*. Mackenzie to Edgar, March 26, 1878.
17 *Mackenzie Letterbooks*, Vol. VII, p. 502. Mackenzie to Pelletier, March 4, 1878.
18 *Joly Papers*. Mackenzie to Joly, March 20, 1878.
19 Parliamentary Debates, p. 1878ff., April 1, 1878.
20 *Mackenzie Papers*, p. 1895. Mackenzie to Brown, April 12, 1878.
21 Halifax *Reporter*. Quoted in Sarnia *Observer*, May 17, 1878.
22 *Mackenzie Letterbooks*, Vol. VII, p. 559. Mackenzie to Letellier, April 22, 1878.
23 Parliamentary Debates, March 13, 1878.
24 Ibid., p. 137ff., March 22, 1878.
25 G. W. Ross, op. cit., pp. 131-2.
26 Parliamentary Debates, p. 2386, May 1, 1878.
27 Ibid., May 3, 1878.
28 Ibid., May 26, 1878.
29 Ibid., May 8, 1878.
30 Ibid., May 10, 1878.
31 Ibid., April 11, 1878.

32 W. Buckingham and G. W. Ross, op. cit., pp. 491-2.
33 *Mackenzie Papers*, p. 1914. Mackenzie to Chas. Mackenzie, May 12, 1878.
34 W. Buckingham and G. W. Ross, op. cit., pp. 500-1.
Mackenzie Letterbooks, Vol. VII, p. 510. Mackenzie to Holton, May 15, 1878.
Joly Papers. Mackenzie to Joly, May 2, 1878.
35 *Cartwright Papers*. Mackenzie to Cartwright (no date), 1878.
36 *Mackenzie Letterbooks*, Vol. VII, pp. 578-9. Mackenzie to Dufferin, May 11, 1878.
Dufferin Papers, Film No. 1144. Mackenzie to Dufferin, June 14, 1878.
37 Ibid., Film No. 1140, p. 215. Dufferin to Hicks-Beach, May (no date), 1878.
38 Ibid., Film No. 1140, p. 193. Dufferin to Hicks-Beach, April 2, 1878.
39 Ibid., Film No. 1140, p. 217. Dufferin to Hicks-Beach, May 23, 1878.
40 Ibid., Film No. 1140, p. 225. Dufferin to Hicks-Beach, May 27, 1878.
41 Ibid., Film No. 1144, Mackenzie to Dufferin, June 14, 1878.
42 Ibid., Film No. 1142, Hicks-Beach to Dufferin, May 10, 1878.
43 *Mackenzie Papers*, p. 1914. Mackenzie to Chas. Mackenzie, May 12, 1878.
44 Ibid., p. 1923. Jeremiah Allan to Mayor of Montreal, May 14, 1878.
45 *Mackenzie Letterbooks*, Vol. VII, p. 599. Mackenzie to Sir John Rose, May 17, 1878.
46 *Dufferin Papers*, Film No. 1144, Mackenzie to Dufferin, June 14, 1878.
47 Ibid., Film No. 1147, p. 144. Col. J. B. Strange to Dufferin, June 12, 1878.
48 Ibid., Film No. 1144, Mackenzie to Dufferin, June 14, 1878.
49 *Mackenzie Papers*, p. 1925. Mackenzie to Chas. Mackenzie, May 20, 1878.
50 Ibid., p. 1927. Mackenzie to C. R. Black, May 22, 1878.
51 *Globe*, May 30, 1878.
52 Ibid., May 31, 1878.
53 Sarnia *Observer*, June, 7, 1878.
54 Buckingham and G. W. Ross, op. cit., p. 502.
55 Ibid., p. 585.
56 *Mackenzie Papers*, p. 1956. Mackenzie to Brown, June 18, 1878.
57 W. Buckingham and G. W. Ross, op. cit., p. 503.
58 *Mackenzie Letterbooks*, Vol. II, p. 71ff. Mackenzie to Jas. Bennett, District Orange Grand Master, July 8, 1878.
59 Ibid., Vol. II, p. 34ff. Mackenzie to Mayor Beaudry, July 3, 1878.
60 Ibid., Vol. II, p. 56. Mackenzie to Acting Manager, Grand Trunk Railway, Montreal, July 6, 1878.
61 *Dufferin Papers*, Film No. 1142, p. 17. Hicks-Beach to Dufferin, June 22, 1878.
62 Ibid., Film No. 1141, Mackenzie to Dufferin, July 6, 1878.
63 Ibid., Film No. 1147, p. 170ff.
64 *Mackenzie Papers*, p. 2005. District Master David Grant to Mackenzie, July 12, 1878.
65 *Dufferin Papers*, Film No. 1140, p. 33. Dufferin to Hicks-Beach, Sept. 4, 1878.
66 Ibid., Film No. 1140, p. 236. Dufferin to Hicks-Beach, May 31, 1878.
67 Ibid., Film No. 1140, p. 217. Dufferin to Hicks-Beach, May 23, 1878.
68 Ibid., Film No. 1144. Mackenzie to Dufferin, July 3, 1878.
69 *Blake Papers*, Film No. M241, p. 271. Mackenzie to Blake, July 2, 1878.
70 Toronto *Mail*, Aug. 7, 1878.
71 Ibid., Aug. 8, 1878.

72 Ibid., Aug. 19, 1878.
73 R. M. Hamilton, op. cit., John A. Macdonald to Goldwin Smith. Quoted by Goldwin Smith in letter to *Globe*, Sept. 23, 1895.
74 Sarnia *Observer*, Aug. 19, 1878.
75 *Buckingham Papers*. Mackenzie to Buckingham, Sept. (no date), 1878.
76 *Dufferin Papers*, Film No. 1144, p. 159. Mackenzie to Dufferin, Sept. 19, 1878.
77 Donald Creighton: *The Old Chieftain*, p. 243.
78 *Dufferin Papers*, Film No. 1149, p. 74. Dufferin to Lorne, Aug. 22, 1878.
79 Ibid., Film No. 1140, p. 45. Dufferin to Hicks-Beach, Sept. 20, 1878.
80 W. Buckingham and G. W. Ross, op. cit., p. 516.
81 *Mackenzie Letterbooks*, Vol. II, p. 404. Mackenzie to Senator Thibaudeau, Sept. 21, 1878.
82 *Brown Papers*, p. 2548. Mackenzie to Brown, Sept. 24, 1878.
83 *Edgar Papers*. Mackenzie to Edgar, Sept. 24, 1878.
84 Ibid.
85 *Mackenzie Letterbooks*, Vol. II, p. 470. Mackenzie to W. Darling, Sept. 30, 1878.
86 *Mackenzie Papers*, p. 2121. Dufferin to Mackenzie, Oct. 6, 1878.
87 *Mackenzie Papers*, p. 2134. Cartwright to Mackenzie, Oct. 6, 1874.
88 Ibid., p. 2138. Mackenzie to Dufferin, Oct. 9, 1878.
89 W. Buckingham and G. W. Ross, op. cit., pp. 529-30.
90 Donald Creighton: *The Old Chieftain*, p. 244.

CHAPTER 18

The Shades of Opposition

1 *Mackenzie Letterbooks*, Vol. II, p. 547. Mackenzie to Huntington, Dec. 9, 1878.
2 *Jones Papers*. Mackenzie to Jones, Dec. 6, 1878.
3 *Dufferin Papers*, Film No. 1144, p. 161. Mackenzie to Dufferin, Oct. 23, 1878.
4 *Mackenzie Papers*, p. 2122. Brown to Mackenzie, Oct. 1, 1878.
Joly Papers. Joly to Mackenzie, Sept. 26, 1878.
5 *Mackenzie Papers*, p. 2129. Brown to Mackenzie, Oct. 3, 1878.
6 Ibid., p. 2146. Thos. Hodgins to Mackenzie, Oct. 9, 1878.
7 Ibid., p. 2179. Mackenzie to Mary Thompson, Nov. 1, 1878.
8 Ibid.
9 David Lee: "The Dominion General Election of 1878 in Ontario". Published in *Ontario History*, Summer Edition, 1959.
10 *Buckingham Papers*. Mackenzie to Buckingham, Oct. 22, 1878.
11 *Mackenzie Letterbooks*, Vol. II, p. 569. Mackenzie to David Thompson, Dec. 11, 1878.
12 Ibid., Vol. II, p. 547. Mackenzie to Huntington, Dec. 9, 1878.
13 Ibid., Vol. II, p. 554. Mackenzie to Pelletier, Dec. 19, 1878.
14 Ibid., Vol. II, p. 561. Mackenzie to Holton, Dec. 11, 1878.
15 Ibid., Vol. II, p. 580. Mackenzie to Blake, Dec. 31, 1878.
Ibid., Vol. II, p. 582. Blake to Mackenzie, Jan. 2, 1879.
16 Buckingham and G. W. Ross, op. cit., p. 538. Mackenzie to Miss Biggar, Jan. 25, 1879.
17 Ibid.

18 *Mackenzie Papers*, p. 2235. Mackenzie to Mary Thompson, Feb. 9, 1879.
19 *Parliamentary Debates*, Feb. 13, 1879.
20 *Mackenzie Papers*, p. 2252. Mackenzie to Mary Thompson, Mar. 6, 1879.
21 Ibid.
22 Ibid.
23 *Macdonald Papers*, Vol. 204. Chapleau to Macdonald, Sept. 19, 1878.
24 *Parliamentary Debates*, March 11, 1879.
25 Ibid., March 14, 1879.
26 *Buckingham Papers*. Mackenzie to Buckingham, March 15, 1879.
27 *Parliamentary Debates*, March 14, 1879; April 7, 1879; April 9, 1879.
28 Ibid., April 22, 1879.
29 Ibid., p. 1079. April 8, 1879.
30 Ibid., p. 1645. April 30, 1879.
31 Ibid., p. 1886. May 10, 1879.
32 Ibid., May 7, 1879.
33 *Joly Papers*. Mackenzie to Joly, April 6, 1879.
34 *Mackenzie-Thompson Papers*. Mackenzie to his wife, May 5, 1879.
35 Ibid.
36 *Mackenzie Papers*, p. 2262. Mackenzie to Lorne, May 3, 1879.
37 A. Mackenzie, op. cit., p. 140.
Brown Papers, p. 2595. Lorne to Brown, May 22, 1879.
Ibid., p. 2613. Brown to Lorne, June 21, 1879.
38 W. Buckingham and G. W. Ross, op. cit., pp. 541-2.
39 *Joly Papers*. Mackenzie to Joly, June 28, 1879.
40 *Buckingham Papers*. Mackenzie to Buckingham, Sept. 12, 1879.
41 Ibid.
42 Ibid.
43 Ibid.
44 *Mackenzie Papers*, p. 2337. Mackenzie to Mary Thompson, Jan. 31, 1880.
45 *Le Vrai Canard,* Feb. 28, 1880.
46 *Parliamentary Debates*, p. 15ff., Feb. 12, 1880.
47 Ibid., p. 559ff. March 9, 1880.
48 *Mackenzie-Thompson Papers*. Mackenzie to his wife, Feb. 25, 1880.
49 Ibid., Mackenzie to his wife, March 2, 1880.
50 Ibid.
51 Ibid., Mackenzie to his wife, March 15, 1880.
52 *Parliamentary Debates*, p. 649, March 15, 1880.
53 A. Mackenzie, op. cit., p. 141ff.
54 Ibid., p. 142.
55 *Brown Papers*, p. 2658. Mackenzie to Mrs. Brown, April 20, 1880.
56 *Mackenzie Letterbooks*, Vol. II, p. 673ff. Mackenzie to Hon. L. H. Davies, May 20, 1880.
57 O. D. Skelton, *Life and Letters of Sir Wilfrid Laurier*, 1921.
58 *Parliamentary Debates*, p. 1815, April 27, 1880.
59 Ibid., April 29, 1880.
60 *Mackenzie Papers*, p. 2742. May 5, 1880.

CHAPTER 19

"O Take Me Home"

1 W. Buckingham and G. W. Ross, op. cit., p. 634.
2 *Mackenzie Papers*, p. 2356. Mackenzie to C. R. Black, May 20, 1880.
3 *Mackenzie Letterbooks*, Vol. II, p. 689ff. Mackenzie to Rev. John McKinnon, Georgetown, P.E.I., May 25, 1880.
4 Ibid., Vol. II, p. 673ff. Mackenzie to Hon. L. H. Davies, May 20, 1880. Ibid., Vol. II, p. 685ff. Mackenzie to N. D. Stewart, May 25, 1880.
5 *Mackenzie Letterbooks*, Vol. II, p. 708ff. Mackenzie to John Menzies, Edinburgh, Scotland, June 25, 1880.
6 Ibid., Vol. II, p. 698ff. Mackenzie to W. Waller, Ottawa, June 19, 1880.
7 J. Pope: *Correspondence of Sir John Macdonald*, p. 277. Letter from Mackenzie to Macdonald, Oct. 26, 1880.
8 *Mackenzie Papers*, p. 2366. Mackenzie to Rev. J. Thompson, Nov. 28. 1880.
9 Ibid., p. 2370. Mackenzie to C. R. Black, Dec. 20, 1880.
10 *Mackenzie Papers*, p. 2368. Sir John Rose to Mackenzie, Dec. 3, 1880.
11 *Parliamentary Debates*, p. 389ff. Jan. 12, 1881.
12 *Buckingham Papers*. Mackenzie to Buckingham, Jan. 26, 1881.
13 *Parliamentary Debates*, March 1, 1881.
14 *Mackenzie-Thompson Papers*. Newspaper report of anecdote recounted in 1892 by Hon. L. H. Davies.
15 W. Buckingham and G. W. Ross, op. cit., p. 564. Mackenzie to Jas. Young.
16 *Mackenzie Papers*, p. 2386. Lorne to Mackenzie, April 26, 1881.
17 *Mackenzie Papers*, p. 2388. Mackenzie to Lorne, April 30, 1881.
18 *Buckingham Papers*. Mackenzie to Buckingham, May 31, 1881.
19 W. Buckingham and G. W. Ross, op. cit., p. 576. Mackenzie to Chas. Mackenzie, June 3, 1881.
20 *Mackenzie Papers*, p. 2390. Mackenzie to Chas. Mackenzie, June 9, 1881.
21 Ibid., p. 2392, Mackenzie to Chas. Mackenzie, June 20, 1881.
22 *Buckingham Papers*. Mackenzie to Buckingham, July 6, 1881.
23 Ibid.
24 W. Buckingham and G. W. Ross, p. 582.
25 *Buckingham Papers*. Mackenzie to Buckingham, Sept. 7, 1881.
26 Ibid., Mackenzie to Buckingham, Sept. 23, 1881.
27 *Mackenzie Papers*, p. 2413. Mackenzie to C. R. Black, Feb. 28, 1882.
28 *Blake Papers*, Film No. M241, No. 274, Mackenzie to Blake, Feb. 23, 1882.
29 *Parliamentary Debates*, p. 243ff. March 7, 1882.
30 Ibid., p. 1089ff. April 21, 1882.
31 Donald Creighton: *The Old Chieftain*, p. 335. *Globe*, June 9, 1882.
32 *Parliamentary Debates*, p. 1209ff. April 28, 1882.
33 W. Buckingham and G. W. Ross, op. cit., pp. 588-9. *Globe*, May 20, 1882.
34 *Globe*, May 29, 1882.
35 *Globe*, June 12, 1882.

36 Ibid.
37 *Globe*, June 12 and 17, 1882.
38 *Mackenzie Papers*, p. 2425. Wm. Murray to Mackenzie, June 22, 1882.
39 Ibid., p. 2424. J. E. Rose to Mackenzie, June 21, 1882.
40 Ibid., p. 2425. Wm. Murray to Mackenzie, June 22, 1882.
41 Ibid., p. 2432. Hugh Mackay to Mackenzie, July 24, 1882.
42 *Mackenzie Letterbooks*, Vol. II, p. 858. Mackenzie to Hugh Mackay, July 31, 1882.
43 *Mackenzie Papers*, p. 2434. Mackenzie to Mary Thompson, Aug. 29, 1882.
44 W. Buckingham and G. W. Ross, op. cit., pp. 601-2.
45 *Mackenzie-Thompson Papers*. Mackenzie to his wife, Aug. 18, 1882.
46 Ibid.
47 A. Mackenzie, op. cit., Preface.
48 *Parliamentary Debates*, p. 596ff. April 13, 1883.
49 *A. E. Byerly Papers*. Mackenzie to Buckingham, May 1, 1883.
50 *Mackenzie Papers*, p. 2452. Mackenzie to Chas. Mackenzie, June 20, 1883.
51 Ibid.
52 W. Buckingham and G. W. Ross, op. cit., p. 607.
53 *Mackenzie Papers*, p. 2454. Mackenzie to Mary Thompson, July 11, 1883.
54 W. Buckingham and G. W. Ross, op. cit., pp. 604-7.
55 *Parliamentary Debates*, p. 328. Feb. 15, 1884.
56 Ibid., p. 534. Feb. 26, 1884.
57 Ibid., p. 569ff. Feb. 28, 1884.
58 Ibid., p. 1157. March 26, 1884.
59 *Mackenzie Papers*, p. 2458. Geo. Stephen to Mackenzie, July 3, 1884.
60 Ibid., p. 2466. Mackenzie to Mary Thompson, Aug. 4, 1884.
61 Ibid.
62 Ibid.
63 Manitoba *Free Press*, Aug. 29, 1884; Sept. 2, 1884.
64 Ibid., Sept. 2, 1884.
65 W. Buckingham and G. W. Ross, op. cit., pp. 609-10.
66 *The Nor'Wester*, Sept. 3, 1884.
67 Manitoba *Free Press*, Aug. 29, 1884.
68 Ibid., Sept. 2, 1884.
69 W. Buckingham and G. W. Ross, op. cit., p. 608.
70 *Mackenzie-Thompson Papers*. Newspaper account.
71 *Mackenzie Papers*, p. 2468. Geo. Stephen to Mackenzie, Oct. 3, 1884.
72 C. Biggar, op. cit., Vol. I, pp. 425-6.
73 *Mackenzie Papers*, p. 2472. Mackenzie to Rev. J. Thompson, Nov. 13, 1884.
74 Ibid., p. 2474. Mackenzie to Mary Thompson, Feb. 5, 1885.
75 *Parliamentary Debates*, p. 111ff., Feb. 13, 1885.
76 Ibid., p. 133, Feb. 17, 1885.
77 Ibid., p. 994, April 10, 1885.
78 Ibid., p. 2930, June 30, 1885.
79 Donald Creighton: *The Old Chieftain*, p. 426.
80 *Mackenzie Papers*, p. 2476. Mackenzie to C. R. Black, June 18, 1885.
81 Ibid., p. 2480. Mackenzie to C. R. Black, May 18, 1886.
82 Ibid., p. 2484. Mackenzie to Rev. J. Thompson, July 15, 1886.
83 Edward Blake Campaign Speech at Wingham, Ontario. Pamphlets Section, Public Archives of Canada.

84 *Parliamentary Debates*, p. 445. May 16, 1887.
85 *Cartwright Papers*. Mackenzie to Cartwright, Sept. 27, 1887.
86 *Parliamentary Debates*, p. 65. March 5, 1888.
87 Ibid., April 26, 1888.
88 *Mackenzie Papers*, p. 2496. Mackenzie to Mary Thompson, April 13, 1888.
89 Ibid., p. 2498. Mackenzie to Mary Thompson, Oct. 17, 1888.
90 W. Buckingham and G. W. Ross, op. cit., pp. 631-2.
91 Ibid., pp. 630-1.
92 C. Biggar, op. cit., p. 586ff.
93 *Parliamentary Debates*, May 1, 1891.
94 W. Buckingham and G. W. Ross, op. cit., pp. 633-4.
95 W. Buckingham and G. W. Ross, op. cit., p. 634.
96 Ibid., p. 635.
97 *Senate Debates*, April 27, 1892.
98 Ibid.
99 *Parliamentary Debates*, April 19, 1892.
100 W. Buckingham and G. W. Ross, op. cit., pp. 643-4.
101 *Mackenzie-Thompson Papers, Globe* report.
102 Ibid., Toronto *Mail* report.
103 Ibid., *Grip*, April 30, 1892.

APPENDIX

THE MACKENZIE MINISTRY (1)

November 7th, 1873 to October 9th, 1878

(From: *Guide to Canadian Ministries since Confederation, July 1, 1867 - January 1, 1957)*

PRIME MINISTER

The Honourable Alexander Mackenzie

THE MINISTRY

Minister of Public Works

Hon. Alexander Mackenzie .... Nov. 7, 1873—Oct. 9, 1878

Minister of Justice and Attorney General

Hon. Antoine-Aimé Dorion (2) .... Nov. 7, 1873—May 31, 1874
Hon. Sir Albert James Smith .... June 1, 1874—July 7, 1874
(Acting Minister)
Hon. Télesphore Fournier (3) .... July 8, 1874—May 18, 1875
Hon. Edward Blake (4) .... May 19, 1875—June 7, 1877
Hon. Radolfe Laflamme .... June 8, 1877—Oct. 9, 1878

Minister of Marine and Fisheries

Hon. Sir Albert James Smith .... Nov. 7, 1873—Oct. 9, 1878

Minister of Agriculture

Hon. Luc Letellier de St. Just .... Nov. 7, 1873—Dec. 14, 1876
(5) (Senator)
Hon. Isaac Burpee .... Dec. 15, 1876—Jan. 25, 1877
(Acting Minister)
Hon. Charles Alphonse Pantaléon Pelletier .... Jan. 26, 1877—Oct. 9, 1878

Minister of Finance

Hon. Richard John Cartwright .... Nov. 7, 1873—Oct. 9, 1878

Minister of the Interior and Superintendent General of Indian Affairs

Hon. David Laird (6) .... Nov. 7, 1873—Oct. 6, 1876
Hon. Richard William Scott .... Oct. 7, 1876—Oct. 23, 1876
(Acting Minister)
Hon. David Mills .... Oct. 24, 1876—Oct. 9, 1878

---

(1) On November 5th, 1873, Sir John A. Macdonald resigned and on the same day the Governor General invited Mr. Mackenzie to form a government. On November 7th, 1873 the Mackenzie Ministry was sworn to office. Mackenzie resigned on Oct. 8th, 1878, effective Oct. 9th. During the Second Ministry no Orders in Council were passed recording the appointment of ministers to office. This practice could be supported on the theory that ministerial appointments were the prerogative of the Prime Minister and as such did not require the approval of the Governor in Council. Note that in 1953 this practice was again introduced.

(2) Dorion appointed Chief Justice of the Court of Queen's Bench for Quebec, June 1st, 1874.

(3) Fournier appointed Postmaster General, May 19th, 1875.

(4) Blake appointed President of the Privy Council, June 8th, 1877.

(5) St. Just appointed Lieutenant-Governor of Quebec, Dec. 15th, 1876.

(6) Laird appointed Lieutenant-Governor of the Northwest Territories. Oct. 7th, 1876.

Secretary of State of Canada		
Hon. David Christie (7) (Senator)	Nov. 7, 1873	Jan. 8, 1874
Hon. Richard William Scott (Senator)	Jan. 9, 1874	Oct. 9, 1878
Minister of Customs		
Hon. Isaac Burpee	Nov. 7, 1873	Oct. 9, 1878
Postmaster General		
Hon. Donald Alexander Macdonald (8)	Nov. 7, 1873	May 17, 1875
Vacant	May 18, 1875	
Hon. Télesphore Fournier (9)	May 19, 1875	Oct. 7, 1875
Vacant	Oct. 8, 1875	
Hon. Lucius Seth Huntington	Oct. 9, 1875	Oct. 9, 1878
Receiver General		
Hon. Thomas Coffin	Nov. 7, 1873	Oct. 9, 1878
Minister of Inland Revenue		
Hon. Télesphore Fournier (10)	Nov. 7, 1873	July 7, 1874
Hon. Félix Geoffrion (11)	July 8, 1874	Nov. 8, 1876
Hon. Radolfe Laflamme (12)	Nov. 9, 1876	June 7, 1877
Hon. Joseph Edouard Cauchon (13)	June 8, 1877	Oct. 7, 1877
Hon. Wilfrid Laurier	Oct. 8, 1877	Oct. 9, 1878
Minister of Militia and Defence		
Hon. William Ross (14)	Nov. 7, 1873	Sept. 29, 1874
Hon. William Berrian Vail (15)	Sept. 30, 1874	Jan. 20, 1878
Hon. Alfred Gilpin Jones	Jan. 21, 1878	Oct. 9, 1878
President of the Privy Council (16)		
Vacant	Nov. 7, 1873	Jan. 19, 1874
Hon. Lucius Seth Huntington (17)	Jan. 20, 1874	Oct. 8, 1875
Vacant	Oct. 9, 1875	Dec. 6, 1875
Hon. Joseph Edouard Cauchon (18)	Dec. 7, 1875	June 7, 1877
Hon. Edward Blake (19)	June 8, 1877	Jan. 17, 1878
Vacant	Jan. 18, 1878	Oct. 9, 1878
Minister without Portfolio		
Hon. Edward Blake (20)	Nov. 7, 1873	Feb. 13, 1874
Hon. Richard William Scott (21)	Nov. 7, 1873	Jan. 8, 1874

(7) Christie appointed Speaker of the Senate, Jan. 9th, 1874.

(8) Macdonald appointed Lieutenant-Governor of Ontario, May 18th, 1875.

(9) Fournier appointed Puisne Judge of Supreme Court of Canada, Oct. 8th, 1875.

(10) Fournier appointed Minister of Justice, July 8th, 1874.

(11) Geoffrion resigned from Ministry, Nov. 8th, 1876.

(12) Laflamme appointed Minister of Justice, June 8th, 1877.

(13) Cauchon appointed Lieutenant-Governor of Manitoba, Oct. 8th, 1877, effective Dec. 2nd, 1877.

(14) Ross appointed Collector of Customs, Halifax, Sept. 30th, 1874.

(15) Vail resigned from Ministry, Jan. 20th, 1878.

(16) See First Ministry, note (18). It is of interest to note that, during this ministry, in the absence of the President of the Privy Council, the presiding Councillor signed the Minutes of the Committee as "Acting President". In similar circumstances in the First and Third Ministries the presiding Councillor signed as "Senior Councillor". Apparently, in this respect, the Macdonald governments carried on the spirit of Section V of the 1867 Instructions. From the assumption of office by the Fourth Ministry in 1891, under Sir John Abbott, the term "Acting President" was generally used.

(17) Huntington appointed Postmaster General, Oct. 9th, 1875.

(18) Cauchon appointed Minister of Inland Revenue, June 8th, 1877.

(19) Blake resigned from Ministry, Jan. 17th, 1878.

(20) Blake resigned from Ministry, Feb. 13th, 1874; subsequently reappointed to the Ministry as Minister of Justice, May 19th, 1875.

(21) Scott appointed Secretary of State, Jan. 9th, 1874.

BIBLIOGRAPHY

Biggar, C. R. W.: *Sir Oliver Mowat,* 2 Vols. Toronto 1905

Boyd, John: *Sir Georges-Etienne Cartier; His Life and Times.* Toronto 1914

Buckingham, William and Ross, Hon. George W.: *The Honourable Alexander Mackenzie; His Life and Times.* Toronto 1892

Campbell, R. E.: *George Brown's Attempted Reciprocity Treaty of 1874.* University of Toronto Thesis 1936

Careless, J. M. S.: *George Brown and the Toronto Globe.* Ph.D. Thesis Harvard University

Careless, J. M. S.: *Brown of the Globe,* Vol. I. Toronto 1959

Cartwright, The Rt. Hon. Sir Richard: *Reminiscences.* Toronto 1912

Casgrain, P. B.: *Letellier de St. Just et son Temps.* Quebec 1885

Creighton, Donald: *John A. Macdonald; the Young Politician.* Toronto 1952

——*John A. Macdonald; the Old Chieftain.* Toronto 1955

Dent, John Charles: *The Last Forty Years,* 2 Vols. Toronto 1887

Dufferin, Lady Harriet: *My Canadian Journal.* London 1891

Farr, David M. L.: *The Colonial Office and Canada, 1867-87.* Toronto 1955

Grant, Sir James A.: *Recollections.* Typed Manuscript in Parliamentary Library

Innis, Harold A.: *A History of the Canadian Pacific Railway.* Toronto 1923

De Kiewiet, C. W., and Underhill, F. H.: *Dufferin-Carnarvon Correspondence, 1874-78.* The Champlain Society, Toronto 1955

Kreutzweiser, Erwin: *The Red River Insurrection.* Gardenvale, Quebec 193—

Lauriston, Victor: *Lambton's Hundred Years, 1849-1949.* Sarnia 1949

Lee, David: "The Dominion General Election of 1878 in Ontario". Published in *Ontario History,* Summer issue, 1959

Leggo, William: *The History of the Administration of the Right Hon. Frederick Temple, Earl of Dufferin.* Toronto 1878

Lower, Arthur: *Colony to Nation.* Toronto 1946

Mackenzie, Hon. Alexander: *The Life and Speeches of the Hon. George Brown.* Toronto 1882

——*Political Points and Pencillings.* Toronto 1878

——*Reform Government in the Dominion.* Toronto 1878

——*Speeches.* Toronto 1876

Mackinnon, Frank: "The Supreme Court of Canada". Published in *Canadian Historical Review* 1946

McEachern, R. A.: *Canadian Discussion on the Imperial Relationship.* University of Toronto Thesis 1933

Morton, A. S.: *A History of the Canadian West to 1870-71.* London 1939

Ormsby, Margaret: *British Columbia, A History.* Toronto 1958

——"Prime Minister Mackenzie—The Liberal Party and the Bargain with British Columbia". *Canadian Historical Review,* June 1945

Pacaud, L.: *Sir Wilfrid Laurier.* Toronto 1935

Phelan, Josephine: *The Ardent Exile.* Toronto 1951

Pope, J.: *Correspondence of Sir John A. Macdonald.* Toronto 1921
Preston, W. T. R.: *My Generation of Politics and Politicians.* Toronto 1927
Ross, George W.: *Getting into Parliament and After.* Toronto 1913
Rumilly, Robert: *Histoire de la Province de Québec*, 6 Vols. Montreal 1941 & 1942
Saywell, John T.: *The Office of the Lieutenant Governor.* Toronto 1957
Skelton, Isabel: *The Life of Thomas D'Arcy McGee.* Gardenvale, Quebec 1925
Skelton, O. D.: *The Life and Times of Sir Alexander Tilloch Galt.* Toronto 1920
Smith, W. H.: *Canada: Past and Present.* Published by Thomas MacLean 1852
Splane, R. B.: *The Upper Canada Reform Party 1867-78*, Vols. I & II. University of Toronto Thesis 1948
Stanley, G. F. G.: *The Birth of Western Canada.* London 1936
Thomas, L. H.: *The Struggle for Responsible Government in the North West Territories 1870-97.* Toronto 1956
Underhill, Frank H.: "Edward Blake, The Supreme Court Act, and the Appeal to the Privy Council 1875-76". Published in *Canadian Historical Review* 1938
——"Edward Blake's Interview with Lord Cairns on the Supreme Court Act, July 5, 1876". Published in *Canadian Historical Review* XIX, Sept. 1938
——"Edward Blake, the Liberal Party and Unrestricted Reciprocity". Published in *Canadian Historical Review* XX, March 1939
——"Edward Blake and Canadian Liberal Nationalism". Published in *Essays in Canadian History* by R. Flenley. Toronto 1939
——"Political Ideas of the Upper Canada Reformers 1867-78". *Report* of the Canadian Historical Association 1942
Wade, Mason: *The French Canadians 1760-1945.* Toronto 1955
Willison, Sir J.: *Reminiscences, Political and Personal.* Toronto 1919
Young, James: *Public Men and Public Life in Canada*, 2 Vols. Toronto 1912

Parliamentary Debates 1854-1892 (For the period prior to 1870 the Library of Parliament has collections of newspaper reports of the debates.)

*Newspapers**

Canadian Illustrated News, 1869-83. Public Archives of Canada
Canadien, Le, 1806-89. Public Archives of Canada
Grip, 1874-94. Public Archives of Canada
Lambton Shield, 1853-54. 1st edition in Sarnia Public Library
Liberal, The, 1875. Public Archives of Canada
Mackenzie's Weekly Message, 1852-60. Public Archives of Canada
Montreal Gazette, 1785-1892. Public Archives of Canada
Montreal Herald, 1811-92. Public Archives of Canada
Nation, The, 1874-76. Public Archives of Canada
Ottawa Citizen, 1859-92. Public Archives of Canada
Ottawa Free Press, 1875-92. Public Archives of Canada
Sarnia Observer, 1853-78. Public Archives of Canada

*These collections are not necessarily complete for the dates mentioned.

Toronto Examiner, 1840-55. Public Archives of Canada
Toronto Globe, 1844-92. Public Archives of Canada
Toronto Leader, 1853-59. Public Archives of Canada
Toronto Mail, 1872-92. Public Archives of Canada

Collections of Private Papers

Blake, Edward, *Papers*. Ontario Public Archives; Microfilm in Public Archives of Canada
Brown, George, *Papers*. Public Archives of Canada
Buckingham, William, *Papers*. Public Archives of Canada
Byerly, A. E., *Papers*. Ontario Public Archives
Campbell, Alexander, *Papers*. Ontario Public Archives
Cartwright, Sir Richard, *Papers*. Ontario Public Archives
Dufferin, Earl of, *Papers*. Microfilm in Public Archives of Canada
Edgar, James, *Papers*. Ontario Public Archives
Fleming, Sir Sandford, *Papers*. Public Archives of Canada
Gzowski, Sir Casimir, *Papers*. Ontario Public Archives
Hodgins, Thomas, *Papers*. Ontario Public Archives
Jones, A. G., *Papers*. Nova Scotia Public Archives; Published in 1952 Report of the Nova Scotia Public Archives
Laurier, Sir Wilfrid, *Papers*. Public Archives of Canada
Lotbinière, Joly de, *Papers*. Joly de Lotbinière Estate, Leclercville, Quebec
Macdonald, Sir John A., *Papers*. Public Archives of Canada
Mackenzie, Alexander, *Letterbooks*. Public Archives of Canada
Mackenzie, Alexander, *Papers*. Queen's University; Microfilm in Public Archives of Canada
Mackenzie-Thompson *Papers*. In possession of Mrs. B. Morgan, 238 Powell Avenue, Ottawa
Mackenzie, William Lyon,– Lindsey *Papers*. Ontario Public Archives
Mills, David, *Papers*. University of Western Ontario
Morris, Alexander, *Papers*. Ontario Public Archives
Smith, Marcus, *Papers*. Public Archives of Canada
Tupper, Sir Charles, *Papers*. Public Archives of Canada

INDEX

REDEEMER COLLEGE LIBRARY
3 2758 00033 0493